INTRODUCTION TO LOGIC AND CRITICAL THINKING

INTRODUCTION TO LOGIC AND CRITICAL THINKING

Sixth Edition

MERRILEE H. SALMON
University of Pittsburgh

WADSWORTH
CENGAGE Learning·

Australia • Brazil • Japan • Korea • Mexico • Singapore • Spain • United Kingdom • United States

WADSWORTH
CENGAGE Learning™

Introduction to Logic and Critical Thinking, Sixth Edition
Merrilee H. Salmon

Publisher: Clark Baxter

Senior Sponsoring Editor: Joann Kozyrev

Development Editor: Ian Lague

Assistant Editor: Joshua Duncan

Editorial Assistant: Marri Straton

Media Editor: Katie Schooling

Marketing Program Manager: Sean Foy

Manufacturing Planner: Mary Beth Hennebury

Rights Acquisitions Specialist: Shalice Shah-Caldwell

Production Management and Composition: PreMediaGlobal

Senior Art Director: Jennifer Wahi

Cover Designer: Michelle DiMercurio

Cover Image: Shutterstock / ©Vlade Shestakov

For product information and technology assistance, contact us at **Cengage Learning Customer & Sales Support, 1-800-354-9706**

For permission to use material from this text or product, submit all requests online at **www.cengage.com/permissions** Further permissions questions can be emailed to **permissionrequest@cengage.com**

Library of Congress Control Number: 2011940454

Student Edition:

ISBN-13: 978-1-133-04975-3

ISBN-10: 1-133-04975-3

Wadsworth
20 Channel Center Street
Boston, MA 02210
USA

Cengage Learning is a leading provider of customized learning solutions with office locations around the globe, including Singapore, the United Kingdom, Australia, Mexico, Brazil, and Japan. Locate your local office at **www.cengage.com/global**

Cengage Learning products are represented in Canada by Nelson Education, Ltd.

To learn more about Wadsworth, visit **www.cengage.com/ wadsworth**

Purchase any of our products at your local college store or at our preferred online store **www.cengagebrain.com**

Instructors: Please visit **login.cengage.com** and log in to access instructor-specific resources.

Printed in the United States of America
Print Number: 06   Print Year: 2019

In Memory of
WBH
and
WCS

PREFACE TO THE SIXTH EDITION

This book, for students with no prior training in logic, provides tools to develop critical-thinking skills. It does so by:

(1) guiding students through the fundamental principles of inductive and deductive logic; and

(2) showing them how to use these principles to sort what is valuable from what is worthless in the daily flood of information that reaches them.

In the five years since the 5th edition of this book was published, the amount of information easily available to students has exploded. Computers with Internet access are now standard equipment for freshmen in college. All the Web has to offer can be reached from mobile devices as well. Constant exposure to this largely unedited information as well as to various media, which are edited but often with strong political or social bias, makes critical thinking more important than ever. **This new sixth edition through many of its explanations, examples, and exercises recognizes these new ways of acquiring information.**

This book differs from others with similar goals in several respects:

(1) *A wealth of examples and exercises taken from newspapers, magazines, the Web, literature, history, law, politics, math, science, medicine, and the arts.* If principles of logic and critical thinking are to be used in real life after students leave the classroom, the principles must be applied to real-life examples during the learning process. The exercises range in difficulty from fairly easy to challenging. Many stretch the vocabulary of students and lead them into new areas of knowledge. Enough background information is provided to enable students to solve all of the exercises. There are approximately **850 exercises** in the book, **45 percent of them new to this edition**. Answers for even-numbered exercises are provided at the back of the book so that students can check their work and learn from any mistakes.

(2) *Special attention to the language of arguments.* The second chapter of the book is devoted to issues that are important to students' understanding of ordinary-language arguments. Discussions of vagueness, ambiguity, and of various types of definition and their uses are intended to raise students' sensitivity to the richness of language. Students will learn how appropriate language can clarify ideas and strengthen arguments. They will also learn to see through obfuscating and ambiguous language that can make fallacious arguments seem convincing. **Examples and exercises new to this edition take account of new vocabulary that has entered the language as a result of social media.**

(3) *Expanded treatment of inductive logic.* Most of the arguments that students encounter in ordinary life are inductive—that is, ones in which premises offer less-than-conclusive evidence for their conclusions. This book explains the structural features of various types

of inductive arguments and the different criteria for evaluating them. Special attention is given to statistical reasoning and probabilities so that even students with minimal facility for mathematics can understand the criteria for judging arguments based on samples. A chapter on causal arguments discusses the classical causal analyses of David Hume and John Stuart Mill and relates these to the modern use of controlled experiments and to notions of probabilistic causation. **Exercises and examples new to this edition draw on reports of experiments concerning dangers of cell-phone use, environmental issues, health problems, and other topics of special interest to young adults.**

(4) *Organization of the book.* After a general introduction to arguments, a chapter on language, and a chapter on the characteristics of each of the three broad classes of arguments (inductive, deductive, and fallacies), the next four chapters are devoted to inductive arguments. Although most introductory logic books take up inductive arguments after deductive discussion, I believe that careful work on inductive arguments is a better way to begin the study of logic because students are more familiar with inductive arguments and because it is easier to find examples of them in everyday contexts. Once students become familiar with the structural features of inductive arguments, they are better able to understand the importance of the form of an argument and to appreciate its all-important role in determining the validity of deductive arguments. When they are introduced to the symbolism of formal deductive logic at this point, they see it as a helpful tool rather than a total mystery, and more quickly grasp the use of truth tables and Venn diagrams for proving validity. For teachers who prefer a more traditional route, however, the book is designed so that deductive arguments can be taught before inductive ones by skipping from chapter 3 directly to chapters 8, 9, and 10—and to Appendix 1 for a system of natural deduction, if desired—and then returning to chapters 4 through 7.

(5) *Treatment of fallacies.* Most fallacious forms of reasoning occur with a violation of some standard of correct reasoning. For example, the fallacy of hasty generalization involves drawing a conclusion on the basis of inadequate evidence, typically a generalization on the basis of a sample that is too small. Instead of treating all the fallacies in a separate chapter, this book discusses each in context with the correct form of argument that it superficially resembles. This treatment makes it easier to see how to avoid fallacies as well as to understand why we are sometimes tempted to commit them. **In light of the current popular usage of "begs the question" to mean "raises the question," the new edition includes a brief discussion of the fallacy of begging the question.** For easy reference, Appendix 2 provides an index of fallacies with brief definitions of each.

Pedagogical aids for this book include in each chapter many relevant examples and exercises that illustrate how the general principles of logic and critical thinking apply to everyday life. Answers to even-numbered exercises are provided at the end of the book. **A website for the sixth edition includes outlines of each of the chapters,**

new additional exercises, and interactive tests. A manual for teachers with additional instructional material and answers to questions is also available. Instructors who wish to create their own, **customized version of this text** have access to a vast library of content. The all-new **CengageCompose** site lets instructors quickly review materials to pick what they need for specific courses. Site tools let instructors easily assemble modular learning units in the order they want and immediately provides an online copy for review. Additional content, such as case studies and exercises are also available. Instructors can contact their local Cengage Learning sales representative for pricing and ordering information.

Acknowledgements: The author is grateful to all the students and teachers who have used earlier editions of the book and have offered useful and insightful comments. She is particularly grateful to John Burn, of Wayne State University; Philip Cronce, of Chicago State University; S.E.A. Hughes, of Chaffey College; Karlin Luedtke, of the University of Virginia; Michael Fletcher Maumus, of Brooklyn College; Daniel Yeakel, of Wayne State University; Ellen Kaplan-Maxfield; and several anonymous reviewers for their generous help with this edition.

Merrilee H. Salmon
Pittsburgh, 2011

TABLE OF CONTENTS IN BRIEF

TABLE OF CONTENTS

INTRODUCTION TO LOGIC AND CRITICAL THINKING

Chapter One

INTRODUCTION TO ARGUMENTS

I. INTRODUCTION

We live in the Information Age. Computers that are connected to the Internet allow us to gather information quickly about almost anything. One or two keystrokes will bring up the latest news, biographies of famous and not-so-famous people, details of historical events, sources of quotations, and instructions for cooking food or building furniture. Locating consumer goods and reviews of them is simple. We now take for granted the easy access to information that in the past was difficult to acquire, even for those who had government archives or the finest university library at their disposal.

Moreover, the Internet is not our only source of information. We still read newspapers, books, and magazines. We attend lectures, watch television, listen to the radio, and talk with friends off-line.

All this information, if it is to be useful to us, must be processed—understood, sorted for relevance, checked for accuracy and completeness, balanced against competing information, organized coherently, and analyzed for its implications. If we plan to act on information, we also need to consider how our actions will affect others.

This is where logic and critical thinking come in. They are tools that allow us to navigate the flow of information, to sort out the good from the bad, to find patterns, to combine apparently unrelated bits, and to figure out how information can enrich our intellectual lives and help us manage our practical affairs.

Logic and critical thinking are not new to you. You could hardly have come this far in life without them. Many of the most important logical principles are embedded in language, and you learn them when you learn how to use such terms as *and, or,* and *not.* You use logic and critical thinking when you organize materials to write term papers, try to persuade others to share your beliefs, convince friends to see one movie rather than another, and defend your words and actions against critics. You are using critical thinking when you recognize that many Internet postings are unbelievable nonsense. Some Internet observers say that without editorial filtering of content, 95 percent of what is offered as information on the Internet is garbage. You also recognize that opinions, rumors, and fantasies can slip through editorial filters even when the media are behaving responsibly. You are aware that the source of information matters, and you are cautious about accepting the self-interested statements of politicians and advertisers.

Do you enjoy reading police procedural novels or watching movies based on them, such as *The Girl with the Dragon Tattoo?* Do you watch television programs about investigations of crime scenes? Using logic and critical thinking to figure out these stories is important to your enjoyment of them. You examine the evidence along with the investigator, follow the questioning of witnesses, notice when something that at first seemed insignificant turns out to be relevant, and finally put all the clues together to solve the crime.

You probably also apply your critical thinking skills when you look at photographs in newspapers or on the Internet. Pictures, when they are used to convey information, need critical examination. Photoshopping can digitally enhance and change pictures in deceptive ways. People used to say "pictures don't lie," but that was not strictly true even before the days of photoshopping. Photos could always be retouched, cut, and pasted to create an illusion. Moreover, any photograph, like any story—even a true one—begins from a point of view, establishes a context, and ignores some aspects of a setting to focus on others. Critical thinkers who are aware of this can use their knowledge both to avoid being deceived and to appreciate better the artistry of storytelling and photography.

Did you take an ACT or SAT exam before entering college? These examinations test logic and critical thinking skills. Other examinations, such as the GRE, the LSAT, the GMAT, and the MCAT, which are used to rank students who want to enter graduate or professional schools after college graduation, also have a critical thinking component. The results of these tests are supposed to show whether students will perform well at various levels of education in different fields.

Tests of critical thinking are used also to measure how much students learn when they are in college. In *Academically Adrift,* Richard Arum and Josipa Roksa examine results of testing college students for critical thinking skills as they progress from their first to their fourth year. Their study looked at the scores of thousands of college students who took the Collegiate Learning Assessment exam and found that the critical thinking ability of 45 percent of students did not improve after two years of college. Even after four years, 36 percent did not improve. Educators, shocked by these findings, have tried to explain the poor scores. Arum, one of the authors of the study, blames a lack of academic rigor. He believes that college courses have been so dumbed down that students no longer have to work hard to get good grades. Because students are not sufficiently challenged, he says, they do not spend enough time studying, reading, and writing to improve their critical-thinking skills. Other educators believe, however, that a more likely reason that students did not improve was because they already had high levels of skill when they entered college. Still others say that this type of test does not accurately reflect what students learn in college. Despite differences in how to account for the students' poor performance on the Collegiate Learning Assessment exam, however, all the educators agree that skill in critical thinking is an essential attribute of an educated person.

The aim of this book is to develop students' skill in logic and critical thinking by offering an organized approach to the subject matter and providing skill-building exercises. We begin by characterizing our subject matter.

Critical thinking refers to many different activities and abilities. The following list includes some of the important ones:

- Analyzing the meaning of information;
- Checking information for accuracy and completeness;
- Putting various pieces of information together in a coherent way;

- Comprehending instructions and advice;
- Following directions;
- Solving problems;
- Judging what information is relevant to a particular issue and whether that information is evidence for the truth of some assertion;
- Questioning matters that do not make sense;
- Attempting to avoid mistakes in thinking (fallacies);
- Marshaling relevant information (evidence) when this is needed to support some statement (constructing arguments);
- Judging whether purported evidence supports a conclusion (recognizing and evaluating arguments); and
- Making decisions and plans in light of the best available information or evidence.

We are especially interested in (1) analyzing meanings; (2) recognizing arguments and evaluating their strengths; (3) recognizing and avoiding fallacies; and (4) making decisions in light of available information or evidence.

(1) We need to interpret information to determine whether we understand it. Interpreting verbal information requires special sensitivity to language, which is the topic of the second chapter of this book.

Critical thinking involves paying careful attention to what we hear and read so that we can understand and respond appropriately. So far, we have mostly been concerned with language that transmits information, usually in declarative sentences, such as "Thirty students are in the critical thinking class." When the transmitted information is questionable, it makes sense to ask for evidence—that is, information that supports or undermines the truth of some assertion.

However, language is not always used to provide information. We engage in small talk just to "stay in touch" with others. We *express* our feelings of joy, sorrow, sympathy, anger, hope, and fear in language. We ask *questions*, make *requests*, and issue *warnings* ("Heads up!") and *commands* ("Do not write in this book."). Asking for evidence for expressions of feeling, questions, commands, and the like would not be appropriate.

To understand meanings, we need to pay attention to the circumstances or context in which words are spoken or written. In casual conversation, for example, comments about unpleasant weather can serve to open a conversation or keep it alive. In contrast, if you are interested in weather because you are planning to fly in a small plane, it makes sense to determine whether information that is presented is correct.

When your close friend tells you that her head hurts or that chocolate ice cream is wonderful, she is expressing her feelings, and you don't ask for her to provide evidence for how she feels. In a different context, such as a survey conducted by a company selling painkillers or ice cream, seeking further information to support what people say about their pains and preferences makes sense.

Even though information is often conveyed in songs and poetry, we chiefly pay attention to their expressive content. When we read an epic poem, such as Homer's *Iliad,* we can respond aesthetically to the poem without raising the question of whether Helen of Troy existed and whether her kidnapping by a Trojan prince caused a war between the Greeks and Trojans. The *Iliad* is a work of art and can be valued as such without raising questions of factual accuracy.

It is possible, however, to shift attention from the aesthetic value of works like the *Iliad* and read them for historical clues as well. In fact, many expeditions have been mounted to find evidence for the Trojan War, and scholars debate whether and to what extent the *Iliad* was based on actual historical events. When the focus is on the information contained in the poem rather than on its expressive features, questions about evidence arise.

(2) As these examples show, context and interest guide how we analyze what is said and under what circumstances we need to look for further information to verify the truth of what is said. Context and interest also influence the amount and type of information that is required. If someone cries "Fire!" in the office building where you are working, you don't look for evidence; you get out of the building as soon as possible. If you learn that a building where you used to work burned today, you might check it out before accepting what you have been told.

Being misinformed can result in costly mistakes, but gathering information to use as evidence can also be costly. Costs can be measured in time, money, and even goodwill. We risk offending people, for example, by questioning their accuracy or invading their privacy. Before we decide whether to collect evidence, we have to balance the costs of doing so against the costs of being wrong.

As noted, information that is relevant to the truth of some assertion and presented in support of it is called evidence. The popularity of television series about crime scene investigators (CSI) has made "evidence" a familiar term. In CSI shows, the opening scene usually focuses on the aftermath of some brutal crime, often a murder. A team of investigators descends on the scene to collect information that will allow them to identify the victim, to determine what happened, and to find the person who committed the crime.

Crime scene investigators are experts in forensic science; they focus primarily on physical evidence but also gather verbal evidence when they collect statements from witnesses and examine documents. Using such verbal evidence, they construct arguments to prove who committed a crime. Some, but not all, verbal evidence consists of descriptions and summaries of physical evidence. In many sciences, such as prehistoric archaeology, geology, and chemistry, physical evidence is the primary focus of scientific research. In other disciplines, such as history and many of the social sciences, verbal evidence is more important. Documents, for example, are the focus of most historical work and provide the basic information for constructing arguments about the causes of important historical events.

But historians also look at physical evidence, such as when they determine a date for a document from the composition of its paper and ink. Prehistoric archaeology is concerned with what material remains can tell us about human life before there were written records or where no written records survive. Here physical evidence is paramount. Historical archaeology, however, studies material remains of humans who also kept written records. For example, archaeologists and historians both conduct intense studies of the United States Civil War. Historians use correspondence, military orders, and other documents to build their arguments about what happened and why. Archaeologists survey and dig to find physical remains of fortifications, weapons and other traces of battles, troop movement, and the like. Sometimes the written records do not agree with the physical findings. Either type of information may be misleading. A soldier's eyewitness account of a battle may not give an accurate account of the number of troops engaged or the area of the battlefield; an archaeologist may be misled about the size of a battle because of soil movement and erosion or degradation of battle debris. So we cannot say that one type of evidence always trumps another. In each case of conflict between verbal and physical evidence, arguments for either side must be examined carefully.

(3) Fallacies are mistakes in reasoning, such as thinking that some irrelevant information supports the truth of a statement. Avoiding such mistakes is an important objective for a critical thinker. Most of us are suspicious of exaggerated statements made in advertisements and by politicians, and are apt to ask why we should believe them. Sometimes, however, we do not ask for evidence, or we accept the flimsiest sort of reasons, in support of things that we want to believe anyway. We are especially vulnerable to mistakes in reasoning when our minds are clouded by desire, fear, greed, or other strong emotions.

We often do not look for evidence when information comes from friends and various "authorities," such as teachers, television newscasters, and newspaper reporters. When we trust a source, we accept what that source says. Trust, however, should not always override a need for further information. If a friend tells you that some substance produces a safe high, you would be wise to seek further evidence. The amount of evidence you require depends in part on what could happen if the friend's assertion turns out to be false.

Sometimes we use or accept means other than evidence to persuade people to do things. This is not always wrong. It is appropriate, for example, to appeal to people's sense of compassion to persuade them to aid victims of poverty or oppression. But it is not appropriate to believe, on the basis of such compassion alone, that a particular group is responsible for the oppression, that one type of aid is more appropriate than some other type, or that the democratic government of the impoverished people will collapse if the aid is withheld. To fail to distinguish between nonevidential persuasion and evidence that would support an assertion is to commit a fallacy.

(4) In addition to the critical tasks already mentioned, we need to think critically about our decisions. When we are trying to decide on some action, we want to consider the consequences for ourselves and others. We should examine not only what the various results of our action would be but also how probable each outcome is, and the relative benefits or costs of these outcomes. Would you, for example, invest $5 in a lottery ticket if the winning ticket pays $5,000, but your chance of winning is only one in a million? There are just two outcomes to consider in this case: you win or you don't. But not winning is the outcome with a much higher probability, and you must figure out whether the cost of $5 is worth the risk.

Real-life decisions are rarely so straightforward as the decision whether to purchase a single inexpensive lottery ticket. Many criminals are in jail because—aside from their indifference to moral considerations—they believed correctly that the probability of being apprehended for their crime was small but failed to balance that low probability against the severe cost of being caught.

Sometimes just being aware of the pitfalls of not thinking critically spurs us to more careful thought. As in many other areas of life, however, practice is the best way to improve critical-thinking skills.

Exercise Set 1.1

These exercises are designed to raise your awareness of the need to interpret information, to distinguish between unsupported assertions and arguments providing supporting evidence, and to recognize when evidence must be provided to support what is asserted or to take some recommended action.

1. Many people argue that President Obama is not a native citizen of the United States because his father was Kenyan. His father was in fact from Kenya. Is any further information needed to show that Obama is not a native citizen?

2. Suppose a friend tells you that taking Professor Cyril's class is certain to boost your GPA. Would you decide to take the course based on that statement? What information would you look for to support what your friend says?

3. Suppose you tell your professor that you missed an examination because you were ill. How could you support that assertion?

4. Can you name two disciplines in addition to history in which verbal evidence is usually more important than physical evidence?

5. Recently a reality-show producer announced that he was teaming up with AOL to produce comedic videos of classic works by Shakespeare and others, based on *Cliffs Notes*. The producer says the idea is to bring classic works of fiction to the online masses, including students. Suppose that "Twelfth Night" is the first show produced and a professor asks his Shakespeare class to view it. Does the professor's assignment mean that his Shakespeare course is being dumbed down?

6. You are interested in buying a used 2008 automobile. The salesman at the used-car lot says the former owner was a little old lady who drove the car only on Sundays. Would you base your decision to buy or not on his word? If not, what sort of evidence would you seek?

7. You read the following in a nonfiction travel book about the Greek island Corcyra (Corfu):

> Climb to Vigla in the time of cherries and look down. You will see that the island lies against the mainland roughly in the form of a sickle. On the landward side you have a great bay, noble and serene, and almost completely landlocked. Northward the tip of the sickle almost touches Albania and here the troubled blue of the Ionian is sucked harshly between ribs of limestone and spits of sand. Kalamai fronts the Albanian foothills, and into it the water races as into a swimming pool; a milky ferocious green when the north wind curdles it.
>
> —L. Durrell, *Prospero's Cell*

Durrell says that from a given vantage point (Vigla) in summer (the time of cherries), you can see the sickle shape of the island. He describes (makes further assertions about) Corfu's location with respect to surrounding geographical features, states, and towns. His language is expressive (for example, "the troubled blue . . . is sucked harshly between ribs of limestone") and is designed to convey the feelings of both serenity and untamed beauty that the island inspires.

   a. Does the author offer any evidence for the assertions he makes?
   b. Suppose you are reading this book to acquire some information about the island because you hope to visit it as a tourist. Should you gather evidence to support the accuracy of Durrell's descriptions?
   c. Suppose you are a military commander who plans an invasion of the island. Should you seek evidence for the truth of Durrell's descriptions?

8. You read by a recognized expert on mushrooms about *Amanita verna*, a type of wild mushroom. He says this mushroom looks much like a variety commonly found in grocery stores. It is pure white (when fresh) and very beautiful. Then he says the following:

> Edibility: Deadly poisonous. The symptoms are delayed, making applications of first aid almost useless. Never eat a white *Amanita*.
>
> —A. H. Smith, *The Mushroom Hunter's Field Guide*

   a. What assertions does Dr. Smith make in the quoted passage?
   b. Why do you think Dr. Smith mentioned the similarity between *Amanita verna* and grocery-store mushrooms?
   c. Is "Never eat a white *Amanita*" an assertion?
   d. Would you seek further information before following Dr. Smith's advice?

9. President Abraham Lincoln wrote the following sentence in a letter to a friend:

    If slavery is not wrong then nothing is wrong.

    How would you interpret what Lincoln says? (That is, what does he mean? Does he think slavery is wrong?)

10. In the spirit of saving the planet, the method of shallow cultivation is offered as an alternative to the use of poisonous herbicides to control weeds:

    Shallow cultivation is an effective way to control weeds. Experiments have shown that hoeing or tilling only the top 2–4 inches of soil before seed sprouts can set eventually exhausts most of the vast supply of weed seeds that lie dormant in the soil.

    —P. H. Johnson, "Make Your Soil Smile," *Organic Gardening*, March 1987

    a. What does the author mean by "shallow cultivation"?
    b. Is evidence (physical or verbal) presented for any assertions?
    c. If you are a backyard gardener trying to save money and avoid poisons, would you seek further evidence before trying shallow cultivation instead of herbicides to control weeds?
    d. If you are a truck farmer whose only income depends on the success of your crops, would you seek further evidence that shallow cultivation is an effective means of weed control?

11. A reporter for the University of Arizona's student newspaper conducted telephone interviews with insurance agents from four major companies. She inquired into auto insurance rates for a twenty-year-old male college student who had no history of automobile accidents. Specifying the same automobile make, model, and year in each interview, she found that some identical auto insurance policies cost as much as $200 more per year than others. Her closing line for her story:

    It pays to shop around and research the various types of coverage in order to get the best deal.

    —B. Medlyn, *Arizona Daily Wildcat*

    What evidence supports the author's assertion that it pays to shop for the best deal in auto insurance?

12. Proponents of legalizing marijuana say it is not so dangerous as alcohol insofar as the latter is responsible for thousands of deaths in America annually. They also say that smoking marijuana is safer than smoking tobacco, which is responsible for several fatal diseases.

    a. Describe what evidence, if any, is offered for the assertion that marijuana is less dangerous than alcohol.
    b. Describe what evidence, if any, is offered for the assertion that marijuana is safer than smoking regular cigarettes.
    c. If marijuana really is no more dangerous than alcohol or cigarettes, is that a good enough reason to believe that marijuana should be legalized? Why or why not?

13. Smart phones and tablets will soon handle the majority of our personal computing needs because we want to be mobile while staying connected with the people and things we care about.

Does this argument strongly support the claim about smart phones and tablets? Do you agree that mobility trumps the strengths of laptops—which are semimobile—and desktop computers? What do you consider the biggest disadvantage of mobile devices?

14. In the last act of the play, Lear holds the lifeless body of his daughter Cordelia in his arms. He says the following:

I know when one is dead and when one lives;
She's dead as earth.-- Lend me a looking-glass;
If that her breath will mist or stain the stone,
Why then she lives.

—Shakespeare, *King Lear*

The grief-stricken Lear first admits Cordelia is dead and then hopes in vain that she is still alive. What evidence does he call for to settle the matter?

15. In a memo concerning whether commercial speech is protected by the First Amendment [which guarantees freedom of speech], Supreme Court Justice Harry Blackmun wrote that false or misleading advertising could be regulated

not because it is commercial or pecuniary in purpose but because [regulation] prevents commercial injury and without it commerce would be impossible.

—L. Greenhouse, *Becoming Justice Blackmun*

What reason does Justice Blackmun give for restricting false advertising? Can you clarify the reasoning involved?

16. It is a sobering thought that overexposure to lead was probably a factor in the decline of the Roman Empire. . . . Romans lined their bronze cooking, eating, and wine storage vessels with lead. They thus avoided the obvious and unpleas-ant taste and symptoms of copper poisoning. They traded them for the pleasant flavor and more subtle poisoning associated with lead. Lead was also common in Roman life in the form of paints, and lead pipes were often used to carry water. Examination of the bones of upper-class Romans of the classical period shows high concentrations of lead—possibly one cause of the famous decadence of Roman leadership. The lower classes lived more simply, drank less wine from lead-lined containers, and thus may have picked up far less lead.

—P. Ehrlich, *The Population Bomb*

Ehrlich portrays a decadent upper class suffering from lead poisoning, leading Rome to ruin. However, he does not say whether any bodies of lower-class Romans have been examined for levels of lead.

    a. Assume it is true that the lower classes lived more simply and drank less wine from lead-lined containers. Does this persuade you that they picked up far less lead than the upper classes? Why or why not?

    b. What evidence might support the assertion that the lower classes were exposed to just as much lead? *(Hint: Who was mining the lead, working with lead paints and lead pipes, and manufacturing lead-lined containers for wine?)*

17. On a recent sports news show on television, a football player comments on whether college football players should be paid for playing ball:

Football players should be paid because they work five or six hours a day, and have to play—work again—on Saturdays. It is just like a real job.

    a. The player asserts that playing college football is just like a real job. Does he give any evidence for this?

    b. Can you think of any important differences between playing college football and working at a real job? *(Hint: To answer this you may have to clarify the meaning of "real job.")*

    c. Is it obvious that anyone who works five or six hours a day and again on Saturdays should be paid for that work?

II. ARGUMENTS AND LOGIC

In Exercise Set 1.1, many questions concerned information that can support the truth of some assertion. Such information, or evidence, as already noted, can be either verbal or physical. When you return damaged goods to a store to prove their condition, you present physical evidence to support your claim that the goods are damaged. Similarly, detective stories tell us that without a body (or other physical evidence), it is difficult to support claims that a murder has been committed. Some, but not all, verbal evidence describes physical evidence. To establish the birth date of George Washington, for example, the evidence you seek is verbal—the words, spoken or written, of some authoritative source.

Arguments are sets of sentences consisting of an assertion to be supported and the verbal evidence for that assertion. When we support some sentence by offering verbal evidence for it, we are **arguing** for that sentence.

The terms *argument* and *arguing* are frequently used in another way: *argument* to refer to a dispute or disagreement and *arguing* to refer to the activity of disagreeing. These different meanings are related in the sense that when we are involved in a disagreement or dispute, we often try to show that our position is correct by stating evidence to support it.

In terms of critical thinking, the word *argument* most commonly refers to a set of sentences related in such a way that some purport to provide evidence for another, without any suggestion of dispute or disagreement.

Logic is the field of study concerned with analyzing arguments and appraising their correctness or incorrectness. Thus it plays an important part in critical thinking. Logic, however, is broader than critical thinking because it does not confine itself to examining particular arguments but is a formal systematic study of the principles of valid inference and correct reasoning. For the purposes of this text, we can think of logic and critical thinking as disciplines that are separate but overlapping. We are especially interested in the area of overlap.

Arguments are made up of sentences. The sentences that state the evidence are **premisses**; the sentence being argued for is the **conclusion**. An argument can have any number of premisses, but (by definition) it can have only one conclusion.

The following argument has just one premiss, which is written above the line that separates it from the conclusion:

> Mary has a twin sister.
> _____
> Therefore, Mary is not an only child.

The next argument has two premisses:

> Abortion is the same as murder.
> Murder is wrong.
> _____
> Therefore, abortion is wrong.

Many arguments have more than two premisses. Charles Darwin once said that his entire book, *The Origin of Species,* was just one long argument for a single conclusion: the truth of evolution.

Whether a particular sentence is a premiss or a conclusion depends on the role it plays in a given argument. The sentence "Abortion is the same as murder," which is a premiss in the above argument, might be the conclusion of a different argument:

> Abortion is the deliberate killing of a human fetus.
> Human fetuses are persons.
> Any deliberate killing of a person is murder.
> _____
> Therefore, abortion is murder.

We could continue to develop other arguments with new premisses to support any of the premisses of the above argument, particularly if its truth is challenged. For example, is every deliberate killing of a person murder? Can you think of an exception?

Although it is almost always possible to doubt the premises of an argument and to ask for other arguments to support those premises, this process normally ends when the interested parties find premises that they can agree upon as a starting point. Sometimes this happens quickly, especially when premises state what is easily observed to be true. But when the arguments concern important issues, such as the morality of abortion, it may be hard to agree on premises that are less controversial than the proposed conclusions. Sometimes disagreements are so deep that it is impossible for opponents to find any acceptable premises they can share.

Usually the point of an argument is to support the truth of its conclusion. Demonstrating the truth of a conclusion requires both:

1. the truth of all the premises;[1] and
2. the right type of support by the premises for the conclusion.

Logic pays special attention to the second point—the relationship between the premisses and the conclusion. To determine the *logical* strength of an argument, the question of whether the premises are actually true may be set aside in favor of answering whether the premises *would* support the conclusion *if* they were true. Although the actual truth of premises is relevant for critical thinking, it is important to recognize that the truth of premises and the support they would provide for a conclusion if they were true are two separate issues.

Premises and conclusions of arguments are usually **declarative** sentences, which present information and make assertions. Declarative sentences—unlike ordinary questions and commands—can be either true or false.

Occasionally you will find that a special kind of question called a *rhetorical question* serves as a premiss or conclusion of an argument. The following excerpt, taken from an editorial, argues against using female American soldiers to sexually humiliate detainees during interrogations at military prisons, as described in a Pentagon report.

> Does anyone in the military believe that a cold-blooded terrorist who has withstood months of physical and psychological abuse will crack because a woman runs her fingers through his hair suggestively or watches him disrobe? If devout Muslims become terrorists because they believe Western civilization is depraved, does it make sense to try to unnerve them by having Western women behave like trollops?
>
> —Editorial Page, "The Women of Gitmo," *The New York Times*, 7/15/2005

In this argument the premises have the grammatical form of questions. But these are rhetorical questions, which means they are devices to emphasize the only suitable response. The writer implies that these questions demand resoundingly negative answers. Thus such questions, unlike ordinary questions, are used to "state the facts."

---

[1] An exception to this requirement for true premises occurs in a form of reasoning called indirect argument.

Using rhetorical questions instead of declarative sentences as premises or conclusions of arguments is a dramatic and often persuasive way to make a point.

Example

Your friend says to you, "You're not going to wear *that* shirt to the party, are you?" (Rhetorical question.)

III. RECOGNIZING ARGUMENTS

Before learning how to classify and evaluate different types of arguments, we want to distinguish arguments from other patterns of language, such as unsupported assertions. In arguments, a sentence that is asserted is supported by other sentences. It makes no sense to accuse someone of presenting a poor argument for a case if no argument at all is offered. The most we can reasonably do in such circumstances is to say that an argument *should* be given to support the assertion.

When we are trying to identify an argument, the first question to ask is what point the author or speaker is making. When we have identified the sentence that makes the point (the conclusion, if it is an argument), then we can ask what assertions, if any, are intended as support or evidence (premises) for that point.

Examples

1. Cigarette smoking is a serious health hazard. Statistical studies show that cigarette smokers are not only at much greater risk for contracting lung cancer but also have higher incidences of emphysema and heart disease.

In this example, the claim that cigarette smoking is a serious health hazard is the conclusion, and citing statistical studies showing that smokers have higher rates of certain types of serious illness than nonsmokers supports it.

2. Marijuana should not be legalized because it is potentially dangerous and not enough is known about its long-term effects, and because use of marijuana leads to use of hard drugs.

Even though this argument is stated in a single sentence, we can divide that sentence into parts that are themselves sentences and that stand in the relationship of premises and conclusion. The conclusion of this argument is the declarative sentence: "Marijuana should not be legalized." The three premises, conjoined in a compound declarative sentence, are: "it is potentially dangerous," "not enough is known about its long-term effects," and "use of marijuana leads to use of hard drugs." Each of these component sentences is an assertion, the truth of which can be questioned. For this argument to establish the truth of its conclusion, all of these premises must be true, *and* together they must provide reasons for accepting the conclusion.

Sometimes special words called **indicator words** introduce the premises or the conclusion of an argument. In several arguments presented already, the word *therefore* served to introduce conclusions. This is a very common use of the term in English. Other terms that often introduce conclusions of arguments are *thus, and so, consequently, necessarily, hence, it follows that,* and *for that reason.* Words that frequently indicate premises are *because, since, for,* and *for the reason that.*

In the following arguments, the indicator words are italicized:

1. There is no difference in the dedication or productivity of men and women office workers. *Therefore,* men and women office workers in comparable positions should be paid the same.

In the above argument for equalizing pay between men and women office workers, the indicator word *therefore* introduces the conclusion of the argument. The premises are stated before the conclusion.

2. Regarding Wael Ghonim's use of Facebook and Twitter in promoting the Egyptian revolution:

> There [is] nothing new about revolutions being social and involving media, *for* in the American Revolution, a pamphlet published in 1776, "Common Sense," by Thomas Paine was second only to the Bible in readership and inspired the colonists to take action against their British ruler. Besides being widely read in private, "Common Sense" also was featured in readings in taverns and coffee houses.
>
> —L.G. Crovitz, *The Wall Street Journal*, 2/14/2011

In the argument above, the conclusion is stated first without an indicator word. The word *for* introduces the premises.

Although these indicator words often signal premises or conclusions of arguments, they have other uses as well. Thus when we see these words, we cannot take for granted that we have identified an argument. *Since,* for example, is sometimes used to indicate passage of time, as in "Every week since Harry has been away at college, he has received his hometown paper in the mail."

Because is frequently used to express a causal connection between two events rather than to offer evidence. An example occurs in the sentence "Tony Blair became unpopular because of his role involving Great Britain in the war in Iraq."

Here no attempt is made to prove that Tony Blair, the former British prime minister, became unpopular. Presumably that is so widely known that it needs no support. The sentence asserts, but does not argue, that the reason for his unpopularity was his conduct regarding the war in Iraq. If we want to *argue* that leading Britain into the war caused his unpopularity, we would present evidence that Blair enjoyed popularity before he acted on questionable information about the danger Iraq posed to Britain. We might gather evidence that people were angry with his sending soldiers into a war based on false assertions. Or the argument might try to eliminate other possible causes of his unpopularity, such as slanderous attacks by Blair's political enemies.

When a subject matter is unfamiliar, it can be difficult to distinguish a causal assertion from an argument. If, for example, someone were to tell me that the National Collegiate Athletic Association (NCAA) will soon rule that football players can be paid by colleges for playing ball *because* there has been so much pressure in favor of this move, I would not know whether she was presenting evidence for the assertion that the rule will be changed or whether she was explaining why the rule will be changed. Because I don't keep up with football news, I don't know which rulings have been made or are being contemplated.

If I am being told that pressure for paying players is a *reason to believe* that the ruling will change, the passage is intended as an argument. If I am being told that the new rule going into effect is a result of pressure that was exerted, the passage is a causal explanation. In many cases we must ask questions, examine the context for clues, or make "educated guesses" about the intent of a set of sentences before we can decide whether it argues for a conclusion or makes a causal assertion.

The indicator terms *for, since, thus,* and *therefore* are also used in causal explanations of why something happened: "He was invited to the wedding since he's my mother's favorite cousin." "My dog ran away; therefore I am putting up this sign to ask for help in finding him." "She sets high goals for herself; thus she was disappointed to place third in the marathon."

Although sentences that assert a causal connection are not themselves arguments, they can be premises or conclusions of arguments, as in the following example.

> Improper handling of raw poultry is a major cause of salmonella poisoning.
> Salmonella can be controlled by cooking poultry throughly and disinfecting or
>   cleaning with hot soapy water any surfaces that have been in contact with raw poultry.
> _____
> Therefore, if you want to avoid infecting your family with salmonella poison,
>   you will clean all surfaces that have been in contact with raw poultry.

In addition to their use in causal statements, *thus* and *therefore* sometimes introduce an example or an important point, as in "Not all mammals give birth to live young. *Thus* the platypus is an egg-laying mammal." Closely related to this meaning of *thus* is its use as a synonym for "in this way": "Every day during the last school term, I read over what I had written the previous day, crossed out the rough parts, and rewrote bits of it. Thus I learned to write a decent essay."

Although indicator words can alert us to the presence of an argument, because of their other uses they are not absolutely reliable. Moreover, some arguments lack any indicator words. In these cases, we depend on the context as well as the meanings of the sentences to determine whether someone is presenting an argument or instead a series of unsupported assertions.

Here is an argument that has no indicator words:

> A judgment of acquittal by reason of insanity is appropriate only when a jury verdict of guilty would violate the law or the facts. We cannot say that this was the situation in Washington's case. The district court did not err in its refusal to enter a judgment of acquittal by reason of insanity.

—United States District Court of Appeals,
(District of Columbia; Bazelon, *Washington v. United States*)

The context (a decision by a court of appeals) is helpful in determining that the above is an argument, because court rulings are supposed to be supported by reasons. The last sentence of the passage asserts that the district court's judgment was not in error, and the reasons for this (the premises) are given in the first two sentences. To decide whether an argument is present, we should ask ourselves (1) "What point is being made?" and (2) "What evidence is offered to support it?" In this case, we can spot the conclusion if we know that it is the business of district courts of appeals to decide whether lower court rulings are correct. Without background knowledge, however, it can be difficult to decide whether a given sentence is intended to be a premiss or a conclusion.

When no indicator words are present, try to insert them (premiss indicators before suspected premisses and conclusion indicators before conclusions) to see whether the passage makes sense when reconstructed in this way. This method will not always work, because if we are unsure of the context we may be unable to see whether one way of constructing the passage makes more sense than another. Assuming that the district court of appeals was ruling on whether the lower court was correct, if we insert indicator words in the previous example, it reads like this:

> *Since* a judgment of acquittal by reason of insanity is appropriate only when a jury verdict of guilty would violate the law or the facts and *since* we cannot say that this was the situation in Washington's case, *therefore* the district court did not err in its refusal to enter a judgment of acquittal by reason of insanity.

The meaning of the original passage is not changed when the indicator words are inserted; this supports our view that an argument is present and that we have identified its premisses and conclusion correctly.

When we insert indicator words to mark the premisses and conclusion of an argument, we must pay attention to stylistic variations in the way arguments are presented in ordinary language. Frequently, for emphasis, the conclusion of an argument is stated before the premisses, but it is stylistically awkward to begin an argument with *therefore*. If we want to insert indicator words and at the same time have the passage retain correct English style, we sometimes have to reorder the sentences, putting the conclusion sentence last.

In summary, it is helpful, when trying to decide whether an argument is present, to consider the context carefully and to ask the following:

- What point is the speaker or writer trying to make?
- Is the speaker or writer presenting evidence to support the truth of some assertion?
- Is the speaker or writer trying to explain why something happened rather than arguing that it did happen?
- Is an example or illustration—rather than an argument—being presented?

Exercise Set 1.2

PART I. In each of the following arguments:

Use the indicator words to help identify the premisses and the conclusion.

Rewrite the argument in *standard form*. That is to say, write each premiss on a line by itself. Underneath the last premiss, draw a line, and write the conclusion beneath the line. Although in standard form premisses are written above the conclusion, it is advisable to identify the conclusion first. Consider the following example. The conclusion is enclosed in parentheses, and each premiss is underlined:

> (The earth is spherical in shape.) For <u>the night sky looks different in the northern and southern parts of the earth</u>, and <u>this would be so if the earth were spherical in shape.</u>
>
> —Aristotle, *de Caelo*

In standard form the argument, which has two premisses, looks like this:

> The night sky looks different in the northern and southern parts of the earth.
> This would be so if the earth were spherical in shape.
> ———————————————————————————
> The earth is spherical in shape.

1. Since identical twins, who have the same genes, are more likely to have the same blood pressure than fraternal twins, who share half the same genes, we can conclude that high blood pressure is inherited.

2. People who say that America is facing inevitable decline as a world power are wrong because the serious problems the U.S. faces, such as massive debt, poor education and political impasse, all have solutions.

3. In England under the blasphemy laws it is illegal to express disbelief in the Christian religion. It is also illegal to teach what Christ taught on the subject of non-resistance. Therefore, whoever wishes to avoid being a criminal must profess to agree with Christ's teachings but must avoid saying what that teaching was.

   —B. Russell, *Skeptical Essays*

4. A coin has been tossed twelve times and has shown a *head* each time. Thus it is very likely that the next time this coin is tossed it will also show a *head*.

5. In poker, a flush beats a straight, and a full house beats a flush, so a full house beats a straight.

6. Moral philosophy is an indispensable first step in that larger political campaign [for restricting smoking] because we need to be persuaded that something *ought* to be done before there is any hope whatsoever that it will.

—R. E. Goodin, *No Smoking*

7. The poet ought always to seek what is necessary or likely in characters as well as in the construction of the incidents, so that it is either necessary or likely that a character say or do such things as well as necessary, or likely that this incident arise with that one. It is apparent, therefore, that the solutions of plots ought to happen as a result of the plots themselves and not from a contrivance.

—Aristotle, *Poetics*

8. **Background:** *Feng shui*, sometimes called "geomancy," refers to traditional Chinese beliefs concerning the manipulation and flow of energy (*qi*).

A building facing a vacant lot on the south is good geomantically because in China, during the summer, the south winds are refreshing and bring good ventilation or cosmic breath.

—E. Lip, *Feng Shui for the Home*

9. Over a period of two years now, I have tested my instrument [the newly invented telescope]—or rather dozens of my instruments—by hundreds and thousands of experiments involving thousands and thousands of objects, near and far, large and small, bright and dark; hence I do not see how it can enter the mind of anyone that I have simplemindedly remained deceived in my observation.

—Galileo, cited by D. Boorstin in *The Discoverers*

10. Since creationism can be discussed effectively as a scientific model, and since evolutionism is fundamentally a religious philosophy rather than a science, it is clearly unsound educational practice and even unconstitutional for evolution to be taught and promoted in the public schools to the exclusion or detriment of special creation.

—H. Morris, *Introducing Creationism in the Public Schools*

11. Evolutionary theory merits a place among the sciences for . . . [i]t offers a unified set of problem-solving strategies that can be applied, by means of independently testable assumptions, to answer a myriad of questions about the characteristics of organisms, their interrelationships, and their distributions.

—P. Kitcher, *Abusing Science*

12. In the cast of a die [one of a pair of dice], the probability of ace is one-sixth, because we do actually know either by reasoning or by experience, that in a hundred or a million of throws, ace is thrown in about one-sixth of that number, or one in six times.

—J. S. Mill, *A System of Logic*

13. All those who have been president of the United States have worked hard and tried their best to make our nation as good as it can be. Thus, we should view any of their actions that brought harm to the country to be the result of bad decisions and mistakes rather than an evil intention to weaken America.

14. Last night how they'd [FBI agents searching for a kidnapped baby] figured it was: People who *buy* babies black market don't talk about it. But, okay, eventually they do have to buy *things*. So, if the Graves baby is alive, somewhere, maybe in Ohio, maybe far from Pittsburgh—could be in Switzerland, for God's sake—it got handed over or is about to be handed over to someone who might buy a stroller or some health insurance.

—K. George, *Taken*

PART II. In each of the following arguments, the conclusion is enclosed in parentheses. Try to insert appropriate indicator words before sentences that are premises or conclusions, and see whether the passage makes sense. With some choices of indicator words, the sentences need to be rearranged.

1. Women tend to do better on essay tests than on timed multiple-choice tests. Men tend to do better on timed multiple-choice tests than on essay tests. SAT tests are timed multiple-choice tests. (SAT tests are biased in favor of men.)

2. (The human mind is not the same thing as the human brain.) The human body, including the brain, is a material thing. The human mind is a spiritual thing. Nothing is both a material thing and a spiritual thing.

—K. Campbell, *Body and Mind*

3. (The year 1859 is perhaps the most important one in the history of biology to date.) In that year Charles Darwin published his theory of evolution by natural selection, which has deeply affected not only biology, but other branches of human thought as well.

—L. C. Dunn and T. H. Dobshansky, *Heredity, Race and Society*

4. (A mortgage-backed security has a prepayment risk.) If a homeowner decides to pay off a mortgage ahead of schedule, i.e., prepay the mortgage, the mortgage-backed security containing that particular mortgage does not receive all the anticipated interest payments.

—*Investment Forum*

5. With no legal, regulated disposal facilities available, illegal dumping becomes more attractive. Far more damage will be done to the environment from illegal dumping than from regulated, legal disposal. (Hazardous-waste disposal facilities are essential to the protection of Pennsylvania's environment.)

—F. Kury, *Pittsburgh Post-Gazette*

6. Bernard Madoff, imprisoned after being convicted of defrauding investors of billions of dollars in a giant Ponzi scheme, claimed in an interview that some

of the banks he dealt with knew what he was doing but chose to ignore it. The banks denied any knowledge of the fraud.

Experienced news reporters commenting on this interview said that Madoff had done nothing but lie over the decades while he was committing the fraud, so (why would anyone believe him now?)

7. Since women tend to live longer than men and on average earn less than men and have less pension coverage than men, (women need to invest more for retirement).

8. (Poker is one of the finest exercises for keeping gray matter alive.) "Poker involves mathematics, planning, and strategy—all complicated mental processes—and these are exactly what imparts the benefit of producing more brain neurons," says Paul D. Nussbaum, Ph. D., a neuropsychologist and an expert in Alzheimer's disease at the University of Pittsburgh School of Medicine. Further, a regular activity must be both novel and mentally challenging to prevent dementia, and poker can provide both forms of brain stimulation.

—R. Lederer, "We All Speak Poker," *AARP Magazine*, July–August 2005

PART III. In each of the following, the *indicator words* are italicized. Try to determine whether an argument is offered or whether the *indicator words* are used as part of a causal explanation, to indicate passage of time, or for some other purpose:

1. In some parts of the country, parents have objected to high-school classes requiring students to read ROMEO AND JULIET, by William Shakespeare, *because* it portrays teen lust, drug use, and suicide.

2. Blessed is the man that walketh not in the counsel of the ungodly, nor standeth in the way of sinners, nor sitteth in the seat of the scornful. *For* the Lord knoweth the way of the righteous; but the way of the ungodly shall perish.

—Book of Psalms

3. President Nixon resigned *because* of the scandal associated with the Watergate break-in and his desire to avoid impeachment.

4. *Since* Peter the Great, there has been a long, distinguished list of non-Westerners who have sought to bring the ideas of the West to their countries.

—F. Zakaria, *The Post-American World*

5. Man disavows, and Deity disowns me:
   Hell might afford my misery a shelter;
   Therefore hell keeps her ever hungry mouths all
   Bolted against me.

—W. Cowper, "Lines Written During a Period of Insanity"

6. This promotion of colleges to universities is consistent with the long-honored American custom of "raising" a thing by adding to the number of syllables used to describe it. For example, rain is raised to precipitation. College has only two syllables, and even seminary only four. But university, with five syllables, adds distinction. *Thus*: University of Montevallo, Alabama . . . Upper Iowa University . . . Midwestern University, Texas.

—P. Fussell, *Class*

7. *Since* our laws of logic are derived from our practical experience, our reasoning can be valid only so long as we apply it to our environment as it is here and now, so to speak. Should our environment change, we would have to change our logic accordingly.

—N. A. Court, *Mathematics in Fun and in Earnest*

8. To air one's views at an improper time may be in bad taste. If you have received a letter inviting you to speak at the dedication of a new cat hospital, and you hate cats, your reply, declining the invitation, does not necessarily have to cover the full range of your emotions. You must make it clear that you will not attend, but you do not have to let fly at cats. The writer of the letter asked a civil question; attack cats, then, only if you can do so with good humor, good taste, and in such a way that your answer will be courteous as well as responsive. *Since* you are out of sympathy with cats, you may quite properly give this as a reason for not appearing at the dedicatory ceremonies of a cat hospital. But bear in mind that your opinion of cats was not sought, only your services as a speaker. Try to keep things straight.

—W. Strunk, Jr. and E. B. White, *The Elements of Style*

9. In Richard Strauss's tragic opera *Elektra*, Elektra is obsessed with revenge against her mother Klytämnestra and her mother's lover Aegisth, because the two of them murdered Elektra's father. She waits for her brother Orest to return home to help her, but when she hears that he is dead, she seeks the help of her younger sister, Chrysothemis. Chrysothemis shrinks from the deed, but Elektra says (sings):

You must help me kill Klytämnestra *because* she murdered our father.

—R. Strauss, *Elektra*

10. In the same scene of the opera, Elektra also sings:

You must help me kill Klytämnestra *because* Orest is not here to help me do it.

—R. Strauss, *Elektra*

IV. EXTENDED ARGUMENTS

Thus far, we have looked at arguments that offer one or more premises in support of a single conclusion. Frequently, however, in real life, we meet not only arguments like this but also a series of interrelated arguments—sometimes in a single paragraph or even a single sentence. We call these **extended arguments.** Some extended arguments attempt to establish a conclusion by stating premisses and, in addition, by producing evidence for those premisses. Thus, the premisses of the main argument are conclusions of subsidiary arguments. Some arguments display both the pros and cons of a position and present arguments for each side before selecting one conclusion. Other extended arguments present several different arguments in support of the same conclusion. Still others argue for several closely related conclusions. The techniques for analyzing these more complicated extended arguments—that is, for identifying premisses and conclusions—are just the same as for simpler arguments, with slight "bookkeeping" modifications.

First of all, as before, it is helpful to try to discover the main point the speaker or writer is making and to identify the reasons offered in support of that point. Then we can begin to investigate whether any of the premisses of that argument are supported by reasons. If they are, we can say that the main argument contains *subarguments*, which can be investigated as well. This procedure can be messy. But our goal is to understand complicated arguments by reducing them to simpler parts.

Example

Women need to invest more for retirement, for several reasons.

1. According to the National Bureau for Health Statistics (2009), women tend to live an average of 5 years longer than men, and thus spend a longer time in retirement.
2. On average, women earn less than men. According to Bureau of Labor Statistics (2010) women who worked full-time, year-round earned only 80 cents for every dollar earned by men. Because women earn less money, they have less money to invest.
3. Women have less pension coverage than men. According to the Social Security Administration, while earning lower wages, women also work fewer years than men, often because they are caring for children or elderly parents. They thus earn fewer credits for social security. In addition, women are less likely than men to work for companies that provide 401-K or other private pension plans.

In the above extended argument, the main conclusion is stated first, followed by three reasons for accepting the conclusion. Each of the reasons is supported by statistical evidence taken from information provided by U.S. government agencies.

Example

Since there can be no talk of an independent ideology formulated by the working masses themselves in the process of their movement, <u>the only choice is either bourgeois or socialist ideology</u>. There is no middle course. Hence {to belittle the socialist ideology in any way, to turn aside from it in the slightest degree means to strengthen the bourgeois ideology}.

—V. I. Lenin, *What Is to Be Done?*

In the above extended argument, the main conclusion is stated last, following the conclusion indicator word *hence.* The premiss that supports this conclusion is underlined and is itself supported by the sentence following the premiss indicator word *since.* In this example, as in many extended arguments, a conclusion of a preliminary argument is restated in simpler terms ("There is no middle course") when it is used as the premiss of the next argument.

Exercise Set 1.3

Isolate the arguments in each of the following passages and identify their premisses and conclusions. Write each argument in standard form.

1. We have seen that the capacity to be alone is a valuable resource. It enables men and women to get in touch with their deepest feelings; to come to terms with loss; to sort out their ideas; to change attitudes. In some instances, even the enforced isolation of prison may encourage the growth of the creative imagination.

   —A. Storr, *Solitude*

2. Because publishers are aiming at a national market, the number-one criterion for any textbook is avoidance of controversy. Since they must respond to a variety of specific criteria from their buyers, this has resulted in what has been called the "dumbing down" of textbooks.

   —C. Holden, *Science* 235 (1987)

3. **Background:** This passage describes the popular energy behind the movement that ousted Egyptian President Hosni Mubarak in early 2011. Free, or open, trade is a policy that allows trade across international boundaries without interference, such as imposing special taxes or duties.

   There is a wholly political argument for open trade with Egypt. That energy we saw on TV can go only in a few directions. Egyptians can pour their energies into building a 21st-century economy for Egypt and with it a more productive and peaceful Middle East. Or, if the Egyptian economy falters, they will redirect that energy into grievance and blame seeking, which in our time is a straight path to joining Islamic jihad against the West. . . . In short, we should want them to make money, not war. For now it looks like that is exactly what most of the faces of Egypt's remarkable revolution want to do.

   —D. Henninger, *The Wall Street Journal,* 2/17/2011

4. Through analytic techniques of diverse kinds, through group therapies and encounter groups, by means of hypnosis, drug therapy, and brain stimulation, self-disclosure [the revealing of personal secrets] is aided and interpreted. But the therapeutic value of any one of these techniques is far from established; and the

need for caution in choosing persons best qualified to listen to personal revelation is increasingly clear…. The caution is well founded. One cannot trust all who listen to confessions to be either discreet or especially capable of bringing solace or help. In addition, the act of confessing can in itself increase the vulnerability of persons who expose their secrets, especially in institutionalized practices. Studies have shown that when self-revelation flows in one direction only, it increases the authority of the listener while decreasing that of the speaker. In ordinary practices of confiding, the flow of personal information is reciprocal, as the revelations of one person call forth those of another; but in institutionalized practices, there is no such reciprocity. On the contrary, therapists and others who receive personal confidences are often taught to restrain their natural impulse to respond in kind.

—S. Bok, *Secrets*

5. The grouping of these drugs [LSD, DOM, DMT, psilocybin, mescaline] is not arbitrary or simply for the sake of convenience. They can be considered members of the same drug class for two important reasons. First, they elicit a common set of effects: sensory perceptual (distorted time sense; altered sensations of colors, sounds, and shapes, ultimately developing into complex, often multimodal hallucinations; and synesthesia, or mixing of the senses); psychic (dreamlike feelings; depersonalization; and rapid and often profound alternations of affect such as depression or elation); and somatic (dizziness, tingling skin, weakness, tremor, nausea, and increased reflexes). Second, and perhaps more important, these drugs display cross-tolerance—that is, a decreased efficacy of one drug taken shortly after another drug. Thus, if a person has a full-blown hallucinatory experience following ingestion of LSD, the normal hallucinatory response to mescaline or DOM taken the next day will be dramatically blunted or abolished. Therefore, even though it may be argued, and perhaps correctly so, that drugs such as marijuana and PCP should also be classified as hallucinogenic, they do not belong to the class of LSD-like drugs since they show no evidence of cross-tolerance with them.

—B. L. Jacobs , "How hallucinogenic drugs work," *American Scientist 75*
(July–August 1987):386

6. **Background:** Steve Jobs, founder of Macintosh, dropped out of college but stayed on campus, sitting in on courses that interested him. Fascinated by calligraphic work on campus posters and labels, he sat in on a calligraphy course to see how it was done.

None of this had even a hope of any practical application in my life. But 10 years later, when we were designing the first Macintosh computer, it all came back to me. And we designed it all into the Mac. It was the first computer with beautiful typography. If I had never dropped in on that single course in college, the Mac would have never had multiple typefaces or proportionally spaced fonts. And since Windows just copied the Mac, it's likely that no personal computer would have them. If I had never dropped out, I would never have dropped in on this calligraphy class, and personal computers might not have the wonderful typography that they do.

—Steve Jobs, 2005 Commencement Address at Stanford

V. RECONSTRUCTING ARGUMENTS

1. INCOMPLETELY STATED ARGUMENTS

We have already considered the problem of identifying premises and conclusions when there are no indicator words to help us recognize the parts of an argument. In addition, many arguments in English are incompletely stated, which is to say that some premisses and even the conclusion of an argument may be omitted. Once we recognize the presence of an argument, we frequently have to reconstruct it by supplying missing parts before we can evaluate its strength. In ordinary language, arguments may be stated incompletely to avoid boring a listener or reader with the obvious.

Suppose you are wondering whether Jeb, your lab partner in a chemistry class who was worried about paying a tuition bill, settled his account. Another friend who works in the registrar's office says, "Jeb must have come up with the money, since his application to graduate on Sunday has been approved." The approval of Jeb's application to graduate convinces you that his bill has been paid because, as every student knows, degrees are not granted to those with unpaid tuition bills. Even though "No student with an unpaid bill can graduate" is unstated, this is a premise of the argument that supports the conclusion that Jeb's tuition was paid. Without this premise, there is no clear connection between bill paying and graduation. Because you and your friend are both aware of the relevance and the truth of this premise, however, there was no need to mention it.

Many, but not all, unstated premisses are, like the one just mentioned, **generalizations.** Sentences that say that *all* or *no* members of one class are members of another class are **universal generalizations.** "No student with an unpaid bill can be graduated" is an example of a (negative) universal generalization. "All tuition bills must be paid before graduation" is an example of an affirmative universal generalization.

"The Washingtons are probably wealthy, since they drive a new Cadillac" is another example of an argument with a missing—but presumably obvious—premise: "Most families who drive new Cadillacs are wealthy." Generalizations that state that some proportion of members of one class are members of another class are **statistical generalizations.** The universal generalization *"All* families who drive new Cadillacs are wealthy" would not be a good choice for the missing premise in this argument because driving an expensive automobile is not an infallible mark of wealth. "Most families who drive new Cadillacs are wealthy" is more likely to be true than "All families who drive new Cadillacs are wealthy." An indication—not always present—that a statistical generalization is implicit in the above argument is the word *probably*.

Statistical generalizations are sometimes stated numerically, as in "Fifty-three percent of American voters voted for Obama in the 2010 presidential election," or "Fourteen infants out of one hundred born to mothers with HIV are also infected with HIV." Universal generalizations can be thought of as limiting cases of statistical generalizations. That is to say, a generalization is statistical if its percentage is greater than 0 percent and less than 100 percent; otherwise a generalization is universal. As we have seen, not all statistical generalizations are stated numerically; *most, usually, seldom, frequently*, and *rarely* can indicate a statistical generalization. Statistical generalizations, like universal generalizations, provide a link between the particular facts mentioned in the stated premisses of an argument ("the Washingtons drive a new Cadillac") and the conclusion ("the Washingtons are wealthy").

In the context of an ordinary conversation or informal presentation of an argument, it is appropriate to omit premisses that are obviously true. However, if we are concerned with checking the correctness of an argument, it is good to state that argument as completely as possible. This means that we must occasionally spell out even what is obvious to everyone.

Another reason for seeking out the implicit or assumed, but unstated, premisses in an argument is that when some hidden premisses are exposed, they turn out not to be obvious after all. Consider the following extended argument offered by a student who is trying to persuade a classmate of the benefits of nuclear power:

> Well, I'm for it because, first of all, we're eventually going to use up all our fossil fuels. And, if we don't do that soon, we're going to have really bad problems with acid rain, which we already have. The Canadians definitely feel the effects of acid rain. But we don't think about that because we [in the United States] don't feel the effects right now. And eventually we're not going to have an ozone layer left. Even though there are definite costs to nuclear power—I mean a disaster like there was at Chernobyl would be a nightmare—but if the plants were safely managed and operated, then a disaster like that would be less likely. . . .

At this point, the other student in the discussion interrupted to point out that nuclear power is not the only alternative to fossil fuels. Other sources of power, such as wind, hydroelectric, and solar, are available, she said. In this discussion (which was recorded in a study of how students reason in ordinary conversation), the first student had not said anything like "The only choice is between fossil fuels and nuclear power," but the second student correctly understood that this was a hidden premiss in her argument. The first student's argument for the use of nuclear power focused on problems with fossil fuels, but this line of reasoning would support nuclear power only if other alternatives were not available or were not adequate to meet our energy needs.

After the hidden premiss (which in this case was not a generalization) was pointed out and challenged, the first student revised her argument. She conceded the point that solar, wind, and hydroelectric power might eventually be feasible alternatives to nuclear power and fossil fuels but said that, at the present stage of technological development, the alternatives could not supply the nation's energy needs.

In the give-and-take of conversation, which is where most of us learn to develop our skills at critical thinking, premisses that are implicit (unstated) are most easily recognized when they are not shared by all participants. The first student in the conversation knew about wind, solar, and hydroelectric power, but she did not consider them real alternatives to nuclear and fossil fuels. The second student was more optimistic about the development and use of alternate power sources, and so she was unwilling to accept the unstated premiss of the first student: that one has to choose between the dangers of nuclear power and the depletion of fossil fuels, with their attendant pollution.

The mistake of basing arguments on a premiss (either stated or unstated) that only two choices are available when a wider range of alternatives exists is common enough to be labeled a *fallacy*. The fallacy has several names: *black-and-white thinking*, *false choice*, *false dilemma*, and *false dichotomy*. This fallacy can be difficult to recognize when the premiss concerning the choice of alternatives is not stated.

An unstated premiss shared by participants in a conversation can sometimes be recognized by noting when it is referred to later as if it has been stated. For example, in another recorded discussion of nuclear power, one student argued for nuclear power on the basis that it costs less than fossil fuels. Although this stated premiss was challenged by another student, he did not challenge the unstated assumption (which both students shared) that the *least costly alternative should be chosen*. Later, however, when the second student pointed out that nuclear power actually costs more when the costs of nuclear waste disposal (currently borne by the U.S. government) are included, he remarked that because the first student thought the least costly alternative should be adopted, he therefore should not support nuclear power. Although the first student had not actually said that the least costly alternative should be adopted, he accepted the second student's remark as if he had said it, indicating this was indeed an unstated premiss in his argument for the use of nuclear power.

The following two arguments depend on unstated generalizations that are somewhat more difficult to detect than the unstated premisses in the examples just mentioned.

The first argument is taken from *Crime and the Criminal Law* by Barbara Wootton, one of the first female members of the British Parliament.

> To punish people merely for what they have done would be unjust, for the forbidden act might have been an accident for which the person who did it cannot be held to blame.

The conclusion of Wootton's argument is that it is unjust to punish people without taking into account their intentions as well as their actions. The reason she offers for this conclusion is that the forbidden act might have been a blameless accident. The unstated premiss, required to connect blameless actions with ones for which they should not be punished, is a generalization: No persons should be punished for acts for which they do not deserve to be blamed.

Is this general principle correct? In the British system of law, as in the American, actions committed with an evil intent or a "guilty mind" *(mens rea)* are distinguished from accidental actions. Most of us would agree that people should be *blamed* only for acts they intended to do, or at least were negligent in failing to prevent. But both the American and British legal systems sometimes do punish people for "accidental" acts, even when no blame is warranted.

Example

If you are caught in an elevator stuck between floors for an hour and, as a result, find a parking ticket when you return to your car, you are not to blame for overparking. Nevertheless, you probably still have to pay the fine because the law treats this as a case of **strict liability**. In other words, the law recognizes no excuses. Many considerations can be offered to justify strict liability laws. In the case of parking fines, strict liability is justified by appealing to the good use the city makes of money collected from this source, the minor nuisance of paying a small fine even when the violator is not to blame, and the excessive court costs of allowing defenses for simple parking violations.

If we accept the principle of strict liability for some kinds of action, we cannot accept the general principle that connects punishment with blame in an unqualified way. The apparent conflict between strict liability and the principle that conduct should be punished only if it is blameworthy can be resolved by restricting the application of strict liability to **noncriminal** cases. Wootton's book, *Crime and the Criminal Law,* is clearly concerned with criminal justice, and her remarks can be taken to apply in this context. The principle connecting punishment with blameworthiness is well established in Anglo-American criminal law.

Example

> Since reason alone can never *produce* any action or give rise to volition [desire], I infer that the same faculty [reason] is incapable of *preventing* volition or of disputing the preference with any passion or emotion.

> —D. Hume, *A Treatise of Human Nature*

Hume, writing in the eighteenth century, was concerned with the nonrational aspect of human life—the area of feelings and emotion. One of his famous sayings is "Reason is and ought only to be the slave of the passions." Hume's words are less startling when we realize that "passions" in those days referred in a general way to human feelings, not specifically to sexual passion. Hume believed that human morality must be founded on the sort of goodness that human beings—with all their biological limitations, natural feelings, and sympathies—are able to achieve, rather than on some intellectual view of an ideal form of goodness.

In this argument for "natural morality," Hume's conclusion is that "reason is incapable of preventing volition or of disputing the preference with any passion or emotion." The words "I infer that" indicate a conclusion is being drawn. Hume offers as evidence the claim that "reason" (the human intellect) cannot by itself produce or cause our desires and wishes. The hidden premiss in this argument seems to be the claim that a general connection exists between the lack of power to cause something and the lack of power to prevent that same thing:

> Nothing that is powerless to cause an activity or event of a certain sort is powerful enough to prevent that activity or event.

Does this premiss seem obviously true to you? A wall can stop a rolling ball, but it cannot set the ball in motion. Sometimes it seems that just looking the wrong way at machines prevents them from operating properly, yet only a trained repair person can cause those same machines to work the way they should. You can prevent your antique watch from operating by dropping it into dishwater, but you probably cannot build a new watch or repair the damaged one.

Perhaps we could restate or qualify Hume's missing premiss so that it appears more plausible. If, for example, Hume was referring not to individual human capacities but to what humans in general can do, the example concerning your watch is no longer applicable because human beings can both produce and destroy watches. Can you think of a case in which humans in general have no power to cause or produce something but do have the power to prevent its operation?

When we are reconstructing arguments, such as when we are determining whether an argument is being offered, careful attention to context—written, spoken, or implied—is crucial. If we intend to deal seriously with Hume's or Wootton's arguments, we must consider them in the larger context of these authors' works and use whatever information we can gather to supply missing premisses. When we are engaged in a discussion with someone who presents an argument, we should ask questions to clarify any unstated premisses. When we are presenting arguments of our own, we should be aware of any hidden premisses that could undermine these.

When we are reconstructing arguments in situations that provide inadequate contextual information, we should supply the missing premisses that are the most plausible under the circumstances. This means that they should have "the ring of truth." That is, they should be premisses that, although they may not actually *be* true, at least are not known to be false or are not wildly unbelievable. The missing premisses should also be sentences we could reasonably expect the proponent of the argument to accept.

A particularly insidious form of assuming the truth of an unstated premiss gives rise to the fallacy of **Begging the Question**. This fallacy occurs when some point is assumed to be true, in the absence of any justification for its truth and often in the absence of any agreement about its truth by the parties involved. The logical meaning of "to beg a question" is not the same as "to raise a question" or "to ask a question," although the phrase is sometimes used this way in ordinary speech. The "question" in "begging the question" refers to the issue that is contested, and "begging" means "assuming." The use of the term can be confusing because sometimes a question is begged at the same time a different but related question is asked, as in "Have you stopped beating your dog?" Whether you answer yes or no to such a question, you appear to admit to having beaten your dog. The unwarranted assumption (the question begged) behind the question being asked is that you beat you dog in the past.

Identifying and exposing the missing premisses of arguments is a fussy business, complicated by the need to understand the context in which an argument occurs, the information available to the person who presents the argument, the intentions of that person, the purpose of the argument, and other possible factors. Learning more about the structure of different types of arguments will aid our task of finding missing premisses.

Exercise Set 1.4

PART I. Identify each of the following sentences as:

1. a universal generalization; or
2. a statistical generalization.

In some of the exercises, you must depend on common sense or general background knowledge to determine the correct interpretation.

1. Few college ball players become professional athletes.
2. College graduates earn more than those who have never been to college.
3. Fifty-five percent of students on the Dean's List are women.
4. Today's students must borrow money to finance their college education.
5. Only the good die young.
6. He who is not thrashed is not educated.
   —Menander
7. Whales are mammals.
8. Politicians are honest.
9. People who eat whole grains tend to have normal weight.
10. Computers are not immune to viruses.

PART II. In each of the following, an unstated generalization is required to connect the premises with the conclusion of the argument. Try to supply a plausible generalization to complete each argument. If no plausible generalization will make the argument succeed, explain why.

1. Female office workers work just as hard as male office workers and are just as productive. Therefore, office workers who are women should receive the same pay as men in comparable positions.

2. Nuclear power should not be used because there is no government plan for the safe disposal of spent fuel.

3. Nuclear power should be used because it is less threatening to the environment than fossil fuels.

4. Using drugs is wrong because people addicted to drugs neglect their duties.
   —William Bennett

5. Marijuana should be legalized because it is no more dangerous than alcohol, which is already legal.

6. The current mayor should be reelected because he promises to reduce taxes.

7. The use of fluorescent light bulbs should be mandatory because these require less energy than incandescent bulbs.

8. Tomatoes will be expensive in late winter because growers in Florida were hit by a hard freeze in December.

9. Joseph failed his exam this morning because he was up all night.

10. Your tires will be good for the drive from New York to Los Angeles because they have made it six times before without any trouble.

11. A head will show on the next toss of the coin, for the past six tosses have been heads.

12. Snowdrops are members of the amaryllis family of bulbs and are thus unattractive to rodents.

2. CONTEXTUAL CLUES FOR RECONSTRUCTING ARGUMENTS

We return to the problem of missing premises after we have had more to say about evaluating different forms of arguments. Now we turn to the question of sorting out the components of arguments in contexts that contain sentences that are neither premises nor conclusions.

Sometimes an argument is framed in a context of background information that tells us something about the quality of the evidence, how it was gathered, or why it is relevant to the conclusion. Consider the following passage:

A witty experiment by Philip Goldberg proves what everyone knows, that having internalized the disesteem in which they are held, women despise both themselves and each other. This simple test consisted of asking women undergraduates to respond to the scholarship in an essay signed alternately by one John McKay and one Joan McKay. In making their assessments, the students generally agreed that John was a remarkable thinker, Joan an unimpressive mind. Yet the articles were identical; the reaction was dependent on the sex of the supposed author.

—K. Millett, *Sexual Politics*

Our first clue that this passage contains an argument is the assertion in the opening sentence that something is being proved. To *prove* something is to produce evidence that shows it is true. The conclusion of the argument (the sentence that is proved) is "having internalized the disesteem in which they are held, women despise both themselves and each other." The evidence for this conclusion is contained in the premiss: "the reaction [to the essays identical but for supposed author] was dependent on the sex of the supposed author." Millett's premiss is in turn supported by (is a conclusion drawn from) the outcome of Goldberg's experiment:

> Women undergraduates evaluated identical essays, which differed only in the sexually distinctive names of the supposed authors, as being the work of a remarkable thinker when the supposed author was male, and an ordinary thinker when the supposed author was female.

Additional background information provided in Millett's passage assures us that the conclusion was something already widely known and that the experiment, a simple test, was witty. None of this information is evidence to support the truth of the conclusion, but it does tell us something about the *quality* of the evidence presented and helps us to understand the author's point of view.

Here is another argument stated in a context that contains additional information, by social commentator Andy Rooney:

> Another way to tell a rich person from a poor person is one I learned years ago when I worked for a morning news broadcast. We often had important people on it as guests and I began to notice one thing that the rich men had in common. They never wore overcoats. Nelson Rockefeller must have been on the show five times on different winter days and he never wore an overcoat or carried one. It was a long while before I realized he was so rich he didn't need one. He was never out in the cold because all he did was walk the 10 feet from his chauffeur-driven limousine to the building and anyone can stand that much cold. For all I know Rockefeller didn't even own a raincoat or an umbrella. Most of the restaurants a rich person like him would eat in have canopies extended to the street.
>
> —A. Rooney, *"How to Spot Rich People"*

The conclusion of Rooney's argument is "They [rich men] never wear overcoats." His premisses state that the sample of rich men he observed never wore overcoats. This evidence is strengthened by his suggestion as to why rich men do not need overcoats. The rest of the passage contains information about how Rooney gathered his sample and speculation about rich men's ability to dispense with rain gear as well as overcoats.

Sometimes the context of an argument provides information that indicates something is true, although the argument itself attempts to establish that the situation is a good one or a bad one. In the following argument, philosopher Bertrand Russell, after telling us that rats behave a certain way toward food, argues that they are sensible to do so.

> Rats will eat food that contains rat poison. But if, before eating, they were to subject their food to scientific analysis, they would die of hunger meanwhile, and so they are well advised to take the risk.

Examples that illustrate a point often occur in the context of arguments. Such illustrations are neither premises nor conclusion, but they clarify points and aid understanding by making general ideas concrete. Patrick Lord Devlin does this in the following passage:

> <u>No society can do without intolerance, indignation, and disgust;</u> they are the forces behind the moral law, and indeed it can be argued that if they or something like them are not present, the feelings of society cannot be weighty enough to deprive the individual of freedom of choice. I suppose that there is hardly anyone nowadays who would not be disgusted by the thought of cruelty to animals.
> —P. Devlin, *The Enforcement of Morals*

Devlin supports his conclusion, which is underlined, with the premises that follow in the same sentence. (His argument also depends on a generalization he does not state here but tries to establish elsewhere in his book: No society can live without morals.) Devlin's concrete example of disgust is provided in the last sentence of the quoted passage.

In addition to background information and examples that serve to illustrate and clarify points, arguments often contain remarks intended to put a reader or listener in a *properly receptive frame of mind* to accept their conclusions. Such additional material might convey an atmosphere of humor, fear, seriousness, or any number of other moods. For example, in the argument quoted earlier, Millett tells us that Goldberg's experiment proves "what everyone knows." Such a remark might intimidate a reader who feels inclined to disagree with Millett because it suggests that anyone who does not agree with her conclusion is disputing common wisdom. This sort of statement can distract the reader from a critical examination of the argument under consideration.

When we examine the support that evidence provides for a conclusion, we should separate carefully any additional material from the actual evidence. The extra material may appeal to our emotions and discourage us from taking a close, critical look at the central issue: Does the alleged evidence support the conclusion?

Sometimes arguments repeat, in slightly different words, points already made in a premiss or in the conclusion of the argument. When a conclusion is stated at the beginning of a passage and is followed by reasons for accepting that conclusion, the conclusion may be restated for emphasis at the end of the argument. Restating points when arguments are long and complicated can clarify a presentation by keeping track of where the argument has been and where it is leading. Repetition can help ensure that the reader or listener gets the point.

Less lofty motives, however, also inspire repetition. As advertisers have taught us, repeated exposure to an assertion can convince people that it is true, even when only flimsy evidence, or no evidence at all, has been offered. Thus, an advertising campaign for Brand X soap might call for billboard signs, newspaper and magazine ads, and television and radio spots, all flooding the market with the message "Brand X is the best soap."

A different use of repetition is found when the conclusion of an argument is repeated but modified slightly to make it stronger or weaker.[2] Consider the following passage, taken from *The Odd Woman*, a novel by George Gissing, and try to decide what use is served by repeating the conclusion at the end of the argument after stating it initially:

> It is the duty of every man, who has sufficient means, to maintain a wife. The life of an unmarried woman is a wretched one; every man who is able ought to save one of them from that fate.

Exercise Set 1.5*

Each of the following passages contains at least one argument. Rewrite each argument in standard form. Discuss the role of any additional material in the passages.

1. **Background:** Alexander Hamilton, a Founding Father, author of *The Federalist Papers*, and first U.S. Secretary of Treasury, was killed by Aaron Burr in a duel fought in 1804. Hamilton had participated in earlier duels, which were elaborate forms of conflict resolution in which the duelists usually did not try to kill their opponents but rather intended to demonstrate courage by submitting to the ordeal.

   But with his son Philip's death and his own growing attention to religion, Hamilton had developed a principled aversion to the practice. By a spooky coincidence, in the last great speech of his career Hamilton eloquently denounced dueling. During the Harry Crosswell case [in which Hamilton was attorney for the defense], he argued that [dueling] was forbidden "on the principle of natural justice that no man shall be the avenger of his own wrongs, especially by a deed alike

---

[2]These exercises are demanding. Teachers may wish to defer assigning them until later in the term after various forms of arguments, including categorical syllogisms, have been analyzed

interdicted [i.e., forbidden] by the laws of God and man." In agreeing to duel with Burr, Hamilton claimed to be acting contrary to his own wishes in order to appease public opinion.

—R. Chernow, *Alexander Hamilton*

2. In the past there has been much argument whether, in the strategy of inflation control, one should seek to come to grips with the level of demand or whether one should seek to deal with the wage-price spiral. . . . The proper answer is that both are important. Inflation could be controlled by a sufficiently heavy reduction in the level of demand. It could also be controlled with a less drastic reduction if something could be done to arrest the interreactions of wages and prices, or, to speak more precisely, of wages, profits, and prices.

—J.K. Galbraith, *The Affluent Society*

3. Mobile telephone handsets emit radiation that can be absorbed by the head. There is some worry that this radiation can cause brain cancer, and the World Health Organization has announced that an increased risk of brain cancer from cell phone use is a possibility. But in recent years, although mobile telephone use has increased enormously (there are now more than 5 billion users worldwide), there has not been a corresponding increase in brain cancer, which remains a rare disease. So the fear that using your cell phone will give you brain cancer seems unfounded.

4. If you live in a country like the United States, it is easy to say that population is the major problem [for preserving the environment]. But if you think about it a little more deeply, you could rapidly come to understand that consumption and the kinds of technology that we use are also very important in setting the stage for the world of the future.

    For example, people in rural Brazil or rural Indonesia [like most of their counterparts in developing countries] live at about one-fortieth of the consumption level of people in the United States. If you consider that we've added 135 million people to the population of the United States since the end of World War II, then you realize that the impact of the extra people in the United States on the world—in terms of levels of consumption, levels of pollution, uses of inappropriate technologies that may themselves be destructive—is about equal to the impact on the world of all the entire population of developing countries—4.2 billion people. It is not justifiable to say that population is the only factor. It's our lifestyle and our way of dealing with the world that is truly significant.

—P. Raven, *Bulletin of the American Academy*, Spring 2005

5. "Most people wear some sign and don't know what it's saying. Choose your sign according to your audience," Malloy said. "A good dark suit, white shirt and conservative tie are a young man's best wardrobe friends, if he's applying for a

white collar job in a big range of business and professional categories. They're authority symbols. It's that simple," he said.

—"Fashion," *Chicago Daily News*

6. Envy is, I should say, one of the most universal and deep-seated of human passions. It is very noticeable in children before they are a year old, and has to be treated with the most tender respect by every educator. The slightest appearance of favoring one child at the expense of another is instantly observed and resented. Distributive justice, absolute, rigid, and unvarying, must be observed by anyone who has children to deal with. But children are only slightly more open in their expressions of envy, and of jealousy (which is a special form of envy) than are grown-up people. The emotion is just as prevalent among adults as among children.

—B. Russell, *The Conquest of Happiness*

7. Money is, with propriety, considered as the vital principle of the body politic; as that which sustains its life and motion and enables it to perform its most essential functions. A complete power, therefore to procure a regular and adequate supply of revenue [by taxation], as far as the resources of the community will permit, may be regarded as an indispensable ingredient in every constitution. From a deficiency in this particular, one of two evils must ensue; either the people must be subjected to continual plunder, or the government must sink into a fatal atrophy, and, in a short course of time, perish.

—A. Hamilton, *The Federalist Papers*

8. Even if humans had stopped emitting greenhouse gases starting in 1988, when NASA scientist James Hansen announced to Congress that global warming had arrived, all the changes today resulting from global warming—the melting of Greenland's ice sheet, the slowing of the North Atlantic Gulf Stream, warmer ocean surfaces, and more intense hurricanes—would still be under way. There is so much carbon dioxide and other greenhouse gases in the atmosphere that even if humans stopped emitting new greenhouse gases tomorrow, the planet would continue to heat up for several more decades and probably longer. As surely as the science of climatology tells us that the warming of the earth is caused by humans, it also tells us that a dramatically warmer and transformed climate is almost certainly inevitable.

—T. Nordhaus and M. Shellenberger, *Break Through*

9. Theories, such as those of Peter Tompkins in his book *Mysteries of the Mexican Pyramids,* that link the pyramids of Egypt and Mexico also find little support in the available archaeological data. In fact, the last of the great pyramids at Giza on the Nile were built nearly 3,000 years before the great pyramids of the Sun and Moon at Teotihuacan [Mexico], or the well-known pyramids in the Maya Lowlands. As Kurt Mendelssohn has pointed out, it is difficult to imagine a

boatload of ancient Egyptians arriving in Mexico and introducing a monumental activity that had not been practiced in their homeland for millennia. Moreover, as many writers have argued, it is much more likely that a boatload of foreigners with no nearby support and no clear military or technological advantage would be killed before they got far from the beach rather than that they would be able to introduce a new architectural style all over ancient Mexico. In addition, the structures have major functional differences: the Egyptian pyramids come to a point and serve as tombs, while the Mexican ones are truncated and serve as foundations for temples, although they sometimes housed tombs as well.

—J. Sabloff, *The Cities of Ancient Mexico: Reconstructing a Lost World*

10. Inevitably historians are involved in selecting from the available sources the material they deem significant in the light of the problems under scrutiny. They never have access to all the facts anyway, and even those to which they do have access are selected to suit their own purposes. There is no history on a mortuary table. The "facts" therefore do not simply "speak for themselves"; the historian stage-manages their performance on the contemporary scene.

Selection, then, is inescapable.

—D. Livingstone, *The Geographical Tradition*

VI. REVIEW

The purpose of this chapter has been to introduce the subject matter of logic and critical thinking, especially where the two overlap. This is a prelude to more detailed attention to various aspects of reasoning that will help students assess the thinking of others and improve their own reasoning abilities. Some skills that contribute to critical thinking are the following:

1. Sensitivity to different uses of language;
2. The ability to recognize when evidence is required to support an assertion;
3. Awareness of the distinction between the truth of sentences and the support they would provide for some other sentence *if* they were true;
4. The ability to recognize arguments, to identify their parts, to supply unstated premises, and to sort the premises and conclusion of an argument from the context in which it is stated; and
5. The logical skill of evaluating an argument in terms of how well the premises support the conclusion.

All of these critical-thinking skills are useful and important in our everyday lives. Our language reflects what is important in human culture; as with other vitally interesting aspects of human life, a special vocabulary has developed for discussing issues in logic and critical thinking. Because some of this vocabulary may be new to you, or is used in a new way, it is helpful to review the definitions of the most important terms:

Argument   A set of sentences related in such a way that some of the sentences are presented as evidence for another sentence in the set.

Conclusion   The sentence in an argument that is supposedly supported by the evidence.

Declarative Sentence   Declarative sentences—as opposed to questions, commands, requests, and exclamations—assert that something is the case.

Evidence   Evidence is information that is offered in support of some assertion. It may be physical evidence, as when damaged goods are presented to support a claim that they are defective; or it may be verbal, in which case some sentences are offered to support the truth of another sentence.

Fallacy   A mistake in reasoning, in particular, of supposing—or pretending—evidence has been presented in support of an assertion, when some form of nonevidential persuasion has been used instead.

Fallacy of Begging the Question   A mistake in reasoning that occurs when some assumption is taken to be true without justification. For example, to say that a particular herb cannot be harmful because it is found in nature begs the question of whether all natural things are harmless.

Fallacy of Black-and-White Thinking   A mistake in reasoning that occurs when it is supposed that only two alternatives are available although in fact others are possible. For example, "It cannot be white; therefore, it must be black" ignores the whole range of shades of gray.

Indicator Words   Words commonly used to signal premises or conclusions of arguments. Examples of premiss indicator words are *for, since, because,* and *for the reason that.* Examples of conclusion indicator words are *hence, thus, therefore, and so, it follows that,* and *for that reason.*

Logic   The formal systematic study of the principles of valid inference and correct reasoning, and the application of those principles to the analysis and appraisal of arguments.

Premiss   A sentence that is offered as evidence in an argument.

Statistical Generalization   A sentence that states that some proportion of members of one class are members of another class. Common forms of these sentences are: "Most . . . are . . ." and "Most . . . are not . . . ." Statistical generalizations may also be expressed numerically, as in "x percent of . . . are . . . ."

Universal Generalization   A sentence that states that all or none of the members of one class are members of another class. Common forms of these sentences are: "All . . . are . . . " and "No . . . are . . . ," where the blanks are filled in by terms that denote classes of individuals.

The terms in boldface above are the most important ones introduced in chapter 1 and are used throughout this text. Two other terms that are part of the standard vocabulary of logic and critical thinking are so often misused that they should be mentioned here:

Infer   To infer is to conclude from something known or assumed. This is a mental activity that may be—but need not be—expressed in language.

For example, on the basis of the dark circles under a friend's eyes, you might *infer* that your friend did not get enough sleep last night, but you would not say anything at all. If you *argue* that your friend did not get enough sleep, you *state* the evidence (cite the dark circles) and the conclusion. Arguing, unlike inferring, is an activity that requires the use of language. When you state your reasons for drawing an inference—when you express in language the premises and the conclusion—you transform the inference into an argument.

Imply   To imply is to provide a basis from which an inference may be drawn. Words, actions, looks, appearances may all "have implications"—that is, they may provide a basis for someone to infer something from them. It is also appropriate to speak of a person's implying something, through words, silence, looks, or some other feature. *Imply* also has another special meaning, in the context of deductive logic: To say that one sentence implies another means that the second sentence follows from or is a consequence of the first. *Infer* is sometimes confused with *imply,* as in "Your scowls infer that you disapprove of Mary Ann." A scowl can imply disapproval but not infer it. As Fowler, in his *Dictionary of Modern English Usage,* says of *imply* and *infer,* respectively: "Each word has its own job to do, one at the giving end and one at the receiving."

The best way to review this type of subject matter is to work more exercises. If you can complete the exercises in the following section successfully, you will know that you have mastered the material covered in chapter 1. Some of these exercises are difficult, so do not be discouraged if they require a lot of effort. Moreover, because these arguments are stated in ordinary language—which is not always as precise as we would like—and because the selected passages are taken out of broader contexts, different interpretations of a given passage are possible. In a given case, for example, it may be unclear whether the author is providing an argument or a causal explanation, or whether providing just one argument or several. If a premise seems to be missing, the most plausible missing premise to supply might not be clearly identifiable. Whenever you think more than one interpretation is plausible, mention this and give your reasons for each interpretation. If the skills of logic and critical thinking you are developing in this course are to be useful in the ordinary situations you encounter in everyday life, you must practice with examples taken from such contexts.

Exercise Set 1.6

For each of the following passages:

- (a) Indicate whether or not the passage contains an argument (or several arguments).
- (b) Write the argument(s) in standard form.
- (c) If an argument depends on a missing generalization as an implicit premiss, supply the generalization.
- (d) Discuss any cases in which nonevidence, such as a threat, might be mistaken for evidential support.
- (e) Indicate what role any additional material not part of the premisses or the conclusion plays in the passage.

1. At best, though, there is very little chance of a longtime future in smokejumping. [Smokejumpers fight forest fires by using parachutes to get close to the fire and attempting to quench it.] To start with, you are through jumping at forty, and for those who think of lasting that long there are only a few openings ahead, administrative or maintenance.

    —N. Maclean, *Young Men and Fire*

2. Since no man has a natural authority over his fellow man, and since force is not the source of right, convention remains as the basis of all legitimate authority among men.

    —J-J. Rousseau, *The Social Contract*

3. Scientifically, it [Captain James Cook's first voyage to the South Pacific] was a hugely successful venture. The transit of Venus was accurately observed and recorded, kangaroos were discovered, ethnographic studies of indigenous peoples carried out, the New Zealand coastline was charted, and a vast amount of material collected and shipped back to the Royal Society—thousands of plants, five hundred fish preserved in alcohol, five hundred bird skins and hundreds of mineral specimens.

    —D. Livingstone, *The Geographical Tradition*

4. Suppose Achilles [the famous Greek warrior] runs ten times as fast as the tortoise [a very slow moving animal] and gives him a hundred yards start. In order to win the race, Achilles must first make up for his initial handicap by running a hundred yards; but when he has done this and has reached the point where the tortoise started, the animal has had time to advance ten yards. While Achilles runs these ten yards, the tortoise gets one yard ahead; when Achilles has run this yard, the tortoise is a tenth of a yard ahead; and so on, without end. Achilles never catches the tortoise, because the tortoise always holds a lead, however small.

    —M. Black, "Achilles and the Tortoise," in W. Salmon, Ed., *Zeno's Paradoxes*

5. Poetry, indeed, cannot be translated, and therefore it is the poets who preserve languages; for we would not be at the trouble to learn a language when we can have all that is written in it just as well in translation. But, as we cannot have the beauties of poetry but in its original language, we learn it.

—S. Johnson

6. Adam was led to sin by Eve and not Eve by Adam. Therefore it is just and right that woman accept as lord and master him whom she led to sin.

—St. Ambrose

7. IBM's computer, Watson, defeated two champion human players at Jeopardy. This victory led some people to claim that the machine possessed powers of understanding on a level with humans. Against this view, philosopher John Searle argued that the machine did not and could not understand anything. It merely did what it was designed to do, namely, to simulate understanding. Computers can store vast amounts of information that they can retrieve with great speed on the basis of appropriate clues. But, Searle argues, computers are incapable of understanding, in the literal sense of the term.

8. [Some] Christians seem to think that they have a right to use the law to enforce Christian morality on divorce, abortion, contraception, assisted procreation, suicide and so on. I am myself a Christian and I have always thought that, while upholding their own moral values, Christians should also be especially concerned to uphold the value of personal autonomy. There has been a long tradition of Christian theological thought . . . which emphasizes the primacy of the individual "conscience." St. Thomas Aquinas says, for example, that it is a sin to go against the dictates of one's conscience. Again, it has always been a tenet of traditional Christianity that it is a sin to coerce non-Christians into the Christian Church, and one may legitimately infer that it is similarly against Christian faith to use the law to coerce non-believers in respect of moral matters.

—M. Charlesworth, *Bioethics in a Liberal Society*

9. [The] vision of a society of autonomous moral agents choosing freely for themselves, and willingly tolerating a situation of moral or ethical pluralism, on the basis of their commitment to the value of liberty or moral autonomy, has been subjected, over the last thirty years, to a sustained critique from various quarters. There have been, first, attacks on the notion of autonomy itself: for example that it grossly overestimates the capacity of people to make decisions for themselves and neglects the degree to which every human decision is influenced by both external and internal (psychological) factors. Thus it has been said that we are inescapably part of a particular community and that communal values and practices largely set our ethical goals for us. We discover them and do not directly choose them. This is especially the case in so-called "traditional" societies where the whole idea of autonomous individuals choosing their own life

projects and engaging in what Mill calls their own "experiments in living" is, so it is claimed, absurd.

—M. Charlesworth, Bioethics in a Liberal Society

10. Hair analysis has been found to be a good test in screening large groups of people for exposure to toxic trace metals. It is not as widely used as blood analysis, but studies have shown that concentrations of lead, cadmium, arsenic, and mercury in hair provide a good record of exposure.

    Also, since the metal grows out with the hair, lengthwise sections of hair can show the approximate time when a short, intense exposure occurred.

    Chromium is essential for the hormone insulin to work properly. Thus, in time, it may be that measurements of chromium in hair will be useful in identifying people with diabetes and in monitoring the course of the disease.

— J. Mayer and J. Goldberg, "Food for Thought"

11. My suggestion for a wine to accompany chocolate desserts is different [from wines made from the muscat grape]. I prefer a rich, slightly sweet red wine. Indeed, it was a chocolate dessert that led me to change my mind about late-harvest zinfandels.

    The proper use for those alcoholic, full-fruited wines with considerable residual sugar is with chocolate. The very strength of the wine cuts through the rich heaviness of the chocolate.

—P. Machamer, "Wine," Pittsburgh Post-Gazette

12. "Public schools must improve or face extinction," says the president of the American Federation of Teachers.

    Albert Shanker, leader of the 600,000 member union, said here yesterday the future of public education is threatened by the prospect of tuition tax credits and vouchers for parents who send their children to private and parochial schools.

    With the student exodus, "Ultimately, we would have the end of public education in this country. Public schools could become like the poorhouse or the charity ward of a hospital. . . . "

    "Tuition tax credits is not a disease you feel right away. It's not like a toothache. . . . It's like a creeping cancer," Shanker said.

    Some of the problems with public education that would cause parents to choose nonpublic schools are discipline and academic standards, he said.

—Pittsburgh Press

13. The thought tends to wrap itself in a joke because in this way it recommends itself to our attention and can seem more significant and more valuable, but above all because this wrapping bribes our powers of criticism and confuses them. We are inclined to give the thought the benefit of what has pleased us in the form of

the joke; and we are no longer inclined to find anything wrong that has given us enjoyment and so spoil the source of the pleasure.

—S. Freud, *Jokes and Their Relation to the Unconscious*

14. It is incontestable that sense perception plays a crucial role in the natural sciences. It serves as the sole means through which we can gather information about the world around us. Knowledge of general laws is posterior, in the empirical sciences, to knowledge of particular instances, and for the latter the evidence of the senses is required.

—R. Swartz, *Perceiving, Sensing, and Knowing*

15. If a person is known to lie occasionally, it is not reasonable to accept something *simply* on the ground that he testifies to it. Similarly, once the senses have been discovered to be capable of deception, it is not reasonable to regard a belief as solid or permanent *merely* because it is based on sensory evidence. For it may turn out that the occasion on which the senses provided the evidence for the belief was one on which the senses were deceptive; and then, of course, the belief would have to be abandoned. Despite this, however, it may still be reasonable to regard some sensory beliefs as permanent and indubitable, if occasions on which the senses are absolutely reliable can be distinguished from those on which they are likely to deceive.

—H. Frankfurt, *Demons, Dreamers, and Madmen*

16. Noting the diversity of Paraguayan languages, Dobrizhoffer comments: "Truly admirable is their varied structure, of which no rational person can suppose these stupid savages to have been the architects and inventors. Led by this consideration I have often affirmed that the variety and artful construction of languages should be reckoned among the other arguments to prove the existence of an eternal and omniscient God."

—M. Harris, *The Rise of Anthropological Theory*

17. The first ten amendments ("The Bill of Rights") to the United States Constitution grant certain rights to all citizens to protect them from certain kinds of interferences from their own government. One citizen cannot violate the constitutional rights of another citizen for the purely logical reason that constitutional rights are rights against the government, not rights against other individuals.

—J. Murphy and J. Coleman, *The Philosophy of Law*

18. My position has been that savage ignorance is just as rational as civilized knowledge. Magic and religion, to many people, are a part of common sense. As a part of common sense it is reasonable for them to hold it. If another part of their common sense is an uncritical attitude towards belief, an acceptance of the received or traditional ideas, then their belief in common sense is reinforced and doubly rational. In our society superstition and elementary popular science are all mixed up. But part of common sense in our society is the attitude of being critical

towards traditional or received ideas. Once one becomes critical, and establishes standards of being critical, then I personally believe that it is no longer reasonable to hold on to the more simple-minded magico-religious beliefs in prayers and spells. So I can provide a reason why I accept western science and not magic in, say, the matter of farming. At the same time I can insist that, within his common sense, or frame of reference, the savage is also being reasonable.

—I. C. Jarvie, *The Revolution in Anthropology*

19. Despite abundant literature on the subject, the occurrence of human cannibalism in Old World prehistory remains an open question. We are concerned here with dietary cannibalism—the use of humans by humans as food—evidence for which is found in patterns of bone modification and discard. The key features of dietary cannibalism involve close, detailed similarities in the treatment of animal and human remains. If it is accepted that the animal remains in question were processed as food items, then it can be suggested by analogy that the human remains, subjected to identical processing were also eaten.

—P. Villa et al., "Cannibalism in the Neolithic," *Science 233 (1986)*

20. By the snapping of twigs, and the rustling of leaves, [the Deerslayer knew that] Hetty had evidently quitted the shore, and was already burying herself in the forest. To follow would have been bootless, since the darkness, as well as the dense cover that the woods everywhere afforded, would have rendered her capture next to impossible; there was also the never-ceasing danger of falling into the hands of their enemies. After a short and melancholy discussion, therefore, the sail was again set, and the ark pursued its course toward its habitual moorings.

—J. F. Cooper, *The Deerslayer*

21. So we have lots of uncertainty about [human cloning], and that is precisely why it is so problematic to justify a ban on harm-prevention grounds. The usual legal standard requires clear evidence of serious harm, at the least. Here we do not come close to meeting it. If we were to wait a bit, and see what happens, then we could form our judgments with greater knowledge as to how the practice did impact the lives of the newly cloned and their immediate families. At that point, we might learn things that support the worst fears of the opponents of cloning, and if so, then we can use hard evidence, not abstract fears, to decide what form of ban (whole or partial, conditional or absolute) to impose on the practice.

—R.A. Epstein, *Clones and Clones*

22. The Catholic Church had a deep investment in controlling the calendar. The Counter-Reformation movement saw an increasing tightening of days and dates both inside and outside the Lenten season. Under the circumstances, determining Easter was as much a sign of ecclesiastical authority as it was of natural astronomical rhythms. By the sixteenth century, the tables for calculating its annual date no longer synchronized with the lunar cycle and in 1582, Pope Gregory XIII signed a papal bull designed to reconcile the discrepancies. But in canceling ten

days of October of that year he put Italy and other Catholic countries out of step with Protestant and Orthodox countries which continued to follow the old style Julian calendar (England only shifted in 1752, Russia in 1918 and Greece in 1923). The new Gregorian calendar made it clear that accepting a way of judging the date [of Easter] was a matter of accepting papal supremacy.

—E. Welch, *Shopping in the Renaissance*

23. Describe the "argument" the author uses to convince Maria that free will does not exist:

We were eating cold fruit-soup. The soup was served in a huge tureen. It was a beautiful piece of china, and Maria was particularly fond of it. She hated things being broken, even a Woolworth tumbler. The veranda was surrounded by large polished panels of glass. I got up, by now trembling with anger, and lifted the tureen up from the table. I said:

"Look, Maria, let us settle this problem in an empirical way, once and for all. If you continue to assert that I have a Free Will, you will thereby enrage me to the point when I cannot help smashing this tureen against the windowpane, for my actions are determined by your words. If you recognize that there is no such thing as a Free Will, the tureen will automatically be safe. But what is a tureen compared to the problem we are trying to settle?"

"It is *my* tureen," Maria said, watching my hands with anguish.

"I give you ten seconds to decide." I started counting—one-two-three, in a cold rage. . . . At the count of nine, Maria said:

"All right, you win, put it down."

"You admit that I have no Free Will?" I asked, to make quite sure.

"*You* certainly haven't."

—A. Koestler, *The Invisible Writing*

24. [B]ecause the . . . rules are designed to benefit all and because the punishments prescribed for their violation are publicized and the defenses respected, there is some plausibility in the exaggerated claim that in choosing to do an act violative of the rules an individual has chosen to be punished.

—H. Morris, "Persons and Punishment," 1968, *The Monist* 52

25. And although it is utterly true that God's existence is to be believed in because it is taught in the Holy Scriptures and, on the other hand, that the Holy Scriptures are to be believed because they have God as their source (because, since faith is a gift from God, the very same one who gives the grace that is necessary for believing the rest can also give us the grace to believe that he exists); nonetheless, this cannot be proposed to unbelievers because they would judge it to be a circle.

—R. Descartes, "Letter to the Dean and Doctors of the Faculty of Sacred Theology of Paris"

Chapter Two

PAYING SPECIAL ATTENTION TO THE LANGUAGE OF ARGUMENTS

I. INTRODUCTION

II. AMBIGUITY

> Exercise Set 2.1

III. VAGUENESS

> Exercise Set 2.2

IV. DEFINITIONS

1. Ostensive Definition
2. Verbal Extensional Definition
3. Intensional Definition
    i. Definitions That Show How a Word Is Commonly Used
        > Exercise Set 2.3
    ii. Definitions That Introduce a New Word into the Language
    iii. Definitions That Reduce Vagueness
        > Exercise Set 2.4
    iv. Definitions for Theoretical Purposes
        > Exercise Set 2.5
    v. Definitions Designed to Transfer Emotive Force
        > Exercise Set 2.6
4. Syntactic Definitions and Implicit Definitions
    > Exercise Set 2.7
5. Operational Definitions
    > Exercise Set 2.8

V. USE AND MENTION

> Exercise Set 2.9

VI. REVIEW

> Exercise Set 2.10

I. INTRODUCTION

Understanding arguments requires paying special attention to language. Before we can decide whether the premises of an argument support its conclusion, we must understand what its premises and conclusion mean.

The problem of linguistic meaning is complex. Linguists, philosophers, scholars of literature, historians, and poets all study aspects of meaning. The power and effectiveness of language challenge us to understand how languages originated and developed. We want to understand how language captures, transmits, preserves, and loses meanings. Experts disagree about even such basic matters as which elements of language are the primary units of meaning—words, phrases, sentences, or longer texts. In this chapter, we consider only a few issues concerning this vast subject matter. We focus on problems that arise when we try to understand and evaluate arguments.

II. AMBIGUITY

Ambiguity—the capacity of being understood in two or more ways—can occur at any meaningful level of language. Words, phrases, sentences, paragraphs, and longer works, such as poems and plays, can all be ambiguous. Because language is a relatively compact instrument for expressing meanings, the quality of having two or more distinct meanings is useful. In literature, particularly poetry and drama, ambiguity allows for a richness of interpretations and readings. Consider, for example, Shakespeare's *Twelfth Night*. This frequently performed play has been adapted to other media, including musical comedy. Ambiguities begin when the principal characters, twins Viola and Sebastian, are separated in a shipwreck. Viola, disguised as a male, enters the local duke's service, falls in love with him, but maintains her disguise. The duke, in love with Olivia, assigns Viola (whom he knows as Orsino) to plead his case. Olivia is not interested in the duke but is attracted to Viola/Orsino, whom she takes to be a young man. The language that the two women use with one another is loaded with ambiguities that reflect this situation. In the end, Viola weds the duke, and Olivia ends up with Viola's male twin, Sebastian.

Less fortunate is Olivia's steward Malvolio, who can be interpreted as either a self-deceiving fool or a tragic character. The ambiguous language in a forged letter causes Malvolio to think that Olivia is in love with him. The letter persuades him to wear strange clothes and engage in odd behavior. Olivia, unaware of the letter, interprets his strange behavior as an illness and suggests that he go to bed. Malvolio interprets the suggestion as a lover's invitation, and so it goes until he finds himself in prison. Since Shakespeare's subtle and richly textured language allows various readings for the play as a whole and for the speeches of all the play's characters, ambiguity is essential to our enjoyment of this work of art.

Despite the value of ambiguity, it can get in the way of communicating information. We do not appreciate ambiguity in directions for finding locations, cooking food, or operating machinery. Yet we are aware that even when we are trying to be precise, we can slip into ambiguity or fail to recognize it.

Ambiguity complicates the understanding of arguments. When we examine arguments, we should note whether expressions have the same sense each time they occur in the argument. Using an ambiguous expression in more than one way in the context of a single argument compromises the ability of the premises to support the conclusion. Consider the following argument, written in standard form:

> Mad men should not be permitted to make important decisions concerning the
>   lives of others.
> My father is mad.
> _____
> My father should not be permitted to make important decisions concerning the
>   lives of others.

Suppose that this argument is offered in the following context: My father is mad at (angry with) me because I took a curve at a reckless speed and wrecked his car. He has refused to let me drive his car in the future.

The first premiss is plausible if the term *mad* means *not mentally competent.* But as we understand the context of this argument, *mad* in the second premiss means the same as *angry.* In this argument, the term *mad* is supposed to be the crucial link between the two premisses (the technical name for this link is "the third term"), but the connection fails because "mad" refers to one property in the first premiss and a different property in the second. The line of reasoning in this argument is a joke, but more problematic examples of the mistake can occur.

Using multiple meanings of an ambiguous term to confuse or deceive is called *equivocation.* The **fallacy of equivocation** occurs when the force of an argument depends on shifts of meaning, even when there is no intent to deceive. Bertrand Russell in *Problems of Philosophy,* for example, accuses Bishop Berkeley of committing this fallacy. Berkeley is famous for his idealist argument that things can exist only in the mind of a perceiver. His work is the source of the puzzle that asks whether a tree falling in the forest really makes a sound if there is no one around to hear it crash. Russell says that Berkeley fails to recognize that the term *idea* is ambiguous: It can refer to something perceived or to an act of perception. According to Russell, Berkeley apparently confuses these two meanings, and this leads him to think that things must be ideas in the mind of a perceiver in order to exist.

In the preceding examples, equivocation occurs on a single ambiguous word—*mad* in the first case and *idea* in the second. The possibility of equivocation, however, can also involve the ambiguity of a whole sentence or larger unit of language. Consider the following extract from the *Journal* of John Wesley, the founder of Methodism.

> 1751. London. I was carried to the Foundery and preached, kneeling (as I could not stand) on part of the Twenty-third Psalm.

Wesley had sprained his ankle and preached in a kneeling position. His text was the Twenty-third Psalm. However, the sentence could be understood to mean that he knelt on a copy of the psalm as he preached.

The ambiguity in Wesley's sentence is the result of ambiguous sentence structure instead of a single ambiguous term. This kind of ambiguity is called **amphiboly**. Amphibolies can occur when commas or modifiers are omitted or misplaced. For example, "He has two grown sons and a daughter in the nunnery" is a puzzling sentence, for it suggests that the sons as well as the daughter are in the nunnery. The ambiguity is resolved when a comma is placed after *sons*. Another example is "The guards and prisoners who refused to join in the prison break were tied and left behind," which suggests there were guards who refused to break out of prison. Commas surrounding the phrase "and prisoners who refused to join in the prison break" would help to clarify the meaning of the sentence. Another ambiguous sentence is "They have brown and green eyes." This could mean that the persons referred to have multicolored eyes, but it is probably an attempt to express "Some of them have brown eyes, and some have green eyes."

Sometimes ambiguities arise through the use of adjectives and adverbs that are **relative terms**, such as *small* and *large*. The term that the relative adjective or adverb modifies is important to understanding it. A large mouse is not a large animal. A small skyscraper is probably not a small building.

Ambiguity can also result from shifting the **accent** or emphasis on certain words when a passage is read or spoken. Boswell, in his *Journal*, criticized a fellow lawyer for inferring that it was all right to lie *for* his client because the Ninth Commandment, which prohibits lying, actually says "Thou shalt not bear false witness *against* thy neighbor."

No recipes exist for detecting and avoiding fallacies of equivocation. But when we recognize that words can have more than one meaning, that grammatical constructions can be misleading, and that shifts in emphasis can change the meaning of a passage, we stand a chance of preventing the most serious mistakes. Sometimes to prevent misunderstanding we need to define our terms. (We discuss techniques for definition later in this chapter.)

When our primary purpose is to present or to evaluate evidence, we should try to resolve ambiguities and make all assertions as clear as the context demands. We should avoid ambiguity when giving or receiving instructions, or transferring crucial information.

At the same time, we must remember that conveying information is not the only purpose of language. In other uses of language, ambiguities play important and valuable roles. We have already looked at Shakespeare's use of ambiguities. Poets use ambiguous words and expressions to evoke multiple images and to convey several meanings. The expressive power of poetry depends on such compact use of language. Puns and other forms of humor also depend on ambiguity. Language would be greatly impoverished without such ambiguities.

Exercise Set 2.1

Discuss the ambiguities on which the following seven arguments depend.

1. Ben is a person who is a good quarterback. Therefore, Ben is a good person.

2. Nuclear power is environmentally safer than other types of energy because it does not increase atmospheric carbon.

3. All dissidents are not revolutionaries. Lenin was a dissident. Therefore he was not a revolutionary.

4. Among all primates, only man is capable of producing great music. Sarah Chang (a famous concert violinist) is not a man. Therefore, Sarah Chang is not capable of producing great music.

5. All material things are made up of atoms and molecules, which have space between and within them. Therefore, objects that appear to be solid, such as tables and chairs, are not really solid.

6. God must exist, because only God can perform miracles, and it is a miracle that I passed my physics exam.

7. Alzheimer's [disease] is common; the Queen is not common. Therefore the Queen has not got Alzheimer's.

—A. Bennett, *The Uncommon Reader*

8. The only answer the Greek holy of holies gave [to Croesus, king of Lydia, who had asked the Delphic oracle whether he would succeed in a war against Persia] was that by going to war he would destroy a great empire. It happened to be his own, but, as the priestess pointed out, she was not responsible for his lack of wit.

—E. Hamilton, *The Greek Way*

Discuss the ambiguity on which Croesus's inference depended.

9. An ambiguity in the term *normal,* which can mean either "average or usual" or "healthy, correct, without fault," is sometimes the basis for fallacies of equivocation. Consider the following argument for the safety of nuclear power and decide whether it depends on this ambiguity.

All of us are exposed to a certain amount of background radiation from natural causes. Such background radiation forms part of normal atmospheric conditions that humans have lived with for ages. Thus, since nuclear power plants are responsible for increasing atmospheric radiation only by a factor of two, this is within the range of normal and should not be condemned.

10. Do you think that parents who are very concerned with their child's educational progress would be satisfied with being told their child was normal? How are they likely to understand *normal*? What question do you think they would ask the child's teacher?

11. How does ambiguity figure in the following conversation?

Algernon: I don't think there is much likelihood, Jack, of you and Miss Fairfax being united.

Jack: Well, that is no business of yours.

Algernon: If it was my business, I wouldn't talk about it. It is very vulgar to talk about one's business. Only people like stockbrokers do that, and then merely at dinner parties.

—Oscar Wilde, *The Importance of Being Earnest*

12. Do the ambiguities in the following involve an amphiboly or a single word with more than one meaning?
    a. A young woman told comedian Groucho Marx that she went to a college for girls. He replied, "That's the reason I'd want to go too."
    b. Michael saw a dog running through the field with his binoculars.

13. The ethical theory called *Psychological Egoism* maintains that people always act selfishly so as to seek their own satisfaction or good. Consider this argument:

Yes, we do things for others, but we get satisfaction out of doing them, and this satisfaction is our end for doing them. Doing them is only a means to this satisfaction. Hence, even in doing "altruistic" things for others, like taking them to see the ocean, we are seeking our own good.

—W. Frankena, *Ethics*

Discuss whether this argument of the egoist depends on an ambiguity.

14. Many popular songs have ambiguous titles and contain lines that are ambiguous. For example, consider Pink Floyd's "We Don't Need No Education." Find an example of an ambiguous line or song title and discuss its several meanings.

15. Discuss the sources of ambiguity in the following examples from Fowler's *Modern English Usage*:
    a. Please state from what date the patient was sent to bed and totally incapacitated by your instructions.
    b. Miss Pickhill grasped the pince-nez which hung from a sort of button on her spare bosom.
    c. No force was used beyond that necessary to put an end to the uproar by the stewards.

16. Headline writers delight in ambiguities. Consider the following headline for a review of a book about Claude Shannon, the founder of information theory: "Little Bits Go a Long Way."

Discuss the ambiguity here. Try to find an ambiguous headline in a newspaper or magazine.

17. Discuss the following example of ambiguity, from Lewis Carroll's *Through the Looking Glass*:

"I see nobody on the road," said Alice.

"I only wish *I* had such eyes," the King remarked in a fretful tone. "To be able to see Nobody! And at that distance too! Why it's as much as *I* can do to see real people, by this light!"

III. VAGUENESS

Vagueness occurs in many forms; we consider three.

1. An expression is **vague** if borderline cases for its application occur.

Example

The term *middle-aged* clearly applies to those who are fifty years old, and *young* to those who are twenty. It is less clear at what age *young* is no longer applicable and *middle-aged* is.

Vagueness differs from ambiguity in that an ambiguous term has at least two distinct, *nonoverlapping* meanings. Many English words, such as *kid,* are both ambiguous and vague. *Kid* is ambiguous because it can refer to a young goat or a child. In the first sense, *kid* is not vague, for goats are no longer kids when they reach their first birthday. However, no clear cutoff point determines when a person is no longer considered a kid. We ignore possible ambiguities of the terms discussed in this section in order to concentrate on vagueness.

A standard example of a vague term with borderline cases of application is *bald.* A person with no hair at all is bald; a person with a full head of hair is not bald. But there are cases in which it is unclear whether the term *bald* is applicable. Other examples of terms that are vague in this sense are *old, happy, hip, rich,* and *thin.* Most color terms in ordinary language are vague.

2. Vagueness also arises when several criteria exist for application of a term, with no specification of how many criteria have to be fulfilled or to what degree. When a term is vague in this sense, it is similar to an ambiguous term in having more than one meaning but is distinct in that the meanings overlap.

Example

Consider the expression "Terry is a good friend." What are the criteria for being a good friend? Can a good friend let you down sometimes? How often or in what ways can someone let you down and still be a friend? Can a good friend take something from you without permission? Some would say yes, but others would not agree, and most would say "It depends. . . ."

Vague terms, like ambiguous terms, can cause difficulties in arguments. For example:

> Jason seldom attends religious services.
> _____
> Jason is not religious.

The argument fails because attending services is only one criterion among several for being religious. Other criteria might include belief in a supernatural being; membership in an organized religion; adoption of an ethical code or set of altruistic values; performance of acts of devotion or piety; and a sense of reverence toward fellow humans, other living things, or the universe. It is appropriate to call a person "religious" when all, or only some, of these criteria are applicable.

Insofar as *religious* is a vague term, it is unclear just how many of these criteria must be met in order to say that someone is religious. If all of them are applicable to a particular person, that person is religious. If none of the criteria that constitute being religious apply, the person is not religious. Evidence that someone does not attend religious services appeals to only one of the criteria and does not strongly support the conclusion that the person is not religious.

3. Lack of specificity is a third form of vagueness. Suppose that you ask where Larson lives, and someone answers "Ohio" without specifying further details. If you are interested only in the state of residence—for example, if you want to ensure that certain states are represented in a meeting of delegates—this answer is adequate. If, however, you want go to Larson's house for a party, you need more specific information. Judging the level of specificity appropriate for a given situation is an important communicative skill. We should aim at being specific enough for the purpose at hand while avoiding irrelevant details.

Vagueness is a pervasive, important, useful, and ineliminable feature of language. Ordinary conversation needs such comfortable but vague expressions as "See you soon" and "How have you been?—Just fine." International diplomacy depends heavily on vague language. Diplomats can convey strong disapproval by using expressions as "The government has warned that it will take strong measures if its territorial waters are violated," without giving away any secrets or risking loss of face.

Reducing vagueness is crucial, however, in some circumstances. For example, although the vagueness of the term *religious* is unproblematic in most contexts, some situations demand a precise definition of this term.

Example

When all young men in the United States were subject to the draft, conscientious objectors to military service who professed a religion were treated differently from nonreligious conscientious objectors. Religious objectors were assigned to alternate nonmilitary service. Nonreligious objectors went to jail.

When something as serious as a prison sentence is at stake, it is important to state precisely the conditions under which the penalty will be applied. In this situation, we need a definition of *religion* to reduce its vagueness. In the next section, we will discuss various techniques for defining terms as well as several types and purposes of definition, including definitions to reduce vagueness.

Exercise Set 2.2

1. Have you ever argued with anyone about whether a tomato is a fruit or a vegetable? What are the criteria for whether something is a vegetable or a fruit? Can you think of a situation in which it would be important to clarify these vague terms?

2. Discuss any elements of vagueness (not ambiguity) in each of the following terms:
   a. student
   b. misdemeanor
   c. free trade
   d. patriot
   e. war crime

3. Can you think of any common nouns in the English language that are not at all vague?

4. What role does vagueness play in the following argument?

Lord Caversham:	Good evening, Lady Chiltern! Has my good-for-nothing young son been here?
Mabel Chiltern:	(coming up to Lord Caversham): Why do you call Lord Goring good-for-nothing?
Lord Caversham:	Because he leads such an idle life.
Mabel Chiltern:	How can you say such a thing? Why he rides in the Row at ten o'clock in the morning, goes to the Opera three times a week, changes his clothes at least five times a day, and dines out every night of the season. You don't call that leading an idle life, do you?

   —Oscar Wilde, *An Ideal Husband*

5. How does vagueness figure in the following somewhat plausible but actually *incorrect* argument?

   Paint sample A looks the same color as paint sample B.
   Paint sample B looks the same color as paint sample C.
   _____

   Therefore, paint sample A looks the same color as paint sample C.

IV. DEFINITIONS

In this section, we touch briefly on the problems of definition, again focusing on how meanings affect the way we understand and evaluate arguments. Various ways of defining words (i.e., giving their meanings) serve different purposes.

1. OSTENSIVE DEFINITION

Often the best way to define a term is to draw attention to the objects the term refers to by pointing to or displaying them. Parents teach many words to their infants by pointing to baby's eyes, nose, ears, and so forth while uttering the words that refer to those things. This technique is called **ostensive definition.** Many philosophers regard ostensive definition as fundamentally important for learning language and for establishing a link between words and the objects that words denote.

Useful as it is, ostensive definition has limits. Sometimes attention is directed to the wrong object. A baby may notice the pointing finger rather than the nose when the word *nose* is uttered. Or the baby may suppose that the whole face or the whole person is meant by *nose.* We can ostensively define general terms, such as *eye,* only by pointing to particular eyes, thus creating the possibility that some special feature of the particular eyes, such as their color, will be mistakenly attached to the general term *eye.*

Ostensive definition is further limited when no objects of the right type are available. In midtown Manhattan, ostensive definitions of skyscrapers are easy, but not in the New Guinea highlands—unless some appropriate pictures are available. Abstract objects, such as the Gross National Product, resist ostensive definition because they cannot be pointed to or displayed. Despite these limitations, ostensive definition is important and useful in many circumstances.

2. VERBAL EXTENSIONAL DEFINITION

Ostensive definition is sometimes called **nonverbal extensional definition**. The **extension** of a term is the set of individuals, objects, or events to which the term can be correctly applied. For example, the extension of *dog* is the set of all dogs; the extension of *prizefighter* is the set of all prizefighters. In ostensive definition, as we have seen, some member or members of the set to which the term applies are pointed to, pictured, or displayed in some way.

Verbal extensional definitions also select members of the set to which a term applies, but they do this verbally by naming members of the set instead of pointing to them. In this way, *prizefighter* might be defined by naming some prizefighters, such as Muhammad Ali, Joe Louis, Evander Holyfield, and Sonny Liston.

Verbal extensional definitions have limitations. Common nouns, such as *prizefighter,* refer not only to all present and past prizefighters but also to future prizefighters. In such cases, it is impossible to provide a complete verbal extensional definition that lists all members of a class. With only a partial listing the focus might be on properties that belong to members of the list but not all to whom a term applies. For example, Ali, Louis, Holyfield, and Liston are not only all prizefighters; each is also male, a heavyweight, a world champion, and an African-American. Yet Rhonda Luna is a female featherweight prizefighter.

It is also difficult to list members of sets when the members have no names. Sometimes subsets (instead of members) of the set that is the extension of a term can be listed, and this may work to convey meaning. For example, we could define *marsupial* extensionally by naming various kinds of marsupials, such as opossums, kangaroos, wallabies, and wombats. But it would be very difficult to formulate a verbal extensional definition of *kangaroo*. Few individual kangaroos have names, and various types of kangaroos are not known by terms sufficiently familiar to convey their meaning to someone who does not know already what a kangaroo is.

3. INTENSIONAL DEFINITION

The **intension** of a term is the set of all and only those properties that a thing must possess for that term to apply to it. For example, a person must possess the property of being a professional boxer for the term *prizefighter* to be correctly applicable. When a term is given an **explicit intensional definition**, a phrase equivalent in meaning to the term is stated, as in "prizefighter" means "a professional boxer." All intensional definitions are verbal. We can distinguish several types of explicit intensional definitions by recognizing that definitions have various purposes.

i. Definitions That Show How a Word Is Commonly Used

Most dictionary definitions, such as the intensional definition of *prizefighter* just given, are of this type, called **lexical definitions**. *The Professor and the Madman,* a book by S. Winchester about the construction of the massive *Oxford English Dictionary,* states the criteria for success:

> Defining words properly is a fine and peculiar craft. There are rules—a word (to take a noun as an example) must first be defined according to the class of things to which it belongs (mammal, quadruped), and then differentiated from other members of that class (bovine, female). There must be no words in the definition that are more complicated or less likely to be known than the word being defined. The definition must say what something is, and not what it is not. If there is a range of meanings of any one word—*cow* having a broad range of meanings, *cower* having essentially only one—then they must be listed. And all the words in the definition must be found elsewhere in the dictionary—a reader must never happen upon a word in the dictionary that he or she cannot discover elsewhere in it. If the definer contrives to follow all these rules, stirs into the mix an ever-pressing need for

concision and elegance—and if he or she is true to the task, a proper definition will probably result.

In accord with the standards stated above, a lexical definition should be neither too narrow nor too broad. That is to say, the definition should state the set of properties possessed by all things to which the term applies, and only to those things. For example, the following definition:

"Knife" means "an instrument for cutting"

is too broad. Some instruments for cutting, namely scissors, are not knives. The definition:

"Table" means "a piece of furniture consisting of a flat top set horizontally on four legs"

is too narrow. Some tables have fewer than four legs, and some tables have more.

A definition can be both too broad and too narrow. For example:

"Cat" means "domestic animal"

is too broad, because "domestic animal" applies to livestock, dogs, and various other pets as well. The definition is also too narrow, because many wild animals belong to the cat family.

In addition to being neither too broad nor too narrow, lexical definitions should not be circular. A **circular definition** incorporates the term being defined, or some variant of that term, in the definition. For example, many universities distinguish between full-time and part-time students with respect to fees and privileges. If we ask for the meaning of "full-time student" in this context, the answer:

"Full-time student" means "a person who is enrolled full time in school"

is a circular definition. Presumably, the person asking the question knows that a student is someone enrolled in school.

Sometimes circularity is not so obvious because the circle is large enough to include several definitions. Consider the following pair of definitions, taken from a recently published dictionary (*not* the *Oxford English Dictionary*):

"Grazing" means "feeding on growing grass."
"Grass" means "any of various green plants that are eaten by grazing animals."

What we learn from these definitions is little more than that grazing animals feed on growing grass and grass is what is eaten by grazing animals. This pair of definitions comes close to being circular. We must remember, though, that because English is a mixed language that incorporates words derived from Norman, Anglo-Saxon, and German roots among others, definitions that provide synonyms are not necessarily circular.

From one point of view, to say that "dormitive" means "causing sleep" looks circular, but this is an example of defining a medical term with a Latin root by giving a synonym in plain English. Context determines whether a synonym is a close-enough variant of the term being defined to make the definition circular.

Exercise Set 2.3

1. We have said that abstract objects such as numbers cannot be ostensively defined. But numerals, which are conventional representations of numbers, can be ostensively defined.
    a. Give an ostensive definition of the Roman numeral that represents the number three.
    b. Give an ostensive definition of the Arabic numeral (base 10) for the number seven.
    c. Give an ostensive definition of the binary numeral (Arabic, base 2) for the number two.
2. Give a verbal extensional definition of either (1) "winners of the World Series (U.S. baseball) since 2010" or (2) "World Cup (soccer football) winners since 2010."
3. What is wrong with each of the following lexical definitions?
    a. "Politically" means "in a politic manner."
    b. "Mouse" means "a small animal."
    c. "Fork" means "a utensil for eating foods."
    d. "Whale" means "an aquatic mammal."
    e. "Land grant" means "a grant of land made by the government."
4. Many slang terms are on their way to becoming a standard part of a language. Since meanings of these terms are somewhat fluid, a dictionary does not always present the best account of current usage. Look up the meaning of the slang term "cool" in a dictionary (an online dictionary will probably offer the most up-to-date definition). Discuss whether the definition you find accords with your sense of the term.

ii. Definitions That Introduce a New Word into the Language

When new situations or interests arise, we may need to introduce a new word into the language. The definitions that introduce new words are called **stipulative definitions**. For example, *social media* is a relatively recent introduction:

> "Social media" means "websites and applications used for social networking."

Until a few years ago, websites and applications for social networking did not exist. Thus, the language did not require a special term to refer to them. Sometimes new words are taken over from another language, as when Europeans adopted the Nahuatl Native American *chocolate,* for a food unknown in Europe before Spaniards brought it back from Mexico in the sixteenth century. Sometimes we form new words by combining parts of old words, as in "locavore," which means "one who eats mostly locally grown food." We also stipulate new meanings for old words. "Friend," an old noun, is now also a verb that means "to add to a list of personal associates on a website." Some new words, especially technological words, are fresh constructions (e.g., *byte*).

The **conventional** nature of language is most apparent in stipulative definitions. Expressions in a language do not acquire their meanings as a result of some natural connection between the words and the things in the world that the words denote. The connection between the word *thunder* and the meteorological phenomenon of thunder is conventional, unlike the natural connection between thunder and lightning. This is true even when a word such as "thunder" can evoke or resemble the sound of the natural phenomenon. After all, the word for thunder is different in different languages.

Most words have the meanings they do as a result of the widespread and sometimes unconscious decisions to use them in a certain way. We do not believe that the first humans who used language explicitly stipulated the meanings of all their original expressions. Such a scenario seems highly unlikely, even though the true origins of language remain shrouded in mystery. Nevertheless, given what we do know about the development of languages—the ways in which new words are added and words that are no longer useful are discarded—the conventional nature of language is indisputable. Different human languages use different vocabularies to refer to many of the same features of the world because the development of each involved the adoption of different conventions. No language is more correct or true to the world than another language.

Stipulative definitions must meet at least the following two requirements if they are to be acceptable:

1. A term that is stipulatively defined should not already have a widely accepted standard meaning.

In Lewis Carroll's *Through the Looking Glass,* Humpty Dumpty says that he is the master of words—words mean what he chooses them to mean. Alice protests because Humpty is stipulating new and different meanings for words that already have established senses. Alice is justified in her complaint. Confusion obviously results from Humpty Dumpty's attitude toward words with established usage. We do not need a new term to denote highways, for example, but we did need a new term to denote the new feature of the world that we call a "website."

2. A term that is stipulatively defined should be a useful addition to the language.

Making up new words and offering stipulative definitions for them can be amusing, but unless the new words serve some useful purpose, they will not become part of the language. Special interests often require the stipulation of a new vocabulary. The Internet, which has prompted the introduction of many new terms, is a case in point. The danger looms, however, that mere **jargon**—terminology that is incomprehensible to those outside a special-interest group—might replace ordinary language even when the special interest requires no new concepts and could use language with standard meanings. Stipulative definitions of this type are unfortunate because, while they might satisfy members of the special-interest group, they hinder rather than help successful communication with those outside the group.

iii. Definitions That Reduce Vagueness

For some purposes, the meaning of a vague term must be clarified and made more precise. Definitions that do this are **precising definitions**. *Full-time university student* is a vague term. In ordinary usage, it means roughly "a person who devotes a major part of his or her energies to acquiring some type of knowledge or skill through university courses." However, the vagueness of the term poses a problem for universities that assign fees and benefits on the basis of whether students are full-time or part-time. Universities typically solve this problem by offering a precising definition of *full-time student* in their catalogs. Here is one university's definition of *full-time student:*

> "Full-time student" means "student who is carrying a course load of at least twelve units a semester."

Note that this precising definition is not the same as a stipulative definition. It does not introduce a new term or assign a completely new meaning to a term already in use. This precising definition eliminates borderline cases of the vague expression *full-time student* for the special purpose at hand by making a course load of at least twelve units per semester the criterion for being a full-time student (at that university). This definition sorts students at the university into just two categories: those who are full-time and those who are not.

Another type of precising definition assigns a special or technical meaning to be used in a particular context. Our text contains many examples of such definitions that occur in the study of logic. *Argument* and *fallacy* are just two examples. In music, *beat* and *tempo* are technical terms; their technical meanings are different from the senses they carry in ordinary contexts. All disciplines employ some technical vocabulary that those who want to understand the field must master.

Not all cases of reducing vagueness are as simple as the precising definitions mentioned so far. When a term, such as *religion*, is vague because of a number of different criteria for its application, it can be difficult to specify just which criteria are most important or how many criteria must be met in order to apply the term. Recent debates concerning the definitions of *death of a person* and *beginning of life of a person* make us aware of the complexity of the problem. Even when new definitions are set forth in judicial rulings that take into account public debates and studies by experts, the definitions do not go unchallenged. This is because the proposed definitions have grave and far-reaching social consequences. The definitions in these cases not only reduce vagueness but also involve a theoretical account of what it means to be a person. As such, the definitions are appropriately classed as theoretical.

Theoretical definitions, which are discussed in the next section, differ from technical definitions. Although a technical definition specifies the meaning of a term as it is used in some area of study, such a definition does not necessarily carry with it any commitment to the truth of a theory. Consider the term *sonnet*. The technical definition of the term is "a fixed verse form of Italian origin consisting of fourteen lines that are typically five-foot iambics rhyming according to a prescribed scheme" (*Merriam-Webster's Collegiate Dictionary, Tenth Edition*). This definition does not carry with it any commitment to a view of the nature of poetry in the way that the definition of *death of a person* carries a commitment to a theory of what it means to be a person.

Exercise Set 2.4

1. *Adult* (as applied to humans) is a vague term. For what purposes might a precising definition of *adult* be required? Discuss some of the problems that arise in formulating such a definition.

2. "All men are mortal" is a generalization. Is it also vague in the sense of lacking specificity?

3. Most state universities charge residents and nonresidents of the state different tuition fees for the same educational programs. Suppose you are a state legislator assigned to a committee to define *resident* for the purpose of charging tuition fees. What considerations would guide your attempt? What definition would you propose? Alternatively, how is *resident* defined by state universities in your state?

4. What are some important technical terms in your major field of study (or a major you are thinking of choosing, if you have not yet done so)? Can you give an acceptable definition of one of these?

5. The following nouns are relatively new to English: "staycation," "frenemy," "bromance," and "vuvuzela." Do you know what they mean? Where can you find definitions of these terms?

6. Sometimes when celebrating with excess enthusiasm a football championship, students are arrested for disorderly conduct. What does "disorderly conduct" mean? What sort of definition of the term is required in these circumstances?

7. Do you think the stipulative definition of "friend" as a verb violates the first principle for successful stipulative definition—that the term not already have a widely accepted standard meaning? Why or why not?

8. The Food and Drug Administration (FDA) and the US Department of Agriculture (USDA) are the agencies that govern food labels in the US. Here is one of their regulations: "To qualify for the label "fat-free," a food must have less than 0.5 grams of fat, with no added fat or oil."

   The FDA defines "fat-free" in this regulation. What type of definition is this?

9. Can you find an example of jargon?

iv. Definitions for Theoretical Purposes

We have already introduced the concept of a theoretical definition, in contrast to a technical definition. The term *theory* has several meanings, two of which concern us here. In one sense, *theory* refers to a general approach to, or belief about, some subject matter that is expressed in a set of interrelated statements concerning the nature of the subject. In this sense, we can speak of a theory of justice. A theory of justice might include such statements as "Justice requires that all persons be treated similarly under similar circumstances," "Justice requires that individuals in a society be given equal opportunities and access to the good things in that society," or "Justice demands that punishments should be tailored to the nature of the offense."

The definition:

"Death of a person" means "cessation of that person's brain functions"

involves a theory in this sense—that is, a set of interrelated statements concerning the special character of human life. This theory accepts the view that a human body that has totally and irreversibly lost the use of its brain is no longer a person, even if machines can maintain the body's circulatory, respiratory, and other systems. The term *vegetable* is sometimes applied in such situations to mark the transformation of the body from the time that it was the body of a person, capable of thoughts and feelings, to its passive state after loss of brain function. One who holds this theory of what it means for a person to die would, for example, probably agree that it is not immoral to remove a body that has lost all brain function from machines designed to maintain respiration. In addition, the theory supports the view that no harm is done to the *person* if vital organs from that body are removed for transplanting. (While the person lives, he or she may direct how his or her body is to be used after death, just as the person directs the use of his or her personal property.)

A second sense of *theory* refers to scientific theories—that is, to sets of general, but not vague, interrelated statements about the nature of society or the physical world that are subject to testing and proof. Einstein's theory of relativity and Darwin's theory of evolution are two examples. Such theories often refer to things, such as subatomic particles, that cannot be directly observed. Statements about these theoretical entities form the basis for other statements that can be confirmed or disconfirmed by observing the behavior of relevant features of the world. Frequently, scientists take a term from ordinary language, or from another theory, and redefine it for some new theoretical purpose. For example, in classical mechanics, *work* is defined as "the product of force and distance," and *momentum* is defined as "the product of mass and velocity." In classical mechanics, as in many physical theories, these terms are defined explicitly by means of other terms in the theory.

Other terms, such as *force*, are not explicitly defined. Although classical mechanics tells us how to calculate force (mass times acceleration), no expression synonymous with *force* is presented in the theory. Instead of being defined explicitly, the meanings of such terms are given implicitly in the fundamental generalizations (or *laws*) of the theory. Sir Isaac Newton's three laws of motion all say something about how forces act on bodies: They describe the effects of forces with respect to such other theoretical features as mass, acceleration, momentum, and distance. In a sense, we can say that the theory tells us what force is insofar as it tells us how forces operate under various circumstances.

Theoretical definitions are similar to precising definitions in that both reduce vagueness. However, in addition to reducing vagueness, theoretical definitions connect the term being defined with other terms in the theory. A complete understanding of the theoretical meanings of explicitly defined terms, such as *work*, and implicitly defined terms, such as *force*, is gained only through an understanding of the theory.

Exercise Set 2.5

1. The following argument used by John Rock, who was a principal designer of the (birth-control) Pill, depends on the meaning of *natural*. What theoretical considerations enter into the definition of *natural*?

   In nature, during pregnancy, progestin is produced to block the release of additional eggs.
   The Pill is progestin in tablet form.
   _____
   Therefore, the Pill is a natural method of birth control.

2. Many herbal supplements are promoted on the basis of being "natural," that is to say they do not have any chemical additives. Should we take "natural" in this sense to mean the same as "not harmful" or "good for you"? Why or why not?

3. Some people criticize the conduct—particularly sexual conduct—of others as being wrong because it is unnatural. What does "unnatural" mean in cases of moral condemnation?

4. Formulate a definition of either "liberal" or "conservative" in the political sense of those terms. Discuss the theoretical significance of your definition and some of the problems associated with framing your definition. (You may use a dictionary to get started.)

5. Identify and discuss a theoretical definition of some term in a discipline that interests you, such as your major field of study, politics, health care, or the law.

v. Definitions Designed to Transfer Emotive Force

Persuasive definitions are designed to transfer emotive force, such as feelings of approval or disapproval. Like other explicit intensional definitions, a persuasive definition should state the properties that a thing must possess for the term to apply. However, persuasive definitions also convey an attitude toward what is being defined. For example, the definition:

> "Homosexual" means "one who has an unnatural desire for those of the same sex."

conveys, through use of the term *unnatural,* a negative or disapproving attitude toward homosexuals. An attitude of approval—although more subtle than the disapproving attitude in the above definition of *homosexual*—is conveyed by the following definition:

> "Democracy" means "the acceptance and practice of the principle of equality of rights, opportunities, and treatment; lack of snobbery."

An attitude of approval is present in this definition because most people place a positive value on equality of rights and lack of snobbery. Perhaps the emotive force of this definition of *democracy* can be seen more clearly if we contrast it with another definition:

> "Democracy" means "rule by majority."

Most people would not regard this definition as persuasive. Its emotive force seems neutral and does not engender the same degree of approval as do appeals to equality of rights and lack of snobbery. Some people, including Plato however, have associated rule by majority with mob rule. When this is so understood, defining *democracy* as "rule by majority" conveys negative emotive force.

As often happens when more than one definition of the same term is offered, these two definitions of *democracy* differ in their statement of intension as well as in their emotive force. "Rule by majority" and "the acceptance and practice of the principle of equality of rights, opportunities, and treatment; lack of snobbery" do not refer to the same properties of a democracy.

Whether persuasive definitions are appropriate depends on the context in which they occur. Nothing is intrinsically wrong with trying to persuade others to share our attitudes. Insofar as the attitudes themselves are immoral or inappropriate in some way, however, trying to persuade others to share them may deserve punishment, blame, or milder forms of criticism.

Persuasive definitions are often meant to be humorous. For example, *philosophy* has been defined as "a doubt which lives in one like a hookworm, causing pallor and lack of appetite." In this definition, as in many designed to amuse, the intension of the term—the properties a thing must have if the term is to apply—is partially or completely ignored. When entertainment is the point, this is acceptable. But if we want to define a term to make its standard use known, then a persuasive definition is probably inappropriate and can be deceptive or misleading.

Familiarity with the technique of persuasive definition increases our awareness that words that refer to the same objects may differ sharply in emotive force. It does not require much sensitivity to recognize the difference in attitudes conveyed by the terms *woman* and *bitch* or *black* and *nigger* or *white* and *honky*. Objectionable slang terms that are disrespectful to various ethnic, racial, and religious segments of the population are regrettably all too common.

Sometimes the negative emotive force of an expression is less obvious. Calling an airplane race in which the pilots are women a "powder-puff derby" conveys an attitude that such races are to be taken less seriously than races in which men are the pilots. Calling a woman who writes poetry a "poetess" suggests she is not quite up to the standards of a poet.

We should be especially sensitive to the emotive force of any expressions used in arguments, for emotively charged terms can lead us to accept or reject conclusions when that is not warranted by the evidence.

Exercise Set 2.6

1. Discuss the different emotive forces (if such a difference exists) for each of the following pairs of terms. Aside from emotive force, do both members of each pair have the same intensional meaning? (That is, does each member of the pair refer to the same things?)
   a. Fragile—Weak
   b. Public servant—Bureaucrat
   c. Native American—Indian
   d. Sweat—Perspire
   e. Chairman—Chairperson
   f. Cop—Police officer
   g. Boy—Young man
   h. Actor—Actress
   i. House—Home
   j. Estate tax—Death tax
   k. College—University
   l. Psychiatrist—Shrink
   m. Man—Gentleman
   n. Tolerance—Permissiveness

2. Give a persuasive definition of some form of popular music (for example, rap, swing, neosoul, death metal, etc.).

3. The following is taken from the work of William McDonough, a "green" architect. Comment on the difference in emotive force between Ralph

Waldo Emerson's statement about his return voyage and McDonough's characterization of the voyage:

> In the 1830's, when [Emerson's] wife died, he went to Europe on a sailboat and returned in a steamship. He remarked on the return voyage that he missed the "Aeolian connection."[1] If we abstract from this, he went over on a solar-powered recyclable vehicle operated by craftpersons, working in the open air, practicing ancient arts. He returned in a steel rust bucket, spilling oil on the water and smoke into the sky, operated by people in a black dungeon shoveling coal into the mouth of a boiler. Both ships are objects of design. Both are manifestations of our human intention.

4. Discuss the persuasive force of "natural foods" and "natural medicines." What is the intension of these terms?

5. A former governor of California once called his critics "girlie men." How would you define this term? Is your definition a persuasive definition? Is it possible to give an emotively neutral definition of "girlie men"?

6. "Freedom's just another word for nothing left to lose" (Kris Kristofferson). How would you classify this definition?

4. SYNTACTIC DEFINITIONS AND IMPLICIT DEFINITIONS

Thus far, with the exception of implicit theoretical definitions and purely humorous persuasive definitions, we have defined terms by giving their intensions or extensions in an explicit manner. For the most part, the terms defined in this way have been common nouns and adjectives. Some words, such as prepositions, articles, and conjunctions, do not have an intension or an extension: They do not refer to things, events, persons, or activities, although they do have meanings and play an essential role in language.

The meanings of these terms are primarily grammatical or **syntactic**. Examples of such words are *not, and, or,* and *if . . . then.* We can sometimes define them explicitly, by presenting synonyms that have the same grammatical function ("and" means "also; in addition to; moreover; as well as"). More often, however, the definition states the grammatical function of the term along with examples of contexts in which the term occurs. For example, one dictionary implicitly defines *or* as "a *coordinating conjunction* that introduces an alternative, as in 'I'll offer him beer or wine.'" Another implicit definition of *or* is "a word that connects sentences in such a way that the compound sentence that is formed is true whenever either of the sentences it connects is true, but is false otherwise." Truth-table definitions of the logical connectives (see chapter 6) are implicit definitions of this type.

---

[1]Aeolus was the Greek god of the wind.

Contextual definitions offer yet another implicit way to define syntactic terms. For example, *unless* is contextually defined in the following: "We'll have a picnic unless it rains" means the same as "If it doesn't rain, then we'll have a picnic." In this sort of contextual definition, no single expression synonymous with *unless* is presented. Instead, the defining expression is synonymous with the whole expression in which *unless* occurs.

Exercise Set 2.7

1. Give a syntactic definition of *and*, and give an example that shows how it is used.

2. Give a syntactic definition of *but*, and give an example that shows how it is used.

3. Give an implicit contextual definition of *neither . . . nor . . .* by providing an expression in which the words occur and another equivalent expression in which they do not occur.

5. OPERATIONAL DEFINITIONS

In addition to ostensive definition, one other type of nonverbal definition, called **operational definition**, is especially important to scientific studies. A Nobel prize-winning physicist named P. W. Bridgman (*The Logic of Modern Physics,* 1927) first introduced the technique. Bridgman was aware that words could cause confusion because of their ability to carry various emotive and referential meanings. As a scientist, he was concerned about variations in the meanings of *scientific* terms as a result of different associations and contexts of use. He wanted to establish the meanings of scientifically important terms in a way that guaranteed that any scientist who used these terms would employ them in exactly the same way. Bridgman proposed fixing the meanings of scientifically important terms by specifying public and repeatable operations, with specific outcomes, to determine whether a term was applicable in a particular situation.

Example

"Each side of my table is three feet long" means that when a standard yardstick is lined up with each side of my table (the operation), the ends of the yardstick coincide with the ends of my table (the outcome).

The technique of operational definition is not intended to offer verbal definitions of abstract terms, such as *length*. Instead, a public and repeatable physical operation (such as laying a standard yardstick along the edge of a table) is specified for determining whether or not a sentence containing specific expressions such as "is three feet long" can be applied correctly to a situation. Nothing is lost, Bridgman believed, by refusing to consider *length* in the abstract, because scientists use the concept of length only in specific contexts. Once we understand how to use sentences in which expressions like "three feet long" occur, then we understand what such expressions mean. Since the operation of measuring with a standard yardstick is public and repeatable, this operational definition guarantees that scientists will all use the expression "three feet long" in exactly the same way.

With suitable scientific instruments, many of the terms used by scientists can be defined operationally. For example, "This flame is blue" can be operationally defined as meaning that when subjected to analysis by a spectrometer, the flame registers between 4,240 and 4,912 angstrom units of wave length. (Notice that this operational definition also eliminates any borderline cases of application of the color term.) Operations other than measurement can also be used in operational definitions. For example, "The liquid in this jar is acid" means that when a piece of litmus paper is placed in this liquid, the litmus paper turns (or remains) pink. All that is required is a high degree of agreement among various observers as to the outcome of the operation and that the operation be repeatable.

The technique of operational definition has problematic features. For example, when we refer to the temperature of a body, we tend to ignore the fact that there are several different types of instruments and operations available for measuring temperature and no operation for coordinating the various results. In such cases, we cannot, strictly speaking, refer to "the temperature" of a particular object but only, for example, to "the mercury thermometer reading" or "the alcohol thermometer reading." In addition, some measuring instruments cannot be used throughout the full range of a quantity. For example, alcohol thermometers cannot be used to measure extremely hot things. These problems with instruments of observation and measurement introduce some awkwardness into scientific discourse. However, many scientists are willing to pay this price in order to specify the meanings of terms by tying them to observations and measurements.

More serious problems arise in trying to define operationally some highly theoretical terms used by scientists. *Electron,* for example, does not refer to anything that can be directly observed or measured. Electrons are unobservable entities that scientists invoke to account for certain kinds of observed behavior. Scientists infer the existence and behavior of electrons on the basis of highly sophisticated ideas about the causes of reactions in various physical experiments. Electrons play a fundamental role in high-level physical theories about the nature of matter. Attempts to reduce terms such as *electron* to terms that can be operationally defined have not been successful.

As things stand now, in light of the various difficulties surrounding operational definition, the program offers little hope of providing such definitions for *all* the important terms used by physical scientists. Nevertheless, this form of definition is regarded as important in standardizing meanings of many scientific terms by establishing operational criteria for their application.

Even though operational definitions were first proposed for the physical sciences and have encountered serious difficulties there, many social scientists remain enthusiastic about the possibility of constructing operational definitions for the terms that occur in their own disciplines. Behavioral psychologists, for example, believe that operational definitions are the best way to handle so-called mental terms, such as *intelligence, belief, anxiety,* and *fear.* They have tried to specify publicly observable features of behavior or physiology in order to define particular concrete uses of such terms.

Examples

"John Jones is afraid of the dark" means that whenever Jones is in a dark place, he breaks out in a cold sweat and begins to tremble.

"Maria Garcia is very intelligent" means that Garcia scored above 135 on the Stanford-Binet (IQ) test.

Although Bridgman allowed for symbolic operations (such as pencil-and-paper operations that have test scores as their outcomes) along with physical operations, attempts to define mental terms operationally are highly controversial. Two types of objections prevail. One has to do with the obvious problem of how to quantify concepts such as *intelligence.* Measuring someone's intelligence is much less straightforward than measuring that person's height, just as monitoring the movement of the electrons in a body is less closely tied to direct observation than measuring a body's temperature. Critics object that intelligence tests depend on specific cultural backgrounds and ignore many features that we believe human intelligence includes. Similarly, physiological manifestations of fear, anxiety, and other mental states vary from person to person and culture to culture, making it difficult to specify the publicly observable criteria for the presence of such states.

A second objection cuts deeper into the program of operational definition. An operational definition of a mental property equates that property with the outcome of some operation. Many people say, however, that even if we devised satisfactory tests for measuring intelligence, intelligence itself could not be the score on the test. The test score, these objectors say, might be a good *indicator* of the degree of intelligence possessed by a person, but it would not be the *same thing* as intelligence. In other words, critics of operationalism assert that the *meaning* of someone's being in a particular mental state cannot be equated with the outcome of any measurement.

Despite these difficulties, some strong supporters of operational definition maintain that a term is scientifically meaningful only insofar as it can be operationally defined. They say that terms that cannot be defined operationally are of no use to science and that things amenable to operational definition are the only suitable objects for scientific study. Others take the more moderate view that although operational definitions play an important role in any science, their usefulness is limited, and it is inappropriate to demand operational definitions for *every* term used in a discipline.

Exercise Set 2.8

1. Try to formulate *operational definitions* for each of the following:
    a. The term "sour" in "This lemon tastes sour."
    b. The expression "weighs 120 pounds" in "Joan weighs 120 pounds."
    c. The expression "believe that Crosby is the National Hockey League's most valuable player" in "The Penguins believe that Crosby is the National Hockey League's most valuable player."
    d. The term "elastic" in "These bandages are elastic."

2. Social scientists often use questionnaires to formulate operational definitions. For example, they might be interested in arriving at an operational definition for the term *alcoholic* if they wanted to correlate alcoholism with some other social phenomenon, such as working in a particular profession or being subjected to the stresses of student life. Try to formulate a questionnaire (using about ten questions) that would operationally define whether or not the person who answers the questionnaire is an alcoholic. Mention any difficulties involved in devising such a questionnaire.

V. USE AND MENTION

Careful readers of this chapter will have noticed that whenever we mention words (that is, talk about the words themselves) rather than use words to refer to other objects in the world, we either enclose the word that is mentioned in quotation marks or we italicize it. These are two standard conventions for forming the name of a word so that we can talk about it, and they signal when a word is being mentioned rather than used. A third convention is to display the linguistic item that is mentioned on a separate line.

Example

Consider the difference between the following two sentences:
   "Alcoholism" has ten letters.
   Alcoholism is a serious social problem in the United States.

Normally, as in the above example, the context makes clear whether a term is being used or mentioned, but using the name of a word to talk about that word adds a degree of clarity. We should be careful to use the quotation names of words (or the italic names) when we want to emphasize that we are mentioning (not using) inappropriate words, such as ethnic slurs. For example, in discussions of the book *Huckleberry Finn*, we can use quotation names to refer to any objectionable terms, making it clear that we are mentioning the language for purposes of critical discussion rather than using racist language.

Exercise Set 2.9

1. Using quotation marks to form the names of linguistic expressions, punctuate each of the following in such a way that the resulting sentence is true.
    a. Kim is a name used for both males and females.
    b. Premiss is sometimes spelled with a single s and a final e.
    c. You can find the definition of stereotype in any college dictionary.
    d. Engravers use burin differently from archaeologists.
    e. To swallow something hook, line, and sinker means to believe it completely.
2. Numerals are linguistic expressions that are the names of numbers. Bearing this in mind, and using quotation marks to form the names of linguistic expressions, punctuate each of the following in such a way that the resulting sentence is true. (Some of the sentences may not need further punctuation.)
    a. The Roman numeral M represents one thousand.
    b. The winning number is 77777.
    c. Only two distinct symbols, 0 and 1, are used in binary numerals.
    d. The Arabic decimal, Roman, and binary representations of the number three are, respectively, 3, III, and 11.
    e. $7 + 4 = 11$.

VI. REVIEW

In this chapter, we have looked at how language serves various purposes and how definitions capture different aspects of meaning. Most definitions are verbal, but two important types of definition (ostensive and operational) are nonverbal. Nonverbal definitions are especially important for providing a link between language and the world. Verbal definitions serve a number of purposes, such as providing a standard meaning of a term; introducing a new term into the language; reducing vagueness; enhancing a point of view; and advancing a theory. When we are aware of the different types and purposes of definitions, we are able to state our ideas more clearly, evaluate arguments more carefully, and avoid some common mistakes in reasoning. New terms introduced in this chapter include the following:

Ambiguous   A word or expression is ambiguous when it has several distinct, nonoverlapping meanings. An ambiguity that results from grammatical structure is an **amphiboly**. An ambiguity of **accent** arises from a shift in emphasis.

Equivocation   Equivocation is the use of an ambiguous expression in more than one of its senses in a single context. When an argument depends on equivocation to establish a conclusion, the **fallacy of equivocation** is committed.

Extension   The set of objects to which a term refers.

Implicit Definition   In implicit definitions terms are defined by showing how they are used in a given situation or situations. Examples include implicit definitions of theoretical terms and definitions that present an expression in which the defined term occurs, along with a synonymous expression in which it does not.

Intension   The intension of a term is the set of all and only those properties a thing must possess for the term to apply to it.

Intensional Definition   Defining a term by stating the properties a thing must possess for the term to apply to it is intensional definition. All intensional definitions are verbal. Further distinctions among intensional definitions take into account the various purposes of definition:

> **Lexical Definition**   To present the accepted standard use of a term is the purpose of lexical definition.

> **Stipulative Definition**   To introduce a new term into the language is the purpose of stipulative definition.

> **Persuasive Definition**   The purpose of persuasive definition is to express or evoke an attitude, such as approval or disapproval, toward things referred to by the term.

> **Precising Definition**   Precising definitions reduce the vagueness of a term.

> **Theoretical Definition**   To construct a theory is the purpose of a theoretical definition. These definitions may be explicit, in which case terms are defined by giving synonymous expressions formulated in the vocabulary of the theory, or implicit, in which case terms are defined according to their use in the laws or generalizations of the theory.

Operational Definition   This type of definition specifies a publicly observable and repeatable operation with a specified outcome that determines whether a sentence containing the expression is correctly applicable to a given situation.

Ostensive Definition (or nonverbal extensional definition)   This type of definition is a nonverbal form of definition in which pointing or some other way of indicating the extension of a term is used to give the meaning of the term.

Syntactic Definition (or grammatical definition)   Terms without an intension or extension are sometimes defined by indicating their syntactic or grammatical role in a language. These definitions are often supplemented by presenting a context in which the term occurs. (Example: A is an indefinite article used in such expressions as "A dog ran out into the road.")

Vagueness   A term is vague if there are borderline areas in which it is unclear whether or not the term applies, or if it has several overlapping meanings. *Vague* also refers to language that is general rather than specific. Vagueness is a useful feature of language, but definitions that reduce vagueness are required in some circumstances.

Verbal Extensional Definition   Defining a term by listing or naming members of its extension is verbal extensional definition.

Exercise Set 2.10

PART I. Classify each of the following definitions as to type:

1. "Communism" means "an economic theory or system of ownership of all property by the community as a whole."

2. "Communism" means "a form of government characterized by rigid state planning and control of the economy, ruthless suppression of all opposing political parties, suppression of individual liberties under a dictatorship, and expansion by military action and subversion."

3. "Embryonic stem cell" means "unspecialized cell extracted from four- to five-day-old embryos that have the capacity to develop into almost any type of tissue in the body."

4. "NFL team" means "Pittsburgh Steelers, Green Bay Packers, New England Patriots, Philadelphia Eagles, Dallas Cowboys, New York Jets, Minnesota Vikings, and New Orleans Saints."

5. "Monotreme" means "platypuses and echidnas."

6. "Monotreme" means "egg-laying mammal."

7. "Romantic" means "impractical in conception or planning."

8. "Carl is obese" means "Carl's BMI [body-mass index] measures 31."

9. In the report filed with the Department of Justice, "EPA" means "Environmental Protection Agency."

10. Just as "I believe in God" often means "I prefer not to think," so does "I love you" often mean "I want to own you."

    —J. Fowles, *Daniel Martin*

11. "Not both soup and salad" means "either no salad or no soup."

12. Two psychiatrists and a sports scientist (in the June 2005 issue of *The Physician and Sportsmedicine*) use the term "obligatory exerciser" to refer to those "who feel obligated or compelled to continue exercising despite the risk of adverse physiologic or psychological consequences, such as social isolation and injuries caused by overtraining. For obligatory exercisers, exercise is an addiction not a free choice."

13. "Egregious" means "flagrant."

14. "The" is a definite article that is used to refer to a particular person, place, or thing.

15. "LBD" means "little black dress."

16. "Black tie" when written on an invitation means "men are required to wear semiformal evening clothes to this event."

17. Philosophy: a discipline that deals with unintelligible answers to insoluble problems.

—H. Adams

18. "Markov chain" means "a discrete stochastic process in which the probabilities of occurrences of various future states depend only on the present state of the system or on the immediately preceding state."

19. "State university" means "an institution of higher learning that grants advanced degrees and is supported by taxes."

20. "Abortion" means "the deliberate murder of a human fetus."

PART II. What sort of definition is needed to settle each of the following issues?

1. Should a travel trailer or camper be assessed as a mobile home?

If the camper and travel trailers are considered to be mobile homes, the property tax must be paid in the same year that they are assessed. If the assessor considers the camper to be a recreational device and actually a part of the owner's personal property, the camper is considered in the same category as a boat or an automobile, and the tax is not paid until the year after it is assessed.

—Editorial, *The Indianapolis Star*

2. According to some philosophers, the ideal or ethical law is grounded in nature, and the various interpretations that have been placed on *nature* have generated different forms of natural-law theory. A serious problem, then, is how to define *nature*.

PART III

1. The definition of "abortion" in Part I, Exercise 20, has negative emotive force. Can you find a definition of "abortion" that is neutral with respect to emotive force?

2. Business people and advertisers recognize that the name of a company can have a positive or negative influence on the success of the company. For example, the brand name "Spanx" was chosen by the company owner/ inventor of a line of lycra foundation undergarments for women (and now men also). What is your opinion of this name? Choose some company that you believe has a "success-inducing" name, and discuss why that is so.

3. The following definition of "marriage" can be found in Webster's Ninth *New College Dictionary*: "the institution whereby men and women are joined in a special kind of social and legal dependence for the purpose of founding and maintaining a family."

   Although this definition is found in a dictionary (lexicon), is it only a lexical definition? Some people have argued on the basis of this definition that same-sex marriages must not be legal. Comment on whether a definition such as this has the ability to determine laws concerning marriage.

Chapter Three

DEDUCTIVE ARGUMENTS, INDUCTIVE ARGUMENTS, AND FALLACIES

I. INTRODUCTION

The premisses of any argument are put forth as reasons for accepting its conclusion. Two questions thus arise:

1. Are the premisses true? We should doubt a conclusion based on premisses known to be false.
2. Is the argument logical? That is to say, would the premisses, if true, provide strong support for the conclusion?

To decide whether premisses are true, we need information about the world, about the meanings of words, or both. For example, suppose a financial analyst argues that the stock market will go up because the Federal Reserve Bank is going to reduce interest rates. To know whether the Fed intends to reduce rates, we need to know whether there has been an official announcement by the Fed or whether the analyst is depending on an insider's tip or hunch.

The analyst's argument relies also on an unstated premiss about the connection between falling interest rates and a rising market. This correlation often holds, but there are important exceptions. In some circumstances, reducing rates will not stir a sluggish market.

Example

In standard form the analyst's argument is:

> The Fed will reduce interest rates.
> Very often, when interest rates fall, the market rises.
> _____
> The market will rise.

Our study of arguments focuses on the question of whether the premisses would, if true, support the conclusion. We can do this without knowing whether the premisses are actually true. The analyst's argument is logical, which is to say that if the analyst has the facts straight (if both premisses are true) and if other relevant information is not being ignored, then probably the market will rise.

To investigate the logical strength of ordinary-language arguments, we look at the contexts in which they occur, the meanings of the terms in the argument, and certain structural features of the arguments. We can analyze structures, or forms, of arguments in a general way, without reference to specialized factual knowledge. In the sample argument above, for example, an important structural feature is that the claim made in the first premiss is linked with the claim made in the conclusion by a generalization that states that two types of things (falling rates and rising markets) regularly go together. This structural feature occurs in many arguments and can be discussed without reference to the factual content of the arguments. We can thus examine in a general way the structures that various arguments share as well as how structural features strengthen or weaken arguments.

In this chapter we begin to address such structural questions by distinguishing three types of arguments. To do this we ask whether the premises of an argument, if true, (1) guarantee the truth of the conclusion, (2) make it probable that the conclusion is true, or (3) fail to provide support for the conclusion. We can perform triage on arguments in this way without knowing whether their premises and conclusions are actually true.

An argument in the first category is **deductive**. An argument is deductive when its premises and conclusion are related in such a way that the truth of the premises guarantees the truth of the conclusion. Such an argument is sometimes called a **valid**, or deductively valid, argument to distinguish it from the fallacies that superficially resemble deductive arguments but lack the essential characteristic of preserving truth. A relationship of **deductive support** holds between the premises and conclusion of a deductive argument. In a deductive argument, *if* the premises are all true, then the conclusion *must* be true.

The second type of argument is **inductive**. In such an argument, the premises provide a different kind of support for the conclusion. In an inductive argument, *if* the premises are all true, then *probably* the conclusion is true, but it might be false. **Inductive support** provides good reasons but not conclusive reasons to accept the conclusion.

Into the third category fall the **fallacies**. In a fallacy, or **fallacious argument**, the alleged evidence offers only very weak support or is irrelevant to the conclusion. We have already seen that in the fallacy of equivocation, the premises are irrelevant to the conclusion because of a shift in meaning of some crucial term. Fallacies also occur when the premises make some irrelevant appeal to our emotions instead of providing evidence for the truth of the conclusion. Still other fallacies have structures that resemble those of deductive or inductive arguments while violating some standard of deductive or inductive reasoning. These pretenders can be called *deductive fallacies*, or *invalid arguments,* when they resemble deductive arguments or *inductive fallacies* when they resemble inductive arguments. The premises of fallacious arguments, even if true, do not guarantee or even make it probable that the conclusion is true. The conclusion of a fallacious argument might be true, but its premises are not good reasons to believe it.

Arguments (either deductive or inductive) that provide the proper kind of support for their conclusions and also have all true premises are called **sound arguments**. (Terminology on this point varies. Some writers prefer to apply the term *sound* only to deductive arguments and use a different term, such as *cogent,* to refer to an inductive argument with all true premises.)

In this chapter, we look at examples of deductive and inductive arguments to learn more about the differences between them. Recognizing each type is important because different standards apply for evaluating inductive and deductive arguments. This chapter also discusses some general characteristics of fallacious arguments and considers a few examples of fallacies.

II. DEDUCTIVE ARGUMENTS

In a deductive argument, if all the premisses are true, the conclusion cannot be false. This guarantee—that true premisses will yield true conclusions—is the outstanding characteristic of deductive arguments, and it is obviously a valuable feature. How is the truth of the premisses preserved? The conclusion of a deductive argument puts together or restates information that is contained in the premisses without adding new information about the world. For example, the conclusion of the argument might depend on the definition of some expression in the premisses:

> Jack is a bachelor.
> _____
> He has no wife.

The conclusion of this argument makes explicit something about the meaning of *bachelor* rather than telling us something new about Jack. Because the truth of the conclusion depends solely on the truth of the premiss, given conventional linguistic meanings, the conclusion contains no new information about the world.

The conclusion of a deductive argument might be an instance of a general principle that is stated in the premiss:

> Addition is commutative.
> _____
> $3 + 4 = 4 + 3$

Again, to see that the conclusion cannot be false if the premiss is true, we need only to understand the meaning of the premiss (that is, reordering the terms to be added does not change the value of the sum) and to understand that the conclusion says the sum of 3 and 4 is the same as the sum of 4 and 3. Alternately, the conclusions of some deductive arguments follow as a result of connections drawn among the premisses by important logical terms, such as *and, or, not, all,* and *some*:

Examples

> 1. Either Jeb is not graduating, or he has paid his tuition bill.
> But he is graduating.
> _____
> He has paid his tuition bill

> 2. All whales are mammals.
> All mammals are warm-blooded.
> _____
> All whales are warm-blooded.

The next argument is as old as the first text in logic—written more than 2,300 years ago.

All men are mortal.
Socrates is a man.
———————————
Socrates is mortal.

The first premiss is a universal generalization. It contains the information that all members of one class, or type of thing (the class of men), are also members of another class (the class of mortals). The second premiss provides the information that the individual whose name is Socrates is a member of the class of men. The conclusion of the argument combines the information contained separately in the two premisses. Strictly speaking, the conclusion contains no new information not already present in the premisses. Neither premiss says explicitly (in just those words) what is said in the conclusion, but the information in the conclusion is implicit in the premisses. Moreover, this is true not only for the simple arguments in the three examples above but also for every argument in which the conclusion follows deductively from its premisses.

Deductive arguments **preserve truth** because they recombine and restate information that is contained at least implicitly in the premisses. Whereas the conclusion of a deductive argument can restate or recombine information, put it together in novel ways, and thus make explicit what was formerly only implicit, such a conclusion cannot go beyond what was already present, at least implicitly, in the premisses to advance our knowledge of what the world is like. Deductive arguments preserve truth, but they cannot extend factual knowledge.

If deductive arguments cannot give us any new information that was not already present in the premisses, what purpose do they serve? Why should we bother to state a conclusion if all of the necessary information is already provided in the premisses? If all arguments were as simple as the example about Socrates, there would be little reason to state conclusions. The mere statement of both premisses together would be sufficient for most people to get the point or "to put two and two together." Sometimes such simple arguments are presented without their conclusions. For the same reason that premisses can be omitted, conclusions can also be unstated. It is boring to dwell on the obvious.

Not all deductive arguments are simple, however. Sometimes the chain of reasoning that connects the premisses to the conclusion is long and complex. When this is so, even though the conclusion contains no new information (in the sense that it only selectively *recombines* information stated in the premisses), the conclusion will seem new because we had not put together the information in the premisses in just that way. Even the person constructing the argument might be surprised to see where the premisses lead, because although the premisses jointly imply the conclusion, the conclusion is not merely a restatement or specific instance of one of the premisses. Thus, although the conclusion of a correct deductive argument cannot yield new information, it can put information together in ways that might not have occurred to anyone before. We can and do deduce conclusions that are new from a psychological standpoint. Even when the conclusions of deductive arguments are novel, surprising, or startling in this sense, however, they can only draw out what was already there in the premisses.

Example

In the following example, Smith's deductive argument reaches a conclusion that is psychologically new and surprising to Jones, even though its conclusion contains no new information. Jones commutes from his suburban home to a job in the city. Smith wants to demonstrate to Jones that he is spending three weeks of every year riding a commuter train.

Jones: Three weeks a year—that's ridiculous!

Smith: No, it's a simple matter of logic. You ride the train to and from work, one hour each way, five days a week, for a total of forty-nine weeks a year, allowing for your vacation and holidays. Using simple arithmetic, that comes to a total of 490 hours per year on the train. There are twenty-four hours in a day, and if you divide 490 by 24, you get 20 and 10/24 days. That's almost twenty-one days, or three weeks a year you spend on the train.

Jones: Ouch.

The reasoning in this argument is mathematical, and its deductive character depends on the calculations by which the conclusion is reached. Mathematical proofs are primary examples of deductive reasoning. Although mathematicians may believe on inductive grounds that a particular theorem holds in every case because it holds in every case tested so far, they do not regard the theorem as proven until it has been established as the conclusion of a deductive argument. Deductive arguments pervade our everyday lives, especially in our use of mathematics, including simple arithmetic. Balancing checkbooks, counting change, and setting up a budget all require deductive reasoning. Although you probably do not use geometry much in your everyday life now, if you studied it in high school you were intensely involved in constructing and evaluating deductive arguments. You began the course in geometry with a set of first principles—axioms, postulates, and definitions—and then proceeded to derive theorems (conclusions) on the basis of those principles. This was an exercise in deductive reasoning, and, as you no doubt remember, some parts of it were subtle. Even though you had the required premisses in hand, it was not always obvious how to combine those premisses to deduce the theorem you were supposed to prove.

All other areas of mathematics, including those that, unlike geometry, are not formulated as axiomatic systems, essentially depend on deductive arguments. All mathematical proofs, including proofs in statistics and mathematical probability, are deductive arguments. Furthermore, we can regard mathematical proofs as the purest form of deductive reasoning because even the premisses contain no information about what the real world is like. The mathematical principles that form the basis for mathematical proofs are themselves usually considered to be true by definitions of the terms involved or to be true claims about abstract constructions of the human mind, such as numbers or geometric figures. This is what Bertrand Russell (1959) was referring to when he said "I fear that, to a mind of sufficient intellectual power, the whole of mathematics would appear trivial, as trivial as the statement that a four-footed animal is an animal."

Russell does not believe that all mathematics is trivial to our minds, for our intellectual powers are limited. When we apply mathematical reasoning to factual claims, as we did in the preceding example about Jones's commuting time, the results may seem surprising—just as the results of a complicated mathematical proof may seem surprising. The point is that the use of mathematical calculations in an argument does not introduce any information about the world that goes beyond what is already stated in the premisses.

Exercise Set 3.1

For each of the following sets of premises, write a conclusion that follows deductively.

1. Hero Bicycles is the world's biggest bicycle manufacturer. Hero Bicycles is located in the Punjab, India.

2. Each cake requires five eggs. We need to make four cakes.

3. In the game of poker, four of a kind beats a full house, and a full house beats a straight.

4. The probability of rolling an ace with a fair die is 1/6. The probability of rolling two aces with a pair of fair dice is the probability of rolling an ace on the first die times the probability of rolling an ace on the second.

Many arguments concerning ethics, in which a proponent attempts to show that an action is right or wrong or that a moral principle is acceptable or unacceptable, are deductive. A standard way to establish that some kind of action is right (or wrong) is to show that all actions of that type are right (or wrong) because they fall into a broader class of right (or wrong) actions.

Example

All deliberate killing of helpless persons is wrong.
Euthanasia (mercy killing) is a deliberate killing of a helpless person.

Euthanasia is wrong.

In this argument, if the premisses are true, then the conclusion cannot be false. Whether the premisses are true (or acceptable, if one objects to regarding moral claims as true) is an important and interesting question, but the deductive character of the argument is independent of the answer to that question.

Other arguments in ethics attempt to show that some moral principle is not acceptable because it would condone or permit actions that we consider immoral. This pattern of argument is more complicated than the last one, for it contains subarguments within a larger argument. The following example is an argument of this type.

Example

First subargument:

> Whatever is done as an expression of love is morally acceptable.
> Mrs. X, who believed her child's soul was possessed by demons that
>   could be driven out only by beating the child, beat her child severely
>   because she loved him.
> _____
> Mrs. X did something morally acceptable when she beat the child.

Second subargument:

> The conclusion of the argument in the first part is obviously false.
> But that argument is deductive. (If all its premisses are true, then its conclusion
>   as well is true.)
> _____
> At least one of the premisses of the first argument is false.

Third subargument:

> At least one of the premisses of the first argument is false.
> The second premiss states a fact about Mrs. X's behavior, and its truth is not
>   in question.
> _____
> The first premiss is false. (It is not true that whatever is done as an expression
>   of love is morally acceptable.)

This method of proving that a sentence is false—taking it as a premiss and showing that it, either alone or in combination with other premisses whose truth is not in doubt, leads deductively to an obviously false conclusion—is fairly common, not only in ethical arguments but in mathematics and many other fields as well. It may seem odd to begin an argument with a premiss that is believed to be false. Nevertheless, this often happens in dialogues, when one person makes a statement and the other person tries to show that it is false.

Example

> *He:*   You don't love me anymore.
> *She:* Don't be silly. Suppose that I don't love you. If a woman doesn't love a man,
>   she doesn't care what happens to him, she doesn't want to spend time with
>   him, and she doesn't give him presents. But I do care what happens to you,
>   I do want to spend time with you, and I do give you presents. So you see,
>   I do love you.

This way of arguing is called **indirect proof**. (Mathematicians sometimes call it *proof by contradiction*.) We will look more carefully at the logical structure of this useful form of deductive argument in later chapters.

Example

Judge Richard A. Posner uses an indirect argument ("Bad News," *New York Times Book Review*, 7/31/2005) to support his claim that people do *not* consume news and opinions to become well informed about public issues.

He begins by assuming that becoming well informed about public issues does motivate the consuming of news. But then he says, "Were this so then liberals would read conservative newspapers and conservatives liberal newspapers, just as scientists test their hypotheses by confronting them with data that may refute them." But, obviously, that is not the case. Liberals tend to read liberal papers and magazines, and conservatives likewise consume news and opinions that tend to support rather than undermine their views, and so each side is unable to test its opinions against counterarguments.

Exercise Set 3.2

Whole numbers that can be divided evenly only by themselves and 1 are called "prime." For example, 1, 2, 3, 5, and 7 are all prime; 4, 8, 9, and 10 are not prime.

1. What would be the first premiss you would use in an indirect argument to establish the conclusion: The next prime number after 11 is 13?

2. Can you complete the argument that proves 13 is the next prime number after 11?

An important feature of some ethical arguments is that they apparently acknowledge exceptions to general principles of morality, such as the general prohibition against killing humans. It might seem that, because there are exceptions to general principles of morality, these principles are not universal generalizations. An examination of how exceptions are treated, however, clarifies those cases in which moral principles are regarded as universal generalizations and reveals when ethical arguments employing them have a deductive structure.

For example, although the deliberate taking of human life is morally unacceptable, exceptions are recognized. If Jones deliberately kills Smith in self-defense, this act is not necessarily considered wrong. Such actions are permissible according to a different general principle that allows killing in self-defense. The important point about such exceptions is that they too are governed by universally general principles, which may be somewhat more limited in their application. Thus, to show that a particular killing was not a wrongful act even though it was deliberate, we might show that the circumstances surrounding the act make it a case of "killing in self-defense" rather than another sort of killing. Then according to the principle that killing in self-defense is morally justifiable, the act would not be considered morally wrong. When an apparent exception to some accepted moral principle is encountered, another deductive argument, based on a different acceptable general principle, can be invoked to handle the exception.

In addition to recognizing that some types of arguments, such as those in ethics, depend heavily on deductive reasoning, we can look for other clues to alert us to the presence of deductive arguments. Because in a deductive argument if the premises are true the conclusion *cannot* be false, certain words and phrases mark the strong support provided in these arguments. Expressions such as *must, it must be the case that, necessarily, inevitably, certainly,* and *it can be deduced that* frequently indicate that an argument is deductive. The terms *entail* and *imply* also signify a deductive connection between premises and conclusion.

The indicator terms for deductive arguments are not absolutely reliable, however, because they sometimes occur in strong inductive arguments—that is to say, when a conclusion is supported strongly by evidence, but the truth of all the premises is nevertheless compatible with the falsity of the conclusion. To test whether an argument is really deductive, ask the following question: Is it impossible for the conclusion to be false if the premises are true? To answer this question for any except the simplest arguments, however, we need to know how to judge the nature of the relationship between premises and conclusion, and we need to understand the meaning of *impossible* in this context. The clues provided here regarding the contexts in which deductive arguments are normally used and the special words used to indicate the presence of a deductive argument offer some guidance. If the proponent of an argument intends it to be deductive (here again we may need to grasp the context to see this), we can judge the argument by the standards for deductive arguments.

Our task can be complicated when arguments in ordinary language are stated incompletely. Then it is especially difficult to tell whether, for example, a missing premise is a universal or a statistical generalization. Contextual clues for judging whether arguments are deductive are particularly useful at this stage because they suggest the appropriate type of missing premise. If a missing premise is to provide nontrivial support for the conclusion, it should be more plausible than the conclusion itself. If we ignore this caution about plausibility, we could transform any argument into a deductive argument by adding some suitable premise. (For example, adding the conclusion itself as an additional premise would make the argument deductive.)

Occasionally, terms such as *necessarily* make an argument look stronger than it is. For example, in this time of economic hardship many leaders of business argue against government interference with market forces, such as providing bailouts and regulating corporate practices like executive pay. They agree that economic change is desirable but argue that private business is necessarily in the best position to effect change because of its intimate connection to and knowledge of the marketplace.

Private business is indeed closely tied to what people buy and sell, which might provide a good reason to believe that it is the most effective instrument of economic change.

Nevertheless, the linkage to the marketplace is hardly compelling. The government, with its power to control the money supply, interest rates, taxes, import duties, and other aspects of the economy, for example, might be a far more effective instrument of economic change than private business, even though the latter is more closely tied to the marketplace. It is true that many large private corporations would prefer that government refrain from using those powers and let a free market determine the state of the economy. The preferences of the corporation, however, are irrelevant to how strongly the premisses of the argument support its conclusion.

In Arthur Conan Doyle's stories about master detective Sherlock Holmes, arguments are characterized as deductive although the truth of their premisses does not guarantee the truth of the conclusions. We can recognize and admire the impressive logical powers of Holmes in these stories, but we should realize that most of what he calls "deductions" are really strong inductive arguments, as logicians define the terms. That is to say, if the premisses of Holmes's arguments are true, then very probably his conclusions are true. Consider the following passage from "A Scandal in Bohemia," in which Dr. Watson visits Holmes after a long absence. Although Watson has not told him so, Holmes figures out that Watson has returned to the practice of medicine.

"And in practice again, I observe. You did not tell me that you intended to go into harness."

"Then, how do you know?"

"I see it, I deduce it. How do I know that you have been getting yourself very wet lately, and that you have a most clumsy and careless servant girl?"

"My dear Holmes," said I, "this is too much. You would certainly have been burned [as a witch] had you lived a few centuries ago. It is true that I had a country walk on Thursday and came home in a dreadful mess; but, as I have changed my clothes, I can't imagine how you deduce it. As to Mary Jane, she is incorrigible, and my wife has given her notice; but there again I fail to see how you work it out."

He chuckled to himself and rubbed his long nervous hands together.

"It is simplicity itself," said he; "my eyes tell me that on the inside of your left shoe, just where the firelight strikes it, the leather is scored by six almost parallel cuts. Obviously they have been caused by someone who has very carelessly scraped round the edges of the sole in order to remove crusted mud from it. Hence, you see, my double deduction that you had been out in vile weather, and that you had a particularly malignant boot-slitting specimen of the London slavey. As to your practice, if a gentleman walks into my rooms smelling of iodoform, with a black mark of nitrate of silver upon his right forefinger, and a bulge in the side of his top hat to show where he has secreted his stethoscope, I must be dull indeed if I do not pronounce him to be an active member of the medical profession."

The fiendishly clever Holmes is right on all counts, as usual, and his "deductions" might be convincing in a court of law. It is possible, however, that Watson cleaned his own boots and that the signs of medical practice were the result of Watson helping out in an emergency rather than setting up his own practice. In some cases, we might want to analyze arguments such as the ones Holmes gives here as if they were intended to be deductive arguments in which a universally general premiss has been left unstated. Here, however, such an approach is unlikely to work because the required premisses, such as "Every pair of boots scored by cuts was cleaned by a clumsy servant," are no more plausible—in fact, less plausible—than the conclusion. Holmes's conclusion goes beyond a clever recombination of the information he states in his premisses, and so his argument, although ingenious and persuasive, is not a truth-preserving deductive argument.

As we all know, linguistic usage varies and Holmes is entitled to call his inferences "deductive." In studies of logic, however, the term has a more restricted use. Despite general agreement among logicians about the truth-preserving character of deductive arguments, they use the term *deductive argument* in slightly differing ways. *Deductive argument* in this text refers to arguments that contain premisses that, if true, lead to a conclusion that cannot be false. Sometimes, the proponent of an argument intends it to be deductive, but the premisses are not related to the conclusion in the right way. An argument may also seem to be deductive when it contains expressions that indicate that necessarily the conclusion follows from the premisses even though this is not the case. Accordingly, some texts define *deductive arguments* as arguments in which the premisses purport to or are intended to provide deductive support for the conclusion. Then a further distinction is made between *valid* arguments, those that are truly deductive, and *invalid* arguments, those that fall short of the deductive standard. Other texts, including this one, define *deductive arguments* as those in which the premisses (including implicit premisses) actually provide the appropriate level of support. Each way of defining the term *deductive argument* has advantages and disadvantages. The disadvantage of defining the term as "an argument in which, if all the premisses are true, the conclusion cannot be false" is that deductive arguments are valid by definition, so the expression *valid deductive argument* is redundant. Moreover, a common way of referring to fallacies that mimic deductive arguments as "invalid deductive arguments" is awkward. An advantage of our definition is that it does not suggest that *inductive* arguments are defective because they lack the defining characteristic of deductive arguments. The structure and perspective of this textbook reflects the belief that it is better to recognize inductive arguments as a separate type of argument with a special role and value instead of viewing them as failed or weak versions of deductive arguments.

Exercise Set 3.3

PART I. If we define a deductive argument as one in which it is impossible for the conclusion to be false if all the premisses are true, which of the following sentences are true?

1. A deductive argument can have a false premiss.

2. A deductive argument can have a false conclusion.

3. A deductive argument can have all false premisses and a false conclusion.

4. A deductive argument can have all false premisses and a true conclusion.

5. A deductive argument can have all true premisses and a false conclusion.

6. A deductive argument can have one true premiss, several false premisses, and a true conclusion.

7. A deductive argument can have one false premiss, several true premisses, and a false conclusion.

8. A deductive argument can have the same sentence as one of its premisses and as its conclusion.

PART II. For each of the following arguments, indicate in a general way the definitional or structural features that make it deductive. If the argument requires the addition of an obviously true but unstated premiss, say what that premiss is.

1. John and Mary are siblings. Therefore, Mary has a brother.

2. Mary is Michael's mother. Therefore, Michael is Mary's son.

3. Black swans live in Australia. Therefore, not all swans are white.

4. Every senior owns a smart phone. Carlos does not own a smart phone. Therefore, Carlos is not a senior.

5. The student council meeting began at 11 A.M. and ended at 2 P.M. Thus, the council meeting lasted three hours.

6. If unrest persists in the Middle East then oil supplies will be disrupted. If oil supplies are disrupted, then gasoline prices will rise. And unrest will persist in the Middle East, so gas prices will go up.

7. Graduation ceremonies will be held in the stadium, which seats 1,500 people. Four tickets to the graduation ceremony are reserved for each graduating senior. There are 400 graduating seniors. So if all the ticket holders show up for graduation, there won't be enough seats for everyone.

8. A person should not be judged guilty of murder if he was certified as insane at the time of the act of killing another person. The court has accepted the doctor's certification of Smith's insanity at the time of killing. Therefore, Smith should not be judged guilty of murder.

9. Joe paid $3,000 to have 500 copies of his drawing printed for online sale and will have to pay a 15% commission for each print he sells. Because he is

charging only $50 for each print, he will need to sell at least 71 to recover his costs.

10. Poisonous plants and plant parts, such as some mushrooms and the beans of castor plants, occur in nature. Therefore, it is incorrect to conclude that a substance is beneficial to your health just because it is natural.

11. If we can prevent something bad without sacrificing anything of comparable significance, we ought to do it.
    Absolute poverty is bad.
    There is some absolute poverty we can prevent without sacrificing anything of comparable moral significance.
    _____

    We ought to prevent some absolute poverty.

    —P. Singer, *Practical Ethics*, 1993

12. "Where is he, then?"
    "I have already said that he must have gone to King's Pyland or to Mapleton. He is not at King's Pyland. Therefore he is at Mapleton."

    —A. C. Doyle, *"Silver Blaze"*

PART III. None of the following six arguments is deductive. Describe a situation in which the conclusion of each of the following arguments could turn out to be false even though the premises are all true.

1. Every political survey has indicated that the next governor of the state will be a Republican. Therefore, the Republican candidate will win the governor's seat in the next election.

2. Every senior can register for this class. Sally is not a senior. Sally cannot register for this class.

3. Greer was rushed to the hospital yesterday, apparently suffering from heat exhaustion. Therefore, Greer will not win the marathon today.

4. Every student admitted to this college has the ability to perform well in college classes. You have been admitted to this college. Thus, you will perform well in this logic class.

5. Many studies have shown that reduction in smoking among teenagers is correlated with raising the price of cigarettes. Now David Leonhardt, writing in the *New York Times,* says a similar effect on beer drinking among teenagers happens when either the cost of beer or the penalties for underage drinking are raised. He cites lower rates of teenage drinking in the several states that have adopted those policies.

6. In Shakespeare's *Hamlet*, Polonius gives the following advice to his son Laertes:

    This above all, to thine own self be true,
    And it must follow, as the night the day,
    Thou canst not then be false to any man.

III. INDUCTIVE ARGUMENTS

Inductive arguments can have false conclusions even when all the premisses are true and support the conclusion in the sense of contributing to or upholding its probability. Inductive arguments lack the definitive and valuable truth-preserving feature of deductive arguments. This apparent shortcoming, however, is more than offset by a feature of inductive arguments that is lacking in deductive arguments. Inductive arguments can extend or amplify our factual knowledge. For this reason, we call inductive arguments **ampliative**. Conclusions of inductive arguments amplify or go beyond the information found in their premisses. Conclusions of ampliative arguments contain new information that is not present, even implicitly, in their premisses. Although the field of mathematics is well suited to the almost exclusive use of deductive reasoning, in all other fields of human endeavor—natural science, the social sciences, history, literary criticism, the practical knowledge of everyday affairs, and even ethics—inductive inferences and arguments are indispensable.

Inductive arguments figure strongly in reasoning about causes. Many of Holmes's arguments that impressed Dr. Watson supported claims about causes. Thus, Holmes inferred that the cause of the bulge in Dr. Watson's top hat was a hidden stethoscope and that the cause of Watson's carrying a stethoscope was a return to medical practice. The following argument, which is the opening passage in Charles Darwin's *The Origin of Species,* is also causal:

> When we compare the individuals of the same variety or sub- variety of our older cultivated plants and animals, one of the first points which strikes us is, that they generally differ more from each other than do the individuals of any one species or variety in a state of nature. And if we reflect on the vast diversity of the plants and animals which have been cultivated, and which have varied during all ages under the most different climates and treatment, we are driven to conclude that this great variability is due to our domestic productions having been raised under conditions of life not so uniform as, and somewhat different from, those to which the parent species had been exposed under nature.

Darwin noted differences among members of the same species of domestic plants and animals, such as dogs. The range of types from Chihuahuas to Great Danes is far more varied than that found in wild species such as elephants, which come only in two varieties (African and Asian). Darwin concluded that differences within a single species occur because humans breed plants and animals under a much greater variety of conditions than the conditions to which wild species are exposed. Humans have bred dogs for centuries in almost every part of the world—for sport, show, work, and a variety of other purposes. Elephants flourish in highly specialized environments in only a few places.

Causal arguments are among the most common inductive arguments. Other familiar types of inductive arguments include the following:

1. Arguments that conclude something about the future on the basis of what has happened in the past.

> That a stone will fall, that fire will burn, that the earth has solidity, we have observed a thousand and a thousand times; and when any new instance of this nature is presented, we draw without hesitation the accustomed inference.
>
> —D. Hume, *Dialogues Concerning Natural Religion*

Philo, the speaker in this passage of the dialogue, does not actually state the obvious conclusion—that in the future, stones will continue to fall, fire to burn, and the earth to be solid—but his meaning is clear.

2. Arguments that conclude something about the past on the basis of present evidence.

> Pollen grains, though microscopic, are preserved in peat bogs in a remarkable manner for hundreds and even thousands of years. Since the pollen of every plant has its own special form, it is possible with the microscope to establish what plants were growing at different points in time. The distinct layers in peatbogs thus become, as it were, the pages of a great picture book illustrating the changing flora of the land through the ages.
>
> —P. V. Glob, *The Bog People*, 1971

Here the pollen, which is observed in the present, provides the basis for reconstructing the types of vegetation that grew in prehistoric times. Historians, geologists, archaeologists—all who are concerned with knowledge of the past—use inductive reasoning in this way.

3. Arguments that generalize on the basis of a sample of observations or experiments.

This is the type of inductive reasoning that is used in public opinion polls to determine the popularity of a political candidate or to learn about the public's attitude toward a particular piece of legislation. You have seen or heard such arguments, particularly in election years. Here is another example of this form of reasoning:

> Various researchers have studied the different effect of divorce on men and women. One study of 3,000 divorces, based on Los Angeles county records from 1977–78, showed that when marital property was divided equally in a divorce, men's standard of living improved by 42% on average during the first year following the divorce, while women's dropped by 73%. Later analysis of the same

data by Richard Peterson showed that because of mistakes in recording information, the true figure was closer to a 10% increase for men and a 27% decline for women.

The statistical information shows that a policy designed to be fair (50–50 division of property in divorce settlements) has unexpected implications. This information may have an influence on future financial calculations for divorce settlements. Generalizing on the basis of samples is one of the most useful ways in which we extend our knowledge through inductive reasoning.

4. Arguments that conclude something about a particular case on the basis of what happens usually or frequently, but not always.

The following passage, taken from Mark Twain's *Notebook*, is an amusing example of this common form of inductive argument.

> At bottom I did not believe I had touched that man. The law of probabilities decreed me guiltless of his blood, for in all my small experience with guns I had never hit anything I had tried to hit. And I knew I had done my best to hit him.
>
> —Mark Twain, *Notebook*

5. Arguments that conclude that a further similarity holds on the basis of known similarities between two types of things.

This form of reasoning is often used in making a decision to buy a particular brand of merchandise on the basis of good performance by other items of the same brand. Similarities in materials, methods of manufacturing, and other product qualities provide evidence to support some further, as yet unobserved similarity, such as durability, in a new product. This kind of reasoning also provides the focus for much of our medical research. Investigators observe the effects of various substances on experimental animals, which are similar to humans in certain respects, and conclude that those substances will affect humans in similar ways. Here is an example:

> Marian C. Diamond, professor of anatomy at the University of California at Berkeley, warned recently that birth control pills may inhibit development of the brain.
>
> Dr. Diamond said that research reveals that female sex hormones contained in birth control pills limit growth of the cerebral cortex, a part of the brain which regulates intelligence.
>
> Dr. Diamond has been working with female rats into which she has injected a hormone equivalent to a birth control pill. Such rats showed less growth of the cerebral cortex than rats not injected with the hormone.
>
> —*Parade Magazine*

Recognizing contexts in which inductive arguments are appropriate will help to determine whether a given argument is inductive or deductive, but the real test of a deductive argument is to ask the following: Would the premisses, if true, make it impossible for the conclusion to be false? In an inductive argument, the falsity of the conclusion is compatible with the truth of the premisses, but the premisses should make it *probable* or *likely* that the conclusion is true as well. As in deductive arguments, special terms draw attention to the inductive nature of the link between the premisses and the conclusion. These terms include *probably, usually, tends to support, likely, very likely,* and *almost always.* When Mark Twain said "The law of *probabilities* decreed me guiltless," he indicated that his argument was inductive. The terms *may* or *might* sometimes point to the tentative nature of an inductively drawn conclusion, as in Dr. Diamond's claim that "birth control pills *may* inhibit development of the brain."

An important difference between deductive and inductive arguments is that whereas deductive support is an all-or-nothing affair (either the truth of the premisses is incompatible with the falsity of the conclusion or not), inductive support may vary in strength. The terms used to indicate that an argument is inductive can provide information about the degree of strength of the argument. For example, *may, might,* and *possibly* indicate weak or moderate support; whereas *almost always, highly probable,* and *very likely* indicate strong support. The expressions *with practical certainty* or *with moral certainty* indicate a very high degree of inductive support. They are appropriate when the evidence is overwhelmingly strong. Nevertheless, despite the meaning of the term *certain,* this support is different from that demanded in deductive arguments. The phrase *beyond all reasonable doubt* often indicates a strong inductive argument, but it can signal a deductive argument as well.

A further difference between inductive and deductive arguments concerns how additional information can affect the strength of the argument. Suppose you have received $1,000 from the estate of a distant relative. You want to invest it in a mutual fund, and your main objective is preservation of capital with reasonable income from your investment. You select a fund that has paid a dividend every quarter for forty years and that has shown moderate growth. Your decision was based on the following argument:

> Fund X has a 40-year record of paying regular dividends while
>   maintaining a slow growth of capital.
>
> My investment objectives are regular income and preservation of capital.
> _____
> Fund X is a suitable investment for me.

Suppose you later learn that Fund X has just undergone a reorganization and that the new managers have a reputation for picking speculative stocks with aggressive growth potential. With the addition of this new information to your original argument, the support for the conclusion is considerably weaker.

Alternatively, additional information can strengthen an inductive argument. Consider some recent research on the role of heredity in alcoholism. On the basis of a 10-year study of 202 alcoholic men, Dr. T. Reich, at the Alcohol Research Center at Washington University, learned that 38 percent had alcoholic fathers, 21 percent had alcoholic mothers, 57 percent had alcoholic brothers, 15 percent had alcoholic sisters, 32 percent had alcoholic sons, and 19 percent had alcoholic daughters. When we realize that in the general population, alcoholism develops in only 3 percent of women and 8 to 10 per cent of men, this information supports the conclusion that hereditary factors are important in the development of alcoholism. Additional information from Swedish studies of adopted children—which clearly showed that the children of alcoholics are four times more likely than other children to become alcoholics even if the children are adopted early in life by people who do not abuse alcohol—makes the argument in support of the hereditary character of alcoholism even stronger.

Thus as these examples show, additional information can either strengthen or weaken an inductive argument. In contrast, if a deductive argument is already valid, then the addition of premisses cannot strengthen the argument or weaken it in the sense of making it invalid. The truth of its original premisses is incompatible with the falsity of its conclusion. Because *if* the premisses in the original argument were true, then the conclusion would be true as well; adding anything (even a false premiss) to the premisses cannot change that relationship. Premisses of inductive arguments, however, can offer a range of support—from very strong to moderate to weak—for their conclusions. So additional premisses can make an argument either stronger or weaker. When the support in an inductive argument is extremely weak but the argument superficially resembles a correct inductive argument, the argument is called an inductive fallacy.

Some arguments, particularly those used in science, combine inductive and deductive elements. An argument used by Louis Pasteur is an example. Pasteur is well known for his method of pasteurization, a gentle heating process that destroys harmful organisms in fresh milk. Before Pasteur tried pasteurizing milk, he suggested the process as a solution to the problem of wine turning sour during the aging process. Yeast cells, which are living organisms, are responsible for the fermentation necessary to make wine. Using a microscope, Pasteur discovered that there were several types of yeast in wine. He hypothesized that after the fermentation yeasts had done their work, some of the other yeasts caused the wine to sour during the aging process. He reasoned that if all remaining yeast cells in the wine were destroyed by gentle heating *after* fermentation was completed, the wine could age without souring. His method worked and earned him the enthusiastic thanks of the wine industry in France.

The deductive part of Pasteur's argument is:

> Yeast cells are the cause of souring in wine.
> Gentle heating destroys yeast cells.
> ——————————————————
> Gently heated wine does not sour.

After experiments showed that heated wine did not sour, Pasteur *inductively* concluded that his belief about yeast *causing* the wine to sour was correct. This conclusion follows inductively rather than deductively; although the yeast cells were killed by heating, it is *possible* that some other agent that also could be destroyed by heating was the causal factor in wine spoilage. Even with a deductive component, arguments of this type have an overall inductive structure because the conclusion about the *cause* does not follow with certainty from the premises concerning the success of the experiment. Arguments of this type are fundamental to scientific reasoning.

Exercise Set 3.4

PART I. Find an example of an inductive argument in a newspaper, magazine, or other contemporary source. Reconstruct the argument in standard form and tell whether it falls into any of the six categories described in this section.

PART II. Identify the premises and the conclusion of each of the following inductive arguments. If the argument belongs to one of the six common types of inductive argument discussed in this section, identify which one.

1. Waynesburg, a small town in Pennsylvania, celebrates "Rain Day" on July 29 each year. Records show that it has rained on July 29 in Waynesburg on 108 of the last 130 years. It is very likely that rain will fall in Waynesburg on July 29 next year.

2. The problem of obesity has reached epidemic proportions in America. Yet an article published by the Department of Agriculture suggests that people freely choose to overeat and that government efforts to combat obesity will not work. Paul Krugman (*The New York Times*, 7/8/2005) argues that because "the history of government interventions on behalf of public health, from the construction of sewer systems to the campaign against smoking, is one of consistent, life-enhancing success," government action could help significantly to overcome obesity, America's fastest-growing health problem.

3. Researcher K. Palazoglu of the University of Mersin, Turkey, showed that microwaving French fries before cooking reduces acrylamide, a harmful chemical.

   In the experiment, potato strips were fried after a microwave precooking step. Acrylamide in the potato strips was reduced by 36%, 41%, and 60% when frying at 150, 170 and 190 degrees C, respectively.

   —based on a report in *Science News*

4. Although the bay upon whose shores Cerros (Mexico) now sits is a fairly choppy body of water, the archaeological discovery of certain plant and fish remains at the site indicates that, in the late Preclassic, Cerros lay on the shores of a calm lagoon.

   —J. Sabloff, *The Cities of Ancient Mexico*, 1989

5. Stanford University scientist K. Deisseroth implanted optical fibers in mouse brains and used them to manipulate nerve cells to cause or ease anxiety.

Neuroscientist and psychiatrist Kerry Ressler says that the results bring us closer to understanding anxiety and other psychiatric disorders in humans.

—Based on a report in *Science News*

6. [The Assistant Secretary of Health for the Department of Health and Human Services] released the results of the National Household Survey on Drug Abuse, which examined a national sample of Americans over age 12, and the High School Senior Survey.

    The surveys showed that one out of three Americans over age 12 has tried some kind of illicit substance.

7. Guillain-Barre (GBD) is a rare and serious disease of the peripheral nervous system, often associated with ascending paralysis. Some people claim that it can be brought on by flu vaccine.

    A recent study though, reported in the *New England Journal of Medicine*, showed that for 90 million doses of the vaccine in China during the 2009 swine flu epidemic, there were only 11 cases of GBD. This rate of the disease is actually lower than the percentage of GBD in the general population in China, and no other adverse side effects were noted. So we can conclude that receiving the flu vaccine does not raise the risk of contracting GBD.

8. There are events which are foreknown by persons who have applied their observation to that end. Of this kind are tempests and gales of wind, produced by certain aspects of the Moon, or the fixed stars, towards the Sun, according to their several courses, and the approach of which is usually foreseen by mariners. . . .

    Since it is thus clearly practicable, by an accurate knowledge of the points above enumerated, to make predictions concerning the proper quality of the seasons, there also seems no impediment to the formation of similar prognostication concerning the destiny and disposition of every human being. For by the constitution of the Heavens, at the time of any individual's primary conformation, the general quality of that individual's temperament may be perceived . . . [and] an event dependent on one disposition of the Heavens will be advantageous to a particular temperament, and that resulting from another unfavorable and injurious. From these circumstances, and others of similar import, the possibility of foreknowledge is certainly evident.

    —from Ptolemy's *Tetrabiblos*, cited in P. Suppes,
    A Probabilistic Theory of Causality, 1970

9. When the elaborate methods of preparation of some of the plants used to break down the monotony of life are studied, it becomes quite evident that primitive man must have possessed something other than chance to reveal to him the properties of food and drug plants. He must have been a keen observer of accidents to discover fermentation, the effects and localization of alkaloids and toxin resins, and the arts of

roasting and burning a product to gain from it the desired narcotization or pleasing aromas (coffee).

—O. Aimes, cited in L. Mumford *technics and Human Development*, 1966

10. It is clear that our *Iliad, Odyssey, Erga,* and *Theogony* are not the first [hexameter poems]. These ostensibly primitive poems show a length and complexity of composition which can only be the result of many generations of artistic effort. They speak a language out of all relation to common speech, full of forgotten meanings and echoes of past states of society; a poet's language, demonstrably built up and conditioned at every turn by the needs of the hexameter metre. There must therefore have been hexameter poems before our *Iliad*.

—G. Murray, *The Literature of Ancient Greece*, 1956

IV. FALLACIES

Fallacies, or **fallacious arguments**, appear to support their conclusions, but appearances can deceive. Committing a fallacy is different from making a factual error. Although in ordinary language, the term *fallacy* can refer to false beliefs (particularly those that we believe because they are attractive to us), studies of logic reserve the term for mistakes in reasoning. From this standpoint, we can be mistaken about something without committing a fallacy. To believe, for example, that Thomas Jefferson did not own slaves is erroneous but not fallacious. The person who does not believe that Jefferson owned slaves is ignorant of certain facts, but that person's logical ability to draw conclusions on the basis of evidence may not be at fault. To commit a fallacy, we must offer or accept nonevidence as evidence for a claim.

Two familiar fallacies are the fallacy of black-and-white thinking and the fallacy of equivocation. The first occurs in arguments that base a conclusion on a limited set of alternatives—such as a choice between loving and hating someone—when a broader range of possibilities is available. The fallacy of equivocation involves using an expression, such as "mad," in one sense in one of the premisses and a different sense in another premiss or in the conclusion of an argument. If the premisses state that someone is "mad" in the sense of "angry" and the conclusion uses the term in the sense of "crazy," we cannot use the term to connect premisses and conclusion. Many other fallacies arise as a result of violating logical standards for valid deductive arguments and strong inductive arguments.

Fallacies can mislead us for many reasons. Sometimes our emotions interfere with our power to make unbiased judgments. A conclusion can be so attractive that we are ready to accept almost anything offered as evidence in support of it. Swindlers and confidence men present preposterous "evidence" for the reliability of their money-making schemes, but they count on the desire for money to cloud the judgment of their victims. Alternatively, an assertion may be so repugnant that we will accept almost any statement as evidence against it. (How can I believe that someone I love has betrayed me?) Critical thinking requires us to separate the psychological desire to believe or deny a claim from considerations of how well supported that claim is.

In other cases, we feel a strong like or dislike, or respect or disapproval, for the person who makes a claim. This can so prejudice us that we fail to consider the strength of the evidence. Fond parents, for example, are notorious for their willingness to accept a child's word as sufficient evidence. Although sometimes the authority of a person making a statement is a legitimate reason for accepting it, critical thinking requires that we not let emotional feelings about the person making the statement mislead us.

When someone presents a claim in the context of a threat or an enticement, we may fail to notice the lack of evidence. An "argument" that substitutes a threat of force for evidence has, like many fallacies, a special name. It is called **"appeal to force,"** or (in Latin) *ad baculum*. This fallacy appeals to an emotion (fear) rather than to our reasoning ability. Although a threat may be a good reason (in the sense of serving your best interests) to do something, it should not be confused with evidence for the truth of a statement. In a totalitarian regime, for example, threats against one's life are good reasons not to openly disagree with the party line but are not evidence for its truth. Totalitarian societies are not alone in employing fear to achieve their ends. Leaders of democratic societies have sometimes used fear to win citizen support for unjust or unnecessary wars.

Another fallacy that plays on emotions is called **"appeal to pity,"** or *ad misericordium*. This occurs when we confuse feeling sorry for someone with evidence for the truth of an assertion that is made by or about the person who is to be pitied. A well-known scientist, a victim of terminal cancer, made an appeal to pity when he said in response to challenges to a theory he was trying to defend: "I can say these things . . . because this is my last hurrah, and I have to tell the truth." Although the scientist's illness certainly deserves our sympathy, it is not a reason to believe his theory. Sometimes lawyers defend their clients against criminal charges by saying that the client was ill, was mistreated, or has suffered enough. Any of these claims might be relevant to alleviating the punishment inflicted on the criminal, if convicted. Such claims are probably not, however, relevant to the issue of whether the defendant committed the crime. To suppose that they are would be fallacious.

Aside from exerting emotional pressure, a fallacy can deceive us by its resemblance to a correct form of argument. One of the reasons for studying the formal structure of arguments, as we do in the following chapters, is to be able to recognize such fallacies. A few examples will suffice here.

1. Since things that are causally connected with one another occur together in a regular way, the premises of causal arguments often include statements that such regularities have been observed. But to argue for a causal connection *merely* on the basis of the fact that things have occurred together occasionally in the past is to argue fallaciously. The observed co-occurrences could be coincidental. All sorts of things happen together without any causal connection existing between them. For example, in 1993 Hanna Gray ended her tenure as president of the University of Chicago, and Mike Ditka ended his tenure as coach of the Chicago Bears. Neither announced any definite plans for the following year. Yet, it is unlikely that these matters are causally linked and even more unlikely that, as a Chicago alumnus suggested, "Hanna Gray is Coach Mike Ditka in disguise."

2. In Woody Allen's *Love and Death,* the hero offers this argument to demonstrate his skill in logic:

> All men are mortal. Socrates is mortal. Therefore, all men are Socrates.

The transparent way in which this fallacious argument parodies the classic example of deduction makes it amusing rather than deceptive. Life would be simpler if all fallacies were so easy to detect.

Sometimes, as in the fallacy of black-and-white thinking, relevant evidence concerning alternatives is ignored. Ignoring relevant evidence can also result from thinking in terms of *stereotypes*—fixed, rigid, or conventional mental patterns that leave little room for noting individual variations in information received or for classifying new information appropriately.* A blatant example of this kind of fallacy would be to argue that a person was intelligent—or stupid—solely on the basis of the fact that he or she was a member of some racial or ethnic group. Arguing on the basis of such an inaccurate generalization ignores the well-known fact that individual members of every ethnic or racial group vary considerably in intelligence and that variations among groups as a whole are negligible compared to variations within groups. Prejudicial judgments of this type are a particularly invidious form of thinking in terms of stereotypes.

Stereotypic thinking is not always this obvious (or obnoxious). Psychologists have demonstrated that fallacious reasoning involving stereotypical thinking is common even in the absence of any racial or other type of prejudice. Two psychologists presented the following problem to several student groups and professional colleagues (Tversky, A., & Kahneman, D. (1974). Judgments under uncertainty. *Science, 185,* 1124).

Persons to whom the problem was presented were told that the following had been drawn at random from a collection of 100 personal descriptions (30 of lawyers and 70 of engineers):

> John is a 39-year-old man. He is married and has two children. He is active in local politics. His favorite hobby is the collecting of rare books. He is competitive, argumentative, and articulate.

The problem is to tell whether John is an engineer or a lawyer.

---

* Note the negative persuasive character of this definition of *sterotype,* and contrast it with another definition in Exercise Set 3.6, Exercise 21.

A large majority answered "lawyer," even though no specific information about John's profession occurs in the description and descriptions of engineers outnumbered descriptions of lawyers by more than two to one. It is thus much more likely that a description drawn at random from such a collection would be a description of an engineer, but almost everyone simply ignored this evidence and instead concentrated on the description itself, although it contained little helpful information.

On the basis of the results of this and similar experiments, the psychologists who conducted the study concluded that people are the captives of certain stereotypes pertaining to lawyers and engineers. Presumably, the general stereotype of a lawyer is formed by the media's representation of high-powered trial lawyers, who are competitive, argumentative, and articulate. Collecting rare books can be an expensive hobby, and prominent lawyers earn large incomes. In addition, many high-level political offices are held by men and women trained in the law. None of the information presented in the description is incompatible with the engineering profession, however, and a large number of lawyers lead less glamorous lives than those lawyers who exemplify the stereotype. If the solid information is ignored that descriptions of engineers in the sample far outnumber those of lawyers, then a judgment that a lawyer (not an engineer) is being described could be accounted for by stereotypical mental pictures of lawyers and engineers.

Exercise Set 3.5

Point out the fallacious reasoning in each of the following:

1. Although the evidence is overwhelming that Mr. J. has skimmed almost a million dollars from public funds entrusted to him for the city's regatta, he shouldn't be convicted of that crime because he is over 70 years old and has just completed a series of treatments for pancreatic cancer.

2. In college, you can either be a serious student or establish beneficial social contacts. In later life, however, who you know is more important than what you know, so you would be well advised to let your studies slide in favor of an active social life.

3. The current mayor of your city is just as concerned about gang violence as you are. Therefore, if you want to see gang violence reduced, you should vote for her.

4. Of course the governor lost her temper and got emotional when she learned that some top officials in the state were taking graft—she's a woman, isn't she?

5. Vaccinating children against measles is a leading cause of autism. I know this is so because most of the children in my son's school program for autistic children were vaccinated.

6. Despite reporters' incriminating testimony to the grand jury, the president maintains that his chief-of-staff is not guilty of any wrongdoing. The president dismisses the charges, saying that he has known the man and has been his friend for more than 30 years.

7. A 74-year-old grandmother was arrested on suspicion of having stolen $50,000 worth of jewelry and silver from families who had employed her as a nurse for newborn children. Police said that the alleged victims of the woman have been reluctant to press charges because "she's such a sweet, nice lady. . . . It's just like she's your grandmother."

—*Pittsburgh Post-Gazette*

8. Proof that every horse has six legs:

Behind they have two legs and in front they have fore legs. This makes six legs.

—adapted from J. Cohen, in R. A. Baker (Ed.) *A Stress Analysis of a Strapless Evening Gown*, 1967

V. REVIEW

In this chapter, we have learned the distinguishing characteristics of deductive and inductive arguments as well as the general nature of fallacies. Once it becomes apparent that an argument is being presented, the pertinent logical questions to ask and to answer are as follows:

1. What is the conclusion?
2. What evidence is offered in support of the conclusion?
3. Is it possible for the premises to all be true while the conclusion is false?
4. If the answer to the third question is unclear, look at the context in which the argument is offered.

    a. Is the context mathematical? Does the reasoning in the argument depend on mathematical calculations?
    b. Is the context one of ethical reasoning in which a particular kind of action is shown to be an instance of a general principle, or a general principle is challenged because it permits obviously immoral behavior?
    c. Does the reasoning depend largely on drawing out the meanings of terms in the argument?

Arguments of type (a), (b), and (c) are all likely to be deductive.
If the argument does not fall into any of the categories above:

    d. Is it an argument that tries to establish something about the future or the past on the basis of present evidence?
    e. Is it an argument designed to show that something is the cause of something else (a causal argument)?
    f. Is the argument based on a sample study?
    g. Is the argument based on what usually happens (or does not happen)?
    h. Does the argument conclude that two things are similar in some respects on the basis of other similarities?

Arguments of type (d), (e), (f), (g), and (h) are probably inductive.

Remember, as well, to look for conclusion-indicator words such as *probably* and *necessarily* because they can indicate the type of argument.

If the argument bears some resemblance to a correct deductive or inductive argument but has premisses that do not in fact support the conclusion, the argument is fallacious. We study types of fallacies because awareness of them helps to avoid committing and being deceived by them.

The most important new terms introduced in this chapter are defined below.

Appeal to Force   An appeal to force is a fallacious form of reasoning in which a threat of force is inappropriately put forth or accepted as evidence for a conclusion

Appeal to Pity   An appeal to pity is a fallacious form of reasoning in which sympathy or pity for the circumstances of a particular person is inappropriately put forth or accepted as evidence for a conclusion.

Deductive Argument   A deductive argument is constructed such that, if all the premisses are true, the conclusion cannot be false.

Factual Information   This type of information is concerned with what the world is like, in contrast to what is true merely by definition of the terms involved or true by the principles of mathematics.

Fallacy   (fallacious argument) A fallacy is an argument in which the premisses provide only very weak support, or no real support, for the conclusion.

Indirect Proof   Indirect proof is a type of argument that shows that a contradiction or an obviously false sentence follows deductively from an assumption that a statement to be proved is false. Since a deductive argument with a false conclusion must have at least one false premiss, this method can be used to show that an original assumption that a statement is false is itself false, or that the statement is true.

Inductive Argument   An *ampliative* argument in which the premisses, if true, make it probable that the conclusion is true as well is an inductive argument.

Sound Argument   A sound argument is a deductive or inductive argument in which all the premisses are true.

Valid Argument   A valid argument is a correct, successful, or genuine deductive argument—that is, an argument in which the premisses, if true, guarantee the truth of the conclusion.

Exercise Set 3.6

Reconstruct each of the arguments in the following passages by first identifying the conclusion of the argument and then its premisses. Write the arguments in standard form, and then categorize them as inductive or deductive. Try to identify and supply any obvious missing premisses, such as generalizations that link a premiss with the conclusion. If you use any clues from the context of the argument to identify the type of argument and/or any missing premisses, be sure to identify them.

1. Conversation enriches the understanding, but solitude is the school of genius; and the uniformity of a work denotes the hand of a single artist.

   —Edward Gibbon

   Gibbon is surely right. The majority of poets, novelists, composers, and, to a lesser extent, of painters and sculptors, are bound to spend a great deal of their time alone, as Gibbon himself did.

   —A. Storr, *Solitude*, 2005

2. [Concerning the beginnings of spoken language] the possibility is there that language did not emerge just once. Rather, like writing, making pottery, controlled use of fire and other great inventions, language could have emerged at different places at different times. From strictly probabilistic considerations, it is more likely for language to have had several points of origin, given that there were many independent human populations from which the emergence of language was possible.

   —W. S.-Y. Wang, *The Emergence of Language*, 1972

3. A lawyer offers the following argument in a burglary case to prove the defendant's innocence:

   Assume that the defendant was burglarizing the store at 7:30 P.M., on Friday the 13th of October. This is the time that the burglar alarm sounded. No fewer than six of his coworkers can testify that he was at his job from 4 P.M. until midnight on that day. In order to break into the store, he would have had to have been in two places at the same time.

4. Handling numbers in daily business has to be easy because it was invented by regular people to make things easy.

   —E. Ruedy and S. Nirenberg, *Where Do I Put the Decimal Point*, 1990

5. Pleasure and pleasure alone is desired as an end [that is, not as a means to something else].

   What is desired as an end and only what is desired as an end is good as an end.

   Therefore, pleasure and pleasure alone is good as an end.

   —W. Frankena, *Ethics*, 1973

6. Skin hue is neither a necessary nor a sufficient condition for being classified as black in our culture. That looking black is not in our culture a necessary condition for being black can be seen from the phenomenon of passing. That it is not a sufficient condition can be seen from the book *Black Like Me*, by John Howard Griffin, where "looking black" is easily understood by the reader to be different from being black.

   —R. A. Wasserstrom, "Racism, Sexism, and Preferential Treatment" 1977,
   UCLA Law Journal, 3

7. Based on a study published in *The Journal of Addictive Medicine*, researchers concluded that about 40% of high school students have tried marijuana.

   The study polled 1,906 boys and 2,191 girls, all students in Connecticut schools in grades 9–12. Forty percent reported that they had smoked marijuana in the past month.

8. Arab countries are not as advanced economically as Western countries. Recently economic historians have argued that Islamic beliefs and practices cause this retardation of business. But this cannot be so, for Turkey, Indonesia and Malaysia—all overwhelmingly Muslim countries are economically vibrant.

9. In 1977, the Supreme Court of the United States heard arguments on an important reverse-discrimination case: *Regents of the University of California v. Bakke*. Allan Bakke, a white applicant, who was denied admission to the university's medical school at Davis, claimed that the university discriminated against him by reserving for minority students 16 of the 100 slots in the entering medical school class. In deliberating whether this use of racial criteria was fair, Justice Harry Blackmun noted to himself that the role of the judiciary "is to protect against unfairness." He said that the university's approach was not unfair because in it, "race is used to enhance the fairness of the system. . . . We have seen that the mere neutrality is often not enough."

   —Adapted from the account by L. Greenhouse,
   Becoming Justice Blackmun, 2005

10. Within Western civilization, there developed several sources of moral authority . . . Canon Law [based on the authority of God], Roman Law [based on the authority of a perceived natural moral order in the universe], English common law [based on social custom and tradition], and the social contract theory [based on the individual in a state of nature concerned primarily about his or her own safety and happiness]. Each of these systems of law was, consequently based on a different type of ethical system and each focused primarily on a different facet of human nature.

    —James H. Rutherford, *The Moral Foundations of United States
    Constitutional Democracy*, 1992

11. We can also infer [from the novel *Middlemarch*] the view that imagination governs perceptions, but that desires govern imagination; so that, ultimately, desires govern perception.

    —P. Jones, *Philosophy and the Novel*, 1975

12. From a report of an excavation of a Mesolithic site in Ireland, inhabited approximately 9,000 years ago:

    At what times of year were the Mount Sandel huts occupied? Could the site have served as a year-round settlement? Our excavations have uncovered much evidence with seasonal connotations. For example, the salmon bones are evidence of summer occupation. Today the main salmon run up the Bann is in mid-summer: June, July, and August. In Mesolithic times there may also have been an earlier run, say in April or May. Although the lower water temperatures [at that time] make it unlikely that the salmon run would continue beyond the fall, eels do run downstream in the fall: September, October, and November are the best months of the eel run. Hence the eel bones at the site are evidence of fall residence. So is the presence of hazelnuts, which are ready for picking by mid-fall, and of water-lily seeds, which are best collected in September.

—P. C. Woodman, "A Mesolithic Camp in Ireland," 1981,
Scientific American 2

13. Economically stagnant Arab countries, such as Egypt, are demographically similar to China in the sense that they have a huge labor pool of young adults. China has achieved great economic success by using this source of labor to build a large export market. Therefore, it is likely that the Arab countries could also achieve economic success if they can similarly develop a large export market.

14. "Mathematics," said the American physicist Gibbs, "is a language." If this be true, any meaningful proposition can be expressed in a suitable mathematical form, and any generalization about social behavior can be formulated mathematically.

—K. J. Arrow

15. Scott McKinney and Jeffrey Ellenbogen, two scientists who study sleep, have investigated the role of alpha waves—brain waves that help us keep in touch with our surroundings when we are awake but seem to disappear while we sleep. To investigate the role of alpha waves, they kept track of the EEGs of 13 subjects in Massachusetts General Hospital's sleep lab. When subjects were asleep, the investigators played noises at increasing decibel levels and observed the responses of the subjects. The investigators reported their results online in PLoS ONE. They said that when it took louder noises to wake subjects they were in a very deep phase of sleep, but when they stirred to softer noises, they were in a light sleep. The investigators found that alpha waves, though often hidden, unlike theta and delta waves, did not disappear entirely in sleep. Hidden alpha waves were strongest in the light sleep stage. They concluded that the strength of a person's alpha waves could predict how easily the person could be awakened.

16. The question of nutrition is closely related to that of locality and climate. None of us can live anywhere; and he who has great tasks to perform, which demand all his energy, has, in this respect, a very limited choice. The influence of climate upon the bodily functions, affecting their retardation or acceleration, is so great, that a blunder in the choice of locality or climate may not merely alienate a man from his duty, but may withhold it from him altogether, so that he never comes face to face with it. . . . Enumerate the places in which men of great intellect have been and are still found; where wit, subtlety, and malice are a part of happiness; where genius is almost necessarily at home: all of them have an unusually dry atmosphere. Paris, Provence,

Florence, Jerusalem, Athens—these names prove this: that genius is dependent on dry air, on clear skies—in other words, on rapid organic functions, on the possibility of continuously securing for one's self great and even enormous quantities of energy.

—F. Nietzsche, *Ecce Homo*

17. A layman seldom sets out the premises from which he is arguing, so it is generally impossible to tell whether some false conclusion is the result of thinking illogically about true premisses, or the result of thinking logically about false premisses. Or both!

—G. A. Miller, citing John Stuart Mill, "Is Scientific Thinking Different?" 1983, February, *Bulletin of The American Academy of Arts and Sciences.*

18. Paleolithic inhabitants who decorated the [Lascaux] cave were predominantly right-handed. Not only do the majority of the animals face right (an orientation generally preferred by right-hand draftsmen) but also the "fossilized" rope depicted . . . was obviously the work of a right-handed individual. Since the natural twisting motion involves the overhand rotation of the thumb away from the body, the twist in this case must have been imparted by the right hand.

—Letter from T. A. Reisner, 1982, *Scientific American* 4

19. Although incest taboos do possess social functions, these cannot account for their origins, because it is impossible to believe that early men who instituted these rules could have known their possible social advantages.

—A. de W. Maalfjit, *Images of Man*, 1974

20. Yes, and if oxen and horses and lions had hands, and could paint with their hands, and provide works of art, as men do, horses would paint the forms of gods like horses, and oxen like oxen, and make their bodies in the image of their several kinds.

The Ethiopians make their gods black and mule-nosed; the Thracians say theirs have blue eyes and red hair.

—Xenophanes, *Fragments*

21. Stereotypical thinking, long considered a source only of mistakes in reasoning, has recently been redefined and defended by some psychologists. The following argument defends stereotypes as thought-efficient starting points for understanding other cultures and social groups. Lee believes that we cannot do without stereotypes, but that we need to develop more accurate stereotypes to avoid unjustified prejudices and to understand better other cultures.

Stereotypes are probabilistic beliefs we use to categorize people, objects, and events. We have to have stereotypes to deal with so much information in a world with which we are often uncertain and unfamiliar.

—Yueh-Ting Lee, cited by B. Bower, 1996, *Science News, 149*

22. "Markets Misjudge Japan Risks" was written a week after Japan's disastrous earthquake, tsunami, and nuclear reactor problems.

    Even Japanese stocks may bounce back. In the weeks after the January 1995 earthquake that struck Kobe the Nikkei [stock exchange] fell as much as 25%. It recovered the losses by year end, finishing slightly higher.

    —D. Reilly & J. Jannarone, "Heard on the Street," *Wall Street Journal,* March 16, 2011

23. If a man's destiny is caused by the star under which he is born, then all men born under that star should have the same fortune. But masters and slaves and kings and beggars [whose fortunes differ greatly] are born under the same star at the same time. Thus, astrology—which claims that a man's destiny is caused by the star under which he is born—is surely false.

    —Pliny the Elder, *Natural History*

24. The real justification (perhaps a cynical one) for progressive taxation is that the wealthier receive more benefits from government and, therefore, ought to pay more. This may not be true in a strict accounting sense; the middle and upper classes don't use food stamps. But in this country, the essence of government is to preserve the social order. The well-off benefit from this far more than do the poor.

    —P. Samuelson, "Economic Focus," *Pittsburgh Post-Gazette*

25. The World Cancer Research Fund recently published a study that linked excessive body fat (Body Mass Index >30) with six different types of common cancer, including breast, bowel and pancreas. Their study covered 40 years of research and examined more than 7,000 studies.

26. The American Dental Association passed a resolution to oppose oral piercing, which it considers a public health hazard. "There can be [lifelong] nerve damage that affects the way you talk and swallow," said Dr. Timothy Rose, president of the association. . . . Our chief concern is beyond whether [tongue piercing] is crazy or not," Dr. Rose continued, trying not to be judgmental. "To have someone stick a needle, clean or dirty, through a vascular part of your body—the risk of disease has to be immense," he added.

    —*The New York Times*, January 26, 1999

Chapter Four

A CLOSER LOOK AT INDUCTIVE ARGUMENTS

I. INTRODUCTION

II. STATISTICAL SYLLOGISMS

1. Form of Statistical Syllogisms
2. Standards for the Strength of Statistical Syllogisms
    Exercise Set 4.1
3. The Fallacy of Incomplete Evidence
    Exercise Set 4.2
4. Special Types of Statistical Syllogism
    i. Arguments from Authority
        Exercise Set 4.3
    ii. Arguments against the Person (*Argumentum ad Hominem*)
    iii. Arguments from Consensus
5. Missing Premises in Statistical Syllogisms
6. An Incorrect Form of Inductive Argument
    Exercise Set 4.4

III. ARGUMENTS FROM ANALOGY

1. Form of Arguments from Analogy
2. Standards for the Strength of Analogical Arguments
3. Fallacies Associated with Analogical Arguments
4. Analogy in Archaeology and in Legal and Moral Reasoning
    Exercise Set 4.5
5. Analogy and the Slippery Slope
    Exercise Set 4.6

IV. ARGUMENTS BASED ON SAMPLES

1. Preliminary Account of the Form of Inductive Generalizations
2. Standards for Correct Inductive Generalizations
3. Fallacies Associated with Inductive Generalizations
4. The Revised Form of Inductive Generalization
    Exercise Set 4.7

I. INTRODUCTION

In this chapter, we take a closer look at specific types of inductive arguments. Generally, the aim of any argument is to establish its conclusion. By definition, however, the conclusions of inductive arguments might be false even when all the premises are true. The premises of an inductive argument should make it probable that the conclusion will be true. The very least we can expect from an inductive argument is some measure of how likely we are to be correct if we draw a conclusion on the basis of the evidence presented.

Our study of inductive arguments begins by classifying them according to form. The **form of an argument** refers to its structural features, without regard to its subject matter or content. Although you may not have thought about forms of argument before, the term *form* in this sense is not new to you. You have undoubtedly been concerned with structures in many real-life situations.

For example, most secondary schools require a civics course in which various forms of government are discussed. The United States has a democratic constitutional form of federal government composed of three main branches—executive, judiciary, and legislative. The powers and responsibilities of each of these branches are outlined in the U.S. Constitution.

The British form of government, in contrast, is a constitutional monarchy composed of a legislative branch (Parliament), a judiciary branch, and a crowned king or queen, who—except in cases of abdication—holds office for life. The head of government is the prime minister, but unlike the president of the United States, the prime minister is not the head of state. The powers and responsibilities of the various branches of the British government are also outlined in a constitution.

Forms of government other than constitutional democracies and constitutional monarchies exist. North Korea, for example, has a dictator. Forms of government can be studied abstractly, without notice of the individuals who fill the positions that are determined by the form of government. When we study forms of government in this way, we learn something about their parts and how these parts are related to one another. Similarly, when we study forms of arguments, we learn something about their parts and how they relate to one another.

In the sections that follow, we identify several forms of inductive argument and consider standards for determining how well the premises in the various argument forms support the conclusions. Form is not the only relevant factor in judging inductive arguments, however. The correctness of an inductive argument depends on content as well. Inductive arguments occur against a background of information that provides a source for unstated premisses as well as other considerations that affect the ability of the premisses to support the conclusion. Inductive arguments are also open-ended in the sense that additional information can weaken or strengthen them. Thus, considerations of context are particularly important in the evaluation of inductive arguments—a point that is emphasized in the examples presented in this chapter.

II. STATISTICAL SYLLOGISMS

The word *syllogism* is derived from the Greek and literally means "a putting together of ideas." The use of the term in logic is related to this meaning. **Syllogisms** are arguments with (usually) two premisses and a conclusion that "puts together" information presented in the premisses. The following argument is an example of a deductive form of syllogism:

> All men are mortal.
> Socrates is a man.
> ———
> Socrates is mortal.

The **statistical syllogism** is an inductive form that closely resembles the deductive form of syllogism, but its general premiss is a statistical generalization rather than a universal generalization. The following argument is an example of a statistical syllogism:

> Ninety percent of freshmen at State University are residents of the state.
> Elena is a freshman at State University.
> ———
> Elena is a resident of the state.

We use statistical syllogisms when we argue that what is generally, but not universally, true (or false) is also true (or false) for a particular case. The statistical generalization in the premisses is not always numerical. *Almost all, most, very often, almost never,* and other terms can occur instead, as in the following example:

> Hardly any freshmen had a philosophy course in high school.
> Oscar is a freshman.
> ———
> Oscar did not have a philosophy course in high school.

Many authors distinguish inductive arguments from deductive arguments in the following way: In deduction, one goes from general premisses to a particular conclusion, whereas in induction, one goes from the particular to the general. Statistical syllogisms are exceptions to this popular (but incorrect) characterization of inductive arguments. As you can see, statistical syllogisms proceed from a generalization in the premiss to a claim about a particular individual in the conclusion. Because arguments of this form may have false conclusions even though their premises are all true, they cannot be deductive. As with other inductive forms of argument, statistical syllogisms vary in strength.

Reasoning in the form of a statistical syllogism is common in everyday life and guides many of our decisions and beliefs. We do not plan outdoor picnics in Chicago in January because the weather will usually not be favorable. If we are fortunate enough to travel to southern France, we expect to find good food at country inns because that is usually the case. We dread a summons for an audit of our tax return because audits of tax returns tend to be costly and unpleasant.

1. FORM OF STATISTICAL SYLLOGISMS

With the preceding examples in mind, we are ready to look at the abstract form of statistical syllogisms:

> X percent of all Fs are Gs.
> a is an F.
> _____
> a is a G.

In this form of argument, F and G represent classes of individuals or properties that determine those classes. The lowercase letter a represents an individual person, place, or thing. The class denoted by F is the **reference class,** which is the class that the individual mentioned in the second premise is **referred to** or belongs to. The class denoted by G is the **attribute class.** Members of this class have the property **attributed to** the individual in the conclusion. In the above argument about the individual Oscar, the reference class is *freshmen* and the attribute class is *persons who have had a philosophy course in high school.*

2. STANDARDS FOR THE STRENGTH OF STATISTICAL SYLLOGISMS

The most obvious standard for judging the strength of a statistical syllogism is the closeness to 100 percent (or 0 percent in the negative case) of the statistical premiss. If the premiss in the preceding sample argument had stated that 99 percent instead of 90 percent of the freshmen at State University were state residents, a stronger case would be made for the conclusion that Elena is a state resident. Similarly, the argument would have been weaker if only 85 percent rather than 90 percent of all the freshmen were state residents. If only 51 percent of all freshmen were state residents, the argument would be so weak that we would reject it. When the statistical premiss is not expressed numerically, other terms indicate the strength of the argument. For example, "Almost all Fs are Gs" supports the conclusion that a, who is an F, is also a G more strongly than "A sizable majority of Fs are Gs."

A second criterion of strength of statistical syllogisms is whether all available relevant evidence has been considered in selecting the reference class. This requirement, which is called the **rule of total evidence,** is designed to address problems that arise as a result of individuals belonging to an indefinite number of classes. Elena, for example, belongs not only to the class of freshmen but also to the class of women students, and many other classes as well. Assume that we have the following information about Elena:

> Besides being a freshman at State, she has brown hair, is 18 years old, supports equal rights for women, works part-time in an office, and belongs to the Foreign Students' Club.

Each of these properties of Elena marks a class to which she belongs. In constructing an argument with the conclusion "Elena is a state resident," we must take into account *every* class that Elena belongs to that might affect the probability that she is a state resident. Suppose, for example, we know that only 2 percent of the members of the Foreign Students' Club are state residents. If we assign Elena to this reference class, ignoring all the other information, we can construct the following argument with true premisses:

> Two percent of all members of the Foreign Students' Club are state residents.
> Elena is a member of the Foreign Students' Club.
> _____
> Elena is *not* a state resident.

Both this argument and the original argument have true premisses, and their statistical premisses are very close to 100 percent and 0 percent, respectively. So, if we were to use only the standard that requires a strong statistical generalization, both arguments would appear to be strong. Yet their conclusions cannot both be true because they contradict one another. The conclusion of the first argument says that she is a state resident; the conclusion of the second says that she is not. Following the **rule of total evidence** can help us avoid this unfortunate situation. This rule requires us to assign Elena to a reference class of freshmen at State who are members of the Foreign Students' Club and who are also members of *any other classes relevant to state residency* to which she belongs and for which information is available.

Background knowledge plays an all-important role in helping us to decide which classes are relevant. On the basis of common background information, for example, we know that her hair color and age are irrelevant. (Her age would be relevant, however, if she were much older than the average college freshman.) Working in an office *might* be relevant, because some residence restrictions may apply to student eligibility for such jobs. If we do not know or cannot find out about that, however, the information is not available and cannot figure into our construction of the proper reference class. Suppose that the only classes for which information relevant to state residency is available are the class of freshmen and the class of Foreign Students' Club members. A check of school records for past years shows that about 5 percent of freshmen members of the Foreign Students' Club during that period were state residents. We are now in a position to construct the appropriate statistical syllogism that embodies all available relevant evidence:

> Five percent of all freshmen at State University who are members of the Foreign Students' Club are state residents.
> Elena is a freshman member of the Foreign Students' Club.
> ___
> Elena is *not* a state resident.

If the statistical premise of a statistical syllogism is assumed to be part of our common background knowledge, we may not bother to state it. For example, the following argument:

> The student who sits next to me in logic class is not registered, for his name was not called at roll call.

could be reconstructed as a statistical syllogism with the implicit premise, "Most people who are not called at roll are not registered." When we are concerned with evaluating such arguments, however, we should try to state any implicit premises. Sometimes when implicit premises are exposed, we find that they are questionable or fail to represent all available relevant evidence. When the implicit premise in this argument is exposed, we realize that the student could be known to the teacher, who marks him present when she sees him in class. If this is so, then the argument is weak because the reference class in the implicit premise violates the requirement of total evidence.

Exercise Set 4.1

PART I. Each of the following arguments is or can be reconstructed as a statistical syllogism. (a) Identify the reference class and the attribute class, and (b) assess the strength of the argument, using the criteria discussed in this section.

1. Fewer than 30 percent of eligible young people (ages 18–29) vote in midterm elections. Jake is an eligible 23-year-old citizen, so probably he did not vote in the last midterm election.

2. Since fewer than 30 percent of eligible young people vote in midterm elections, Marta, who is a junior and head of Young Republicans, was not a voter in the last midterm election.

3. Joan, a 23-year-old, did vote in the last midterm election, and since 58 percent of young voters voted Democratic, she voted a Democratic ticket.

4. Apple pie almost always comes out on top in polls asking for America's favorite dessert. So if you serve apple pie at your party, Picky Patty won't complain.

5. Because most German shepherds are easy to train, your German shepherd puppy should do well in dog-training school.

6. Stocks typically outperform bonds in the first recovery year after a recession. Since this is such a year, stocks should outperform bonds.

7. The adverse health effects from cigarette smoking account for an estimated 443,000 deaths, or nearly one of every five deaths, each year in the United States. So even though I smoke, it probably won't kill me.

8. Most standard homeowners' theft-and-casualty policies extend coverage to students living away from home. Therefore, your parents' homeowners' policy will probably cover the computer that was stolen from your dorm room.

PART II. Each of the following passages gives advice based on a statistical syllogism. In each case, reconstruct the argument in standard form, and explicitly state the statistical premiss, the premiss that refers to a particular individual, and the conclusion.

1. Always remember that the odds in this hobby [mushroom collecting] are heavily against the collector. He is gambling the price of a mess of mushrooms against the doctor and hospital bills. With such odds in mind it is up to the collector to be critical of what he collects.

   —A. H. Smith, *The Mushroom Hunter's Field Guide, 1958*

2. *Dear Dr. Molnar:*   I am 56 and considering an operation. Would you advise against it? I've had a loss of hearing since about age 12. On a recent checkup my doctor said two bones have grown together in the middle ear. He thinks there is an 85 percent chance of improvement to "very good;" 10 percent chance of no improvement; 5 percent chance of further damage.

   Answer: Why should I advise against the operation? Only one chance in 20 of being worse off; 17 chances in 20 of being better off. There are few if any operations in which 100 percent success can be guaranteed. If I were the patient in such a case, I'd take the 17 to 1 odds.

   —"Doctor Molnar," syndicated newspaper columnist

3. At a Democratic committee meeting, the incumbent prosecuting attorney loses his party's endorsement. He considers running as an Independent, but his advisers tell him not to because hardly any Independents could receive enough votes to win an election in that city.

4. Take your umbrella when you go out today because there is a 70 percent chance of rain in your area.

5. More than two thirds of the students who enter this college earn their degrees. So don't bother studying for your finals tonight; come to the party with us.

6. Don't be too discouraged at the rejection of your short story by three different magazine editors. Most great writers had some early work rejected many times before it was accepted for publication.

7. Since only 10 percent of qualified applicants are admitted to your first-choice law school, you shouldn't count on getting in.

8. Since only 10 percent of qualified applicants are admitted to your first-choice law school, you shouldn't bother to apply.

9. That cat will probably never learn to use a litter box because when she was two weeks old, she was separated from her mother and was not mothered by another cat.

10. Find an example using a statistical syllogism to predict an outcome in sports.

3. THE FALLACY OF INCOMPLETE EVIDENCE

When the reference class (the class denoted by F in "X percent of Fs are Gs") in a statistical syllogism is not based on all available relevant evidence, the argument is fallacious. *Relevant evidence* is "any evidence that might influence the probability that the individual (a) has the property (G) attributed to it in the conclusion." We need suitable background knowledge to determine what sort of evidence is relevant. For example, if we are trying to infer how a member of Congress will vote on a bill to increase price supports for farm products, relevant evidence would include not only the member's voting history on such bills, but also whether the member's home district is in an agricultural region of the country. Information about the size of the member's family or the brand of automobile the member drives is irrelevant to this issue. Common sense helps us judge what is relevant, but statistical studies can also determine relevancy. Statistics gathered by insurance companies, for example, indicate that the age and sex of a driver are relevant to whether that driver will be involved in a serious automobile accident.

It is difficult to say what *available evidence* means in this context. How much research is required to be sure we have accounted for all available relevant evidence? Obviously, we are seldom in a position to spend years of our lives—or even hours—acquiring evidence that is "available" in the sense that it is part of the storehouse of human knowledge. Often we must make judgments and take actions (such as agreeing to a medical procedure) in the absence of evidence that may be "available" but that we are unable to obtain because we lack time or money. The requirement of total evidence is not intended to place unrealistic restrictions on reasoning. It only demands a reasonable effort to find appropriate reference classes. To follow the rule of total evidence, we must not ignore—through carelessness, prejudice, or laziness—evidence that is within our reach, and we must not suppress evidence that is known to be relevant.

Consider the following example of a fallacy in the form of a statistical syllogism:

Ninety-eight percent of *Fortune* 1,000 corporation CEOs are men.
Anne Mulcahey was CEO of Xerox, a *Fortune* 1,000 corporation.

Anne Mulcahey is a man.

This argument appears to be a strong one only if we ignore the well-known fact that *Anne* is a name rarely given to a male. If we accept the argument as it stands, we will be more likely to accept a false conclusion than a true one, for the probability that a CEO named Anne is male is quite low. Even though we do not have exact figures to assign a probability to the proper reference class (male CEOs named Anne), we can see that this additional evidence is relevant and that it undermines the original argument.

The argument that a movie star has no home telephone because she is not listed in the phone directory ignores the information that many celebrities have unlisted numbers. Similarly, it would be a violation of the requirement of total evidence to infer that your bus for work, which is normally on time, will be on time when the city streets are covered with ice.

In statistical syllogisms, the requirement of total evidence is designed to ensure that we select an appropriate reference class. The requirement of total evidence more broadly understood applies to all other forms of inductive argument as well. To construct good inductive arguments, we must take account of any available relevant information that could affect the truth of the conclusion of the argument. The rules of critical thinking do not permit us to construct arguments in which we selectively choose evidence that supports our conclusions while we ignore available evidence that would undermine them.

Exercise Set 4.2

PART I. Each of the following arguments commits the fallacy of incomplete evidence. In each case, discuss what relevant information is ignored.

1. Most Chinese do not speak English, so the newly appointed ambassador of the People's Republic of China to the United States probably does not speak any English.

2. Most Americans under 30 years of age do not earn over $200,000 a year. Justin Bieber is an American under the age of 30, so he probably does not earn over $200,000 annually.

3. Only about 2 percent of college football players ever play professional ball after college, so the Heisman trophy winner will probably not play pro ball after he is out of college.

4. Few American women who are older than 65 engage in regular physical exercise. Because Cher is in that age group, she probably no longer exercises.

5. The widow of the heir to the Johnson Wax fortune probably had to reduce her standard of living after her husband died because most widows find themselves unable to maintain the standard of living they had when their husbands were alive.

PART II. Suppose that Lee Washington is a freshman who entered your university this academic year, but that it is too early in the year to have any information about how Lee is doing in classes. What sort of evidence is relevant to constructing an appropriate reference class for drawing a conclusion about whether Lee will graduate?

4. SPECIAL TYPES OF STATISTICAL SYLLOGISM

A number of special uses of statistical syllogism are so common that they, and the fallacies that resemble them, have standard names.

i. Arguments from Authority

We all rely on the advice and counsel of others. Sometimes when we present arguments, we appeal to what experts have said on the matter instead of presenting direct evidence for claims. Critical thinking allows this, for it would be difficult and wasteful to always repeat arguments already made by experts. Thus, many arguments that appeal to a legitimate authority are strong inductive arguments. Some arguments that appeal to authority are fallacious, however. The principle that guides the difference between correct and incorrect uses of authority is based both on the nature of the authority's expertise and on the nature of the subject matter.

It is reasonable to take the word of an authority if both:

(i)   The authority is an expert on the matter under consideration.
(ii) There is agreement among experts in the area of knowledge under consideration.

Authorities achieve their status through training, talent, and experience. These qualities enable them to understand and evaluate evidence in areas that are not easily accessible to others. Condition (i) is designed to rule out taking the word of an authority in one field about matters outside the authority's area of expertise. Speaking as an authority outside of one's area of expertise happens rather frequently. We should remember that expertise in physics, chemistry, or another one of the physical sciences does not make a person an authority on social matters or ethics. Expertise in sports or the arts does not make a person an authority on world peace, urban renewal, or the various commercial products athletes and actors are often called upon to endorse.

Condition (ii) recognizes that some areas of knowledge are so controversial that persons with comparable training, experience, and all other credentials of a genuine authority disagree with one another. Appeals to authority in such circumstances are feeble because different "authorities" give conflicting opinions on the matter. Although economists, for example, agree in some areas of their discipline, expert economists may hold conflicting views about ways to stimulate the economy, defeat inflation, increase employment, and other such matters. In psychiatry, also, qualified doctors disagree. Thus in criminal trials, when both prosecutor and defense attorney call expert witnesses to support their opposing positions, the prosecutor's expert psychiatrist might pronounce the defendant sane at the time of the crime, whereas the defendant's expert psychiatrist will testify to the defendant's insanity.

When both conditions for an authority are fulfilled, we can accept as correct most of what the authority on a particular subject says about that subject. In such a case, the **argument from authority** is a statistical syllogism of the following form:

> Most of what authority a has to say on subject matter S is correct.
> a says p about S.
> ———————————————————————————————
> p is correct.

The first premiss is a statistical generalization; the second premiss is a statement about a particular assertion (a member of the reference class of assertions in the authority's field of expertise); and the conclusion attributes the property of being correct to that assertion.

Arguments from authority are rarely presented in this explicit form of a statistical syllogism. Usually the authority is merely cited or quoted in support of some conclusion. For example, a point in the theory of relativity might be argued for by quoting Einstein's view on the matter; a claim concerning the best way to bake a soufflé might cite Julia Child. Sometimes a group of authorities, rather than an individual authority, is cited: "All leading physical scientists agree that the earth is more than four million years old." Regardless of the way arguments from authority are stated, these arguments are acceptable only when conditions (i) and (ii) are fulfilled.

Because arguments from authority are inductive, the conclusion of an argument from authority can be false even when the premisses are true and the conditions for authority are satisfied. In a correct argument from authority with true premisses, however, probably the conclusion will be true. Nevertheless, in using arguments from authority, it is wise to remember that history, including the history of science, offers many examples of expert authorities who were mistaken in their beliefs and were proved wrong in the light of new evidence. This should not be surprising because new evidence must be assimilated (often a slow process) before experts in the field recognize its significance and change their opinions. Despite these cautions about their use, arguments from authority have an important place in both scientific and everyday reasoning.

Fallacious arguments from authority occur when the alleged authority lacks expertise in the area of concern or the experts in the area disagree with one another. Such arguments can deceive us in several ways.

First, when someone is a genuine expert in a particular field of knowledge or has achieved success in a difficult and highly competitive enterprise, that person is properly entitled to prestige and recognition for his or her accomplishments. Such people are often asked to express their views on a wide variety of issues, many of which lie completely outside their field of expertise. Famous physicists state their opinions on moral questions; a football hero endorses one brand of panty hose. Their statements cannot carry the weight of a legitimate appeal to authority, for they are speaking about subjects outside their area of expertise. We should resist the temptation to accept arguments that rely on the glamour or prestige of an authority in one field to support the truth of claims in another, unrelated area of knowledge.

Second, some persons set themselves up as authorities—or their followers set them up—when they lack the expertise of a genuine authority. Authoritative knowledge of modern science, for example, requires years of training and study under the supervision of experts. Yet some people claim to have achieved such knowledge through self-study of obscure texts, visions, inspirations, revelations, or other questionable means. They claim to have found cures for diseases that have eluded standard medical research, or they claim to be able to explain major cosmic events in ways that defy the truth of well-accepted scientific theories. These people, called "cranks" by all but their followers, are not reliable authorities in the subject areas in which they profess expertise. We should not accept arguments that appeal to such "authorities" and must scrutinize these "authorities" with special care when we wish that their conclusions—such as a new cure for a hitherto incurable disease—were true.

Finally, in many branches of knowledge, widespread disagreement separates those who have all the right academic and professional credentials. Economics and psychiatry, already mentioned, are just two examples. It is probably no exaggeration to say that in every discipline in which scholars are actively engaged, there are some areas in which the experts disagree. The U.S. Civil War, for example, has been extensively studied and analyzed by historians, and there is widespread agreement about many aspects of this conflict. To settle a noncontroversial point, an appeal to a distinguished historian of that period would suffice. Nevertheless, different schools of American history dispute the precise role of slavery as a causal factor in the War Between the States, and so appeals to authority on that topic are weak. Scientists avidly debate whether birds are descendants of dinosaurs, as most paleontologists believe, or whether, as some ornithologists hold, the two developed along parallel evolutionary paths. The evidence presented by the experts can be considered and evaluated on its own merits by those qualified to judge. When such evidence is considered and evaluated, however, the form of argument is not that of an argument from authority but some other type.

In determining whether an argument from authority is fallacious, background knowledge helps to determine whether an alleged authority is genuine and whether the area of knowledge is one in which experts disagree.

Exercise Set 4.3

1. Creation scientists, who claim that scientific evidence supports the biblical account of creation more strongly than it supports evolutionary biology, argue for their view by listing the many supporters of creationism who hold doctoral degrees in various branches of science, from earth science to chemistry to nutrition. These lists rarely include any professional biologists, however.

Critics of creation science say that the creationists are using a fallacious argument from authority. On what grounds do they make this claim?

2. Many nuclear scientists argue that Americans should be willing to live close to nuclear power plants because American plants are more carefully monitored than the plants of similar design that failed at Fukushima. They say that many safety features of American plants make the probability of such a nuclear disaster very small. Critics of nuclear power who do not dispute the nuclear scientists' estimates of the probability of nuclear accidents nevertheless say that the people who must live with the risk are the ones to say what risk they will tolerate. Thus, we can say that whereas the critics are willing to accept the argument from authority for the amount of nuclear risk, they reject the argument from authority for the acceptance of nuclear-power risk. Which of the two conditions does the rejected argument violate?

3. For some kinds of cancer, such as prostate cancer in elderly men, most radiologists favor radiation therapy, whereas surgeons usually urge a surgical procedure, and still other doctors argue for nonintervention and careful watching of the progress of the disease. Why is it, thus, difficult to construct an argument from authority for a "best" treatment for prostate cancer?

4. "Gibson's Law" states that "for every Ph.D., there is an equal and opposite Ph.D." This "law" is sometimes invoked in discussions of public policy formation, law, and scientific research. How is this law related to our criteria for successful arguments from authority?

ii. Arguments against the Person (*Argumentum ad Hominem*)

Arguments against the person (also known by the Latin name *argumentum ad hominem*) are the inverse of arguments from authority. Arguments against the person conclude that a statement is false because it is made by a particular person or group of persons. Such arguments are legitimate only when there is reason to believe that most of the claims made by the individual or group on a particular aspect of that subject matter are false. Like arguments from authority, correct arguments against the person can be construed as statistical syllogisms:

> Most of what individual a says about a particular subject matter S is false.
> a says p about S.
> ───────────────────────────────────
> p is false.

Although the forms of argument from authority and argument against the person are similar, we are not often in a position to claim that most of what an individual says about a subject is false. Whereas many genuine authorities exist, few individuals lie about or are almost always wrong about a subject. Truth telling, rather than lying, is the normal mode of communication. Indeed, communication would soon break down if this were not so. Moreover, people do not usually make pronounce-ments about subjects on which they are more often wrong than right. For these reasons, special care should be exercised when arguments against the person are encountered.

With this warning, some circumstances in which legitimate arguments against the person can occur should be mentioned. One concerns the pronouncements of scien-tific cranks whose views conflict with the collected wisdom of scientists. In the area of their weird theories, cranks are more apt to be wrong than right. Similarly, the exagger-ated claims made by high-pressure salespersons regarding certain products are prob-ably more often false than true, especially when the products are made by companies that have bad records with the local chamber of commerce. Such companies have a history of failing to live up to their promises. The performance records of some stock-brokers are so poor that their clients would be advised to hold off when those brokers say "Buy." Arguments against the person are also made by lawyers who want to attack the credibility of witnesses. If a lawyer can show that a witness has already committed perjury when questioned about the subject at issue and can also show that a lie would benefit the witness, the argument may be strong.

Arguments that a claim is false on the grounds that it was made by a particular individual or group are fallacious unless most claims made by the individual or group on that subject are false. This statistical premiss, as we have seen, is hardly ever true, so legitimate cases of arguments against the person are rare. Fallacious *ad hominems* are fairly common. We might commit this fallacy, or be taken in by it, for several reasons. We may dislike the person who is making the claim, or we may disapprove of the per-son's looks, clothing, views, habits, religion, ethnic origin, or some other personal char-acteristic or association. Obviously, such prejudices should not be allowed to intrude on our critical judgments of the evidence for truth or falsity of claims.

A second reason why we are sometimes misled by fallacious arguments against the person is our desire to deny the claim made by the person. When we disagree with a claim someone makes, we might, in the absence of any counterevidence, try to discredit this claim by attacking the person's character or qualifications, however irrelevant they may be to the issue. An old joke advises lawyers who have no case to "abuse the per-son." In a sophistical (misleading, but clever) bit of reasoning, Samuel Johnson defends the fallacious use of argument against the person in such cases:

> "When there is a controversy concerning a passage in a classic, or concerning a
> question in antiquities, or some such subject, one may treat an antagonist with
> politeness and respect. But where the controversy is concerning the government
> or religion of my country, it is of such vast importance to have the better, that the
> person of the opponent is not to be spared. If a man firmly believes that religion is a
> great treasure, he will consider a writer who endeavors to deprive mankind of it as
> a robber; he will look on him as odious even though the infidel may think himself in
> the right. . . . "

> Dr. Johnson said that when a man voluntarily engages in an important controversy, he is to do all he can to lessen his antagonist, because authority from personal respect has much weight and often more than reasonings. "If," said he, "my antagonist writes bad language, though that may not be essential to the question, I will attack him for his bad language."
>
> —J. Boswell, *The Ominous Years*

Johnson is probably correct in saying that people are more often moved by their respect (or lack of respect) for a person than by the strength of argument. Unfortunately, people often pay less attention to reasons than to the person who provides them. Nevertheless, as critical thinkers, we do not want to be deceived by such ploys.

When an argument against the person (an *ad hominem* argument) attacks the character of an individual, the argument is called an "abusive *ad hominem*." When an argument attacks not the person *per se* but some circumstances of the person, such as religion, nationality, or membership in a political party, the argument is called a "circumstantial *ad hominem*."

Another variant of *ad hominem* arguments is called "*tu quoque*," which can be translated "you too." This occurs when someone counters an attack on a position by accusing the person who offers it of being in a position similar to that being criticized. Example: "You cannot call me slow or lazy because you have not finished any of the work you were assigned to do either." *Tu quoque* arguments cannot be cast easily into the form of a statistical syllogism and are almost always fallacious.

Regrettably, fallacies of all these types occurred in an interchange among distinguished scientists. The focus of the discussion was the contention by Dr. Luis W. Alvarez, a Nobel prize winner in physics for his work on nuclear particles, and his son, Dr. Walter Alvarez, a geologist, that the impact of a large comet 65 million years ago was responsible for the extinction of the dinosaurs. The main evidence for the comet's impact is a layer of metallic iridium found in sedimentary rock all over the world. The evidence that this impact caused the extinction of dinosaurs is far from conclusive, and many paleontologists (scientists who specialize in fossil evidence for extinct life forms) reject the Alvarezes' theory that a single catastrophe caused the extinction. The paleontologists say the fossils show that the extinction took place over a very long period. This controversial situation has all of the features that promote the use of fallacious arguments from authority and fallacious arguments against the person: a distinguished expert in one field (L. Alvarez, a nuclear physicist) speaking in an area (paleontology) outside his field of expertise, and disagreement even among expert paleontologists about the nature of fossil evidence.

In the quoted portions of this report from the *New York Times*, fallacies are identified in square brackets:

> Dr. Luis Alvarez also criticizes three earth-sciences professors at Dartmouth College, Charles B. Officer, and his colleague Charles L. Drake as well as Robert Jastrow, who all reject the cometary impact hypothesis. "It is now clear," Dr. Jastrow said in an

interview, "that a catastrophe of extraterrestrial origin had no discernible impact on the history of life as measured over a period of millions of years."

Dr. Alvarez responded: "There isn't any debate. There's not a single member of the National Academy of Sciences who shares Jastrow's point of view." (Dr. Alvarez is himself a member of the Academy.) [Fallacious appeal to authority: Members of the academy are scientists distinguished in many different fields but do not constitute a legitimate authority in paleontology.]

He added: "Jastrow, of course, has gotten into the defense of Star Wars, which for me personally indicates he's not a very good scientist. In my opinion, Star Wars doesn't stand a chance." [Circumstantial *ad hominem*: Jastrow's conclusion about extinction is rejected because Jastrow has aligned himself with supporters of the government's Strategic Defense Initiative.]

In rejoinder, Dr. Jastrow noted that Dr. Alvarez had personally flown on the nuclear raid that destroyed Hiroshima, and that in 1954, Dr. Alvarez had been one of only five physicists willing to appear before the Atomic Energy Commission to denounce J. Robert Oppenheimer as a security risk. . . . [*Tu quoque*: In response to Alvarez's accusation that Jastrow is aligned with questionable government science policy, Jastrow points out Alvarez's own connection with other questionable government science-related activities.]

In his public barbs at Dr. Officer, Dr. Alvarez asserted that the Dartmouth geologist was laughed to scorn at a 1985 meeting of the American Geophysical Union and that the incident had shorn Dr. Officer of scientific credibility [abusive *ad hominem*]. . . . Dr. Officer responded: "This is a misstatement. There was no outburst of laughter following Walter's brief comment, and no direct or implied derision of me as a scientist by the audience. . . . "

Closer to home, Dr. Alvarez has harsh words for some of his colleagues at Berkeley. Among them is Dr. William A. Clemens, a paleontologist who recently reported in *Science* that he had found abundant dinosaur fossils along Alaska's North Slope. The dinosaurs would not have faced the danger of freezing since temperatures were much milder then, but at such high latitudes, total darkness must have persisted for several months each winter, thereby halting the growth of plants and curtailing food supplies.

That the dinosaurs nevertheless survived such conditions, Dr. Clemens contends, undermines the comet theory because a cometary impact would not have blocked sunlight for nearly as long as the polar winter.

Dr. Alvarez responds by saying that he considers Dr. Clemens inept at interpreting sedimentary rock strata and that his criticisms can be dismissed on grounds of general incompetence [abusive *ad hominem*], a charge Dr. Clemens rejects.

—M. W. Browne, *The New York Times*, January 19, 1988

iii. Arguments from Consensus

In an **argument from consensus** (in Latin, *ad populem*), some assertion is held to be correct, or incorrect, on the grounds that most people believe, or reject, the assertion. An automobile advertisement argues that one brand of car is best by stating "50 million

Americans can't be wrong!" Advertisers, politicians, and others try to persuade people to act by stating that "everyone" does it. Such arguments, when they are correct, can be cast in the form of a statistical syllogism:

> Usually, when most people agree on a statement about a subject matter S,
> the statement is true.
> p is a statement about S that most people agree on.
> _____
> p is true.

The similarity between this argument form and that of the argument from authority is easy to see. On what topics, we need to ask, is consensus (which means "agreement, especially in opinion") an authority? Background knowledge is essential to know whether the subject matter is understood by enough people in the group being polled for an argument from consensus to work. For example, most graduates of New York high schools know that the state capital is located in Albany. If a large group of New York high school graduates were asked about the state capital, the consensus would probably be the correct answer. Consensus of the same group on the capital of New Mexico or of Slovenia ("no opinion" rather than a systematic error in naming the capital city would probably be the result of attempting to find a consensus) would not be so reliable. Moreover, even in the cases where consensus is a reliable authority, running an opinion poll might not be the most efficient way to argue for a claim. Such factual matters as the location of capitals are relatively easy to settle by checking reference books or asking a single reliable authority.

Unless consensus is a reliable authority on a subject matter, an appeal to consensus is fallacious. Fallacious appeals to consensus often depend on prejudice: "Everybody knows those people are cannibals [or witches, thieves, infidels, and so forth]."

Statements about the most popular brand of beer or the current favorite sport of young people are commonly supported by appeals to consensus. In these cases, however, the arguments are deductive, because they are grounded in a definition ("popular" means "what is liked by the people or by most people"), rather than inductive. Such an argument could fail to have a true conclusion only if it had a false premiss. In contrast, to argue on the basis of popular appeal that a given product is most nutritious, most healthful, or best in some other feature is fallacious if the consensus is just a popularity contest. Majority opinion can deductively support a statement about what is most popular but might not even provide weak inductive support for other claims.

In some other instances besides popularity contests, majority opinion *by definition* validates the truth of a statement. One example is suggested by the recent judicial ruling that a movie is pornographic if it violates local standards of decency (that is, if most people in that community would consider it pornographic). Under these circumstances, the following argument would be correct:

> A movie is legally pornographic if most people consider it pornographic.
> Most people consider movie M pornographic.
> _____
> Movie M is legally pornographic.

Careful examination of this argument reveals that it does not have the same form as the argument from consensus. One of the premisses states something that is true as a result of a definition (in this case, the legal definition of *pornographic*). The other premiss, although it is a statistical generalization, states that the circumstances for the application of the definition have been fulfilled for the movie in question; the conclusion states that the movie belongs to the class of pornographic things thus defined. If the premisses of this argument are true then, necessarily, the conclusion is true. The argument is not inductive but deductive. The argument is neither a fallacy nor an argument from consensus.

If we turn our attention to the statistical premiss in such an argument and ask how it is supported, then we appeal to another sort of inductive argument, called **inductive generalization,** which is discussed in Section IV later in this chapter.

5. MISSING PREMISSES IN STATISTICAL SYLLOGISMS

Once the form of an argument is identified, it is easier to identify any missing premisses required to complete the argument. We have already noted that the statistical premiss in a statistical syllogism is frequently suppressed, particularly when it represents a claim that is widely known. In such cases, we appeal to general background information as well as to what is stated to form a plausible and relevant statistical generalization. As critical thinkers, we construct and evaluate arguments because we want to arrive at true beliefs on the basis of what we already know. Thus, we try to minimize ignorance and maximize knowledge. In arguments from authority, arguments against the person, and arguments from consensus, the statistical premiss is frequently suppressed. We need to supply this premiss to evaluate those arguments because their correctness depends on whether most of what an authority says is right, whether most of what a person says about a subject is false, or whether majority opinion on a subject is reliable. Once the suppressed premiss is stated, we can call upon background knowledge or gather evidence to assess its truth. The acceptance of fallacious arguments can often be prevented merely by exposing their suppressed premisses.

6. AN INCORRECT FORM OF INDUCTIVE ARGUMENT

As we saw at the beginning of this chapter, the statistical syllogism resembles a correct form of deductive argument. The inductive form differs from the deductive in substituting "X percent" for "all," where X is greater than zero and less than one or some nonquantitative expression such as *most* or *a high proportion.*

Deductive Form	Inductive Form
All *F*s are *G*s.	*X* percent of *F*s are *G*s.
a is an *F*.	*a* is an *F*.
a is a *G*.	*a* is a *G*.

The form of deductive argument that the statistical syllogism resembles is called a **quasi-syllogism.** This form is **valid,** which means that if an argument has this form it cannot have all true premises and a false conclusion. The structural features of the quasi-syllogism are sufficient to guarantee that any argument with that form is deductive, regardless of the content of the argument or any background information. No form of an inductive argument is valid. That is to say, inductive forms alone can never guarantee—or even make it probable—that the conclusion of arguments in this form will be true if their premises are true. Unlike deductive arguments, inductive arguments depend on more than form for their strength. As we have seen, arguments in the inductive form of statistical syllogism may have true premises and a false conclusion. However, if background knowledge assures us that the reference class is correctly chosen and if the percentage in the statistical premiss is appropriately high (or low in the negative case), we can say that in these arguments probably the conclusion will be true if the premises are true. Given these qualifications, the statistical syllogism is a correct inductive form of argument.

The following deductive argument is an example of another kind of syllogism, called a **categorical syllogism**:

> All humans are mammals.
> All mammals are animals.
> _____
> All humans are animals.

Letting uppercase letters represent class terms, we can exhibit the form of this argument as follows:

Deductive Form

> All *F*s are *G*s.
> All *G*s are *H*s.
> _____
> All *F*s are *H*s.

This particular form of the categorical syllogism is valid, which means the consistent substitution of any class for each occurrence of the letters *F, G,* and *H* will result in a deductive argument.

If we replace *all* with *most* in the form of this categorical syllogism, the following form results:

> Most *F*s are *G*s.
> Most *G*s are *H*s.
> _____
> Most *F*s are *H*s.

This form is not inductively correct, however. Even when we are careful to take account of all available relevant evidence, this form of argument is not likely in general to lead us from true premisses to true conclusions. Consider the following argument:

> Most physicists are men.
> Most men are nonphysicists.
> _____
> Most physicists are nonphysicists.

Despite its true premisses, the conclusion of this argument is a self-contradiction. This incorrect form exemplifies the danger of supposing that all correct inductive argument forms are just slightly weakened versions of deductive forms.

Exercise Set 4.4

PART I. Reconstruct each of the following arguments. Identify those that are instances of a correct inductive form and those that are fallacious. If the background knowledge required to evaluate the argument is missing, discuss what would be needed.

1. I want to take a daily vitamin supplement, and my favorite American League pitcher recommends one brand. But I am reluctant to take his advice because so many major league players apparently lied about taking steroids.

2. In March 2011, the *Washington Post* conducted a poll asking whether the (Afghanistan) war was no longer worth fighting. Two thirds of those polled answered yes. My roommate was one of the people polled, so she probably agreed that the war was no longer worth fighting.

3. Many prisoners have complained that conditions in the county jail are overcrowded and unsanitary. However, these persons are all criminals, so we do not need to believe what they say about the jail.

4. Both the American Medical Association and the American Dental Association have formally endorsed fluoridation of drinking water. Therefore, fluoridation promotes dental welfare and is not generally harmful to people's health.

5. Most advertisers agree that it is not dishonest to present their products in the best possible light, even if that means making exaggerated claims about the worth of the products. Therefore regulators should not try to enforce "truth in advertising" standards too strictly.

6. For at least 30 years, even as oil has more than doubled and tripled in cost, economic advisers to both major political parties have agreed that the best way to make consumers conserve energy is to impose taxes, ranging from $0.50 per gallon of gas to $5.00 a barrel on imported oil. Therefore, higher taxes on gas and oil use will be the best way to encourage conservation.

7. At several points in the history of the United States, mothers of soldiers have organized to pressure the government to cease waging wars. The government

can reasonably ignore their petitions, however, because as women the protestors cannot be expected to take a rational view of the situation.

8. When a captured pirate was brought before Alexander the Great and asked by the mighty conqueror what he meant by keeping hostile possession of the sea, he replied:

> "[The same as] what thou meanest by seizing the whole earth; but because I do it with a petty ship, I am called a robber, whilst thou who dost it with a great fleet are styled emperor."

> —St. Augustine, *The City of God*

   Which type of *ad hominem* argument is the pirate using in his answer?

9. Osiander [writing in 1540] pointed out how little real evidence there was for [the myth of Jewish slaughter of Christian children]: even Jewish converts to Christianity, always ready to blacken the character of Judaism, had never made a single accusation of child-murder against their former faith. Predictably, his enemies said (wrongly) that he was a Jew himself, which as far as they were concerned annulled any force in his arguments.

> —D. MacCulloch, *The Reformation*, 2006

10. The following argument by a fictional character supports the use of folk medicines:

> I know they have been well reported of and many wise persons have tried remedies providentially discovered by those who are not regular physicians, and have found a blessing in the use of them. I may mention the eminent Mr. Wesley [the founder of Methodism], who, though I hold not altogether with his Arminian doctrine, nor with the usages of his institution, was nevertheless a man of God.

> —George Eliot, *Felix Holt*

11. Miss Manners says that the socially correct thing for a vegetarian guest to do at a dinner party is to be perfectly happy eating salad, bread, and any vegetable. Therefore, the behavior she describes is the socially correct thing to do.

12. What kind of argument is Wicker using against North? Is Wicker justified?

> After so much lying, even for purposes North considers patriotic, his protestations that he now only wants to tell the truth aren't worth much. Why should he be considered believable, even under oath, when he testified under oath that he had so often considered other values more important than truth?

> —Tom Wicker, *The New York Times*, July 8, 1987

PART II. In this passage, the author attempts to defend creationism against the charge that it is unscientific. Identify the type of *argumentum ad hominem* committed here.

> Thus, for a theory to qualify as a scientific theory, it must be supported by events, processes or properties which can be observed, and the theory must be useful in

predicting the outcome of future natural phenomena or laboratory experiments. An additional limitation usually imposed is that the theory must be capable of falsification. That is, it must be possible to conceive some experiment, the failure of which would disprove the theory.

It is on the basis of such criteria that most evolutionists insist that creation be refused consideration as a possible explanation for origins. Creation has not been witnessed by human observers, it cannot be tested experimentally, and as a theory it is nonfalsifiable.

The general theory of evolution also fails to meet all three of these criteria, however.

—D. Gish, *Evolution? The Fossils Say No!* 1979

PART III. Background: Although we normally consult a dictionary to check the standard pronunciation of some unfamiliar or disputed word, the linguists who construct dictionaries base their entries on how most people pronounce the word. Thus, the way most people pronounce the word constitutes the standard for how it should be pronounced. Shifts in the standard pronunciation of many words account in part for the need to revise dictionaries from time to time.

With the preceding as background information, consider (1) whether the argument with the premiss that most English speakers pronounce the word *otiose* as ó-shi-ós inductively supports the claim that this is the correct pronunciation. (In other words, is this an argument from consensus?) (2) Is the premiss itself supported by inductive or deductive reasoning? (3) Have you heard "nuclear" pronounced in more than one way? How do *you* say it? Which pronunciation is recommended in the most up-to-date dictionary you can find?

PART IV. One of the most famous (and puzzling) general premisses for an *ad hominem* argument occurs in St. Paul's letter to Titus, an assistant helping him spread the gospel of Christ. Warning Titus of people from Crete, Paul says

They are all liars, as one of their own has said,

—Titus 1, 12–13a

The "one of their own" was the philosopher Epimenides, a Cretan, who said "All Cretans are liars."

This is the basis for the paradox of the liar. Can you see what the puzzle is?

PART V. In Section 6, an example was given of an argument with true premisses and a false conclusion in the following form. Construct another example of an argument with true premisses and a false conclusion in this form:

Most Fs are Gs.
Most Gs are Hs.

Most Fs are Hs.

(Hint: Choose classes in such a way that F is a much smaller class than G, so that it is possible for most Fs to be Gs and most Gs to be Hs, whereas few or even no Fs are Hs because the Hs could be just all the things that are not Fs.)

PART VI. Identify the fallacy being attacked in the following:

> One of the hardest things to remember is that a man's merit in one sphere is no guarantee of his merit in another. Newton's mathematics don't prove his theology. Faraday was right about electricity, but not about Sandemanism. Plato wrote marvelously well, and that's why people still go on believing his pernicious philosophy. Tolstoy was an excellent novelist; but that's no reason for regarding his ideas about morality as anything but detestable, or for feeling anything but contempt for his aesthetics, his sociology, and his religion. In the case of scientists and philosophers this ineptitude outside their own line of business isn't surprising. Indeed, it's almost inevitable. For it's obvious that excessive development of the purely mental functions leads to atrophy of all the rest. Hence, the notorious infantility of professors and the ludicrous simplicity of the solutions they offer for the problems of life.
>
> —A. Huxley, *Point Counter Point*, 1928

III. ARGUMENTS FROM ANALOGY

When we point out an observed similarity between two things or two types of things, we draw an **analogy** between them. In everyday life, we often notice and comment on similarities. A great boxer—Muhammad Ali—claimed to "float like a butterfly and sting like a bee." Analogies that are unusual and surprising are the stuff of which literature, especially poetry, is made. Thus, James Boswell (*In Search of a Wife*) draws an analogy between his character and a kind of fabric: "I am a weaker man than can well be imagined. My brilliant qualities are like embroidery on gauze." Chugan Egetsu wrote in the fourteenth century: "Confusianism and Buddhism are like two faces of a coin. Their arguments are like two identical jewels." Open almost any page of Shakespeare and you will find beautiful analogies, which in literature are called *similes* and *metaphors*:

> How far that little candle throws his beams! So shines a good deed in a naughty world.
>
> —Shakespeare, *The Merchant of Venice*

On the subject of analogy, the mathematician G. Polya (1957) has said, "Analogy pervades all our thinking, our everyday speech and our trivial conclusions as well as artistic ways of expression and the highest scientific achievements." When, on the basis of analogies, we conclude that items similar in observed ways are also similar in some further, as yet unobserved respect, we employ an **argument from analogy**. For example, analogical reasoning from the observed effects of the birth-control hormone on rats (which are physiologically similar to humans) has been used to conclude that birth-control pills may affect human brain development.

Not every use of analogy is an argument from analogy. For an argument to be present, a conclusion must be drawn on the basis of an analogy. The examples from Ali, Boswell, Egetsu, and Shakespeare are not arguments from analogy; the analogies that are stated are not used to support some further unobserved similarity. Instead, these analogies enhance our ability to see the world in new ways by directing our attention to interesting similarities. Analogies, even when they are not part of arguments, can influence how we reason about the world. Several important examples of the power of analogy were shown in experiments conducted by P. Thibodeau and L. Boroditsky at Stanford University. They presented two reports about a crime, one describing crime as "a wild beast preying on the city" and the other describing the identical crime but using the analogy "virus affecting the city."

Responses to how to deal with crime varied from strong law enforcement and punishment from the group that read the wild beast analogy to a much greater emphasis on social reforms from the group that read the report with the virus metaphor.

1. FORM OF ARGUMENTS FROM ANALOGY

Although arguments from analogy are stated in various ways, many can be reconstructed to exhibit the following basic form:

> Objects of type X have properties F, G, H, and so on.
> Objects of type Y have properties F, G, H, and so on and also an additional property Z.
> _____
> Objects of type X have property Z as well.

Both premises of these arguments mention the respects (F, G, H, etc.) in which the two types of objects have been observed to be similar. The second premiss also mentions a property (Z) that has been observed in one type of object. The conclusion states that the other type of object has that property as well.

In the argument that concludes that birth-control pills may affect human brain development, the properties F, G, H, and so on—although unspecified in the premises—are the physiological properties that humans (objects of type X) and rats (objects of type Y) have been observed to share. Rats are used in medical experiments because they possess these properties. That the further property Z of brain development is affected by the birth-control hormone has been observed for rats and is inferred to hold for humans as well.

In the absence of sufficient information about the effects on humans of potentially harmful substances, experiments are performed on animals. The animals' reactions lead us to conclude (inductively) that humans would react in similar ways. This form of reasoning is understood not only by scientists but also by the general public. In view of widespread familiarity with the role of experimental animals, the similarities between these animals and humans are not always stated explicitly. When the conclusions of such arguments are challenged, however, mention is often made of relevant dissimilarities (differences) between the animals used in the experiment and human beings. The results of tests on laboratory rats, for example, can be challenged on the basis of the disparity in size between rats and humans.

When we reconstruct analogical arguments to judge their strength, we should try to state explicitly any *implicit* points of analogy contained in the premises. Specialized knowledge may be needed to state the implicit similarities. For example, most of us do not know enough physiology to be able to state precisely how various experimental animals resemble humans. We must then rely on experts' claims that the similarities are present, but we should at least be aware that the nature of these similarities is crucial to the argument.

2. STANDARDS FOR THE STRENGTH OF ANALOGICAL ARGUMENTS

The strength of an argument from analogy, or an **analogical argument**, depends heavily on the **relevance** of the similarities mentioned in the premises to the similarity stated in the conclusion. One feature is relevant to another if the presence of the first increases (is positively relevant to) or decreases (is negatively relevant to) the probability that the second feature will also be present.

The definition of *relevance* does not tell us how to determine whether some feature is relevant in a given context. For this we need background information. For example, the color of a car's finish is relevant to its aesthetic appeal and to whether it shows dirt but not to its durability. Other properties of the car, such as the materials used in its frame, are relevant to its durability but not to its aesthetic appeal or resistance to dirt. In the argument about birth-control pills, the conclusion states that the birth-control hormone will produce a physiological effect in humans similar to the physiological effect it produces in rats. The implicit premise asserts the existence of physiological similarities between rats and humans. The similarities employed in the implicit premiss are relevant to the similarity drawn in the conclusion because similar physiological features are relevant to whether or not the same substance will produce a similar physiological effect.

As noted, however, there are many dissimilar physiological features between rats and humans. Rats are smaller; their brains are less complex; and undoubtedly other important (relevant) differences distinguish rats from humans. Such dissimilarities account in part for the tentative nature of the conclusion of this argument, which is indicated by the use of the term *may*.

The **degree** of relevant similarity (or relevant dissimilarity) between the objects mentioned in the premises and the conclusion is also important in judging the strength of analogical arguments. Obviously, the greater the degree of relevant similarity the two types of objects share, the stronger the argument that the feature mentioned in the conclusion will also be shared. For this reason, the results of experiments on our closest mammalian relatives—the large primates—are considered more likely to apply to humans than results obtained through experiments on rats. By the same token, the greater the degree of relevant dissimilarity, the weaker the argument.

Consumer decision making frequently employs arguments from analogy. You may, for example, decide to buy another car from the manufacturer of your reliable old car. If your conclusion that the new car will be reliable is based on a suitable degree of analogy between the old car and the new one and if there are few relevant dissimilarities, your argument will be strong.

Some features we believe relevant to automotive reliability are incorporated in the type of engine, braking system, transmission, and suspension systems. If these features are similar in the new car and the old, the conclusion that the new car will be reliable may be strongly supported. If, however, the new car has many innovations (perhaps a different type of fuel-injection system and a redesigned starter) or if your old car is a sedan and the new car is a sports model with radically new design features, your argument from analogy will be weakened by these relevant dissimilarities. Not every feature of a car is relevant to reliable performance. The location of the antenna and the style of upholstery probably make little difference.

Other criteria for determining the strength of analogical arguments are the number and variety of instances mentioned in the premises or, in other words, the number and diversity of instances that form the basis for the analogy. (There is a close relationship between many arguments from analogy and arguments based on samples, which are discussed in Section IV in this chapter.) A larger and more varied set of instances helps us to recognize which similarities are relevant. If the similar properties mentioned in the premises and in the conclusion go together in a variety of otherwise dissimilar circumstances, we have reason to believe their connection with one another is not accidental—that a causal connection or some other real connection exists between the properties mentioned in the premises and the property mentioned in the conclusion.

Suppose, for instance, that you owned not just one reliable car made by the manufacturer but had owned and driven six cars, in various models and styles. Your argument that another car made by this manufacturer will be reliable is strengthened because the additional evidence tends to show that the manufacturer produces a variety of reliable cars and that the model you owned was not just a fortunate exception.

Similarly, if experiments showed that birth-control hormones had an adverse effect on brain development not only in rats but also in rabbits, pigs, and other experimental animals, then the conclusion that birth-control hormones have an adverse effect on humans is strengthened. The additional evidence tends to show there is not something special about the reaction of rats that makes them relevantly dissimilar to other mammals (and possibly to humans) in their response to the hormone.

The principle that a variety of cases strengthens an analogical argument might seem to conflict with the principle that says relevant dissimilarities between instances in the premises and the instance in the conclusion weaken an analogical argument. There is no real conflict between these two principles, however. The instances mentioned in the premises can have properties that differ in irrelevant ways yet also be similar in ways that are relevant to the property inferred in the conclusion.

3. FALLACIES ASSOCIATED WITH ANALOGICAL ARGUMENTS

Arguments that have the form of analogical reasoning but fail to meet the standards for strong analogical arguments are fallacies. Some fallacious arguments attempt to establish a conclusion on the basis of irrelevant analogies. In *A System of Logic* (first published in 1843), John Stuart Mill named this fallacy the **fallacy of false analogy**. For example, to argue that Joan is probably lazy because her brother John is lazy is fallacious, for the similarities between Joan and John that are implicit in the premiss (whatever similarities siblings typically share) are not particularly relevant to the property of laziness. Many families have both lazy and industrious children.

One of Mill's own examples of this fallacy is the argument that a paternalistic form of government is superior to other forms of government because paternalistic governance works well in families, and families and states resemble one another in many ways. Mill points out that the relevant qualities for a successful paternalistic governance of a family—affection of the parents for the children and parental superiority in wisdom and experience—are conspicuously absent in most paternalistic forms of state government. States and families are therefore relevantly dissimilar to one another with respect to how they should best be governed.

Many examples of false analogy are found in early anthropological studies of tribal cultures. Because scholars falsely assumed that certain aspects of tribal cultures were similar to our own, they viewed the behavior of individuals in tribal societies as perverse or bizarre. For example, observers noted that in some aboriginal societies the words for *mother* and *father* refer not only to the biological parent but also to the parent's siblings. Because the observers believed that in our own society children would use names in this way only if they were confused about the identity of their biological parents, they concluded that the same was true in these societies. Because the people they observed did not seem confused, the observers inferred that at some time in the past there had been a system of group marriage in which the terms that mean *mother* and *father* were applied to a variety of persons because the child could not know which members of the group were actually the biological parents. Later, more detailed anthropological studies—notably those of A. R. Radcliffe-Brown—showed that the kinship terminologies used in our society and in tribal societies are relevantly dissimilar but equally systematic ("logical") and useful in their own contexts. It is no more mysterious for a child in a society with a different kinship terminology to call his or her mother's sister *mother* than it is for a child in our own society to use *aunt* to address his or her mother's sisters, father's sisters, father's brother's wife, mother's brother's wife, elderly female cousins, and even mother's friends.

4. ANALOGY IN ARCHAEOLOGY AND IN LEGAL AND MORAL REASONING

We have already discussed the use of analogical arguments in medical research. Archaeology is another science that depends heavily on arguments from analogy. Archaeologists study humans by examining the material remains of the things they made.

Because the people who made these objects are no longer alive, archaeologists cannot directly observe how these things were used by their makers. Written records are of little help in the study of prehistoric peoples because, as the term *prehistoric* indicates, these people had no writing system, left only fragmentary records, or wrote in languages that we do not yet understand.

Archaeologists note, however, that other people who are now living or whose lives are historically documented use or once used items **similar in form** to those found in archaeological excavations. On the basis of these observed similarities, archaeologists infer by analogy that the prehistoric items were **used for similar purposes.** Archaeologists working in caves in Oaxaca, Mexico, for example, found awl-like objects made from sharpened deer bones that were analogous in virtually every relevant respect (including patterns of wear) to bone tools used by contemporary Oaxacan farmers. Because the farmers used these tools to scrape kernels from corn, the archaeologists, who found remains of corn in the caves as well, unhesitatingly attributed the same function to the prehistoric artifacts.

Legal arguments frequently invoke analogical reasoning. Judges rule on the legality of actions and cases brought before them in hearings and trials. In a civil court, for example, a trial might be held to determine whether a proposed merger between two companies involves a violation of antitrust laws. To rule on such actions, judges must be aware of any laws that are applicable to the particular case being tried before them. In addition to being guided by laws—which are usually broadly stated and difficult to apply to complex cases—judges are guided in their rulings by **precedent.** Legal precedents are previous judicial rulings (interpretations of the law for particular cases).

Analogical reasoning plays an important role in the legal process with regard to the use of precedents. For example, lawyers who are arguing that a corporate merger should be declared illegal will examine previous rulings on mergers. In particular, these lawyers will look for a decision important enough to constitute a precedent. If such a "controlling case" ruled against a merger, the lawyers will try to present relevant similarities between the case they are arguing and the controlling case in which a merger was denied. Lawyers who are arguing in favor of the merger will try to point out the absence of analogy (relevant dissimilarities) between the controlling case and the case in question.

In the absence of a controlling case, lawyers on both sides will search through reports of court decisions on mergers and argue relevant similarities between their case and those decisions that are favorable to their position. They will also point out relevant dissimilarities between their case and those decisions that are unfavorable to their position. The judge, after hearing the arguments, decides whether the case in question should be regarded as relevantly similar to the mergers that were denied or permitted in the past.

Analogy plays an important role in moral as well as legal reasoning. When we claim that a given act deserves blame, for example, we may try to show that the act is relevantly similar to other actions that are classified as blameworthy. If we can conclude that the act is relevantly similar to other blameworthy acts, then we can use the ethical principle that like acts should be treated similarly to argue deductively that the act in question deserves blame. Or someone might argue analogically, for example, that a particular case of promise breaking is relevantly similar to other cases in which ignorance was an important excusing factor. Then a further deductive argument (not an argument from analogy) would conclude that this case of promise breaking should be excused because it occurred under conditions of ignorance that generally excuse fulfilling promises.

We use analogical reasoning also to attribute characteristics, motives, desires, and feelings to other people. For example, we might judge a politician too weak to handle the stresses of high office because he had behaved irresponsibly in situations of similar, but less severe, stress. You might not criticize a friend for behaving crossly if she had all four wisdom teeth pulled the day before for you could not help your own bad temper the day after your wisdom teeth were pulled. We infer that other persons, who are similar to us in many observable respects, share similar hopes, fears, and feelings when confronted with situations that would inspire those hopes, fears, or feelings in ourselves.

Exercise Set 4.5

Reconstruct the analogical arguments contained in each of the following passages. Identify the points of analogy in the premises—including any unstated premises—and the analogies argued for in the conclusions. Assess the strength of the arguments on the basis of the criteria presented in this section. Discuss any cases in which further background knowledge is required to determine relevance.

1. In 2010 USC appealed penalties, including a two-year postseason ban, imposed by the NCAA.

   "We disagree with many of the findings in the report from the NCAA Committee on Infractions and assert that the penalties imposed are too severe for the violations identified and are inconsistent with precedent in similar cases," said Todd Dickey, USC's senior vice president for administration.

2. My last pair of Brand X running shoes were comfortable, gave excellent support to my feet and ankles, and lasted a long time. I expect my new pair of Brand X running shoes, which have the same design, to give the same kind of service as my old pair.

3. "It's not fair," said Marianne to her mother. "When my sister was my age, you let her drive your car after school every day. My grades are just as good as hers were, and I am just as responsible. You should let me have the car after school when you are not using it."

4. Lawyer Jeffrey Ramer presented an argument to the Greenwich Board of Assessment Appeals for reducing the assessment to a lower rating from the present highest (S-6) rating because his client's 16,913 square-foot mansion, valued by the town at $5.7 million, is only half complete.

"You have to keep in mind that the palace at this point is plywood and two-by-fours," Ramer told the appeals board. He said the mansion lacks the amenities of a palatial estate, from bidets to steam baths to crown molding. He said the house doesn't even have plumbing fixtures yet.

—www.greenwichtime.com, May 3, 2010

5. Wives, be subject to your husbands as to the Lord, for the husband is head of the wife as Christ also is the head of the church; as the church is subject to Christ, so wives are to be subject to their husbands in every respect.

—St. Paul, Ephesians 5:22

6. Technology was once thought to be a uniquely human attribute, but the discovery of tool use in apes, otters, birds, and even wasps has scotched that. Nevertheless, the extent and nature of tool use among apes remains a subject of considerable importance in relation to the development of technology among the earliest members of the human family, the hominids. William McGrew of Stirling University, Scotland, therefore decided to survey what has been observed among our simian cousins. . . . "For most of my career I've worked with chimpanzees," he said, "and I have tended to generalize from chimps to the other apes. Great apes [gorillas, orangutans, gibbons] have usually been considered to be of similar intelligence, and I expected similarities in tool use to what I had known about chimps."

—*Science* 236 (1987)

7. The force that binds planets to the sun (gravity) obeys the same general form of law as the electrical force that binds electrons to the nucleus of an atom. (Both gravity and electricity decrease in strength with the square of the distance between the bodies or particles.) Therefore, the electron particles, which have negative charges, when attracted by the positive electricity of the nucleus, should move around it in the same way that the planets move around the sun.

(This was British physicist Ernest Rutherford's argument in favor of an arrangement of parts of the atom offered in opposition to a "plum pudding" model, which held that the electrons were arranged randomly throughout the atom like raisins in a pudding.)

8. Nitrogen dioxide gas is produced from sources that burn fossil fuels. Gas-burning stoves and unvented space heaters can produce high levels (0.2–0.5 ppm) of this gas in houses.

Studies of human populations suggest that young children exposed to nitrogen dioxide at home may have an increased incidence or severity of respiratory infections. These findings are supported by laboratory investigations, showing that mice are more susceptible to bacterial respiratory infections after exposure to nitrogen dioxide. Susceptibility to respiratory tract infection is influenced by the effectiveness of the lung's defense mechanisms.

—research by J. Davis, M. Davidson, and T. Schoeb at University of Alabama at Birmingham, reported to National Center for Environmental Research.

9. **Background information:** In the case of *Langridge v. Levy* (1837), the court allowed recovery to the plaintiff, who said that the defendant sold his father a defective gun. The gun had blown up in the plaintiff's hand, and the court ruled that the seller had falsely declared the gun safe when he knew it was defective.

In *George v. Skivington* (1869), a chemist who compounded a secret hair wash was liable to the wife of the purchaser for injuries caused by the wash. . . . [The court] thought that the imperfect hair wash was like the imperfect gun in the *Langridge* case. It chose to ignore the emphasis in the *Langridge* case on the purported fact that the seller knew the gun was defective and lied. It said, "substitute the word 'negligence' for 'fraud,'" and the analogy between *Langridge v. Levy* and this case is complete.

—E. H. Levi, *An Introduction to Legal Reasoning*, 1970

10. Master Kao said, "Men's nature is like a current of water. If you open a channel for the current to the east, it will flow east. If you open a channel to the west, it will flow west. Men's nature makes no distinction between the good and the not good, just as water makes no distinction between east and west."

Master Meng replies, "Water can be trusted not to make a distinction between east and west; but is this so in relation to up and down? Men's natural tendency towards goodness is like the water's tendency to find the lower level. Now if, for example, you strike the water and make it leap up, it is possible to force it over your head. . . . But this surely is not the nature of water, and it is only if force is applied that it acts in this way. That men can be made to do evil is due to their nature also being like this.

—E.R. Hughes (Ed.) *Chinese Philosophy in Classical Times*, 1954

11. Johnson told me that he went up thither without mentioning it to his servant when he wanted to study, secure from interruption; for he would not allow his servant to say he was not at home when he really was. "A servant's strict regard for the truth (said he) would be weakened by such a practice. A philosopher may know that it is merely a *form* of denial [that is, a 'little white lie'], but few servants are such nice distinguishers. If I accustom a servant to tell a lie for *me*, have I not reason to apprehend that he will tell many lies for *himself*?"

—J. Boswell, *Life of Johnson*

Reconstruct the argument that Johnson believes his servants would use if he allowed them to lie for him.

12. After President Clinton admitted lying to his wife about an extramarital affair, Franklin Graham (son of evangelist Billy Graham) wrote in an opinion article in the *Wall Street Journal*:

> If he will lie to or mislead his wife and daughter, those with whom he is most intimate, what will prevent him from doing the same to the American public?
>
> —Peter J. Boyer, *The New Yorker*, August 22, 2005

13. In the following passage, an analogy is drawn between shade trees and knowledge, or the habit of intellectual activity. The analogy is used to argue for the importance of educating persons during their youth. Discuss the relevance of the similarities.

> Knowledge is a comfortable and necessary retreat and shelter for us in an advanced age; and if we do not plant it while young, it will give us no shade when we grow old.
>
> —Lord Chesterfield, *Letters*

14. 'Tis education forms the common mind;
    Just as the twig is bent, the tree's inclined.

    —A. Pope

15. It seems that the Latin races are far more deeply attached to their Catholicism than we Northerners [that is, Northern Europeans] are to Christianity generally, and that consequently unbelief in Catholic countries means something quite different from what it does among Protestants.

    —F. Nietzsche, *Beyond Good and Evil*

16. Now, pro-life folk need to understand that just as it can be said that some highly civilized folk believed that slavery was a normal human institution (St. Paul, John C. Calhoun) so some people feel that way about abortion. And as long as people feel that way, they are perplexed, indignant and outraged at condemnations of their behavior, let alone efforts to restrict it.

    It is for this reason that one should be no more tempted to scorn a woman who terminates a pregnancy by abortion than one would have been to associate with Thomas Jefferson, a slaveowner.

    —W. F. Buckley, Jr., former syndicated newspaper columnist

17. The anti-climatic fact is that, as a matter of general opinion, scientists concluded years ago that sexual orientation is not chosen. How? The answer seems startlingly low tech: basically the same way they concluded that left-handedness is not chosen, through common sense. Left-handers tell us they don't choose to be left-handed. Aspects of left-handedness, like homosexuality, almost universally appear in early childhood.

    —C. Burr, *The New York Times*, Op-Ed, August 2, 1993

18. The following argument is offered against D. Gish's antievolutionary claim that no transitional forms exist between reptiles and mammals.

Imagine that we have a sequence of color patches, forming a continuous gradation from yellow through orange into red. For purposes of convenience, we divide them into two classes, the red ones and the yellow ones, by choosing some criterion of demarcation. (We might pick, for example, some wavelength in the middle of the orange range.) It would be absurd to object that we do not have a continuous sequence of colors on the grounds that all of the patches in the yellow class fail to satisfy the criterion for being in the red class.

This analogy is easily applied to the reptile-mammal transition. The fossil record supplies a sequence of organisms showing gradual changes into a number of characteristics. For taxonomic purposes, zoologists want to split these organisms into two classes, the reptiles and the mammals. Paleontologists are aware that they are imposing a division on a continuum. . . . The series is divided by using the criteria of jaw mechanics, ear structure, and features of the teeth.

—P. Kitcher, *Abusing Science: The Case Against Creationism*, 1982

19. Wyman (1874) listed four reasons underlying his conclusions [that human remains from aboriginal Floridan middens indicated prehistoric cannibalism]:
    1. The bones . . . were not deposited there at an ordinary burial of a dead body.
    2. The bones were broken as in the case of those of edible animals, as the deer, alligator, etc.
    3. The breaking up of the bones had a certain amount of method.
    4. There is no evidence that the bones were broken up by wild animals.

    —T. White, *Prehistoric Cannibalism at Mancos 5MTUMR-2346*, 1992

20. What use of analogy is made in the following legal decision (*Paton v. British Pregnancy Advisory Service Trustees*, 1979)?

In the discussion of human affairs and especially of abortion, controversy can range over the moral rights, duties, interests, standards and religious views of the parties. Moral values are in issue. I am, in fact, concerned with none of these matters. I am concerned and concerned only with the law of England as it applies to this claim. My task is to apply the law free of emotion or predilection. . . .

The foetus cannot, in English Law, in my view, have a right of its own at least until it is born and has a separate existence from its mother. That permeates the whole of the civil law of this country . . . and is, indeed, the basis of the decisions in those countries where law is founded on the common law, that is to say, in America, Canada, Australia. . . .

—Sir George Baker P, as cited in *Embryo Experimentation*,
Singer et al. (Eds.), 1990

5. ANALOGY AND THE SLIPPERY SLOPE

Several of the exercises in Exercise Set 4.5 are concerned with making distinctions (or failing to make distinctions) among analogous things. Johnson believes, for example, that his servants will not be able to distinguish social lies told for his convenience from lies they want to tell for their convenience. Kitcher criticizes creationists for thinking that an evolutionary continuum does not exist just because scientists have divided life forms into taxonomic classes. Sir George Baker interprets English law to say that before birth a fetus has no rights of its own and after birth it acquires those rights.

Many persons involved with the moral issues surrounding abortion, *in vitro* fertilization, and experiments on human embryos are concerned with identifying a developmental stage in the life of the embryo that marks the point at which the embryo should be treated as a person with the full complement of human rights. Sir George Baker represents one extreme view on when this status is achieved—birth is the marker event. The Roman Catholic Church represents the other extreme—the moment of conception is the marker event. Other markers that have been proposed are segmentation (the point when twinning can no longer occur); the end of first trimester of pregnancy; the end of the second trimester; the development of the fetal nervous system; "quickening," or the mother's awareness of movement in the womb; and viability, or the capacity to live outside the womb. Whereas all of the proposals have something to be said for them, none is entirely satisfactory, for fetal development is a process in which there are no sharp divisions. Even conception and birth are not instantaneous events but are themselves processes that extend over some time. Nevertheless, despite the difficulty of drawing nonarbitrary distinctions at any point along the continuum of fetal development, it would be fallacious to conclude that no meaningful distinctions could be drawn between the beginning of the process and the end, or between early, middle, and late stages in fetal development. To argue in that manner is to commit the **fallacy of the slippery slope**. Moreover, it is consistent with a "pro-life" position to recognize a nine-month fetus as far more similar to a newborn in morally relevant ways than to a newly fertilized human egg. Other questions may be raised about the legitimacy of destroying early-stage embryos besides their similarity to late-stage fetuses or the continuity of the process of fetal development.

Johnson, in saying "few servants are such nice distinguishers," sees them as sliding down a slippery slope—telling white lies for him will lead to telling other sorts of lies for themselves. Franklin Graham raised a similar question about President Clinton. Kitcher accuses the creationists of the opposite mistake—they suppose that because a taxonomic distinction has been drawn an evolutionary gap exists.

The slippery slope is an ancient form of fallacious reasoning. According to van Fraassen (*The Scientific Image*), Sextus Empiricus argued nearly two millennia ago that incest is not immoral, on the grounds that "touching your mother's big toe with your little finger is not immoral, and all the rest differs only by degree." Van Fraassen is concerned with the slippery slope character of arguments that challenge the distinction between observable and nonobservable objects. This topic and the closely related distinction between observable and theoretical entities in science are subjects of intense debate in contemporary philosophy of science. Here is the argument that van Fraassen criticizes:

> There is, in principle, a continuous series beginning with looking through a vacuum and containing these as members: looking through a windowpane, looking through glasses, looking through binoculars, looking through a low-power microscope, looking through a high-power microscope, etc., in the order given. The important consequence is that, so far, we are left without criteria which would enable us to draw a non-arbitrary line between "observation" and "theory."
>
> —G. Maxwell, cited in van Fraassen, 1980

In trying to decide what import such arguments have, it is useful to examine the notion of an "arbitrary" distinction. The term *arbitrary* in this connection can mean that no justification at all can be given for drawing the distinction or it can mean that different justifications can be given for various ways of drawing the distinction, and that the choice of where to draw the distinction is to be justified by the purpose of the distinction. Thus, although achieving the age of 18 years is no clear marker of having reached the level of maturity required to vote, serve in the armed forces, and take on other adult responsibilities, by that age a great many people have matured sufficiently to qualify as adults. For all kinds of practical reasons, some age must be chosen to mark the age of majority. Therefore, the choice of 18 is arbitrary in the second sense—19 years might serve the purposes mentioned as well as 18—but not in the first sense of the term.

The form of slippery slope arguments can be represented in the following way:

> There is some continuum between X and Y.
> In terms of that continuum, X and Y differ only by degree.
> _____
> Therefore, no meaningful distinction can be drawn between X and Y.*

The employment of the slippery slope often occurs in cases of moral or legal reasoning, in contexts in which decisions can have a lasting impact on people's lives and well-being. For this reason, the arguments need to be examined carefully to determine the sense in which considerations of analogy, or similarity, support drawing distinctions and to determine the purposes those distinctions are intended to serve as well as the effects of any actions taken on the basis of such distinctions.

Exercise Set 4.6

1. The following argument against abortion at any stage of fetal development has been called a slippery-slope argument:

---

* This form was suggested by Professor Michel Janssen, University of Minnesota.

> Since it is clearly wrong to kill a human being the day it is born, and since the fetus is the same person the day before it is born as the day it is born, it is also wrong to kill it on that day, and on the day before, and the day before that, and so on back to the first moment of that being's life.

Some opponents of euthanasia ("mercy killing") support their position by a slippery-slope argument. Try to construct such an argument, and then criticize it. Remember that showing that a particular argument against euthanasia is fallacious is not the same thing as showing that euthanasia is morally correct.

2. Some people argue against legalizing medical marijuana on the grounds that "you let the camel's nose into the tent, pretty soon the whole camel will be inside."

   Fill in details and explain how this is an example of slippery-slope reasoning.

3. Referring to Dolly, the first cloned sheep:

   > The queasiness many people feel over the news that a scientist in Scotland has made a carbon copy of a sheep comes down to this: If a cell can be taken from a human being and used to create a genetically identical double, then any of us could lose our uniqueness. One would no longer be a self.

   > —George Johnson, "Soul Searching"

   Is this a slippery-slope argument?

IV. ARGUMENTS BASED ON SAMPLES

Arguments based on samples share a common form called **inductive generalization.** Other names for the same form are **simple induction, induction by enumeration,** and **statistical generalization.** Inductive generalizations are arguments from the particular to the general. They have the characteristic that has been inaccurately attributed to all inductive reasoning. As we have seen, statistical syllogisms draw particular conclusions from general premises. Nevertheless, the premises of inductive generalizations are about particular cases (the cases that make up the sample), though their conclusions are generalizations about a population. Moreover, inductive generalization is such a common form of inductive argument that those who define induction as arguing from the particular to the general might be excused for focusing on this one important type.

Inductive generalization is the argument form political pollsters use to forecast election results. Before an election, poll takers interview a sample of the population of registered voters, and on the basis of what members of the sample say about how they will vote, the pollsters predict how the population will vote. The statistical information contained in the premisses is extended in the conclusion to apply to the entire population. Such an argument looks like the following:

Twelve hundred (60 percent) of the 2,000 voters polled plan to vote for the incumbent.
_____
60 percent of all voters plan to vote for the incumbent.

Although the predictions based on such polls are often incorrect, their overall record of success is impressive. Such success motivates us to understand how this powerful type of argument works.

Quality-control studies also use inductive generalization. Suppose that a manufacturer wants to know what proportion of its products are defective. The company can employ an inspector to examine a portion of the items as it comes off the assembly line. If, for example, during a one-year period, a plant produces approximately 5,000 stereo receivers (the population) and 100 receivers are inspected (the sample), with only two showing defects, the following argument can be constructed:

Ninety-eight out of 100 (98 percent of) receivers that were examined were without defects.
_____
Ninety-eight percent of the receivers produced at the plant are without defects.

Many scientific studies use inductive generalizations. New drugs are tested by giving them to selected individuals; if the members of the sample suffer no ill effects, the drugs are deemed safe for the general public. The functions of various features of animals, such as distinctive patterns of coloration, are studied by performing experiments on a sample group and noting the effects. The findings are then generalized to apply to all animals of that type. Investigators recently used this form of reasoning when they used black paint to mask high-contrast wing stripes on tropical butterflies and noted that masking did not cause wing damage or affect survival.

You have probably noticed that inductive generalizations are similar in some ways to arguments from analogy. Indeed, in strong inductive generalizations a high degree of relevant analogy exists between a sample and the population it represents. We can distinguish between the form of inductive generalizations, in which a general claim is based on what happens in a sample, and the form of analogical arguments, in which a conclusion about an unobserved similarity is based on similarities that have been observed. In ordinary language, however, because arguments are often incompletely stated, many could be reconstructed in either form. Relevant similarities are crucial to the evaluation of both types of arguments.

Generalizations that are the conclusions of arguments from samples can be either universal or statistical. **Universal generalizations** state that all (100 percent) or none (0 percent) of the members of a class have a certain property. **Statistical generalizations** state that some percentage less than 100 percent, but more than 0 percent, of the members of a class have the property. Recall also that statistical generalizations can be stated non-numerically, using such terms as *most, almost all,* and *very few.* Whether the conclusion of an inductive generalization should be statistical or universal depends on the information contained in the premises. If all members of a sample exhibit the property in question, then the conclusion that all members of the population exhibit that property may be appropriate—provided certain other conditions are satisfied.

1. PRELIMINARY ACCOUNT OF THE FORM OF INDUCTIVE GENERALIZATIONS

Here is a preliminary version of the abstract form of arguments based on samples:

> X percent of observed Fs are Gs.
> _____
> X percent of all Fs are Gs.

The letters F and G in this form represent expressions such as *voters, voters for the incumbent, receivers,* and *items without any defects,* which refer to classes of individuals or to properties possessed by all members of a class. The conclusion of an inductive generalization states that the percentage of Fs that are Gs in the **population** is the same as the percentage in the **observed sample.**

2. STANDARDS FOR CORRECT INDUCTIVE GENERALIZATIONS

When are arguments with true premises in this form likely to lead to true conclusions? The answer depends largely on whether the sample mentioned in the premiss is **representative** of the population referred to in the conclusion. When a sample is representative of the population from which it is taken, the conclusion based on the sample is strongly supported. To say that a sample is representative is to say that the features of the population that concern us in an argument (for example, features that determine how people will vote) are reflected in the sample. When this is the case, what is true of the sample will probably be true of the population as well. Traditionally, the following criteria are required for representative samples:

1. The sample must be large enough.
2. The sample must contain sufficient variety.

Background information about the subject matter of an argument determines whether a sample has sufficient size and variety. If we have reason to believe that a population is highly uniform with respect to the properties that interest us, a small sample could support a strong generalization. With larger, more diverse populations, we usually need a large sample to capture that diversity. A sample of only five voters, all of whom say they will vote for the incumbent, will not support the conclusion of a landslide victory for the incumbent in a national election. Such a sample is so small that it is almost worthless. A sample of five voters, all family members, however, might well support the conclusion that Smith will be elected chairman of a small family-owned company. In a kitchen located on top of a mountain, a cook who wants to determine the boiling point of water at that altitude can use a sample of just one pan—or, to check the reading, perhaps two pans—of water, because that population is highly uniform with respect to the property of boiling point.

Noticing that a small sample may be adequate to represent a large but uniform population suggests the importance of taking varied samples when a population is not uniform. Indeed, even very large samples can lack suitable variety. In a national election, a sample of 100,000 voters would not be representative if all members of the sample were wealthy business executives. Nevertheless, in some circumstances, sufficient size can be viewed as an important (and in some conditions the most important) aid in achieving appropriate variety in samples. A sample that is too small automatically fails to provide the requisite variety.

We now turn to the problem of generating representative samples. A sample taken haphazardly from a population may, through luck, closely resemble that population with respect to the properties that interest us in an argument. However, arguments based on samples gathered without attention to sufficient size and variety do not form a basis for strong arguments. Several methods are used to obtain representative samples. These methods do not *guarantee* that a sample will be representative, but their use increases the probability that it will be so.

A sampling method called *random sampling* is often used. In random sampling, each member of a population has an equal chance of being chosen as a member of the sample. A random sample of students at a university can be generated, for example, by printing each student identification number on a different ticket, mixing the tickets in a rotating drum, and performing a blind drawing of tickets to select a sample of the desired size. A random sample of registered voters in a district can be constructed by assigning a number to each registered voter and using a randomizing device, such as that used to select lottery winners, to generate the sample.

The value of selecting samples that are "sufficiently large" can be shown by taking random samples from an ordinary deck of playing cards, in which one half of the population is red and the other half is black, and considering how much information that samples of various sizes give us about this population. Keeping the cards face down, shuffle the deck so that each card has an equal chance of being selected for the sample. Then select a sample of two cards, replacing the card drawn and shuffling after each draw. There are four possible outcomes of such a selection (or trial): The first card is red (R) and the second is black (B); the first card is black and the second is red; both cards are red; or both cards are black.

(i) RB   (ii) BR   (iii) RR   (iv) BB

In just two of the four possible outcomes (half the time) do we get a sample that is truly representative of the population.

Now suppose that we start again, only this time our sample consists of four trials. Now there are sixteen possible results:

(i) RRRR	(v) RBRR	(ix) BRRR	(xiii) BBRR
(ii) RRRB	(vi) RBRB	(x) BRRB	(xiv) BBRB
(iii) RRBR	(vii) RBBR	(xi) BRBR	(xv) BBBR
(iv) RRBB	(viii) RBBB	(xii) BRBB	(xvi) BBBB

In only six of the 16 possible outcomes (three eighths of the draws), exactly half of the cards are red and half black. However, and this is critical, in all but two outcomes (seven eighths of the draws), a mix of black and red cards occurs, and in only one eighth of the outcomes (as opposed to one half in the smaller sample) could we be misled into thinking the deck contains cards of only one color. So when our sample size is four instead of two, we are more likely to get an answer that is *close to* half red cards and less likely to get an answer that the deck is all red or all black. In general, as our sample size increases, a proportion of red and black cards occurs that is *closer* to the true proportion in the deck. This is so even though as the sample size increases, our chances of getting *exactly* the true proportion (one half) gets smaller. (When the sample size is two, half the possible outcomes are exactly half red; when the sample size is four, three eighths of the possible outcomes are half red; in a sample size of 10, only one fourth of the possible outcomes are exactly half red. But, with a sample size of 10, two thirds of the possible outcomes are between 40 percent and 60 percent red cards.) Thus, as sample sizes increase, we can be more and more confident that a randomly selected sample will resemble the population from which it is drawn.

A special type of random sampling is called *stratified random sampling*. This form of random sampling is useful when information is available about the nature of variation in a population. When we know something about how segments of the population would be apt to differ with respect to the property that interests us in the conclusion (such as voter preference) and when we also know the proportion of each segment in the population, we can *stratify* the different layers in the population and then select randomly within each layer. We know, for example, that voting preferences are often shared by persons of similar social class, occupation, and religious or ethnic background. If we also know the proportion of each of these groups in the population of voters, we can sample randomly *within* the groups to construct a sample that "matches" those proportions. The method of taking stratified random samples has been refined by professional poll takers to permit the construction of relatively small representative samples for huge populations. The Gallup Poll and the Harris Poll, for example, are reliable indicators of voter preference in national elections and other matters of public opinion, even though their samples, which represent hundreds of millions of eligible voters, usually consist of fewer than 2,000 persons.

Random sampling and stratified random sampling are very good ways to generate representative samples and constitute an ideal standard for premises of strong inductive generalizations. Unfortunately, however, theoretical and practical barriers prevent using these techniques in many cases. Gathering statistics costs time and money. Sometimes decisions must be made and actions taken before the best information can be gathered and processed. For this reason, "quick and dirty" samples, which make use of easily available information, are often used. For example, suppose a reporter for a student newspaper, working on a deadline, must turn in a story about students' opinions on building a new sports arena. The reporter does not have time to construct a sample that uses all student identification numbers to generate a random sample and to contact each student. Instead, the reporter waits at the entrance to the library for as long as it takes to question 50 students who walk by. Can you think of some reasons why a sample gathered in this way is less likely to be representative than one that uses the random method?

From what we have said thus far, we can see the importance of background knowledge when we try to assess the strength of an inductive generalization. We not only have to examine the premises of the argument; we also have to consider whether the sample is representative, and this requires information that is not contained in the premisses. When we cannot tell whether a sample is large enough or varied enough, we cannot tell whether an inductive generalization is strong. This dependence on background knowledge—on information that is not a part of the premises—is a feature of all inductive arguments. Success at critical thinking does not demand that we acquire the background knowledge to judge every case. It demands instead that we be aware that certain questions must be raised and know how the answers to these questions affect the arguments that we construct or evaluate.

In thinking critically about arguments, it is important to keep separate the truth of a conclusion from the strength of an argument. Bad or weak arguments may turn out to have true conclusions, and good or strong arguments may turn out to have false conclusions. In inductive logic, the standards for correctness are designed to make it probable that if the premises of the argument are true, the conclusion will be true as well. If we adhere to these standards, conclusions based on true premises will usually, but not always, be true.

3. FALLACIES ASSOCIATED WITH INDUCTIVE GENERALIZATIONS

Several fallacies are associated with inductive generalizations. One arises from failing to meet the requirement of obtaining a large enough sample. This fallacy has a number of common names: the **fallacy of insufficient statistics, hasty generalization,** and **leaping to a conclusion.**

If a friend snaps at you when you ask a question, you commit a fallacy of hasty generalization if you conclude that this one instance of unfriendly behavior shows he is no longer your friend. If you conclude that no one likes artichokes because none of your friends do, this too would be a hasty generalization. The psychological reasons for leaping to a conclusion are fairly obvious in these cases. In the first, hurt feelings may color your judgment; in the second, personal interest in opinions of friends may obscure the fact that they are only a small part of the population. To avoid making hasty generalizations, we should dispassionately consider the size of the sample before we draw any conclusion from it. If feelings are not clouding our judgment, but we lack the appropriate background information to decide whether a sample is large enough, we should try to acquire the information. If this is not possible, it is better to suspend judgment than to jump to a conclusion.

A second fallacy associated with inductive generalizations is the **fallacy of biased statistics.** To say that statistics are biased means that the sample lacks proper variety. Biased samples are not representative; they fail to capture, or represent, the variety present in the population from which the sample is taken. Again, background information is required to judge whether a sample is sufficiently varied. Knowing, as we do, that business executives are apt to think alike on political matters, a set of statistics generated by a sample of voters that comprises only business executives (no matter how large the sample is) would be considered biased if these statistics were being used to infer the outcome of a national election.

A recent example of biased statistics, taken from a newspaper, reported a study in which an investigator tried to show that usually when a person is falling in love with someone, the other person is likely to reciprocate the affection. But the investigator's sample was biased, for the group he questioned consisted entirely of couples who had recently become engaged.

In another newspaper story, a reporter surveyed residents of a large city to see whether they would object to having a bus line out of service for several months while a new subway was being built. Every person questioned objected to the plan, but all the persons surveyed were riding that bus line during the hours when most riders are going to work or returning from their jobs. Riders who depend on that bus line for getting to and from work do not constitute a representative sample of city residents.

Still another fallacy associated with inductive generalization consists of rejecting a generalization strongly supported by premises that cite sufficient and unbiased statistics. This sometimes happens when we acquire new information that apparently conflicts with the statistics. The following case provides an example.

Someone is planning to buy a new car and carefully collects all the appropriate statistical information. The statistics include comparisons of thousands of automobiles in terms of performance, safety, repair bills, and other important features. On the basis of these statistics, the prospective buyer concludes that a certain brand of automobile is the best buy. Before the purchase is made, however, this person announces the decision to a friend at a party and is informed that the friend's brother bought the same model of car, which turned out to be a real lemon. The friend describes in vivid detail all the things that went wrong with the car. If the person then rejects the conclusion that the chosen brand is the best buy, a fallacy is committed. Can you see why?

It is not that new information should be ignored. Additional information—either in the premises themselves or in the form of new background information—can strengthen or weaken inductive arguments. But this new information concerns only one case, and one new case cannot outweigh all the statistical information that has been collected. The statistics already take account of defective automobiles. The information that some cars of the chosen brand are lemons is recognized, but presumably this brand comprises relatively fewer lemons than other brands. This is what the statistics say, and no reason has been given to doubt their reliability.

Psychologists R. Nisbett and L. Ross (*Human Inference*, 1980) have studied instances of this fallacy, which David Hume noticed and commented on in the eighteenth century. The psychologists agree with Hume's explanation of why the fallacy occurs. The problem, they say, is that new information received about a car from a friend at a party is more vivid than an impersonal collection of statistics. When you actually know someone (or someone who knows someone) to whom the lemon belongs, the information seems more startling and impressive than a "mere statistic." The vividness of the new information about a single car psychologically cancels the far more complete, but less vivid, information about thousands of cars. The expense and inconvenience of owning a lemon is brought home to the prospective buyer in an alarming way that tends to override the better information. It is a fallacy, nevertheless, to allow a single vivid case to outweigh strong statistical data. This mistake in reasoning can be called the **fallacy of misleading vividness.**

This fallacy, which is sometimes characterized as focusing on easily available evidence while ignoring good statistics, is very common. Any good speaker or writer knows that well-chosen concrete anecdotes are far more convincing to most people than the sort of general information conveyed in statistical reports. When anecdotal evidence is used to bolster and vivify bland statistical information, no fallacy is committed. When anecdotal evidence that contradicts strong statistics is allowed to outweigh the statistical information, however, fallacious reasoning is the result. So many high-level business executives commit this fallacy that some analysts regard it as the most common logical error in business decision making. If you read the articles in *Fortune* magazine devoted to the reasons executives fail, you will find many examples. When executives commit the fallacy of misleading vividness, they fail to keep the big picture in mind. In business this can be fatal.

4. THE REVISED FORM OF INDUCTIVE GENERALIZATION

Thus far, we have discussed two criteria for evaluating inductive generalizations (size of sample and variety in the sample), the fallacies resulting from the failure to meet these criteria, and the fallacy of ignoring good statistical information when faced with meager but vivid conflicting information. A further criterion for evaluating the strength of inductive generalizations applies to all other forms of inductive reasoning as well.

This criterion is concerned with the strength of the conclusion relative to the strength of the premises in an argument. Remember that an argument is a whole that is composed of parts (the premises and the conclusion). The strength of the whole is determined by considering how much support the premises provide for the conclusion. Thus, an argument can be strengthened by providing better premises (a larger or less biased sample) to support the original conclusion. An argument can also be strengthened, however, by weakening the conclusion while leaving the premises unchanged. A statement is said to be weaker when it is qualified or guarded in such a way that it presents less information, or less specific information, than the original statement.

Suppose, for example, a poll is taken by a student newspaper to determine the outcome of a student-body election. The reporter lacks the resources to construct a truly random sample but tries to avoid bias by talking to beginning and advanced students and members of fraternities and sororities as well as unaffiliated students and students in other special-interest organizations. The reporter interviews 100 of the approximately 2,000 students who are expected to vote in the election. Of those interviewed, 40 (40 percent) say they will vote for the Student Conservative Party, and 60 (60 percent) say they will vote for the Student Liberals. The following argument could be constructed:

> Sixty percent of those interviewed said they would vote for the Liberals.
> ___
> Sixty percent of the students will vote for the Liberals.

Based on our discussion of random samples from a deck of cards, we know it is unlikely that the percentage of Liberal voters in the population of students will be *exactly* the same as the percentage in the sample. Thus, it is common to build into the conclusion of inductive generalizations a **margin of error.** Such deviation in the conclusion from the percentage in the sample by a little less or a little more is an example of "weakening" the conclusion relative to the premises. The altered argument might look like the following:

> Sixty percent of those interviewed plan to vote for the Liberals.
> ___
> Sixty percent (plus or minus 10 percent) of the students will vote Liberal.

In this example, the margin of error is 10 percent on either side of 60 percent. Because the sample size was 100 students (and because we can make certain reasonable assumptions about the nature of voting behavior), this margin of error makes it very probable (about 95 percent probable) that reasoning in this way will lead to a true conclusion.

If 500 students were sampled, then we could choose a smaller margin of error, about plus or minus 5 percent, and be just as confident (with 95 percent probability) that our method will lead to a true conclusion. Alternatively, if our sample was small, say only about 30 students, then to achieve the same confidence level we would have to increase the margin of error to roughly plus or minus 20 percent.

Statisticians have calculated the margins of error associated with various sample sizes for estimating percentages in populations with various probabilities of reaching true conclusions (confidence levels). Their calculations are based on random sampling and some reasonable assumptions about how properties are distributed in a population. Whereas some of the arithmetic can be complicated, the basic idea is the same as that discussed in our example with the playing cards in Section 2. Assuming that the property we are interested in is distributed normally in the population and that the sample is chosen randomly, the larger the sample size, the more likely it is that what is true of the sample will also be more or less true of the population. The confidence level is a measure of the likelihood that use of the method leads to a true conclusion. The margin of error is a measure of how much (more or less) the sample resembles the population.

Margin of error, confidence level, and sample size are intimately related to one another. How much **sampling error** to take account of in an inductive generalization depends on the desired confidence level for reaching true conclusions. If you want to be almost certain of being correct, you are better off with a wider margin of error. You pay for the extra certainty, however, with a loss of precision. If you are willing to accept a lower confidence level (that is, a greater chance of being wrong), then you can adopt a smaller margin of error for a comparable sample size. So, using the sample of 100 students in the example above, we might have concluded that between 55 and 65 percent of the students would vote Liberal, but then our confidence level in the method would only be about 70 percent rather than 95 percent. This means that in 10 arguments similar to this one, we would draw a true conclusion about seven times. If we want to retain the higher confidence level (95 percent) *and* reduce our margin of error to a plus or minus 5 percent, then we must increase our sample size to about 500.

Confidence levels and margins of error are sometimes stated informally rather than numerically. For example, if all members of a large sample have some property, the conclusion might be that *almost* all the members of the population will have this property, and the confidence level might be expressed by some other phrase such as "It is very likely that . . ." Or, if half the members of the small sample have the property, the conclusion might state that *roughly* half the members of the population have the property, and the confidence level could be "It is probable that . . ."

Because samples, no matter how carefully constructed, rarely present an *exact* picture of a population, the conclusion of any inductive generalization should include some allowance for a margin of error. In light of this ever-present possibility of sampling error, we will represent the form of inductive generalization in the following way:

X percent of observed Fs are Gs.
_____
X plus or minus z percent of all Fs are Gs.

In this form, z represents the degree of departure in either direction from the observed percentage in the sample. It is possible to measure precisely the margin of error in some carefully conducted statistical studies, and margins of error are sometimes stated in reports of political surveys and other polls. You should be aware, however, that these quantities need not be expressed numerically in every inductive generalization.

Exercise Set 4.7

Decide whether each of the following arguments is an acceptable inductive generalization or a fallacy. Identify the premises and the conclusion of each argument. In the case of a fallacy, explain what is wrong. Discuss what sort of additional background information, if any, is needed.

1. Lei is a graduate student in astronomy who cooks for himself. He knows the proverb:

   Boiling water's not so hot
   Way up on the mountain top.

   The first night he cooks dinner at the mountain-top observatory, he finds that his rice takes 30 minutes to cook, instead of the usual 25 minutes it takes at the base of the mountain. The second night he gets the same result. From then on, he reasons that he needs to allow 30 minutes for cooking rice at the observatory.

2. A nationwide poll the day after a presidential election called registered voters on their landline phones to ask whether they had voted, and 60 percent answered yes. Thus, between 59 percent and 61 percent of registered voters actually voted.

3. A poll of cellphone users who do not have landlines showed that 55 percent of them have no objections to gay marriage. Thus, more than half the population do not object to gay marriage.

4. All the members of my fraternity have tickets to our school's football game this weekend. Therefore the game is sure to be sold out.

5. Studies show that users of cell phones while driving, even of phones not handheld, have impaired responses to traffic and have more accidents than when not using cell phones. One study, reported in the March 2003 issue of *Experimental Psychology: Applied,* involved 110 undergraduates at the University of Utah. Using a Driver Training Simulator, the students "drove" for 40 minutes on a simulated freeway, responding to brake lights on passing cars. Even while using hands-free cell phones, the students took longer to brake, rode the brakes longer, and took longer to accelerate again after slowing down. Three rear-end "crashes" occurred in that group, whereas no crashes occurred in the group not using cell phones. The study also showed little or no difference in the distraction level between talking on the phones or just listening.

6. At the University of Pennsylvania, psychiatrists conducted a study to determine the social factors that affect the well-being of coronary patients.

There were 93 patients in the study; slightly more than 50 percent of them had pets of some kind (dogs, cats, fish, and one iguana). At the end of a year, one third of the patients who did not own pets died, but only three animal owners succumbed. The psychiatrists concluded that pet ownership may have a positive effect on the health of humans.

7. There is no overestimating the importance of pets to people it seems. Katcher [the psychiatrist in charge of the study mentioned in Exercise 6] reported that in one questionnaire, on which people were given the opportunity to indicate whether they thought their pet was an animal or a human member of the family, 48 percent responded that the animal was a human family member.

—"Human-Animal Relationship under Scrutiny," *Science, 214* (1981)

8. Jonathan has to travel to New York from Chicago. He is a nervous traveler, so he compares statistics over the past 10 years on accidents involving buses, trains, automobiles, and planes on routes between the two cities. Jonathan determines that a bus is safer in terms of fewer lives lost than any of the other forms of travel. As he is about to purchase his ticket, however, he sees a newspaper story about a bus accident in which six people died. Jonathan decides not to buy the bus ticket and to fly instead.

9. An American student in Russia reported on some of the ways that Russian students try to achieve success in exams:

They do not wash or cut hair on the day of the exam to prevent all "right" and "clever" thoughts from leaving the head.

If you will go around students' dormitories at midnight before an exam, you will hear plaintive cries from open windows. With magic words "Freebie, be caught" students try to attract Freebie and Fortune. The louder students cry, the more possibly the freebie will come. And it works. I know many a one who has succeeded!

10. EPA statement released two weeks after the Japanese 9.0 earthquake and tsunami:

WASHINGTON – During detailed filter analyses from 12 RadNet air monitor locations across the nation, the U.S. Environmental Protection Agency (EPA) identified trace amounts of radioactive isotopes consistent with the Japanese nuclear incident. Some of the filter results show levels slightly higher than those found by EPA monitors last week and a Department of Energy monitor the week before. These types of findings are to be expected in the coming days and are still far below levels of public health concern.

EPA's samples were captured by monitors in Alaska, Alabama, California, Guam, Hawaii, Idaho, Nevada, Saipan, Northern Mariana Islands and Washington state over the past week and sent to EPA scientists for detailed laboratory analysis.

11. Women are believed to talk too much. Yet study after study finds that it is men who talk more—at meetings, in mixed group discussions, and in classrooms where girls or young women sit next to boys or young men. For example, communications researchers Barbara and Gene Eakins taperecorded and studied seven university faculty meetings. They found that, with one exception, men spoke more often, and without exception, spoke for a longer time. . . .

When a public lecture is followed by questions from the floor, or a talk show host opens the phones, the first voice to be heard asking a question is almost always a man's. And when they ask questions or offer comments from the audience, men tend to talk longer. . . . [A study by M. Swicker is cited. The mean was 23.1 seconds for women, 52.7 for men.]

—D. Tannen, *You Just Don't Understand*, 1991

12. Most labs test [for rabies] only bats that are submitted because they are rabies-suspect. Results are often reported in a manner that implies that these bats are representative of bats in general. An extreme case involved a claim that 50% of a state's bats were rabid because one of only two bats examined tested positive.

—M. Tuttle, *America's Neighborhood Bats*, 1992

V. EXTENDED INDUCTIVE ARGUMENTS

In real life, the various forms of inductive arguments frequently occur in combination. Different forms of argument can support the same conclusion. No inductive argument provides conclusive support, and no combination of inductive arguments can provide conclusive support either. A conclusion can be more strongly supported, however, when several types of favorable arguments can be mustered for it. Arguments against the person, arguments from authority, and arguments from consensus are often presented in combination with other arguments.

Sometimes the conclusion of an inductive generalization serves as the premise of a statistical syllogism. For example, a person might read a report citing statistics about the dangers of off-road bikes and conclude that most off-road bikes are unsafe. Then, using that generalization as a premise, the person might conclude that the off-road bike that she or he owns is unsafe, even though it has not given any trouble so far. No new techniques are needed for evaluating these extended arguments, beyond sorting out the different components and applying the appropriate standards to each.

VI. PRO AND CON ARGUMENTS

Frequently we confront not just one argument, or an extended argument, to support a single conclusion but rather some "pro" arguments for a conclusion and "con" arguments against the same conclusion. This can happen when participants in a debate disagree about the truth of premisses. Not surprisingly, different sets of premisses can lead to different conclusions. In still other cases, different (and conflicting) conclusions can be drawn because of different views about how evidence should be interpreted.

Consider, for example, the pro and con arguments centering on the career of Casanova. He was an eighteenth-century libertine whose 12 volumes of *Memoirs* present detailed accounts of his seduction of hundreds of women from all walks of life—noblewomen to servants and nuns to prostitutes. From the first publication of *Memoirs* (nearly a quarter of a century after Casanova's death), historians have questioned the veracity of the work, citing inconsistencies as well as the use of many pseudonyms. Recently, however, a former American diplomat, J. R. Childs, published a book in which he argues that Casanova was telling the truth. He tries to show that the pseudonyms can be matched to real people, that the apparent inconsistencies in time and place can all be explained, and that the *Memoirs* provide us with a valuable piece of social history. He also says that if Casanova were not telling the truth he would never have presented himself in such an unflattering light.

In a review of Childs's book, however, Angeline Goreau (*The New York Times*) contends that in order for Childs to identify real persons with the pseudonyms, we must assume that Casanova was telling the truth in the first place—but this is just what is denied by his critics. Goreau points out that in the *Memoirs*, the author himself repeatedly proclaims his powers of deceit and his ability to deceive "without the slightest qualm of conscience." Goreau also says that even if Casanova is not trying to dupe us in his autobiography, we must place his *Memoirs* in the context of the times in which works of this sort were written. She says that such documents are dubious as social history because they were designed rather to make some religious or philosophical point (Casanova was preaching the philosophy of moral relativism) or to justify the author in the eyes of posterity.

Neither side in this dispute denies the basic premisses: Inconsistencies and pseudonyms abound in the *Memoirs*, and Casanova presents himself as a deceiver. However, these premisses are used in different ways. On both sides, the arguments employed are inductive. Childs uses inductive generalizations when he tries to go from individual instances of Casanova's truth telling (supported by identifications of pseudonymous characters) to a general claim that Casanova was telling the truth. Statistical syllogism is used when Childs argues that most persons who lie, unlike Casanova, do not present themselves in an unflattering light, so Casanova is not a liar. Goreau uses analogical reasoning when she argues that Casanova's *Memoirs* are similar to other autobiographies of his time in their propensity to promote some religious, philosophical, or justificatory theme; these other autobiographical works are not reliable guides to social history, so Casanova's work is not a reliable guide either. She also accuses Childs of committing the **fallacy of circular reasoning,** because he assumes as a premiss just what his book is supposed to prove as a conclusion, namely, that Casanova was telling the truth.

Circular arguments are deductively valid, in the sense that their conclusions cannot be false if all their premisses are true. Accusations of circular reasoning are usually directed at arguments based on premisses no more plausible than the conclusions they support. Such circular arguments fail to convince those who doubt their conclusions, for the truth of the premisses is contested.

In trying to decide which conclusion about Casanova to accept, readers can try to assess the evidence for both sides according to the information available to them. They should also try to keep an open mind when doubts can be raised about the correctness of either the evidence or the conclusion. Additional evidence can sometimes resolve the issue, as can new arguments about how the evidence should be interpreted, but some disputes remain insoluble.

People who are faced with important business decisions, such as where to open a new restaurant, must consider arguments both for and against a particular location. For example, is it sensible to open a new restaurant in a district that already has a number of similar restaurants? Although competition for customers would be greater in a restaurant district and workers might leave for a job across the street, benefits from that location would include increased customer traffic, convenience in dealing with suppliers, and the greater availability of workers.

VII. REVIEW

In chapter 4, we have examined three important and commonly used forms of inductive argument:

1. **Statistical syllogisms**
2. **Arguments from analogy**
3. **Inductive generalizations** (arguments based on samples)

In evaluating arguments in these forms, a number of criteria have been suggested. Some of these criteria apply only to particular forms; others apply to all forms of inductive reasoning.

The strength of inductive generalizations depends on whether the sample described in the premiss is representative of a population. Two factors are important here: the size of the sample and the degree of variety in the sample. **Random sampling,** in which each member of a population is equally likely to be a member of the sample, and **stratified random sampling,** in which relevant variety in a population is proportionately matched in the sample, are two good methods for obtaining representative samples.

The strength of **arguments from analogy,** or **analogical arguments,** depends crucially on whether the similarities mentioned in the premisses are **positively relevant** to the similarity inferred in the conclusion. Such relevance is the case if the similarity mentioned in the premiss increases the probability that the similarity in the conclusion will obtain. Whether analogies are relevant depends on background information that is not usually contained in the premises of an argument. The **degree** of relevant similarity and relevant dissimilarity, as well as the **variety** in the instances cited in the premises, are also important determinants of the strength of these arguments.

Statistical syllogisms are judged on the basis of the strength of their statistical premisses and also on whether they meet the requirement of **total evidence.** In statistical syllogisms, the requirement of total evidence demands that we choose the appropriate **reference class** in the premises of the argument. Background knowledge is required to select the reference class.

A number of special cases of statistical syllogism—**argument from authority**, **argument against the person** (*argumentum ad hominem*) in its various forms: abusive *ad hominem,* circumstantial *ad hominem,* and **argument from consensus**—have also been discussed. In their correct form, these arguments depend on a statistical premise to the effect that in most cases dealing with the subject matter under consideration, the arguer speaks truthfully (authority), or falsely (against the person), or that the majority opinion is correct (consensus). *Tu quoque* (you too), another form of argument against the person, does not fit the form of statistical syllogism and is usually fallacious.

In evaluating any inductive argument, we must consider the strength of the premisses relative to the strength of the conclusion. Adding supporting evidence, such as a larger or more varied sample for an inductive generalization, additional relevant analogies in an argument from analogy, a stronger statistical premiss, or a more appropriate reference class in a statistical syllogism strengthens arguments. Weakening the conclusions of arguments while keeping their premises the same also strengthens arguments. Because the strength of an argument is determined by how well the premises support the conclusion, a conclusion that is qualified by allowing a margin of error or is weakened in some other way, relative to the same evidence, will result in a stronger argument.

The requirement of total evidence applies to all inductive arguments. In statistical syllogisms, the requirement of total evidence obliges us to choose the reference class that embodies all available relevant evidence about the individual mentioned in the conclusion. When we construct inductive generalizations, the requirement of total evidence forbids us to ignore or disregard any relevant evidence in selecting a sample. In an argument from analogy, relevant dissimilarities cannot be ignored.

A number of fallacies superficially resemble these correct forms of argument. In each case, a fallacy occurs when some standard is violated. Not every fallacy has a special name, but many do. A list of common inductive fallacies follows.

Fallacious Argument against the Person   This fallacy occurs when there are no good grounds to believe that a statement is false because a particular individual says it is false. (The appropriate statistical premise—most of what the individual says about a particular subject matter S is false—cannot be accepted.) Fallacious *ad hominems* are frequently identified by special names: abusive *ad hominem*, circumstantial *ad hominem*, and *tu quoque*.

Fallacious Argument from Authority   This fallacy occurs when the authority cited is not a genuine expert in the field of concern, when the authority is speaking outside his or her field of expertise, or when experts in the area of concern disagree among themselves.

Fallacious Argument from Consensus   This fallacy occurs when majority opinion does not constitute a good reason to believe the truth or falsity of a statement.

Fallacy of Biased Statistics   This fallacy occurs when the sample is not sufficiently varied to represent a population, usually through failure to approximate a random sample.

Fallacy of Circular Reasoning   This fallacy occurs when the truth of the conclusion is already assumed in the premisses that are supposed to support that conclusion.

Fallacy of False Analogy   This fallacy occurs when the types of objects in the premisses of an analogical argument are relevantly dissimilar to the object in the conclusion.

Fallacy of Hasty Generalization   (also called **insufficient statistics** or **leaping to a conclusion**) This fallacy occurs when the sample in an inductive generalization is too small to be representative.

Fallacy of Incomplete Evidence   This fallacy occurs when the requirement of taking account of all relevant available evidence is violated.

Fallacy of Misleading Vividness   This fallacy occurs when a small amount of particularly vivid information is allowed to outweigh a substantial amount of statistical support for a conclusion.

Fallacy of Slippery Slope   This fallacy occurs when it is claimed that no distinction can be made on the grounds that any distinction would be an arbitrary break in a continuum of similar things.

In addition to the names of the forms of arguments and fallacies discussed, you should be familiar with the meanings of the following terms:

Attribute Class   This is the class represented by G in the statistical premiss of the form "X percent of all Fs are Gs" in a statistical syllogism. The conclusion claims that the individual mentioned in the argument is (or is not, in negative cases) a member of this class.

Reference Class   This is the class represented by F in the statistical premiss of the form "X percent of all Fs are Gs" in a statistical syllogism. The other (particular) premiss claims that the individual mentioned is a member of this class.

Syllogism   A syllogism is a type of argument, first studied by Aristotle, with two premisses.

Exercise Set 4.8

1. Is this a strong inductive argument? Why or why not?

   The Pew Global Attitudes Survey [Pew surveys are considered very reliable] released in June 2005 asked people in 16 countries whether they had a favorable impression of the United States. A stunning 71 percent of people from India said yes. Only Americans had a more favorable view of America (83 percent) The numbers are somewhat lower in other surveys, but the basic finding remains true: Indians are extremely comfortable with and well disposed toward America.

   —F. Zakaria, *The Post-American World, 2008*

2. Rasmussen Reports has a very good record of success predicting presidential election results. The following is an excerpt from an account of their methodology.

   Comment on various statements in this account with respect to how they are designed to avoid fallacies of inductive generalization.

   Data for Rasmussen Reports survey research is collected using an automated polling methodology. Field work for all Rasmussen Reports surveys is conducted by Pulse Opinion Research, LLC.

   Generally speaking, the automated survey process is identical to that of traditional, operator-assisted research firms such as Gallup, Harris, and Roper. However, automated polling systems use a single, digitally-recorded, voice to conduct the interview while traditional firms rely on phone banks, boiler rooms, and operator-assisted technology.

   For tracking surveys such as the Rasmussen Reports daily Presidential Tracking Poll the automated technology insures that every respondent hears exactly the same question, from the exact same voice, asked with the exact same inflection every single time.

   All Rasmussen Reports' survey questions are digitally recorded and fed to a calling program that determines question order, branching options, and other factors. Calls are placed to randomly-selected phone numbers through a process that insures appropriate geographic representation. Typically, calls are placed from 5 pm to 9 pm local time during the week. Saturday calls are made from 11 am to 6 pm local time and Sunday calls from 1 pm to 9 pm local time.

   After the calls are completed, the raw data is processed through a weighting program to insure that the sample reflects the overall population in terms of age, race, gender, political party, and other factors. The processing step is required because different segments of the population answer the phone in different ways. For example, women answer the phone more than men, older people are home more and answer more than younger people, and rural residents typically answer the phone more frequently than urban residents.

For surveys of all adults, the population targets are determined by census bureau data.

For political surveys, census bureau data provides a starting point and a series of screening questions are used to determine likely voters. The questions involve voting history, interest in the current campaign, and likely voting intentions.

Rasmussen Reports determines its partisan weighting targets through a dynamic weighting system that takes into account the state's voting history, national trends, and recent polling in a particular state or geographic area.

3. Samuel Johnson presents the following case supporting the right of a schoolmaster to beat his pupils. What kind of arguments does Johnson employ? Does he commit any fallacies?

The government of a schoolmaster is somewhat of the nature of a military government; that is to say that it must be arbitrary according to particular circumstances. A schoolmaster has the right to beat, and an action of assault and battery cannot be admitted against him unless there is some great excess, some barbarity. Pufendorf [an outstanding legal scholar] maintains the right of a schoolmaster to beat his scholars.

—J. Boswell, *Boswell for the Defense*

4. In the following passage, what form of argument is the author using? Identify the premisses and the conclusion of the argument.

The fundamental right of parental autonomy [the right of parents to share in the companionship, care, custody, and management of their minor children] arguably is identical both within the traditionally recognized nuclear family unit and outside that traditional family unit so long as the relationships maintained outside the unit are "family-like" in the previously specified sense [both parents have an active interest in making parental decisions, and neither is prevented from doing so by reasons of distance, disability, or any other incapacitating factor]. Since the state's right to interfere with these rights within the family is limited by a principle far more restrictive than "the best interest of the child," it is hard to see why state interference should become any less restricted after divorce. Normally, the state may interfere with parental rights only to prevent harm or abuse to the child. . . . Why should a comparable limitation on state judicial power not be present after divorce as well?

—E. Canacakos, "Joint Custody as a Fundamental Right," *Arizona Law Review*, 1982

5. For centuries people have been interested in how to determine the sex of a fetus. Food choices loom large in these investigations. Evaluate the following argument:

WebMD Health News reported a study of 740 newly pregnant British women who did not know the sex of their fetuses. The women answered questionnaires about their diets at the time of conception. Researchers also asked them about their diets in the year preceding conception and asked them to keep a food diary in their fourth month of pregnancy.

The collected data showed that 59 percent of women who ate the most calories at the time of conception delivered boys, in contrast to 45 percent who ate the fewest calories but also delivered boys.

The study also showed that women who delivered boys consumed foods higher in nutrients, including potassium.

The mothers who delivered boys consumed about the equivalent of a large banana in terms of calories and potassium, compared to the mothers who delivered girls.

Despite the differences reported, the overall male-female birth ratio in the group studied was close to 50–50.

Conclusion: Mom's diet may influence baby's sex.

In Exercises 6 through 11, identify the form of argument used and evaluate each argument according to the standards for that form.

6. The pope, the spiritual leader of millions of Roman Catholics who believe that he speaks infallibly on matters of faith and morals, has—as have previous popes—proclaimed abortion to be a form of murder. Therefore, abortion is murder.

7. The Zagats of *Zagat Restaurant Surveys* usually tell people who are thinking of opening a restaurant not to do it. Their research shows that 60 percent of new restaurants fail within three years.

8. In a *Wall Street Journal/NBC News* poll of 1,000 adults during the week before a federal budget crisis, 53 percent said that Medicare is fine the way it is or needs only minor changes. It reported a margin of error of plus or minus 3.1 percent. Therefore, between 49.9 percent and 56.1 percent of adults feel this way about Medicare.

9. Most people who break an arm can go back to work in a week or so. Therefore, the Red Sox pitcher who broke his arm in last Saturday's game should be back on the mound next weekend.

10. A study conducted in China by Professor Tong Chen showed that strawberries can fight cancer. Chen's team recruited 36 patients with mild to moderate precancerous lesions in the esophagus. Biopsies were taken before and after the six-month study. Patients consumed 60 grams of freeze-dried strawberries dissolved in a glass of water each day. At the end of the study, 29 of the 36 participants showed improvement. Chen said that a larger controlled study was needed to confirm the results.

11. In the outbreaks of human poisoning from methylmercury in Japan and later in Iraq, one of the most consistent signs in adults was deficits in visual function. . . . The visual system of macaque monkeys resembles that of humans and exhibits the same signs and pathological lesions as that of humans when exposed to

methylmercury. Macaques are therefore excellent models for testing the effects of methylmercury on the visual system.

—D. C. Rice and S. G. Gilbert, "Early Chronic Low-Level
Methylmercury Poisoning in Monkeys Impairs Spatial Vision," *Science, 216* (1982)

12. What steps would you take to find an unbiased sample if you wanted to conduct a poll to determine student opinion at your college or university about the legalization of marijuana?

13. What kind of argument supports the conclusion that is stated in the first sentence of the passage below?

Over wide areas of Australia the tame dingo was by no means an effective hunt-ing dog and it contributed relatively little to the Aborigine's larder.

At Warburton, the Aborigines denied ever having used dingoes in hunting, especially when pursuing large animals, and this view was echoed by Jankunt-jara [in South Australia, at the southeastern end of the Western Desert] infor-mants interviewed by Hamilton. Nor were dingoes ever used for hunting by the desert-dwelling Aborigines we observed in the Clutterbuck Hills-Tikatika region in 1966–1967 or at Pulykara, near Mt.Madley, in 1970.

—R. A. Gould, *Living Archaeology,* 1980

14. Can you think of any plausible example in which the opinions of most Americans would constitute the basis for a nonfallacious argument from consensus?

15. Researchers in Israel looked at student performance from 1993 to 2005 in 264 high schools, 395 middle schools and 1,000 elementary schools. In all categories, classroom performance of both boys and girls improved when the proportion of girls to boys in the classrooms increased.

In a set of tests given to 10th graders, for example, the average score for girls was 69 and for boys 63. But when the percentage of girls in the classroom was in-creased by 20 percent, the boys' score went up 1.6 points and the girls' 1.3.

The scale of improvement is about the same as that brought about by other educational reforms, such as reducing class size.

—based on research by V. Lavy and A. Schlosser,
American Economic Journal: Applied Economics

16. The following passage is taken from a letter to the editor of *Science News* (June 12, 1993) concerning land use in the Americas prior to CE. 1500. Name the mistake in reasoning that the author is worried about. Tell what form of argument the author uses against the argument he criticizes.

Data from one lake in central Mexico are extrapolated to Native Americans in general. Given the diversity and complexity of Native Americans, this is astonishing.

Could a parallel assertion be made, for instance, after researching long-term erosion patterns into Lake Como in Italy and then issuing a blanket statement about the land use practices of Eurasian peoples? Most researchers would not be so foolish as to make such a pronouncement.

—Philip Snyder

17. In the following, name the mistake in reasoning that the author of the letter accuses Gajdusek of making. Also tell what form of argument Schryer employs against Gajdusek.

I must question the relevance of Gajdusek's argument that "the whole of Australia knows these people are cannibals." . . . [This] may well be true, but proves nothing. At one time virtually the whole population of Europe and much of Britain and America "knew" that witches existed and countless persons were not only arrested but put to death for allegedly practicing witchcraft. Nevertheless, it is now generally acknowledged that witches, defined as persons with supernatural powers of diabolical origin, do not exist and never did. Gajdusek may or may not have other proof for the existence of cannibalism in New Guinea, but he does his case no good by arguing, in effect, that if a lot of people, including civil authorities, believe in the occurrence of some questionable practice then it must be so.

—Letter from D. R. Schryer in *Science,* 233 (1986)

18. The following is taken from a letter to the editor of *Science News* (August 7, 1993). Identify the fallacy that the author of the letter suggests the person who wrote the article commits.

You make statements about alcoholics in general on the basis of a study using entirely male samples. My experience as a member of Alcoholics Anonymous, however, has suggested that there are significant differences between female and male alcoholics. This is particularly noticeable with regard to the incidence and severity of depression.

—Anita A.

19. Discuss the pro and con arguments in the following:

A new review of 130 studies "strongly suggests" playing violent video games increases aggressive thoughts and behavior and decreases empathy.

The results hold "regardless of research design, gender, age or culture," says lead researcher Craig Anderson, who directs the Center for the Study of Violence at Iowa State University in Ames. His team did a statistical analysis of studies on more than 130,000 gamers from elementary school age to college in the USA, Europe and Japan. (published in Psychological Bulletin)

But Christopher Ferguson, an associate professor at Texas A&M International University in Laredo, says in a critique accompanying the study that the effects found "are generally very low." He adds that the analysis "contains numerous flaws," which he says result in "overestimating the influence" of violent games on aggression.

Ferguson says his own study of 603 predominantly Hispanic young people, published last year in *The Journal of Pediatrics*, found "delinquent peer influences, antisocial personality traits, depression, and parents/guardians who use psychological abuse" were consistent risk factors for youth violence and aggression. But he also found that neighborhood quality, parents' domestic violence and exposure to violent TV or video games "were not predictive of youth violence and aggression."

Anderson says his team "never said it's a huge effect. But if you look at known risk factors for the development of aggression and violence, some are bigger than media violence and some are smaller.

—Sharon Jayson, *New Analysis Reasserts Video Games' Link to Violence,*
www.usatoday.com/news/health/2010-03-01

20. Discuss the forms of argument used in the following discussion of banning tobacco advertising and tobacco products:

Advertising bans can be particularly helpful in reducing cigarette consumption among adolescents, with whom we should be especially concerned on grounds of "informed consent." There is good evidence that cigarette advertising in general, and sport sponsorship in particular, appeals to children [several statistical studies are cited]. Conversely, banning advertising of cigarettes in Norway in 1975 led to a sharp decline in the percentage of teenagers who subsequently have become daily smokers [again, statistical studies are cited]. . . .

Against bans on the use or sale of tobacco, the Prohibition analogy is standardly urged. Already we have evidence of substantial "bootlegging" (or "butt-legging") of cigarettes between states with low cigarette taxes and those with high ones. Any more serious ban on sale or use of tobacco would no doubt lead to even more illicit activity of this sort. Even accepting such slippage, however, this strategy is still bound to reduce smoking substantially. Whether more would be lost in terms of respect for the law than would be gained in terms of public health remains an open question.

—R. E. Goodin, *No Smoking,* 1989

Chapter Five

CAUSAL ARGUMENTS

I. INTRODUCTION

Many of the inductive arguments discussed thus far are causal arguments. The conclusions of such arguments state that a causal relationship holds (or fails to hold) between two types of things or events. For example, one argument based on experiments on rats concluded that birth-control hormones may affect brain development. Another concluded that obliterating the high-contrast wing stripes on tropical butterflies does not affect wing damage or survival.

Statements about causes occur as the conclusions of different forms of argument. Some causal arguments are inductive generalizations; others are arguments from analogy. Arguments from authority, which, when correct, are statistical syllogisms, are also used to support causal conclusions. In this chapter, we pay special attention to a variety of ways of establishing causal relationships. We call any argument in which the conclusion states a causal relationship a **causal argument**, but we should remember that this expression does not refer to any single form of argument.

Causal connections are a focus of concern in everyday life. When cars break down, when buses are late, when classes are canceled, when we do poorly in an examination, or when personal relationships take a turn for the worse, we look for causes.

Research by psychologists R. Nisbett and L. Ross (*Human Inference*) shows that people readily generate causal accounts of events on the basis of little evidence. Nisbett and Ross also found that spontaneous causal analysis occurs frequently in ordinary conversation. In one experiment, the investigators "bugged" thirteen haphazardly selected conversations at singles' bars, at a picnic for economically underprivileged senior citizens, and at student bull sessions. Using a set of categories that included "gives information," "gives evaluation," "gives advice or suggestions," "makes prediction," and "gives causal analysis," they classified each utterance of the speakers. Statements expressing or requesting causal analysis accounted for roughly 15 percent of all utterances recorded. Even though, as the investigators admit, their sample was not random, the proportion of ordinary speech devoted to causes was impressive. The search for causes is not confined to scientific investigations; it is also important in our daily lives.

In this chapter, we look closely at some methods that have been proposed as aids to discovering causes and supporting statements about causes. Although the *discovery* of causes is an important part of science and everyday life, critical thinking is more particularly concerned with the *justification* of causal statements than with how causes can be discovered. Inadequate evidence for causal conclusions should be challenged or supplemented. Thus, we need to know how to evaluate arguments with causal conclusions. We should also be aware of common mistakes in causal reasoning (causal fallacies) and learn to avoid them.

II. MILL'S METHODS FOR ESTABLISHING CAUSES

Justifying causal statements is primarily a problem in *inductive* logic. The reasons in support of a causal connection are usually not conclusive, although some causal arguments are better than others. Inductive logic is a much newer branch of knowledge than deductive logic. The latter has been studied continuously since it was first developed by the Greek philosopher Aristotle twenty-three hundred years ago. (This is not to say that no one reasoned logically before Aristotle, but he was the first to formulate *principles* of logical reasoning.) In the nineteenth century, John Stuart Mill—the author of *Utilitarianism, On Liberty,* and *On the Subjection of Women*—tried to spell out the rules of inductive logic, just as Aristotle had done for deductive logic.

Mill recognized that knowledge of scientific laws is based on inductive reasoning and that reasoning about causes is central to acquiring such knowledge. He was distressed with the flimsy basis for many causal statements put forward by scientists of his own day. To correct the problem, he formulated standards that he believed represented sound scientific practice and that could serve as guidelines for reasoning about causes. Mill believed that causal statements should be based on careful observation and experiment; he thought that if he could formulate some rules about how to use observation and experiment to gain knowledge of causes, then people could become more skilled at causal reasoning. The methods that Mill outlined, although they do not always measure up to his exaggerated claims for their success, still provide an important basis for scientific reasoning.

Mill's methods are also useful in ordinary causal reasoning. He outlined and discussed five methods that we examine in this chapter. Mill presented his methods both as aids to discover causes and instruments to justify causal statements. Scientists in fact use them both ways.

1. THE METHOD OF AGREEMENT

Shortly after a flight from Japan landed in Copenhagen, 144 passengers were hospitalized. Another 51 were treated but did not require hospitalization. All of the affected passengers exhibited symptoms of a gastrointestinal disorder. Doctors immediately suspected food poisoning. The passengers had eaten food taken aboard during a refueling stop in Anchorage. All those who later became ill had eaten omelets prepared by a cook who worked for the airline's catering service in Anchorage. During a two-week investigation, it was learned that this cook had an infected sore on his finger. Officials concluded that bacteria from this infection had been the source of contamination and the cause of the food poisoning suffered by the passengers.

The investigators' pattern of causal reasoning, as described here, exemplifies Mill's **Method of Agreement**. When we use the Method of Agreement to identify the cause of some event or condition, we look at *antecedent circumstances* (the events or conditions that occurred earlier) to see whether some antecedent circumstance is common to each occurrence of the event for which a cause is sought. If only one common antecedent circumstance can be identified, then it is likely to be the cause—or a part of the cause—of the event or condition under investigation.

Not every common antecedent circumstance is a cause, however, for many antecedent circumstances are causally irrelevant. In this case, for example, all the passengers who became ill boarded the plane in Tokyo, but we have no reason to believe that boarding a plane in a particular city causes gastrointestinal illness. Causal reasoning is guided by general background knowledge about the types of causes that bring about the condition or event in question. In the airline incident, the illnesses were diagnosed as food poisoning. This diagnosis structured the search for a cause. It is well known that food poisoning is caused by bacterial contamination of food. Contamination can occur in several ways. Food can become contaminated through contact with unclean utensils or unclean hands. Harmful bacteria multiply when susceptible foods are not stored at the proper temperature. This background information led to the discovery of the cook's infected finger.

Schematically, the Method of Agreement can be presented in the following form, where e represents the event or condition for which the cause is sought, and S through Z represent a selection, guided by general background information, of antecedent conditions. The left-hand column numbers each separate case in which e occurs.

Case	Antecedent Circumstances	Event for Which Cause Is Sought
1	X, Y, Z	e
2	X, U, V, Y	e
3	X, W, S	e
4	X, T, Z, W	e
etc.	$X, \ldots$	e

In this schematic representation, X is the only antecedent circumstance in which all occurrences of e agree. Thus, the use of Mill's Method of Agreement supports X as the cause—or a part of the cause—of e. Applying the scheme to our example, the number of cases is 195—the total number of cases of food poisoning (e). The antecedent circumstance X represents the circumstance of eating an omelet prepared by the cook with an infected finger. The other letters represent various other antecedent circumstances that were possible causes of the disease. In our example, these antecedent circumstances included foods and beverages, other than the cook's omelets, that were consumed by passengers who became ill.

The use of the Method of Agreement does not guarantee discovery of a cause. Because we face an unlimited number of antecedent circumstances in most cases of causal inquiry, the Method of Agreement cannot be applied mechanically. Using background knowledge, we need to confine our attention to those antecedent circumstances that are possible causal agents. Unless an investigator has some idea of the type of cause sought, the Method of Agreement is nearly useless.

Moreover, the method does not guarantee that the *suspected* cause is the *real* cause of the illnesses. (Mill's Methods are inductive, not deductive, forms of reasoning.) The investigators could have overlooked the true source of contamination, and the cook with the sore finger might have been only coincidentally connected with the illnesses. However, this investigation of food poisoning was thorough, so officials felt there was little room for doubt.

One limitation of the Method of Agreement is that ignorance or error might lead to a possible cause being overlooked when constructing the list of antecedent circumstances. Sometimes the true cause may go unnoticed because of a failure to identify the causal agent in a complex situation. Consider a drunk who concludes that soda is the source of his hangovers because the hangover occurs whenever soda is drunk with scotch, bourbon, brandy, gin, or vodka. If the true cause is not identified on the list, the Method of Agreement will not disclose it, and the method may lead to a false conclusion. An additional problem arises with the use of this method because both the so-called antecedent circumstance and the effect could be effects of some common underlying cause. Although fever usually precedes the red spotting in a case of measles, the fever is not the cause of the spots. Both fever and spots are caused by the disease. This problem of a common cause is a general problem of causal reasoning, not just for the use of Mill's methods. It is discussed in greater detail in Section VI later in this chapter.

Mill's methods are most likely to lead to a true conclusion when we possess general information about the types of causes that bring about the condition or event in question. We can use this information to narrow the search for a cause within that general framework or **causal theory**. In our example, the causal theory that guides the search for a cause of the passengers' illnesses is the general information about the symptoms and causes of food poisoning. We know that vomiting, stomach cramps, and diarrhea can occur several hours after eating contaminated food. Also, harmful bacteria multiply rapidly in foods typically cooked at low temperatures—such as omelets, custards, and cream sauces. Such foods receive special scrutiny during investigations of food poisoning. Furthermore, harmful bacteria can be introduced into foods from cuts, unwashed hands, and the like. All of this background information, not just the use of Mill's methods, helped to solve the problem of the passengers' illnesses.

Exercise Set 5.1

For each of the following situations, suggest some possible common antecedent circumstances that you might investigate to find the cause of the event described.

1. The lights in your room at home and your computer go dark just as you are completing a term paper. You leave the room to search for the circuit breaker and notice that all your house lights and those of your neighbors are out as well.

2. Every Wednesday this term the Food Court where you usually have lunch is so crowded that you can hardly find a place to sit.

3. Although it is early summer, all of the trees in the woods near your home are turning brown.

4. You and all of your friends are having problems with your new smart phones, all purchased within the last three months.

5. You are in Chicago's O'Hare Airport waiting for a flight to arrive from New York. An announcement says that the flight will be delayed by several hours. When you look at the arrivals' board, you see that all flights from Boston and other cities in the northeastern part of the United States are delayed as well.

6. Three students in a class turn in identical term papers.

7. An unusually high number of students from your former high school earn scholarships at major universities year after year.

2. THE METHOD OF DIFFERENCE

Although the newspaper report from which the food poisoning example was taken did not present all the details, it was likely that the investigation to find the cause of the illnesses used another of Mill's methods, the **Method of Difference**, to eliminate some possible causes of the disease. Once the illnesses were tentatively diagnosed as food poisoning, the search for a cause concentrated on foods eaten by the various passengers. According to the report, everyone in the first-class section of the plane was served an omelet prepared by that cook, but many of the tourist-class passengers were not. The cook prepared between 207 and 215 omelets, but only 195 passengers became ill. No one however, who had not eaten an omelet prepared by the cook with the infected finger became ill.

Mill's Method of Difference tells us that to find the cause of an event or condition e, we should try to find two cases—one where e occurs, and one where it does not—that are similar in all respects but one in their antecedent circumstances. Then, the antecedent circumstance that is present when e is present, and absent when e is not, is the cause of e. Schematically, the Method of Difference can be represented as follows:

Case	Antecedent Circumstances	Event for Which Cause Is Sought
1	X, S, R, U, V, W	e occurs
2	S, R, U, V, W	e does not occur

Suppose, for example, that a husband and wife were on the same flight and were served identical meals. Suppose further that the wife was allergic to eggs, so she did not eat the omelet, although she ate all the other foods and—except in that one respect—ate the same things as her husband. If she did not become ill and her husband did, the omelet would be judged to be the cause of the food poisoning according to Mill's Method of Difference. The only difference between e's occurring and failing to occur is the presence of X (eating an omelet) in the antecedent circumstances of e. Under these conditions—because unless X occurs, e fails to occur—Mill's Method of Difference states that X is the cause, or an indispensable part of the cause, of e.

The Method of Difference has the same limitations as the Method of Agreement. If the real cause is not listed in the antecedent circumstances, the method cannot detect it. Similarly, the method works best when the choice of antecedent circumstances is guided by a causal theory. In our example, a well-established causal theory suggests possible causes of food poisoning. In the presence of such causal theories, Mill's methods provide strong evidence for causal statements. A further, and very significant, limitation on the use of the Method of Difference is the difficulty of finding two cases exactly similar except in one respect in their antecedent circumstances—one in which the effect occurs and the other in which it does not.

Exercise Set 5.2

For each of the following situations, suggest some antecedent circumstances that might account for the presence of the effect on the one hand and its absence on the other.

1. Your favorite team in the NCAA Basketball Final scored only 53 points after scoring 70 points against the same team earlier in the season.

2. You are enrolled in the local electric company's "budget plan," whereby the company calculates a monthly average payment for you. You have been paying $60 a month for two years. This month, however, the company tells you that beginning next month, your monthly budget bill will increase to $65.

3. Last week your efforts to impress a particular person seemed to be going well; this week that person ignores you completely.

4. The night before last you fell asleep as soon as your head hit the pillow, but last night you lay awake for at least two hours before you fell asleep.

5. Your new cotton shirt fit perfectly the first time you wore it two weeks ago, but it is now too tight around the collar and its sleeves are an inch too short.

6. You and a friend submit identical solutions to a puzzle contest. He wins a prize, but you do not.

7. Last year you got a big tax refund; this year you owe the government money.

8. Your dog refuses to eat the brand of food that he ate so happily the previous night.

3. THE JOINT METHOD OF AGREEMENT AND DIFFERENCE

In many causal investigations, we do not find a pair of cases to which the Method of Difference applies. This method requires two cases that are exactly similar except for the presence or absence of a single antecedent circumstance. Such situations are rare. Mill proposes another method, called the **Joint Method of Agreement and Difference**, to identify cases in which the presence or absence of some antecedent circumstance determines whether the effect occurs. In this method, which has been used in many important investigations, the Method of Agreement is applied to all cases in which the condition occurs and again to all cases in which the condition does *not* occur; the two sets are then compared, in the same manner as the two individual cases in the Method of Difference.

Cases	Antecedent Circumstances	Event for Which Cause Is Sought
1	X, S, T, U	*e* occurs
2	X, S, T	*e* occurs
3	X, T	*e* occurs
4–*i*	X, S	*e* occurs
j	S, T, U, V	*e* does not occur
j + 1	S, T	*e* does not occur
j + 2	T, U	*e* does not occur
n	S, U, V	*e* does not occur

In the schematic representation, the cases (1–*i*) in which *e* occurs are grouped together. (In our example, these cases would be the 195 cases of food poisoning.) The cases (*j*–*n*) in which *e* does not occur are also grouped together.

The newspaper report from which our example was taken did not specify the number of cases in which passengers did not become ill, but the plane was a jumbo jet and carried many such persons. The letters *S* through *V* represent foods eaten by each passenger. The letter *V* might represent an alternative food to *X* (for example, a different type of main dish).

Because it is so powerful and so often applicable, the Joint Method of Agreement and Difference is widely used to study the causes of and cures for diseases. For example, if just two persons are given a flu vaccination and one escapes the flu but the other is stricken, we know little about the effectiveness of the flu vaccine. In some cases, apparent exposure to a cause does not produce the effect. The person who did not get the flu may have had a natural immunity or may not have been exposed. If everyone in an isolated community receives a flu vaccine and little or no flu occurs, use of the Method of Agreement would tell us the vaccine was effective. But we cannot be confident about this result, for the community may simply not have been exposed to the flu virus. If, however, hundreds of students are vaccinated for the flu at the student health clinic and only a few of them get the flu, but a very large proportion of the hundreds of unvaccinated students at the same school get the flu, the Joint Method of Agreement and Difference tells us there is good reason to believe the vaccine is effective in preventing flu.

Although Mill's methods are most effective when they are applied within the structure of a specific causal theory to provide evidence for causal statements they can also be used to guide and restrict the search for causes when no specific causal theory is available. In this way, Mill's methods help investigators formulate causal theories that can be subjected to further testing. Early studies of cholera, discussed by B. MacMahon and T. Pugh (*Epidemiology*), illustrate this point. Even before the germ theory of disease was developed, observers in the nineteenth century noted that cholera spread when persons came into contact with infected persons and that the occurrence of cholera was associated with poverty, overcrowding, refuse, and filth. General causal theories of the time suggested that the common factor was exposure to the fecal matter from cholera patients, but there was disagreement about whether the disease was transmitted through the air or carried by water.

In 1854 a perceptive observer, John Snow, noticed that during a severe cholera epidemic in London, the frequency of the disease was much lower in some areas of the city than in others. Five years earlier, in 1849, all groups in London had been uniform with respect to frequency of the disease. Using the Joint Method of Agreement and Difference, Snow looked for antecedent circumstances that would account for the different frequencies of cholera present in the two groups in 1854. He discovered that families in the area were served by two different water companies. Those supplied by the Southwark and Vauxhall Company had a much higher incidence of cholera than those supplied by the Lambeth Company. In the years between 1849 and 1854, the Lambeth Company had changed its source of supply—which had been near the area where the Southwark and Vauxhall Company obtained its water—to a place farther upstream on the Thames River. As a result of its move, the Lambeth Company no longer drew its water from an area where large amounts of sewage entered the river. Snow believed this confirmed his suspicion that waterborne fecal contamination was the cause of cholera.

In the wake of Snow's investigations, efforts were made to provide the citizens of London with clean drinking water, and the incidence of cholera declined significantly, even though the exact cause of the disease (the specific germ) was not known until forty years later. Snow's use of Mill's methods was an important step in the development of the germ theory of disease.

The search for causes and cures of disease often begins when investigators notice differences in the geographic distribution of a disease. When a disease is prevalent in one area and much less common in another area, it is natural to look for causes in such general features as differences in diet, soil (which affects food grown there), and water supplies.

Not all attempts to use Mill's methods as aids in discovering causes have been so successful as Snow's work on cholera. Samuel Pepys reported a incident in his *Diary* that shows the perils of using Mill's methods in the absence of a causal theory.

During an epidemic of the bubonic plague in London in the 1660s, not a single London tobacco seller died of the plague. On these grounds, reasoning by what is now called the Joint Method of Agreement and Difference, tobacco was believed to prevent the plague. Accordingly, at Eton—a boarding school located outside London—all the school boys were ordered to smoke tobacco. Eton is one of the few boarding schools in history where boys were flogged for failing to smoke. Unfortunately, smoking did not prevent the occurrence of bubonic plague at Eton; the use of tobacco was apparently unrelated to avoidance of the disease. Whatever spared the London tobacconists remains unknown; their escape from the plague may have been a coincidence. We now know that the bubonic plague virus is transmitted through fleas that are carried on rodents. After the rats die of the disease, the hungry fleas begin migrating to other hosts; when they bite people, the disease is transmitted into the human population. The great plague episodes in England during the seventeenth century resulted when rats escaped from ships that had brought them—and the disease—from foreign ports. This causal connection between rats, fleas, and the plague was not discovered, however, until a hundred years after the worst plague epidemics—and only much later was the immediate cause, a specific virus, isolated.

In our own time, medical research expends many resources to discover causes and cures for cancer, AIDS, and other scourges. Mill's methods are frequently applied at various levels of research. It was observed some time ago, for example, that cervical cancer was almost nonexistent among nuns, although it was a rather common form of cancer among women in general. Use of the Joint Method of Agreement and Difference led investigators to suspect that some aspect of sexual activity or the reproductive process is causally related to cancer of the cervix. We now know that many cervical cancers are caused by a form of the sexually transmitted human papilloma virus (HPV), against which a vaccine has been developed.

4. THE METHOD OF CONCOMITANT VARIATION

The Method of Difference and the Joint Method of Agreement and Difference apply only when we can observe the suspected causal source in some cases and not in others. In the investigation of the cause of food poisoning, the suspected foods were eaten by some passengers but not by others. In the study of cholera, London households received water from distinct sources. In these cases, as in all cases for which the Method of Difference and the Joint Method of Agreement and Difference apply, we can distinguish between exposure and nonexposure to the suspected cause.

As in the cholera example, the event or condition that results from the cause can be an increased or decreased rate or relative frequency of occurrence in a group of persons rather than an occurrence of the condition corresponding to each exposure to the suspected cause. Cholera was not present in each case in which the suspected cause (contaminated water) was present. Nevertheless, the water supply was judged to be the cause (or part of the cause) of cholera because a greater proportion of customers of Southwark and Vauxhall contracted the disease than did customers of the Lambeth

Company. Background knowledge informs us that some people are more susceptible to disease than others and also that people drink water from sources other than the pumps in their own neighborhoods.

Although Mill did not discuss rates or frequencies in his methods, he designed the methods to find and justify partial causes. His methods have long been used by scientists to discover causes of different rates or frequencies of effects under investigation.

Sometimes when we want to investigate a causal question, we face circumstances in which the effect and the suspected cause are always present to some extent. This inhibits use of the Method of Difference and, consequently, the Joint Method. The Method of Agreement may be used, but if there are several common antecedent circumstances, this method may not distinguish among them. If, however, the condition or event under investigation varies in degree or strength from one case to another, the **Method of Concomitant Variation** can be a useful aid in discovering causes and justifying causal statements. Mill's idea behind this method was that a change in the strength of the effect is to be accounted for by a change in the strength of the cause. Thus, to find the cause of an effect that varies, look for an antecedent condition that varies. The variation in the effect can be in direct or inverse proportion to variation in the suspected cause. The following example demonstrates the method.

High blood pressure (hypertension) is a major contributor to fatal heart attacks. According to recent statistics published by the American Heart Association, about 75 million Americans over age 20 (one of every three adults) suffer from high blood pressure. However, the frequency with which fatal hypertension attacks the population varies from place to place. Two scientists noted that the death rate from hypertension-related heart attacks in Tucson, Arizona, was 41 percent below the national average. They suggested that the lower hypertension-related death rate resulted from a relatively high content of selenium in Arizona soil. Selenium is a metal found in small quantities in almost all soils and, like other trace minerals, finds its way into the human body in minute amounts through the food chain.

Current physiological theory acknowledges the role of some trace minerals in preventing diseases. The scientists studied 45 cities. They used the selenium levels measured in grazing food or forage crops as a gauge for amounts of selenium present in state soils. Tucson was among nine cities in seven Western states with high selenium levels and relatively low hypertension-related death rates. The death rates attributed to high blood pressure in selenium-poor states (Connecticut, Illinois, Ohio, New York, Oregon, Massachusetts, Rhode Island, Pennsylvania, Indiana, and Delaware) are three times greater than these rates in selenium-rich areas.

In this example, the association between selenium levels in the soil (the antecedent circumstance) and death rates from high blood pressure (the condition for which a cause is sought) suggests that selenium may be a causal factor in the prevention of fatal high blood pressure. The method used to discover this connection—or to justify the existence of a causal connection between higher selenium levels in the soil and lower incidence of fatal high blood pressure—is Mill's Method of Concomitant Variation. Following is a schematic representation of this Method:

Cases or Groups	Antecedent Circumstances	Event or Condition for Which Cause Is Sought
1	$X+, Y, Z, \ldots$	$e+$ (or $e-$)
2	$X-, Y, Z, \ldots$	$e-$ (or $e+$)

The first column represents individuals, events, or circumstances—or groups of the same—classed according to the severity or degree of strength of the condition under investigation. There may be more than two such groups. For example, instead of dividing the individuals into two groups according to whether a condition is present in severe or mild degree, we might divide the individuals into three groups—severe, mild, and moderate. The letter X represents the antecedent circumstance that varies in strength—either in the same direction as the condition under investigation or in the opposite direction. In our example, the death rate from hypertension decreased ($e-$) as the selenium level increased ($X+$). The letters Y, Z, and so on represent any other common antecedent circumstances suspected of being causally connected with the condition under investigation. In the newspaper report from which our example is taken, no other antecedent circumstances—such as different trace minerals or average hours of sunshine per day—were mentioned. Presumably, the scientists decided to focus on the role of selenium in this study.

Another study of disease provides a classic example of the use of the Method of Concomitant Variation. Every day in large cities, people die from respiratory problems. Although nowadays smog or ozone alerts keep people inside in times of heavy air pollution, until recently people were unaware of the close connection between fatal respiratory events and air pollution. This changed with a dramatic discovery in the early 1950s. In counting the number of deaths in London that occurred during a time of severe atmospheric pollution (formerly called "London fog") from November 29 to December 16, 1952, it became apparent, based on Mill's Method of Concomitant Variation, that the intense smog had caused approximately 4,000 deaths. Information concerning the antecedent circumstances (pollution measured in parts per million of sulfur dioxide, SO_2) and the event whose cause is sought (increase in number of deaths) is reproduced in Figure 5.1. This graph shows clearly that the increases and decreases in the number of deaths ($e+$) almost exactly match the increases and decreases in parts per million of sulfur dioxide in the atmosphere ($X+$).

The Method of Concomitant Variation, like Mill's other methods, is most useful within the framework of a specific causal theory. Such a causal theory provides guidance as to which antecedent circumstances among an indefinite number of available antecedents are plausible candidates for causes. If little is known about the specific causal

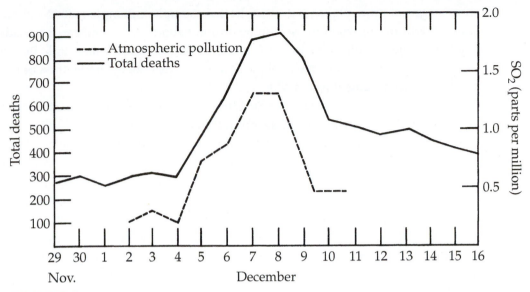

FIGURE 5.1

Atmospheric pollution (in parts per million of sulfur dioxide) and numbers of deaths per day in London, from November 29 to December 16, 1952. *Source:* B. MacMahon, T. Pugh, and J. Ipsen, Epidemiologic Methods (Boston: Little, Brown, 1960), p. 6. Copyright © Lippincott Williams & Wilkins. Reproduced by permission.

nature of a widespread disease, such as cancer or hypertension, and different frequencies appear to be present in different geographic areas, investigators use the Method of Concomitant Variation to select broad environmental features that vary with intensities that match the variation in frequency of the disease. In doing this, the search for causes is narrowed, and sometimes it is possible to bring a disease under control even when the precise causal agents are unknown.

5. THE METHOD OF RESIDUES

Mill's **Method of Residues** recognizes that in some situations many causal forces may be interacting and offers a way to separate those components in causal analysis. Suppose, for example, that you have planted a dogwood tree that is not growing well. You consult a knowledgeable neighbor, who suggests a number of causes for poor growth. She asks if the tree has been getting enough water and informs you that the tree requires at least an inch of water every week during the growing season. You have been giving the tree adequate water, however, so that is not the problem. She then asks whether the proper amount of fertilizer has been used—too little or too much can harm the tree. But you have followed the recommended dosage of feeding once a year. She inspects your tree and notices that grass is growing right up to its trunk. She tells you that this is known to inhibit dogwood growth. You, therefore, clear a circle of two feet around the trunk of the tree and keep the grass away from it. In the next growing season, the tree shows signs of more vigorous growth. In this example, a complex effect—abnormally slow growth of dogwood trees—can be brought about by several causes: inadequate water, improper fertilization and turf cover growing right up to the trunk. But the slow growth in your tree is not a result of the first two causes, so, by the Method of Residues, the third cause is judged responsible.

A famous use of the Method of Residues occurs in the history of astronomy. From ancient times until late in the eighteenth century, astronomers thought there were just six major planets in our solar system. After Herschel discovered the seventh planet Uranus in 1781, astronomers noted that its orbit was irregular. That is to say, the path of the planet was not exactly the sort of ellipse that would result from the combined gravitational pull of the sun and Uranus's "nearest" neighbors in the solar system, the planets of Jupiter and Saturn. For a while, the irregularity was suspected to be the result of an error in calculation. But when a young astronomer, H. Leverrier, verified the calculations, he suggested that a different cause—the gravitational pull of a still more distant eighth planet—would account for the irregular orbit. At Leverrier's suggestion about where to look for this planet, an observational search was made, which resulted in the discovery of Neptune in 1846.

The Method of Residues works by using known causes to account for as much of the complex effect as possible and then invoking an additional cause to account for the remainder. This method is verified by identifying the postulated new cause, if possible. Schematically the Method of Residues can be characterized as follows:

Components of Causal Complex	Complex Effect
$X, Y, Z, ?$	e_1 & e_2 & e_3 & e_4
X accounts for	e_1
Y accounts for	e_2
Z accounts for	e_3
$?$ accounts for	e_4

Exercise Set 5.3

In each of the following exercises,

a. Identify the condition or event for which a cause is sought. Be sure to tell whether specific occurrences or rates (relative frequencies) of occurrence are being investigated.

b. Identify all antecedent circumstances mentioned in the example.

c. State which of Mill's methods is being used.

d. Identify the cause, according to the use of Mill's methods.

Note that some of the exercises are taken from newspaper reports and that less than complete information is available. If more background information is required to make a judgment, discuss why this is so. Being aware of what is needed to pass critical judgment on a problem is part of critical thinking. The evidence we receive in newspapers, magazines, and other sources is often incomplete with respect to the conclusions stated there.

1. Scientists, working under the direction of J. Higham, showed that male Rhesus macaques are better at recognizing fertility signals in female macaques that they know than in females from other groups. When the scientists presented images of female macaques during fertile and infertile periods, the males who knew the females looked at the fertile females longer. (Fertile females have darker faces.) The males who looked at unfamiliar fertile females did not gaze longer at them.

2. Alzheimer's disease is a serious form of senility that afflicts between 5 and 10 percent of all persons over age 65. Recently, researchers discovered that patients who die of Alzheimer's disease have much smaller amounts of a particular enzyme in the cortexes of their brains than persons the same age who do not suffer from the disease. The loss of this enzyme activity has been suspected as a cause of the lesions found on the brains of Alzheimer's patients. In postmortem examinations of five Alzheimer's patients and five people without the disease, it was found that all the diseased patients had lost neurons from the nucleus basalis (a tiny area deep in the brain whose function is not understood by neurologists), whereas all the people without the disease had the normal number of cells in this area. Scientists who conducted this study believe that the loss of neurons from the nucleus basalis may be responsible for the decreased activity in the cortex.

3. A working paper, "Rainfall, Human Capital, and Democracy" by S. Haber and V. Menaldo, demonstrates a relationship between rainfall levels and types of regimes in the world since 1945.

    The authors discovered that among regions with less than 21.5" annual rainfall, there are only 2 democracies (Cyprus and Israel) but 14 autocracies. In regions with moderate rainfall (21.5–51") there are 18 democracies and 7 autocracies. In regions with greater than 51" annual rainfall there are 6 democracies and 11 autocracies.

    Apparently open societies (democracies) need just the right amount of rain to flourish.

4. Background information: We now know that the disease beriberi is caused by a dietary deficiency in the B complex of vitamins, particularly vitamin B_1. Whole grains provide a common source of this vitamin. The episode described here occurred before anything was known about vitamins. The research was conducted in an asylum for the insane. Cured rice is rice that has been treated to preserve some of the outer hull. Uncured rice (now usually called "polished rice") is rice from which the outer hull—which contains most of the vitamins—is removed.

    The lunatics are housed in two exactly similar buildings on opposite sides of a quadrangle surrounded by a high wall. On December 5, 1905, all the lunatics at that time in the hospital were drawn up in the dining shed and numbered off from the left. The odd numbers were subsequently domiciled [housed] in the ward on the east side of the courtyard, and no alteration was made in their diet. They were still supplied with the same uncured rice as in 1905. The even numbers were quartered in the ward on the west of the quadrangle and received the same rations as the occupants of the other ward with the exception that they were supplied with cured rice. . . . On December 5, there were 59 lunatics in the asylum; of these, 29 were put on cured rice and 30 on uncured rice. The next patient admitted to the asylum was admitted to the cured rice ward, and the one admitted after him to the uncured rice ward, the next to cured, and so on alternately to the end of the year.

In the middle of the year, the patients in the east ward were moved to the west ward and those in the west ward to the east, but they continued to receive the same diets. By the end of 1906, among 120 patients eating uncured rice, there had been 34 cases of beriberi and 18 deaths. Among the 123 patients assigned to cured rice, there had been only 2 cases and no deaths, and both cases had been manifested at the time the patients were admitted to the asylum.

—B. MacMahon and T. Pugh, *Epidemiology*

5. Film star Geena Davis (*Thelma and Louise*) founded an institute to study gender in media when she noticed how few females had roles in G-rated movies. Children viewing these films see three to five males for each female role.

   When asked in a *Wall Street Journal* interview whether the TV and movies kids watch have an effect on them, Ms. Davis answered that, based on the research conducted by the Institute, "The more hours of television a girl watches, the fewer options she believes she has in life. And the more hours a boy watches, the more sexist his views become."

6. The National Minimum Drinking Age Act, signed into law by President Reagan in 1984, required every state to set 21 years of age as the legal minimum for the purchase and public possession of alcohol. Strong support for the law came from those who believed that raising the minimum legal drinking age (MLDA) to 21 would greatly reduce alcohol-related traffic deaths. Many studies have been conducted to test this thesis.

   The American Medical Association reported that studies by Wagenaar (1993) and Jones (1992) showed that the 21-year-old MLDA saves the life of over 1,000 youth each year. They also showed that when the MLDA is lowered (as it was in Massachusetts in the 1970s), motor vehicle crashes and deaths among youth increase. The AMA says that at least 50 studies have evaluated this correlation.

7. Despite the evidence above (Exercise 6), some people object to the MLDA of 21, particularly for college students.

Issue: Nineteen- and twenty-year olds are drinking anyway. If we legalize it, at least they'll be drinking in supervised settings, such as a bar or nightclub, rather than in cars or at unsupervised parties.

Reply: Data show bars and nightclubs are not safe, controlled locations. Studies have repeatedly shown that a majority of alcohol outlets regularly break the law, for example by selling alcohol to minors or selling to intoxicated patrons. When the legal age is lower than 21, teens purchase the majority of their alcohol at liquor stores where it is cheaper than getting it at bars. They then consume this alcohol in homes, cars or parks. These areas are very difficult to control.

—A. Wagenaar and T. Toomey, "Effects of Minimum Drinking Age Laws"

8. Because of an increase in both obesity in youth and sports injuries over the past 25 years, many more people develop osteoarthritis at a relatively early age. Glucosamine/Chondriton supplements, offered as an over-the-counter treatment for osteoarthritis, is an $850 million a year business.

The largest study of the effectiveness of these products involved about 1,600 participants in 2006. Twenty-two percent who suffered from moderate to severe knee pain showed statistically significant relief.

There was no difference in pain relief compared with a placebo ("fake" pills that only look like the real thing) for 78 percent of the participants with mild pain.

A follow-up study in 2008 showed similar results.

9. Headline: Do zinc lozenges shorten common colds?

Researchers gave 25 people zinc acetate dihydrate lozenges within 24 hours of the onset of a cold; 23 others received an inert substitute. Both lozenges tasted of peppermint. Neither researchers nor participants were told who was receiving zinc until afterward. Participants took a lozenge every 2 to 3 hours for 4 or 5 days.

People getting 80 mg of zinc a day reported their overall cold symptoms abated in less than 5 days, compared with 8 days on average for the group getting the substitute lozenges.

—*Annals of Internal Medicine*, reported in *Science News, 158*

10. In a study at Vipeholm, a mental institution in southern Sweden, 436 adult patients on a nutritionally adequate diet were observed for several years. They were found to develop caries [cavities] at a slow rate. Subsequently, the patients were divided into nine groups to compare the effect of various changes in their carbohydrate intake. Sucrose was included in the diet as toffee, chocolate, or caramel, in bread, or in liquid form. Caries increased significantly when food containing sucrose was ingested between meals. Not only the frequency but the form in which sucrose was ingested was important: sticky or adhesive forms were more cariogenic [cavity-producing] than forms which were rapidly cleared from the mouth. After two years on the test diets, the patients were again placed on the control diet, and the caries activity reverted to the pretest pattern.

—E. Newburn, *Science* 217 (1982)

11. A research team, led by Dr. Wancai Yang, has shown that black raspberries can prevent intestinal cancers.

    Researchers genetically engineered two types of mice to test the benefits of black raspberries. One type was engineered to develop intestinal tumors, and the other type was engineered to have an inflammation of the large intestine that can lead to colorectal cancer.

    For 12 weeks, all mice were fed a "high-risk" diet—which was high in fat and low in calcium and vitamin D—and some were also given a supplement, so 10 percent of their calories came from freeze-dried black raspberry powder.

    Both types of mice that ate the black raspberry powder had fewer tumors than the mice not given the supplements.

    Among mice engineered to have intestinal tumors, the growth of new tumors decreased by 45 percent, and the total number of tumors in the mice decreased by 60 percent, the study said. The black raspberries stopped tumors from developing by suppressing a protein that binds to the gene that the scientists genetically modified in the mice, the researchers said.

    In the mice engineered to have the intestinal inflammation, new tumors and number of tumors were reduced by 50 percent because the black raspberries worked to reduce inflammation, according to the study.

    —Based on a report by Amanda Chan in *Health News*

12. Pheromones are discrete chemicals produced by insects to communicate with other members of their own species. Insects signal the presence of food, enemies, or willing mates by ejecting pheromones. The chemicals can be produced in laboratories and sprayed on crops to confuse the insects that produce the chemicals naturally. Scientists who are concerned about damage to the environment hope that the use of pheromones will provide a safer alternative to toxic pesticides.

    In the Finger Lakes region of New York, growers sprayed five plots of wine grapes with pheromones and five plots adjacent to each of these with conventional insecticide. At harvest time damage from grape berry moth was less in plots sprayed with pheromones in four of the five comparisons.

    The plot in which the pheromone spray was less effective was at the edge of a forest with a lot of wild grape growing, and consequently a much larger population of moths.

    —Based on a report by Dennehy, Clark, and Kamas, *New York Life Science Bulletin*

13. Sir Richard Doll, who died in 2005 at age 92, studied links between smoking and many ailments. One of his important studies focused on comparing mortality rates for smokers and nonsmokers. He followed a group of more than 40,000 British male doctors born from 1900 to 1930 for the half-century between 1951 and 2001. The mortality rates for the two groups began to diverge before the doctors reached age

50. By age 60, there was a 10 percent difference between the two groups. By age 70, 81 percent of nonsmokers were still alive, but only 58 percent of smokers lived to age 70. More than 60 percent of nonsmokers lived to age 80, whereas only about 25 percent of smokers celebrated their 80th birthdays. By age 90, more than 20 percent of nonsmokers were still alive while fewer than 5 percent of smokers lived that long.

—Based on a graph published by the *Medical Research Council* in 2004

It is never too late to quit, however! According to Sir Richard's obituary in the *New York Times* (2005, July 26), he also found that people who stopped smoking, regardless of age, could reduce the danger.

14. Banning deer boosts numbers of migratory birds.

In a 9-year test, excluding deer raised the populations among some bird species, such as hooded warblers. Populations of other birds, such as chipping sparrows (who prefer open fields) decreased. In this test, the researchers used fences about 10 feet high surrounding four plots, each about 10 acres in size to exclude deer, and allowed deer to enter four other 10-acre plots. The no-deer zones grew dense with plants, attracting birds who prefer mature forests, such as the warblers.

—*Science News,* 2000, August 12

15. Researchers said a biopsy of the brain of nine-year NFL veteran Tom McHale, who died of a drug overdose at age 45, showed that he suffered from a severe degenerative brain disease called chronic traumatic encephalopathy. It was caused by repeated concussions.

The biopsy was the sixth out of six performed on deceased NFL players between the ages of 25 and 50 that showed evidence of such severe damage. All six men suffered emotional and behavioral problems after their playing days were over, often culminating in erratic behavior, drug abuse and suicide or overdose.

Dr. Ann C. McKee of Boston University's Center for the Study of Traumatic Encephalopathy, who performed the biopsy on McHale, said she had found similar damage in the brain of a recently deceased 18-year-old who had suffered multiple concussions playing high school football—the youngest age at which it had ever been observed.

The damages in both cases were similar to those observed in boxers who have taken severe beatings to the head, McKee said. Although they are also similar to the changes seen in Alzheimer's disease, she added, "they represent a distinct disease with a distinct cause, namely repetitive head trauma."

—T.H. Maugh II, *Los Angeles Times*

16. N. Volkow [the director of the National Institute on Drug Abuse] wants to know why some people can't seem to close the fridge. "Is the signal [to eat] really stronger in overeaters, or is the part of the brain controlling these urges not normal?"

she asks. She and her collaborators began to answer this question in 2001, when they studied differences between the brains of normal-weight and of obese people.

In previous research that had focused solely on drug abusers, Volkow and other researchers found that many addicts had a deficiency in a particular type of receptor for dopamine, one of the brain's feel-good chemicals. Most drugs of abuse reward their takers, "and reinforce the habit," by flooding the brain with more dopamine than normal. So, the researchers theorized that some drug users become addicts as a way of making up for a shortage of dopamine receptors.

Scientists have known for decades that eating also floods the brain with dopamine. When Volkow and her colleagues looked at the brains of 10 obese people, the team found a dopamine-receptor deficiency identical to that in drug addicts. Volkow stresses that obesity seems to be a significantly more complex disorder than drug abuse because many unrelated factors, such as glandular problems, lack of exercise, or a genetic predisposition to storing fat, can lead to weight gain. However, the brains of several of the obese volunteers in Volkow's study seemed to be telling another story: "These people were compulsively driven to eat as if food were their stimulus of choice," she says.

—From "Food Fix," *Science News Online*, 2005, September 3

17. Find an example of the use of one of Mill's methods in some current newspaper or magazine, and analyze it in the manner of Exercises 1–16.

III. CONTROLLED EXPERIMENTS

Several of the preceding exercises describe **controlled experiments** that scientists use to establish causal relationships. Controlled experiments usually draw upon Mill's Joint Method of Agreement and Difference or the Method of Concomitant Variations. In a controlled experiment, the investigator studies two or more groups that are similar to one another, except for their exposure to the suspected cause.

For example, in a controlled experiment to study the effects of a birth-control hormone on brain development in rats, two groups of 100 laboratory rats are selected from a relatively uniform population. The two groups are treated the same in all respects except that the food of one group (the experimental group) is supplemented with doses of the birth-control hormone and the food of the other group (the control group) is not supplemented. If retarded brain development (or a higher frequency of retardation) occurs in the experimental group but fails to occur in the control group, the experiment supports the statement that the birth-control hormone is the cause of retardation in laboratory rats. If after this treatment, however, the two groups do not differ significantly with respect to retardation, the experiment does not support a causal relationship.

When scientists perform controlled experiments to establish causal statements, they also use the argument form of inductive generalization. The experimental group of rats in the study just described is randomly selected from the population of laboratory rats and thus represents the population from which it is drawn. Because this is so, what happens to the experimental group in the experiment provides a basis for generalizing to what *would* happen to any population of laboratory rats if all were exposed to the hormone. Similarly, the control group is another randomly selected representative sample of rats, and the results obtained from the experiment can be generalized to what would happen to the population of laboratory rats if they were not exposed to the hormone. Being able to say what *would* happen under various circumstances is especially important in causal reasoning, for when we say that one sort of thing causes another (for example, birth-control hormones cause brain damage in rats), we mean not merely that taking hormones was *correlated* with brain damage in the rats that were studied but also that, *if* any population of rats were exposed to the hormone, then those rats would suffer a greater rate of brain damage than a population not so exposed. Correlation between events can be established by observation, and statistical studies can be used to prove that such correlation exists. But when we want to say that one event is the cause of another, we need to go beyond observation to what would happen in unobserved cases. Controlled experiments provide us with inductive support for such causal statements.

Some types of controlled experiments are better than others. The type of controlled experiment performed on the rats in the hormone study is called a **randomized experimental study**, the gold standard for controlled experiments. In such studies, both the experimental group and the control group are selected randomly from the population they represent prior to being manipulated for the purposes of the experiment.

In the physical sciences, it is relatively easy to obtain experimental and control samples to perform randomized experiments. Any bit of pure sodium, for example, is a representative sample of that metal, so that investigators can take any samples of pure sodium to perform controlled experiments to discover the causal properties of sodium. (Sometimes, however, it is difficult to isolate the substance to be investigated. Nobel Prize winner Marie Curie had to handle tons of pitchblende to isolate enough radium to perform her experiments on radioactive materials.)

When animals are the subject of randomized experiments, experimenters must be concerned about such matters as the purity of the genetic lines of the laboratory animals, the proper maintenance of the animals, the control of extraneous influences that might affect the outcome of the experiments, and the humane treatment of the experimental animals.

When humans are studied, randomized experiments are subject to severe moral and legal restraints. Although these restraints are not relevant to whether experimental studies support causal statements, they are extremely important to the ethics of science. Perhaps you felt uneasy when you read about the treatment of "lunatics" in the beriberi experiment described in the last section. How cruel to compel a group of helpless people to eat a diet suspected of causing a serious disease like beriberi! In fairness to the researchers who first suspected that diet was the cause of beriberi, however, a diet of polished rice was not unusual for many people outside institutions during that time. Nevertheless, restrictions on scientific and medical research would not allow such an experiment today. The government—with some unfortunate lapses—enforces strict guidelines for any experiments involving human subjects, with the result that experiments in which humans are forced to participate are less likely to occur. Federal regulations also require that subjects who volunteer for experiments be informed about any suspected dangers so that they can give informed consent. Some of the same protections against harming experimental subjects are extended to animals. Animal-rights activists have raised serious questions about the treatment of experimental animals and have protested acts of apparent cruelty.

Not all controlled experiments involve manipulation of subjects. In some types of studies no treatment at all is imposed, and the "experiment" consists primarily of recording observations. In **prospective studies**, for example, the experimental group is drawn from individuals who choose to expose themselves to the suspected causal factor. These subjects are said to be "self-selected." The control group in a prospective study is then matched to the experimental group in features thought to be relevant to occurrence of the effect (except the causal factor under consideration). Instead of manipulating the experimental group, as in a randomized experimental study, experimenters observe and wait to see what happens. This type of controlled study has been used to investigate the harmful effects of smoking. A sample of persons who already smoke (the experimental group) is matched for such features as age, sex, occupation, place of residence, ethnic background, and history of disease with a sample (control group) of nonsmokers, and researchers observe both groups over a period of time to see whether rates of various illnesses (or death rates from those illnesses) are different in the two groups. Such studies can be very costly because of the time required for the effects to develop but are important for gathering useful information about the course of a disease and the adequacy of various forms of treatment. Ongoing studies, for example, compare the long-term cure rate of mastectomy (removal of the breast) and lumpectomy (removal only of diseased tissue) for similar forms of breast cancer. Prospective studies are also used to study the outcomes of various social and educational reforms, such as how educational programs in prisons affect recidivism (the tendency to return to criminal behavior after leaving prison), how preschool education for the children of impoverished families influences later academic performance, and whether distribution of free hypodermic needles to drug addicts reduces incidence of AIDS.

When prospective studies would be too costly or would take too long to gather urgently needed information, **retrospective studies** are sometimes employed. In a retrospective study, the experimental group is chosen from a population that already exhibits the effect for which a cause is sought. Obviously, this group is not randomly selected. The experimental group is matched to a control group (again, not randomly selected) that lacks the effect but is similar in other relevant respects—such as age and sex. Then a backward-looking study of the histories of the two groups is conducted to find some difference in antecedent circumstances between the two groups and to justify maintaining that the difference is causally related to the observed effect.

A recent retrospective study investigated the cause of a particular type of disturbed sleep in some of the infants in a maternity ward of a hospital. The experimental group of 28 newborn infants all showed more rapid-eye-movement sleep and less quiet sleep than the 30 newborns in the control group. The infants who slept quietly were children of mothers whose age, nutrition, care during pregnancy, and other properties believed to affect the welfare of newborns were similar to the mothers of infants in the experimental group. It was found that the infants in the experimental group, however, had all been exposed while still in the womb to low doses of methadone. Their mothers were former heroin addicts on a methadone maintenance program. None of the mothers in the control group had taken drugs during their pregnancies.

Although prospective studies and retrospective studies avoid some of the moral and legal objections to randomized experimental studies on humans (and animals), they do not avoid all objections. Forming matched control groups can involve intrusive questioning that forces patients to expose personal histories they would prefer to conceal. The benefits to persons in the control groups in these studies are unclear. Both prospective and retrospective studies are flawed by selection bias, which compromises their scientific value. Because the samples in both types are *not* randomly selected, they are not likely to be representative. In prospective studies, for example, the apparent self-selection of the experimental group can mask some other underlying cause that gives rise to the effect. As the tobacco companies remind us, smokers may be drawn to smoke because of some underlying condition. That, in turn, might contribute to an illness that the study suggests is smoking-related. Control groups that are matched to a nonrandom sample are likewise nonrandom. Retrospective studies have an added problem of possible errors in the records and reports used to reconstruct antecedent circumstances.

Many prospective and retrospective studies of human disease draw on hospital patients as subjects, but this practice is almost sure to produce biased samples. Depending on their locations, some hospitals attract patients from one economic group of the population; others, from different economic classes. People who enter a hospital for the treatment of one disease might be more susceptible than the general public to other diseases. In evaluating the effects of curative or preventive treatments, it is important to know the medical history of a patient's family, but hospital records that contain such information are confidential and can be inaccurate. For these reasons, medical scientists are cautious about projecting the results of studies of hospital patients onto the general population.

Another possible source of bias associated with controlled studies of humans is the difficulty of obtaining large enough samples. In the study that concluded that the sleep of newborn infants was affected by methadone absorbed in the womb, experimenters were able to select a group of babies with similar prenatal histories and different sleep patterns, but both the experimental group and the control group were very small. It is often difficult to obtain samples that are large enough to be representative of even a special subgroup of the human population, such as the subgroup of newborns.

When we are able to study the difference between a control group that is a representative sample of a population, none of whom are exposed to the suspected causal agent, and an experimental group that is a representative sample of a population, all of whom are exposed to the suspected causal agent, then we are justified in concluding that the results of the study will yield reliable information about what *would* happen if the population were exposed to the suspected causal agent. Insofar as samples are not representative, conclusions are less strongly supported.

Studies performed on experimental animals often come close to the ideal conditions of a randomized experimental study. Laboratory animals are bred for uniform characteristics so that almost any group of them is a representative sample of the population. Such animals are not, however, representative of the *human* population. If we want to use the results of animal studies to draw conclusions about humans, we need to construct arguments from analogy. Any relevant differences between the experimental animals and humans weaken the conclusions of such studies.

One further problem that should be mentioned in connection with controlled studies is the need to eliminate psychological influences that might affect the purity of the results. It is well known that human illnesses often improve when a patient believes in the treatment being administered. The technique of a **double-blind experiment** attempts to eliminate such psychological influences in judging the effectiveness of possible cures. In an experiment to test a new drug, for example, members of the control group receive some inert substance (called a *placebo*) such as a sugar pill, whereas members of the experimental group get the drug. The people receiving these substances do not know whether they are members of the control group or the experimental group; they are "blind" to the type of substance they receive. In addition, the investigators dispense the drugs and placebos blindly. That is to say, the substances are coded, and those performing the study cannot tell the placebo from the drug at the time of the experiment. In this way, the experimenters are better able to make unbiased judgments about the success of treatment in each case because they learn who received the drug and who received a placebo only after the experiment is completed and its outcome is registered.

Double-blind experiments are used in most drug tests and in other tests as well. In the 1980s, the U.S. government completed a three-year study of the effectiveness of cloud seeding for enhancing rainfall. The technique of seeding clouds involves flying over them and sprinkling them with fine particles of silver iodide. None of the experimenters in the study "knew at the time on which days they were actually seeding clouds with fine silver iodide particles, and on which they were merely sprinkling them with an inert sand 'placebo'" (R. A. Kerr, "Test Fails to Confirm Cloud Seeding Effect," *Science* 217 [1982]). Neither those who decided which clouds to seed nor those who judged the amounts of rain that fell from seeded clouds knew whether the clouds had been seeded with silver iodide or sand. After three years, a locked vault that held the secret record of the silver iodide seeding was opened. The experimenters were disappointed to find that this particular double-blind experiment failed to confirm the effectiveness of cloud seeding, but they planned further, more refined experiments and were convinced that researchers must continue to use such controlled experiments to test the effectiveness of various weather-modification procedures.

Despite all the problems with controlled experiments, such studies of both humans and animals play an extremely important role in causal investigations. Controlled experiments are among the best ways we have of distinguishing causal relationships from mere coincidental connections.

Exercise Set 5.4

1. Review the set of exercises at the end of the previous section on Mill's methods and note any that exemplify controlled experiments. When you identify the controlled experiments, describe the experimental group and the control group and say whether the study is randomized experimental, prospective, or retrospective in design.

2. Which of Mill's methods is used in the following study that links concussions to brain disease? Is this a controlled experiment?

   The National Football League commissioned a telephone survey of 1,000 retired players that was released just two weeks ago. The study found that players under the age of 50 were 19 times more likely to have been diagnosed with dementia, Alzheimer's and other memory-related diseases, compared to the general public.

   —CBS 60 minutes (2009, October 11)

3. What is the type of the controlled experiment described below?

   A study published in the *Journal of Periodontology (JOP)*, the official publication of the American Academy of Periodontology (AAP), demonstrates that including flossing as part of one's routine oral care can actually help reduce the amount of gum disease-causing bacteria found in the mouth, therefore contributing to healthy teeth and gums.

   The study, conducted at New York University, examined 51 sets of twins between the ages of 12 and 21. Each set was randomly assigned a two-week treatment regimen, with one twin brushing with a manual toothbrush and toothpaste and the other twin brushing with a manual toothbrush and toothpaste and flossing. At the end of the two-week trial, samples were taken from both pairs of twins and compared for levels of bacteria commonly associated with periodontal disease.

The study findings indicated that those twins who did not floss had significantly more of the bacteria associated with periodontal disease when compared to the matching twin who flossed in addition to tooth-brushing with toothpaste.

"This study illustrates the impact flossing can have on oral health. The twins experimental model is a powerful tool to help sort out genetic and environmental factors that often confound the interpretation of treatment studies. This study demonstrates that flossing can have an important and favorable impact on an individual, as compared to that of a non-flossing individual with similar genetics and possibly similar habits," explains Dr. K. Kornman, editor of the *Journal of Periodontology*. "Twins tend to share the same or similar environmental factors such as dietary habits, health and life practices, as well as genetics. In this case, the only difference was flossing, and the outcome was significant. Flossing may significantly reduce the amount of bad bacteria in the mouth."

—Retrieved August, 2008 from http://www.perio.org

4. What type of controlled experiment is described below?

Alpa Patel, PhD and a team of scientists, analyzed responses to questionnaires from 123,216 people, of which 53,440 [were] men and 69,776 women. These individuals had no record of cancer, stroke, heart attack or lung disease, and they took part in the American Cancer Society's Cancer Prevention II study in 1992. The time spent sitting and physical activity related to mortality from 1993 to 2006 was analyzed. Results showed that longer sitting time is related to higher mortality risks, especially in women. Women reportedly sitting more than six hours a day had 37 percent more chances of dieing [sic] during the considered period than women who sat less than three hours a day. As for men, those who sat more than six hours a day were 18 percent more likely to die than those sitting less than three hours a day. After adding individuals' physical activity level to this data, results remained rather proportional: women and men who sat more and had little or no physical activity had 94% and 48% chances of dieing [sic], compared to those that sat less and were more active.

Dr. Patel said that "several factors could explain the positive association between time spent sitting and higher all-cause death rates. Prolonged time spent sitting, independent of physical activity, has been shown to have important metabolic consequences, and may influence things like triglycerides, high density lipoprotein, cholesterol, fasting plasma glucose, resting blood pressure, and leptin, which are biomarkers of obesity and cardiovascular and other chronic diseases."

—"The more you sit the sooner you die," *Softpedia*, 2010, July 20

5. In what ways does the study described in the following fall short of a randomized experimental design?

"There's a lore in Alcoholics Anonymous," [Harriet de Wit] continues, "that a single drink can lead to a drinking binge." But no one had ever shown—under controlled conditions—if this was true for the so-called average drinker. Earlier this year, de Wit and her coworkers decided to find out. In a double-blind study, the researchers gave a placebo drink or a little bit of alcohol to a small group of volunteers—mostly graduate students—who were "light to moderate drinkers." A short while later, the team asked the volunteers to choose between a second drink or a small amount of money—usually about $10. The people who had received the alcohol "pre-load" were twice as likely to choose alcohol.

—*University of Chicago Magazine* (1991, August)

6. Find a description of a controlled experiment in an outside reading source. (Some good sources are the magazines *Science, Science News,* and *Nature* as well as the *Science* sections of newspapers and weekly newsmagazines. Other possible sources are newspaper stories and Sunday supplements, such as *Parade Magazine.*) Characterize the important features of the experiment (whether it was double-blind, how the control group was matched to the experimental group, and so on).

7. Critically discuss the features of the experiment reported below:

Oxytocin, a hormone associated with social bonding, seems to make people more inclined to trust strangers with their cash. In a game in which 58 volunteers could invest money with anonymous trustees, economist Ernst Fehr of the University of Zurich and his colleagues dosed half the subjects with a whiff of oxytocin and the others with an inert placebo nose spray. After sniffing oxytocin, investors were roughly twice as likely to invest all their funds and on average the oxytocin group put in nearly 20 percent more than placebo subjects.

—Charles Q. Choi, *Scientific American* (2005, August)

8. Have you heard people say that using a cell phone can cause brain tumors? Most attempts to answer this question by performing controlled experiments have said no. Controlled studies that try to link a rare disease, such as brain cancer, with an extremely common suspected cause, such as cell-phone usage, are particularly challenging to design. Can you give one or more reasons why this is so? A group of Danish neuroscientists, led by H. C. Christensen, provided evidence against any causal link between cell-phone use and brain cancer. Describe the important features of their experiment, taken from a report in *Neurology* (2005) 64.

The authors looked at records of all cases of glioma and meningioma (two types of brain tumors) diagnosed in Denmark between September 1, 2000 and August 31, 2002.

They enrolled 252 persons with glioma and 175 persons with meningioma aged 20 to 69. They also enrolled 822 control subjects, randomly sampled from the population and matched for age and sex with the persons with tumors. They obtained information from personal interviews, medical records containing diagnoses, and the results of radiologic examinations. They matched cases (tumor patients) and controls on socioeconomic factors and tested their memory ability, using the Mini-Mental State Examination.

For a small number of cases and controls, the authors monitored the number of ingoing and outgoing calls, rather than relying on reports from memory. Using standard statistical tests, the authors found no association between cell phone use and risk for glioma or meningioma.

9. Characterize the type of each of the following controlled experiments to determine whether dietary fiber protects against colorectal cancer (CC).

   a. In 1992, G. R. Howe and associates collected records of 5,287 patients with CC and 10,470 patients without. After analyzing patients' intake of fiber, vitamin C, and beta carotene, the study concluded that risk decreased as fiber intake increased.

   b. In 1980, Charles S. Fuchs and associates asked 88,657 women with no history of cancer, polyps (a precursor to cancer), or bowel disease to complete a diet questionnaire in 1980. After following the women for 16 years, the researchers concluded that there was no association between the intake of dietary fiber and the risk of CC.

   c. In 2000, Arthur Schatzkin and associates published the results of a study in which 2,079 patients who had recently had colorectal polyps removed were randomly assigned to eat diets low in fat and high in fiber fruits and vegetables or to follow their usual diets over four years. The study concluded that adopting a diet high in fiber and low in fat does not influence the risk of recurrence of polyps.

   d. In 2000, David S. Alberts and associates randomly assigned 1,429 people who recently had polyps removed to eat low-fat, high-fiber dietary supplements or to eat placebo foods that looked and tasted the same but were low in fiber. After three years they concluded that a dietary supplement of wheat-bran fiber does not protect against recurrent polyps.

   —Information taken from *The New York Times* (2005, September 28)

IV. DIFFERENT USES OF "CAUSE"

For want of a nail, the shoe was lost,
For want of a shoe, the horse was lost,
For want of a horse, the battle was lost,
And all for the want of a horseshoe nail.

—Nursery rhyme

Our references to "the cause" of some event or condition conceal different meanings of the word *cause* and the complexity of most causal situations. How we use *cause* depends on how much we know about a situation and on our practical or theoretical interest in a causal relationship.

Consider a murder trial in which the defendant is accused of shooting the victim. The prosecutor, who is interested in showing that the defendant is legally responsible for the gunshot wound that led to the victim's death, says that the defendant's action was the cause of death. But the medical examiner has a different interest. If the victim died immediately after being shot, for example, the cause cited might be "massive internal bleeding." If the victim did not die immediately but was taken to surgery and suffocated after an allergic reaction to an anesthetic, the medical examiner's report would cite suffocation as the cause of death. The causal accounts given by the lawyer and the coroner, although different, do not conflict with one another; even though suffocation was the *proximate* physical cause of death (the causal physical circumstance closest to the event), the action of the defendant was an important earlier part of the causal chain that led to the suffocation. The law is interested in one part of that chain (*who* is to blame), and the medical specialist is interested in another (which of the body's systems stopped working).

The causal chain leading to the victim's death undoubtedly contains more links. The ambulance that took the victim to the hospital may have been delayed by traffic. The anesthetist may have failed to check the victim for allergies. The shooting may have been provoked (caused) by a quarrel resulting from the victim's attentions to the defendant's spouse; the victim's attentions might have been encouraged by the spouse; and so on. All of these events and conditions can be a part of the complex causal process leading to the death of the victim. Only a special interest in some part of the complex set of events and processes (such as who is legally responsible or what should be put on the death certificate) leads us to refer to this as "the cause."

Even this account of the *chain* of causal events that results in the death of the victim is oversimplified, for it fails to consider various other chains of events that might be interwoven with these events and that could reinforce or counteract them. Thus, the analogy of a "causal network" rather than a "causal chain" is more appropriate.

Diverse interests of the lawyer and the medical examiner lead them to focus on different aspects of the causal network. The lawyer wants a conviction; the medical examiner must determine the physical events leading to the victim's death. In other circumstances, such as a scientific investigation of a disease, a feature is singled out as "the cause" because it is more susceptible to control than other aspects of the causal process. In the story of the defeat of yellow fever, for example, the anopheles mosquito is usually cited as "the cause" of the disease. Although the mosquito plays a causal role by transferring the disease from one human to another, the specific yellow-fever virus must be present in the bloodstream for the mosquito bite to cause the disease.

Nevertheless, the discovery of the insect vector of the disease, and the realization that the disease was not transmitted by physical contact with a victim of yellow fever or other common sources of contamination were of crucial importance in control of the disease. Even though a vaccine for yellow fever was developed in the 1930s, programs to control the disease, like those to control malaria, are still primarily aimed at eliminating mosquitoes rather than controlling the specific virus.

The importance of naming the part of the causal process that is susceptible to our control as the "cause" is apparent when we compare how we identify the cause of diseases in some plants and in humans. Many humans have natural immunities to diseases. All of us have known some of those lucky ones who never catch colds even when almost everyone around them is sneezing and coughing. We do not, however, try to control the spread of human infectious diseases through selective breeding, and a lack of natural immunity is rarely cited as the cause of human disease. In contrast, when a disease-resistant strain of some useful plant is discovered, plant breeders immediately try to propagate the new strain and market it for this valuable property. Breeding resistant strains rather than attacking the specific organism responsible for the disease is an accepted and effective method of controlling diseases in plants. Because of this, we sometimes say that a plant succumbed to disease *because* it lacked the immune characteristic.

In studying types of causes, it is useful to distinguish between necessary causal conditions and sufficient causal conditions. The mosquito carrier of yellow fever is a **necessary causal condition** of the disease. Without the mosquitoes, the disease does not survive in nature. A condition is called "necessary" if the effect cannot occur without that condition. The presence of oxygen (or hydrogen), for example, is a necessary causal condition for the existence of fires. Our attention most often focuses on causally necessary conditions when we are interested in eliminating some undesirable effect. When medical scientists try to eliminate a disease, they look for some necessary causal condition, such as the mosquito carrier of yellow fever. No one, however, would think of trying to prevent forest fires by reducing the oxygen in the atmosphere near forests, though this would be effective. Unlike the mosquito in the yellow-fever example, oxygen is never referred to as "the cause" of forest fires, even though, like the mosquito, it is a causally necessary condition. The difference between the two cases is that the mosquito is something we can eliminate to prevent the problem; oxygen is not.

When we are interested in bringing about some effect, rather than in eliminating an effect, we often look for a **causally sufficient condition** that we can control. A condition is "causally sufficient" for some effect if, whenever the condition is present, the effect must occur. Vaccination is sufficient for the prevention of smallpox. Decapitation of a person is a causally sufficient condition for that person's death. Scientists search for wonder drugs ("magic bullets") that will bring about causally sufficient conditions for curing human diseases.

It is unusual, however, to be able to isolate a single causally sufficient condition. Frequently, the term *sufficient condition* refers instead to some important causal factor that, against a background set of necessary conditions, is especially proximate, interesting, or easy to control. For example, it is reasonable to say that bringing water up to a temperature of 100° Celsius is sufficient to make that water boil. This is true, however, only when certain necessary background conditions, such as normal atmospheric pressure and relative freedom of the water from impurities, are operative. Turning a light switch to the "on" position suffices to produce light only when power is available, the lamp is in working order, the bulb is not burned out, and so forth. When the background conditions are fairly standard, are not subject to great fluctuation, or are not usually under our direct control, we typically ignore them and use the term *sufficient causal condition* to refer somewhat loosely to an event or process that we can control directly and that under standard background conditions, will produce the desired effect.

Sometimes we say that a set of causal conditions is "individually necessary and jointly sufficient" for some event to occur. The conditions individually necessary and jointly sufficient to cause germination in viable grass seed, for example, are (1) adequate water, (2) suitable temperature, (3) oxygen, and (4) light. When all of these conditions are present jointly in the appropriate degree (proportions vary for different types of grasses), germination occurs.

Frequently, however, even when we know a lot about the causes of some type of event, we are unable to specify individually necessary and jointly sufficient, complete sets of conditions. An example follows.

Dental caries, the localized destruction of tooth tissue by microorganisms, is a process familiar to most of you, and this process is well understood by medical scientists. Three main causal factors are (1) the hosts (saliva and teeth), (2) the microorganisms (particularly one called *Streptococcus mutans,* which is found in dental plaque), and (3) the diet.

Experiments have shown that rats fed through stomach tubes do not develop cavities even when the caries-producing *S. mutans* is present. Similarly, rats do not get cavities when they are fed orally if their mouths are kept sterile. It would seem then that the presence of teeth, microorganisms, and food are individually necessary and jointly sufficient for cavities in rats. However, rats do not *always* develop cavities under these circumstances—although groups of them do develop cavities at "the normal rate." Some rats, like some humans, apparently are able to resist cavities better than others. For this reason, we cannot say that the presence of the three necessary conditions (teeth, microorganisms, and a food supply) jointly form a sufficient causal condition for the disease.

Further necessary conditions might be specifiable in this case (for example, lack of fluoride protection and genetic susceptibility to the disease), but frequently the causal situations are too complex to permit us to identify a complete set of conditions. The effort that medical scientists are willing to expend in search of additional necessary conditions for a particular type of event depends largely on practical concerns, such as how much knowledge is necessary to control the causal process. Although diet, especially sugar consumption, receives emphasis in some studies of dental caries, other research focuses on host factors (fluoride treatment of teeth and drinking water) and on microorganisms (the possibility of immunization).

We have been looking at some of the different ways in which the term *cause* is used. The point of this discussion is that there are a number of correct uses of the term. Different uses of *cause* are suitable in different circumstances. It is important for us to understand the various ways that *cause* is used so that we can identify and understand important causal relationships.

We especially want to be aware that there can be a cause that is neither a sufficient nor a necessary causal condition for an effect. Cigarette smoking, for example, is neither necessary nor sufficient for contracting lung cancer. You might get lung cancer even if you do not smoke. Likewise, you might escape lung cancer even if you are a heavy smoker. Nevertheless, it would be foolish, with all the evidence now available, to deny that smoking causes lung cancer. Smoking is a probabilistic cause of the disease. We call a causally antecedent condition a **probabilistic cause** when its presence makes the occurrence of the condition under investigation more probable than it would be in the absence of the antecedent condition. Strong evidence points to smoking as an antecedent condition that is related to lung cancer in this probabilistic way. Many of the controlled experiments examined in this chapter provide evidence for assigning probabilistic causes. We have already mentioned that Mill did not think of causes in terms of frequencies, but his methods are widely used in modern research to study the variations in frequencies that provide a basis for probabilistic causal statements.

The following example, taken from a syndicated newspaper medical advice column, shows the danger of confusing probabilistic causes with sufficient causal conditions:

> Dear Dr. Steincrohn: Thinking about premature death has caused a serious depression in my husband. Although only 38, and, according to our doctor, physically sound he lives in fear of dying early.
>
> He blames it on his poor heredity. His father died of a coronary attack at the age of 59 and his mother had a stroke at about the same age. One uncle suffers from extremely high blood pressure.
>
> With that kind of family history, he asks, "What chance have I got?" As a result he smokes too much. Drinks a lot. Has let himself get fat.
>
> He figures how he lives won't make any difference. Have you run into similar problems?

In answering this letter, the doctor correctly notes that "there may be a hereditary disposition to stroke and heart attacks," but he points out that the man is not inevitably doomed to an early death. He cites records of patients who had good family histories and poor living habits who died earlier than their counterparts who had bad heredity traits. The husband, at least if his wife's description of the situation is accurate, seems to regard his poor heredity traits as causally sufficient for an early death rather than as factors that increase the probability of early death. As a result of this misunderstanding, he ignores other factors, such as not smoking, which could counteract a possible predisposition to cancer, stroke, or heart attack.

Exercise Set 5.5

For each of the following causal statements, discuss whether "cause" is used in one or more of the following ways:

a. A proximate or nearest cause in a chain or network of causes

b. An agent causally responsible for some action or event

c. A necessary causal condition

d. A sufficient causal condition

e. A sufficient causal condition against a background of accepted, stable necessary conditions

f. A probabilistic cause

1. Martha failed the exam because there wasn't enough time to finish it.

2. Jason will graduate with his class in May because he finally paid his library fines.

3. William went to the party because Jean invited him.

4. Arson was the cause of the fire at the museum.

5. The house burned down because oily rags were stored in a closet.

6. Tom crashed the party because he didn't have an invitation.

7. Sara didn't get the flu this spring because she got her flu shot in November.

8. The crops are poor this summer because there hasn't been enough rain.

9. Lei won the competition because he practiced eight hours a day to prepare for it.

10. The ice on the sidewalk is melting because salt was thrown on it.

11. Ari is depressed because he didn't get the job he wanted.

12. The nuclear disaster at Fukushima in 2011 has caused slowing or canceling development plans for nuclear power plants in other parts of the world.

13. The assassination of Archduke Ferdinand at Sarajevo in August 1914 was the cause of World War I.

14. The heavy penalties imposed by the Allies on the Germans after the First World War caused the Second World War.

15. According to the U.S. Government Accountability Office (GAO), over the past twenty years college-textbook prices have risen at double the rate of inflation.

The GAO blames the large increases on the costs of developing supplemental materials such as CD-ROMs. Yale law professor Ian Ayres, however, says the real problem is the lack of price competition. Through a series of mergers, the five largest publishers now control 80 percent of the college-textbook market.

16. Working conditions of air traffic controllers were investigated as a result of a number of incidents of controllers sleeping on the job when planes were trying to land at major airports.

17. A bare foot in direct contact with the ground depends more on the four small toes for traction and weight distribution than it does when supported by a shoe. Thus the small toes of the habitually unshod become stronger and bigger than those of the habitually shod.

—Caitlin E. Cox (based on research by Erik Trinkaus), *Natural History,*
2005, September

18. Fear of public speaking caused Rosa to abandon a promising career in government.

19. Because the state has reduced the amount of money it previously awarded to university education, an increase in tuition is inevitable.

20. Of the usual clinical tests for assessing the fertility of a male—sperm number, morphology (shape) and motility (movement)—only sperm motility is correlated with fertilizing ability. If a sperm sample contains less than 20 [percent] motile sperm, fertilization will not occur.

—K. Dawson, *Embryo Experimentation,* (Singer et al., Eds.)

V. HUME'S ANALYSIS OF CAUSATION

Thus far in our discussion, we have not proposed a definition of *cause* that would cover the various uses of the term. Even though we all have some understanding of the term, it turns out to be difficult to define *cause* precisely. In the eighteenth century, David Hume offered an analysis of the meaning of statements of the general form "*A* causes *B*." Hume was trying to solve the problem of how to justify causal inferences. To keep things simple, he analyzed the type of causal relationship that holds between two uncomplicated events or types of events (the striking of two billiard balls and their movement after the collision). Hume said that he could find nothing in the *ideas* of striking and subsequent motion to connect the two events. That is to say, the concepts of striking and of motion are not related through their meanings in the way that synonyms (such as *bachelor* and *unmarried male*) or mathematical equalities (2 + 2 and 4) are to one another. It is certainly possible to conceive of a ball being struck without subsequent motion.

Failing to find what he called "a relation of ideas" (such as a definitional connection), Hume turned to experience (matters of fact) for a better understanding of causes. The features he could *observe* in such relationships were the following:

1. *A* and *B* are joined with one another in space and time. ("No action at a distance.")
2. *B* follows *A*. (The "effect" does not precede the "cause.")
3. Whenever *A* occurs, *B* occurs. ("Constant conjunction.")

Hume realized that all three of these relationships might be observed between two events that were only coincidentally connected with one another. (Remember the London tobacconists' avoidance of bubonic plague.) Hume, therefore, felt that his analysis of the observable features of causal relationships failed to uncover any "real"—as distinguished from coincidental—connection between the two events. The only additional feature he could find to connect *A* to *B* in such cases was a habit of expecting *B* when presented with *A*. Hume's analysis pushed the matter still further, for he showed that there is no logical reason—no correct noncircular deductive or inductive argument—to support the view that constant conjunctions that have been observed in the past will continue to hold in the future.

Hume was not satisfied with his attempts to understand causal reasoning, and he challenged others to find a "real connection" between cause and effect. But his own conclusion was skeptical: The inference from cause to effect is based on a psychological habit of expectation, formed as a result of observing such connections in the past. The inference, Hume said, is apparently not grounded in *reasoned* knowledge of real connections but in habit or custom. Because we tend to think that our knowledge of causes, especially what we have learned from scientific investigations, is based on more than mere habit, Hume's well-argued and startling conclusion has troubled all who have thought seriously about this problem.

Hume's arguments have been the subject of many philosophical works as various authors have attempted to solve the problems he raised. Many reluctantly accept Hume's skeptical conclusion that there is no logical reason to support the view that constant conjunctions that have been observed in the past will continue to hold in the future. Nevertheless, most people also believe that genuine causal connections can be understood as something more than the habit of expecting repetitions of these same conjunctions.

We should understand that Hume was not recommending that we cease our causal investigations or that we give up causal reasoning. He thought this would not only be foolish but also psychologically impossible. A number of philosophers and scientists have adopted the following pragmatic stand in view of Hume's analysis:

Although we have no logical reason for believing that the future will
resemble the past, if it does, then our causal judgments that are based on

observations of continued regularities (using controlled experiments and reasoning of the sort recommended by Mill) will be the ones that provide useful and important information about the world. If the world changes in such a way that the present regularities no longer hold, no other method now available can give us any better information about what regularities—if any—we can expect in the future.

You may have noticed that in this presentation of Hume's analysis of "*A* is the cause of *B*," a cause is understood to be a "causally sufficient condition." This is expressed in the third statement of his analysis: "Whenever *A* occurs, *B* occurs." Causally sufficient conditions are sometimes called "deterministic" causes. A **deterministic cause,** unlike a probabilistic cause, inevitably results in its effect.

Determinism is the philosophical principle that everything that happens is a result of causally sufficient conditions. Determinism does not say that we know, or even that we will someday know, what these conditions are in each case. Determinism is a view about what the world is like, not a view about the knowledge we can obtain about that world. According to the principle of determinism, the fundamental causal structure of the world is deterministic, and references to probabilistic causes reflect our ignorance of some part of the causal complex—some "hidden factors" that, if understood, would complete the causal story.

Whether all fundamental causes are deterministic is another difficult—and, as yet, unanswered—philosophical question. If the causal structure of the universe is fundamentally deterministic, then our talk about probabilistic causes may simply reflect our ignorance of unknown, deterministic causal factors. In Hume's time, the most advanced science of the day was Newtonian physics. Newton's genius had formulated an impressive set of deterministic causes: expressed in his Law of Universal Gravitation and his three Laws of Motion. In view of Newton's successes, it was widely believed that future scientific advances would uncover more and more deterministic causes in cases where previous knowledge had been probabilistic.

Consider our view that smoking is a probabilistic cause of lung cancer. It is certainly possible that further scientific investigation may uncover a hidden factor, such as a genetic property present in some but absent in others, that predisposes humans to lung cancer when they smoke heavily. Medical scientists might someday be able to specify a set of individually necessary and jointly sufficient causal conditions for the disease.

Nevertheless, in some areas of modern science, particularly quantum physics, the best theories available not only lack deterministic causes at the most fundamental level but also could not even accommodate the discovery of "hidden factors." This point is difficult to understand without an appropriate background knowledge of quantum physics. Nevertheless, it is so important that some scientists have considered it the most revolutionary feature of modern science—comparable to Newton's great discoveries in the seventeenth century. Many scientists hope that eventually a different—and, to their minds, a more satisfactory—deterministic theory of quantum physics will be discovered. But they recognize that the present theory cannot be expanded or modified to become a deterministic theory without giving up some firmly held principles about causality, such as *an effect cannot occur earlier than its cause*. The finest experimental results currently available cannot be accounted for by a deterministic causal theory. The most advanced theory of physics in the twenty-first century depends on probabilistic knowledge.

Thus, quantum physics differs from medical science. Medical scientists have discovered that specific microorganisms are causally responsible for such diseases as cholera, plague, tuberculosis, and Legionnaires' disease, and that deficiencies in specific substances (vitamins) are causally responsible for such diseases as beriberi, rickets, and scurvy. Medical theory is heavily committed to the discovery of such specific causal agents, which when present or absent—against a standard background of necessary causal conditions—are sufficient for the occurrence of specific diseases. In other words, the history of medical science can be viewed in terms of searches for deterministic causes and success in finding such causes. With the ever-growing importance of understanding the genetic component of disease, however, this deterministic approach might be modified. Biologists now know that genetic changes (mutations) can be caused by cosmic radiation, which is subject to the indeterministic laws of quantum phenomena.

Probabilistic causation would remain important even if all fundamental causes were deterministic, for at any point in the investigation of a subject area, probabilistic knowledge may be the most accurate or accessible knowledge available. Furthermore, the search for deterministic causes is frequently guided and motivated by the observance of probabilistic (statistical) regularities. In the practice of science as well as in everyday life, we continue to be concerned with probabilistic causes.

One final remark: Hume's worries about causation are not solved by replacing a deterministic notion of causality with a probabilistic one. His arguments apply to conjunctions that hold with probability as well as to constant conjunctions.

VI. CAUSAL FALLACIES

Mistakes in causal reasoning, or causal fallacies, can arise when some important aspect of the causal relationship is ignored or distorted. Hume's analysis of the causal relationship maintains that causes are regularly connected with their effects. This feature of the causal relationship holds whether we are talking about causally necessary conditions, causally sufficient conditions, proximate causes, or probabilistic causes. We expect causes and their effects to occur together with some degree of regularity. Hume also maintained that no cause occurs later in time than its effect. The following three causal fallacies normally occur because of insufficient attention to or misunderstanding of these features.

1. CONFUSING COINCIDENTAL RELATIONSHIPS
WITH CAUSES (*POST HOC*)

Sometimes people focus on the second standard feature just mentioned and infer that *A* is the cause of *B* simply because they observe that event *B* occurs later than event *A*. To reason this way is to commit a causal fallacy. The fallacy is common enough to be given the special name *post hoc,* which is derived from the first two words of the Latin expression that describes the fallacious pattern of reasoning: *Post hoc, ergo propter hoc* ("after this, therefore because of this").

Ordinarily, we would not say that one event caused another merely on the grounds that the second occurred later than the first. We constantly observe successions of events without drawing causal connections between them. But sometimes when the events are striking, unusual, or important to us, we mistake a coincidence for a true causal connection, particularly if such a connection fits roughly within some accepted causal framework. If, for example, an air conditioning unit breaks down the day after it receives routine maintenance service, we might suspect that the tinkering of the person who worked on the unit was responsible. But to draw a causal conclusion on the basis of such evidence would be *post hoc.* Further investigation could show that, for example, a worn-out timing switch was the cause of the breakdown. Mechanical systems can go wrong in many ways that are unrelated to the maintenance work, so drawing a causal conclusion would be premature in this case. In our critical moments—when we are free from the annoyance of having to pay for a second service call—we realize that the observed succession of events might be coincidental. *Post hoc* fallacies arise under circumstances similar to those that promote hasty generalizations. When a conclusion is attractive to us, laziness, prejudice, fear, hope, or some other strong psychological motivation tempts us to accept it without evidence. Conclusions of *post hoc* reasoning can turn out to be true, but reasoning *post hoc* does not justify such conclusions.

Post hoc reasoning underlies many superstitious beliefs. If, for example, you eat eggs for breakfast when you usually have cereal and then perform brilliantly on a math examination, it would be a *post hoc* fallacy to conclude that the different breakfast was the cause of your performance. If you receive bad news on three successive Wednesdays and conclude that Wednesday is your unlucky day (that this day of the week somehow causes you to receive bad news), you are committing a *post hoc* fallacy. An article in the *New York Times Magazine* citied numerous disturbing events that occurred during August, the traditional month for presidential vacations, and asked "What is it about August?" The fallacy was part of the humor of the piece. Not much effort is required to recall momentous events that have occurred in other months of the year.

Another source of *post hoc* fallacies is a belief that effects resemble their causes— or that a cause must somehow contain whatever is in its effect. Mill was especially scornful of this mistake, which he considered an undesirable holdover from crude medieval attempts to reason scientifically by reading signs present in nature. He maintained that proponents of the resemblance theory of causation might as well argue that pepper had to be in the cook because there was pepper in the soup. Belief in the efficacy of many folk medicines is based on this kind of reasoning, which is associated with the teachings of Paracelsus (born c. 1493). Herbal cures were selected on the basis of resemblance between the form of plant and the afflicted part of the body. The leaves of the wildflower Hepatica (Liverwort) are shaped something like the human liver, so the plant was used as a cure for liver ailments. The leaves of Pulmonaria (Lungwort) resemble human lungs and were, therefore, considered to be an effective lung medicine. The "medicine" seemed to work in some cases. Because, however, many human illnesses clear up regardless of treatment—or lack of treatment—we should not believe a cure has been found simply because improvement follows treatment in a few cases.

Controlled experiments are the best way to distinguish coincidental from causal relationships. When a controlled experiment is impossible or impractical, we should continue to observe to determine whether the connection, for example between "medicine" and cure, persists. After smoking tobacco failed to prevent the plague at Eton in the seventeenth century, for example, observers realized that the connection between using tobacco and avoiding the plague had been coincidental. Mill understood that it was important to use his methods repeatedly and in conjunction with one another to test suspected causal connections. His views are reflected in the modern use of controlled experiments and observations. Besides checking for repetition of connection between suspected cause and effect, controlled experiments are designed to eliminate factors irrelevant to the causal process. In the absence of opportunities for checking the persistence of regularities, critical thinkers want to suspend judgment about whether a connection is coincidental or causal. Consider, for example, Exercise 12 in Exercise Set 5.3 that linked black raspberries to cancer prevention. In the absence of a strong medical theory to support such a connection, it would be wise to conduct further studies.

2. IGNORING A COMMON CAUSE

Even when observation and experiment assure us that a regular connection exists between a suspected cause and some effect, we need to distinguish among various direct and indirect causal connections. For example, when archaeologists excavate sites in Central and North America, they find that sites that contain pottery frequently have fragments of grinding stones (used for grinding corn) as well. But they do not conclude that the presence of pottery causes the presence of grinding stones or that the presence of grinding stones causes the presence of pottery. To do so just because the two are found in conjunction with one another would be committing **the fallacy of ignoring a common cause.** Pottery fragments and grinding stone fragments are not directly causally related to one another. Their joint occurrence is a result of an underlying common cause, namely human habitation of those sites.

Regular associations that depend on a common cause occur often; thus, if we ignore this possibility, we are liable to commit a causal fallacy. "Symptoms" often refers to regularly associated events that depend on an underlying common cause. Measles—a serious disease now controlled by vaccination—presents itself in the patient with red spots and a high fever. But the underlying cause is the measles virus, and merely treating the spots or the fever will not cure the disease. In medicine and medical research, ignoring a common cause can have serious consequences for the physical well-being of humans.

A well-known common cause, namely, a sharp drop in atmospheric pressure, accounts for the regular association between stormy weather and falling barometers. Another example of a common cause occurred when the tips of many pine trees in a major U.S. city turned brown. Investigation by the forestry department showed that this happened not because of infection spreading from one tree to others but as the result of an atmospheric inversion that allowed atmospheric fluorides to concentrate in the foliage of the pines.

When two or more events are causally related to one another through an underlying common cause, they are sometimes said to be indirectly causally related. "Indirect causal relationship" also refers, however, to the relationship between events that are part of the same causal chain but are separated from one another by one or more intervening links. In this latter sense, for example, we say that the "want of a horseshoe nail" indirectly caused the loss of the battle.

When adequate causal theories are available, they can be used to identify common causes and to distinguish these from their multiple and indirectly related effects. Given what we know about measles and about weather, for instance, we know that treating the symptoms will not cure the disease and that placing barometers in pressurized cabins will not prevent storms. But sorting out symptoms from common causes in many other situations requires the use of controlled experiments or other sophisticated forms of inductive reasoning. As we have seen, the results of controlled experiments themselves are sometimes puzzling enough to suggest a common cause may be at work. In the late 1970s, for example, a well-conducted retrospective study of more than 100,000 women found that those who smoked more than 25 cigarettes a day were at four times the risk of suicide as nonsmokers. Here, it is reasonable to suspect the operation of a common cause, such as anxiety or depression, that would lead both to cigarette smoking and to suicidal tendencies. Further investigation is certainly appropriate in such cases.

3. CONFUSING CAUSE AND EFFECT

A third causal fallacy, the **fallacy of confusing cause and effect,** arises when evidence supports a direct causal relationship between two types of events, but the *direction* of the relationship is not given adequate consideration. An example of this mistake occurs in one of Graham Greene's spy novels, *The Human Factor.* In one part of the book, two secret agents discuss a method to "eliminate" a colleague suspected of leaking secrets. One of the agents suggests using peanuts as a weapon and offers the following account to his baffled coworker:

> "Peanuts when they go bad produce a mold. Caused by *aspergillus flavus*—but you can forget the name. It's not that important, and I know you were never any good at Latin."
>
> "Go on, for heaven's sake."
>
> "To make it easy for you I'll concentrate on the mold. The mold produces a group of highly toxic substances known collectively as aflatoxin. And aflatoxin is the answer to our little problem."

The condescending spy in this episode mistakes a cause for its effect. The peanuts do not produce a mold when they go bad. The mold attacks the peanuts and is the cause of their going bad. The mold, in other words, is a cause—not an effect—of spoiled peanuts.

Because effects cannot precede their causes, paying careful attention to the *temporal order* of two events that have a direct causal relationship to one another helps to avoid this fallacy. For example, it is well known that the rise in the incidence of lung cancer and the increase in cigarette smoking have been regularly connected over the past fifty years. Most people believe there is a direct causal relationship between these two events—the increase in tobacco use is the cause, and the increase in cancer is the effect. However, some people have said that the rise in the incidence of lung cancer may have caused the increase in smoking, because having cancer may create a craving for tobacco. This seems to be a case of the fallacy of confusing cause and effect, for most smokers who develop lung cancer have smoked heavily for years. Their smoking habits were fixed long before they contracted the disease. No evidence indicates that people who contracted lung cancer increased their smoking thereafter.

Although the question of which came first—smoking or lung cancer—seems clear, in many situations sorting earlier from later parts of a causal complex is not simple. For example, archaeological evidence shows that certain areas of the southwestern United States were occupied for a prolonged period by one group of people (Anasazi) whose abrupt disappearance was succeeded by the presence of a different ethnic group (Athabascans). The agreed-upon temporal order of this series of events is subject to various causal interpretations. The invasion of the newcomers might have caused the former residents to abandon these areas, or the influx of the newcomers might have been caused, or partially caused, by the decision of the former residents to depart, thus leaving an area open for occupation.

In some cases, further observation or controlled experimentation that attempts to interfere with some part of the causal process can enable us to determine the direction of a causal relationship. On the basis of many studies of the development of lung cancer and the smoking history of victims of this disease, we can reject the view that cancer causes an increase in smoking.

In their studies of prehistoric pueblos in the Southwest, archaeologists look for evidence of warfare and of unfavorable conditions for agriculture, as well as for other evidence—such as the exact dates of leaving and arrival of the different groups—that would help them to decide whether invasion by new people was the cause of pueblo abandonment or an effect of the abandonment.

Although no effect can precede its cause, the complexity of many causal relationships hampers a proper causal ordering of all their components. Multiple interacting causes reinforce and counteract one another to such a degree that isolating the various parts in order to observe or control them separately may not be feasible. In such situations, awareness of the possibility of an underlying common cause, or of the possibility that cause and effect may be confused with one another, can at least prevent us from accepting inadequately supported causal statements.

4. GENETIC FALLACY: REASONS AND CAUSES

Genesis means *origin*. The **genetic fallacy** is a mistake in reasoning that occurs when some factor concerning the origin or causal source of a belief is offered or accepted as evidence for its truth.

Unlike the three causal fallacies just considered, the genetic fallacy does not involve misunderstanding the evidence required to support a causal statement. To avoid the genetic fallacy, we need to understand the differences between the cause of holding a belief and the evidence for the truth of that belief.

In a logically correct argument, the premises that state the evidence are reasons for accepting the conclusion as true. That is to say, if the premises are true, and the argument is a correct inductive argument, the conclusion is probably true. In correct deductive arguments, the conclusion cannot be false if the premises are all true. Sometimes, however, beliefs are not based on reasons but arise from various psychological factors. These factors include devotion to the person from whom the belief was acquired, social pressures to conform to some set of beliefs, and the implantation of a belief at an early age. Any of these factors can be a causal source of a belief and can be cited in an explanation of why someone holds the belief. They do not, however, constitute evidence for the truth of the belief.

An adult who is afraid of the dark may believe that he will suffocate if he is alone in a dark room. This belief may be the result of being locked in a closet as a child. The frightening childhood experience is part of a (correct) causal explanation of that person's fear of the dark. We have good evidence that cruel treatment of children causes fears that persist into adulthood. However, none of this is evidence that being in the dark will suffocate the person. To confuse the causal explanation of the belief with reasons (in the sense of evidence) for its truth is to commit the genetic fallacy.

Fallacious appeals to authority, fallacious appeals to consensus, and fallacious *ad hominem* arguments can be considered variants of the genetic fallacy, for they involve mistaking some feature of the genesis of a statement (the person who is its source) as evidence for (or against) its truth. If you argue that your senator's description of some proposed legislation is false because he is a pompous windbag, then your so-called argument is a fallacious, abusive *ad hominem,* and you also commit the genetic fallacy. (This is so even if the windbag's account is in fact false.)

5. CONFUSING THE HARM OR BENEFITS THAT RESULT FROM HOLDING A BELIEF WITH EVIDENCE FOR IT

Closely related to accepting or rejecting a statement because of its source (rather than because of evidence) is accepting or rejecting one because of its consequences—the harm or good that might be caused by holding the belief. This fallacy can occur when our desires interfere with our reasons for belief. Suppose, for example, you are a heavy smoker and you want very much to continue smoking. If you can make yourself believe, despite all the evidence, that cigarette smoking will not harm you, then why should you give up smoking? Holding the belief that smoking will not harm you has the apparent benefit of continuing your pleasure in smoking, and because of that, you believe it. The situation just described is a form of wishful thinking. Of course, smoking is harmful, whether you believe it or not, and continuing to smoke cannot be counted overall as a benefit. In this case, confusing—or replacing—the apparent benefit of holding a belief with evidence for the belief can be dangerous as well as fallacious.

Swindlers and confidence men offer preposterous statements about easy money schemes and depend on the greed of their "marks" to override any evidence against the truth of those statements. If we very much want the prize that would result if a promise were true, we find it more difficult to pay attention to evidence against it.

Some fundamentalist religious groups have rejected Darwin's theory of evolution not because of evidence against it, but because they believe that if the biblical account of creation is not accepted as literal truth, the standards of morality will decline. Darwin's own cousin held similar views and wrote to him that she hoped he was wrong about evolution but that, if he was not, she hoped at least that people would not learn about his ideas. Although we may be legitimately concerned about the consequences of a statement concern for consequences should be kept distinct from evidence for it. Moreover, we should look for evidence that a belief will in fact have the consequences some fear it will have. The supposed relationship between the truth of evolutionary theory and a lapse in moral standards is hardly self-evident, for example.

Holding beliefs is not always cost free. If you believe that a friend is loyal, you enjoy a benefit. If someone presents you with evidence that the friend has betrayed you, you have a problem. If you admit that the friend has betrayed you, you pay the price of lost or diminished friendship. It is not hard to understand why you do not want to pay that price. But if you take avoiding that cost as a justification (in the sense of evidence) for denying the betrayal, you confuse the effect of holding a belief with a reason for the belief, and you engage in fallacious reasoning.

To avoid the genetic fallacy, we must distinguish the source of a belief from reasons for it. Similarly, we have to distinguish the resultant harm or benefit of holding a belief from reasons to avoid this fallacy of confusing the truth of a belief with possible consequences of its being true.

Before closing the subject of causal fallacies, we should note that the fallacies described in this section treat only some of the most common errors in causal reasoning. Because of the complexity of causal arguments and of the many forms they take, causal reasoning can go wrong in a wide variety of ways. Being able to recognize the most common fallacies should help us to avoid the hazards of causal reasoning.

VII. REVIEW

The aims of chapter 5 have been to increase understanding of causal reasoning, to offer standards for assessing causal arguments, and to point out some common causal fallacies. New terminology included the names of Mill's five methods for discovering causes and justifying causal statements: the **Method of Agreement,** the **Method of Difference,** the **Joint Method of Agreement and Difference,** the **Method of Concomitant Variation,** and the **Method of Residues.** Look again at Section II, in which these methods are discussed, to be sure you are able to recognize examples of these methods.

In our discussion of the term *cause,* several types of causes were distinguished:

Necessary Causal Condition   "*A* is causally necessary for *B*" means that without *A, B* will not occur.

Sufficient Causal Condition   "*A* is causally sufficient for *B*" means that whenever *A* occurs, *B* will also occur.

Deterministic Cause   This cause is a sufficient causal condition.

Probabilistic Cause   *A* is a probabilistic cause for *B* if the presence of *A* increases the probability that *B* will occur.

Proximate Cause   This is the causal condition in a causal complex that is nearest in time or space to the event caused.

Another important concept is a **controlled experiment.** In a controlled experiment, an experimental group is subjected to a suspected causal agent and a control group is not. The controlled experiment provides a context for the application of Mill's Joint Method of Agreement and Difference or the Method of Concomitant Variations. The technique is especially valuable when we can be reasonably confident that the control group and the experimental group differ with respect to the suspected causal agent but are similar in most other relevant respects. In one type of controlled experiment, the **randomized experimental study,** the control group and the experimental group are selected to form representative samples of a population. Thus, it is reasonable to infer by inductive generalization that what happens to these groups in the presence or absence of the suspected cause would also happen to the population they represent. Because it can be immoral to subject humans to unpleasant and possibly harmful causal agents, these randomized experimental studies are often performed on experimental animals. If we want to infer what would happen to humans on the basis of these animal studies, we need additional analogical arguments.

Another type of controlled study is a **prospective** (forward-looking) **study,** in which an experimental group that has already been exposed to the suspected cause is matched with a control group that has not been exposed. The experimenter then watches to see what happens in each group. These experiments are inferior to randomized experiments for demonstrating causal statements because there is reason to believe that the experimental and control groups are not representative samples. Nevertheless, these studies provide valuable information. Because humans self-select themselves into the population from which an experimental group is drawn, these studies avoid some of the moral objections to performing randomized experiments on humans. They also circumvent the need for additional analogical arguments to draw conclusions about humans.

Retrospective (backward-looking) **studies** are another type of controlled study. In these, the experimental group is chosen from individuals who already exhibit the effect. A matched control group that lacks the effect is chosen, and the histories of the two groups are examined to see whether a difference in past exposure to the suspected causal factor can be found. These studies suffer from many of the problems of prospective studies and introduce additional bias into the samples. They are the weakest form of controlled study, but because they give quicker results than prospective studies, they can provide useful information, such as early warnings about the dangers of some medical treatment. They can also be used to gain information for conducting a more thorough prospective study.

Causal fallacies discussed in this chapter include the following:

Post Hoc   *Post hoc* is the fallacy of arguing that *A* is the cause of *B* just because *B* comes later than *A*. A relationship that is coincidental is judged—on the basis of insufficient evidence of a regular connection—to be causal. Many superstitious beliefs involve this fallacy.

The Fallacy of Ignoring a Common Cause   When evidence supports the view that there is a regular connection between two events or types of events, the nature of the connection must be investigated before making a causal judgment. *A* and *B* might be regularly connected through some common underlying cause *C*. In such cases, neither *A* nor *B* directly causes each other. Both *A* and *B* are effects of a common cause.

The Fallacy of Confusing Cause and Effect   When two events or types of events are regularly connected and do not result from a common cause, care must be taken to define which is cause and which is effect. Effects cannot occur earlier than their causes. In complex causal relationships, however, the temporal order of the various parts of the complex may be difficult to investigate.

Genetic Fallacy   This fallacy occurs whenever something about the genesis (origin, source, or cause) of a statement or a belief is taken as evidence for its truth.

Fallacy of Mistaking Some Consequence of a Belief with Evidence for It   The name describes the fallacy. In some instances, the fallacy involves wishful thinking.

Exercise Set 5.6

PART I

1. With new noninvasive imaging technology, researchers are able to observe formerly hidden features of the human brain in action. This has led to many new proposals about the relationships between brain and behavior.

   Lisa F. Barrett scanned brains of 58 volunteers and found that those with an amygdala (an area deep in the brain that serves as a kind of command center for many functions) that was larger than normal tended to socially interact more with family and friends. But Dr. Barrett warned that further study was needed to sort out whether socializing a lot created a larger amygdala or whether the larger amygdala led to greater sociability.

   What fallacy was Dr. Barrett avoding?

2. InstaPundit blogger G. Reynolds writes that the government tries to increase the size of the middle class by providing college education and home ownership to people who haven't earned and saved for these things. But he says that owning homes and attending college do not cause people to enter the middle class; these are merely markers of qualities such as self-discipline and delayed gratification that allow people to enter and stay in the middle class.

   What fallacy does Prof. Reynolds accuse government subsidizers of committing?

3. A retrospective study of 163,000 patients who entered the hospital for heart bypasses or to remove damaged sections of lungs or colons showed that patients who were not operated on the day they were admitted were more likely to develop serious infections such as pneumonia. For bypass patients, the infection rate was 6 percent for same-day surgery, 9 percent for delays of two to five days and 18 percent for delays of six to ten days.

   If we say on the basis of this evidence that extended waiting time for surgery is the cause of the higher rate of infection, what causal fallacy might we be committing?

PART II. Identify any fallacies involved in the following arguments:

1. The night before my last math exam, I partied with friends instead of studying. I pulled an *A* on that one, so I won't be studying for this one either and count on another *A*.

2. If you look at any study of "wealthiest Americans," you can see that most of their wealth comes not from wages or salaries but from ownership of stocks, bonds, and real estate. Therefore, if you aspire to membership in this group, you should begin building your stock portfolio as soon as possible.

3. If you want a good catch on your next fishing trip, wear a copper bracelet. It always works for me.

4. Even though scientists are always searching for signs of life in other parts of the universe, they won't find any. If there were extra-terrestrial life, it would mean that we are not the unique creation of the Almighty.

5. It has been widely observed that when young children who are usually well behaved become irritable and difficult, they exhibit the symptoms of a cold or viral infection the next day. It is clear that their misbehavior causes these illnesses.

6. During the looting and rioting in Detroit in the summer of 1967, the items most commonly stolen were color television sets. Some people argued that one way to prevent such riots would be to distribute free color television sets to those who want them.

7. Tom is being reasonable when he regards all his co-workers with suspicion for fear they are trying to take over his responsibilities. After all, he grew up in a tough situation and had to fight for everything he has achieved. He became convinced at an early age that others were out to get him.

8. Statistics show that in the United States during the past 50 years, the amount of greenhouse gas and the state of public health have both increased dramatically. We can conclude that greenhouse gases have been good for public health.

9. A number of legislators are opposed to legalized abortions on the grounds that women undergoing abortions may be damaged psychologically. We can dismiss the truth of their statements, however, for these legislators are Catholic, and everyone knows the Catholic Church is opposed to abortion.

10. A football coach trying to bring his team out of a slump studies the statistics of past games. His research on several teams over a number of years shows that many more passes and attempted passes are almost always made by the losing team than by the winning team. From this information, the coach infers that he can make his team win by restricting the number of passes they throw.

11. Since modern civilization came into being through Christianity, it would not survive once its supernatural basis were removed.

—Evelyn Waugh

12. Computers cannot really *think,* because if we were to admit that there are thinking machines, that would mean we humans might be mere machines as well, a very degrading situation.

13. In the biblical account of the expulsion of the First Family from Paradise, Eve took a bite of the forbidden fruit before offering it to Adam. Thus Eve is the cause of the fall from Paradise.

PART III. The following examples are taken from Friedrich Nietzsche's *Twilight of the Idols,* in which he discusses errors in causal reasoning. Identify the fallacy that Nietzsche criticizes in each of these examples.

1. Everybody knows the book of the famous Cornaro in which he recommends his slender diet as a recipe for a long and happy life—a virtuous one too . . . . The worthy Italian thought his diet was the *cause* of his long life, whereas the precondition for a long life, the extraordinary slowness of his metabolism, the consumption of so little, was the cause of his slender diet.

2. The church and morality say: "A generation, a people, are destroyed by license and luxury." [I] say: when a people approaches destruction, when it degenerates physiologically, then license and luxury *follow* from this (namely, the craving for ever stronger and more frequent stimulation, as every exhausted nature knows it).

3. This young man turns pale early and wilts; his friends say: that is due to this or that disease. I say: that he became diseased, that he did not resist the disease, was already the effect of an impoverished life or hereditary exhaustion.

4. The newspaper reader says: this [political] party destroys itself by making such a mistake. [I] say: a party which makes such mistakes has reached its end; it has lost its sureness of instinct.

PART IV. In each of the following, identify the mistake in causal reasoning that is pointed out or avoided.

1. Has sodium been getting a bum rap? For a decade, health organizations, government agencies, and physicians have urged everyone to cut back on the intake of all forms of sodium.

    R. Curtis Morris, Jr., of the University of San Francisco's General Clinical Research Center, thinks such recommendations may be wrong. "It has never been demonstrated," he says, "that any form of sodium other than sodium chloride [table salt] can raise blood pressure." This means, for example, that the sodium ingested as sodium bicarbonate in baked goods or antacids probably does not affect blood pressure and should not be lumped together on food labels with the sodium of sodium chloride.

—Scientific American, 258, 1988

2. Breast cancer patients are more likely to survive the disease if they have a happy, positive frame of mind than if they feel hopeless and depressed, according to a study by a team of scientists at the University of Pittsburgh and Yale University.

   [Dr. Sandra] Levy emphasized that the findings do not necessarily mean that cancer can be cured by making patients happy. The scientists don't know whether happy feelings cause longer survival, perhaps through an enhancing effect on the body's own healing process, or whether the patient's positive feelings are simply an effect, possibly resulting from an inherent stamina.

   —H. Pierce, *Pittsburgh Post-Gazette*

3. Women who had a greater severity of alcoholic symptoms were far more likely to experience depression compared to women who had lesser degrees of alcoholism. More important, the severity of symptoms of depression or alcohol misuse at the start of the study "predicted" the severity of the other, one year later. The relationship between depression and alcohol is quite strong, especially among women. When women experience symptoms of depression, they are at increased risk for alcohol dependence subsequently.

   This finding is important because many people, including health professionals, tend to view depression and alcoholism as separate problems, when in fact, they are related to one another.

   As for the association between depression and alcoholism, one explanation is that depression may, in part, stem from the continued depressive effects of alcohol while the person is drinking. Another factor contributing to the relationship between alcohol and depression can also be attributed to the environment in which the individual lives. Finally, the role of genetics must also be considered. Individuals may be vulnerable to both depression and alcoholism because of their genes.

   The positive relationship between alcohol and depression argues strongly for a comprehensive approach to treatment. This means not only paying attention to the problem of alcohol, but to also take into consideration the treatment of depression—which can call for anti-depressant medications and/or psychotherapy. Such a comprehensive approach will help to ensure a better outcome for the patient.

   —Isabel C. Murphy, *http://www.SoberRecovery.com*

4. A large (525 participants for four years and 184 more for eight years) prospective study established a significant link between hypertension (high blood pressure) and sleep-disordered breathing (SDB), or apnea, the most common sign of which is snoring.

   SDB occurred in 30 percent of hypertensive subjects. Treatment of apnea often improves blood pressure and ignoring apnea has been shown to increase cardiovascular mortality (death by heart attack). Whether SDB contributes to the onset of hypertension is unclear. Although researchers in the study controlled for body-mass index and other anthropomorphic measures (such as neck size and waist size), it is possible that obesity is the underlying cause of both SBD and hypertension.

—http.//www.RepiratoryReviews.com

5. [S. E. Hyman's] plagiarism charge [against Edmund Wilson] was nonsense. Wilson wrote the first American review of "The Waste Land"—after the poem had appeared in *The Dial* but before Eliot published the notes in the book edition which have guided interpreters ever since—and he wrote one of the first reviews anywhere of "Ulysses." Wilson did not borrow from anyone when he wrote those reviews because there was, at the time, no one to borrow from.

—Louis Menand, "Edmund Wilson's Critical Life," *The New Yorker*, 2005, September 8 and 15

6. Many social critics bemoan the gap in lifetime earnings between those who graduate from college and those who do not. They usually say that a lack of education contributes to the lower income. But Frieda A. Stahl writes in a letter to *The New York Times* that "the gap in college degrees is the outcome of the disparity in wealth, not the cause." She goes on to point out how ever-increasing college costs make a college education unaffordable for increasing numbers of students.

7. "Evidently, children who've been raised with night-lights in their rooms end up having some vision problems. Their eyes don't get enough rest is the hypothesis."

"Or maybe," Rebecca said, "the children don't see well to begin with, and there's some biological connection between fear of the dark and bad eyesight; ever thought of that?"

—A. Tyler, *Back When We Were Grownups*

Chapter Six

PROBABILITIES AND INDUCTIVE LOGIC

I. INTRODUCTION

In an inductive argument, true premises and a correct form make it probable that the conclusion is true as well. We know that inductive arguments vary in strength. Evidence presented in some make it highly probable that their conclusions are true; others provide a lesser degree of support. The probabilities that we are talking about here refer to the degree of support premises provide for a conclusion, not to the conclusion itself, even though we sometimes (loosely) say, "Given the evidence, the conclusion is probably true." So far, we have relied on a common-sense understanding of the words *probable* and *probability.* In this chapter, we take a closer look at the concept of *probability* and its relationship to inductive logic.

We have noted that the statistical premiss of a statistical syllogism can be stated numerically, as in "Ninety percent of all first-year students are state residents." On the basis of such information, and assuming that the reference class embodies all relevant information, it is natural to say "With a probability of 90 percent, or 0.9, a randomly selected first-year student [for example, Maria] is a state resident." When we want to invest money or place a bet, we have a practical interest in knowing how to assess probabilistic support in a precise, numerical way. Consider, for example, the sentence "A blind draw from a standard deck of cards will result in a nonheart" (that is, a spade, a diamond, or a club will be drawn). We can argue for that conclusion using the following statistical syllogism:

> Most cards in a standard deck are nonheart cards.
> *a* is a card drawn "blind" from a standard deck.
> _____
> *a* is a nonheart card.

This argument is reasonably strong. If, however, we are interested in placing a fair *bet* that a nonheart will be drawn, we prefer to assign a numerical probability to "*a* is a nonheart." For this purpose, we use background information about standard decks of cards. A deck has 52 cards divided evenly among four suits (13 hearts and 39 others that are not hearts). Thus, the first premiss can be stated quantitatively: "The nonhearts are $^{39}/_{52}$ (that is, ¾ or 75 percent) of the cards." With this information—which encompasses all relevant available information when a card is drawn blindly—we can say that the probability a nonheart will be drawn is 0.75, or ¾.

This probability determines proper betting odds. In an even-money bet, the amount won or lost is equal to the "stake" (the amount put at risk). An even-money bet is proper when, as in the toss of a fair coin or the draw of a red card from a standard deck, two equally likely outcomes are possible. If you win such a bet, your stake is returned along with an equal amount, so that you double your money. If you lose, you forfeit your original stake. In such cases, the odds are even, or 1 to 1. When the probabilities of various outcomes are not equal, the betting odds can be altered in an appropriate way to assure fairness. For example, betting odds of 3 to 1, in which the return for a winning bet is three times the stake, are fair for an outcome with a probability of ¼, or 0.25. In such a case, there are three times as many ways of losing as there are of winning. *Odds* refers to the difference in favor of one side and against the other. For an outcome with a probability of ¼, such as blindly drawing a heart from a standard deck, the odds are 3 to 1 *against* winning. A payoff of 3 to 1 balances this disadvantage and makes the bet fair. For an outcome with a probability of ¾ (drawing a nonheart), the odds against winning are only 1 to 3, so an accordingly smaller payoff balances this advantage.

We often use numerical probabilities to assess the strength of inductive generalizations. We have noted that by increasing the sample size, we can reduce the margin of error while retaining the same confidence level in the conclusion of an inductive generalization. Alternatively, by increasing the sample size and retaining the same margin of error, we can increase the confidence level. The confidence level can be understood as the minimum probability that arguing in this way will lead to a true conclusion. Under some circumstances, we can state these probabilities numerically. In one example, we looked at a random sample of 100 students to predict voting behavior. Based on the information that 60 percent of the sample planned to vote for the Liberals, we concluded, with a confidence level of 0.95, that between 50 percent and 70 percent of the student population would vote for the Liberals. Assigning this confidence level is equivalent to saying that the use of this statistical method of reasoning will lead to a true conclusion at least 95 percent of the time. Probabilities play an important role in judging the outcomes of controlled studies, for as we have seen, such experiments use information about what happens in the experimental and control groups to tell us what probably would happen in populations.

We know that the properties of random samples rarely match exactly the properties of the populations from which they are selected. But within a margin of error, samples should resemble the population most of the time. Let us look at some examples that involve tossing a fair coin and counting the number of times it comes up heads and tails. Begin a series of tosses. Stop after five tosses. This series is your sample. Suppose the sample contains no heads (TTTTT). This does not happen often, but it is possible. Table 6.1 displays all 32 possible outcomes of a series of five tosses. Only one of these contains no heads. When the numbers involved are not large, we can display all the possible arrangements and count the favorable cases. Alternatively, the mathematical theory of combinatorials provides a formula for calculating the number of possible combinations of x things taken n at a time: x^n. Since we are concerned with two things (HT) taken five at a time, the number of possible combinations is 2^5, or 32.

By counting cases, we can see that the probability of getting no heads in five tosses of a fair coin is ⅟₃₂ (slightly more than 3 percent). Your sample of five tosses of a coin that resulted in all tails is said to be **statistically significant** at the 0.05 level because it is the kind of sample you would expect less than 5 percent of the time with a fair coin. Statistical significance is obviously dependent on sample size. In a series of two tosses of a fair coin, an outcome of no heads would *not* be significant at the 0.05 level—heads fail to turn up about 25 percent of the time (HH, HT, TH, TT).

Table 6.1
Outcomes of five tosses of a fair coin

There are thirty-two possible outcomes:

5 Heads	4 Heads, 1 Tail	3 Heads, 2 Tails	2 Heads, 3 Tails	1 Head, 4 Tails	5 Tails
HHHHH	HHHHT	HHHTT	TTTHH	TTTTH	TTTTT
	HHHTH	HHTHT	TTHTH	TTTHT	
	HHTHH	HHTTH	TTHHT	TTHTT	
	HTHHH	HTTHH	THHTT	THTTT	
	THHHH	HTHHT	THTTH	HTTTT	
		HTHTH	THTHT		
		THTHH	HTHTT		
		THHHT	HTTTH		
		THHTH	HTTHT		
		TTHHH	HHTTT		
1	5	10	10	5	1

Statistical significance is an important concept in scientific studies because statistically significant results can occur for different reasons. In the first place, a sample could be the sort that occurs infrequently. Improbable things do happen; a series of five tails in five tosses of a fair coin is a somewhat improbable occurrence. In the second place, however, the unusual outcome could indicate a mistaken assumption about the population from which the sample is taken. Perhaps the assumption that the coin is fair is incorrect.

Although traditionally a criterion of statistical significance at the 0.05 level (corresponding to a 95 percent confidence level) is adopted for many scientific studies, use of statistical significance at the 0.01 level is also common. A result is statistically significant at the 0.01 level if the probability of obtaining such a result is less than $\frac{1}{100}$, or 1 percent. A series of ten tosses of a fair coin that results in no heads has a probability of less than $\frac{1}{1000}$. A sample composed of such a series would be statistically significant at the 0.001 level and could be used to challenge the assumption that the coin is fair.

A branch of mathematics, called *the probability calculus,* is the basis of statistical reasoning. It provides rules for calculating unknown probabilities when some probabilities are known. If we know, for example, that the probability of obtaining a head on a single toss of a fair coin is ½, then we can use the mathematical theory of probability to calculate the probability of obtaining all heads on two, three, or more tosses of a fair coin. Because the method of calculating unknown probabilities on the basis of known probabilities is a part of mathematics, it belongs properly to deductive logic rather than to inductive logic. However, the probability calculus has such important applications for inductive reasoning that all serious studies of inductive logic include some treatment of probabilities.

The mathematical theory of probability was developed during the seventeenth century in two different places to solve two different types of problems. On the European continent, where gambling with cards and dice was a major form of amusement for the nobility, an interest in setting fair betting odds motivated probability studies.

What does *probability* mean in such a situation? Most games of chance assume a set of equally possible alternatives (for example, each card is equally likely to be drawn from a deck; each face on a die has an equal chance of showing) and identify *probability* with the **ratio of favorable to possible outcomes**. In coin tossing, if the coin is fair, there are two equally possible outcomes: heads or tails. Either can be chosen as the favorable outcome. The ratio of favorable to possible outcomes in a fair coin toss is therefore ½. In dice games, each die has six sides. Assuming the die is balanced, the outcome of a particular face showing in a roll of a single die is ⅙. In card games, a standard deck contains 52 cards divided into four suits, each containing 13 cards. The probability of blindly drawing a particular single card from a well-shuffled deck is ¹⁄₅₂; of drawing any card of a particular suit, ¹³⁄₅₂ (¼); of drawing a particular denomination, such as an ace, ⁴⁄₅₂ (¹⁄₁₃).

Remember that the mathematical calculus of probability is used to calculate probabilities on the basis of some initially known probabilities. The method of counting cases can be used for solving some simple probability problems, such as calculating the probability of throwing two sixes on a single throw of a pair of fair dice. Considerable mathematical skill is required, however, to use the known probability of obtaining a six on a single toss of a fair die to determine how many times a pair of dice must be tossed to yield a probability equal to or greater than ½ of throwing at least one double six. In working out answers to problems such as this—posed by the Chevalier de Méré—Pascal, Fermat, and other French mathematicians constructed the foundations of the mathematical theory of probability. The usefulness of their results goes far beyond helping gamblers to assess fair payoffs. The techniques developed to solve de Méré's problem are also used, for example, to figure out the relationship between size of sample, margin of error, and confidence level in experimental studies.

At about the same time that an interest in gambling prompted French mathematicians to develop probability theory, a different interest motivated probability studies in England. There, the problem was not how to figure fair betting odds for games of chance but rather to determine the fair costs of insurance to cover burial expenses. This was the beginning of **actuarial science**—the calculation of risks and associated insurance premiums.

The Great Plague struck London in 1664. Previous epidemics of this disease (bubonic plague, sometimes called "the black death") had wiped out between one-fourth and three-fourths of the population. Although people did not know how to prevent the plague, when it arrived this time, they formed associations to share the burden of funeral and burial expenses. Even after the plague ended, interest in this type of insurance continued. To determine the fair costs of membership in burial associations, it was necessary to know, for example, the probability that a prospective member would survive another five, ten, fifteen, or twenty years. The gamblers' understanding of *probability* as a ratio of favorable to possible outcomes was not appropriate in these circumstances. Years of life are not dealt like cards from a deck, with any year considered an equally possible year for death to occur. A different concept of probability was required.

Probability in this actuarial context is concerned with the observed **relative frequency** with which events of a certain type occur. Information on the ages at which death had occurred for persons living in various areas who were engaged in assorted occupations was available in church records. Burial associations compiled the information in "mortality tables," which were used to determine the relative frequency with which persons in given situations survived to reach various ages. On the basis of the information in a mortality table, for example, it could be observed that 90 percent of the 25-year-old carpenters living in London during a specified period of time had survived their 30th birthdays. A burial association might then use this information to assign a probability of 0.9 that Hawkins, a 25-year-old carpenter from London, would be able to pay dues in the association for at least five years and could be charged accordingly for his five-year membership.

Insurance companies still use mortality tables to figure the probabilities that determine the cost of life-insurance premiums. The information in modern tables is far more extensive than the data contained in seventeenth-century tables. Similar tables, based on records of automobile ownership and accidents, determine automobile-insurance premiums. Records show, for example, that males under 25 years of age have more accidents than females in the same age category. Before insurance companies were challenged on the basis of sex discrimination, they had used this information to charge young male drivers correspondingly higher rates. Health-insurance costs also are based on actuarial tables that record the frequency of various illnesses and the costs associated with their treatment.

From these historical examples, we see that *probability* has at least two different meanings: the ratio of favorable to other equally possible outcomes, and the relative frequency of events of a particular type in some reference class of events. Both senses of *probability* lend themselves naturally to **quantitative** (numerical) expressions of probability values. When probabilities are expressed quantitatively, the probability of a sentence that describes an event is stated as a single real number (integer, fraction, or irrational number) between 0 (the lowest possible value) and 1 (the highest possible value). A probability can be expressed as a ratio between two numbers (¼), as a decimal fraction (0.25), or as a percentage (25 percent).

Probability is commonly used another way. Suppose, for example, you assign a very low probability to the statement that your grandmother will go to a Lady Gaga concert if she ever performs in her city; *probability* here does not mean *ratio of favorable to possible outcomes.* Your probability assignment is not based on the relative frequency of her attendance at Lady Gaga concerts. Instead, probability is used as a measure of the **degree to which it is rational to believe certain statements**. Your belief that your grandmother will not go to a Lady Gaga concert is based on your knowledge of her taste in music, her level of interest in pop culture, her dislike of crowded places, and a lot of information about how she prefers to spend her leisure time. The "degree of rational belief" concept of probability can be expressed numerically, but it does not lend itself so naturally to quantification as do the other meanings of *probability*. If numerical values are assigned to these degrees of rational belief, however, the mathematical rules for calculating unknown probabilities on the basis of known probabilities can be applied to them as well.*

II. THE RULES OF PROBABILITY

Before examining the mathematical rules, we should note that any assignment of a probability value is based on general background information or on evidence regarding specific conditions. Probability assignments are always **conditional** on the assumed truth of some such information. Thus, the probability of "A coin toss results in heads" being equal to ½ is conditional on the coin having the usual design and being balanced in the usual (fair) way. Using the examples considered in the last section, the probability of the 25-year-old carpenter's surviving his 30th birthday, for instance, is conditional on there being no evidence that he has a fatal disease; the low probability of your grandmother's attending the Lady Gaga concert is conditional on no one's offering her a large sum of money to go.

Statements of probability values are standardly written as follows:

$$\mathbf{Pr}(h \mid e) = n$$

which can be read, "The probability of a statement h, on evidence e, is equal to n." Sometimes, however, when it is clearly understood that a probability value is conditional on general background information and not on any special evidence, we write

$$\mathbf{Pr}(h) = n,$$

omitting any reference to evidence.

Rule 1

The value n in a sentence of the form

$$\mathbf{Pr}(h \mid e) = n$$

must be a single real number between 0 and 1, inclusive.

---

* For further discussion at an elementary level of different meanings of *probability* and related matters, see W. Salmon's *Foundations of Scientific Inference* (1967). For a more advanced, but still accessible, discussion, see M. C. Gulavotti's *Philosophical Introduction to Probability* (2005).

This rule expresses the convention of using 0 and 1 as the lower and upper limits of probability values and of assigning a unique probability value to any sentence in a given context. In view of rule 1, the following assignments of probabilities are improper:

Pr(Jones will win the Sweepstakes | Jones bought a Sweepstakes ticket) = −1.

(No probability values can be negative numbers.)

Pr(The Democrats will win the next presidential election) = 1.25.

(No probability value can be greater than 1.)

Rule 2

If h follows deductively from e, then

$$\mathbf{Pr}(h|e) = 1$$

To say that h follows deductively from e means that if e is true, then h must be true also. If this is so, then the probability of h, on evidence e, takes the highest possible value—that is, 1.

Examples

    a. **Pr**(Mrs. Jones is married | Mrs. Jones has a spouse) = 1.
    b. **Pr**(A black or a red card is drawn | A card is drawn from a standard deck) = 1.

In (b), e is "A card is drawn from a standard deck" and h is "A black or a red card is drawn." If a card is drawn from a standard deck, that card will be either black or red; no other possibilities exist. Thus, $n = 1$.

The probability value of 1 is not reserved exclusively for sentences that follow deductively from the available evidence. Sentences that are certainly true ("sure things") are assigned a probability equal to 1. The type of certainty involved here may be practical certainty, rather than certainty based on strict relationships of deductive logic.

Example

Pr(A six-year-old child, using materials found in an ordinary home workshop, cannot build a spaceship that will reach Mars) = 1.

Notice that no statement of evidence (e) is given in this example, but the probability is conditional on general background information. This sentence is so likely to be true on the basis of everything we know (i.e., it has "practical certainty") that the assignment of 1 is appropriate.

The lowest probability value (0) is assigned to sentences that either are inconsistent with the evidence sentence or are false as a matter of "practical certainty."

Examples

    a. $\mathbf{Pr}$(Five aces are drawn | Five cards are drawn from a standard deck, without replacing the cards in the deck after they are drawn) = 0.

Here, the sentence "Five aces are drawn" is inconsistent with evidence the cards are taken from a standard deck, without putting them back into the deck after they are drawn. (Standard decks contain only four aces.)

    b. $\mathbf{Pr}$(A human being, without any artificial aids, can leap tall buildings in a single bound) = 0.

Given our background knowledge of human physiology, we have "practical certainty" that this sentence is false.

Rule 3

If two sentences h_1 and h_2 are **mutually exclusive** (if they cannot both be true), then, on the same evidence in both cases, the probability that their *disjunction* (h_1 or h_2) is true is equal to the sum of their individual probabilities.

A **disjunction** is a compound sentence with *or*, or an equivalent connective, such as *unless*, as its major connective. Examples: "The coin came up heads, or the coin came up tails," or "The coin came up heads unless the coin came up tails." Symbolically, rule 3 can be expressed

$$\mathbf{Pr}(h_1 \text{ or } h_2 | e) = \mathbf{Pr}(h_1 | e) + \mathbf{Pr}\,(h_2 | e)$$

Although this rule is stated for two mutually exclusive sentences, it can be generalized to any number of mutually exclusive sentences. It allows us to calculate the unknown probability of a disjunction when each disjunct is incompatible with all the others and the probabilities of all the individual disjuncts are known.

Examples

    a. Using as evidence the claim that a fair die is tossed a single time, we know that the probability of throwing a six is equal to ⅙ and that the probability of throwing a two is ⅙. Since the sentences "A six is thrown" and "A two is thrown" are mutually exclusive for a single throw, rule 3 tells us that the probability of "A six is thrown, *or* a two is thrown" is (⅙ + ⅙), or after performing the addition (²⁄₆) and reducing the fraction, ⅓.

    b. Conditional on the same evidence as in (a), the probability of "A six *or* a two *or* a three is thrown" is equal to (⅙ + ⅙ + ⅙), or ½

    c. Conditional on the same evidence as in (a), what is the probability of "An even number of dots will show on the uppermost face of the die"? The sentence that an even number of dots will show means the same as "Either two dots or four dots or six dots will appear uppermost," and this sentence is a disjunction composed of three mutually exclusive disjuncts, each with a probability of ⅙. To calculate the probability of the disjunction, use rule 3 and add the individual probabilities: (⅙ + ⅙ + ⅙) = ½.

Rule 4

The probability of the **conjunction** of two sentences is equal to the probability of the first sentence multiplied by the probability of the second sentence on the condition that the first sentence is true.

A conjunction is a compound sentence with its major components connected by *and* or some other expression, such as *moreover* or a semicolon, which indicates that the sentence as a whole is true just in case all of its components are true. "A six showed on one of a pair of dice, and a five showed on the other" is an example of a conjunction. Rule 4 allows us to calculate the probability of a conjunction when the probabilities of the individual conjuncts are known. Symbolically, rule 4 can be expressed as follows:

$$\mathbf{Pr}(h_1 \text{ and } h_2 \,|\, e) = \mathbf{Pr}(h_1 \,|\, e) \times \mathbf{Pr}\,(h_2 \,|\, e \text{ and } h_1)$$

In English, the rule says the probability that a conjunction is true is equal to the product of the probability of the first conjunct and the probability that the second conjunct is true if the first one is true. Like rule 3, rule 4 can be generalized to any number of cases, but for simplicity here we state it to cover only two conjuncts. When more than two conjuncts are involved, calculations become more complicated because the probability of each successive conjunct is conditional on the truth of all the preceding conjuncts.

Examples

a. Suppose that a fair coin is tossed twice (the evidence sentence). What is the probability that both tosses yield a head?

Rule 4 tells us to multiply the probability the first toss will yield a head (½) by the probability that the second toss will be a head on condition the first toss yields a head. This probability is also ½, because what happens on the first toss has no effect on the second toss. (The probability of a head on the second toss is ½ regardless of whether the first toss is a head or a tail—the outcomes of the first and second tosses are **independent** of one another.) Multiplying ½ by ½ gives us ¼, which is the probability that "two heads appear on two tosses of a fair coin."

b. Suppose that two cards are drawn blindly from a standard deck and placed in a drawer together (the evidence). What is the probability that both cards are aces? We want to know the probability of the conjunction "The first card is an ace, *and* the second card is an ace." The probability that the first card is an ace is ⁴⁄₅₂.

(There are four aces in a standard deck of 52 cards.) The probability that the second card drawn is also an ace, if the first card drawn is an ace, is $3/51$. (At the time of the second draw, the deck contains 51 cards; if the first card drawn is an ace, only three aces remain in the deck.) The product of $4/52$ and $3/51$ is $12/2{,}652$. This fraction can be reduced to $1/221$, which is the probability of drawing two aces from a standard deck in two draws (without replacing the first card drawn).

In example (b), unlike in example (a), the probabilities are not the same for the first and second conjuncts. When a fair coin is tossed, what happens on a second or a third toss is independent of what happens on any previous toss. When cards are drawn from a deck without replacement after each draw, the probabilities of drawing a particular card are not the same for successive draws. The deck is different after each draw. What happens on the second draw is not independent of what happens on the first draw. If, however, the cards are replaced and the deck is shuffled after every draw, the outcome of each draw is independent of previous draws from the deck.

c. What is the probability of drawing three aces in three draws from a standard deck without replacement?

Here, we want to apply rule 4 to more than two conjuncts. The probability that the first draw is an ace is $4/52$. The probability that the second draw is an ace, given that the first card drawn is an ace, is $3/51$. The probability that the third card is also an ace, given that the first and second cards drawn are aces, is $2/50$. Multiplying these three probabilities (a calculator is helpful for such problems), we find that the probability of drawing three aces from a standard deck in three draws without replacement is equal to $24/132{,}600$. This fraction can be reduced to $1/5{,}525$.

In these examples of the application of rule 4, it is easy to tell whether the events being considered are independent or not. Tosses of coins and rolls of dice are independent events. Draws from a deck of cards, when cards previously drawn are replaced and the deck is reshuffled, are also independent. When cards drawn from a deck are not replaced (as in games such as 21, or Blackjack, where cards that are exposed are then placed on the bottom of the deck and the deck is not reshuffled), successive draws are not independent. In applying rule 4 to real-life situations, we must pay attention to whether events are independent. For example, suppose that the probability of getting a busy signal when calling any one of your close friends without "call waiting" is 0.05. The probability of getting a busy signal when you call one friend and then getting another busy signal when you call a second friend immediately afterwards is *not* equal to 0.05×0.05 if those two friends are also friends of one another, because the busy signals would not be independent events. If your first friend is on the phone, this raises the probability that you will also get a busy signal when you try to call the second friend. It can be difficult to assign probabilities to descriptions of events that are not independent of one another, but we should at least be aware of how a lack of independence can affect the calculation of probabilities.

Rules 1 through 4 form the entire basis of probability theory, just as the axioms of Euclidean geometry form the basis of that area of mathematics. We take notice of one useful theorem that makes calculations simpler than they would otherwise be:

Theorem

If $\mathbf{Pr}(h \,|\, e) = n$, then $\mathbf{Pr}(\text{not } h \,|\, e) = 1 - n$.

Here, "not h" is the negation, or denial, of the sentence h. For example, h could be "A card drawn from a standard deck is red." Then "not h" is "A card drawn from a standard deck is not red." Because these two sentences are mutually exclusive and jointly exhaustive (the truth of one and the falsity of the other exhaust the possibilities), the sum of the probabilities of h and "not h" is equal to 1. But this means that the probability of either of the sentences is equal to 1 minus the probability of the other.

Examples

   a. What is the probability of not drawing an ace from a standard deck when a card is drawn blindly?

Since the probability of drawing an ace is $4/52$, the probability of not drawing an ace is $1 - 4/52 = 48/52 = 12/13$.

   b. What is the probability of obtaining at least one head in two tosses of a fair coin?

Rule 3 is not applicable to this problem because "a head occurs on the first toss" and "a head occurs on the second toss" are not mutually exclusive sentences. Heads could occur on both tosses. If we were (mistakenly) to add the probabilities of obtaining a head on the first toss and of obtaining a head on the second toss, the probability would be equal to 1. Obviously, this is incorrect, because it is by no means certain that a head will occur in two tosses. However, the sentence "At least one head occurs in two tosses of a fair coin" is equivalent to the sentence "Tails do not occur on both tosses of a fair coin." We can use rule 4 to calculate the probability of obtaining tails on both tosses ($\frac{1}{2} \times \frac{1}{2} = \frac{1}{4}$). Then, we can use the theorem to calculate the probability of not obtaining a tail on both tosses ($1 - \frac{1}{4} = \frac{3}{4}$).

The *Rasmussen Report*, issued in 1975—before the accidents at Three-Mile Island, Chernobyl, and Fukushima, was considered the most complete study by the U.S. government on the safety of nuclear power. The report, which has been criticized by those opposed to nuclear power, offers an interesting and important application of this theorem. Critics (K.S. Schrader-Frechette) say the report misrepresents the probability of a serious accident at a nuclear-power plant.

According to federal government figures, the probability of a serious accident in the United States is $1/17,000$ per year, per reactor. "Serious accident" in this context refers to a core melt that, again according to government estimates, would be equivalent to one thousand Hiroshimas. The probability of $\frac{1}{17,000}$ per year per reactor may sound like a very low probability. However, critics point out that each reactor presently operating at 65 nuclear-power plants has an estimated lifetime of 30 years. The critics feel we should be concerned with the probability that a serious accident will occur at any one plant during its 30-year lifetime.

We can apply the preceding theorem twice to calculate the probability that a core melt will occur in at least one of these 65 nuclear-power plants over its 30-year lifetime. This probability is equal to 1 minus the probability that there will be no serious accidents in any of these 65 plants during their 30-year lifetimes. Using the government probability of $\frac{1}{17,000}$ per year per reactor that there will be a serious accident and assuming that the events (core melts per year per reactor) are independent, the probability that there will be no core melts is equal to

$$\left[1 - \left(\frac{1}{17,000}\right)\right]^{65 \times 30},$$

or

$$\left(\frac{16,999}{17,000}\right)^{1,950},$$

which is equal to 0.8916.

We can then apply the theorem a second time to determine the probability that there will be at least one serious accident. "There will be no serious accidents (core melts)" is the denial of "There will be at least one serious accident." To calculate the probability that there will be at least one serious accident, we subtract the probability that there will be no serious accidents (0.8916) from 1:

$$1 - 0.8916 = 0.108$$

Thus, using the data available at the time of the Rasmussen Report, the probability that the United States will be faced with a nuclear-power disaster equivalent to one thousand Hiroshimas is, according to the government's own figures, more than 10 percent. Given the present state of nuclear power in the United States, however, with 104 reactors operating and more than half of them more than 30 years old, the 10 percent estimate is too low.

In considering the probability of a serious nuclear accident, difficulties in applying the probability calculus to life situations become apparent. First of all, we can ask whether it is reasonable to assume that the probability of a serious accident in a nuclear-power plant is the same throughout each of its 30 or more years of use. In addition, an assumption of independence per year, per reactor core melts is probably false. Nuclear reactors are built along similar designs and have almost identical safety devices. Thus, if the threat of a serious accident is connected with the design of the reactor itself or the failure of its protective devices, such accidents could not be considered independent. Another possible source of serious accidents is sabotage. We might judge an isolated instance of a sabotage-caused accident as independent of other such acts, but the sabotage could be part of a terrorist campaign against nuclear-power reactors. Another factor that would undermine an assumption of independence is that publicity about the sabotage at one plant could be a causal factor in other instances.

An additional difficult question is whether the lack of independence would **raise** or **lower** the estimate of the probability that an accident will occur in at least one plant during its 30+-year lifetime. Some critics of nuclear power have also objected that the figure of $1/17,000$ is an unrealistically low estimate of the probability of a serious accident per year per reactor.

Such questions cannot be answered by simply applying the rules to calculate probabilities. The assignment of initial probabilities and the determination of whether events are dependent or independent require us to assemble and evaluate evidence, using means far beyond the probability calculus. With suitable evidence in hand, however, many of the argument forms—inductive generalizations, statistical syllogisms, and analogies—can be useful in assigning appropriate initial probabilities.

Exercise Set 6.1

1. What is the probability of obtaining either a heart or a diamond in a single blind draw from a standard deck of cards?

2. What is the probability of not obtaining either a heart or a diamond in a single blind draw from a standard deck of cards?

3. What is the probability of obtaining three heads in three tosses of a fair coin?

4. What is the probability of obtaining at least one head in three tosses of a fair coin?

5. What is the probability of obtaining either a head or a tail in a single toss of a fair coin?

6. What is the probability of drawing two aces in two blind draws from a standard deck of cards without replacement?

7. Suppose you are playing a card game in which four cards are dealt to each person. What is the probability that you will be dealt four aces? What is the probability that you will be dealt four kings or four queens or four jacks?

8. a. A family has two children. What is the probability that one child is a girl and the other a boy?

   b. If the family has four children, what is the probability that the oldest and the youngest children are boys?

9. Consider a health club with 100 members (60 men and 40 women). Each member uses the club for just one favorite activity, and men and women are equally likely to engage in any of the activities. Of the members of the club

20 are swimmers; 30 play racquetball; 24 take aerobic exercise classes; 16 lift weights; and 10 play indoor tennis.

    a. Suppose a member of the club is randomly selected:
        1. What is the probability that the member selected is a weight lifter?
        2. What is the probability that the member is either a swimmer or takes aerobic exercise classes?
        3. What is the probability that the member selected is either a tennis player, a racquetball player, or a weight lifter?
        4. What is the probability that the member selected is a female weight lifter?
        5. What is the probability that the member selected is a man who takes aerobic exercise classes?
    b. Suppose that two members of the club are randomly selected:
        1. What is the probability that both are tennis players?
        2. What is the probability that the first one selected is a tennis player and the second one selected is a racquetball player?
        3. What is the probability that a tennis player and a racquetball player are selected?

10. You and your best friend share a birthday and are both 20 years' old. Actuarial tables published by the Social Security Administration say that slightly more than half (.51) of 20-year-olds will live to celebrate their 80th birthdays. What is the probability that both of you will see your 80th birthday?

11. Assuming that you know what day your birthday is but do not know what your professor's is, what is the probability that you both share the same birthday (day only—not year)?

12. Suppose three friends are asked to choose blindly, and with replacement, one ball from an urn containing one each of the following colors: red, blue, yellow, green, orange, purple, and black. What is the probability that

    a. All will draw the same color?
    b. At least two will draw the same color?

13. Suppose that you hold three aces and two different small cards in a game of draw poker. If you discard the two small cards, what are your chances of improving your hand on the draw? The hand will be improved either by drawing another ace and any other card or by drawing a pair. (*Hint: Because this is a fair game and you do not know what cards are in the other players' hands, treat their cards as if they were part of the deck.*)

14. If your chances of being apprehended for committing some crime are 0.7, your chances of being convicted if apprehended are 0.6, and your chances of serving time if apprehended and convicted are 0.5, what is the probability that you will serve time if you rob the local grocery store?

15. You are taking a true-false test that has ten questions, and you need a score of 70 percent to pass. You know the answers to only six of the questions. For the other four, you toss a coin and answer *true* if it comes up heads and *false* if it comes up tails.

    a. What is the probability that you will pass the exam? (Think about this as the probability of getting at least one right answer in four tries—or one minus the probability of getting four wrong answers.)

    b. Can you think of a better method than the coin tossing described here to get a passing grade?

III. USING PROBABILITIES TO PLAN A COURSE OF ACTION—DECISION THEORY

"Probability," as Bishop Butler remarked in the eighteenth century, "is the very guide of life." None of us can see what the future holds. We make most choices, decisions, and plans with limited knowledge about what the state of the world will be and what others will do. We can, however, assign probabilities to various possible outcomes before we make decisions. For example, if we care about seeing a movie from the beginning, we try to arrive at the theater before the show is scheduled to begin because it will probably start on time. We pursue our college education because we believe that what we learn in college will probably enhance the quality of our lives.

The probability that some event or condition will occur is not the only consideration on which we base our decisions to act. We are concerned with costs and benefits as well. In Exercise 14 in Exercise Set 6.1, the surprisingly low probabilities given for apprehension, conviction, and incarceration are based on government crime statistics. Nevertheless, although the probability that someone would actually serve time for robbing a store is low, even an immoral or antisocial person who contemplates such an act should reflect not only on the probability of serving time but also on the unpleasantness of imprisonment. It is prudent to avoid even a fairly small risk of being incarcerated. Conversely, if some potential benefit is very attractive, it is reasonable to expend great effort to achieve it, even though the probability of attaining it is small. Many athletes, for example, make significant sacrifices to achieve a place on an Olympic team, although for most, the probability of making the team is very low.

The term *utility* refers to the desirability (*positive* utility) or undesirability (*negative* utility) of a situation. The term *value* (which can also be positive or negative) is sometimes used as well. Thus, when contemplating an action that could result in a prison sentence, the negative utility of serving time in prison should be considered along with the probability of serving time.

Decision theory is the study of reasonable decision making in contexts that vary with respect to the knowledge available. (Here, a *decision* is a decision to take some action.)

The goal of decision theory is to develop criteria for rational (reasonable) decision making. In a brief look at decision theory, we consider three general contexts in which decisions occur:

1. **Decisions under risk**: Contexts in which we can assign probabilities to states of the world that we believe are relevant to our actions. Our knowledge in these contexts is said to be partial or incomplete.
2. **Decisions under certainty**: Contexts in which the relevant state of the world is assured. In these contexts, our knowledge of states relevant to our actions has "practical certainty."
3. **Decisions under uncertainty**: Contexts in which various relevant states of the world are possible but of unknown probability.

1. DECISIONS UNDER RISK

Consider the example of a patient whose doctor suggests an ear operation. The patient is faced with making a decision under risk. If the patient decides to have the operation, three different states of the world or conditions are relevant, each associated with a probability (the condition of improved hearing to "very good": 0.85 [85 percent]; the condition of no improvement: 0.10 [10 percent]; the condition of further damage to ear: 0.05 [5 percent]). The probabilities in this case are relative frequencies based on statistics gathered from similar operations. No utilities for the various outcomes are mentioned, though clearly the first outcome has the greatest utility as well as the highest probability; the second outcome has a lower utility (the hearing problem is unimproved, and the patient must endure the pain and expense of an operation); and the third outcome has the lowest utility. If the patient decides against the operation, it is almost certain that the ear condition will stay about the same. The utility of this outcome ranks higher than the utilities of having an unsuccessful operation (with an outcome of no improvement or further damage) but ranks lower than the outcome of an operation that results in hearing improvement. Should the patient have the operation or not? The decision problem can be represented in the following array, which displays the states of the world and the probabilities associated with them in the light of the two actions:

	States of the World		
	Improved Hearing	No Change	Worse Off
Actions			
1. Have operation	0.85	0.10	0.05
2. Refuse operation	(almost) 0	(almost) 1	(almost) 0

In light of the information available to the patient, several guides to action can be considered. The patient could act as if the most probable result of the operation will occur and choose the operation. However, "Always act as if the most probable state will occur" is a poor decision-making rule because it ignores the utilities of various states, and it will lead to some apparently irrational decisions. Following this rule, for example, would lead an immoral criminal to hold up the local grocery store on the grounds that the most probable result of the action would be to escape a prison sentence. Following this rule would also lead a homeowner to refuse to purchase fire insurance, even at a favorable price, because the probability (based on statistics) that a given house will catch fire is very low.

Another possible decision rule is "Always choose the action that could result in a state of affairs with a higher utility than any other possible state of affairs." If the patient follows this rule, the operation will be chosen, for a restoration of hearing is clearly the state with the highest utility, and this condition is possible only if the patient has the operation. But this rule ignores the known probabilities involved in making a decision under risk, and like the rule "Always act as if the most probable state of affairs will occur," it can lead to decisions that most of us would regard as foolish.

To illustrate the shortcomings of this rule, consider the following case. Suppose that Hilary has $20,000 to cover college costs. She places a high utility on having money but also strongly desires a college education, and college would be out of the question if this $20,000 were lost. Someone offers Hilary a chance to invest that $20,000 for a possible return of $100,000 within a year. There is a 10 percent probability that the $20,000 investment will return a profit of $100,000, but the probability that the original $20,000 stake will be lost is 90 percent. What action should she take? Given the high value placed on a college education, most people would consider it unreasonable to risk the $20,000 under these circumstances, even though one possible state of affairs associated with this action (money for education and a lot left over for other things) has the greatest utility.

To evaluate correctly these decisions under risk, a rule that accounts for both utilities and probabilities is required. "Choose an action that maximizes **expected utility**" is such a rule. This rule, although not flawless, is a good way to think about decision problems and works well for many decisions. To understand the rule of maximizing expected utility, we need to know how to calculate expected utilities. To do so, we first need to quantify, or measure, utilities, because calculation requires numbers. Measuring utilities is by no means simple. How can we assign numbers to the value of hearing properly or undergoing an unsuccessful operation or losing one's hearing? Objectivity is not the issue here. The measurements of utilities need not be objective in the sense that the assigned quantities would be acceptable to any reasonable person. All that is required is that the person confronted with the decision assign his or her own utility values, but even that can be difficult.

Studies of decision theory usually begin with examples of monetary decisions, such as decisions concerning bets or investments. An investment that will return $30,000 seems—all other things being equal—three times as desirable as (has three times the utility of) an investment that will return $10,000. If dollars are correlated in this manner with units of utility, it is easy to assign a measure of the utility of various amounts of money lost or won, for money already comes in measurable units. Before returning to the problem of the ear operation, we consider a decision about spending small amounts of money on games of chance to illustrate how expected utilities work.

Suppose you attend a school fair to benefit the library and want to spend $2 playing a game of chance. You have to decide whether to risk $2 on a punchboard or on a dice game. If you choose to play the punchboard, four states of the world are relevant to your action: the state in which you win $10, the state in which you win $5, the state in which you win $2, and the state in which you win nothing. Given the way the punchboard is designed, the respective probabilities associated with these states are 0.05, 0.10, 0.20, and 0.65. If you play the dice game and roll any matched pair, you win $10; otherwise you win nothing. To assure that units of utility correspond to the amounts of money won or lost, you assume that the dice game is no more or no less amusing than the punchboard and that you desire to gain as much money as possible from your $2 play.

The expected utility of a $2 punch can be calculated by letting each dollar equal one unit of utility, multiplying each payoff with its associated probability, summing the results, and subtracting the cost of playing the game:

$$[(10 \times 0.05) + (5 \times 0.10) + (2 \times 0.20) + (0 \times 0.65)] - 2,$$

which is equal to

$$(0.50 + 0.50 + 0.40 + 0) - 2 = -0.60.$$

Thus, in dollars and cents, the expected utility of a $2 punch is −60 cents.

In the dice game, the expected utility is similarly calculated by multiplying payoffs with their associated probabilities, summing the results, and subtracting the $2 cost. In general, the rule for calculating the expected utility of some decision is to multiply the probability of each relevant state of affairs by the total units of utility associated with that state. The sum of these products minus the initial cost (also measured in units of utility), if any, is the expected utility of that decision.

In the dice game, the probability of rolling two matched dice is $\frac{1}{6}$. This probability can be calculated in several ways. The probability of rolling any particular pair is $\frac{1}{36}$. You can win by rolling any of six mutually exclusive pairs, and $(\frac{1}{36} + \frac{1}{36} + \frac{1}{36} + \frac{1}{36} + \frac{1}{36} + \frac{1}{36}) = \frac{1}{6}$. Or the problem can be viewed another way. The first die shows some number on its face. The probability that the second die will show the same number is $\frac{1}{6}$, and this is also the probability that you will roll a pair.

The utility (the payoff) associated with rolling a pair is $10, or 10 units of utility. The probability of *not* rolling a pair is $\frac{5}{6}$ (1 minus the probability of obtaining a pair). The payoff for not rolling a pair is 0. Because $10 \times \frac{1}{6} = 1.67$ and $0 \times \frac{5}{6} = 0$, we sum these amounts and subtract the $2 cost ($1.67 + 0 - 2 = -0.33$). Thus, the expected utility (measured in money) of a play on the punchboard is −$0.60, and the expected utility of the dice game is −$0.33. If you followed the rule of maximizing expected utilities, you would choose the dice game and thereby cut your losses.

Let us return to the problem of measuring the utilities associated with the ear operation. Remember that the measures assigned are for demonstration purposes only. You might assign values differently and could not be criticized for doing so. The units assigned here are just "units of utility." The arithmetic operations of addition, subtraction, multiplication, and division can be performed on these units of utility, but the units need not—and perhaps cannot—be translated into monetary amounts.

i. Units of utility of three states associated with decision to undergo operation (probabilities are enclosed in parentheses):

Hearing improvement to "very good": 10 (0.85)
No improvement: −2 (0.10)
Further damage: −10 (0.05)

(Notice that the three states are mutually exclusive and exhaust the possible relevant states; thus the sum of their probabilities is equal to 1.)

ii. Units of utility associated with the only state with nonzero probability relevant to the decision not to undergo the operation:

No change: 0 (1)

Using these figures, the expected utility of the operation is $[(10 \times 0.85) + (-2 \times 0.10) + (-10 \times 0.05)] = 7.8$. The expected utility of not having the operation is $(0 \times 1) = 0$. The "cost" of the operation was not calculated separately here; it was "figured in" when the utilities were assigned to various states of the world. Following the rule of maximizing expected utility, if you were the patient, you would most likely choose the operation.

In considering candidates for the best rule to follow when making decisions under risk, different rules can lead to the same decision in some cases. In this example, the most probable state of affairs after the operation was also the state with the greatest utility. But the rule "Choose the action that maximizes expected utility" is adequate when other proposed rules appear to offer unreasonable advice. This happens frequently when a state with a low probability has a very high utility or when a state with a high probability has a very low utility. That is why the rule for maximizing expected utility is generally accepted as a good rule for rational decision making when the probabilities of the various states are known. This rule is applicable when other rules would lead to decisions that seem unreasonable.

Exercise

Cellular phone service providers offer a bewildering variety of plans to users. These range from pay-per-call to a monthly fee (on a two-year contract) for calling anywhere in the country. Compare any two plans that appeal to you, and decide between them on the basis of your probable use of cell phone minutes and cost of each program. Assume that units of utility can be measured in dollars. You may also assume, if you prefer, that you already own a good cell phone, or you can consider plans that include a new phone.

2. DECISIONS UNDER CERTAINTY

In some situations, we choose among various actions when each action is associated with only one state of affairs. These decisions are called **decisions under certainty**, but this is something of a misnomer because the future is never absolutely certain. The world around us might change in an unpredictable way between the time of the decision and the completion of the action. For example, you are deciding between studying for a test in your room and studying for a test in the library. Ordinarily, only one state is relevant to each choice in a decision under certainty—you study in your room if that is your decision or study in the library if that is your choice. It is, however, possible that before you study in the library, it closes because of an unusual and unexpected electrical power failure. In general, when we talk about decisions under certainty, we simply ignore such unusual possibilities.

The probability associated with the single state of affairs relevant to the action in a decision under certainty is (almost) 1. Thus, there is no need to calculate probabilities of various outcomes. The rule to apply when making decisions under certainty is simple: "Choose an action with the highest utility." If no single action has the highest utility, it is reasonable to choose any of the actions that have the highest utility.

Even though calculating probabilities for decisions under certainty poses no problems, assigning and comparing utilities can be difficult. For example, some products (such as automobile tires and batteries) are sold at prices that depend on the length of the guarantee period. If you buy tires with a two-year guarantee at a specified price, you can calculate the costs per year and compare these costs to the costs per year of tires with a three-year guarantee. But other factors might enter into the decision. How long will you keep your car? How much trouble is it to replace worn tires? Are both sets of new tires equally safe throughout their guarantee period? Suppose the tires are identical; only the guarantee is different. Is it worthwhile to pay for the longer guarantee period as a kind of insurance against having to pay for new tires? Comparing utilities almost always involves more than monetary considerations, and these additional factors should not be ignored just because they make the decision more difficult. In many cases (as in the tire-buying decision), the consideration of additional factors involves probabilities that can change a decision under certainty into a decision under risk. For example, it can be possible to assign a probability to your car lasting two years and a different probability to its lasting three more years.

Because no probability calculations are involved in decisions under certainty, utilities can simply be ordered by rank (highest, second highest, and so on). In other words, in a decision under certainty, we do not need to assign units of utility. We need to assign units of utility in decisions under risk because we perform arithmetic operations, such as multiplication and addition, on probabilities and utilities. Decisions under risk require arithmetic calculations, whereas decisions under certainty do not and are simpler in this respect.

Exercise

Suppose that an improbable event has occurred: You have won first prize in a lottery. The prize is an all-expense-paid week in Hawaii for two, valued at $10,000, but the winner can choose instead a cash prize of $3,000. Which would you choose? Explain how you assigned units of utility to guide your decision.

3. DECISIONS UNDER UNCERTAINTY

In **decisions under uncertainty**, as in decisions under risk, our knowledge is incomplete. In decisions under risk, however, we at least can make judgments about the probability of various states of the world. When we face decisions under conditions of uncertainty, we are aware that different states are relevant to our decisions, but we are unable to assess the probabilities of the various states. We cannot even say whether one relevant state is more likely, less likely, or just as likely to occur as any other. Such situations may be unusual; in most cases, we have sufficient knowledge to make at least very rough assignments of probabilities on the basis of past experiences or information gathered from other sources. If we can make even crude probability judgments, we should follow the rule for making decisions under risk (choose the action that maximizes expected utility). For the sake of completeness, however, and because of some interesting problems associated with decisions under uncertainty, most accounts of decision theory discuss these decisions.

In the absence of information about probabilities, we must base our choices entirely on the utilities that are associated with various states of affairs. In many cases of decision under uncertainty, a rank ordering of utilities is sufficient. Some decisions under uncertainty are simple, for one of the actions will have a better outcome than the other actions for each state of the world. For a simple decision between two actions, each associated with two states, this situation can be represented as follows:

	States of the World, Ordered by Rank (1 is highest)	
	I	**II**
Actions		
I	4	3
II	2	1

In the preceding table (or **decision matrix**), two possible states of affairs are associated with Action I. These are ranked lowest (fourth) and second-lowest (third) in utility.

Action II also has two associated states, ranked highest (first) and second-highest (second) in utility. In this situation, Action II is said to **dominate** Action I. Assuming that a decision has no effect on the probabilities of the states of the world, it would seem irrational to choose Action I because either state associated with Action II is better than either state associated with Action I.

In the following case of a decision under uncertainty, one action **dominates**. Mark, a football player, is offered two nonathletic scholarships—one at State University and one at Out-of-State University (OSU). The information he has regarding the schools does not allow him to assign any probabilities of making either football team. He would like to play ball, but he wants the best education possible, regardless of whether he plays ball, and he believes the academic program at State is better. His utilities are ranked (1) play ball at State, (2) do not play ball at State, (3) play ball at OSU, and (4) do not play ball at OSU. Thus, he will be better off at State, whether or not he plays ball. Going to State is the rational decision for him.

	States of the World, Ordered by Rank (1 is highest)	
Actions	**Make the Team**	**Do Not Make the Team**
Go to State	1	2
Go to OSU	3	4

Suppose, however, that Clark, another football player, has also won scholarships. He really wants to play ball and perceives State as the best place to play. If, however, he cannot play ball, he would prefer an easier academic program so he will be free to pursue other interests. Faced with the same offers as Mark, his ranking of utilities are (1) play ball at State, (2) play ball at OSU, (3) do not play at OSU, and (4) do not play at State.

	States of the World, Ordered by Rank (1 is highest)	
Actions	**Play Ball**	**Do Not Play Ball**
Go to State	1	4
Go to OSU	2	3

In this decision under uncertainty, neither action dominates. Going to State is associated with the most highly valued state, but also with the lowest value. Because no dominant action is available, the next question is whether there is just one **satisfactory action**—an action that is not associated with any unacceptable states of affairs. If Clark were satisfied with a utility ranked three or higher but were not satisfied with a utility ranked lower than three, then choosing State would not be a satisfactory action for him to take. He should follow the rule: "Choose the action that is satisfactory," and go to OSU.

Alternatively, suppose that no utility is completely unacceptable to Clark. He could accept being a nonplayer at State, although for him that outcome has the lowest utility. The rule for choosing *the* satisfactory action does not apply if there is *more than one* satisfactory action. At this point, he can consider several other strategies (rules for decision). Which rule Clark follows will depend in part on his tolerance for risk. Decision theorists categorize three different types of decision-making personality:

1. **The Gambler:** In situations in which only one action is associated with the state of affairs with the highest utility, one decision strategy is to take that action. The gambler is willing to take a chance to get the best. If Clark is a gambler, he will go to State.

2. **The Cautious Player:** The cautious player focuses on the lowest, rather than the highest, utility of each outcome. The choice is based on which action is associated with the **highest of the low utilities**. The cautious player wants to protect against losses, to "maximize the minimum." Using this maxi-min strategy, Clark will choose OSU, for the lowest utility associated with that action is 3, whereas the lowest utility associated with State is 4.

3. **The Calculator:** The calculator is not willing to gamble or to be satisfied with maximizing the minimum. In an effort to steer between these two, the calculator tries to choose the action associated with the **highest average utility**. An average utility cannot be determined merely on the basis of a rank ordering, however, for calculating an average requires assigning units to utilities. In addition, the calculation also requires assigning some probability value to each outcome. By definition, however, there are no known probabilities associated with the various possible states of the world—if there were, this would be a decision under risk. The calculator responds to this difficulty by simply assuming that each state is equally likely.

If Clark is a calculator, one possible assignment that is consistent with his rank orderings would be the following: play at State (10); do not play at State (2); play at OSU (8); do not play at OSU (6). The average utility of an action can now be calculated by adding the utilities of each possible outcome for that action and dividing the total by the number of possible outcomes. The average utility of the decision to go to State is then $(10 + 2)/2 = 6$, and the average utility of the decision to go to OSU is $(8 + 6)/2 = 7$. Following the rule of choosing the action with the highest average utility, our player will go to OSU.

In the calculator's decision-making rule, which assigns average utilities, the decision under uncertainty is really transformed into a decision under risk. This is so because each possible state of affairs is regarded as having the same probability value as any other. This method thus introduces an unsupported assumption (the claim that the various states of the world are equally likely) into the decision problem.

The method would not be appropriate if available information indicated that one state were actually less or more likely than another. In these situations, the problem should be treated as a decision under risk, and probabilities should be assigned in a suitable way. Even when no available information indicates that one state is more likely than another, however, the assumption that each can be treated as equally likely is dubious because in effect it transforms a lack of information into a statement that probabilities are equal. It is very important to recognize the difference between "no information about probabilities" and "all states have the same probability." Nevertheless, the calculation strategy that allows this transformation is regarded as rational by some decision theorists.

In thinking about the choices open to the football players, we can see the importance of assuming that one's decision does not affect the probabilities of relevant states of the world. Sometimes this assumption is fair; our decisions have no effect on states of the world. Although we may jokingly say that if we plan a picnic for Saturday, it is sure to rain that day, our decision to schedule a picnic has no effect on whether it rains. The (perhaps unknown) probability of rain remains the same whatever is decided. For the decision of the football players, however, the assumption might not hold. If Mark decides to go to State, and Clark learns this, then Clark may go to OSU to avoid competing with Mark for a position on the team. If Clark goes to OSU, then Mark's chance of making the team at State might be improved because Clark is no longer a competitor, so the state of the world "Mark plays ball at State" has a higher probability as a result of Mark's decision to attend State. In such ways, decisions can affect probabilities of states and even result in canceling the dominance of an action. Such problems take us into the area of game theory, which looks at how decisions by interacting players affect the payoffs for the other players.

4. THE PRISONER'S DILEMMA

An interesting game-theoretic puzzle involving decisions under uncertainty is entitled the **Prisoner's Dilemma**. Following is one version of this much-discussed problem:

A man and a woman are arrested on suspicion of operating a ring of burglars. The police have sufficient evidence to make the arrests, but the district attorney doubts there is enough evidence to convict the pair. In an effort to obtain further evidence, the prisoners are prevented from consulting with one another, and the district attorney offers the following to each of them:

> Confess to the crime. If your partner does not confess, you will receive a
> light sentence of one year in prison, but your partner will receive the maxi-
> mum sentence of five years.

Each prisoner wants to know what will happen if both partners confess. The district attorney tells each prisoner that if both confess, each will receive a three-year sentence.

The district attorney also reveals that if neither partner confesses, the burglary case will collapse although there is sufficient evidence to convict both partners of a lesser crime, for which they will each receive the maximum sentence of two years.

In making such a bargain, the district attorney is confident that both partners will confess, even though each would be better off if neither partner confessed. Can you see why this is so?

The formulation of the problem assumes that neither partner can assign a probability to whether the other partner will confess. Thus, each partner is faced with a decision under uncertainty. If units of (negative) utility are correlated with the length of possible prison terms, each prisoner is faced with the following choices of actions and the utilities associated with the possible outcomes of those actions. (Utility rankings are shown in parentheses—remember that 1 is the highest rank.)

	Partner Confesses	Partner Does Not Confess
Confess	−3 (3)	−1 (1)
Do Not Confess	−5 (4)	−2 (2)

Each prisoner must consider two different states of the world. In the state of the world in which the partner confesses, the prisoner is better off by confessing (and getting a three-year term) than by not confessing (and getting a five-year term). In the state of the world in which the partner does not confess, the prisoner is better off confessing (a one-year term) than not confessing (a two-year term). Each prisoner is faced with the same choices and penalties. The district attorney feels that each partner will make a rational decision. As we can see from the matrix, however, the act of confessing dominates and is the only rational choice.

The Prisoner's Dilemma raises interesting problems about decision rules. It is crucial to note that separating the partners, thereby preventing their communication and cooperation, affects their decisions. A condition of the problem prevents the partners from working out a solution between themselves that would benefit both. Even if they were able to communicate with one another, each partner would be faced with the problem of whether the other partner could be trusted to carry out the jointly agreed-on plan. If each partner's decision as to whether to trust the other partner is a decision under uncertainty, the dilemma arises again.

The Prisoner's Dilemma is an artificial problem, but decision problems that resemble the dilemma can arise in real life. Consider, for example, a group of similarly prosperous manufacturers with factories located along a river into which they dump wastes. The river is in danger of becoming severely polluted as a result of their behavior, and if pollution levels rise significantly, the manufacturers will be charged stiff penalties. Moreover, each plant is considering expanding its operations, a move that would add to the pollution. The profits of each manufacturer would increase only if its plant could expand without paying a penalty. If most of the manufacturers expand, the pollution levels will be high enough to result in penalties, which will reduce profits below present levels for all of them.

Assuming that each manufacturer acts independently and without knowledge of the other manufacturers' actions, we can frame the decision problem in the following way. The board of directors of Plant X is considering expansion. The members of the board figure that if its plant is the only manufacturer to expand, the pollution levels will not rise noticeably, and Plant X can count on a 10 percent increase in profit. If Plant X does not expand but the other plants do, then Plant X not only will have to pay a share of the penalty but, unlike the other plants, will not accrue any additional revenue from an expanded facility to help offset this loss. In such a case, the profits (P) of Plant X would sink 10 percent below the present level, whereas the profits of the other (expanded) plants would sink to only 5 percent below the present level. In the absence of information regarding the other manufacturers' plans, the board members of Plant X are making a decision under uncertainty and are in a situation similar to the Prisoner's Dilemma because each manufacturer considering expansion is in the same state as Plant X.

	Others Expand	Others Do Not Expand
X Expands	$P - 0.05P$ (3rd best)	$P + 0.10P$ (best)
X Does Not Expand	$P - 0.10P$ (worst)	P (2nd best)

Problems like this, in which decisions that seem rational according to the rules result in less-than-optimal states of the world, have challenged both ethicists and decision theorists to think carefully about such issues as free will, cooperation, and individual utilities versus what is most valuable for a social group, and whether "rational choice" means the same thing in decisions under uncertainty and decisions under risk. These problems can arise anytime there is some shared common good that will not be appreciably harmed by one or a few overusing it but will be destroyed if everyone with access to it abuses the privileges of use. (See B. Skyrms, *The Dynamics of Rational Deliberation*, especially chapter 1, for a brief history and outline of a proposal to resolve these issues.)

5. THE PETERSBURG PARADOX

Another famous problem in the history of probability and expected utilities, the **Petersburg Paradox**, raises questions about decision rules and about how to assign units of value, even in situations in which the payoff is money. The problem arises in the context of a game of chance with clearly defined probabilities and payoffs. It was formulated in the seventeenth century by the Swiss mathematician Daniel Bernoulli. Bernoulli, one of the scholarly guests of the Empress Catherine the Great at her court at St. Petersburg, offered a solution to the problem.

The game can be played this way: Begin by tossing a fair coin and continue to toss until a tail appears. As soon as a tail shows, the game is over. If the first toss is a tail, the game is over and there is no payoff. If one head shows before a tail appears, the payoff is $4. If two heads show, the payoff is $8. If three heads show, the payoff is $16, and the payoff doubles for each successive head that occurs before a tail appears.

The paradoxical aspect of the game arises when we attempt to determine a fair price to play the game. Normally in games of chance, a price is considered fair if it is equal to or reasonably close to the expected value of a play of the game. If units of value are equated with dollars, the expected value of a play can be calculated in the usual way—by multiplying the probability of each relevant state of affairs by the associated payoff for that state and summing the results. The mutually exclusive states relevant to a play of the Petersburg game are "Game ends after one toss"; "Game ends after two tosses"; and so forth, for an indefinite number (n) of tosses. The probability that a game will end after one toss (that a tail will appear on the first toss) is ½, and the associated payoff is $0; the probability that a game will end after two tosses (HT) is ¼, and the payoff is $4; the probability that a game will end after three tosses (HHT) is ⅛, and the payoff is $8; and so on. In other words, the expected value in dollars is

$$(1/2 \times 0) + (1/4 \times 4) + (1/8 \times 8) + (1/16 \times 16) + \cdots + (1/n \times n)$$

Each of the terms after the first term in this series is equal to 1, and because there is no mathematical limit to the number of tosses, the mathematical sum of the series is an infinite number of dollars. It would seem that the game is worth playing no matter how much a play costs, for any finite cost would be less than the infinite expected utility of the game.

An endless coin-tossing game is unrealistic, but the situation is hardly less puzzling if some reasonably large limit is placed on the length of a game. For example, let us say that the maximum number of tosses in a play is 1,001 tosses. The expected value of that game is $1,000; however, only the most reckless gambler would pay $1,000 to play such a game. How much would you pay?

Many different solutions to the Petersburg Paradox have been proposed. You might be able to think of one yourself. Bernoulli's solution is particularly interesting for introducing a concept that remains important in contemporary economic theory—the diminishing marginal utility of money.

Bernoulli distinguished the *physical* value of money from its *moral,* or *practical,* value to explain why the addition of a certain fixed amount of money to a large fortune has less value (except to a miser) than the addition of the same amount of money to a small fortune. The principle of the diminishing marginal utility of money can be stated as follows:

> If a certain gain is added to an initial fortune f, the utility of this gain decreases as f increases.

According to this principle, a person whose initial fortune is $100 will place a greater value on an additional $100 than a person whose initial fortune is $100,000. The physical value of the $100 is the same in both cases, but the *moral,* or *practical,* value is much greater in the first case than in the second. In deciding what price to pay to play the Petersburg game, a reasonable person who is aware of the decreasing marginal utility of money will consider the moral value, as well as the physical value, of the expected winnings and will also consider the moral value of the money that must be risked to play the game. In terms of moral value, the loss of even a small amount of money can be very hard on a poor person; the win of a large amount might not mean much to a rich one. Bernoulli even offered a plausible formula for calculating the moral value of increases or subtractions from an initial fortune. (See J. M. Keynes, "The Application of Probability to Conduct," in J. R. Newman's *The World of Mathematics,* for further discussion of solutions to the Petersburg Paradox.)

A more practical application of the principle of the diminishing marginal utility of money occurs in a homeowner's decision to purchase fire insurance at the usual price charged by an insurance company. The probability of losing a house to fire in any given year is very low, about 0.001. Suppose your house is worth $200,000. The insurance company offers to cover the loss for an annual premium of $600. Should you purchase the insurance? If you think of insuring the house as a sort of bet that you will get a payoff of $200,000 with a probability of 0.001, then an objectively fair price for the bet would be only $200 ([0.001 × $200,000] + [0.999 × $0]). Yet the insurance company wants to charge three times that price, so you have to ask yourself what it is worth to you to have the insurance. If the value of your house is the major part of your fortune—as it is for most people who own a house—it seems worth more than $200 for you to avoid the loss of that fortune. According to the formula devised by Bernoulli (see R. Carnap, 1962), if your whole fortune, including the house, is only about 1 percent greater than the value of the house ($220,000), then you should be willing to pay an even larger sum than $600 for the insurance—about $900. If you are a millionaire, however, with a fortune greater than ten times the value of the house, you might reasonably decide the premium is about $400 higher than it is worth to you and prefer to carry the risk yourself, essentially acting as your own insurance company. Many people make decisions similar to that of the millionaire homeowner when they decide not to carry collision insurance on an old car.

6. THE LAW OF AVERAGES AND THE GAMBLER'S FALLACY

If a fair coin is tossed repeatedly, then "on average" roughly half the tosses will result in heads, and as the series of tosses grows longer (that is, the sample grows larger), the proportion of heads continues to hover around one-half. Suppose you toss a coin and get a head on the first toss and tails on the next eight tosses. Should you use the law of averages to argue that the next toss will be a head? Many people not only argue this way but bet money accordingly.

Another tail in the series just described would be the ninth in a row. A series of nine tails in nine tosses has a low probability ($\frac{1}{2}^9 = \frac{1}{512}$). Nevertheless, such series do occur (about one in five hundred times). If the coin is fair, the probability that the next toss will be a head is 0.50, the same as for any other toss. What happens on earlier tosses has no effect on the next toss, because the events are independent. The law of averages tells us that if the series of tosses is long enough, the eight tails in a row will eventually become insignificant. After a thousand tosses, for example, there might still be a slight excess in the proportion of tails to heads, but the proportion will be roughly half and half. The law of averages does not predict what happens in the tosses that immediately follow the improbable series of eight tails. To suppose otherwise is to commit the **gambler's fallacy**.

The preceding account of how to understand the law of averages assumes that the coin is fair and that the tosses are independent. Suppose those assumptions are false. Then would it be reasonable to assign a high probability to the next toss being a head? If the coin is weighted (unfair), but the tosses are independent, then the evidence that eight tails have appeared in succession makes the probability that the next toss will be a head *less* than 0.50. The evidence suggests that the coin is weighted for tails. If the coin is cleverly designed so that a hidden magnet controls which side lands up and is programmed so that after a certain number of tails, a head appears, then not only is the coin unfair, but also the tosses are not independent. Without information about how this magnet is adjusted, it is not reasonable to assign a probability of greater than 0.50 to heads on the next toss.

Another instance of the gambler's fallacy occurs when statistical records are misused in the following way: Suppose your favorite baseball player has ended his past four seasons with batting averages that range between 0.330 and 0.340. This means that he gets hits "on average" about one out of three times at bat. It is now about the middle of the season; his average so far this year is 0.330, but he is in a slump and has not had a hit in his last ten times at bat. Unlike the coin tosses, hits are not independent events. Psychological factors such as a burst of confidence after several hits or physiological factors such as an injury that becomes progressively more painful each time the batter takes to the box can affect the probability of the next hit. If we are going to use past performance as our guide to the future, then we must take account not only of the published statistics but also the hot streak or the slump. We commit the gambler's fallacy if we think the batter has somehow used up his allotted number of failures after a certain point will have proportionately more (or fewer) hits from now on to keep his average intact.

IV. REVIEW

In chapter 6 we have considered applications of the mathematical calculus of probability to inductive logic. The term *probability* has been used to refer to the ratio of favorable to possible outcomes of some action or event, to the relative frequency with which events of a certain type occur in some series of events, and to the degree to which it is rational to believe certain statements. Whatever interpretation of *probability* is adopted, however, numerical probabilities should behave in accord with the mathematical rules of probability. These rules allow us to calculate unknown probabilities when some probabilities are known.

Probabilities play an important role in everyday decision making. Decision theory offers an analysis of decisions and criteria for making rational decisions. Several rules or strategies for making decisions in the face of less-than-complete knowledge have been proposed in this chapter. The rule "Choose an action that maximizes expected utility" is the most acceptable rule for choosing among actions when the probabilities of the various possible states associated with these actions are known. The rule for decisions under certainty, "Choose an action that maximizes utility," is reasonable when facing several actions each of which is associated with a single known state of affairs. In deciding among actions that are associated with more than one state when the probabilities of such states are unknown, the rule "Choose the dominant action" should be followed if such an action is available. If no action dominates, but one satisfactory action is available, it should be chosen. If neither of these rules applies reasonable decisions can be made using either the gambler's strategy, the cautious strategy, or the calculating strategy.

Decision theory offers criteria for making reasonable decisions, depending on the type of information available, but it cannot provide the information required for making reasonable decisions. Many decisions are inappropriate and even dangerous in the absence of accurate information. Unfortunately, in times of economic stress, many people who are desperate to support their families risk what little money they have on schemes that promise great returns for an initial investment that might exhaust their resources. The advertisements for such schemes are deceptive in various ways.

In one example, an online ad promises (for a $995 fee) to help set up an importing and online distribution business that will provide access to millions of dollars' worth of profit. For $995, takers get an instruction manual, advice about what to import and sell, a "business package" with templates for invoices and other business forms, and advice for setting up a Web site. All the real information, excluding the dubious advice, is available for free at any public library.

In this scheme, a person is asked to risk $995 for some unspecified and unguaranteed large gain without any hint of what the probability of actually making any money is.

When the stakes are so high (as they are in this case), it is imprudent—and a violation of the principles of critical thinking—to make decisions on the basis of such poor sources of information. Advertisements, paid for by profit-seeking organizations, cannot be considered authoritative sources of information. When available evidence allows us to frame strong inductive generalizations, statistical syllogisms (including legitimate appeals to authority), or arguments from analogy, probability judgments are reasonable and useful. Without reliable probabilities, high-utility decisions can be perilous.

A list of some important terms introduced in chapter 6 follows:

Conjunction   A compound sentence that is true just in case all its major components (conjuncts) are true. *And* is commonly used to conjoin the elements of conjunctions. Other words in English, such as *moreover, in addition to,* and *but* are also used to form conjunctions. These words differ in rhetorical force from *and* (for example, *but* suggests a contrast between the elements it conjoins); nevertheless, they all have the logical force of conjoining elements in such a way that the truth of the whole depends on each element's being true.

Decisions Under Certainty   Decisions in which a single state of the world is associated with each action.

Decisions Under Risk   Decisions in which the probabilities of the various states associated with the actions are known.

Decisions Under Uncertainty   Decisions in which the probabilities of the various states associated with the actions are not known.

Disjunction   A compound sentence that is true if any of its major component sentences (**disjuncts**) is true, but false if all disjuncts are false. *Or* is commonly used to join sentences to form a disjunction; *unless* is also used.

Dominating Action   In a decision under uncertainty, if one action has a better outcome than any other action for each state of the world, that action dominates.

Expected Utility   The utility of some event is its value or desirability, which can be positive or negative. To make decisions that require calculations involving probabilities and utilities, we need to assign units of utility to various states of the world associated with actions. The expected utility of an action is calculated by multiplying the probability of each state associated with the action by the utility associated with that state and summing the results.

Gambler's Fallacy   This fallacy occurs when one appeals to "the law of averages" to infer that an unusual series of events will be reversed in the short run. For example, if a series of five coin tosses has been all heads, the "law of averages" cannot be used to infer that the next toss will be a tail. If the coin is fair and the tosses are independent, the probability of a tail on the next toss is ½. If the coin is not fair, and the tosses are still independent, the series of five heads supports the claim that the coin is altered in such a way as to land heads.

Independent Events   Events are independent of one another when the occurrence of one event does not affect the probability of the occurrence of another event. Tosses of a coin are independent of one another; draws from a deck of cards without replacement and reshuffling are not independent of one another.

Mutually Exclusive Events   Events are mutually exclusive if the occurrence of one precludes the occurrence of an another. On a single roll of a pair of fair dice, rolling a total of six points and rolling a total of five points are mutually exclusive events. Sentences are mutually exclusive when the truth of one rules out the truth of the other. If the sentences that form a disjunction are mutually exclusive, only one of them can be true. If one sentence in a disjunction is the denial of another in the disjunction, the disjunction itself must be true and has a probability of 1.

Satisfactory Action   In a decision under uncertainty, if no action dominates but just one action is associated with no states of unacceptable levels of utility, that action is a satisfactory action.

Exercise Set 6.2

1. The state in which you live operates a lottery. The proceeds of the lottery are used to supplement the state's unemployment insurance fund. You can play the lottery for $1 per chance. To play, you choose a three-digit number from 000 to 999, inclusive, and receive an official ticket with that number printed on it. Each evening, a ball is drawn blindly from a container that holds 1,000 balls, each marked with a different three-digit number. If the number on your ticket is selected in the daily drawing on the date you play, you receive $500 for your ticket. Otherwise, you receive nothing.

    a. Suppose you buy one ticket. What is the probability that your number will win?
    b. What is the expected utility (in dollars) of a single play?
    c. Suppose you decide to play three times in one day, and you choose the same numbers each time. (You hold three tickets at a cost of $3.) What is the expected utility (in dollars) of your triple play?
    d. Suppose you decide to play three times in one day, and you choose different numbers each time. What is the expected utility (in dollars) of this triple play?

2. Power Ball is a multistate lottery. Each ticket costs $1. Various prizes can be won, but the jackpot requires the winner to choose correctly five numbers from 1−55 and the power ball number from 1−42. The probability that a single ticket will win the jackpot is 1/195,249,054. The jackpot amount varies, depending on how many tickets are sold and on the amount paid out in the previous drawing. Jackpot accumulations are announced and updated in the days before each drawing. Examples of expected utilities are $0.56 for a $1 play for the minimum jackpot of $20 million and $1.59 for the largest jackpot so far of $365 million. The break-even point (expected utility of $1.00) is about $195 million.

  a. How big does the jackpot have to be for a $1 ticket to have a higher expected utility than the ordinary lottery ticket described in Exercise 1?
  b. How big would the jackpot have to be for you to buy a ticket?
  c. What considerations other than money affect the expected utility you would place on purchasing a ticket?

3. An investor has $1,000 to invest for a year. She can either purchase a Certificate of Deposit for $1,000 and cash it in for $1,050 at the end of the year or she can invest the $1,000 in a stock her broker recommends, even though the stock is slightly overpriced. The broker thinks the stock will rise in value to $1,500 in a year if the company is taken over by an international group. The probability of a takeover is 0.40. If there is no takeover, the stock's price will likely (with 0.90 probability) fall back to $900.

Assume that the probabilities are reliable, that utility can be measured in dollars, and that no other utilities matter in this decision.

  a. What is the probability that no takeover will occur?
  b. What is the expected utility of investing in the Certificate of Deposit?
  c. What is the expected utility of investing in the stock?
  d. Which decision rule should the investor use?
  e. What is the rational decision in this case?

4. You are in charge of organizing a party held for the sole purpose of raising money for a worthy cause. You must decide whether to schedule an outdoor picnic or an indoor buffet supper. This event must be planned so far in advance that you have no way of assigning a probability for rain on the day of the party. On the basis of past events of this type, you have the following information:

If it does not rain, the outdoor picnic will yield a profit of $500, and the indoor buffet supper will yield a profit of $170.

If it does rain, the outdoor picnic will yield a profit of $80, and the indoor buffet supper will yield a profit of $440.

  a. Is this a decision under risk, a decision under certainty, or a decision under uncertainty?
  b. Is it reasonable in this case to correlate units of utility with dollars gained for the worthy cause?
  c. Which decision rule would you follow in this case?
  d. Apply the decision rule, and state which decision you would make. (Show your work.)

5. The same conditions stated in Exercise 4 exist, *except* that on the basis of weather records for the date of the party, you can reasonably assign a probability of ⅓ to rain on that date.

   a. What type of decision are you faced with now?
   b. Which decision rule should you follow?
   c. On the basis of that rule, what is the decision? (Show your work.)

6. You are a restaurant manager who is responsible for planning the "daily specials." You are considering whether to introduce a new Thursday special. If the special is successful, the restaurant will show a profit of $350 for the night; if the special is not successful, the restaurant will lose $50. If you serve the usual Thursday special, the restaurant will show a profit of $100. On the basis of past introductions, you assign a probability of 0.50 that the new dish will be a success. You have been doing a good job at the restaurant, so you are not afraid that you will be fired if you make the wrong decision in this matter. However, you share in the profits, so the decision does affect your pay.

   a. Which decision rule would you use in this situation?
   b. What is your decision? (Show your work.)

7. Someone at a fund-raiser gives you a ticket that he has purchased. Five hundred tickets were sold. You can turn the ticket in for a $10 cash payout or you can enter it in a raffle for a prize of $1,000.

   a. If money is the only consideration, what is the expected value of each of the choices?
   b. What kind of decision is involved?
   c. What are your own utilities in this case?
   d. Which decision rule would you use, and which decision would you take?

8. As an enthusiastic opera fan, you are considering the purchase of a season ticket to the opera. If you buy a $100 season ticket, you can see five operas for the price of four single tickets ($25). Your work schedule is erratic, however, and you figure the probability that you can attend only three is about ⅔; the probability that you can attend at least three is about ⅓. Should you buy a season ticket? In your answer, describe the relevant states of the world and the probability and utility (in dollar cost of tickets) associated with each.

9. A famous problem in decision theory, called "Pascal's Wager," was formulated by the French mathematician and philosopher Blaise Pascal in the seventeenth century. Pascal, who was a devout Christian, offered several formulations of the problem. Here is one way of looking at Pascal's Wager:

There are two possible states of the world: either God exists, or He does not. You are faced with two choices: Believe in God, or refuse to believe. If God does exist and you are a believer, you will be rewarded with infinite happiness in Heaven. If God does not exist and you believe He does, your life will be as usual, without any supernatural benefits or penalties. If, on the other hand, you refuse to believe and God exists, you can expect everlasting punishment in Hell. If you do not believe and there is no God, your life will be the usual rewards of life with no Heaven or Hell to face.

    a. Is this version of Pascal's Wager a decision under certainty, uncertainty, or risk?

    b. If you accept this formulation, does any action dominate?

    c. Do you think this way of presenting the problem is reasonable? To answer, consider, for example, whether there are just two choices and two states associated with each. Is "life as usual" the same for the believer and the nonbeliever? Does Pascal make any assumptions about what God is like? (See I. Hacking, *The Emergence of Probability*, for a discussion of various forms of Pascal's Wager.)

10. Flu immunizations can offer valuable protection against the flu, particularly in an epidemic year. The shots, however, are not entirely unproblematic. Some people experience an allergic reaction from flu shots. This reaction is less severe than a case of flu and lasts a much shorter time. Another problem is that in order to be effective, the flu shot must be administered before it is known whether an epidemic is on the way.

    Suppose you are trying to decide whether to get a flu shot. Public health doctors assign a probability of 0.8 that this year will be an epidemic year in your city. You have never had the flu in a nonepidemic year and believe the probability that you will get flu is 0 if there is no epidemic. If an epidemic strikes your city and you are not vaccinated, your chances of getting the flu are 0.6, and you will be ill with the flu for seven days. If you are vaccinated, there is a probability of 0.01 that you will have a reaction and be ill for two days.

    Flu vaccination is free at the student health clinic, and you do not particularly mind getting shots. Thus, it is reasonable to equate units of (negative) utility of this decision with days of illness.

    a. What is the probability that you will get the flu if you are not vaccinated?

    b. What is the expected utility of not being vaccinated?

    c. What is the expected utility of being vaccinated?

    d. If you follow the rule of maximizing expected utilities, will you get the flu shot?

11. Suppose a person who needs $10,000 to stay in business (the business is the person's only means of support) is offered the choice between a $10,000

interest-free loan for 10 years or a gamble on a prize of $100,000 if any number but a six is rolled on a single throw of a fair die (but nothing if the six shows). Also suppose this person has no other way of obtaining the money needed to stay in business.

    a. Is it rational for this person to choose the gamble rather than the loan?

    b. Why or why not?

    c. What does this problem suggest about the practice of equating units of utility with units of money?

    d. What does this problem suggest about considering risks as well as possible gains when contemplating an action?

12. You shop regularly at outlet stores that reduce prices on unsold items by 50 percent every Wednesday. On Saturday you see a jacket you like that costs $100. You would like to wait until Wednesday, when you could get it for $50, but figure there is a probability of 0.75 that it will be sold before Wednesday. If the jacket is sold before Wednesday, you will purchase a similar one for $125 at another store. Construct a decision matrix to solve your shopping dilemma (to buy now or wait), and make a rational decision.

13. You are buying a new set of tires for your 10-year-old automobile. Identical sets of tires can be purchased for $532 with a six-year warranty or $476 with a four-year warranty.

    Assign probabilities to "keeping your car for at least six years" and "keeping your car for no more than four years."

    Set up a decision matrix for choosing between the six-year and four-year warranties, decide which to choose, and explain why your choice is rational.

14. You are trying to decide whether to purchase collision insurance for your six-year-old automobile. The car has a retail value of $6,000. The price of the insurance for a year, with a $500 deductible, is $300.

    a. What are some of the probabilities and utilities you would consider in making your decision?

    b. Suppose you decide to purchase the insurance. Can you construct a decision matrix that supports this decision?

15. If you were offered the choice between a $10 gift and a ticket with a 0.10 chance of winning $100, which would you choose?

    Explain why.

    Which decision rule did you use?

Chapter Seven

CONFIRMATION OF HYPOTHESES

I. HYPOTHESES

The first time I baked cupcakes, they tasted fine but looked funny. They were cracked, crooked, wobbly, and peaked. When I told an experienced cook about my cupcakes, she said they had been baked in an oven that was too hot. This surprised me, for I had followed cookbook directions carefully, but I decided to test her claim. If she is right, I thought, and if I make the cupcakes the same way but bake them at a lower temperature, they should turn out all right. I baked another batch, lowering the oven temperature 50 degrees. This time the cupcakes looked the way they were supposed to, and I believed the cook was correct in saying that my first cupcakes had been baked in an oven that was too hot.

This experience illustrates the type of reasoning that is examined in chapter 7. To check whether the oven was too hot, I *tested* by making a prediction based on the cook's diagnosis and by observing what happened. Sentences that are tested in this way are called hypotheses. Webster's definition captures this sense of *hypothesis*: "a supposition used as a basis from which to draw conclusions." *Hypothesis* has other related uses in ordinary language. It can mean a guess or suspicion that something is the case, without an accompanying proposal to test the suspicion: "Our *hypothesis* is that the mouse stole the cheese." *Hypothesis* also can refer to a belief that is not supported, or not yet supported, by evidence: "The existence of life on other planets is only a hypothesis." In this chapter, *hypothesis* refers to any sentence that we want to test by determining whether predictions that follow from it are true. Scientists regularly test hypotheses by performing experiments or making observations to check the truth of predictions based on those hypotheses. In the right circumstances, true predictions offer inductive support and are said to **confirm** hypotheses; predictions that turn out to be false **disconfirm**, or inductively undermine, hypotheses. In this chapter, we examine the logic of confirmation, which is an important part of inductive logic.

Hypotheses can be formulated about any subject matter. In an attempt to understand why a presidential candidate made false claims in a debate, a reporter offered the hypothesis that sloppy work by the candidate's staff was the cause. Many hypotheses, such as this one, are causal. Mill's methods, which are closely related to the form of reasoning discussed in this chapter, are helpful for checking the truth of causal hypotheses. Hypotheses can be expressed in various ways. Some have the form of universal generalizations: "All human languages have terms for kinship relations." Some have the form of statistical generalizations: "Forty-nine percent of all Americans approve of the way the president is handling foreign affairs." Other hypotheses are particular rather than general sentences: "A mouse is in the kitchen."

II. THE HYPOTHETICO-DEDUCTIVE METHOD

Many science textbooks for high school and college classes present the following simple version of the **hypothetico-deductive method**:

> To see whether a hypothesis is true, derive some prediction from it. If the prediction is true, then the hypothesis is confirmed. If the prediction is false, then the hypothesis is disconfirmed.

Example

> If the too-hot oven caused the cupcakes to peak, then baking the next batch at a lower temperature will give good results.
> Baking the next batch at a lower temperature gave good results.
> _____
> The too-hot oven caused the cupcakes to peak.

This argument is not deductive. We can see that the premises could be true, but the conclusion false. Even though the cupcakes that were baked at a lower temperature turned out the right shape, the *cause* of the failure the first time might have been something other than the temperature. For example, I might have mismeasured one of the ingredients in the first batch. This argument, as it stands, is not a good inductive argument either. It requires additional premises to provide support for the hypothesis that the high-oven temperature was the cause of the misshapen cupcakes.

In this chapter, we develop an account of reasoning about the truth of hypotheses that better reflects both common-sense reasoning and scientific practice.

The form of reasoning we want to examine can be illustrated with a famous example from seventeenth-century science—Galileo's use of the telescope to check a prediction based on the **heliocentric** (Sun-centered) hypothesis that Earth and other planets revolve around the Sun.

In Galileo's day, the prevailing **geocentric** (Earth-centered) hypothesis was one that had been adopted fourteen hundred years earlier by Claudius Ptolemy, a Greek astronomer. The Ptolemaic hypothesis states that our immobile Earth stands at the center of the universe, with the other planets and the Sun revolving around it. Using this model of the universe and making careful observations, Ptolemaic astronomers were able to calculate and predict accurately the positions of stars and planets at various times of the year. In other words, the geocentric hypothesis had resulted in many true predictions and was regarded as well confirmed. No European scientist challenged its truth.

In 1543 Copernicus, a Polish astronomer, proposed a new heliocentric way of thinking. In his model, the Earth and other planets revolve around the Sun. Copernicus did not base his system on any new observations or incorrect predictions by the Ptolemaic astronomers. His account simplified calculation but did not offer a new description of the universe. Accordingly, his system made the same predictions as the Ptolemaic system regarding the observable positions of visible heavenly bodies. The Copernican system simplified calculating orbits because by considering the Sun at the center of the system, orbits of the planets are more regular and nearly circular in shape. About 50 years after Copernicus's book was published, a Danish astronomer, Tycho Brahe, introduced still another planetary system in which the Earth was motionless, the Sun orbited the Earth, and the other planets orbited the Sun. The geocentric Tychonic system had the same mathematical advantages as the Copernican system—it offered simpler orbits with easier calculations than the Ptolemaic system—and it fit all observational evidence. Moreover, in a time when scripture was considered by many scholars to be relevant to such matters, the Tychonic system agreed with biblical remarks about the Earth's not moving. Psalm 104, for example, says: "O Lord my God . . . who laid the foundations of the earth, that it should not be removed for ever."

All three of these planetary systems—Ptolemy's, Copernicus's, and Tycho's—were proposed before 1609, the year the telescope was invented. Galileo did not invent the telescope, but he built one that same year and was the first to use the instrument for astronomical observations. Soon after he built his telescope, a student suggested that if the Copernican system were correct, then Venus, as it moves in its orbit between the Earth and the Sun, should show a range of phases similar to the phases of the Moon— from almost dark to crescent to nearly full. (See Figure 7.1.) Galileo turned his telescope on Venus, and over a period of several months he was able to observe the phases. (You can observe this yourself with a good pair of binoculars.) He interpreted these data as evidence that the Copernican (heliocentric) system was correct—that the apparently immobile Earth actually revolves around the Sun.

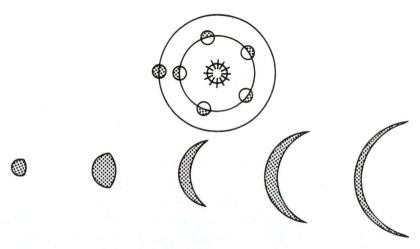

FIGURE 7.1   PHASES OF VENUS

In the Copernican system, Venus can appear nearly full as it passes behind the Sun, and its size varies greatly. Source: Richard S. Westfall, *The Construction of Modern Science: Mechanisms and Mechanics* (Cambridge: Cambridge University Press, 1971). Used by permission of the publisher.

As a first approach to understanding the hypothetico-deductive method, we can follow a science-textbook pattern to reconstruct Galileo's reasoning. His hypothesis is "The Copernican system is correct." On the basis of this hypothesis, Galileo (with the help of his student) deduced a prediction that could be checked by observation and would be true if the hypothesis were true. The prediction in this case is "Venus will show phases." The argument can be stated as follows:

> If the Copernican system is correct, then Venus will show phases.
> Venus shows phases.
> _____
> The Copernican system is correct.

This form of the argument is similar to the argument that concluded that a too hot oven caused the cupcakes to fail. We recall that Tycho's geocentric system, however, also predicts the phases of Venus. Therefore, both premises of the Copernican argument can be true and the conclusion false. Thus, as Galileo was aware, this argument for the Copernican system is not deductive.

Normally, arguments for hypotheses are intended to be inductive arguments, not deductive arguments. The truth of the premises of an inductive argument never guarantees a true conclusion. *Confirmation* refers to positive inductive support rather than to a guarantee of truth. So the question we need to address is whether, in arguments of the (inductive) hypothetico-deductive form, the premises lend probabilistic support to the conclusion. If we consider the hypothetico-deductive argument in its simple form, the answer to this question is "not enough." This answer is less distressing than it might seem, however, because the actual form of reasoning used by scientists to confirm hypotheses depends on additional premises not recognized in this preliminary version of the hypothetico-deductive method.

III. COMPLEXITIES IN THE HYPOTHETICO-DEDUCTIVE METHOD

The name *hypothetico-deductive method* is misleading. The term *deductive* refers not to the overall structure of these arguments but rather to the nature of the connection between the hypothesis and the observable prediction that is deduced from it. To say the connection between the hypothesis and the observable prediction is deductive means that if the hypothesis is true, then the prediction cannot be false. The conditional sentence that states this relationship is but one premise in a confirmation argument, however. Moreover, in many confirmation arguments, the connection between the hypothesis and the observable prediction is inductive rather than deductive. In such arguments, the truth of the hypothesis makes it highly probable that the prediction will be true but does not guarantee the truth of the prediction.

1. AUXILIARY HYPOTHESES

If we turn our attention to the conditional premiss of Galileo's argument, we can see that additional information is required to connect the main hypothesis deductively with the observable prediction. This information consists of sentences that are usually unstated but assumed to be true. These assumptions are called **auxiliary hypotheses**. They form part of a generally accepted theoretical background or standard conditions of the observation or experiment. Although they are assumed to be true in the context of testing the hypothesis for which they are auxiliaries, they can themselves be tested in other contexts. One of Galileo's assumptions (auxiliary hypotheses) was "Venus lies between the Earth and the Sun." Because this assumption was a part of the standard view of astronomy at that time, it was not in question. Another of Galileo's auxiliary hypotheses was "The telescope is a reliable instrument for observing celestial bodies." If these two auxiliary hypotheses were stated, the conditional premiss in Galileo's argument would be:

> If the Copernican system is correct, and if the telescope is a reliable instrument of observation, and if Venus lies between the Earth and the Sun, then Venus will show a complete set of phases.

There are two important types of auxiliary hypotheses. One type has to do with **proper testing conditions.** In general, auxiliary hypotheses of this type are concerned with whether all of the equipment (such as the telescope) and materials used in a test are in proper working order and whether the observers are capable of correctly assessing the outcome of a test.

The second type of auxiliary hypothesis comes from **theoretical background knowledge**. Hypothesis testing is carried out against a background of presumed knowledge, such as the knowledge that Venus is between the Earth and the Sun. Tests of hypotheses concerning the curative powers of drugs assume that certain theories of human physiology and microbiology are true. The physical theory of optics plays a background role in any tests that use microscopes or telescopes. Various theories, or selected parts of theories, function as auxiliary hypotheses when they are assumed to be true in a test of another hypothesis.

Sometimes, especially when a test has a surprising or disturbing outcome, scientists reexamine the auxiliary hypotheses and may subject them to tests. When we recall that Galileo was the first to use a telescope to observe the heavens, we can understand how his auxiliary hypothesis about the reliability of the telescope could be challenged. In the controversy that followed his discoveries (he was criticized, warned, then silenced, and finally tried by the Inquisition and placed under house arrest by the Catholic Church), Galileo suggested his critics look through the telescope to observe what he had seen. With his instrument, he had observed not only the phases of Venus but also the moons of Jupiter and the mountains on our Moon. His critics refused to look through the telescope though, because they believed that telescopes could not be relied on to show what was really there.

In Galileo's time, questions about his telescope were chiefly theoretical. That is to say, the optical principles used to construct telescopes were considered dubious. Intelligent critics thought it implausible that putting together two curved lenses—each of which would distort the appearance of objects—could enable an observer to see far-away objects more clearly. Curved lenses and mirrors were used in those times, as they are now, for distorting images, as, for example, in "fun houses" in amusement parks.

When an entrenched belief is challenged by new test results or new observations, auxiliary hypotheses receive special attention. When things go as expected and widely held beliefs are confirmed by tests, we generally do not bother with investigating assumptions. But those assumptions—auxiliary hypotheses—always are important in hypothesis testing.

Awareness of the role of auxiliary hypotheses in the logic of confirmation requires revision of the simplified form of hypothetico-deductive reasoning. With H denoting the hypothesis that is being tested, $A_1, \ldots, A_n$ representing auxiliary hypotheses, and P standing for the observable prediction, the form of the revised argument is as follows:

> If H and $A_1, \ldots, A_{n,}$ then P.
> P is true.
> ———————————
> H and $A_1, \ldots, A_n$ are true.

This form is an improvement over the first version of an argument for confirmation because it includes the auxiliary hypotheses in the premises and makes the role of these hypotheses in the argument explicit. Further revisions are required, however, for the form of argument to be inductively strong.

2. ALTERNATIVE HYPOTHESES

The form of argument that we have just examined fails to represent the full complexity of the logic of hypothesis testing in part because it does not account for the importance of **alternative hypotheses**. Alternative hypotheses, as their name suggests, are alternatives to the hypothesis that is being tested. That is to say, they are distinct (nonequivalent) hypotheses that have the same observational predictions as the hypothesis that is being tested.

In Galileo's time, three competing planetary systems were proposed by leading astronomers. Whereas Ptolemy's geocentric system did not predict the phases of Venus, Tycho's geocentric system predicted the same phases of Venus that Galileo observed. Thus, the Tychonic hypothesis is an alternative to the Copernican. Tycho's system agreed with the Copernican system in all points of observation that could be obtained using the telescopes of that day. Our previous account of the hypothetico-deductive method of confirmation, even with the added complexity of auxiliary hypotheses, does not say anything about how to choose among incompatible alternative hypotheses with the same observable predictions. Both Tycho's system and the Copernican system predict the phases of Venus, so how do we choose one rather than the other? Before trying to answer that question, we look at another case in which alternative hypotheses accounted for the same observational data. The context is the question of when the first humans arrived in America.

The first American immigrants are believed to have come from Asia, probably crossing the Bering Strait on "bridges" formed either when water froze solidly enough to allow passage by foot between separate islands or when lowered sea levels exposed land bridges connecting the islands. From what is now Alaska, these pioneers (or their descendants) spread all over the North and South American continents. The big question—When did this happen?—is puzzling because much evidence indicates that humans were all over both continents roughly 12,000 years ago. Presumably, this widespread dispersion occurred over a long time. However, before the 1970s there was little evidence that humans were anywhere in North America much before 12,000 years previously, and what evidence there was had been highly disputed.

In the 1970s, two archaeologists made an important discovery that they interpreted as confirmation of the hypothesis "Humans were in Beringia 27,000 years ago" [W. Irving and C. Harrington (1973) "Upper Pleistocene Radiocarbon-Dated Artifacts from the Northern Yukon," *Science* 179]. In what is now Alaska, the archaeologists found mammoth bones that showed traces of having been altered by humans. Bones can be shaped into tools only when they are fresh; after a relatively short time, they become too brittle to work. Although mammoths have long been extinct in North America, we know from finding projectile points (parts of weapons) in mammoth carcasses that human hunters and mammoths did coexist for a time. The worked bones that Irving and Harrington found were subjected to radiocarbon dating, which showed that this mammoth had died approximately 27,000 years ago. (The correctness of radiocarbon dating is an important auxiliary hypothesis.)

Nevertheless, many archaeologists did not accept these bone tools as confirmation of the hypothesis that humans were in America 27,000 years ago. They preferred an alternative hypothesis that could accommodate the dates of the worked bones just as well. This hypothesis states that the bones were from an animal that died 27,000 years ago and subsequently remained frozen in the tundra for another 15,000 years. Then, during a thawing period around 12,000 years ago, the mammoth remains were found by newly arrived humans, who at that point worked the bones. The long freeze had preserved the bones from becoming brittle so that when the animals thawed, their bones could be worked just like fresh bones.

Though this alternative hypothesis may seem far-fetched, in recent times long-frozen mammoths have been heaved from the earth in Siberia during thawing and freezing cycles. Their meat was eaten; their ivory tusks were sold on the market; their stomachs were examined to determine what food they had eaten before they died. Moreover, their bones were worked to make tools. At the time of the discovery of the worked bones in Beringia, no other evidence supported the presence of humans in that region before 12,000 years ago. Thus, many archaeologists regarded as initially more plausible the hypothesis that the bones had been frozen for 15,000 years before being worked than the hypothesis of human occupation 27,000 years ago.*

Let us return to our question of how we choose among alternative hypotheses that have the same observable predictions. We could say, like the archaeologists who rejected the claim that humans were in Beringia 27,000 years ago, that when the same true prediction follows from different hypotheses, then the hypothesis that was more plausible before the test (or had a higher **prior probability**) is the hypothesis confirmed by the test. Before the worked bones were found and dated, the hypothesis that humans were present in America 27,000 years ago was much less probable than the hypothesis that frozen bones can be salvaged and worked. Either hypothesis can account for the presence of worked bones from animals that lived 27,000 years ago. If we think of tests as resulting in an increase or decrease of the probability of a hypothesis rather than as settling its truth or falsity, then a test that supports two alternative hypotheses equally well leaves their probabilities relative to one another unchanged. In other words, since either alternative could account for the result, the one that was more probable before the test observation remained more probable after it.

On this view, the prior probability of a hypothesis—the probability that the hypothesis is true prior to taking account of some test of that hypothesis—is important in the logic of confirmation. Not only do these probabilities help us to decide which hypothesis among several alternatives is confirmed by a particular test, they also help us to decide which hypotheses are worth taking the trouble to test. If a hypothesis is very implausible (if its truth is almost impossible to imagine), scientists are reluctant to spend time, effort, or money on testing it. Furthermore, if a hypothesis has a very high prior probability—such as the geocentric hypothesis in Galileo's time—then, even when tests apparently disconfirm it, efforts are made to "save the hypothesis" by questioning auxiliary hypotheses. The debate between supporters of the heliocentric and of the geocentric systems continued for nearly 100 years after the Copernican system was first published. For much of that time, prior probabilities favored the geocentric hypothesis. The laws of motion formulated by Newton, who was born the year Galileo died, severely undercut the geocentric hypothesis, however. These laws, which almost all scientists accepted soon after Newton published them, showed that Tycho's geocentric system required motions that were impossible. Newton's work was followed in the nineteenth century by new observations (such as stellar parallax), which were made possible by better instruments. All of this evidence drastically reduced the probability of the geocentric hypothesis.

The prior probabilities of hypotheses depend on a number of factors. Previous studies or tests can contribute to the probability of a hypothesis. The prior probability

---

* This situation has changed as archaeologists have continued to search for signs of early human occupation of America. They have found evidence that humans were in Chile 14,000 years ago and in the Eastern United States 16,000 years ago.

that a person new to politics will win an election to a major office is usually lower than the prior probability that a person who has run several successful campaigns will win. The prior probability that a new sitcom will succeed on television is enhanced if the pilot for that sitcom had a good reception.

The prior probability of a hypothesis that is compatible with well-established theories is greater than the prior probability of a hypothesis that conflicts with accepted views. The prior probability of the hypothesis that there was life on Mars, even before NASA's Spirit Mars rover landed there was low because of well-established theories about the absence of life-supporting resources on Mars.

A hypothesis proposed by a legitimate authority has higher prior probability than a hypothesis proposed by a crank. This point is related to the former because hypotheses posed by cranks often conflict with well-established theories. Van Daniken's hypothesis that creatures from outer space created the prehistoric earthworks found in North and South America has a lower prior probability than the hypothesis of established archaeologists, who say the earthworks were made by indigenous people. The prior probability that a particular diet will result in weight loss without endangering health is higher when the source is a trained dietitian than when the source is a person without credentials in the field of nutrition.

Hypotheses that are similar to successful hypotheses in various ways, such as employing similar causal mechanisms, have higher prior probabilities than hypotheses that rely on novel and untried mechanisms. Thus, the hypothesis that dogs could be trained to assist people whose vision or hearing is impaired had a reasonably high prior probability in light of the successful training of dogs to assist humans in herding and other tasks.

In some cases, only rough, nonquantitative estimates of prior probabilities can be made. In others, precise quantitative values can be assigned, as we will see in Section VI on Bayesian confirmation. Nevertheless, even when no numerical values are assigned to prior probabilities, these probabilities are implicit in our judgments of whether hypotheses are confirmed by the predictions that follow from them because the prior probabilities determine the relative standing of competing hypotheses with similar predictions.

3. FORM OF INDUCTIVE ARGUMENTS OF CONFIRMATION

We can now examine the structure of reasoning that is used to confirm hypotheses. It is considerably more complex than the first hypothetico-deductive form, which has only two premises. Showing how the simple hypothetico-deductive structure plays a part in reasoning about hypotheses, this new formulation also exhibits the larger overall inductive structure of these arguments when they are supplemented by additional considerations.

Following, in summary, is the structure of arguments of confirmation:

1. The hypothesis is initially plausible. (It has some degree of prior probability.)
2. If the hypothesis and the auxiliary hypotheses are true, then the observable prediction is true.
3. The observable prediction is true.
4. No alternative hypothesis has as high a prior probability as the hypothesis that is being tested.
5. Therefore, the hypothesis is true.

Arguments of confirmation thus have four premisses. The first premiss states the plausibility of the hypothesis to be tested. The second and third premisses are the same premisses found in the simplified version of the hypothetico-deductive form of reasoning. The fourth premiss again appeals to prior probabilities to compare the hypothesis being tested with alternatives that give rise to the same prediction. If a test confirms several alternative hypotheses, the hypothesis that is best confirmed after the test is the one that started out with the greatest degree of plausibility (prior probability). A positive prediction that follows from several different hypotheses confirms each of them; after the test, however, the hypothesis that was most probable before the test remains most probable. The only way to change this relative ranking is by finding negative (disconfirming) evidence or by introducing a new hypothesis.

Although the conclusion of the argument of confirmation is "The hypothesis is true," we must remember that because the argument is inductive, the strength of support that the premisses can give to the conclusion varies. In a situation, for example, in which several alternative hypotheses have prior probabilities only slightly lower than those of the hypothesis being tested, the argument for the truth of the hypothesis will not be very strong. The hypothesis will be only a little better supported after the test than before. In another case, in which a hypothesis has no plausible rivals to account for the observed results, the argument can be strong. If a hypothesis has an extremely high prior probability, a successful prediction might not raise its probability much. If a hypothesis has a very low prior probability, a successful prediction might not raise its probability enough to make it seem well confirmed.

An important consideration in judging the strength of arguments of confirmation is the nature of a hypothesis itself. On the one hand, a low-level empirical hypothesis, such as "There's a mouse in the kitchen," can be strongly supported by a small amount of the right kind of evidence: If we find mouse droppings on the countertop, and we can rule out any other possible explanations for the droppings, there is little doubt that the hypothesis is correct. On the other hand, a theoretical hypothesis as high-level and wide-ranging as the Copernican hypothesis will not be strongly confirmed by a few observations with a new scientific instrument. Although we have some things to say about the quality of evidence, a discussion of the amount and type of evidence necessary to support broad theoretical hypotheses is beyond the scope of this text. The general framework for confirmation arguments developed here, nevertheless, is intended to apply to both high-level and low-level hypotheses.

Finally, any general conclusions about what the world is like can be revised in light of further evidence. This should be clear from our insistence that inductive arguments can be strengthened or weakened by the inclusion of additional evidence. New archaeological evidence has led many scientists to revise their views about how long humans have occupied the Americas. Geocentric theories were strongly supported for a very long time by all the available evidence. These theories were overturned as new evidence was evaluated and absorbed by a scientific community. The hypothesis that smoking causes lung cancer has become established firmly by a patient accumulation of statistical evidence over many years. The hypothesis that running a four-minute mile was beyond human capability was overthrown by Roger Bannister in a single race. Some of today's best-supported theories will undoubtedly go the way of geocentrism as new ones take their places.

4. CONFIRMING A CAUSAL HYPOTHESIS

Edward Jenner's confirmation of the hypothesis that an attack of cowpox confers immunity to smallpox is a classic in the history of medicine. About 30 years ago, the World Health Organization announced that smallpox, long dreaded for its power to kill and disfigure, was at last completely eliminated; not a single case of the disease remained in the world. Because smallpox spreads only by contact among humans (no other carriers of the disease are known), this was a significant step toward the achievement of worldwide health.

Smallpox is highly contagious. When Columbus's sailors first brought it to America, whole populations of Native Americans, who had never been exposed, were destroyed by the disease. Smallpox epidemics were common in Europe and the Middle East before the twentieth century, and until 30 years ago, as noted, the disease was a serious problem in some parts of the world. In the 1960s, New York City was thrown into near panic when it became known that a foreign traveler with an active case of smallpox had spent several hours in Grand Central Station.

For centuries doctors tried to discover a way to prevent smallpox. It was known that those who survived an attack of the disease were immune to further infection. It was also known that some persons contracted a relatively mild form of the disease. Thus, one method of preventing a severe case of smallpox was to be inoculated—that is, to be scratched with infectious material from a sore of someone with a mild case of the disease. This method of inoculation, widely practiced in China as early as the sixteenth century, was hazardous and could result in the very condition it was designed to prevent.

In England, persons who lived and worked near dairy farms were susceptible to cowpox, a similar but much milder disease that attacked both cows and humans. The disease was never fatal and left only a few faint scars. Jenner—a doctor who lived and worked in the dairy region of Gloucestershire, England—was aware of the belief, commonly held in that area, that an attack of cowpox conferred immunity not only to further attacks of that disease but to smallpox as well.

Jenner decided to test this hypothesis. A report of his test is given by Isaac Asimov:

> In 1796, [Jenner] decided to chance the supreme test. First, he inoculated an eight-year-old boy named James Phipps with cowpox, using fluid from a cowpox blister on a milkmaid's hand. Two months later came the crucial and desperate part of the test. Jenner deliberately inoculated young James with smallpox itself.
>
> The boy did not catch the disease. He was immune.

—I. Asimov, The Intelligent Man's Guide to the Biological Sciences

We can reconstruct Jenner's argument using the model for confirmation provided in the preceding section.

1. The hypothesis "An attack of cowpox confers immunity to smallpox" is initially plausible.

It was widely believed in Gloucestershire that an attack of cowpox produced this benefit. Dairymaids and others who worked around cows, although susceptible to cowpox, never seemed to get smallpox, even during epidemics. The plausibility of the hypothesis was also enhanced by an analogy. Mild attacks of smallpox conferred immunity to further attacks, and cowpox produced symptoms similar to those of extremely mild cases of smallpox. All of this made the hypothesis worth testing.

2. If an attack of cowpox confers immunity to smallpox, then Phipps, who has had cowpox and is inoculated with smallpox, will not contract the disease.

In the preceding conditional sentence, the prediction follows deductively from the hypothesis, with the aid of three auxiliary hypotheses:

(i) The smallpox matter with which Phipps was inoculated had not lost its potency.
(ii) Jenner knew how to inoculate, and he was qualified to observe whether Phipps actually had cowpox and whether he contracted smallpox.
(iii) Persons who are inoculated and who do not contract even a mild case of smallpox are immune.

The first two auxiliary hypotheses refer to the conditions of the test; the third is a theoretical background assumption, based on past experience with the disease.

3. The observable prediction is true. Phipps did not contract smallpox.
4. No alternative hypothesis has as high a prior probability as the hypothesis that is tested.

Jenner's hypothesis is a causal hypothesis (having cowpox *causes* immunity to small-pox). Causal hypotheses are difficult to test because of alternative causes that could account for what is observed. For example, some persons have natural immunities to some diseases. Phipps may have been one of those fortunate few who are naturally immune to smallpox. The alternative causal hypothesis "Phipps has a natural immunity to smallpox" supports exactly the same observable prediction: Phipps did not contract smallpox.

The hypothesis of natural immunity, however, had a lower prior probability than the cowpox hypothesis. Although no exact statistics were available, epidemics of the disease showed that a natural immunity to this highly contagious disease was relatively rare compared with the immunity apparently conferred on dairymaids by prior cases of cowpox.

5. Therefore, an attack of cowpox causes immunity to smallpox.

The hypothesis is confirmed.

Example

> Researchers have long believed that using cocaine greatly increases the risk of a heart attack, even for persons who are otherwise at low risk. A study (reported in *Science News*, June 5, 1999) confirms that cocaine users' risk increases dramatically within minutes of taking the drug. M. A. Mittleman and his research team analyzed records of 3,946 heart-attack patients. Thirty-eight said they had used cocaine in the year before the attack, and nine had used it an hour before the heart-attack symptoms appeared. The researchers concluded that during the hour before the attack, the individuals who used cocaine increased their heart-attack risk by 2,400 percent. The researchers based their figures primarily on the age of the victims (users were an average of seventeen years younger than nonusers who had heart attacks). Other risk factors for heart attacks—the likelihood of being male, nonwhite, and a smoker—were accounted for in the study as well.

In this example, the hypothesis that cocaine use is a serious risk for heart attacks was tested. The prediction was that among heart-attack victims, cocaine users at a lower risk for heart attacks in categories (smoking, age, race, etc.) other than drug use would be at a higher risk after taking the drug. Auxiliary hypotheses have to do with the accuracy of the patients' records and reports of their behavior. The reliability of the statistics used for comparisons is another auxiliary hypothesis. No alternative hypotheses were mentioned to account for the observations, though there might have been some unknown risk factors that the nine cocaine users shared and that caused their attacks. Known risks for heart attacks, such as smoking, race, and gender, were accounted for in the study, so these are not the basis for plausible alternative hypotheses. The prior probability of the cocaine hypothesis is higher than that of the hypothesis of unknown risk because of well-established effects of cocaine, such as increased heart rates.

An impressive feature of this study is that the risk of suffering a heart attack for the cocaine user is extremely high in the hour after the drug is taken—twenty-four times normal.

Exercise Set 7.1

In each of the following:

(a) Identify the hypothesis.

(b) State some observable predictions that follow from the hypothesis. Identify any auxiliary hypotheses that are required for predictions.

(c) Formulate an alternative hypothesis, if possible, to account for what has been observed.

(d) Compare (in a rough, nonnumerical way) the prior probabilities of the original hypothesis with any alternatives. Indicate the sources on which your probability assignments depend. (For example, you might assign a very high prior probability to a hypothesis because it fits well with established scientific theories; or you might assign a very low prior probability to the hypothesis on the basis of past experiences with similar types of hypotheses.)

1. Many Americans—up to 70 percent—do not get enough vitamin D through sunshine, even though the vitamin is in most milk. Lack of vitamin D is associated with various serious medical problems, so researchers suggested fortifying bread with vitamin D yeast. This raised a problem, though, because some thought that the yeast, which contains vitamin D_2, might not have the same effect as vitamin D_3, which comes from the sun and is added to milk.

   However, lab rats when fed the vitamin D_2 bread showed all the expected benefits that come from vitamin D_3. So it looks as if the new type of fortified bread can help to correct the nation's vitamin D insufficiency problem.

2. A plastic surgeon who specializes in face-lifts recently commented that his youngest patients are frequently actresses. He believes that actresses seek face-lifts at an earlier age than other women because actresses' faces "fall" as a result of extensive massaging when they apply and remove their makeup.

3. In 1999 researchers studied the development of myopia (nearsightedness) in 479 children who had slept in various conditions of light when they were infants. Thirty-four percent of those who had slept with a night-light until two years of age showed myopia as opposed to only 10 percent of those who had slept in darkness.

   Some researchers disputed the hypothesis that sleeping with a night-light caused myopia. Their study, based on 1,220 children, indicates that night-lights do not make myopia more likely. In that group, 17 percent of those who had slept with a night-light became myopic, as opposed to 20 percent of those who had slept without one. The researchers in the second study questioned parents about their own myopia, suspecting a hereditary factor for the disease.

4. On the basis of annual data, Mr. Ehrenhalt [regional commissioner for the Bureau of Labor Statistics] said, fewer teen-agers (16 to 19 years old) in proportion to the youth population are working in New York City than in other central cities. While New York is at the bottom in the proportion of its young people actually holding jobs, he said, the city's rate of unemployment for that group has run below that in the major middle western cities hard hit by the recession.

   The seeming contradiction, he explained, stems from the fact that a large element of youths here in the 16- to 19-year-old bracket have not been looking for jobs and, in many cases, have probably not even been thinking about working because jobs for young people are so hard to get here. Consequently, they are not counted as unemployed in population surveys, he said.

   —D. Stetson, *The New York Times*

5. Does incarceration of juvenile offenders cause them to continue criminal activity after their release? A study by R. M. Giguere compared data concerning criminal activity of a sample of incarcerated youth after their release with a group who had engaged in similar activity but who were given probation or assigned to some public service activity instead of being incarcerated. She found that incarceration did not stop further criminal behavior and may have made it more likely.

6. Deterring murder is the reason most often given for the death penalty. (The other main reason is retribution: The murderer should suffer loss of life in retribution for the life or lives taken.) Statistics gathered before 2007, when 14 states had no death penalty, have consistently shown, however, that states with a death penalty have a higher murder rate (5.5 per 100,000) than those without (3.1). Since then, New York, New Jersey, and New Mexico have abolished the death penalty, and several other states are considering abolishing it, in part because of the high cost of prosecuting death-penalty cases. We expect the newest statistics to show a drop in homicide levels in all states that have abolished the death penalty. We are also aware, however, that in recent years there has been an overall decline in homicide rates in the U.S.

7. Germany's celebrity polar bear Knut drowned after collapsing at the Berlin Zoo and falling into a pool of water in front of dozens of witnesses. A necropsy found the bear suffered from encephalitis—brain swelling likely caused by an unnoticed infection. "We believe that this suspected infection must already have been

there for a long time . . . at least several weeks, possibly months," Achim Gruber, a veterinary medicine professor at Berlin's Free University, told the Associated Press.

—L. Johnston, *NY Daily News*

8. In the following excerpt, P. V. Glob refers to studies of three Iron Age men, found in Danish peat bogs, in which they had been buried for nearly 2,000 years. The circumstances of the burials as well as their location showed that the men had been deliberately killed, probably in conjunction with some ceremony. Because bog water, which is saturated with soil acids, prevented deterioration of the bodies, the contents of the stomachs and intestines of the three men were examined and analyzed.

In each of these last meals no trace was found of summer or autumn fruits, such as strawberries, blackberries, raspberries, apples, or hips; nor was there any trace of greenstuffs. There are thus grounds for thinking that all three men met their deaths in winter or early spring, before everything had come into leaf. From this we may conjecture that the deaths took place at the time of the mid-winter celebrations whose purpose was to hasten the coming of spring. It was on just such occasions that bloody human sacrifices reached a peak in the Iron Age.

—P. V. Glob, The Bog People

9. Government health agencies and dermatologists continue to warn young people of the dangers of tanning beds and sun lamps, which they believe cause melanomas, a sometimes fatal form of skin cancer.

Studies show that people who use tanning beds are 75 percent more likely to have melanoma.

Despite such warnings, a survey of 3,800 women between 14 and 22 showed that 40 percent of 18- to 22-year-olds and 22 percent of the 14- to 17-year-olds had exposed themselves to indoor tanning.

10. *Emotional preparation aids surgical recovery*:

A study of 60 men undergoing coronary bypass grafts at the University of Iowa Medical Center was conducted recently. The men were divided into two groups. One group received the hospital's standard preparation for patients about to undergo surgery: a brochure on the procedures and a short visit from a nurse to answer questions. The other group watched a videotape called "Living Proof" that followed a patient through the operation and recovery. While 75 percent of those with the standard preparation suffered after the surgery from acute hypertension—a condition that can endanger coronary bypass patients in the first 12 hours after surgery—only 40 percent of those who viewed the tape had the problem.

—D. Goleman, *The New York Times*, December 10, 1987

11. Attempts to modify weather (usually through cloud seeding) were so unsuccessful that by the late 1980s meteorologists in the United States had almost abandoned trying to make it work. But

> advanced instruments [including Doppler radar and Polarimetric radar] can now pierce the veil of clouds and track the complex processes inside them. New satellite sensors can extend these types of cloud measurements over much of the globe.
>
> With these tools, scientists have documented how rainfall is increased or reduced when natural "seeding" takes place by desert dust storms, smoke from forest fires, sea spray, and even urban pollution. Some of these particles produce large cloud droplets, thus triggering rainfall, while others form many small ones, slowing or stopping precipitation. One scientist has found that dust from the Sahara Desert reduces rainfall, while dust from the salt laden Aral Sea area increases it. These 'inadvertent weather modification' studies have validated some of the basic principles thought to be at work in intentional weather modification.

> —S. Cole, "Weather on Demand,"Invention and Technology (2005, Fall)

12. The *French paradox* is the name given to the observation that despite a French diet that is rich in fat, obesity and heart-attack rates are much lower in France than in countries with "healthier" diets. The French also drink red wine that, according to some, has a neutralizing effect on the saturated fats in the diet.

    Resveratrol, a compound found in grape skins, has received attention as the cause of the fat-busting properties of red wine.

    The Mayo Clinic Bulletin on Health Information reported that in studies of mice resveratrol seemed to offer some protection against obesity and diabetes, both risks for heart disease. But they warned:

> "Most research on resveratrol has been done on animals, not people. Research in mice given resveratrol suggests that the antioxidant might also help protect them from obesity and diabetes, both of which are strong risk factors for heart disease. However, those findings were reported only in mice, not in people. In addition, to get the same dose of resveratrol used in the mice studies, a person would have to drink over 60 liters of red wine every day."

> —www.mayoclinic.com/health/red-wine/HB00089

IV. INCREMENTAL CONFIRMATION AND ABSOLUTE CONFIRMATION

Confirmation in most tests, such as Jenner's test of the cowpox hypothesis and Galileo's test of the heliocentric hypothesis, is relative or **incremental**. This means that the probability of a hypothesis after such a test is greater than it was prior to the test.

A hypothesis is confirmed in the **absolute** sense only when it is so strongly supported by evidence that it is almost certainly true—with a probability close to one. Many tests might have to be performed to confirm a hypothesis-absolutely.

Even when a hypothesis is absolutely confirmed, new evidence could overturn it. Before Europeans learned about platypuses, the hypothesis "All mammals bear live young" was considered absolutely confirmed. When Europeans first heard reports of Australian egg-laying mammals, they assumed the aboriginal Australians who had described these strange animals were either mistaken or dishonest. However, the Australians were correct; platypuses are mammals that lay eggs. There are some types of absolutely confirmed hypotheses that may be immune to later refutation, such as the hypothesis that a certain animal, such as the Giant Panda, has inhabited a certain region of China at a particular time. Once the Giant Panda has been observed in the region at that time, the stated hypothesis is immune to further revision unless the "observation" was a delusion, a hoax, or some other kind of mistake. Any hypothesis that is a universal or statistical generalization instead of a singular description of some event, such as observing a Panda, can be revised in light of further evidence.

Newton's laws of motion, long regarded as universally applicable and absolutely confirmed, are now—in light of Einstein's work on relativity—either regarded as only approximately true or restricted in application to particles either not moving at speeds close to the speed of light or not located in strong gravitational fields. To say hypotheses are absolutely confirmed means they are very strongly supported and no evidence is known to count against them. It does not mean that they cannot be rejected in light of future evidence.

Controlled experiments and Mill's methods can be used to test causal hypotheses. Observable predictions deduced from hypotheses are often predictions about the outcome of controlled experiments. The Method of Difference and the Joint Method of Agreement and Difference can sometimes eliminate alternative hypotheses. In controlled experiments, special attention is paid to auxiliary hypotheses that might affect the outcome of a test. The use of varied samples and the repeated use of Mill's methods contribute to the confirmation of hypotheses, for no important hypothesis is firmly accepted or rejected on the basis of a single test.

Any observable prediction that can be derived from a hypothesis can be used to test it, but some predictions are more important than others. Consider, for example, the hypothesis that the wooly mammoths and other large mammals (megafauna) that once roamed North America and Australia became extinct because humans hunted them to extinction. One prediction that follows from the overhunting hypothesis is that these mammals coexisted with humans over a period of time. Archaeological investigation, which has discovered weapons embedded in mammoth carcasses, supports the truth of this prediction. But this evidence does not confirm the overhunting hypothesis nearly so strongly as would archaeological evidence of places where massive numbers of animals were killed or butchered. No such evidence has been found. In fact, many archaeologists believe the long period of coexistence between humans and these animals counts against the overhunting hypothesis and indicates an ecological balance between the hunters and the hunted.

In general, we can say that the more unlikely it is for a prediction to be true unless the hypothesis is true, the better the truth of that prediction confirms the hypothesis. In some cases, it would be very surprising if a prediction turned out to be true unless the hypothesis that gave rise to it were also true. A long period of coexistence between humans and megafauna would not be particularly surprising or unlikely, even if the animals became extinct as a result of some cause other than overhunting by humans. Although extinction can be attributed to human predation, it can also result from a destruction of habitat—which may be a result of human activities, some natural force such as a severe drought, or a combination of both. Giant Pandas in China are now threatened with extinction because of loss of a suitable habitat, despite human efforts to prevent this. Thus, the evidence of coexistence does not weigh very heavily either for or against the overhunting hypothesis.

Proponents of pseudoscientific theories try to find acceptance for them by pointing to successful predictions based on these theories. An example of this is found in **dianetics**—a pseudopsychological theory that predicts the remission of neurotic symptoms in people who undergo the therapy prescribed by dianetic theory. Many persons who submitted to this treatment did improve, so proponents of dianetics can truly say their predictions were true. Neurotic symptoms frequently disappear without any treatment, however. This process is called *spontaneous remission*. In diseases with a high rate of remission of symptoms, it is difficult to say whether a particular treatment caused the symptoms to go away or there was spontaneous remission. Because many people recover from neuroses with no treatment, the true predictions of dianetics do not constitute strong confirmation for the theory.

Astrology attracts many believers, who faithfully read their horoscopes online or in publications, follow the advice given, and note any of the astrological predictions that turn out to be true. Consider some typical examples of forecasts:

1. What appeared to be immovable will now prove to be flexible.
2. An apparent obstacle actually proves to be a stepping-stone toward goal.
3. Be ready for significant change, which could ultimately result in journey.
4. Member of opposite sex does care, will plainly show it.
5. Many people miscalculate when judging your capabilities.

All of these "predictions" are phrased so vaguely that they can be applied to various situations that are not at all unusual or surprising in the lives of most people. The truth of such "predictions" does nothing to confirm the hypothesis that specific events in our lives are influenced by the positions of the stars and planets.

Exercise Set 7.2

1. For the following example:
    a. Identify the hypothesis at issue.
    b. Identify any mistake in reasoning.

   Margaret won a college scholarship based on her swimming ability. She swims competitively for her school. Lately she has noticed joint pain, which the team doctor diagnosed as arthritis. A friend recommends she wear a copper bracelet to alleviate the symptoms, even though there is no scientific support for this treatment. Just before winter break, Margaret buys one for each wrist (for $19.95) and by the time she returns to school, she feels much better. She now promotes the bracelets as a cure for arthritis.

2. Find an example of a prediction made by some pseudoscientific theory and explain why the prediction either does or does not support the theory.

V. DISCONFIRMATION

We have argued that the simple version of the hypothetico-deductive method of confirmation is inadequate and needs to be supplemented with additional premises to provide a suitable model for confirmation. A different response to the inadequacy of the simple method, found in many science textbooks, is that scientific hypotheses cannot be proved; they can only be **disproved**. This suggests that the goal of hypothesis testing is to eliminate false hypotheses rather than to offer direct support for true hypotheses. Let us examine this suggestion in connection with the heliocentric-geocentric controversy.

According to the Ptolemaic system, Venus will not show a full set of phases; it will always have a crescent appearance, although the crescent will vary somewhat in width (see Figure 7.2).

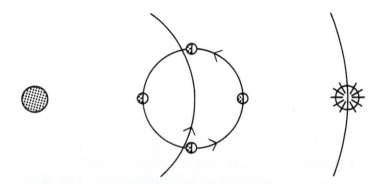

FIGURE 7.2   VENUS, PTOLEMAIC SYSTEM
In the Ptolemaic system, Venus must always appear more or less crescent shaped. Source: Richard S. Westfall, *The Construction of Modern Science: Mechanisms and Mechanics* (Cambridge: Cambridge University Press, 1971). Used by permission of the publisher.

Under the circumstances, Galileo could have used the following argument to disconfirm the hypothesis "The Ptolemaic (geocentric) system is correct." The observable
prediction that follows deductively from this hypothesis is "Venus will not show a full
set of phases."

> If the Ptolemaic (geocentric) system is correct, then Venus will not
>   show a full set of phases.
> Venus does show a full set of phases.
> _____
> The Ptolemaic system is not correct.

As in the argument for confirmation, the first premiss of this argument is a conditional
sentence. A conditional sentence is a compound sentence in which the truth of one of
the clauses (the consequent) is conditional on the truth of the other (the antecedent).
Here, the hypothesis is the antecedent, and the observable prediction, which must be
true if the hypothesis is true, is the consequent. Unlike the simple hypothetico-deductive
argument for confirmation, however, this argument is deductive. (The argument is an
instance of the valid conditional form called *denying the consequent*.) Here is the deductive
form of argument:

> If H, then P.
> P is false.
> _____
> H is false.

Thus, an apparent difference emerges between the confirmation of hypotheses, which
we have said depends on complex inductive reasoning rather than a simple conditional
argument, and the disconfirmation of hypotheses, which can be deductively valid. This
discrepancy accounts for the greater enthusiasm that many scientists express for the
method of disconfirming hypotheses. The method looks particularly attractive when few
hypotheses are available to account for the observed evidence. In such circumstances, one
hopes that the true hypothesis will emerge by elimination of false contenders. For example, if the geocentric hypothesis is rejected deductively, then the heliocentric hypothesis
seems to win by default. However, as we have seen in looking at the geocentric-
heliocentric controversy, proponents of a hypothesis can try to "save" it by rejecting one
or more of the auxiliary hypotheses that are required to connect the hypothesis with the
unfavorable prediction. Although the Ptolemaic system is now rejected by astronomers,
in Galileo's time its prior probability was too great to be outweighed by observations
with an instrument not guaranteed to be reliable. If the disconfirming argument were
fully stated along with the important auxiliary hypotheses, it would read as follows:

> If the Ptolemaic system is correct, if the telescope is a reliable instrument of
>   observation, and if Venus lies between the Earth and the Sun, then Venus
>   will not show a complete set of phases.
> Venus does show phases.
> _____
> Either the Ptolemaic system is incorrect, or the telescope is unreliable, or Venus is not
>   between the Earth and the Sun.

Faced with this set of alternatives, many of Galileo's contemporaries rejected the reliability of the telescope rather than the Ptolemaic system. The general form of this argument for disconfirmation is as follows:

If H and $A_1, \ldots, A_n$, then P.
P is false.
_____
Either H is false or A_1, or $\ldots$, or A_n is false.

In this argument form, the conclusion follows deductively from the premisses, but the conclusion is not simply a rejection of the hypothesis. The conclusion says instead that either the hypothesis is false or one of the auxiliary hypotheses is false.

In scientific practice, it is not appropriate to reject or replace an auxiliary hypothesis just to save a hypothesis that is being tested. Such arbitrary rejection or addition of an auxiliary hypothesis to save a favored hypothesis is called *"ad hoc* reasoning" and is regarded as fallacious. Although arbitrary rejection of auxiliary hypotheses is considered inappropriate, there is not always agreement about whether a particular rejection is arbitrary. Galileo thought his opponents were being arbitrary because they refused to look through the telescope. (See Galileo's own argument for the reliability of his telescope, excerpted in Exercise Set 1.2, Exercise 9.) His opponents did not think they were being arbitrary because they knew that curved lenses distorted images and did not think what they saw through a telescope could support Galileo's case.

When an auxiliary hypothesis is called into question and can be tested, it should be. The methods for testing auxiliary hypotheses are identical to those for testing any other hypothesis. Auxiliary hypotheses cannot be tested in isolation. When an auxiliary hypothesis becomes the focus of attention, still other auxiliary hypotheses have to be called in to connect it with its predictions. An attempt to reach the true hypothesis by eliminating false contenders has drawbacks as well. No theoretical limit can be imposed on the number of possible false hypotheses that have to be eliminated. Although we are not often faced with an abundance of **plausible** hypotheses for testing, we might nevertheless overlook or be unaware of some that should be tested. A situation in which there are only two plausible competing hypotheses and in which the rejection of one "forces" us to accept the other hypothesis seldom occurs. Even if Galileo's arguments could have persuaded his contemporaries to reject Ptolemy's geocentric hypothesis, for example, the Copernican hypothesis is not thereby established, for Tycho's geocentric hypothesis is also compatible with the full set of phases of Venus.

1. CRUCIAL TESTS

Occasionally scientists find themselves in the happy situation of agreeing about auxiliary hypotheses and an observable prediction that confirms one of only two competing hypotheses at the same time that it disconfirms the other. These **crucial tests** have received much attention in the history of science. Jenner's test of the cowpox hypothesis on young Phipps comes close to the ideal situation. The small chance that Phipps was naturally immune to smallpox did not pose a threat in deciding between the following: "Cowpox confers immunity to smallpox," and "Cowpox does not prevent smallpox."

In this case, as in most other examples of crucial testing, the test that seems to settle the question definitively in favor of one of the hypotheses emerges only after prolonged investigation and many "noncrucial" tests. It is unrealistic to call even this kind of scientific reasoning *purely deductive*, for the deductive rejection of one hypothesis is embedded in a series of complex inductive arguments. These inductive arguments serve to support the truth of auxiliary hypotheses, to establish prior probabilities, and to eliminate some alternative hypotheses. Such work is usually necessary before reaching the stage of performing a crucial test. The following section illustrates what typically happens in attempts to disconfirm well-established hypotheses. Like arguments of confirmation, arguments for disconfirmation of a hypothesis involve considerations of prior probabilities and the availability of alternative hypotheses as well as the relation between the hypothesis, auxiliaries, and the observable prediction.

2. DISCONFIRMING A CAUSAL HYPOTHESIS

Different indigenous groups, each with distinct languages and cultures, live in the region of the Amazon river. Some of these groups are constantly engaged in violent warfare with neighboring tribes. The Yanomamö are among the most warlike. Many anthropologists believed that attempts to provide sufficient protein in their diets caused their hostile behavior. The warlike tactics, said those anthropologists, are ecologically advantageous. They enable the Yanomamö to compete for scarce resources in an environment that is inadequately supplied with enough protein for those who live there.

However, when the hypothesis "Warlike behavior among the Yanomamö is caused by a diet deficient in protein" was tested, it was rejected by the two anthropologists who conducted the test (N. Chagnon and Hanes, R. [1979], "Protein Deficiency and Tribal Warfare in Amazonia: New Data," *Science* 203). Chagnon and Hames spent 13 months living with the Yanomamö, carefully recording the foods they ate and calculating the amounts of protein in those foods. They found that the protein intake of the Yanomamö was greater than standard minimum daily requirements. Their diet was not deficient in protein. The argument for disconfirmation can be reconstructed as follows:

1. The hypothesis has initial plausibility.

This hypothesis was the prevailing view among the anthropologists who had studied Amazonian tribal societies. The hypothesis is consistent with one widely accepted theoretic approach to the study of human culture, which views the material conditions in which people live as chief factors in determining their behavior. It is also known that protein deficiencies have various effects not only on human physiology but also on human behavior.

2. If warlike behavior among the Yanomamö is caused by a diet deficient in protein, then the diet of the Yanomamö will exhibit protein deficiency.

The observable prediction of protein deficiency in the Yanomamö diet follows deductively from the hypothesis and the three auxiliary hypotheses that follow:

(i) The methods used by the investigators to measure amounts of available protein in the diet of the Yanomamö were accurate.

(ii) The field study that lasted 13 months was long enough to provide a correct picture of the normal eating patterns of the Yanomamö.

(iii) The "minimum daily requirement of protein" is a good measure of the amount needed to avoid protein deficiency.

The first two auxiliary hypotheses refer to the conditions of the test. The third auxiliary hypothesis is part of generally accepted theoretical knowledge of human nutritional requirements—the theory that is the source of information you see printed on boxes of breakfast cereal.

3. The diet of the Yanomamö is not deficient in protein.

The observable prediction is false.

4. Therefore, warlike behavior among the Yanomamö is not caused by protein deficiency in their diet.

Although the observation that the diet is not deficient in protein disconfirms the hypothesis, it does not conclusively establish that this hypothesis is false. This argument, like the arguments that confirm hypotheses, is inductive—if we regard the falsity of the hypothesis as its conclusion. Deductively, all we can say is that either the hypothesis is false or some auxiliary hypothesis is false.

Some anthropologists have questioned the second auxiliary hypothesis—that is, whether the 13-month study was long enough. Those who study the diets of other people who, like the Yanomamö, live by hunting and gathering have found significant variations in the amounts of available protein from one year to another. Events that do not occur on an annual basis, such as too much or too little rain and epidemic diseases in animals that are hunted, affect the availability of protein-rich food. Hunter-gatherers cannot count on steady supplies of food in stressed environments. The study that formed the basis for disconfirming the protein-deficient diet might have been conducted in an unusually good year for gathering and hunting.

No one denies that the results of this 13-month study are important. However, no single study will convince those who believe that the prior probability of the protein-deficiency hypothesis is very high. Additional tests, carried out over a period of years, could (if the results were similar to the results of the 13-month study) eventually disconfirm absolutely the hypothesis. In this situation, it is difficult to see what sort of crucial test could be devised to help us choose between the hypothesis being tested and some other hypothesis. No other causal hypothesis (except the negative "Warlike behavior is not caused by protein deficiency") was even formulated in this study, although recently some anthropologists have argued that "gifts" of weapons from Americans and Europeans are the cause of the warlike behavior. (See P. Tierney, 2000.) Chagnon continued his studies of the Yanomamö for a number of years without finding evidence for protein deficiency. Nevertheless, many anthropologists regard his work as controversial. In actual practice, a favored hypothesis is rarely rejected despite disconfirming evidence unless there is some feasible hypothesis to replace it.

Exercise Set 7.3

For each of the following, identify the hypothesis that is disconfirmed and construct or reconstruct (insofar as possible) a disconfirming argument, with reference to plausibility, disconfirming observations, and auxiliary hypotheses.

1. Almost every week you and your friends meet for dinner at a small, family-run restaurant. The night before last, you paid with a credit card. You check your account today and find some large, unauthorized charges. Your friend says that the owner-cashier at the restaurant must have "swiped" your card number when you paid for dinner. But you refuse to accept that. How would you argue against your friend's hypothesis?

2. "In 1988, Dr. R. S. Chang from UC Davis and Dr. H. W. Yeung from the Chinese University of Hong Kong published their findings on anti-HIV effects of Chinese herbs. Twelve different species of plants were found to completely stop replication of the virus." [Revivo is an herbal supplement pill.]

—Revivo website

The studies referred to on the Revivo website, were preclinical *in vitro* studies. What this means is that they looked at the effect of different substances on HIV in test tubes. However the evidence that they are providing does not reflect how their product will affect HIV in the body. On the contrary many substances that are effective against HIV in test tube have been ineffective or dangerous in the body.

We can tell little about a substance's effectiveness as an AIDS medicine from how it reacts in test tube. It is therefore necessary to carry out clinical trials on humans to determine whether or not a medicine actually works.

—C. Tomlinson, http://www.quackdown.info/article/
spotting-fake-cures-hiv/ (5/19/2011)

3. Cauterization was the only known treatment [for gangrene]; sometimes the patient was cured by it and sometimes the gray slough would reappear. Most surgeons regarded hospital gangrene and the other septic diseases as inescapable scourges, without troubling to do more than to speculate about their causes. Young Lister [J. Lister, 1827–1912, who revolutionized surgery by the introduction of antiseptics], however,

examined the results of the cautery treatment and reasoned that if some patients recovered and some did not, though all had been exposed to the oxygen in the air which most doctors vaguely assumed to be the cause of the trouble, then oxygen could not be responsible.

—A. Young, *The Men Who Made Surgery*

4. *No Link Found Between Hepatitis B Vaccine and Certain Neurological Disorders.*

WASHINGTON—Based on a review of clinical and population studies, the hepatitis B vaccine does not cause or trigger multiple sclerosis in adults, says a new report from the Institute of Medicine of the National Academies. At present, there is no need for government advisory bodies to review policy that encourages the vaccination of infants, adolescents, and adults at high risk of exposure to the hepatitis B virus, such as health care workers, to protect them against serious liver damage.

"Hepatitis B vaccine policy has been viewed skeptically by some because of concerns about vaccine safety and a perception that the virus itself does not pose a serious risk," said Marie McCormick, chair of the committee that wrote the report, and professor and chair, department of maternal and child health, Harvard School of Public Health, Boston. "However, the committee heard testimony about the seriousness of the disease, especially for young children, and growing evidence of the benefits of the vaccine. Hopefully our report will ease the concerns of adults who need to be immunized against hepatitis B and are worried about the risk for multiple sclerosis."

—News from the National Academies, http://www8.nationalacademies.org/ onpinews/newsitem.aspx?RecordID=10393, May 30, 2002

5. In an attempt to make ecological sense out of a diversity of practices, including food choices and taboos, much attention has been given to protein as a necessity in potentially short supply. These various studies identify a particular potential for protein scarcity in a given situation and seek to demonstrate that the ecologically most important effect of certain aspects of behavior is the alleviation of this scarcity. Support for these interpretations has been offered in the form of the almost universal preference for meat over plant foods, a preference that, while not instinctual, is "biologically and culturally conditioned" and makes good nutritional sense as well.

Yet this general "Protein Hypothesis" faces a number of problems. Proteins per se are not recognized by most peoples of the world and thus are not considered in their evaluations. Furthermore, all meat is not preferred over all plants, and preference orders among animal foods do not correspond to protein contents. Certainly, high-quality protein is a requirement for survival, but since many people can give reasons for their food preferences, and since these reasons do not include the protein content of different foods, it becomes necessary to explore the link between stated preferences and nutritional consequences that include protein intake. One possible link between the two is the suggestion that, for lack of a better name, may be called the "Fat Hypothesis."

There are numerous examples of stated preferences for fat as a major attribute of food desirability. Animal foods are often clearly ranked according to fat content.

—M. A. Jochim, *Strategies for Survival*, 1981

6. After Osama bin Laden was killed by a team of US Navy Seals on May 1, 2011, he was photographed and identified by facial recognition and DNA testing. U.S. officials said that his body was then handled in accord with Muslim burial ritual and buried at sea. Several days later, President Obama announced that the photographs of the dead bin Laden would not be released to the public because they were particularly gruesome, would offend viewers, and could incite reprisals against Americans.

   Law Professor Alan Dershowitz argued against the President's hypothesis by saying that Americans were used to seeing pictures of bloody victims on television and in courtroom trials and could handle this. He also said that photographs of bin Laden would be no more inflammatory to the Muslim community than pictures of the capture and death of Sadam Hussein.

7. In 1678 the Dutch physicist Christian Huyghens suggested [contrary to the accepted theory that light was made up of tiny particles] that light consisted of tiny waves. If it was made up of waves, there was no difficulty about explaining the different amount of refraction of different kinds of light through a refracting medium, provided it was assumed that light traveled more slowly through the refracting medium than through air. The amount of refraction would vary with the length of the waves: the shorter the wavelength, the greater the refraction. This meant that violet light (the most refracted) had a shorter wavelength than blue light; blue, shorter than green; and so on. It was this difference in wavelength that distinguished colors to the eye. And of course, if light consisted of waves, two beams could cross without trouble. (After all, sound waves and water waves crossed without losing their identity.)

   But Huyghens' wave theory was not very satisfactory either. It didn't explain why light rays traveled in straight lines and cast sharp shadows, nor why light waves could not go around obstacles, as water waves and sound waves could. Furthermore, if light consisted of waves, how could it travel through a vacuum, as it certainly did in coming to us through space from the sun and stars? What medium was it moving?

—I. Asimov, *The Intelligent Man's Guide to the Physical Sciences*, 1960

8. Most any textbook tells us that the [pre-Neanderthal] men of Choukoutien cooked meat over hearths, predominantly ate venison, but also ate elephants, rhinoceroses, beavers, bison, and wild pigs, and on occasion one another.

Evidence for the use of fire was summarized by Teilhard de Chardin as so extensive as to need no further comment! In this judgment I must agree, but the evidence hardly justifies the picture one gets from textbooks of early man seated around his hearth roasting meat and carrying on a fireside chat.

The thickest layer of ash, in the upper-middle part of the cave deposit, is up to *six meters* [more than 19 feet] deep. Stone tools and fossilized small vertebrates—rats and bats—were numerous in this layer, *sometimes indeed forming their own layers*. The ash deposit here is not in piles, but spread out in even layers, apparently the result of water movement. In the lower-middle part of the cave deposit, the ash layer is thicker near the south wall. *At its maximum, it is four meters deep*. It was around the fringe of this ash layer that most of the human fossils and stone tools were unearthed.

—Lan-Po, *The Cave Home of Peking Man* (as cited in Binford, 1981)

Note: The emphasis in the quoted passage is Binford's. His alternative hypothesis to the claim that early humans were cave-dwelling hunters of large animals is that early humans were scavengers who used caves but who did not live in them and who feasted mainly on the marrow in bones left by animal predators.

9. Hot water bottles, electric heaters and warm blankets may be no help at all to people suffering the effects of extreme cold, according to six Canadian researchers who found out the hard way. . . . They sat in tubs of ice water for one to two hours, until their body temperatures dropped as much as 8 degrees Fahrenheit, from the normal of 98.6 degrees.

Then they tried three alternative methods of getting their temperatures back up from those dangerously low levels. They sat in front of heaters. They exercised. Or they just shivered.

Shivering warms the body from the inside by letting muscles produce waste heat. It worked surprisingly fast—about three times faster than previous researchers have found.

Surprisingly, external heat appeared to make no difference. "We surmise that the heat blunted the shivering response," said Gordon Giesbrecht [one of the researchers]. "Paradoxically, when we kept the skin cool, it maintained the shivering stimulus and let the body do what it does best."

Exercise, which hypothermia [extreme cold] victims cannot always manage, was best of all, warming the body three times faster than shivering alone.

—J. Gleick, *The New York Times*, February 9, 1988

10. Autism is a serious developmental disease that was considered rare 30 years ago. It is now recognized as covering a spectrum of problems, including Asperger's disease and other milder manifestations. Now by some government estimates autism in some form affects 1 in 100 children.

Many people believe that the widely used childhood vaccine against measles, mumps, and rubella (MMR), and particularly a mercury compound (thimerosal) used as a preservative for the vaccine, are responsible.

Against this view, Dr. J. Baker writes

No one disputes that autism is being diagnosed more frequently than it was twenty years ago. But experts debate to what extent this trend reflects better detection or a real increase in the disorder itself. The definition of autism has been expanded considerably in recent years, and better recognition likely accounts for much of the rise. Indeed, studies of families and twins suggest that genetic factors are of primary importance.

Yet for parents coping with the demands of an autistic child, it is hard not to believe that something in the environment is at fault as well. Many possible causes have been proposed, ranging from food additives to environmental mercury and PCBs. The National Autism Association has focused on the vaccine preservative thimerosal, metabolized to ethyl mercury, as a possible culprit. There is simply no evidence supporting this assertion, however. Denmark removed thimerosal from its vaccines in 1992 and still experienced a subsequent rise in autism. The United States has done the same, and today all of the required childhood vaccines are now available without this preservative. Again, no association with autism has been shown.

—http://www.DukeHealth.org, May 3, 2007

11. Can quicksand suck you completely under?

David Bonn, from the University of Amsterdam, saw signs alerting visitors to the danger of quicksand near the Namak Lake, located in northern Iran. The warnings piqued his curiosity and inspired him to take a sample back to the Netherlands, where he and his colleagues analyzed its composition. Once they had determined the proportions of fine sand, salt water and clay in the quicksand, they mixed up larger batches of the same. Bonn and his colleagues then placed aluminum beads, which had the same density as an average human, on top of their homemade quicksand. The team shook the system, and watched as this action partially submerged the beads.

An object that falls into quicksand can cause the sand particles supported by water to loose their stability and flow downwards in a liquid fashion. Bonn likens the disturbance to the toppling of a stack of neatly arranged oranges.

"An extremely small variation in stress can cause the complete collapse of this material," he says. According to measurements taken from the bead experiments, increasing the physical stress on the particles by just 1% can cause their flow speed to increase by a factor of a million, creating a downward pull. Bonn adds that getting out of the quicksand at this point is tough; the force required to pull out a foot equals that needed to lift a medium-sized car.

"The real danger of quicksand is that you can get stuck in it when the high tides come up," says Bonn. But patience can be a life-saving virtue. If you wait long enough, the sand particles settle and the buoyancy of the mixture will cause you to rise up to the top. As proof, the beads in the experiment did in fact float, and never became more than half submerged in sand. Although each bead measured only four millimeters in diameter, Bonn says that the findings still apply to people, as they have the same density.

—Roxanne Khamsi, *Nature Online*, 2005, September 28

VI. BAYESIAN CONFIRMATION

When arguments for confirmation and disconfirmation are supplemented with considerations of prior probabilities, as suggested in preceding sections of this chapter, and when the requisite probabilities can be expressed quantitatively, **Bayes's theorem**—a theorem of the mathematical calculus of probability—provides a formal model for arguments of confirmation and disconfirmation. In this section, we will look first at Bayes's theorem, and then we will see how arguments similar to those we have already examined can be analyzed along Bayesian lines.

1. BAYES'S THEOREM

The probability calculus is used to calculate unknown probabilities on the basis of known probabilities. Thus, we can use the "multiplication rule" to calculate the probability of a conjunction when the probabilities of individual conjuncts are known:

$$\mathbf{Pr}(h_1 \text{ and } h_2 \,|\, e) = \mathbf{Pr}(h_1 \,|\, e) \times \mathbf{Pr}(h_2 \,|\, e \text{ and } h_1)$$

Example

Suppose we have evidence (*e*) that 40 percent of a population of registered voters are registered Republicans and that 60 percent of the registered Republicans (and no non-Republicans) will vote for the Republican candidate. What is the probability that a voter selected at random from registered voters will vote for the Republican candidate?

$$\mathbf{Pr}(\text{registered Republican and votes Republican} \,|\, e) = 0.40 \times 0.60 = 0.24$$

This example is representative of cases in which we have some information about a "setup," such as the composition of a deck of cards or the composition of a population, and we are interested in the probability of some outcome that has not yet occurred, such as voting for the Republican candidate or drawing an ace from a deck of cards. In other cases, we have already observed an outcome, such as four successive tosses of a coin resulting in a head, and are interested in what kind of setup gave rise to that outcome. (For example, was the coin a fair coin?) Bayes's theorem, which can be derived from the four rules of probability, enables us to calculate these "inverse" or "post-trial" probabilities when certain other probabilities are known. To illustrate the theorem, we consider the question just raised about whether a tossed coin that lands heads four times in a row is fair.

To use Bayes's theorem, some prior probabilities must be known. In our example, we need to know the prior probability that the coin is fair as well as the prior probability that the coin is unfair. (For discussing this problem, let us say that *unfair* means the coin is weighted to land heads up on every toss.) Prior probabilities are usually assigned on the basis of background knowledge or knowledge of earlier experiments. If the coin is received in change from a grocery store, then the prior probability that it is a fair coin is high. But if the coin is in the possession of a person known as a prankster or a gambler whose winnings are suspiciously heavy, we might assign a low prior probability to the fairness of the coin. For the sake of our example, assume a slick gambler holds the coin and the prior probability that it is fair is only 0.1. Then, because the coin is either fair or not fair, the prior probability that it is *not* fair is 0.9 $(1 - 0.1)$.

The next probabilities we need to know are the **likelihoods** that the observed outcome (four heads in a row) would have happened if the coin were fair and if the coin were not fair. If the coin is fair, the probability of obtaining four heads in a row is $(\frac{1}{2})^4$, or 0.0625. If the coin is unfair (weighted to show only heads when it is tossed), the likelihood of getting four heads in a row is 1, because the **evidence statement** (the coin lands heads up) follows deductively from the hypothesis that the coin is weighted to give this result.

In addition, we need to know the probability that the observed evidence would occur in any case—that is to say, without regard to whether the hypothesis is true. This is the **total probability** of the evidence statement. It is based on the prior probabilities of each of the hypotheses that could give rise to the observed evidence as well as the probability that the evidence would occur, given the truth of each of the hypotheses. Suppose, for example, we want to know the probability that a white ball will be drawn (e) when the ball is drawn blindly from either of two jars: (h_1 = the ball was drawn from the first jar) or (h_2 = the ball was drawn from the second jar). Suppose further that each jar has an equal probability of being selected (the prior probability for h_1 is equal to the prior probability for h_2, and both are $\frac{1}{2}$). But suppose the first jar contains 50 white balls and 50 black balls, whereas the second jar contains 75 white balls and 25 black balls. If the ball is drawn from the first jar, the probability that it will be white is $\frac{1}{2}$; but if it is drawn from the second jar, the probability that it will be white is $\frac{3}{4}$. The total probability of drawing a white ball, regardless of which jar is selected is

$$[\mathbf{Pr}(h_1) \times \mathbf{Pr}(e \,|\, h_1)] + [\mathbf{Pr}(h_2) \times \mathbf{Pr}(e \,|\, h_2)],$$

which, in this case, is $(\frac{1}{2} \times \frac{1}{2}) + (\frac{1}{2} \times \frac{3}{4})$. This is equal to $\frac{1}{4} + \frac{3}{8}$, or $\frac{5}{8}$, which is the total probability of "A white ball will be drawn, given that it is drawn from one of the two jars, each with a probability of $\frac{1}{2}$ of being selected, one of which contains $\frac{1}{2}$ white balls and the other of which contains $\frac{3}{4}$ white balls."

Finally, Bayes's theorem is applicable only when the prior probability of the hypothesis that is tested is greater than zero. The reason for this will be clear when we look at the mathematical formulation of the theorem. This limitation does not affect the usefulness of Bayes's theorem as a model of hypothesis-testing because we are not interested in testing totally implausible hypotheses.

We can now assess the fairness of the coin held by the slick gambler. In the following representation of Bayes's theorem, h represents the hypothesis "The coin is fair," let $\sim h$ (not h) represent the other hypothesis "The coin is unfair," and let e represent the evidence "Four heads appeared in four tosses of the coin." Thus, $\mathbf{Pr}(h)$ is the prior probability that h is true, and $\mathbf{Pr}(\sim h)$ is the prior probability that $\sim h$ is true. $\mathbf{Pr}(e|h)$ is the likelihood that four heads will appear if the coin is fair, and $\mathbf{Pr}(e|\sim h)$ is the other likelihood. Finally, $\mathbf{Pr}(h|e)$ is the **inverse probability** that we want to calculate—the probability that the coin is fair, given the evidence of four heads appearing in four tosses.

Assuming that $\mathbf{Pr}(h)$ is not equal to 0,

$$\mathbf{Pr}(h|e) = \frac{\mathbf{Pr}(h) \times \mathbf{Pr}(e|h)}{[\mathbf{Pr}(h) \times [\mathbf{Pr}(e|h)] + [\mathbf{Pr}(\sim h) \times \mathbf{Pr}(e|\sim h)]}.$$

The probability in the denominator is the total probability of e. This is the probability that four heads will occur, regardless of which hypothesis is true. Also, we can see that if $\mathbf{Pr}(h)$ were zero, then the value on the left would be zero as well.

Inserting the values for likelihoods and prior probabilities just assigned into this equation gives us

$$\mathbf{Pr}(h|e) = \frac{0.1 \times 0.0625}{(0.1 \times 0.0625) + (0.9 \times 1)} = 0.0068.$$

The quantity 0.0068, the **posterior probability** of the hypothesis that the coin is fair, is lower than the prior probability of that hypothesis. In other words, after examining the evidence of four heads in a row, the probability that the coin is fair has been reduced from the prior probability of 0.1 to a posterior probability of 0.0068. The hypothesis that the coin is fair is thus disconfirmed.

Exercise Set 7.4

1. Suppose that a population of registered voters contains 40 percent registered Republicans, and that 90 percent of registered Republicans typically vote for the Republican candidate. The Republican candidate is particularly popular and expects to gather 30 percent of the voters who are not registered Republicans. A voter exits from the voting booth and announces truthfully that she has voted for the Republican candidate. What is the probability that she is a registered Republican?

2. Among 400 freshmen attending a small college, 100 are from out of state and 300 are state residents. Cars are owned by 75 of the out-of-state students and by 100 of the state residents.
   a. If a student is selected randomly (if each student has an equal probability of being selected), find the following:
      1. the probability of selecting an out-of-state student without a car
      2. the probability of selecting a state resident without a car
      3. the probability of selecting a student with a car
   b. If the student who is selected randomly has a car, find the following:
      1. the probability that the student is an out-of-state student
      2. the probability that the student is a state resident

3. A total of seven points on a pair of dice can be rolled in six different ways. List the six combinations.
   Suppose you know that someone has rolled a seven (this is the evidence), but you did not see the way the dice came up. What is the probability that four spots showed on one die and three on the other?

4. Two decks of 52 cards have identical backs—a picture of Denali, the highest mountain peak in North America. One deck (A) has ¾ black cards and ¼ red. The other deck (B) has ¾ red cards and ¼ black. Either deck is equally likely to be chosen for a blind draw.
   a. What is the prior probability of drawing a card from the A deck?
   b. What is the prior probability of drawing a red card from the A deck (i.e., the probability that you will choose the A deck and draw a red card from it)?
   c. What is the total probability of drawing a red card (i.e., the probability of selecting a red card no matter which deck is selected)?
   d. What is the total probability of drawing a black card?
   e. Suppose you draw a red card. What is the probability that it was drawn from the A deck?
   f. Suppose you draw a red card. What is the probability it came from the B deck?
   g. Suppose you draw two cards without replacement from a single deck. Both cards are red. What is the probability that they came from deck B?

5. A candidate for state office has a breakfast meeting at one end of the state and is supposed to appear at a dinner in a city at the other end. Her campaign manager goes ahead of her to help with arrangements for the dinner. The candidate plans to fly over in time for the dinner, but her flight is canceled. She figures that if she drives, her chances of arriving on time for the dinner are fifty–fifty (**Pr** = 0.50). Someone offers to fly her in a small plane, but she loathes small aircraft and is reluctant to accept the offer even though it means

she would be practically certain of making the dinner that way. She calls her campaign manager, who tries to persuade her to accept the small-plane ride. He figures his arguments had only about a 40 percent chance of winning her over. He goes to the dinner not really expecting to see her, and she walks in on time. What is the probability that she took the small plane?

6. In Sarah Caudwell's mystery novels, the sex of the main character, Prof. Hilary Tamar, is so cleverly disguised that it is fair to assign even odds to male and female.

Suppose, however, the author had let it slip that Prof. Tamar is color-blind. What then would be the probability that the professor is male?

Background: Color blindness is sex-related, carried on the X-chromosome in about 1 in 100 cases. Men, with only one X-chromosome, have a probability of 0.01 of being color-blind. Women, with two X-chromosomes, have only .01 × .01 chance (0.0001) because having one chromosome without the defect prevents color blindness.

7. Since all but 14 states have passed bicycle helmet laws, some reliable studies set regular helmet use by adult bicycle riders at 0.85. Studies of serious bicycle accidents report that 0.80 of those wearing helmets escape head injury, whereas only 0.20 of those not wearing helmets are so fortunate. Suppose you learn that a friend was in a bicycle accident, suffered head trauma, and is in a coma. What is the probability that your friend was wearing a helmet?

2. USING BAYES'S THEOREM TO TEST A HYPOTHESES

In this section, we see how Bayes's theorem can be used to disconfirm a hypothesis concerning prehistoric agriculture in America: "The diet of people in Ecuador during the Valdivian Period (3800–1500 BCE) was based on intensive maize (corn) agriculture." The prehistoric beginnings of agriculture are of great interest to anthropologists, and the claim that maize agriculture was practiced at this early date in coastal Ecuador has been strongly defended by some investigators. This hypothesis was also initially plausible because the ecological setting in coastal Ecuador is similar to many other areas in which evidence of early agricultural activity is found. Although in this case—unlike the case in which the prior probability of selecting one of the jars depended on the outcome of a toss of a fair die—we have no precise way of assigning a prior probability to the practice of maize agriculture, we do know that the prior probability is rather high; so we will assign 0.7 to it. Then, the prior probability that the diet was not agriculturally based is $1 - 0.7 = 0.3$. Bayes's theorem formally requires that $\mathbf{Pr}(h)$ be greater than zero, and this is reflected in our informal requirement that the hypothesis be plausible.

Anthropologists learn what prehistoric peoples ate by examining their skeletal teeth. Dental caries (cavities), for example, are most frequent and severe in people whose diets are agriculturally based, less severe in gathering-collecting-hunting peoples, and least severe among strictly meat-eating hunters. (This is an important auxiliary hypothesis.)

The agricultural hypothesis was tested by a physical anthropologist, (C. Turner [1978], "Dental caries and early Ecuadorian agriculture," American Antiquity 43). His evidence consisted of a sample of 76 teeth recovered from six crania of individuals who had been buried in a Valdivian-period cemetery. These individuals were judged to have lived to an age at which they would be susceptible to caries (another auxiliary hypothesis). Two additional auxiliary hypotheses were stated by Turner:

(i) Maize, as it is usually prepared for eating, has strong cariogenic potential. (It clings to the teeth and causes cavities.)

(ii) A dental pathology review (T.D. Stewart [1931] *American Journal of Anthropology*) provides a good measure of incidence of dental caries among prehistoric Central American Indians whose diet was agriculturally based. (According to Stewart's review, 15.5 percent of all teeth of these individuals had one or more cavities.)

Using the agricultural hypothesis and these auxiliaries, the observable prediction was that in a sample of 76 teeth, approximately 12 (76×0.155) should have had at least one cavity. However, when the teeth were examined, not a single cavity was found on any of the teeth. (This is the evidence e.)

Using the expected average of 12 bad teeth in a sample of 76 to determine the likelihood of finding no cavities when our hypothesis is true, and making certain assumptions about the randomness of the sample and the normal distribution of cavities in the population, there is only about one chance in 100 of finding no cavities in a sample of 76 teeth: $\Pr(e|h) = 0.01$.

Because our auxiliary hypotheses assure us that the incidence of cavities is much lower when the diet is not agriculturally based, let us assign the likelihood of 0.1 to discovering no cavities if the diet is not agriculturally based:

$$\Pr(e|{\sim}h) = 0.1$$

Now we are ready to apply Bayes's theorem to determine the posterior probability of the hypothesis in light of the evidence:

$$\Pr(h|e) = \frac{0.7 \times 0.01}{[0.7 \times 0.01] + [0.3 \times 0.1]} = \frac{0.007}{0.037} = 0.19$$

The posterior probability that the diet was agriculturally based has been dramatically reduced by this test—from 0.7 to 0.19. The probability that the diet was not agriculturally based (because that is the only alternative) has been correspondingly enhanced—up from 0.3 (its prior probability) to 0.81.

The role of alternative hypotheses, which was not explicit in the first simple formulation of the hypothetico-deductive method, is apparent in the Bayesian model of confirmation. The amount of support that evidence lends to a hypothesis depends on how probable the evidence would be if the hypothesis were false—that is, if some alternative hypothesis were true. To simplify the example, we considered only two alternatives, but we could have treated each alternate hypothesis about subsistence strategy (hunter-gatherer-collector, hunter, and agriculturist) separately by assigning each one a prior probability and considering the likelihood that the evidence would occur for each case.

Bayes's theorem helps us to understand why some tests are more valuable for confirming or disconfirming hypotheses than other tests. Finding no cavities is particularly damaging to the agricultural hypothesis because the absence of cavities would be so unlikely if the hypothesis were true. Furthermore, many hypotheses that we would like to test do not deductively imply any observable predictions even when we invoke auxiliary hypotheses. In these cases, it is reasonable to ask how likely (or probable) a certain prediction would be if the hypothesis were true or if some alternative hypothesis were true. Bayes's theorem helps us to see how these **likelihoods** raise or lower posterior probabilities by various amounts. The posterior probability is changed less by an outcome that is likely to occur whether or not the hypothesis is true than by an outcome that would be surprising unless the hypothesis were true. Thus, this Bayesian pattern, or model, for arguments of both confirmation and disconfirmation seems to agree with our intuition about using the outcomes of predictions to judge whether a hypothesis is true or false.

Exercise Set 7.5

1. Juana, who has just received a postgraduate degree, feels lucky to have found a permanent job in this tough economy. She faced these statistics: Only ⅔ of the graduates of "top-flight" schools and ⅓ of the graduates of lower-ranked schools found permanent jobs within nine months of graduation. The top-flight schools comprise ¼ of the total number. What is the probability that Juana attended a top-flight school?

2. Suppose you see an announcement that all cars of the make and model you own are being recalled to correct a suspension problem. These models were produced at two plants: X and Y. You cannot determine which plant produced your model, but plant X produced about 80 percent of the make and model of your car, whereas plant Y produced only 20 percent. The automobile manufacturer estimates that about 90 percent of the models produced by plant Y have the suspension problem but that only 50 percent of the models produced by plant X have this problem.

    a. What is the probability that the suspension in your car is defective?
    b. Suppose you take your car in to be tested and find out that the suspension is defective. What is the probability that your car was produced by plant X?

3. Based on recent statistics, the probability that a smoker who lives in a rural area will die from lung cancer is 0.00065. The probability that a smoker from an urban area will die from lung cancer is 0.00085. The probability that a nonsmoker from an urban area will die from lung cancer is 0.00015, whereas the probability that a rural nonsmoker will die from lung cancer is 0.00001. Approximately 70 percent of the population live in urban areas, and about 30 percent live in rural areas. Assume that 20 percent of urban dwellers are smokers and that 10 percent of rural dwellers are smokers.

   a. What is the probability that an urban dweller will die from lung cancer?
   b. What is the probability that a person from a rural area will die from lung cancer?
   c. Given only the information that a person died from lung cancer, what is the probability that this person was an urban dweller?
   d. Given only the information that an urban dweller died from lung cancer, what is the probability that this person was a smoker?

4. A murder has been committed, and the police have brought in two suspects on the basis of circumstantial evidence. The suspects are similar in physical appearance, but one is a redhead and the other has dark brown hair. The police feel that one of the two suspects almost certainly committed the crime, but they think there is a greater chance (80 percent) that the redhead, who has a previous record, is guilty. A witness who saw someone running from the scene of the crime says that the person had brown hair, so the brunette is brought to trial. The defense attorney insists that the witness be tested for reliability, and a test is set up. With lighting and other circumstances similar to those in which the crime occurred, the witness is correct about 60 percent of the time in distinguishing redheads from brunettes.

   a. Taking the only performance of the witness into account and accepting the prior probabilities offered by the police, what is the probability that the brunette is guilty?
   b. If the witness had correctly distinguished the redhead from the brunette in only 40 percent of the test cases, what would be the posterior probability that the brunette is guilty?

5. Recently an advisory group of the National Cancer Institute turned down a proposal to study the possible link between breast cancer and fat consumption. The proposal was for a 10-year prospective study of women across the country, 10,000 of them on a low-fat diet to see whether their risk of breast cancer was lower than the additional 22,000 women who would form the control group. The reason the panel of experts gave for the turn-down, according to *Science*, was "The hypothesis that dietary fat is a cause

of breast cancer among women is plausible, but only weakly supported at present." Explain, in terms of the Bayesian model of confirmation, why the consideration raised by the expert critics is important.

6. Cleopatra, Queen of Egypt, committed suicide at the age of 39 in 30 BCE, while she was a captive of Octavian, the future Emperor Augustus. She did not want to be dragged through the streets of Rome in his triumphal march. Tradition, perpetuated by Roman historians and Shakespeare's drama, attribute her death, along with the deaths of her two servants, to the bite of an asp, or Egyptian cobra, hidden in a basket of figs.

   Stacy Schiff, author of *Cleopatra*, argues against the asp hypothesis:

   A woman known for her crisp decisions and meticulous planning would surely have hesitated to entrust her fate to a wild animal. . . . Even the most reliable of cobras cannot kill three women in quick succession and the asp is a famously sluggish snake. An Egyptian cobra . . . puffing itself up to its six-foot splendor, could hardly have hidden in a fig basket, or remained hidden for long. The job was too great and the basket too small. Poison was a more likely alternative, as Plutarch seems to imply with his survey of Cleopatra's experiments. [She was highly educated and interested in science.] Most likely she swallowed a lethal drink or applied a toxic ointment. . . . Assuming she died of the same cause as Charmion [her servant who was barely alive when Octavian found the three], assuming she died in the state in which she was discovered by Octavian [perfectly laid out in her royal robes], Cleopatra suffered little. There were no shuddering paroxysms, which cobra venom would have induced. [Her] toxin's effect was more narcotic than convulsive, the death peaceful, swift, and essentially painless.

   Schiff's reasoning, although non-quantitative, has a Bayesian structure. What are some of the prior probabilities and likelyhoods she considers? What information would we need to assign rough numerical probabilities to the sentences concerning Cleopatra's manner of death in a way that would allow someone to confirm or refute the suicide-by-asp-bite hypothesis?

VII. REVIEW

This chapter provides an introduction to the logic of confirmation. The methodology developed here shows how statements about things that are not directly observable can be inductively supported or undermined by checking the truth or falsity of observable predictions derived from those statements. In scientific reasoning and in everyday life, confirmation employs deductive arguments as well as inductive arguments, but its overall structure is inductive. Because these arguments offer conclusions that go beyond what is observed, future observations might lead us to reject statements that we currently consider to be highly confirmed.

We examined some simple formulations of the hypothetico-deductive method of confirmation. We then supplemented these formulations with additional premises that considered prior probabilities, and we noted the role of alternative hypotheses. Thus supplemented, the hypothetico-deductive method more closely resembles sound scientific practice and can be viewed as an informal and nonquantitative Bayesian model of confirmation. The final section of the chapter discusses Bayes's theorem and the quantitative model of confirmation based on it. Brief definitions of the key concepts examined in this chapter follow.

Ad hoc **Reasoning**   This fallacious form of reasoning occurs when auxiliary hypotheses are rejected (or brought in) arbitrarily, merely to save a favored hypothesis.

Alternative Hypotheses   Hypotheses that are distinct from the hypothesis being tested but that could yield the same observable predictions.

Auxiliary Hypotheses   Auxiliary hypotheses are used in conjunction with the hypothesis being tested to derive observable predictions. The auxiliary hypotheses, not always explicitly stated, are assumed to be true in the context of a test of a main hypothesis. Two chief categories of auxiliary hypotheses are (1) those that claim that the conditions of the experiment or observation are "normal" (that reliable instruments are used by competent observers, and so on), and (2) those (theoretical auxiliary hypotheses) that assume the truth of background theories.

Bayesian Confirmation   A method of confirmation that, like the simpler hypothetico-deductive method, considers the observable predictions derived from the hypothesis and the auxiliary hypotheses. In addition, Bayesian confirmation requires taking into account the prior probabilities not only of the hypothesis being tested but also of the alternative hypotheses. A true prediction confirms one hypothesis, relative to alternatives, if that hypothesis had a higher prior probability than any of the alternative hypotheses. The Bayesian model of confirmation also accommodates observable predictions that follow inductively rather than deductively from the hypothesis and the auxiliary hypotheses. When numerical values can be assigned to the requisite probabilities, **Bayes's theorem** provides a quantitative model for Bayesian confirmation.

Confirmation   Positive inductive support for hypotheses. *Confirmation* is used in both an *incremental* and an *absolute* sense. Hypotheses are incrementally confirmed by tests that raise their probability. Hypotheses are considered to be absolutely confirmed only when they are strongly supported and when no available evidence counts against them. However, it is possible, in light of new evidence, to reject an absolutely confirmed hypothesis.

Crucial Test   A test that confirms one and disconfirms the other of two plausible but incompatible hypotheses that are the only candidates for acceptance.

Disconfirmation   Inductive support for rejection of a hypothesis. Like *confirmation*, *disconfirmation* is used in both an incremental (relative) and an absolute sense.

Hypothesis   A sentence to be tested by checking the truth of a prediction that follows from it.

Hypothetico-Deductive Method   A method of testing hypotheses by deriving an observable prediction from a hypothesis along with any auxiliary hypotheses. The simplest version of the method says that if the prediction is true, the hypothesis is confirmed; and if the prediction is false, the hypothesis is disconfirmed. To provide a realistic account of scientific method, the simple version must be supplemented by considerations of initial plausibility of the hypothesis as well as auxiliary hypotheses and by how the tested hypothesis compares to alternative hypotheses with the same observable predictions.

Likelihood   The probability of a piece of evidence relative to the truth of some hypothesis. Likelihoods are one of the types of probabilities required for using Bayes's theorem as a model of confirmation.

Posterior Probability   The probability that a hypothesis is true after taking into account the results of a particular test. When Bayes's theorem is used as a model of confirmation, the hypothesis is said to be confirmed if its posterior probability is higher than its prior probability, and disconfirmed if its posterior probability is lower than its prior probability.

Prior Probability   The probability of a hypothesis before taking into account the results of a particular test or observation.

Exercise Set 7.6

1. Can a false hypothesis be the basis for a true prediction? Explain your answer, or give an example.

2. Can a true hypothesis be the basis for a false prediction? Explain your answer, or give an example.

3. Which of the following can be used to assign a prior probability to a hypothesis?
    a. Statistical evidence
    b. Personal preference (a gut feeling)
    c. Testimony of some authority on the subject matter
    d. Similarity to other successful hypotheses

4. When different alternative hypotheses have the same observable predictions, how can you choose among them?

5. When, after testing some hypothesis, its probability is lower than it was prior to the test, we say the hypothesis is _____ .

6. In the hypothetico-deductive method, is the argument from the truth of the observable prediction to the truth of the hypothesis deductive or inductive?

7. Usually when testing hypotheses, we ignore auxiliary hypotheses, or assume that they are true. In some situations, though, they demand our attention. Explain why this is so, or give an example.

8. "No matter how carefully a scientific hypothesis is tested, it can be rejected later in light of the discovery of new evidence." If this sentence is true, does it follow that hypotheses can never be confirmed but can only be disconfirmed or rejected?

9. Is it true that in most cases there is only one plausible scientific hypothesis that is compatible with all available evidence? Explain your answer.

10. If a hypothesis has a very strong degree of confirmation, do further successful predictions raise its probability very much? Explain why or why not.

11. Is it always possible to construct and carry out a crucial test to determine once and for all which of two competing hypotheses is correct?

12. Are scientific hypotheses typically a summary of the observable evidence on which they rest?

13. When we are disappointed in the outcome of a test of a hypothesis, should we revise the auxiliary hypotheses to account for the results? Why or why not?

14. Are there any limits to the number of alternative hypotheses we can devise to account for a test result?

15. If the prior probability of a hypothesis is zero, then why is the Bayesian method of confirmation not suitable for testing it?

16. Charles Darwin, famous for arguing that natural selection drives evolution, first observed the *Star of Bethlehem* orchid in 1862. The orchid is about four inches wide with a 12-inch tube-like spur that contains its nectar. In accordance with his evolutionary theory, Darwin predicted that the orchid's survival required a special pollinator with a proboscis long enough to reach the nectar at the bottom of the tube. In 1903 the predicted pollinator, a hawk moth, was discovered, 21 years after Darwin died.

    a. How strongly do you think this discovery confirms evolutionary theory? Give a reason for your answer.
    b. Can you think of an alternative hypothesis to account for the hawk moth's existence and its relationship to the orchid?

17. Einstein's theory of general relativity is almost universally accepted by physicists and has been confirmed in many experiments over the years

since Einstein put it forth in 1916. Recently, Stanford University scientists successfully measured the theory's predicted distortion of space-time by the pull of Earth's mass and how the mass pulls at orbiting objects. The experiment has been "in the works" for 52 years and cost about $750,000,000 to complete. Does this instance of confirmation significantly raise the probability of the theory of general relativity? Why or why not?

18. Suppose you are taking a course in which you have done well on the midterm exams and homework, and you studied for the final and thought you did well in that too. You receive a *D* when your grade report arrives. What can you say about the prior probability of the hypothesis "There was an error in the grade report"?

19. A driver on an isolated stretch of highway runs off the road and is killed in the fire that results from the crash. Police suggest the accident occurred because the driver was drunk. Can you suggest an alternative hypothesis?

20. Your friend texts you that she has won an award for a chemistry project just after she consulted a fortune-teller who predicted that she would win. You do not believe in fortune-telling and long ago assigned the hypothesis "Fortune-tellers have a supernatural ability to predict future events" a very low probability. Discuss the degree to which the successful prediction of the fortune-teller raises the probability of this hypothesis.

Chapter Eight

DEDUCTIVE REASONING— SENTENTIAL LOGIC

I. INTRODUCTION

In a deductive argument, it is impossible for the conclusion to be false if all the premisses are true. Deductive arguments preserve in the conclusion whatever truth is in the premisses because, unlike inductive arguments, they are not ampliative. The conclusions of nonampliative arguments restate or recombine information already present in the premisses. They do not extend factual knowledge. In this chapter, after some preliminary discussion of deductive forms, we focus on one branch of deductive logic: sentential logic.

II. PROPERTIES OF DEDUCTIVE ARGUMENTS: VALIDITY AND THE IMPORTANCE OF LOGICAL FORM

The truth-preserving feature of deductive arguments depends solely on their structures, or **forms**. The study of deductive logic began more than 2,000 years ago, and its development can be characterized as a series of investigations that have extended our understanding of the various forms by virtue of which arguments preserve truth. In sentential logic (or, as it is sometimes called, *propositional* or *truth-functional* logic), the forms by virtue of which arguments are deductive depend on connections among the sentences that make up the arguments. These forms were first analyzed by the Greek logicians of the Stoic school who lived about 2,200 years ago. In chapter 9, we examine forms of arguments that are deductive because of relationships between the subjects and predicates of the component sentences of the arguments. The first work on arguments in which validity depends on intrasentential connections—indeed the first formal study of logic—was carried out by Aristotle, who died in 322 BCE. Medieval and modern logicians have also made important contributions to Aristotelian logic. Finally, in chapter 10 we look briefly at formal properties of arguments that are deductive because of relationships among individuals referred to in the arguments. This area of logic is a relatively recent development. Except for some brilliant work by Leibniz, who died in 1716, the most important contributions to relational logic were made in the late nineteenth and twentieth centuries.

We have seen that the correctness of inductive arguments depends partly on their form but also on other matters, such as background information and the inclusion of all relevant evidence. As noted earlier, the *form* of an argument refers to important structural features that pertain to the argument regardless of its particular subject matter or content. A major difference between inductive and deductive arguments is that in the latter form alone, not content or background information, determines whether the argument is correct.

Examples

1. **Statistical syllogism**	2. **Quasi-syllogism**
(An Inductive Form)	(A Deductive Form)
Most *F*s are *G*s.	*All F*s are *G*s.
x is an *F*.	*x* is an *F*.
x is a *G*.	*x* is a *G*.

Forms, such as (2), that possess the truth-preserving property are said to be **valid**, and by extension any argument in ordinary language that exemplifies (or is an "instance" of) a valid form is valid as well. Strictly speaking, because deductive arguments are defined as truth-preserving, all deductive arguments are valid. Logic textbooks vary in terminology, however; some writers prefer to distinguish two types of deductive arguments: those that are truth-preserving, or valid, and those that are put forth as valid by their proponents but fail to preserve truth. The latter type, that is arguments that merely *purport* to be valid, are sometimes called *invalid deductive arguments*, whereas, this textbook calls them *deductive fallacies*.

The term *valid* has several uses in ordinary English. People speak of valid beliefs, valid reasons, and valid claims. In various contexts, *valid* applies to what cannot be objected to because it conforms to law, logic, or the facts. Thus, you might have a valid claim against your neighbor if a property survey shows that her fence is built on your side of the property line. In this text, however, *valid* and *validity* are reserved for the truth-preserving feature of deductive arguments. Because of this restriction, inductive arguments are never valid, no matter how strongly their premises support their conclusions.

Consider the inductive form of statistical syllogism. Arguments in this form [see Example (1) above] have two premises: a statistical generalization that relates an attribute class to a reference class, and a sentence that says a given individual is a member of that reference class. The conclusion of the affirmative form of a statistical syllogism says that the individual who is a member of the reference class is also a member of the attribute class. When an argument is an instance of this form *and* meets other conditions, such as the requirements for total evidence and an appropriate reference class, it is a strong inductive argument.

In contrast, the validity of deductive arguments depends only on form and meaning. The following deductive argument, which you have seen before, is an instance of a quasi-syllogism [see Example (2) above].

> All men are mortal.
> Socrates is a man.
> _____
> Socrates is mortal.

When we say that Example (2) is a valid form of argument, we mean that any two-premiss argument—in which one premiss says that all members of one class (*F*) are also members of a second class (*G*), and the other premiss says a particular individual is a member of the first class—validly yields the conclusion that the same individual is a member of the second class. It is impossible for an argument that exemplifies this pattern of reasoning (in other words, is an *instance* of this form) to have all true premisses and a false conclusion. Consider another argument in this form:

> All horses are quadrupeds.
> Jaws is a horse.
> _____
> Jaws is a quadruped.

Because Jaws is a shark, the second premiss is false. Obviously, the conclusion in this argument is false as well. Nevertheless, given the form of this argument, the conclusion could not be false if both premisses were true.

Although *validity* refers to the truth-preserving character of deductive arguments, arguments can be valid even when they have false premisses or false conclusions. Paradoxically, an argument can be truth-preserving even when it contains no truth to be preserved. To say that an argument is valid is to claim that in all possible circumstances in which the premisses are true, the conclusion is also true. If an argument—such as the argument about Jaws—is an instance of a valid form, it is valid even though it may contain false premisses and a false conclusion.

Valid arguments in which all of the premisses are true are called *sound arguments*. Soundness is obviously a desirable property of many arguments. If we present a deductive argument in order to persuade someone that its conclusion is true, the argument should not only be valid but should have true premisses as well. As critical thinkers, however, we are sometimes interested in the validity of arguments apart from the truth of their components. We might want to trace the consequences (the conclusions that follow deductively) of a variety of premisses, not all of which can be true. We might ask ourselves what would follow if sentences p and q were both true and, alternatively, what would follow if p were true but q were not. Sometimes we want to identify the consequences of sentences but have no way of determining their truth or falsity at the time the argument is constructed. For example, suppose you are considering whether to cut class on a Friday to drive to a friend's wedding, but you do not know whether there will be a quiz that day in your class. You might want to consider the consequences for your final grade in that class if the teacher gives a quiz and assigns an automatic failing grade for unexcused absences; you might want to consider, as well, the consequences for your friendship if you miss the wedding because of the possibility of a quiz.

In some cases, we can see that a set of premises leads deductively to a false conclusion. When this happens, we know that at least one of those premises must be false. Suppose, for example, that before going on vacation, you arrange to have a leaky roof repaired, and when you return you see no evidence that the work was done. You are annoyed that the landlord did not follow your instructions. On the first night home, however, very heavy rain falls, and the roof does not leak. You can then argue that your premiss was false; the repairs must have been made because otherwise the roof would certainly have leaked.

Because validity depends solely on form, evaluating deductive arguments can be simpler than evaluating inductive arguments. With inductive arguments, we have to take into account all sorts of background information that could affect the strength of the argument. We need to be concerned with the size of samples, the lack of bias, the relevance of analogies, whether any evidence has been suppressed, and other such matters. On the basis of all these considerations as well as the form, we judge whether the premises support the conclusion and, if so, how strong the support is.

In evaluating deductive arguments, we do not need to consider any background information beyond the information required to state implicit premises. If an argument is an instance of a **valid argument form**, then that argument is valid. Moreover, whereas inductive arguments can have varying degrees of strength, validity is an all-or-nothing affair. An argument is either valid or not valid; there are no degrees of validity.

With this reminder of the important general characteristics of deductive arguments, we take a closer look at a group of deductive arguments called conditional arguments. Following a discussion of the nature of conditional sentences, we introduce some common valid forms of conditional arguments and discuss some fallacies associated with them.

III. CONDITIONAL SENTENCES

Conditional arguments are arguments that contain conditional sentences as premises, as conclusions, or both. A **conditional sentence** is a compound sentence in which the truth of one of the clauses (the consequent) is conditional on the truth of the other (the antecedent). In English, the antecedent is frequently introduced by *if* and the consequent by *then*, but stylistic variations are common.

Examples

1. If I study, then I will pass my math exam.
2. Maisie will recover from mono, provided that she takes care of herself.
3. President Obama would not have been elected if he had not been an excellent speaker.
4. You will never pass a math class if you don't do any homework.

1. THE STRUCTURE OF CONDITIONALS

Each of these conditional sentences (or, briefly, **conditionals**) is a compound sentence—a sentence that contains another sentence as one of its parts. A sentence that is not compound is called *simple*. Conditionals are composed of (at least) two sentences—the **antecedent** states the condition, and the **consequent** depends on the stated condition. Antecedents and consequents might themselves be compound sentences. For example, the antecedent of "If I get enough rest and I eat properly, I will soon recover from my illness" is a conjunction.

In Example (1), the antecedent is "I study," and the consequent is "I will pass my math exam." In (2), the antecedent is "she takes care of herself," and the consequent is "Maisie will recover from mono." In (3), the antecedent is "he had not been an excellent speaker," and the consequent is "President Obama would not have been elected." In (4), the antecedent is "you don't do any homework," and the consequent is "you will never pass a math class."

Even this small sample reveals some of the variety of ways in which conditionals are expressed in English. Different verb tenses (past, present, and future) and moods (indicative and subjunctive) occur. Various terms connect the antecedent with the consequent: "if . . . then" and "provided that." Sometimes, as in (1), the antecedent comes before the consequent. In other cases, the antecedent follows the consequent, as in (2), (3), and (4). Subjunctive conditionals, such as (3), usually express what would happen if something else were to occur (a possibility) or what would have occurred if something else had happened, when it did not in fact. These latter subjunctive conditionals are called *counterfactual conditionals*. They are used to talk about events that might once have been possible but which never happened. For example, one can speculate what the outcome of World War II would have been if the Allied invasion of Normandy had failed.

Some conditional sentences indicate that the truth of the antecedent is necessary for the truth of the consequent. If we rule out persons who receive honorary degrees, for example, we can say that being enrolled as a student is a *necessary* condition for receiving a degree from a university. In other words, if someone is not enrolled as a student, then he or she cannot earn a degree. Other ways of expressing this same conditional are "A person can receive a degree from a university *only if* that person is enrolled as a student" or "A person cannot receive a degree from a university *unless* that person is enrolled as a student."

Other conditional sentences indicate that the truth of the antecedent is sufficient for the truth of the consequent. As every student knows, being enrolled as a student is not sufficient for earning a degree. Other conditions, such as earning course credits, meeting distribution requirements, passing grade-point average, and payment of fees and library fines, are also required to earn a degree. The sufficient condition for earning a degree is a conjunction of conditions so complex that several pages in your school's catalogue are devoted to it. In other cases, stating a sufficient condition is easy. For example, being enrolled as a student is sufficient for being eligible to purchase basketball tickets at a student rate. Thus, we can say that *if* someone is enrolled as a student, *then* that person is eligible to purchase basketball tickets at the student rate.

Because the validity of arguments depends on form, and the form of the argument in turn depends to some extent on the forms of the sentences that are its premises and conclusion, we want to be able to represent the form of conditional sentences in a standard way. To do so, we ignore some differences in conditionals as well as some rhetorical features that characterize different ways of stating conditionals in English. Such refinements are suppressed for the sake of focusing on the logical structure of sentences.

The relationship between antecedent and consequent clauses is the crucial logical relationship in conditional sentences, just as the relationship between classes is the crucial relationship in universal generalizations. Thus, it is of primary importance to identify which sentence is antecedent and which is consequent. When conditionals are written in the standard way—"If (antecedent), then (consequent)"—their form is readily apparent. This practice makes it easier to recognize the structure of conditional arguments. Example (1) is already in standard conditional form. We can rewrite Examples (2), (3), and (4) in standard form as well, as follows:

2. If Maisie takes care of herself, then she will recover from mono.
3. If he had not been an excellent speaker, then President Obama would not have been elected.
4. If you don't do any homework, then you will never pass a math class.

Still other ways of expressing conditional sentences in English are given below. Each example is followed by a translation into standard conditional form:

1. Whenever I see a bear, I run. (If I see a bear, then I run.)
2. I run only if I see a bear. (If I do not see a bear, then I do not run.) Note that this is *not* the same as (1), but that it is the same as "If I run, then I see a bear."
3. Given that I see a bear, I run. (Same as (1).)
4. A sufficient condition of my running is my seeing a bear. (Same as (1).)
5. A necessary condition of my running is my seeing a bear. (Same as (2).)
6. I do not run unless I see a bear. (Same as (2).)

Exercise Set 8.1

Rewrite each of the following sentences as a standard-form conditional sentence: *If* (antecedent), *then* (consequent).

1. You can play at Carnegie Hall only if you practice, practice, practice.

2. Unless you brush your teeth twice a day, you won't please your dentist at your checkups.

3. Whenever you want something very much, you will work hard to achieve it.

4. You will be eligible for a scholarship provided that you maintain a 3.3 grade-point average.

5. Without checking your work, you won't find mistakes.

6. In case the teacher asks about her, Jane missed the test because she was ill.

7. You can learn to throw a Frisbee if you really want to do it.

8. Having a grade-point average of C or better is a necessary condition for a student's being graduated.

9. Returning all library books on time is a sufficient condition for avoiding library fines.

10. Only if you care little for your safety will you ride a bicycle without a helmet.

11. Three strikes and you're out.

2. THE TRUTH OF CONDITIONALS

In English, conditionals express various kinds of relationships between the antecedent and the consequent. The conditional "If Maisie takes care of herself, then she will recover from mono," for example, expresses a *causal* connection between Maisie's caring for herself and her recovery. Subjunctive conditionals often express causal relationships: "If Maisie were to take care of herself, she would recover more quickly." Conditionals can also express *logical* and *definitional* connections, respectively, between sentences, as in "If two and two are added, then they equal four" and "If porpoises are aquatic, then they live in water."

The truth of a **causal** conditional depends on whether the situation described in the antecedent stands in the appropriate causal relationship to the situation described in the consequent. If Maisie's taking care of herself is causally irrelevant to her recovery from mono, then that conditional is not a true causal claim. Similarly, a conditional intended to express a logical or a definitional relationship will not be regarded as true unless the appropriate type of connection holds between the antecedent and the consequent.

Occasionally we encounter conditional sentences in which the truth of the antecedent is irrelevant to the truth of the consequent because the consequent could not be false in any case.

Examples

   1. If Jake continues to smoke, he will eventually die.

Jake will eventually die whether or not he continues to smoke—although "eventually" will probably be sooner if Jake smokes than if he does not smoke. Perhaps that is the intended interpretation of the sentence.

   2. If the forecaster predicts rain, then either it will rain or it will not.

In this conditional, the consequent must be true regardless of what the forecaster predicts.

A **material conditional** expresses another type of connection, neither causal nor logical yet similar to other types of conditionals in that it cannot be true if it has a false consequent and a true antecedent. An example of a material conditional is

If humans live on Jupiter, then my great-grandmother was an astronaut.

Although no natural link connects the antecedent and consequent in this conditional, its meaning is clear. The point of this sentence, and others like it in English, is to emphasize that the antecedent is false. It is a way of expressing "No way is there human life on Jupiter."

Although material conditionals are often just humorous ways of stating that something is false, we can draw from them a logically useful principle about interpreting sentential connectives. In a material conditional, the "if . . . then . . ." that connects the component sentences is a **truth-functional** connective. This means that the truth of the conditional sentence is determined completely by (is a function of) the truth of its component sentences. The only circumstance under which a material conditional is false is when it has a true antecedent and a false consequent. That is why the compound sentence "If there's human life on Jupiter, then my great-grandmother was an astronaut" can be used to state the falsity of "there is human life on Jupiter." The consequent of the conditional ("my great-grandmother was an astronaut") is obviously false. Yet the sentence as a whole is understood as true. But if the antecedent were true, then the conditional would be false, for it would have a true antecedent and a false consequent. Thus, a material conditional of the form *If* (antecedent), *then* (consequent) is true unless the antecedent is true and the consequent is false.

It is useful to be able to analyze the logical form of a sentence without regard to its *content* (what it is about, what it says or means). If we use lowercase letters p and q to represent the antecedent and consequent of conditional sentences, then we can ignore the content of p and q and focus on the relationship between the truth of the component sentences and the truth of the compound.

If a sentence has the form "If p, then q," we know the sentence is a conditional, but we cannot tell whether the conditional is a causal conditional, a logical conditional, or a material conditional. Obviously the difference matters for many purposes. From the perspective of grasping the logical relationship between validity and the form of arguments, however, introductory studies consider only the truth-functional relationship. That is, all conditionals are treated as material conditionals. Causal conditional sentences and definitional conditional sentences do resemble material conditionals in the sense that they are false if their antecedents are true and their consequents are false. (For example, the causal conditional "If the match is struck, then it will light" is false when the match is struck and the match does not light.) Causal conditionals, unlike material conditionals, cannot be judged true just because they do not have true antecedents and false consequents. As noted before, the appropriate causal relationship must hold between antecedent and consequent. But knowing whether this relationship holds requires knowledge of the world as well as knowledge of the meanings of the component sentences. More complicated systems of logic have been developed to treat causal conditionals, but they depend on a basic understanding of the material conditionals. Definitional conditionals require additional knowledge as well. To be true, the appropriate relationship must hold between the meanings of the antecedent and the consequent.

Counterfactual conditionals pose special problems because their antecedents are always false. If their antecedents were true, they would not be counter to fact. Thus, we cannot say that they are false whenever their antecedents are true and their consequents are false. Such an interpretation would place us in the difficult position of saying that no counterfactual is false. In using counterfactuals, we want, for example, to be able to recognize the difference between "If the Allied invasion of Normandy had failed, then the Allies would have lost World War II" and "If the Allied invasion of Normandy had failed, then the Allies would still have won World War II." The logic of counterfactual statements requires more apparatus than can be developed here. We avoid the special problems raised by counterfactuals by excluding them from our discussion of conditional arguments. Counterfactual conditionals require more advanced logical analyses, which are beyond the scope of a beginning textbook.

In sentential logic, logicians study the validity of conditional arguments by examining their *forms* and ignore such "extralogical" considerations as the meanings of the component sentences and whether the sentences are related either causally or logically. They examine only what happens when various combinations of truth and falsity are assigned to component sentences. The truth-functional relationship between the antecedent and the consequent in material conditionals serves as a minimal model for other types of conditionals, except for counterfactuals, capturing at least the notion that a conditional cannot be true when it has a true antecedent and a false consequent. We learn important things about validity and the structure of arguments in a simplified system that focuses on material conditionals. This does not mean that all conditionals *really* are material conditionals or that other types of conditionals are unimportant to logicians. The logic of truth-functional connectives, such as the "if . . . then" in a material conditional, does provide a relatively simple introduction to deductive reasoning, however.

In summary, according to the convention adopted for the study of sentential logic, the truth or falsity of a conditional sentence depends only on the truth or falsity of its component parts. There are just four possible combinations, which are listed in the following table:

Antecedent	Consequent	Conditional Sentence
p	q	If p, then q
True	True	True
True	False	False
False	True	True
False	False	True

The only way in which a conditional sentence can be false is for it to have a true antecedent and a false consequent (see the second row in the table).

Exercise Set 8.2

PART I. In the following exercises, the letters p and q represent component sentences in conditionals. Suppose that p is a true sentence and q is a false sentence. Rewrite each conditional in standard form, and state whether the conditional is true or false. (You may refer to the preceding table.)

1. p if q.
2. q if p.
3. q if q.
4. If p, q.
5. p provided that q.
6. q whenever p.
7. p is necessary for q.
8. q is sufficient for p.
9. p unless q.
10. p only if q.

PART II. The difficulty of treating counterfactual conditionals as truth-functional compound sentences has been mentioned. There are other types of compound sentences that are not truth-functional compounds (that is, the truth of the compound does not depend only on the truth of the component parts).

Examples

    a. Jack believes that Obama is the 45th president of the United States.
    b. Frank admired Gloria before he met her.
    c. Rita phoned Larry after she left his apartment.
    d. Frank hopes that Gloria feels the same way about him.
    e. Gloria knows she can never love Frank.
    1. Identify the component sentences in the compound sentences (a), (b), (c), (d), and (e).
    2. A compound sentence is a truth-functional compound only if the truth of the compound depends entirely on the truth of its component parts. We can see that (a) is not a truth-functional compound because that sentence can be true whether or not Obama is the 45th president. Can you say why each of the other sentences (b)–(e) is not a truth-functional compound?

IV. TWO CONDITIONAL ARGUMENT FORMS

In this section, we examine two common forms of conditional arguments. Each has two premisses, one of which is a conditional sentence. In one form, the second premiss affirms the antecedent; in the other form, the second premiss denies the consequent. The character of the second premiss provides the name of each of these argument forms.

1. AFFIRMING THE ANTECEDENT

The following argument is an example of **affirming the antecedent:**

> If we drive nonstop to the coast, we will need two days to recover.
> We are driving nonstop to the coast.
> _____
> We will need two days to recover.

Affirming the antecedent is one of many argument forms that were studied when Latin was the scholarly language of Europe. Affirming the antecedent retains a Latin name, *modus ponens*, which roughly means "the way of putting in place." We can exhibit the form of the argument letting lowercase letters p and q represent the component sentences of the conditional and the same letters for the same sentences wherever they occur in the argument.

> If p, then q
> p
> _____
> q

The English-language argument about driving to the coast is readily seen as valid. If its premisses are true, the conclusion must be true as well. Given our understanding of the material conditionals, we are in a position to prove that any argument that has this structure (form) must be valid. We need only to show there are no circumstances under which "If p, then q" and p are both true while (q) is false.

If the second premiss (p) is true, then the antecedent of the conditional premiss is true. But a conditional with a true antecedent is true only if its consequent (q) is true as well. However, q is not only the consequent of the conditional, it is also the conclusion of the argument. So, if "If p, then q" and p (both premisses) are true, then q (the conclusion) must be true as well.

In showing that this argument form is valid, we did not take into account meanings of the sentences that the letters p and q might represent. Thus, the validity of the form does not depend on the content of the sentences. All that is needed to demonstrate the validity of an argument form is to rule out the possibility that the premisses could all be true while the conclusion is false. Because one of the premisses is a conditional and the other premiss "affirms the antecedent" (claims the antecedent is true) while the conclusion affirms the consequent of the same conditional, it is not possible that the conclusion could be false while both premisses are true.

By showing that this argument form is valid, we have also shown that any argument in English that fits this form, or is an instance of this form, is valid. This means that any argument with two such premisses (one a conditional, the other a sentence that affirms the antecedent) and a conclusion that is the consequent of the conditional is valid.

Examples

1. Paul will go to the concert if Cher will perform. But Cher will certainly perform, so Paul will be there.
2. If Naomi leaves town, Ruth will follow her. So Ruth will follow because Naomi is going.
3. With patience, you will triumph. So you will triumph, for patience is your strong point.
4. A man cannot be robbed unless he can own, spend, claim, or want money. It is impossible for dead men to own, spend, claim, or want money. Therefore, dead men cannot be robbed.

—Reconstruction of Gaffer's argument in Charles Dickens's *Our Mutual Friend*

Exercise Set 8.3

Rewrite each of the four arguments above in standard form, listing the conditional premiss first.

2. DENYING THE CONSEQUENT

The second type of conditional argument, **denying the consequent**, is at least as common as affirming the antecedent and is only slightly more complicated. The Latin name of this form is *modus tollens* ("the way of taking away"). The simplified version of the argument for disconfirming hypotheses has this form.

Example

> If Maryland makes a strong offer, then the coach is going to Maryland.
> The coach is not going to Maryland.
> _____
> Maryland is not making a strong offer.

In this argument, as in affirming the antecedent, one premiss is a conditional. The other premiss denies the consequent or says that the consequent of the conditional premiss is false. The conclusion of the argument says that the antecedent of the conditional is also false. Again, using the letters p and q, we can represent the form of this argument:

> If p, then q
> Not q
> _____
> Not p

As with affirming the antecedent, we appeal to the circumstances under which material conditionals are true or false to show that this argument form is valid. In addition, however, we must consider the logical force of *not*, which turns true sentences into false ones and vice versa. In English, this logical function of **negation** can be accomplished in a number of ways. Sentences can be negated by replacing the main verb of the sentence with the negation of that verb: "You can do this"; "You cannot do this." A verb that means the same as the denial of the verb in the original sentence might be used: "They passed the test"; "They failed the test." The expression "it is not the case that" may precede the sentence to be negated: "You can do this"; "It is not the case that you can do this." Although "it is not the case that . . . " is an awkward phrase, it is favored by logicians because placing it at the beginning of any sentence negates the original sentence without otherwise altering its structure. Different ways of negating sentences are familiar to competent speakers of English, but here are a few examples to remind us of the variety of ways in which negation can be accomplished.

Examples

1. Harry is happy. Harry is unhappy.
2. She will do it. She won't do it.
3. Jack loves Jill. It is false that Jack loves Jill.
4. Students are present. No students are present.

With negations, as with conditionals, we ignore the subtleties of English usage to concentrate on what is logically important. Negation is an operation that changes a true sentence into a false one or changes a false sentence into a true one. This is the feature that is important to the validity of arguments. For this reason, just as conditionals have a standard form, so do negations. To form the negation of a sentence, use *not* in front of the letter that stands for the sentence that is negated ("not p").

Now we are ready to prove the validity of the form of denying the consequent. One premiss of the argument says that the consequent of the conditional premiss is false. If this is so and if the conditional premiss is true, it must have a false antecedent. But the conclusion of the argument simply states that the antecedent of the conditional premiss is false. Therefore, if both premisses are true, the conclusion must be true as well.

> If p, then q
> Not q
> _____
> Not p

Any English-language argument that fits the form (is an instance) of denying the consequent is a valid argument, just as any that fits the form of affirming the antecedent is valid. Following are some examples of arguments in English that are instances of denying the consequent.

Examples

1. If he wants to be a concert pianist, he will practice every day. He must not want to be a concert pianist because he won't practice every day.
2. Stupid savages could not devise complex languages without God's help. The languages of these people are complex. Therefore, God helped to construct the languages.

Example (2) is a reconstruction of Dobrizhoffer's argument that occurred in an earlier exercise (1.6, number 16). Writing this argument as a standard form denying the consequent requires double negation:

> If God did not help to construct the languages of savages, then these
>   languages could not be complex.
> It is not the case that these languages are not complex.
> _____
> It is not the case that God did not help to construct the languages of savages.

Exercise Set 8.4

Rewrite Example (1) above in standard form, showing it to be an instance of denying the consequent.

3. UNSTATED PREMISSES IN CONDITIONAL ARGUMENTS

Because conditional arguments are so common and so well understood, written works and ordinary speech contain many incompletely stated conditional arguments. Either the second (unconditional) premiss or the conclusion might be omitted. Occasionally, both the conclusion and the unconditional premiss are missing, and we must depend on the context to tell us that an argument, rather than just the affirmation of a conditional sentence, is intended. Suppressing premisses and conclusions is acceptable in many situations because it's often better not to bore people by stating what is obvious. For example, in the Bible, St. Paul is obviously arguing for the truth of Christ's resurrection from the dead when he says "If Christ has not risen, vain then is our preaching, vain too is your faith" (I Corinthians 15:14). Paul intends the argument to be interpreted in the form of denying the consequent.

Exercise

Supply the missing premiss for Paul's argument.

When premisses are not actually stated, there is a danger that what is intended as a *modus tollens* may be interpreted as a *modus ponens*. For example, John Wesley (the founder of the Methodist Church), counting on his listeners' faith, is supposed to have said "If you give up belief in witches, then you give up belief in the Bible."

Exercise

Complete Wesley's argument—first as a *modus ponens* (affirming the antecedent) and then as a *modus tollens* (denying the consequent). Which form do you think Wesley intended? With respect to Wesley's conditional, Bertrand Russell once said "I agree." How did Russell, who was not one of the faithful, interpret Wesley's argument?

V. FALLACIES ASSOCIATED WITH THESE CONDITIONAL FORMS

Arguments that are offered as deductive sometimes fail to preserve truth. When these invalid arguments bear a superficial resemblance to valid arguments, they are called **deductive fallacies**. Whether a proponent of an argument intends it to be deductive may be difficult to determine but is an important consideration. Inductive arguments, for example, are not meant to be deductive, and the standards for assessing their strength differ from the standards for evaluating deductive arguments. Although inductive arguments are not truth-preserving, it would be inappropriate to regard all inductive arguments as fallacious.

1. FALLACIOUS (INVALID) FORMS OF ARGUMENT

Before addressing the question of fallacious arguments in English, we consider what it means to say that an argument form is **invalid**. An argument form is invalid (not valid) if it is possible for an instance of that form to have all true premisses and a false conclusion. Invalid argument forms that closely resemble valid argument forms are called *fallacious* forms of argument. The following form, which resembles affirming the antecedent, is an invalid form of argument:

If p, then q

$\dfrac{q}{p}$

To show that this form is invalid, we need note only that if q were true and p were false, the conclusion would be false, but both premises would be true. This is because a material conditional with a false antecedent is true whether its consequent is true or false. Not surprisingly, this fallacious form is called **affirming the consequent**. The simplified version of the argument for confirming a hypothesis has this form. The following argument also is an instance of this form:

If Cincinnati is the capital of Ohio, then Cincinnati is in Ohio.
Cincinnati is in Ohio.

Cincinnati is the capital of Ohio.

The second fallacious form of argument, which superficially resembles denying the consequent, is called **denying the antecedent**.

If p, then q

$\dfrac{\text{Not } p}{\text{Not } q}$

The invalidity of this form is evident if we consider that the second premiss denies the antecedent of the conditional premiss (says it is false). But conditionals are true when their antecedents are false, whether they have false consequents (as the conclusion states) or true ones. Because the truth of the premisses cannot guarantee the truth of the conclusion, the argument form is not valid.

Example

If bats are birds, then bats have wings.
Bats are not birds.

Bats do not have wings.

To show that an argument form is invalid, we need only show that an argument in that form can have all true premises and a false conclusion. As with denying the antecedent, we can do this abstractly by discussing the circumstances under which sentences of a certain form are true or false. Alternatively, we can exhibit an English-language argument that fits the form and obviously has true premisses and a false conclusion. This latter method is called *providing a counterexample*.

2. INVALID AND FALLACIOUS ARGUMENTS

Incorrect arguments are called *fallacious* if they somehow resemble or pretend to be correct arguments. Arguments that resemble deductively correct arguments but are invalid are called *deductive fallacies*. When the premises are all obviously true and the conclusion obviously false, clearly the argument is fallacious. In general, however, showing that a given argument is invalid is more difficult than showing that an argument form is invalid. An argument is invalid only if it is not an instance of any valid argument form. (Of course, no inductive argument, regardless of its strength, is an instance of a valid form. In this discussion of fallacies, we consider only arguments that somehow resemble valid deductive arguments.)

Thus far, we have examined only two valid argument forms—affirming the antecedent and denying the consequent. We cannot prove an argument is fallacious merely by showing that it fails to fit either of these forms. The classic example of a valid argument does not fit either form:

> All men are mortal.
> Socrates is a man.
> _____
> Socrates is mortal.

One problem is that a single English-language argument can fit several different argument forms. Forms capture selected structural features of the argument. Sometimes we are interested in structural (formal) relationships *among* various simple sentences in an argument, as when we analyze conditional arguments. In other arguments, such as the quasi-syllogism about Socrates, validity depends on structural relationships *within* the simple sentences that make up the argument, such as the relationships between the subject and the predicate in a sentence. If the validity of a given argument depends on *intra*sentence structures, we will not prove that it is valid by representing its form in terms of *inter*sentence structure.

If an English-language argument has obviously true premises and an obviously false conclusion, we know that it is invalid, for it could not be an instance of any valid form. For this reason, we can be confident that the examples we presented of English-language arguments that were instances of affirming the consequent and denying the antecedent are fallacious. Deductive validity is a matter of form. When we become more familiar with various argument structures and when we can be reasonably certain we have not overlooked any hidden structure by virtue of which an argument could be valid, we can say it is highly probable that specific arguments are fallacious even though they have true conclusions. For the time being, however, we are on safer ground when we speak of fallacious *argument forms*. When we are presented with an English-language argument that is an instance of one of the better known fallacious forms, we should suspect it of being fallacious. It is reasonable to challenge whoever is presenting the argument to show that it is an instance of some valid form.

Exercise Set 8.5

Each of the following exercises contains a conditional argument. Treat all the conditionals as material conditionals. Assume that all the arguments purport to be deductive, and rewrite each argument (in English) so that its premises and conclusion are on separate lines. If the conditional premiss is not in standard form, rewrite it. Supply missing premisses or conclusions, if necessary. When doing so, be charitable and give the proponent of the argument the benefit of the doubt. Then tell whether the rewritten argument is in the form of affirming the antecedent, denying the consequent, affirming the consequent, or denying the antecedent.

1. If Joan is an actor, then she'll have trouble finding work. She'll have trouble finding work, so she is an actor.

2. Harry will get the role only if he was trained as a method actor. But he wasn't trained as a method actor, so Harry won't get the role.

3. If the TV is not plugged in, it won't work. But the TV is plugged in, so it will work.

4. You can graduate only if your library fines are paid. Your library fines are paid, so you can graduate.

5. Without interesting work, life is tiresome. But life is not tiresome, so there is interesting work.

6. If Freud was correct, then morality is nothing but a set of internalized parental commands. But the notion that morality consists solely of such commands is imbecilic. Freud was surely wrong about morality.

7. Your cellphone bill will be reasonable, provided that you use no more than 200 minutes a month. But according to your past history, you won't exceed the 200-minute allowance, so your cell phone bill will be reasonable.

8. If the ability to live a coherent moral life depended on having an intellectual theory of morality, most people would not live a coherent moral life. So living a coherent moral life does not depend on having an intellectual theory of morality.

9. All forms of pantheism [which involves the belief that man is a part of God] must be rejected, because if man is actually a part of God, the evil in man is also in God. But there is no evil in God.

—Bishop of Birmingham, cited in B. Russell, *Religion and Science*

10. If 2 is not a prime number, then there is a positive integer smaller than 2 and greater than 1 that evenly divides 2. But there is no positive integer smaller than 2 and greater than 1. Therefore, 2 is a prime number.

11. If morals could be taught simply on the basis that they are necessary to society, there would be no social need for religion. But morality cannot be taught in that way.

—Patrick Lord Devlin, *The Enforcement of Morals*

12. We would not be at the trouble to learn a language when we can have all that is written in it just as well in translation. But as we cannot have the beauties of poetry but in its original language, we learn it.

—S. Johnson

13. The earth is spherical in shape. For the night sky looks different in the northern and southern parts of the earth, and this would be so if the earth were spherical in shape.

—Aristotle, *Physics*

14. A judgment of acquittal by reason of insanity is appropriate only when a jury verdict of guilty would violate the law or the facts. We cannot say that this was the situation in Washington's case. Therefore, the district court did not err in its refusal to enter a judgment of acquittal by reason of insanity.

—Bazelon, *Washington v. United States*

15. All history shows that the progress of humanity is accomplished not otherwise than under the guidance of religion. But if the race cannot progress without the guidance of religion—and progress is always going on, and also in our own times—then there must be a religion of our times.

—L. Tolstoy, *What Is Art*

16. One could argue that given raw materials of more-or-less equally ideal qualities for axemaking, a simple utilitarian model would predict a wide but more-or-less even pattern of dispersal of axes in all directions from the quarry source. However, such uniformity of dispersal of greenstone [for making axes] from Mt. Williams is emphatically what one does not find in southeastern Australia.

—R. A. Gould, *Living Archaeology*

17. Because the financial burden of radioactive waste storage is simply taken on by the government [and not by the operators and customers of nuclear power plants], the taxpaying public is the victim of an inequitable practice. . . . If the public as a whole bears the cost of waste storage, but only a subset of society receives the benefits of atomic power, then the costs and benefits of nuclear generation of electricity are not borne equitably.

—K. S. Shrader-Frechette, *Nuclear Power and Public Policy*

18. "What I said was," said Cantrip, "that if it wasn't the Major, then it was the Bruce chap. And it wasn't the Major, so it is the Bruce chap."

—S. Caudwell, *Thus Was Adonis Murdered*

19. A postal regulation requires that sealed letters carry first-class postage. Suppose you are given the task of checking to see whether the regulation has been followed. Obviously, if you see a letter without first-class postage, you must turn it over to see whether it is sealed. Three other possibilities exist: (a) letters stamp-side up with first-class postage; (b) letters back-side up that

are sealed; or (c) letters back-side up that are unsealed. Which of the three types, if any, do you have to turn over to see whether the regulation has been followed? Describe the form of reasoning that you use to answer the question.

20. It is, in fact, a common fantasy, promulgated mostly by the scientific profession itself, that in the search for objective truth, data dictate conclusions. If this were the case, then each scientist faced with the same data would necessarily reach the same conclusion. But as we've seen earlier and will see again, frequently this does not happen. Data are just as often molded to fit preferred conclusions.

—R. Lewin, *Bones of Contention*

VI. ADDITIONAL FORMS OF SENTENTIAL ARGUMENTS

In this section, we continue the analysis of deductive arguments in which validity depends on *truth-functional* connections among sentences. Two sentential connectives— expressed by "if . . . then" and "not" in English—have been introduced. The meanings of these truth-functional connectives are given in the following tables, called *truth tables*, in which *p* and *q* represent any two sentences:

1. *p*	*q*	If *p*, then *q*	2. *p*	Not *p*
True	True	True	True	False
True	False	False	False	True
False	True	True		
False	False	True		

Table 1 can be summarized by noting that the conditional is true whenever the antecedent is false or the consequent is true. Table 2 can be summarized by noting that a negation is false whenever the original sentence is true, and vice versa.

Additional connectives (terms used to form compound sentences)—expressed in English by "or," "and," as well as "if and only if"—can be assigned truth-functional definitions, thereby allowing a large class of English-language arguments to be analyzed in truth-functional terms. Some additional forms of truth-functional arguments are introduced here, followed by a general method for determining the validity or invalidity of any argument form in which validity depends on truth-functional connections among sentences.

Sentential logic, the area of logic concerned with such intersentential connections, is based on two important principles:

1. **The Principle of the Excluded Middle:** Every sentence is either true or false.
2. **The Principle of Contradiction:** No sentence is both true and false.

These principles apply to sentences in a specific context of utterance. For example, the time and place to which the claim "It is raining" refers is either understood or expressed. If spelled out explicitly, the sentence would include a reference to the time and place: "It is raining at 10 A.M. on March 15, 2012, at Washington Square in New York City." The sentence "It is raining" is true when it applies to places and times when it is raining, and it is false when it applies to places and times when there is no rain. When the sentence "It is raining" is understood as referring to a particular time or place, the principles of the excluded middle and of contradiction apply. Some sentences (universal generalizations) are understood as referring to all times and all places ("All men are mortal"). Properly understood, the principles of the excluded middle and of contradiction seem obvious enough, and we accept them in our study of logic.

1. HYPOTHETICAL SYLLOGISMS

The **hypothetical syllogism** is a familiar form of argument, in which both premisses and the conclusion are conditional sentences.

Example

> If inflation can be controlled, then businesses will expand.
> If businesses expand, then unemployment will decrease.
> _____
> If inflation can be controlled, then unemployment will decrease.

As in affirming the antecedent and denying the consequent, the conditional sentences in hypothetical syllogisms are treated as material conditionals. The connective "if . . . then" yields a false compound sentence only if the antecedent is true and the consequent is false. The form of the hypothetical syllogism can be represented by letting p, q, and r stand for the antecedents and consequents in the premisses and conclusion, using the same letter for the same component sentence in each case:

> If p, then q
> If q, then r
> _____
> If p, then r

If this argument form were invalid, it would be possible for the conclusion to be false while both premisses were true. However, this is not possible, because the only way the conclusion could be false would be for p to be true while r is false. But if r is false, then q must also be false for the second premiss to be true. If q is false, however, then p must also be false, or the first premiss will not be true. However, p cannot be false in the premiss and true in the conclusion, for no sentence can be both true and false, so the argument form is valid. The hypothetical syllogism concerning inflation control is an instance of this valid form and is a valid argument.

In offering proofs of validity, we follow this general procedure: Show that it is not possible to assign truth and falsity consistently to component sentences in such a way that all the premisses are true and the conclusion is false.

Hypothetical syllogisms, sometimes called "chain arguments," are often used to demonstrate the truth of a conditional sentence by showing the conditional steps that lead up to it. Consider, for example, the concern that even though cellular phone calls and text messages are carried on different traffic channels, a malicious hacker could use text messages to disable the voice network of cellular telephones. To show that this concern is real, P. D. McDaniel, a security expert, pointed out that if a hacker can direct a network of computers to send thousands of text messages over the Internet to the cellular network, then the hacker can tie up all the network's control channels that direct text messages through some traffic channels and cellular phone calls through others. And, if no control channels are available, then no cellular phone calls can be directed to the traffic channels that carry voice messages. Thus, if hackers send a flurry of text messages, the voice network can be disabled.

2. DILEMMAS

In English, the term *dilemma* usually refers to a choice between two disagreeable alternatives: "Tom is in a dilemma; he must either give up the big party weekend or fail some of his midterms next week." Another meaning of *dilemma* refers to a conditional form of argument with a premiss that states alternatives. The two meanings are connected, for Tom, who is in a dilemma, may confront the following argument:

> If I spend the weekend partying, then I will fail some midterms.
> If I spend the weekend studying, then I will miss out on some good times.
> I will party this weekend, or I will study.
> ———————————————————————————————
> I will fail some midterms, or I will miss out on some good times.

This argument is valid. (Remember that for an argument to be valid, the premisses do not have to be true.)

This **constructive dilemma** is similar to affirming the antecedent. It has two conditional premisses, a third premiss that states that one or the other of the antecedents is true, and a conclusion that states that one or the other of the consequents is true. Using letters to represent simple sentences, this form of argument can be symbolized in the following way:

> If p, then q
> If r, then s
> p or r
> ———————
> q or s

The validity of this argument form depends on the truth-functional meanings of the sentential connectives "if . . . then" and "or." Compound sentences that are connected by *or* are called **disjunctions**. In ordinary language, some disjunctions are **exclusive**, in which case *or* means "one or the other, but not both." When a menu says "Soup or salad is included in the price of the meal," we understand that the disjunction is exclusive. If you want both soup and salad, you must pay extra. Other disjunctions are **inclusive**. In these sentences, *or* means "one or the other, or possibly both." When a road sign says "This bridge is open to automobile or truck traffic," we understand that the disjunction is inclusive. The English word *or* thus has two meanings.

For the purpose of analyzing forms of arguments, it is desirable to eliminate vagueness and ambiguity in the important sentential connectives by agreeing on a single, precise meaning. By convention, logicians have selected the inclusive sense of *or*. The truth-functional meaning of the inclusive *or* is given in the following table, where p and q represent any two sentences:

3.	p	q	p or q
	True	True	True
	True	False	True
	False	True	True
	False	False	False

To summarize: A disjunction is true whenever one or both of its components (**disjuncts**) is true, and false only when both disjuncts are false.

The constructive-dilemma form of argument is valid, for when the truth-functional meanings of "if . . . then" and "or" are adopted and all the premisses are true, the conclusion will be true as well. For the disjunctive premiss "p or r" to be true, at least one of its disjuncts must be true. Then, the conditional premiss that has that disjunct as its antecedent must have a true consequent to be true. But this means that "either q or s" (the conclusion) is true if all of the premisses are true. The English argument concerning Tom's dilemma is valid, because it is an instance of a valid argument form.

Another version of the dilemma, called the **destructive dilemma**, is closely related to denying the consequent (*modus tollens*).

Example

> If the reporter was doing his job, he was present at the political meeting.
> If the reporter is intelligent, he knew what was happening there.
> Either the reporter wasn't present at the meeting, or he didn't know what
>   was happening there.
> _____
> Either the reporter wasn't doing his job, or he isn't intelligent.

The form of this argument is:

> If p, then q
> If r, then s
> Not q or not s
> _____
> Not p or not r

This argument form is valid. (You can convince yourself this is so by applying the same type of analysis used with the constructive dilemma.)

In another variation of the dilemma, the antecedent of one of the conditionals (not p) is the denial of the antecedent of the other conditional (p), and the disjunctive premiss has the form "p or not p." In ordinary language, an obviously true disjunctive premiss, such as this, is usually unstated. In many dilemmas of this type, the conclusion is also unstated.

Example

James Boswell, in his *Journal*, describes an argument offered by Pasquale de Paoli, the "George Washington of Corsica," when Paoli was trying to decide whether or not to marry:

> If he [the commander of a nation] is married, there is a risk that he may be distracted
>   by private affairs and swayed too much by a concern for his family.
> If he is unmarried, there is a risk that not having the tender attachments of a wife
>   and children, he may sacrifice all to his ambition.

Exercise

Can you complete Paoli's dilemma with an appropriate premiss of the form "p or not p" and a conclusion?

In another variant of the constructive dilemma, both conditionals have the same consequent:

> If I win a scholarship, I'll have enough money for tuition.
> If I get a part-time job, I'll have enough money for tuition.
> I'll win a scholarship, or I'll get a part-time job.
> _____
> I'll have enough money for tuition.

This argument shows that dilemmas can present attractive alternatives and conclusions as well as problematic ones.

3. FALSE DILEMMAS

When presented with two choices, we often consider the consequences of each and reason about them using one or another of the dilemma forms. To avoid the fallacy of black-and-white thinking, we must be careful to avoid being misled into thinking that the number of alternatives is always limited to two. Suppose, for example, that a young woman has received two proposals of marriage. Suitor A is charming, but lazy and poor; Suitor B is dull, but rich. The woman might construct the following argument:

> If I marry A, then I'll be poor.
> If I marry B, then I'll be bored.
> I must marry A or B.
> _____
> Therefore, I'll be poor or bored.

The argument is an instance of a valid form. Nevertheless, the woman who reasons in this black-and-white fashion constructs a false dilemma for herself. She can choose not to marry either suitor. Other questionable assumptions underlie this argument. She does not have to assume that her own income is determined by her husband's income. She could tell the lazy charmer that she will consider his proposal when he settles down to work, or she could persuade the other suitor to expand his horizons. If any of these options is available, at least one premiss is false, and thus the conclusion could be false as well.

4. DISJUNCTIVE SYLLOGISMS

In **disjunctive syllogisms**, one of the premisses is a disjunction and the other premiss denies one of the disjuncts. The conclusion affirms the truth of the other disjunct.

> Either the Yankees will win the pennant, or the fans will be unhappy.
> The Yankees will not win the pennant.
> _____
> The fans will be unhappy.

This argument is an instance of the following valid form:

> p or q
> Not p
> _____
> q

If the first premiss is true, then at least one of the disjuncts (p, q) must be true. The second premiss says that one of those disjuncts (p) is false. The conclusion simply says that the other disjunct (q) is true, which must be so if both premisses are true.

A variant of the disjunctive syllogism is as follows:

p or *q*
Not *q*
_____
p

In this valid form, the second disjunct is denied in the second premiss, and the conclusion affirms the truth of the first disjunct.

Because *or* is understood in its inclusive sense, the following argument form, which resembles a disjunctive syllogism, is not valid:

p or *q*
p
_____
Not *q*

Because "*p* or *q*" is true not only when one of the disjuncts is true but also when both disjuncts are true, affirming the truth of one of the disjuncts in the second premiss does not rule out the truth of the other disjunct, as the conclusion states. Nevertheless, the following English-language argument is valid:

Joshua either failed the exam, or he passed it.
Joshua failed the exam.
_____
Joshua did not pass the exam.

In this argument, because of the meanings of *pass* and *fail*, it is impossible for Joshua to both fail and pass the same exam. However, since we have adopted the convention of using *or* in its inclusive sense in the disjunctive syllogism, another form is required to show that the argument is valid. One way to do this is to introduce a new truth-functional connective with the meaning of the exclusive *or*. We could call this new connective "e-or".

4.	*p*	*q*	*p* e-or *q*
	True	True	False
	True	False	True
	False	True	True
	False	False	False

Table 4 can be summarized by noting that an exclusive disjunction is false unless one of its disjuncts is true and the other is false.

We do not really need the special connective for the exclusive meaning of *or*, however, for we can use *or, not,* and *and* in the following way to express *or* in its exclusive sense:

p or *q*, and not both *p* and *q*

The valid form of which the English argument is an instance is:

p or q, and not both p and q

$\underline{p}$

Not q

(The truth-functional meaning of *and*, another important connective, is discussed in the next section.)

Exercise Set 8.6

PART I. Which of the valid argument forms or fallacies discussed in this section best characterizes each of the following English-language arguments?

1. If Roxanne knows that Cyrano speaks to her, she will fall in love with him. If she falls in love with Cyrano, Christian will be disappointed. So Christian will be disappointed if Roxanne knows that Cyrano is speaking.

2. The government must either raise taxes or cut spending for education. If the government raises taxes, citizens will be unhappy, but they will also be unhappy if spending for education is cut. So either way, the citizens will be unhappy.

3. Terry has the choice of playing kickball or soccer, but she said she won't play kickball, so she'll play soccer.

4. If Lyme disease is recognized at an early stage, antibiotics can halt its progress. If antibiotics halt the progress of the disease, the patient can recover completely. So if Lyme disease is recognized at an early stage, the patient can recover completely.

5. If the team wins next week, they'll go to the bowl game. If the team ties next week, they'll win the conference championship. But they will either win or tie next week, so they'll go to the bowl game or win the conference championship.

6. Either you buy a lottery ticket, or you won't win the lottery. But surely you won't win the lottery, so you'll not buy a lottery ticket.

7. There are two ways of carrying on a contest: one by law and the other by force. As the first is often insufficient, it becomes necessary to resort to the second.

   —Machiavelli, *The Prince*

8. If I stay up late to cram for the exam, I'll do poorly because I am so tired. If I don't stay up late to cram, I'll do poorly because I haven't read the material. So it looks as if I'll do poorly on the exam.

9. If I keep up my studies during the term, I won't have to cram for the final exam. If I don't have to cram for the final, I'll do well on it. So if I keep up my studies during the term, I'll do well on the final.

10. Auletes passed down to his daughter [Cleopatra, Queen of Egypt] a precarious balancing act. To please one constituency was to displease another. Failure to comply with Rome would lead to intervention. Failure to stand up to Rome would lead to riots.

—S. Schiff, *Cleopatra*

11. If global warming continues over the next 50 years, glaciers and polar ice caps will continue to melt. If glaciers and polar ice caps continue to melt, sea levels could rise by several feet, pushing Florida's coast inland by 1,000 feet. So if global warming continues, Florida's coast will move inland.

12. Either people must forego such amenities as personal automobiles, air conditioning, and consumption of large quantities of beef, or global warming will continue. But people are not willing to forego their present lifestyles, so global warming will be a fact of life.

13. The neo-Confucianist philosopher Seika writes: If a man's thoughts and prayers are charitable, heaven will recognize them; if they are not charitable, heaven will recognize this also.

14. If [generosity] is practiced in such a way that you will be considered generous, it will harm you [by draining your fortune and eventually causing you to be despised for your poverty]. If it is practiced virtuously [that is, without people knowing you are generous], you will not avoid acquiring a reputation for the opposite vice [that is, it will harm you because you will still be considered miserly].

—Machiavelli, *The Prince*

15. Either one's motives for following the moral word of God are moral motives, or they are not. If they are, then one is already equipped with moral motivations, and the introduction of God adds nothing extra. But if they are not moral motives, then they will be motives of such a kind that they cannot appropriately motivate *morality* at all. So, we reach the conclusion that any appeal to God in this connection either adds nothing at all, or it adds the wrong sort of thing.

—B. Williams, *Morality*

PART II. The fallacy of black-and-white thinking arises when the disjunctive premiss in a disjunctive syllogism or a dilemma rules out legitimate alternatives.

1. Suppose, for example, that you want to buy a car. The person you want to buy the car from wants $1,000 in cash, and you have only $500. You could argue the following:

Either I come up with $1,000, or I cannot get the car.
I cannot come up with $1,000.
_____
Therefore, I cannot get the car.

Whereas this argument is formally valid, the first premiss probably does not represent all the available options. Can you come up with other alternatives?

2. Machiavelli points out a false dilemma in the following passage. Explain his solution.

> A controversy has arisen about this: whether it is better [for a ruler of a state] to be loved than feared or vice versa. My view is that it is desirable to be both loved and feared, but it is difficult to achieve both and, if one of them has to be lacking it is much safer to be feared than loved.

—Machiavelli, *The Prince*

PART III. Complete the following dilemma, posed by a Catholic nun, on the topic of women priests, and evaluate it.

If men and women are the same, why not have women there (in the priesthood).

If men and women are not the same, women must be there.

VII. SYMBOLIZING CONNECTIVES

When validity is treated as a matter of logical form, symbols can be used to represent logical connectives, such as negation, disjunction, and conditionals. This simplifies writing argument forms and reminds us that the truth-functional meanings of connectives are considerably more restricted than the meanings of these terms in ordinary language. The following symbols represent the most important truth-functional connectives:

1. *Arrow* ($\rightarrow$): The connective "if . . . then" is represented by an $\rightarrow$ (called an *arrow*) between two sentences. The arrow joins the antecedent and the consequent of a conditional sentence.
2. *Tilde* ($\sim$): The connective "not" is represented by a $\sim$ preceding the sentence that is negated. The tilde, or negation sign, is regarded as a **connective**, even though it does not connect two sentences. Negation is a unary connective; the other connectives are binary. Because every negated sentence contains another sentence (the sentence that is negated), a negated sentence fits the definition of a compound sentence.
3. *Wedge* (v): The connective "or" is represented by a v between two sentences. The wedge joins two disjuncts in a disjunction.
4. *Dot* ($\bullet$): The connective "and" is represented by a $\bullet$ between two sentences. The dot joins two conjuncts in a conjunction.

In ordinary English, a conjunction with two conjuncts, such as "Casper went to the movies, and Tricia played racquetball," is true just in case both conjuncts are true. Otherwise, it is false. This is the logically important feature of conjunction, and it expresses the whole of the truth-functional meaning of *and*, as shown in the following table. ("True" and "False" are represented by "T" and "F"):

5.	p	q	$p \cdot q$
	T	T	T
	T	F	F
	F	T	F
	F	F	F

Other conjunctions in English include "also," "but," "furthermore," "moreover," and "while." A semicolon can conjoin two sentences as well. Different conjunctions differ in connotation. For example, "but" and "while" suggest a *contrast* between the two sentences that are conjoined ("Jane won the election, but John lost"). "And" sometimes connotes *temporal succession* in the sense of "and then" in addition to its conjunctive force ("Rosie finished the marathon and went to a dance that night"; "Susan married and had a baby"). As with the other logical connectives, however, we ignore these rhetorical subtleties to concentrate on the logical force of conjunction as it affects the validity of arguments. The preceding truth table defines the • by stating conditions under which sentence forms connected by the dot are true or false.

The following three truth tables completely define the other truth-functional connectives introduced thus far:

6.	p	$\sim p$	7.	p	q	$p \rightarrow q$	8.	p	q	$p \vee q$
	T	F		T	T	T		T	T	T
	F	T		T	F	F		T	F	T
				F	T	T		F	T	T
				F	F	T		F	F	F

One other truth-functional connective—the **material biconditional**—will be used. In English, the expression closest in meaning to this connective is "if and only if." The sentence "The roof leaks if and only if it is raining" means that if the roof leaks, then it is raining *and* if it is raining, the roof leaks. Thus, the material biconditional is equivalent to the conjunction of two material conditionals, in which the antecedent of one is the consequent of the other, and vice versa. Since this is so, we could use the arrow and the dot to express the material biconditional: "$(p \rightarrow q) \cdot (q \rightarrow p)$." The left conjunct represents "p only if q," and the right conjunct represents "p if q." However, the relationship represented by the material biconditional is common enough in argumentation to use a special symbol (double arrow) to denote it. The truth table for the material biconditional is as follows:

9.	p	q	$p \leftrightarrow q$
	T	T	T
	T	F	F
	F	T	F
	F	F	T

A material biconditional states that two sentences have the same truth value. Material conditionals are thus true only when both components have the same truth value (either both are true or both are false).

VIII. SYMBOLIZING ENGLISH SENTENCES

To analyze English-language arguments in which validity depends on truth-functional connections between sentences, let lowercase letters (p, q, r, s, and so on) denote simple sentences, and the symbols ($\rightarrow$, •, v, $\sim$, and $\leftrightarrow$) denote truth-functional connectives. When arguments are symbolized, the resulting expressions are argument forms.

Sentence forms are symbolic expressions that consist of a single letter or letters (for sentences) connected in an appropriate way by logical symbols (for connectives). The relationship between sentence forms and English sentences is analogous to the relationship between argument forms and English-language arguments.

In addition to letters and symbols for connectives, some punctuation is necessary to avoid ambiguity in sentence forms. In English, various punctuation marks (commas, dashes, semicolons) serve to eliminate ambiguity. Special terms in English, such as *either, neither,* and *both,* also perform this function. Formal sentential logic has just one means of punctuation—parentheses. These work in the same way as they do in arithmetic and algebra.

For example, the mathematical expression

$$7 + 5 \times 3$$

is ambiguous, because one value (36) is obtained when we add 7 to 5 and then multiply the sum by 3, but a different value (22) is obtained when we add 7 to the product of 5 and 3. When the expression is written

(1) $7 + (5 \times 3)$

the value is clearly 22. When the expression is written

(2) $(7 + 5) \times 3$

the value is 36. Parentheses indicate which expressions belong together and which arithmetic operations to perform first. To determine a numerical value for an expression, we perform the operation **within** parentheses first and the operation that is indicated by the **main connective** last. Parentheses indicate that the sign for addition in expression (1) and the sign for multiplication in expression (2) are the main connectives. In a similar way, parentheses indicate the main connective in sentence forms, telling us whether the sentence form in question is a conditional, disjunction, conjunction, biconditional, or negation.

The following examples illustrate how parentheses are used when translating English sentences into sentence forms.

Examples

1. Either Danica Patrick wins the race and the prize money is large, or her backers will not be happy.

   p: Danica Patrick won the race.
   q: The prize money is large.
   r: Her backers will be happy.

(1) $(p \bullet q) \vee \sim r$

In English, *either* often groups the components that precede *or*. Both the occurrence of *either* and the comma prevent us from understanding the sentence in the following way:

(2) $p \bullet (q \vee \sim r)$ (incorrect translation)

As in numerical expressions, a difference in the placement of parentheses can make a difference in the **truth value** assigned to the compound sentence. Suppose that *p* is false, *q* is true, and *r* is false. Then $\sim r$ is true. Because (1) is a disjunction (v is the main connective) with a true disjunct, (1) is true. However, (2) is a conjunction (its main connective is •), and the first conjunct (*p*) is false. With the same assignment of truth values to sentence letters as in (1), (2) is false.

2. Neither rain nor sleet can keep the postman away, but only Superman could deliver mail in this snowstorm.

   p: Rain can keep the postman away.
   q: Sleet can keep the postman away.
   r: Only Superman could deliver mail in this snowstorm.

$$\sim (p \vee q) \bullet r$$

In this sentence, *neither* and the comma indicate that the main connective is *but*, which is a conjunction. "Neither rain nor sleet can keep the postman away" has the same meaning as

   a. "It is not the case that either rain can keep the postman away or sleet can keep the postman away," or symbolically,

$$\sim (p \vee q)$$

Alternatively, the "neither . . . nor" could be rendered

   b. "Rain cannot keep the postman away, and sleet cannot keep the postman away," or symbolically,

$$\sim p \bullet \sim q$$

We see that expressions (a) and (b) are equivalent by examining the following truth table:

p	q	$p \lor q$	(a) $\sim(p \lor q)$	$\sim p$	$\sim q$	(b) $\sim p \bullet \sim q$
T	T	T	F	F	F	F
T	F	T	F	F	T	F
F	T	T	F	T	F	F
F	F	F	T	T	T	T

In this truth table, as in all standard truth tables, the initial columns display all possible truth values of the relevant sentence letters. The only sentence letters in this truth table are p and q. The third column displays the truth value of "$p \lor q$" for each combination of truth values of the sentence letters. The fourth column displays the values of "$\sim(p \lor q)$." The values in this column are opposite to the values in the preceding column because "$\sim$" turns true sentences into false ones, and vice versa. The fifth and sixth columns display values of the negation of p (opposite to values in the first column) and the negation of q (opposite to values in the second column), respectively. The final column, which is identical to the "$\sim (p \lor q)$" column, gives the values of the conjunction of $\sim p$ and $\sim q$. Thus, the table shows that whatever values are assigned to the sentences p and q, expressions (a) and (b) always have the same truth value. When this relationship holds between two sentence forms, the forms are said to be **logically equivalent**.

The logical equivalence of expressions (a) and (b) above is an example of **De Morgan's laws**. The logician Augustus De Morgan (1806–1871) pointed out important similarities between some aspects of logic and ordinary algebra. The laws that bear his name can be stated in English as follows:

1. The negation of a conjunction is logically equivalent to the disjunction of the negations of the conjuncts.
2. The negation of a disjunction is logically equivalent to the conjunction of the negations of the disjuncts.
3. The conjunction of two sentences is logically equivalent to the negation of the disjunction of their negations.
4. The disjunction of two sentences is logically equivalent to the negation of the conjunction of their negations.

In symbols, the laws can be expressed more succinctly as follows:

1. "$\sim(p \bullet q)$" is logically equivalent to "$\sim p \lor \sim q$."
2. "$\sim(p \lor q)$" is logically equivalent to "$\sim p \bullet \sim q$."
3. "$p \bullet q$" is logically equivalent to "$\sim(\sim p \lor \sim q)$."
4. "$p \lor q$" is logically equivalent to "$\sim(\sim p \bullet \sim q)$."

Exercise Set 8.7

PART I. Translate each of the following English sentences into the sentence form that most nearly captures the meaning of the English sentence, using the suggested sentence letters and their assigned interpretations. Be sure to use parentheses when necessary to prevent ambiguity.

p: Logic is easy.
q: Logic is fun.
r: Symbols can be used.

1. Logic is fun, but symbols cannot be used.
2. Logic is not easy unless symbols can be used.
3. Logic is fun only if symbols can be used.
4. Logic is easy, and logic is fun if symbols can be used.
5. Logic is not fun if symbols cannot be used.
6. Symbols can be used, or it is not the case that logic is easy.
7. Logic is fun if and only if it is easy.
8. Logic is neither easy nor fun.
9. It isn't true that symbols cannot be used.
10. Logic isn't easy if and only if symbols cannot be used.
11. Logic is fun, but it isn't easy.
12. Logic is easy; moreover, it is fun.
13. Either symbols can be used, or logic is easy but not fun.
14. Logic is easy, and if symbols can be used, it is fun.
15. Symbols can be used, but logic is neither easy nor fun.

PART II. Using the preceding interpretations for p, q, and r, translate the following sentence forms into English sentences:

1. $p \bullet \sim r$
2. $\sim(p \bullet r)$
3. $\sim(q \vee r)$
4. $q \leftrightarrow \sim r$
5. $p \bullet (\sim r \rightarrow q)$
6. $(p \vee q) \bullet \sim(p \bullet q)$
7. $r \rightarrow (p \rightarrow q)$
8. $(r \bullet p) \rightarrow q$
9. $q \bullet (p \leftrightarrow q)$
10. $(q \rightarrow r) \bullet (r \rightarrow q)$

PART III. Construct a truth table showing that the expressions "$p \leftrightarrow q$" and "$(p \rightarrow q) \bullet (q \rightarrow p)$" are logically equivalent. This will be a four-row truth table, similar to that showing the logical equivalence of "$\sim(p \text{ v } q)$" and "$\sim p \bullet \sim q$." Be sure to include separate columns for "$p \rightarrow q$" and "$q \rightarrow p$."

PART IV. Construct a truth table comparing each of the following pairs of sentences, and indicate whether the two members of each pair are logically equivalent to one another.

1. $p \rightarrow q, q \rightarrow p$

2. $p \rightarrow \sim q, \sim(p \rightarrow q)$

3. $p \rightarrow q, \sim(p \bullet \sim q)$

4. $p \rightarrow q, \sim p \text{ v } q$

5. $(p \text{ v } \sim p) \text{ v r, r}$

6. $p \rightarrow (q \rightarrow p), p \text{ v } \sim p$

IX. DETERMINING THE TRUTH VALUES OF COMPOUND SENTENCE FORMS

The truth values of **compound sentence** forms that are made up of simple sentences joined by truth-functional connectives depend on the truth values of the component simple sentences. Consider the following examples of sentence forms, when it is known that p is true, q is true, r is false, and s is false.

1. "$r \rightarrow (p \bullet q)$" is true.
This sentence form is a conditional with a simple (noncompound) sentence as its antecedent and a conjunction as its consequent. Because its antecedent is false, it is a true conditional. We do not need to consider the truth value of the consequent, because any conditional with a false antecedent is true.

2. "$(p \text{ v } r) \rightarrow (q \text{ v } s)$" is true.
This sentence form is a conditional with a disjunction as its antecedent and another disjunction as its consequent. The antecedent has a true disjunct (p), so it is true. The consequent also has a true disjunct (q), so it is true. A conditional with a true antecedent and a true consequent is true.

3. "$p \bullet (r \text{ v } q)$" is true.
This sentence form is a conjunction. Its first conjunct is a simple sentence (p), which is true. Its other conjunct is a disjunction with one true disjunct (q), so this conjunct is also true. The conjunction of two true sentences is true.

4. "$(p \bullet r) \text{ v } s$" is false.
This sentence form is a disjunction. Its second disjunct is a simple sentence that is false. Its first disjunct is a conjunction with one false conjunct (r), so the conjunction is false. Thus, the disjunction has two false disjuncts and is false.

5. "$p \leftrightarrow \sim q$" is false.

This sentence form is a material biconditional. One of its components is a simple sentence (p) that is true. Its other component is the negation of a true sentence, so that component is false. Thus, the two components of the biconditional have different truth values, and the biconditional is false.

The general method for determining the truth values of compound sentence forms is to work from the innermost parentheses out, considering the sentences connected by the main connective last of all.

Exercise Set 8.8

Suppose that p is true, q is false, r is true, and s is false. What is the truth value (T or F) of each of the following compound sentence forms?

1. $p \vee q$
2. $q \vee s$
3. $p \bullet (q \vee \sim q)$
4. $(p \bullet q) \vee (r \bullet s)$
5. $(p \bullet r) \vee (q \bullet s)$
6. $p \rightarrow (s \rightarrow r)$
8. $p \rightarrow (r \rightarrow s)$
9. $(p \bullet s) \rightarrow r$
10. $\sim(r \bullet s)$
11. $r \rightarrow (p \rightarrow (q \vee s))$
12. $r \bullet (q \rightarrow p)$
13. $\sim(r \vee s)$
14. $q \leftrightarrow s$
15. $(q \leftrightarrow r) \rightarrow p$
16. $p \rightarrow (q \rightarrow p)$
17. $(q \vee \sim q) \rightarrow p$
18. $p \rightarrow (q \vee \sim q)$
19. $(p. \sim p) \rightarrow r$
20. $(p \vee q) \rightarrow (r \vee s)$

X. DETERMINING THE VALIDITY OR INVALIDITY OF ARGUMENT FORMS

Truth tables are used to prove the validity or invalidity of argument forms. Because every valid argument in which validity depends essentially on truth-functional connectives is an instance of a valid truth-functional *argument form*, the truth-table method provides an indirect test of validity for truth-functional *arguments* in English. Consider the following argument:

> If primitive peoples did not cross the Pacific Ocean, there will not be a strong resemblance between Polynesian artifacts and South American artifacts. But there is a strong resemblance, so primitive peoples did cross the Pacific.

Interpret sentence letters p and q in the following way:

p: Primitive peoples crossed the Pacific Ocean.
q: There is a strong resemblance between Polynesian artifacts and South American artifacts.

Then the English-language argument is an instance of the following argument form:

$$\sim p \rightarrow \sim q$$
$$\underline{q}$$
$$p$$

To prove the validity of this form (and the argument that is an instance of the form), we construct a four-row truth table displaying all possible combinations of the truth values of the component sentences (p, q):

(1)	(2)	(3)	(4)	(5)
p	q	$\sim p$	$\sim q$	$\sim p \rightarrow \sim q$
T	T	F	F	T
T	F	F	T	T
F	T	T	F	F
F	F	T	T	T

In addition to the two initial columns for the sentence letters, columns are provided for each premiss and the conclusion of the argument. Additional columns for compound sentence forms that are components of the premisses or the conclusion may also be included. (In this case, a column is provided for $\sim p$ and one for $\sim q$.) With these additional columns, the truth value of "$\sim p \rightarrow \sim q$" can be determined by looking at just those columns.

To check the validity or invalidity of the argument form, look at the premiss columns (5) and (2) and the conclusion column (1). Note any *rows* in which the premisses are *all* true. (The first row is the only row in which both premisses are true.) Now check that row (or rows) to see whether the conclusion is true as well. If the conclusion is true in each row in which *all* the premisses are true, then the argument form is valid. If in some row the premisses are all true but the conclusion is false, then the argument form is invalid. The argument form above is valid. In the first row, the only row in which all the premises are true, the conclusion is true as well.

Because a truth table displays all possible combinations of truth values of the premises and conclusion, an examination of the truth table settles the question of whether it is possible for an argument in that form to have all true premises and a false conclusion. By definition, an argument (also an argument form) is valid if it is not possible for it to have all true premises and a false conclusion.

The following is another example of an argument in English that can be tested by the truth-table method:

> If we drive nonstop to New York, we'll need at least two days to recover; for if we drive nonstop, we'll be on the road for 24 hours, and if that happens, we'll need at least two days to recover from the trip.

The conclusion is stated at the beginning of the argument, which is an instance of a *hypothetical syllogism*. Assign sentence letters p, q, and r the following interpretations:

p: We drive nonstop to New York.
q: We'll be on the road for 24 hours.
r: We'll need at least two days to recover from the trip.

Then the argument is an instance of the following form:

$$p \rightarrow q$$
$$\underline{q \rightarrow r}$$
$$p \rightarrow r$$

This argument form contains three distinct sentence letters, so an eight-row truth table is required to display all possible combinations of their truth values. (In general, a table of 2^n rows is required when there are n distinct sentence letters.) In addition to the three initial columns for the sentence letters p, q, and r, the truth table contains a column for each premise and a column for the conclusion:

(1)	(2)	(3)	(4)	(5)	(6)
p	q	r	$p \rightarrow q$	$q \rightarrow r$	$p \rightarrow r$
T	T	T	T	T	T
T	T	F	T	F	F
T	F	T	F	T	T
T	F	F	F	T	F
F	T	T	T	T	T
F	T	F	T	F	T
F	F	T	T	T	T
F	F	F	T	T	T

In this truth table, columns (4) and (5) display truth values of the premisses, and column (6) displays the truth values of the conclusion. Both premisses are true in the first, fifth, seventh, and eighth rows. The conclusion is true as well in these rows. Thus, no row contains all true (T) premisses and a false (F) conclusion. This argument form is valid, as is any English-language argument that is an instance of this form.

The form of hypothetical syllogism has three distinct sentence letters and, as we have already seen, requires an eight-row truth table to display all possible combinations of those letters. Dilemma arguments can contain four distinct sentence letters and would require sixteen (2^4) rows. To avoid constructing long and cumbersome tables to establish validity, a **shorter truth-table** method can be used.

As we examine the truth table for the hypothetical syllogism, we can see that in the conclusion column (6), F occurs only twice (row 2 and row 4). These are the only rows relevant to assessing invalidity because only in these rows is it possible to have true premisses and a false conclusion. In all other rows, the conclusion is true. Let us use this information to construct another, shorter table that displays just those rows.

Because the conclusion $p \rightarrow r$ is a conditional sentence form, it is false in just those cases in which p is true and r is false. The only other sentence letter in the argument is q, which could be either true or false. Thus we can construct a two-row table, in which p is true and r is false in both rows while q is true in one of the rows and false in the other.

(1)	(2)	(3)	(4)	(5)	(6)
p	q	r	$p \rightarrow q$	$q \rightarrow r$	$p \rightarrow r$
T	T	F	T	F	F
T	F	F	F	T	F

This table shows that in the only possible cases in which the conclusion ($p \rightarrow r$) is false, then at least one of the premisses is false as well. In other words, the argument form is valid because there are no circumstances under which both premisses can be true while the conclusion is false.

Similar considerations apply to the constructive dilemma with premisses $p \rightarrow q$, $r \rightarrow s$, p v r, and conclusion q v s. The conclusion is a disjunction that can be false only when both q and s are false. In those circumstances, p and r could both be true, or both false, or p true and r false, or r true and p false. These combinations can be displayed in a four-row table:

(1)	(2)	(3)	(4)	(5)	(6)	(7)	(8)
p	q	r	s	$p \rightarrow q$	$r \rightarrow s$	p v r	q v s
T	F	T	F	F	F	T	F
T	F	F	F	F	T	T	F
F	F	T	F	T	F	T	F
F	F	F	F	T	T	F	F

In this shorter truth table, the premiss $p \rightarrow q$ is false in the first and second rows, the premiss $r \rightarrow s$ is false in the third row, and the premiss $p \vee r$ is false in the fourth row. Thus there is no row in which all the premisses are true and the conclusion false.

Although shorter truth tables have obvious advantages, constructing them requires special attention to various ways in which a conclusion could be false. For example, if the conclusion is a conjunction, then it will be false if any of the conjuncts is false, and a separate row in the shorter truth table is needed to display each of the possibilities.

Another method—a so-called *natural deduction method,* sometimes called a tree-proof method—for showing that argument forms are valid or invalid is presented in Appendix One. This method consists of a set of rules for eliminating connectives, thus simplifying the argument forms until their validity is obvious.

Truth tables can also be used to demonstrate the invalidity of argument forms. The invalidity of affirming the consequent, a fallacious argument form, is demonstrated in the following table:

(1)	(2)	(3)
p	q	$p \rightarrow q$
T	T	T
T	F	F
F	T	T
F	F	T

Here, the premisses are given in columns (2) and (3) and the conclusion is given in column (1). Note that in this truth table, as in many others, the initial columns do double duty. One of the sentences is a premiss, and the other is the conclusion. In row (3), both premisses are true, but the conclusion is false. The table thus shows that it is possible for an argument of this form to have all true premisses and a false conclusion. Whatever truth-table method we are using, we can stop constructing the table as soon as we find a single row in which all premisses are true and the conclusion is false.

Although the truth-table method can prove the invalidity of an argument *form,* such a proof does *not* show that any English-language argument that is an instance of the form is invalid. Because not all valid arguments are valid truth-functional arguments, the English argument may be an instance of some other valid form. (Some valid forms, remember, depend on *intra*sentence connections rather than on *inter*sentence connections.) To prove that an English-language argument is invalid, it must be shown either that the argument has all true premisses and a false conclusion or that the argument is not an instance of *any* valid argument form.

Truth tables are useful for analyzing **indirect arguments,** or **proofs by contradiction.** Indirect arguments proceed by taking as a premiss the denial of the claim to be proved and then by showing that from this follows either the denial of the assumed premiss (which is the conclusion to be established) or some obviously false sentence, perhaps even an outright contradiction. The Latin name for this type of argument is *reductio ad absurdum*, and is closely related to *modus tollens* (denying the consequent). If the premisses of a valid argument lead to an absurdity, then at least one premiss must be false.

The premiss that denies the conclusion in an indirect argument is frequently supported by an opponent but rejected by the person constructing the argument. Indirect argument is a powerful method of proof in mathematics. Students of higher mathematics encounter this method frequently and recognize that assuming the denial of what they are supposed to prove provides a convenient starting point for constructing many a proof.

Example

To prove that the square root of two is not a positive integer: Suppose that the square root of 2 is a positive integer. If the square root of 2 is a positive integer, then there must be a positive integer smaller than 2, which when multiplied by itself is equal to 2. But this cannot be so because the only positive integer smaller than 2 is 1, and 1 times 1 is equal to 1. Therefore, the square root of 2 is not a positive integer.

This argument can be understood as an instance of the following form:

$$p$$
$$p \rightarrow q$$
$$\underline{\sim q}$$
$$\sim p$$

The first premiss is "The square root of 2 is a positive integer." This is the antecedent of the second (conditional premiss). The conditional premiss, with a consequent represented by q, is true by definition. The third premiss, which is obviously true, denies the consequent of the conditional. But the conclusion of the argument is a sentence that contradicts the first premiss, so that premiss is rejected as false. The following truth table shows that the argument form is valid:

(1)	(2)	(3)	(4)	(5)
p	q	$\sim p$	$\sim q$	$p \rightarrow q$
T	T	F	F	T
T	F	F	T	F
F	T	T	F	T
F	F	T	T	T

Columns (1), (4), and (5) are premiss columns, and column (3) is the conclusion. In this truth table—unlike the others we have considered so far—there are *no* rows in which all the premisses are true. Although this may seem to invalidate the form, in fact it guarantees its validity. If there are no rows in which all of the premisses are true, then there can be no rows in which all the premisses are true and the conclusion is false. There are no rows in which all the premisses are true because the premisses contradict one another; at least one of the premisses must be false. Because the purpose of this argument is to show that the first premiss is false (it is the denial of the conclusion), this should not be too surprising. Any argument in which it is impossible for all of the premisses to be true is valid, for in such arguments it is automatically impossible for all of the premisses to be true and the conclusion to be false.

When an argument of this form has more than one premiss, the argument does not indicate *which* of the premisses is false, only that at least one of them must be false. The preceding valid argument points to the first premiss as false because the other premisses are obviously true. In some proofs by contradiction, however disputes arise concerning the source of trouble in the premisses. The method of proof by contradiction does not provide the answer to this problem.

Exercise Set 8.9

PART I. Use regular or shorter truth tables to determine the validity or invalidity of each of the following argument forms. Be sure to say whether the form is valid or invalid.

1. $p \bullet q$
   p
   $\sim p \lor \sim q$
   ___
   q

2. $(p \lor q) \rightarrow (p \bullet q)$
   $p \bullet q$
   ___
   $p \lor q$

3. $(p \lor q) \rightarrow (p \bullet q)$
   $\sim(p \lor q)$
   ___
   $p \bullet q$

4. $p \rightarrow q$
   $\sim(q \lor r)$
   ___
   $\sim p$

5. $p \rightarrow q$
   $p \rightarrow \sim q$
   ___
   $\sim p$

6. $p \rightarrow q$
   $\sim p \rightarrow q$
   ___
   q

7. p
   ___
   $p \lor q$

8. $p \rightarrow (q \rightarrow r)$
   $q \rightarrow (r \rightarrow s)$
   _____
   $p \rightarrow s$

9. $(p \cdot q) \rightarrow r$
   _____
   $(\sim r \cdot q) \rightarrow \sim p$

10. $\sim p \vee q$
    $\sim q \vee p$
    _____
    $p \leftrightarrow q$

11. $((p \vee q) \rightarrow r) \rightarrow (p \rightarrow r)$
    _____
    $(p \rightarrow q) \cdot (p \rightarrow r)$

12. $(p \vee q) \rightarrow (r \cdot s)$
    $(r \vee s) \rightarrow t$
    p
    _____
    t

PART II. Using sentence letters and connective symbols, symbolize the following arguments and construct regular or shorter truth tables to decide whether the resulting argument forms are valid or invalid.

1. The game has been sold out unless it has been canceled. If it has been sold out, I won't be able to see it, and if it has been canceled, I won't be able to see it. Either way I won't be able to see the game.

2. You can either face your problem or run away from it. If you're brave, you'll face it, so if you're brave, you won't run away from it.

3. If the city leaders have the same passion for classical music that they have for sports, they will strongly promote the symphony orchestra, both locally and at national and international levels. If the leaders sufficiently promote the symphony, then the orchestra hall will be filled to capacity for every performance. So, if the city leaders have the same passion for classical music that they have for sports, then the symphony will be sold out for every performance.

4. If the hockey team is winning most of its games, the arena is sold out. But the arena is sold out, so the team must be winning most of its games.

5. Electric automobiles are selling quickly and that can be true only if their batteries hold a charge for 100 miles of driving. So electric car batteries do have a 100-mile charge capacity.

6. If I buy a new car, I'll be broke (because of the insurance payments). But if I buy an older car, I'll be broke (because of the cost of keeping it in shape). I must buy either a new car or an older car, so I'll be broke.

PART III. Reconstruct the following arguments as truth-functional arguments, using appropriate symbols and following special instructions when indicated.

1. The following passage occurs in *Antigone*. Antigone has admitted burying her brother, against the tyrant Creon's orders, and has been sentenced to death. Reconstruct her argument.

> *Antigone:* This punishment will not be any pain.
> Only if I had let my mother's son
> Lie there unburied, then I could not have borne it.
> This I can bear.

—Sophocles, *Antigone*

2. Reconstruct the following argument:

> Either you have a rival or you don't. If you have one you must set out to please, so as to be preferred to him; if you don't have one you must still please so as to obviate the possibility of having one. In either case the same principle is to be followed: so why torment yourself?

—C. de Laclos, *Les Liaisons Dangereuses* (P. W. K. Stone, Trans.)

3. Reconstruct the following argument of Bertrand Russell, using truth-functional connectives and the suggested interpretations of sentences:

> In England under the blasphemy laws it is illegal to express disbelief in the Christian religion. It is also illegal to teach what Christ taught on the subject of nonresistance. [Therefore], whoever wishes to avoid being a criminal must profess to agree with Christ's teaching, but must avoid saying what that teaching was.

—B. Russell, *Free Thought and Official Propaganda*

p: You express disbelief in the Christian religion.
q: You break the law.
r: You teach what Christ taught on the subject of nonresistance.

4. Consider the following passage from *Middlemarch*:

> Poor Mr. Casaubon was distrustful of everybody's feelings toward him, especially as a husband. To let anyone suppose that he was jealous would be to admit their (suspected) view of his disadvantages; to let them know that he did not find marriage particularly blissful would imply his conversion to their (probably) earlier disapproval. . . . All through his life Mr. Casaubon had been trying not to admit even to himself the inward sores of self-doubt and jealousy.
>
> Thus Mr. Casaubon remained proudly, bitterly silent.

—G. Eliot, *Middlemarch*

Try to cast Mr. Casaubon's reasoning into argument form, stating the premisses and the conclusion. Then select sentence letters, with appropriate interpretations, and construct the argument form that this argument fits. Use a truth table to test the validity of the form.

5. Consider the following argument:

Now either nuclear power is safe and catastrophic accidents are impossible, in which case no limit on liability is needed to protect the nuclear industry from bankruptcy, or on the other hand, nuclear power is not safe and catastrophic accidents are possible, in which case a limit on liability is needed to protect the nuclear industry from bankruptcy. If the limitation is needed, it can only be so because successful claims can be made against the industry. But successful claims can be made against the industry only when injury can be shown to be the result of a nuclear accident. And if this can be shown, nuclear power is not safe. Hence one cannot argue consistently, both that there is a need for a limit on nuclear liability and that nuclear reactors are safe.

—K. S. Shrader-Frechette, *Nuclear Power and Public Policy*

a. Represent the form of this argument, using the following interpretations of sentences:

p: Nuclear power is safe.

q: Catastrophic accidents are possible.

r: A limit on liability is needed to protect the nuclear industry from bankruptcy.

s: Successful claims can be made against the industry.

t: Injury can be shown to be the result of a nuclear accident.

b. How many rows are there in the truth table for this argument form?

6. The following comments were made by the art critic Harriet Monroe on the occasion of the 1913 exhibition of dissident artists, including Cubists, at the famous New York Armory Show. Many critics were outraged, but Ms. Monroe said, "Better the wildest extravagance of the cubists than the lifeless works of certain artists who ridicule them."

Either these pictures are good or they are not. If they are good, they will make their way in spite of objections; if not, they will perish without the aid of objections.

—J. Parisi, S. Young and B. Collins (Eds.) *Dear Editor: A History of Poetry in Letters*

7. After returning from Kitty Hawk in December 1903, where Wilbur and Orville Wright demonstrated (just barely and with a rather clunky plane) that heavier-than-air flight was possible, Wilbur later wrote:

We found ourselves standing at a fork in the road. On the one hand we could continue playing with the problem of flying so long as youth and leisure would permit, but carefully avoiding those features which would require continuous effort and expenditure of considerable sums of money. On the other hand we believed that if we would take the risk of devoting our entire time and financial resources we could conquer the difficulties in the path to success before increasing years impaired our physical activity.

—M. Bernstein, "How the Airplane Learned to Fly," *Invention and Technology*, 2005, Summer

8. If my categories of thought determine what I observe, then what I observe provides no independent control over my thought.

   On the other hand, if my categories of thought do not determine what I observe, then what I observe must be uncategorized, that is to say, formless and nondescript—hence again incapable of providing any test of my thought. So in neither case is it possible for observation, be it what it may, to provide any independent control over thought. . . . Observation contaminated by thought yields circular tests; observation uncontaminated by thought yields no tests at all.

   —I. Scheffler, *Science and Subjectivity*

9. When Boeing tried to move production of its new 787 Dreamliner from its plant in Seattle to one in South Carolina, the National Labor Relations Board (NLRB) tried to block the move to protect unions and their workers. Washington is a union-shop state in which workers can be compelled to join a union; South Carolina is a "right to work" state in which union membership is voluntary. Union-shop advocates claim that their system protects workers and increases prosperity of states. Critics say this isn't so and cite statistics of greater prosperity for all in right-to-work states. Put into truth-functional form the following adaptation of an argument by A. Laffer and S. Moore:

   If union-shop laws are better for the economy, the NLRB does not need to intervene to keep Boeing in Washington. But the NLRB is trying to prevent Boeing from moving its plant to South Carolina. So forced unionism is not better for the state's economy.

10. Supply a conclusion and show the truth-functional form of the following argument:

    If forced unionism is good for the economy of states, then businesses and workers should be moving to those states in great numbers. But instead, businesses and workers are leaving those states in record numbers.

11. On the basis of the following passage from Beryl Markham's *West with the Night*, can you construct a truth-functional argument for the conclusion that elephants dispose of their dead in secret burial grounds? What is the form of the argument?

    There is a legend that elephants dispose of their dead in secret burial grounds and that none of these has ever been discovered. In support of this, there is only the fact that the body of an elephant, unless he had been trapped or shot in his tracks, has rarely been found. What happens to the old and diseased?

12. Translate this Machiavellian argument into a truth-functional form and say whether it is valid or invalid.

    If a ruler who wants always to act honorably is surrounded by many unscrupulous men, his downfall is inevitable. Therefore, a ruler who wishes to maintain his power must be prepared to act immorally when this becomes necessary [i.e., when surrounded by unscrupulous men].

13. I reasoned, however, as follows:
    1. either Kenneth is deeply and sincerely attached to Ned or he is not;
    2. if he is not so attached, then my pursuit of Ned will cause him no distress;
    3. if he is so attached, then either the attachment is reciprocal or it is not;
    4. if it is reciprocal, Ned will reject my advances and my pursuit of him will accordingly cause Kenneth no distress;
    5. if it is not reciprocal, Kenneth will suffer distress whether or not I pursue Ned;
    6. if Kenneth will suffer distress whether I pursue Ned or not, my pursuit of Ned cannot be the cause of Kenneth's distress;
    7. it is therefore logically impossible for my pursuit of Ned to cause Kenneth distress.

    —S. Caudwell, *Thus Was Adonis Murdered*

14. You think the letter may have had some connection with—with the explosion. Good Lord, but of course—I mean, that's rather more up your street than mine, but I should have thought it was obvious. Here's a man gets a letter threatening unpleasant consequences if he doesn't get out. Which he doesn't. So the consequences happen.

    —M. Gilbert, *The Country House Burglar*

15. The question was raised whether Lee Harvey Oswald, J. F. Kennedy's assassin, was motivated by movies about political assassination.

    The Manchurian Candidate is the story of a man programmed to kill at the command of other people. What self-respecting assassin would take such a character for his role model? Either Oswald acted according to his own wishes, in which case he wasn't imitating [the assassin in *The Manchurian Candidate*] or he really was programmed by the Communists, in which case the question isn't whether Oswald saw [the] movie or whether his Communist masters did.

    —L. Menand, "Brainwashed," *The New Yorker*

XI. TAUTOLOGIES, SELF-CONTRADICTIONS, AND CONTINGENT SENTENCES

Some sentences have the interesting property of being true on the basis of their truth-functional structure alone. One example is "If it is snowing, then it is snowing." This sentence is an instance of the form "$p \rightarrow p$," and although it is apparently about the weather, its truth does not depend on what the weather is. Sentences with this structural property are called **tautologies**. Truth tables can be used to determine whether sentence forms are tautologous. If the column under the sentence form contains only

Ts, that sentence form is tautologous. If a sentence is an instance of a tautologous sentence form, then that sentence is a tautology.

Some truth tables of tautologous sentence forms:

1.

p	$p \rightarrow p$
T	T
F	T

2.

p	$\sim p$	$p \lor \sim p$
T	F	T
F	T	T

3.

p	q	$q \rightarrow p$	$p \rightarrow (q \rightarrow p)$
T	T	T	T
T	F	T	T
F	T	F	T
F	F	T	T

Tautologies belong to the class of sentences that are **logically true**. Their truth depends solely on their logical form. A sentence such as "If it is snowing, then it is snowing" tells us nothing at all about the weather, or anything else in the world. *Tautology* in the logician's vocabulary differs from the common usage of the term to refer to any trivial or uninteresting claim. Because of the empty or uninformative nature of logical tautologies, the two senses are related. Although logical tautologies do not provide information about what the world is like, however, they are not insignificant. For example, one widely held philosophical view of the nature of mathematical truths is that they are all tautologies, and few people would deny the importance of mathematics.

In the same way that some sentences are true by virtue of logical structure rather than their ability to describe the world, other sentences are false by virtue of their truth-functional logical structure. These sentences are called **self-contradictions**. In a truth table, the column under a self-contradiction contains only Fs. An example of a self-contradictory sentence form is "$p \bullet \sim p$," as shown by the following truth table:

p	$\sim p$	$p \bullet \sim p$
T	F	F
F	T	F

The English sentence "It is snowing, and it is not snowing" is an instance of this self-contradictory form. Any conjunction that contains one conjunct that is the negation of another conjunct is self-contradictory. Less obvious forms of self-contradictory sentences also occur, such as the following:

$$(p \rightarrow q) \bullet ((q \rightarrow r) \bullet (p \bullet \sim r))$$

The truth tables for such self-contradictory sentence forms display all Fs in the column under the main connective for the sentence.

Sentences that are neither tautologies nor contradictions are **contingent** sentences. The truth values of these sentences depend on (are contingent on) whether their various components are true or false. The truth-table column under a contingent sentence form contains a mixture of Ts and Fs.

The following important relationship holds between the truth-functional validity of arguments and the tautologousness of sentences:

> An argument is valid truth-functionally if and only if its corresponding conditional is a tautology.

The **corresponding conditional** to an argument is a conditional sentence with the following structural properties:

1. The antecedent of the conditional is the conjunction of all the premisses of the argument.
2. The consequent of the conditional is the conclusion of the argument.

The conditional corresponding to the form affirming the antecedent *(modus ponens)* is

$$((p \rightarrow q) \bullet p) \rightarrow q$$

Hypothetical syllogism has as its corresponding conditional

$$((p \rightarrow q) \bullet (q \rightarrow r)) \rightarrow (p \rightarrow r)$$

Exercise Set 8.10

1. Can an argument with a tautologous conclusion be invalid?
2. Can an argument with a self-contradictory premiss be invalid?
3. Can a valid argument have all tautologous premisses and a contingent conclusion?
4. Is the following claim true? "If two sentence forms are logically equivalent, then the statement of their material biconditional is a tautology." Explain.
5. Explain why no simple sentence can be a tautology.
6. Write the corresponding conditionals for each of the following argument forms:

   a. $p \lor q$
   p
   ___
   $\sim q$

   b. $p \rightarrow q$
   $p \lor r$
   $r \rightarrow \sim s$
   s
   ___
   q

   c. $p \lor \sim p$
   ___
   q

7. Construct truth tables for each of the following sentence forms. Say whether each form is tautologous, self-contradictory, or contingent.

    a. $(p \rightarrow q) \rightarrow (q \rightarrow p)$

    b. $p \rightarrow \sim p$

    c. $\sim p \rightarrow p$

    d. $q \rightarrow (p \lor \sim p)$

    e. $(p \rightarrow q) \rightarrow (p \rightarrow (p \bullet q))$

8. Using sentence letters to represent simple sentences in English, translate each of the following into appropriate sentence forms that most closely capture the truth-functional structure of the sentence. Use a truth table to decide whether the sentence *as translated* is a truth-functional tautology, a self-contradiction, or a contingent sentence.

    a. You cannot win unless you try.

    b. The rain falls on the rich and the poor alike.

    c. It never rains but it pours.

    d. You win some, and you lose some.

    e. If you really love her, you'll tell her so.

    f. You are with me or against me.

    g. It is what it is.

    h. He'll win unless he loses.

    i. If you want it, you want it.

    j. If you wait for her at the café, she'll either show up or she won't.

    k. If determinism is true, then humans do not have free will.

XII. REVIEW

Chapter 8 surveys sentential, or truth-functional, logic. It discusses various forms of arguments, how to translate English sentences and arguments into sentence forms and argument forms by using symbols for sentence letters and connectives, and how to use truth-table tests to determine whether sentences are tautologous as well as whether argument forms are valid or fallacious. Definitions and brief comments on some of the most important terms provide a quick review of this chapter.

Compound Sentence   A sentence that contains another sentence as one of its parts.

Conditional Argument   An argument that contains at least one conditional sentence as a premiss. In this chapter, we studied several valid forms of conditional argument: **affirming the antecedent** (or *modus ponens*), **denying the consequent** (or *modus tollens*), **hypothetical syllogism**, **constructive dilemma**, and **destructive dilemma**.

Modus Ponens	*Modus Tollens*	**Hypothetical Syllogism**
$p \rightarrow q$	$p \rightarrow q$	$p \rightarrow q$
p	$\sim q$	$q \rightarrow r$
q	$\sim p$	$p \rightarrow r$

Constructive Dilemma	**Destructive Dilemma**
$p \rightarrow q$	$p \rightarrow q$
$r \rightarrow s$	$r \rightarrow s$
$p \vee q$	$\sim q \vee \sim s$
$r \vee s$	$\sim p \vee \sim r$

We also studied the forms of two fallacies associated with conditional arguments:

Affirming the Consequent	**Denying the Antecedent**
$p \rightarrow q$	$p \rightarrow q$
q	$\sim p$
p	$\sim q$

Conditional Sentence   A compound sentence consisting of an **antecedent** (the sentence that states the condition) and a **consequent** (the sentence that depends on the stated condition). The standard form of a conditional is "If (antecedent), then (consequent)" or "$p \rightarrow q$."

Deductive Fallacy   An invalid argument that bears some resemblance, possibly misleading, to a (correct) deductive argument.

Disjunctive Syllogism   An argument that has the following form:

$p \vee q$

$\sim p$

q

Invalid Argument   (or, in the terminology of some textbooks, *Invalid Deductive Argument*) An argument is invalid if it is meant to be truth-preserving but fails to meet the standards for deductive validity. An invalid argument is not an instance of any valid form of argument.

Invalid Argument Form   An argument form is invalid if it is possible for an argument in that form to have all true premises and a false conclusion. Invalid argument forms that superficially resemble correct forms are called *fallacious* forms.

Logical Equivalence   Two sentences (or sentence forms) are logically equivalent if it is impossible for them to have different truth values. If two sentences are logically equivalent, then the statement of their material biconditional is a tautology.

Material Conditional   A conditional sentence in which the connection between the antecedent and the consequent is truth-functional rather than some "real" causal, definitional, or logical connection. A material conditional is false only when its antecedent is true and its consequent is false.

Self-Contradiction   A compound English sentence is a self-contradiction if it is false by virtue of its logical structure, regardless of its content. A sentence form is a truth-functional self-contradiction if its column in a truth table contains only *F*s.

Tautology   A compound English sentence is a tautology if it is true by virtue of its truth-functional structure, regardless of its content. A sentence form is a tautology if its column in a truth table contains only *T*s.

Truth-Functional Connective   When components of a compound sentence are joined by truth-functional connectives, the truth or falsity of the compound sentence depends entirely on the truth or falsity of its component parts. "If . . . then," when interpreted in the sense of a material conditional, is a truth-functional connective. *Not* is also a truth-functional connective. If a sentence *p* is true, then "Not *p*" is false. If a sentence *p* is false, then "Not *p*" is true. In contrast, "if . . . then" in subjunctive counterfactual conditionals (for example, "If there had not been a merger between Exxon and Mobil, then oil prices would be lower") is not a truth-functional connective. The truth of a counterfactual conditional is not a function of the truth of its component parts.

Valid Argument   An argument is valid if there are no circumstances under which it is possible for all of its premises to be true and its conclusion to be false. *Valid* is the term applied to correct deductive arguments, those that actually preserve truth rather than merely purport to preserve truth. Any instance of a valid argument form is a valid argument.

Valid Argument Form   An argument form is valid if it is impossible for an argument in that form to have all true premises and a false conclusion.

Chapter Nine

CATEGORICAL SYLLOGISMS

I. INTRODUCTION

Discussions of deductive validity in earlier chapters included examples of obviously valid arguments, similar to the following:

a. Every bat is a mammal.
    No bird is a mammal.
    ———————————————
    No bird is a bat.

b. All birds can fly.
    Some mammals cannot fly.
    ———————————————
    Some mammals are not birds.

c. Every president is a politician.
    Some president is a statesman.
    ———————————————
    Some statesman is a politician.

Each is an example of a type of argument called **categorical syllogism**. In ordinary discourse, we rarely encounter arguments that are expressed in the standard form of the above examples. When the arguments are spelled out that way, they look so obvious that it seems pointless to state them, let alone to develop a set of rules to determine whether they are valid or invalid. In fact, a classic seventeenth-century treatise on logic raised doubts as to whether the formal rules of syllogistic reasoning, which the author admitted to be "the only aspect of logic traditionally treated with any care," are "as useful as is generally believed." For, he says, "If any man is unable to detect by the light of reason alone the invalidity of an argument, then he is probably incapable of understanding the rules by which we judge whether an argument is valid—and still less able to apply those rules" (Arnauld, 1662/1964, p. 175). Despite his doubts, however, Arnauld went on to write a long chapter about the subject.

Syllogistic reasoning is worth studying for a number of reasons. Although often incompletely stated, syllogisms pervade day-to-day reasoning. Many children's "why" questions, together with their answers, can be construed as syllogistic arguments.

Examples

1. Why do chickens have feathers?
    Because they're birds, and all birds have feathers.
2. Do all birds fly?
    No, ostriches are birds, but ostriches can't fly.

An understanding of the rules of the syllogism allows us to construct syllogistic arguments as well as to evaluate difficult syllogisms. Mastery of this common, well-understood type of reasoning also provides access to more difficult types.

In this chapter, we analyze the forms of categorical syllogisms and present a method for determining their validity. Categorical syllogisms, like hypothetical syllogisms and disjunctive syllogisms, are arguments with two premisses. However, categorical syllogisms are *not* truth-functional arguments. Although valid categorical syllogisms are valid by virtue of their forms, truth tables cannot show this because such validity depends on the relationships between the subjects and predicates of sentences that make up an argument. Categorical syllogisms (a), (b), and (c) (p. 351) are all valid. If we represent the structure of these arguments by using sentence letters to denote simple sentences, however, each argument would be an instance of the obviously invalid form:

$$\frac{\begin{array}{c} p \\ q \end{array}}{r}$$

The formal (structural) relationships between classes named by the subject terms and predicate terms of categorical sentences cannot be captured in the sentential system of logic but are essential to the validity of categorical syllogisms.

II. CATEGORICAL SENTENCES

If we let the letter S represent the subject term and the letter P represent the predicate term, we can characterize the forms of the four types of **categorical sentences** in the following standard way:

1. Every S is P. (A)   2. No S is P. (E)
3. Some S is P. (I)   4. Some S is not P. (O)

The letters A, E, I, and O have been used since medieval times to denote the four types of categorical sentences. A, which represents the universal affirmative, is the first vowel of the Latin *Affirmo*, or "I affirm." I, which denotes the particular affirmative, is the second vowel of the same Latin word. E, which identifies the universal negative, is the first vowel of the Latin *Nego*, or "I deny," and O, which represents the particular negative, is the second vowel of the same Latin word.

Exercise

Each of these types occurs in Arguments (a), (b), and (c) (p. 352). For example, the first premiss of (a) is an A sentence. Can you identify the type of each of the other premisses and conclusions in the three arguments?

"Every S is P" can also be stated "All S are P." This form of the **affirmative universal generalization** says that all the members of the class denoted by the term S are members of the class denoted by the term P. Another way of saying the same thing is "The subject class is **included in** the predicate class." (The logic of categorical syllogisms is sometimes called *the logic of classes*.)

Example

"Every junior at the university is an undergraduate."

In this affirmative universal sentence, "junior at the university" refers to the subject class, and "undergraduate" refers to the predicate class.

"No *S* is *P*" is the standard form of the **negative universal generalization**. This type of sentence states that no members of the class *S* are members of the class *P*. Alternatively, this sentence could be interpreted as "The subject and predicate classes do not overlap," or "The subject and predicate classes **exclude** one another."

Example

"No professional football player is a ballerina."

"Professional football player" is the subject term, and "ballerina" is the predicate term.

"Some *S* is *P*" is the standard form of an **affirmative particular generalization** or, as it is also called, an **affirmative existential generalization**. This type of sentence is interpreted to mean that at least one individual is a member of the class *S* and also of the class *P*. "Some *S* is *P*" is a general sentence because no member is actually identified; the sentence just says that some such member exists. Another way of stating the same thing is "The subject and predicate classes overlap to the extent that they share at least one member."

Example

"Some dog is brown."

"Dog" is the subject term, and "brown," or "brown thing," is the predicate term.

"Some *S* is not *P*" is the standard form of a **negative existential** (or **particular**) **generalization**. Sentences of this form state that something (at least one thing) that is a member of the class *S* is not a member of the class *P*. That is to say, at least one member of *S* is not identical with any member of *P*. This alternate formulation, although awkward in English, helps us to understand an important feature of the negative existential generalization: In a roundabout way, it says something about each and every member of the predicate class.

Example

"Some dog is not brown" or "At least one dog is not identical with any brown thing."

"Dog" is the subject, and "brown" or "brown thing" is the predicate.

1. RELATIONSHIPS AMONG CATEGORICAL SENTENCES WITH THE SAME SUBJECT AND PREDICATE TERMS—THE TRADITIONAL SQUARE OF OPPOSITION

Syllogistic logic was developed by Aristotle more than 2,300 years ago. Aristotle was the first person to formalize principles of valid arguments. His work was so important that much of what he developed has continued to be studied in logic classes down to the present day. Only the geometry developed by Euclid, at roughly the same time Aristotle achieved his results, has secured a comparable position in Western intellectual history. In addition to his work on syllogisms, Aristotle investigated the various relationships among the four types of categorical sentences when each has the same subject and predicate. These relationships can be considered by displaying the four types of sentences in a square of opposition, shown as follows:

SQUARE OF OPPOSITION

(A) Every S is P.   (E) No S is P.

(I) Some S is P.   (O) Some S is not P.

According to Aristotle's system of logic, the following relationships hold between pairs of categorical sentences:

1. The *A* sentence and the *O* sentence are **contradictory** to one another, as are the *E* sentence and the *I* sentence.

To say that two sentences are contradictories means that one sentence of the pair is the negation of the other sentence. Because every sentence is either true or false and no sentence is both, exactly one sentence of a pair of contradictories must be true and exactly one false. Intuitively, if "Every S is P" is true, then "Some S is not P" must be false. And if "Some S is not P" is true, then "Every S is P" cannot be true. With regard to the *E* and *I* pair of contradictories, if "No S is P" is true, then "Some S is P" is false. Similarly, if "Some S is P" is true, then "No S is P" must be false. The sentence forms that are diagonally opposite one another on the square of opposition are "opposites" in the sense that they logically contradict one another.

2. The *A* sentence and the *E* sentence are **contrary** to one another.

Two sentences are contraries when they could not both be true, although they could both be false. The sentences "Every dog is brown" and "No dog is brown" are contraries that are both false. The sentences "Every college football player is an athlete" and "No college football player is an athlete" are contraries, but only the second sentence is false. The sentence forms that are opposite one another at the top of the square of opposition are "opposites" in the sense that they are logically contrary to one another.

The terms *contradictory* and *contrary* also apply to pairs of sentences that are not categorical. For example, "My only brother weighs more than my only sister" and "My only sister weighs more than my only brother" are contraries, even though neither sentence is categorical. These sentences could not both be true although they could both be false (if my siblings weigh exactly the same).

Referring to truth-functional sentence forms, any pair of the forms p and $\sim p$ is a contradictory pair, regardless of whether p is a categorical sentence. (Remember that a sentence letter can represent any sentence whatsoever.) The sentences "It is raining" and "It is not raining" are contradictories.

For critical thinking, the distinction between contradictory and contrary pairs of sentences is important. It would be a mistake, for example, to conclude that "Sally hates me" from the premiss "Sally doesn't love me." Although the sentences "Sally hates me" and "Sally loves me" are contrary to one another, they are not contradictory. Therefore, we cannot conclude that, because one of the pair is false, the other must be true. They could both be false. The English term *incompatible* is ambiguous when it is applied to pairs of sentences that do not "agree" with one another. *Incompatible* sometimes refers to contraries and sometimes refers to contradictories.

3. The *I* and the *O* sentences could not both be false, but they could both be true.

Sentences that are related to one another in this way are called **subcontraries** (because of their position beneath the contraries in the square of opposition). The English sentences "Some dog is brown" and "Some dog is not brown" are subcontraries; both are true. The pair "Some men are mortal" and "Some men are not mortal" are subcontraries, but only the first sentence is true. The sentences on opposite sides of the bottom of the square of opposition are "opposite" in the sense that they are subcontraries. Unlike contrary pairs of sentences, subcontraries are not usually mistaken for contradictories. When this mistake does arise, however, it can often be traced to confusion about logical differences between particular generalizations and particular sentences about individuals. For example, the following sentences, which contradict one another:

(i) Elizabeth II is the queen of England.
(ii) Elizabeth II is not the queen of England.

are both sentences about a specific person. In Sentence (ii), inserting *not* after the verb has the same logical force as placing "It is not the case that" before Sentence (i). Despite similarities in appearance, particular generalizations are logically different from (i) and (ii), and inserting *not* after the verb has a different logical force from prefixing "It is not the case that." Consider the following pair of sentences:

(iii) Some woman is a queen.
(iv) Some woman is not a queen.

These sentences are not contradictories. They are both true, and they are subcontraries.

4. The *I* sentence is a logical consequence of (is implied by) the *A* sentence; and the *O* sentence is a logical consequence of (is implied by) the *E* sentence (see Figure 9.1).

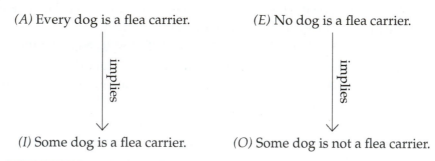

(A) Every dog is a flea carrier.   *(E)* No dog is a flea carrier.

implies   implies

(I) Some dog is a flea carrier.   *(O)* Some dog is not a flea carrier.

FIGURE 9.1   SUBIMPLICATION

It seems reasonable to say that if it is true that every *S* is *P*, then some *S* is *P*. Similarly, if "No *S* is *P*" is true, then it seems to follow that "Some *S* is not *P*." This relationship between the *A* and *I* sentences and between the *E* and *O* sentences is called **subimplication** because the sentences at the top of the square of opposition imply the sentences below them. If the *A* sentence is true, then the *I* sentence must be true as well; if the *E* sentence is true, then the *O* sentence must be true also.

The relationships among categorical sentences in the traditional (Aristotelian) square of opposition can be represented by arrows, as shown in Figure 9.2.

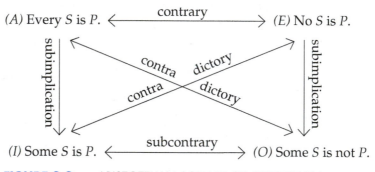

(A) Every *S* is *P*.   ⟵ contrary ⟶   *(E)* No *S* is *P*.

subimplication   contra dictory   contra dictory   subimplication

(I) Some *S* is *P*.   ⟵ subcontrary ⟶   *(O)* Some *S* is not *P*.

FIGURE 9.2   ARISTOTELIAN SQUARE OF OPPOSITION

2. EXISTENTIAL IMPORT AND THE MODERN SQUARE OF OPPOSITION

In order to study the validity of arguments in a formal way, logicians must specify the circumstances under which various sentence forms are either true or false. They do this for sentential logic by assigning truth-functional meanings to connectives and truth values ("true" or "false") to simple sentences. In order to avoid ambiguity in assigning truth-functional meanings to connectives, logicians adopt the convention of interpreting all conditionals as material conditionals, all disjunctions as inclusive disjunctions, and other connectives in the ways specified in treatments of sentential logic. Given these interpretations, the truth value of any compound sentence can be calculated when the truth values of the component parts are known.

Similarly, in syllogistic logic, which studies argument forms in which validity depends on intrasentential connections, some interpretive decisions must be made. The chief interpretive problem in this branch of logic emerges when we consider how to assign truth values to sentences in which the subject class has no members. Consider the following sentences:

A: All unicorns are white.	*E*: No unicorns are white.
I: Some unicorns are white.	*O*: Some unicorns are not white.

How do we understand these sentences? All pictures of unicorns depict them as white, but unicorns are fictional animals—they do not exist. Let us begin by considering the meaning of the *I* and *O* sentences. The first sentence says that there is something that is both a unicorn and a white thing. This seems to be false, however, because there are no unicorns. Similarly, the *O* sentence seems to be false for the same reason. According to the traditional square of opposition, however, these sentences are subcontraries and thus cannot both be false. The problem arises because the *I* and *O* sentences both have **existential import**; when they refer to nonexistent things, both are false. Thus to be consistent, either the interpretation of these sentences must be altered or a part of the square of opposition must be abandoned.

Turning to the *A* and *E* sentences, we have noted that they claim that the subject class is included in (or excluded from) the predicate class. How should we understand *A*? Does it mean that there are unicorns and that they are all white? If so, then *A* has existential import but is false because it is a conjunction with a false conjunct. For various reasons, it is preferable not to interpret the *A* sentence as stating that unicorns exist, at least not in the same explicit way as the *I* and *O* sentences. If we understand *A* to mean that the class of unicorns (regardless of whether this class has any members) is included in the class of white things, then we could interpret the sentence as meaning "If anything is a unicorn, then it is white," while remaining silent on whether there are any unicorns. This seems a good idea when we remember that, if we consider only the forms of sentences and not their content, we cannot know whether members of the subject class exist or not. According to this interpretation, the *A* sentence—unlike the *I* and *O* sentences—lacks existential import. Similar remarks apply to the *E* sentence, which can be understood to mean "If anything is a unicorn, then it is not white." Thus, despite the superficial grammatical resemblance between "Every *S* is a *P*" and "Some *S* is a *P*," the first sentence can be interpreted plausibly as a conditional that lacks existential import, while the second sentence is interpreted as a conjunction with existential import. This is the convention that modern logicians adopt.

The convention of denying existential import to universal sentences accords well with English usage in many cases. Obviously, some sentences that are instances of the (*A*) and (*E*) forms are regarded as true in ordinary language when everyone knows that there are no members of the subject class.

Examples

> *A*: All ghosts are invisible.
> *E*: No ghosts are visible.

Moreover, we sometimes use universal generalizations when we *hope* there will be no members of the subject class.

Examples

> *A*: Every student who fails to meet the deadline for term papers will receive a failing grade.
> *E*: No late papers will be accepted.

For the same reasons that truth-functional conditionals are all interpreted as material conditionals, the *A* and *E* sentences are interpreted similarly. That is to say, a universal sentence is regarded as true unless it has a true antecedent and a false consequent. But this means that every universal sentence with a subject class that lacks members is true. "If anything is a ghost, then it is invisible" is true, because there is nothing that is a ghost. The same sort of reasoning, however, applies to the negative universal generalization "No ghost is invisible," which is also true because it has a false antecedent. ("If anything is a ghost, then it is not invisible.") Interpreted as conditionals, the *A* and the *E* sentences can both be true, so they are no longer contraries. Under the modern interpretation, another relationship from the traditional square of opposition must be abandoned.

Furthermore, the relation of subimplication no longer holds when we adopt a convention that denies existential import to universal sentences. This is so because a premiss that lacks existential import cannot deductively imply a sentence that states that members of the subject class exist. Thus in the modern interpretation of categorical sentences, the square of opposition is drastically simplified. Most of the relationships recognized by Aristotle between forms of categorical sentences with the same subject and predicate terms no longer hold when sentences are considered formally. Only the contradictory relationships between the pairs of categorical sentences diagonally opposite one another remain intact (see Figure 9.3).

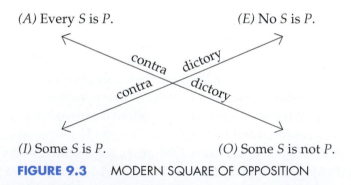

(A) Every *S* is *P*.   *(E)* No *S* is *P*.

contra dictory
contra dictory

(I) Some *S* is *P*.   *(O)* Some *S* is not *P*.

FIGURE 9.3   MODERN SQUARE OF OPPOSITION

It is important to remember that the modern interpretation of universal general-izations is no closer to their "true meaning" than is the interpretation that gave rise to the traditional square of opposition. Each of the two interpretations has costs and ben-efits. The traditional interpretation works well for cases in which the subject class is not empty. In many contexts of ordinary language, we know that members of the subject class exist; in these, the relationships considered by Aristotle hold and are character-istic of good logical thinking. Ultimately, the modern decision to interpret universal sentences as conditionals and existential sentences as conjunctions is justified in logical terms because it facilitates a comprehensive logical system that is able to account for more complex sorts of arguments than the Aristotelian system.*

To summarize of our discussion so far, if we adopt the modern interpretation, then universal generalizations are understood as conditionals:

> *A:* If anything is an *S*, then it is a *P*.
> *E*: If anything is an *S*, then it is not a *P*.

Because both can be true, *A* and *E* are no longer contraries. In addition, the *A* sentence can be true—when there are no *S*s—while the corresponding *I* sentence is false, for the *I* sentence asserts that some *S* is *P*. Similarly, it is possible for the *E* sentence to be true while the corresponding *O* sentence is false. Thus, the relationships of subimplication do not hold. Furthermore, the *I* and *O* sentences can both be false—when there are no members of *S*—so the relationship of subcontraries also fails to hold.

Consider the following four categorical sentences in which "unicorn" is the subject term and "white things" is the predicate term:

> *A*: Every unicorn is a white thing.
> *E*: No unicorn is a white thing.
> *I*: Some unicorn is a white thing.
> *O*: Some unicorn is not a white thing.

Because unicorns do not exist, the *A* and *E* sentences are both true, and the *I* and *O* sentences are both false. The *A* sentence does not imply the *I* sentence; the *E* sentence does not imply the *O* sentence. *A* and *E* are not contraries; *I* and *O* are not subcontraries. However, *A* and *O* are contradictories, as are *E* and *I*; exactly one member of each of these pairs is true, and the other is false.

Logicians' use of sentence forms to represent sentences suppresses the content of those sentences to focus on structural considerations. The logically important feature of categorical sentences is the nature of the relationship between the subject class and the predicate class. Does one class include or exclude the other? Do the two classes share a common member? Does some member of one class fail to belong to the other class? Some advantages of employing sentence forms rather than sentences to analyze

---

*See "Truth-Functional Conditionals and Modern vs. Traditional Syllogistic, " R. B. Angell, 1986, Mind 95 (378): 210–233.

the validity or the invalidity of arguments are already familiar. Later, some previously introduced symbolic techniques will be developed to show how modern treatments of the logic of classes can be extended to more complex systems.

Even though the simpler modern square of opposition is normally used in contemporary formal treatments of syllogistic logic, the relationships among categorical sentences in the traditional Aristotelian square of opposition are important in everyday reasoning in ordinary language. For that reason, they repay our careful attention. Arguments in ordinary language often depend on one sentence being contrary to another, or a subcontrary to another, or a subimplication of another. We should be able to recognize and assess such arguments in ordinary language contexts.

Exercise Set 9.1

PART I. Using Aristotle's account of the relationships between categorical sentences as presented in the traditional square of opposition, answer each question with a categorical sentence in English.

1. What is the contradictory of "All novelists are writers"?

2. What is the contrary of "No novelists are journalists"?

3. What is the contradictory of "Some American automobiles are electric"?

4. What is the subcontrary of "Some automobiles are battery powered"?

5. What sentence must be true if "All electric cars are battery powered" is true?

6. What sentence must be true if "No electric cars are battery powered" is true?

7. What is the contradictory of "Some pro football players are not dancers"?

8. What is the contradictory of "No football players are ballroom dancers"?

9. What sentence is contrary to "All stockbrokers are rich"?

10. What is the subimplication of "No stockbrokers are doctors"?

PART II. Give an English sentence (it need not be categorical) that is contrary to each of the following:

1. It never rains in southern California.

2. Shaq is a tall man.

3. His only pet is a parakeet.

4. Korea's economy is booming.

5. Chocolate desserts are delicious.

6. Dark chocolate is rich in antioxidants.

7. You always complain about work.

8. When it rains, it pours.

9. Reggie is careless.

10. Parrots are long-lived.

PART III. Give an English sentence (it need not be categorical) that is contradictory to each of the following:

1. Peas are not usually eaten with a knife.

2. Lemons are yellow.

3. Baseball is a slow-paced game.

4. Every cloud has a silver lining.

5. The grass is always greener on the other side of the fence.

6. This jewel belongs in the Smithsonian.

7. Mary Stuart was the cousin of Elizabeth I.

8. It never rains, but it pours.

9. Old soldiers never die.

10. The polar ice caps are shrinking rapidly.

III. TRANSLATING ENGLISH SENTENCES INTO STANDARD CATEGORICAL FORMS

With sufficiently clever linguistic manipulation, many sentences that do not appear to be categorical can be adjusted with little or no change in meaning to fit one of the four standard categorical forms. For example, the sentence "It never rains, but it pours" can be "translated" as "Every time of raining is a time of pouring," which is a standard *A* sentence.

1. *A* SENTENCES

Consider the following English sentences:

1. All trespassers are persons who will be prosecuted.
2. Trespassers will be prosecuted.
3. Anyone who trespasses will be prosecuted.
4. If anyone trespasses, that person will be prosecuted.
5. No trespasser will fail to be prosecuted.
6. It is false that some trespassers will not be prosecuted.
7. All persons who will not be prosecuted are not trespassers.

These sentences are all equivalent to one another in the logically important sense that each states that the class of trespassers is included in the class of persons who will be prosecuted. The following remarks about each of these sentences are designed to make this equivalence apparent:

1. Sentence (1) is clearly equivalent to "Every trespasser is a person who will be prosecuted." "Trespassers" denotes the subject class, and "persons who will be prosecuted" denotes the predicate class. "All *S* are *P*" is another standard rendering of the *A* sentence.

2. In English, the **quantifier** ("every," "all," or "some") may be omitted when context shows which quantifier is intended, as is shown in Sentence (2). For example, the sentence "Whales are mammals" is interpreted as "Every whale is a mammal." But the second sentence in "Watch your language. Children are present" is understood to mean "Some child is present." Noun phrases such as "persons who," "things that," and similar expressions can also be omitted from predicate terms.

3. In Sentence (3), "Anyone who trespasses" means the same as "all trespassers."

4. Sentence (4) translates the *A* sentence into a form that makes its conditional nature apparent: "If anything is an *S*, then it is a *P*."

5. Sentence (5) is obviously equivalent to the *E* form: "No trespassers are persons who will not be prosecuted." In addition to changing the "all" in Sentence (1) to "no," the predicate, "persons who will be prosecuted," has been replaced by "persons who will not be prosecuted." In general, an *A* sentence can be transformed to an equivalent *E* sentence in the following two steps:

   a. Replace "every" (or "all") with "no." The change from an affirmative to a negative sentence, or a negative sentence to an affirmative sentence, is called a change in **quality**.

   b. Replace the predicate term of the sentence with its **complement**. The complement of a class is the class of all things that are not in the original class. For example, the complement of the class of cats is the class of noncats; the complement of the class of nonmen is the class of men. The term that refers to the complement class is called the *complement* of the original term.

   The process of changing the quality of a categorical sentence and replacing the predicate term with its complement is called **obversion**. When any categorical sentence (*A*, *E*, *I*, or *O*) is obverted, a sentence that is equivalent in meaning to the original sentence results.

6. Sentence (6) is equivalent to the denial of an *O* sentence: "It is not the case that some trespassers are persons who will not be prosecuted." The *O* sentence that is contradictory to "All trespassers are persons who will be prosecuted" is "Some trespassers are persons who will not be prosecuted." The denial of the contradictory of a sentence is logically equivalent to the original sentence.

7. In Sentence (7), the subject term is the complement of the predicate term in (1), and the predicate is the complement of the subject term in (1). This transformation is called **contraposition**. The contraposition of *A* sentences yields *A* sentences that are equivalent in meaning to the original sentence.

The relationship between subject and predicate in the *A* sentence can be represented graphically in the **Venn diagram*** shown in Figure 9.4.

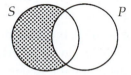

FIGURE 9.4   VENN DIAGRAM OF *A* SENTENCE

Against a background of all the different types of things in the universe, the overlapping circles represent two classes, or types of things, in that universe: *S*s and *P*s. These classes may or may not have members—blank circles do not indicate that a class has no members. Shading indicates the emptiness of a region. Thus, to diagram the *A* sentence, shade the region in the *S* circle that lies outside the *P* circle, for if there are any *S*s, they must lie within the part of the *S* circle that is included in the *P* circle.

2. *E* SENTENCES

Consider the following English sentences:

1. No whales are fish.
2. Whales are not fish.
3. Nothing that is a whale is a fish.
4. None but nonfishes are whales.
5. If anything is a whale, then it is not a fish.
6. All whales are nonfish.
7. It is false that some whales are fish.

Each of these sentences says that the class of whales and the class of fish do not overlap or, in other words, that no members are common to both classes. Comments on each of these sentences follow.

1. Sentence (1) is in standard *E* form.
2. Sentence (2) is equivalent to the categorical *A* sentence "All whales are nonfish." In ordinary English, it is tempting to say "All whales are not fish," but this sentence is ambiguous; it leaves open the possibility that some whales are fish. The original sentence (2), however, denies that any whales are fish. The sentence form "All *S* are not *P*" is not a categorical form and, because it is ambiguous, is not equivalent to the categorical "All *S* are non-*P*," which is a variant of the *A* form.

---

*After John Venn (1834–1923), an English clergyman who made important contributions to mathematics and logic.

3. "Nothing that is a whale" in sentence (3) has the same meaning as "no whales," and "is a fish" agrees better grammatically with this version than "are fish."

4. "None but nonfishes are whales" in sentence (4) means the same as "Only non-fishes are whales" or "If anything is not a nonfish, then it is not a whale." This in turn is equivalent to "If anything is a fish, then it is not a whale." This sentence states that the classes of fish and whales do not overlap (they contain no members in common), which is what the original *E* sentence (1) says.

5. Sentence (5) is the standard translation of the *E* sentence into an equivalent conditional. "No *S* is *P*" becomes "If anything is an *S*, then it is not a *P*."

6. Sentence (6) represents the standard transformation of an *E* sentence into an equivalent *A* sentence by obversion. The quality of the sentence is changed from negative to affirmative, and the predicate term is replaced by its complement.

7. Sentence (7) is the denial of the contradictory of the original *E* sentence (1). In general, the categorical sentence "No *S* are *P*" is equivalent to the noncategorical sentence "It is false that some *S* are *P*."

E sentences (including all the English variants of the standard form of the *E* sentence) can be represented by the Venn diagram shown in Figure 9.5.

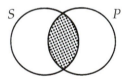

FIGURE 9.5   VENN DIAGRAM OF *E* SENTENCE

As in the Venn diagram of the *A* sentence, the two circles represent the classes *S* and *P*. The shading in the overlapping area indicates that this region is empty. In other words, there is nothing that is a member of both classes.

This Venn diagram is symmetric, unlike the diagram of the *A* sentence. Inspection of the symmetric diagram shows that the sentence forms "No *S* is *P*" and "No *P* is *S*" are equivalent. In other words, the subject term and the predicate term can be interchanged in an *E* sentence without changing the meaning of the sentence. This transformation is called **conversion**. Conversion does not preserve meaning in *A* sentences. For example, "All elephants are mammals" does not mean "All mammals are elephants." Conversion preserves meaning only in sentences with symmetric Venn diagrams.

3. *I* SENTENCES

The following are all English variations of the same *I* sentence:

1. Some logical principles are things difficult to grasp.
2. Some logical principles are difficult to grasp.
3. Some things are both logical principles and difficult to grasp.

4. There are logical principles that are difficult to grasp.
5. Some logical principles are not things that are not difficult to grasp.
6. Some logical principles are not easy to grasp.
7. It is not the case that no logical principles are difficult to grasp.
8. It is not the case that all logical principles are easy to grasp.
9. Some things that are difficult to grasp are logical principles.

Some of these equivalencies are discussed below. The rest are left as exercises for the reader.

1. Sentence (1) is in the standard *I* form.
3. This form in Sentence (3) displays the conjunctive nature of *I* sentences.
5. In Sentence (5), an *O* form that is equivalent to the *I* form can be constructed by changing the quality from affirmative to negative and replacing the predicate term with its complement (obversion).
7. In Sentence (7), the *E* sentence that is the contradictory of the *I* sentence is negated. The resulting sentence is equivalent to the original *I* sentence.
9. Because the *I* Sentence (9) above has the logical form of a conjunction and because the order of the conjuncts is irrelevant to the truth of the conjunction, "Some *S* are *P*" is equivalent to "Some *P* are *S*." As in the *E* sentence, the subject and predicate terms in the *I* sentence may be interchanged without changing the meaning of the sentence. Conversion preserves meaning in *I* sentences.

In constructing the Venn diagram for the *I* sentences, two overlapping circles are again used to represent the classes *S* and *P*. An **x** represents a member (or members) of a class. Because the *I* sentence says that the classes *S* and *P* share at least one member, an **x** is placed in the overlapping region, as shown in the following (symmetric) Figure 9.6.

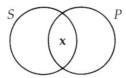

FIGURE 9.6   VENN DIAGRAM OF *I* SENTENCE

4. *O* SENTENCES

The following are all English variations of the same *O* sentence:

1. Some runners are not vegetarians.
2. Some runners are nonvegetarians.
3. Some nonvegetarians are runners.
4. Not all runners are vegetarians.
5. There are nonvegetarian runners.
6. Some nonvegetarians are not nonrunners.

The principles by virtue of which these sentences are equivalent to one another have been introduced already. The first sentence is in standard O form. The second sentence is the obverse of the first sentence. The quality of Sentence (1) is changed from negative to affirmative (that is, from an O sentence to an I sentence), and the predicate term is replaced by its complement. Sentence (3) is the converse of (2), in which the subject and predicate terms of that I sentence are interchanged. Sentence (4) is the denial of the A sentence that is contradictory to the original O sentence. Sentence (5) exhibits the conjunctive nature of the O sentence. Finally, Sentence (6) is the **contrapositive** of Sentence (1). Contraposition preserves meaning in O sentences as well as in A sentences.

Again, using overlapping circles and an **x** to show that a class has some member, the Venn diagram in Figure 9.7 represents all variants of the O sentence. In this case, the **x** is drawn outside the P circle but within the S circle.

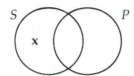

FIGURE 9.7   VENN DIAGRAM OF O SENTENCE

Exercise Set 9.2

For each of the following English sentences, construct an English sentence in one of the four standard categorical forms that captures the meaning of the original sentence. Draw a Venn diagram for each sentence, and clearly label the subject-class circle and the predicate-class circle.

PART I.

1. Only the good die young.
2. If electric automobiles don't have a forty-mile range, they won't sell.
3. The longest mile is the last mile home.
4. Happy is the bride the sun shines on.
5. No one may receive care at VA hospitals except veterans.
6. Not all athletes are graceful.
7. If it isn't genuine, it won't retain its value.
8. The home team always has the advantage.
9. The quickest fix is never the best.
10. Not every good singer is a good actor.
11. American warships are in the Persian Gulf.

12. The easiest course is not always the most satisfying.

13. There's always snow on top of Denali.

14. She brings sunshine everywhere she goes.

15. Nothing in evolution ever happens on purpose.

16. Times like these try persons' souls.

17. It is duty-free only if it is an antique.

18. The last exercise is always the best.

PART II.

Draw a Venn diagram for each of the following opposing views to show how they differ from one another. Label one circle Manga and the other Gekiga:

Takai Saito believed that Manga and Gekiga were entirely different on a technical level, and that the two were mutually exclusive.

Hiroshi believed that they had different readerships, but that since Gekiga's basic components were based on Manga, the former had to be part of the latter.

—Y. Tatsumi, *A Drifting Life*

IV. TESTING FOR VALIDITY WITH VENN DIAGRAMS

Categorical syllogisms in standard form are arguments with two premisses and a conclusion that also have the following properties:

1. Both the premisses and the conclusion are standard-form categorical sentences.
2. Exactly three terms occur in the argument. One term, called the "middle term," occurs once in each premiss; each of the other two terms, called "end terms," occurs once in a premiss and once in the conclusion.

In representing the forms of these arguments, S refers to the subject term of the conclusion, P refers to the predicate term of the conclusion, and M refers to the term that occurs in both premisses.

Recall the definition of formal validity: In all circumstances in which the premisses are true, the conclusion is true as well. In deductive arguments, we say that the information contained in the conclusion is already at least implicitly contained in the premisses. The information contained in categorical sentences can be represented in Venn diagrams. A Venn diagram can show whether one class is included in another, one class excludes the other, classes share a common member, or one class has a member that lies outside the other class (see Figure 9.8).

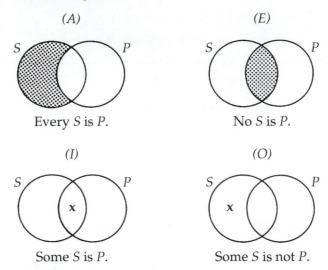

FIGURE 9.8   VENN DIAGRAMS OF THE FOUR TYPES OF CATEGORICAL SENTENCES

To apply the Venn diagram technique to categorical syllogisms, use three overlapping circles—one for each of the three terms in the argument. The circles are arranged in the standard way as shown in Figure 9.9.

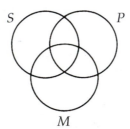

FIGURE 9.9   BLANK VENN DIAGRAM FOR CATEGORICAL SYLLOGISM

To test a syllogism for validity, use shading or **x**'s to mark all the information contained in the premises on this standard blank diagram. Then inspect the diagram to see whether the information in the conclusion sentence is now contained in the diagram. If so, the argument is a valid syllogism. If the conclusion cannot be found in the diagram, then the argument is not a valid syllogism.

Examples

a. All sensitive persons are dreamers.   All S are M.
    All dreamers are poets.   All M are P.
    _____   _____
    All sensitive persons are poets.   All S are P.

In this argument, S is the class of sensitive persons, P is the class of poets, and M is the class of dreamers.

To diagram the first premiss, consider only the two circles labeled S and M. The first premiss is an A sentence, with S as the subject term. Thus, all of the S circle that lies outside the M circle is shaded, as shown in Figure 9.10.

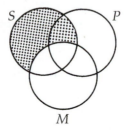

FIGURE 9.10   DIAGRAM OF FIRST PREMISS:
"ALL S ARE M"

To diagram the second premiss, consider the two circles labeled P and M. The second premiss is also an A sentence with M as the subject term, so all of the M circle that does not lie within the P circle is shaded, as shown in Figure 9.11.

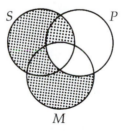

FIGURE 9.11   DIAGRAM OF BOTH PREMISSES:
"ALL S ARE M" AND "ALL M ARE P"

After diagramming these two premisses, inspect the Venn diagram to see whether the conclusion can be found. The conclusion is an A sentence with S as the subject term and P as the predicate term. On the diagram, all of the S circle that lies outside the P circle has been shaded. (A part that lies inside the P circle has been shaded as well, but this does not conflict with the claim that if anything is an S then it is a P; it simply provides the additional information that any of the Ss that are Ps are Ms as well.) Thus, we can read the sentence "All S are P" from the Venn diagram, and the argument is shown to be valid.

b.   All statesmen are honorable persons.   All S are M.
     Some honorable persons are politicians.   Some M are P.
     _____   _____
     Some statesmen are politicians.   Some S are P.

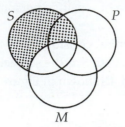

FIGURE 9.12   DIAGRAM OF PREMISS
"ALL *S* ARE *M*"

In Figure 9.12 the first premiss, "All *S* are *M*," is diagrammed by shading the part of the *S* circle that lies outside the *M* circle.

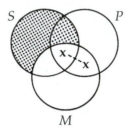

FIGURE 9.13   DIAGRAM OF PREMISSES
"ALL *S* ARE *M*" AND: "SOME *M* ARE *P*"

In Figure 9.13, the information contained in the second premiss, "Some *M* are *P*," is added to the diagram. The overlapping region between the *P* circle and the *M* circle is itself divided into two parts. One part lies within the *S* circle; the other part lies outside. Because the information in the premiss tells us only that there is a member somewhere in this overlap, we cannot locate an **x** definitely in one region or the other. Instead, we use the "floating **x**" (two **x**'s connected by a dashed line) to indicate that a member lies somewhere in that region.

However, when we try to read the conclusion "Some *S* are *P*," we see that the diagram tells us only that an **x** *may* lie in the region overlapping *S* and *P* or that it *may* lie in the region overlapping *P* and *M* but outside of *S*. Thus, we cannot read the conclusion from the diagrammed premisses, and the syllogism is invalid. It is possible for both premisses to be true and the conclusion to be false.

c. No unicorns are black things.   No *S* are *M*.
    Some black things are dogs.   Some *M* are *P*.
    ——————————————————   —————————————
    No unicorns are dogs.   No *S* are *P*.

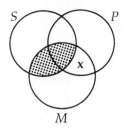

FIGURE 9.14   DIAGRAM OF PREMISSES:
"NO *S* ARE *M*" AND "SOME *M* ARE *P*"

The Venn diagram of the first premiss requires shading the overlapping area between the *S* and the *M* circles. An **x** is then drawn in the overlapping area between the *M* and the *P* circles to represent the second premiss. In this case, as a result of diagramming the first premiss, we can see that the area of overlap between *M* and *P* that also lies within the *S* circle is empty, so a "floating **x**" is not needed. The **x** can only be drawn in the area between *M* and *P* that is not shaded. (Because shading indicates emptiness, no members can be found in a shaded area. The use of floating **x**'s in Venn diagrams can be minimized by diagramming any universal premisses first.) To read the conclusion from Figure 9.14, the area of overlap between the *S* and the *P* circles would have to be shaded completely. Because this is not the case, the syllogism is invalid.

d. No intelligent persons are gluttons.   No *P* are *M*.
    Some famous persons are gluttons.   Some *S* are *M*.
    _____   _____
    Some famous persons are not intelligent.   Some *S* are not *P*.

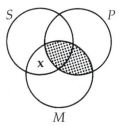

FIGURE 9.15   DIAGRAM OF PREMISSES:
"NO *P* ARE *M*" AND SOME "*S* ARE *M*"

We diagram the first premiss by shading the overlapping region between the *P* and the *M* circles. The second premiss requires placing an **x** in the overlap between the *S* and the *M* circles. The **x** is placed in the unshaded portion. In order to read the conclusion, there must be an **x** in the portion of the *S* circle that lies outside the *P* circle. This is the case, and so Figure 9.15 shows the validity of this syllogism.

e. Some animals are furry.   Some *S* are *M*.
    Some furry things are cats.   Some *M* are *P*.
    _____   _____
    Some animals are cats.   Some *S* are *P*.

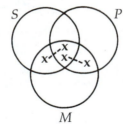

FIGURE 9.16   DIAGRAM OF PREMISSES:
"SOME *S* ARE *M*" AND "SOME *M* ARE *P*"

To diagram the first premiss, place an **x** in the overlap between *S* and *M*. There are two parts to this overlap—one within and one outside the *P* circle (see the preceding figure). The premiss does say where to place the **x**, so a floating **x** must be used. The second premiss says that there is a member of both *P* and *M* but does not say whether this member belongs to *S*. Therefore, another floating **x** is used. The conclusion requires that an **x** be in the overlapping region between *S* and *P*. Because both **x**'s are floating, we cannot tell whether either **x** lies in that region. Thus, the conclusion cannot be read off Figure 9.16, and the syllogism is invalid.

Exercise Set 9.3

PART I. For each of the following syllogisms:

(a) Identify the *S*, *M*, and *P* terms.

(b) Draw a Venn diagram.

(c) Tell whether the syllogism is valid or invalid.

Remember that diagramming will be simplified if universal premisses are diagrammed first. This will minimize the use of floating **x**'s.

1. All animals feel pain. All things that feel pain are able to think. Therefore, all animals are able to think.

2. No nonhuman animals are able to think. Only thinking things feel pain. Therefore no nonhuman animals feel pain.

3. No good persons are cruel to animals. Some children are cruel to animals. Therefore, some children are not good persons.

4. No oil reserves are unlimited. Some power sources are not unlimited. Some power sources are not oil reserves.

5. All new technologies are risky. All new technologies are potentially profitable. Therefore, some risky things are potentially profitable.

6. Some innovators are not well educated. Some persons who are not well educated achieve greatness. Therefore, some innovators achieve greatness.

7. All diets require willpower. No things that require willpower are simple. Therefore, no diets are simple.

8. Some syllogisms are not valid arguments. All syllogisms have two premisses. Therefore, some arguments with two premisses are not valid.

9. No syllogisms are arguments with four terms. Some arguments with four terms are invalid. Therefore, no syllogisms are invalid.

10. Some arguments are invalid. Some invalid arguments are not syllogisms. Therefore, some arguments are not syllogisms.

PART II. Regard each of the following pairs of sentences as premisses. Using an appropriately labeled three-circle Venn diagram, tell what syllogistic conclusion, if any, can be drawn validly from these premisses.

1. No news anchors are inarticulate.
   No reporters are inarticulate.

2. Some rats have fleas.
   Some things with fleas are good pets.

3. No students are boring.
   Some professors are boring.

4. All soldiers are fighters.
   All soldiers are brave.

5. Some tasty foods are nutritious.
   Some nutritious things are not bargains.

6. No valuable thing is free of charge.
   All immunizations at the health center are free of charge.

7. All law-enforcement officers are well trained.
   Some well-trained persons make mistakes.

8. All birds are egg layers.
   Some mammals are egg layers.

9. No birds are cold-blooded.
   All reptiles are cold-blooded.

10. All reptiles are cold-blooded.
    Some dinosaurs are not cold-blooded.

PART III. Suppose we follow the strategic rule of always diagramming universal premisses before particular premisses. This reduces the need for floating x's. If, after diagramming universal premisses, a floating x remains, is the form invalid? Why or why not?

V. DISTRIBUTION OF TERMS—FALLACIES OF DISTRIBUTION

A term is said to be **distributed** in a categorical sentence whenever that sentence says something about every member of the class to which the term refers. In the *A* sentence, for example, the subject term is distributed. The sentence "All logic students are hard-working" says that every logic student is a hard-working person. However, the predicate term in the *A* sentence is not distributed, because that sentence does not say something about every hard-working person.

In the *E* sentence, both the subject and predicate terms are distributed. The sentence "No professional football player is a ballerina" says of every professional football player that he is not a ballerina and also says of every ballerina that she is not a professional football player.

In the *I* sentence, neither the subject term nor the predicate term is distributed. This sentence says only that the two classes share at least one member. The *I* sentence says nothing about every member of either the subject class or the predicate class.

In the *O* sentence, the subject term is not distributed. In *O* sentences, as in *I* sentences, the subject term refers to only some member or members (*some* may mean more than one) of the class, not to every member. The predicate term, however, is understood as distributed in the *O* sentence. The awkward alternate formulation of the *O* sentence presented earlier ("At least one member of *S* is not identical with any member of *P*") illustrates that, in a roundabout way, the *O* sentence says something about each and every member of the *P* class—namely, that at least one member of *S* is not identical with it. Thus, the claim that "Some dogs are not brown" means "At least one dog is not identical with any brown thing," and the latter sentence is regarded as referring to all brown things.

These principles concerning the distribution of terms can be summarized as follows:

> Universal sentences: **S**ubject term is distributed.
> Negative sentences: **P**redicate term is distributed. **(USNP)**

Fallacies of distribution can occur if the distinction between using a term distributively (to refer to every member of a class) and using a term collectively (to refer to a class as a whole) is not recognized. Consider the following arguments, neither of which is a categorical syllogism:

1. I infer that this stew will be delicious because each ingredient that went into it is delicious.
2. Mary's room at college must be large, for she lives in a very large dormitory.

In the first of these arguments, the conclusion that a collective whole (a stew) has a certain property is based on the information that its parts (distributively or individually) have that property. But this type of inference is not reliable. You can put together a collection of individually fine football players and end up with a poor team, and you can gather fine singers into a choir that sings badly. What is true of the parts is not necessarily—or even probably—true of the whole. The mistake of reasoning that what is true of the parts of a whole is also true of the whole, or that what is true of the individual members is true of the class, is called the **fallacy of composition**.

The second argument depends on the principle that what is true of the whole must be true of its parts. But this is also mistaken. Very large machines can be constructed from parts that are individually very small. A herd of cattle can be small even though none of its members is small. The fallacy involved in argument (2) above is called the **fallacy of division**. Like the fallacy of composition, the fallacy of division involves confusing the distributive use of a term with its collective use.

Exercise Set 9.4

1. The following argument occurs in Book V of Lucretius's (c. 100–55 BCE) great philosophical poem *On the Nature of the Universe*. What fallacy does Lucretius apparently commit here?

   In the first place, since the elements of which we see the world composed—solid earth and moisture, the light breaths of air and torrid fire—all consist of bodies that are neither birthless nor deathless, we must believe the same of the world as a whole.

2. Name any fallacies of distribution that occur in the following:

   a. Science tells us that physical objects are made up entirely of tiny particles—electrons, positrons, neutrons, and so on—that are invisible, although their motions can be detected by sophisticated instruments. Science also tells us that these particles are in constant motion and that there are spaces between them. Yet we can see physical objects, feel their solidity, and see that they are not always in motion. So science must be wrong; physical objects cannot be composed of atomic and subatomic particles.

   b. Kyoto has the best tofu in Japan. This tofu is the best in Kyoto. Therefore, this tofu is the best in Japan.

   c. If we want to save fuel, we should all drive our cars instead of taking the bus because, as everyone knows, a bus uses a lot more fuel than a car.

   d. Rust must be good for you because it's iron and oxygen, both of which are essential to life.

   e. Last year's senior class at Central High School had the highest grade-point average recorded in the history of the high school. Therefore each student in the class must have a high GPA.

3. What fallacy occurs in each of the following passages?

   a. What is prudence in the conduct of every private family can hardly be folly in that of a great kingdom.

   —A. Smith, *Wealth of Nations*

b. Every time Max saw Father Mark, he'd rag him about how cheap Catholics were; he reasoned that because the Vatican was rich, all priests, by virtue of being employed by the Vatican, could write checks at will.

— R. Russo, *Empire Falls*

4. What fallacies are referred to in the following passages?

a. Unfortunately, all "Rings" [an art exhibition] really does is prove once more, and in unusually extravagant form, that great artworks do not, by themselves, make great exhibitions.

—R. Smith, *The New York Times*

b. The whole idea of a monolithic, tightly coordinated system rests on a fallacy: that by optimizing every piece of the [strategic defense] system, one optimizes the system as a whole.

—N.M. Waldrop, 1986, *Science* 232:710–713

VI. OTHER WAYS TO TEST THE VALIDITY OF SYLLOGISMS

Venn diagrams provide a general method of determining which conclusions follow validly from premisses in categorical syllogisms. This technique is simple to apply and appeals especially to people who prefer visual representations to verbal descriptions of problems they are trying to solve. Various other techniques are available, however, for determining whether syllogisms are valid or invalid. As we have seen, deductive logicians are less concerned with assessing the validity of particular arguments than with formulating and testing general principles of validity. The truth tables introduced in the previous chapter and the proof method discussed in Appendix One embody such general principles for truth-functional arguments. These systems were devised in the twentieth century to facilitate solving problems in sentential logic that were first studied in antiquity. A number of different systems of principles governing what follows from what in categorical syllogisms has been investigated by many logicians, beginning with Aristotle himself.

Aristotle's treatment of syllogisms differs from the Venn-diagram method. His method resembles to some degree the axiomatic method of Euclidean geometry. To understand Aristotle's approach, the concept of a **figure of a syllogism** must be introduced. In categorical syllogisms, the S term (the subject term of the conclusion) can be either the subject or the predicate of the premiss in which it occurs; similarly, the P term (the predicate term of the conclusion) can be either the subject or the predicate of the premiss in which it occurs. Thus, four possible arrangements, or figures, of the syllogism can be distinguished:

First	Second	Third	Fourth
MP	PM	MP	PM
SM	SM	MS	MS
SP	SP	SP	SP

Because the order in which the premisses of an argument are stated has no bearing on the validity of the argument, variations that depend on this feature can be ignored. Premisses and conclusions of syllogisms are all sentences in *A*, *E*, *I*, or *O* form. There are 64 possible combinations of these four types of categorical sentences taken three at a time (two sentences as the premisses and one sentence as the conclusion), and each of the 64 combinations (called *moods* of the syllogism) can occur in each of the four figures. Thus, only 256 forms of categorical syllogisms exist. Venn diagrams can be used to test each form, and a relatively small number are valid.

Aristotle's own system for testing validity was less tedious than drawing 256 Venn diagrams. He took as axioms those syllogisms in the first figure, such as "All *M* are *P*, and all *S* are *M*; therefore all *S* are *P*," that were obviously valid, and he showed that all valid forms in the other figures could be reduced by obversion, conversion, and contraposition of premisses and conclusions directly or indirectly to obviously valid first-figure forms. To show the invalidity of forms, Aristotle used the method of counterexample, providing ordinary-language arguments in those forms with obviously true premisses and obviously false conclusions.*

Other systems for testing the validity of categorical syllogisms focus on specific features of valid syllogisms and formulate sets of rules that capture these features. If a syllogism violates a rule, it is invalid; otherwise it is valid. Sets of rules for evaluating categorical syllogisms were first devised in the Middle Ages and are still in use today.** Some people find it easier to memorize a few rules than to draw Venn diagrams. Although we will not study any of the sets of rules in this text, we look at one particular rule and the fallacy that results from violating the rule. The rule—which occurs in every set of rules for evaluating syllogisms—says that the middle term must be distributed. The middle term, labeled *M* in our standard formulations of categorical syllogisms, occurs in both premisses but not in the conclusion. Because the distributed term in the *M* premiss says something about each and every member of the class to which it refers, the middle term serves to connect the *S* and *P* terms that are joined in the conclusion. If one of the premisses did not say something about every member of a class, then there might be no connection between the subject term and the predicate term of the conclusion. This connecting function of the middle term is clearly visible in Venn diagrams.

Syllogisms that do not distribute their middle term commit the **fallacy of the undistributed middle**. Consider the following argument:

Some soldiers are sensitive, and all poets are sensitive, therefore some poets are soldiers.

We might be inclined to accept this argument; many fallacies are mistakes in reasoning that are somehow tempting, and in this case we know the conclusion to be true. But when we think carefully about the syllogistic form of the argument, we can see that the

---

*For a discussion of Aristotle's treatment, see B. Mates, *Elementary Logic*.
**A set of rules is presented by W. Salmon in Logic, *3rd ed*. He adapted them from a set given by J. T. Culbertson, *Mathematics and Logic for Digital Devices*.

form is invalid. Moreover, it is not difficult to imagine a situation in which both premisses could be true while the conclusion would be false. Constructing a Venn diagram to show that the argument is invalid is left as an exercise for the reader.

Another way to evaluate categorical syllogisms is found in modern symbolic treatments of predicate logic, which has a scope considerably greater than that of the logic of categorical syllogisms. The symbolic structure of predicate logic is introduced later. Proof methods for some parts of predicate logic are natural extensions of methods like the proof method for sentential logic found in Appendix One.

Syllogistic reasoning is such a common feature of human thought that it has long been studied by developmental psychologists. Now, with new ways of investigating how the brain works (such as functional magnetic-resonance imaging), neuroscientists have begun to study the processes involved in syllogistic reasoning from the "inside."

Exercise Set 9.5

PART I. Identify the premisses and the conclusions of the following categorical syllogisms. Put the premisses and the conclusions into standard categorical form. Use Venn diagrams to determine the validity or invalidity of the arguments.

1. Some horses are nonracers, for Shetland ponies are horses, and all Shetland ponies are nonracers.

2. No persons who are not trained in medicine are doctors; so no fortunetellers are doctors, for all fortune-tellers are persons who are not trained in medicine.

3. Not all children are undisciplined, but some adults are undisciplined, so no adults are children.

4. Some games of Clue are interesting to observe, but no Monopoly games are interesting to observe. Hence, some Clue games are not Monopoly games.

5. Porpoises have lungs, but no fish do; so porpoises are not fish.

6. All Mexican recipes are labor-intensive, but some salad recipes are not labor-intensive; so salad recipes are not Mexican recipes.

7. All feminists support equal treatment of women in military service, but some women do not support equal treatment of women in military service. Hence, some feminists are not women.

8. All rodents are suitable research animals, but no capybara is a suitable research animal, so no capybara is a rodent.

9. Silk flowers never wilt, but roses always do; so silk flowers are not roses.

10. Not all sofas are beds, but some beds are uncomfortable, so some sofas are uncomfortable.

PART II. Some systems of rules for valid syllogisms include the following rule: No syllogistic conclusion can be drawn from two negative premisses.

Provide a justification for this rule. (*Hint: You may provide a proof by cases, using Venn diagrams to support each case. You can eliminate any cases that commit the fallacy of the undistributed middle.*)

PART III. Can there be a valid syllogistic argument with two particular premisses? If yes, give an example. If no, say why not.

VII. REDUCING THE NUMBER OF TERMS IN SYLLOGISMS

By definition, a categorical syllogism cannot contain more than three terms. However, many arguments that do contain more than three terms can be transformed to equivalent categorical syllogisms. Some categorical syllogisms contain more than three terms because **synonyms** occur in the argument. Synonyms, like other rhetorical devices, make the language of arguments more interesting and can increase an argument's persuasive force. When reconstructing arguments to assess their validity, we can reduce the number of terms if we treat synonyms as different occurrences of the same term. In other cases, arguments contain both members of a complementary set of terms. When this happens, try to reduce the number of terms by applying obversion (changing the quality and replacing a predicate term with its complement). Since obversion can reduce the number of terms only when the extra term occurs in the predicate position, it might be necessary to exchange the subject and predicate terms before obverting. (Remember, this exchange is legitimate only in *I* and *E* sentences.) Consider the following argument, in which both premisses are categorical sentences and the conclusion is a categorical sentence, but in which there are four terms:

> All puzzles are interesting.
> All logic exercises are puzzles.
> —————————————————
> No logic exercises are uninteresting.

The terms *interesting* and *uninteresting* are complementary. Obverting the first premiss yields "No puzzles are uninteresting." In this way, we reduce the number of terms to three without changing the meanings of any of the sentences. The syllogism, which now has the following form:

> No *M* are *P*.
> All *S* are *M*.
> —————————
> No *S* are *P*.

can be tested by the Venn-diagram method.

A different way to reduce the number of terms in this English argument is to obvert the conclusion instead of the first premiss. Then the conclusion becomes "All logic exercises are interesting." Again a categorical syllogism results but of the following form:

> All *M* are *P*.
> All *S* are *M*.
> —————————
> All *S* are *P*.

In this form, the *P* term is *interesting*, whereas in the preceding form, the *P* term is *uninteresting*. Is this form a valid form of syllogism?

The following argument contains five terms:

> Some nonbelievers are freethinkers, because no believers are atheists and some atheists are nonfreethinkers.

Letting *P* represent freethinkers, *S* represent believers, and *M* represent atheists, this argument has the following form:

> No *S* are *M*.
> Some *M* are non-*P*.
> _____
> Some non-*S* are *P*.

The second premiss can be obverted: Change the *I* sentence to an *O* sentence, and change non-*P* to *P* ("Some *M* are not *P*").

Next, reduce the pair of terms *S* and non-*S*. Begin by exchanging the subject and the predicate terms in the conclusion. This is legitimate, because the conclusion is an *I* sentence ("Some *P* are non-*S*").

Then this sentence can be obverted to yield the following:

> Some *P* are not *S*.

The reconstructed argument, which contains only three terms, has this form:

> No *S* are *M*.
> Some *M* are not *P*.
> _____
> Some *P* are not *S*.

Is this a valid form of syllogism?

Exercise Set 9.6

Reconstruct each of the following arguments as a categorical syllogism in standard form. Test each syllogism for validity, using Venn diagrams.

1. Genetic diversity in plants protects against blight. Weeds have held on to their diversity and thus to their defenses.

2. Some engineers are artists, but no architects fail to be artists. Hence, some architects are engineers.

3. All modern-style architecture is without ornamentation, but some recently constructed buildings are ornate; so not all new buildings are in the modern style.

4. Some gemstones are nonprecious, for all amethysts are gemstones, and some amethysts are precious.

5. No man is willing to give up his rights, but women are not men; so some women are not unwilling to give up their rights.

6. Researchers' extraction of stem cells from early-stage human embryos destroys human life. Any destruction of human life is not ethical, so stem-cell research is unethical.

7. Early-stage human embryos are balls of cells with no moral status, and only things with moral status are subject to ethical restraints. So early-stage human embryos are not subject to ethical restraints.

8. No use of human embryos that does not respect their unique moral status is ethically sound. Using stem cells obtained from human embryos, which destroys those embryos, to relieve human suffering respects the unique moral status of human embryos. So using stem cells obtained by destroying human embryos is not unethical.

    (Note: Arguments in Exercises 6, 7, and 8 represent different positions in the ongoing debate about the morality of embryonic stem-cell research. The arguments reach opposing conclusions because each begins with at least one controversial premiss that opponents will not accept.)

9. No creatures of habit are easily persuaded to change their routines. All regular exercisers are creatures of habit, so none of them want to change their routines.

Exercises 10 through 12 are from *The Art of Thinking*, also called *Port-Royal Logic*. This seventeenth-century logic text was designed by A. Arnauld to teach a young nobleman everything there was to know about logic in 10 days.

10. That which has no parts cannot perish by dissolution of its parts.
    The soul has no parts.
    _____
    The soul cannot perish by dissolution of its parts.

11. No virtue is offensive.
    Some zeal is not inoffensive.
    _____
    Some zeal is nonvirtuous.

12. All liars are unbelievable.
    Every upright person is believable.
    _____
    All liars are persons who are not upright.

VIII. RECONSTRUCTING ORDINARY-LANGUAGE ARGUMENTS AS SYLLOGISMS

Many arguments that are incompletely stated in English or that contain sentences not in categorical form can be construed as categorical syllogisms.

Examples

a. Consider the following passage:

> In *Plutarch Lied* Pierrefeu rightly says that in war there is no victory which can not be regarded as unsuccessful, for the objective which one aims at is the total annihilation of the enemy and this result is never attained.
>
> —S. de Beauvoir, *The Ethics of Ambiguity*

This argument can be stated in syllogistic form as follows:

All successful victories in war achieve total annihilation of the enemy.
No actual victories in war achieve total annihilation of the enemy.
___
No actual victories in war are successful victories in war.

b. The following argument, from chapter 12 of *What Is Art?*, can also be recast as a syllogism:

> Accustoming people to something resembling art disaccustoms them to the comprehension of real art. And that is how it comes about that none are more dull to art than those who have passed through the professional schools and have been most successful in them. Professional schools produce an hypocrisy of art.
>
> —L. Tolstoy, *What Is Art?*

Syllogistically, this argument can be expressed as follows:

All who have successfully passed through professional schools of art have been accustomed to something resembling art.
All who have been accustomed to something resembling art are persons most dull to real art.
___
All who have successfully passed through professional schools are persons most dull to real art.

c. The next argument is from St. Augustine. We supply an unstated, but obviously intended, premiss marked with an asterisk (*).

> A happy life is not seen with the eye, because it is not a body.
>
> —St. Augustine, *Confessions*, Book X

In syllogistic form, this argument becomes the following:

No happy lives are bodies.
*All things that can be seen with the eye are bodies.
___
No happy lives are things that can be seen with the eye.

d. The fourth example is taken from *The Mismeasure of Man*:

> If I had any desire to lead a life of indolent ease, I would wish to be an identical twin, separated from my brother and raised in a different social class. We could hire ourselves out to a host of social scientists and practically name our fee. For we would

be exceedingly rare representatives of the only really adequate natural experiment for separating genetic from environmental effects in humans—genetically identical individuals raised in disparate environments.

—S. J. Gould, *The Mismeasure of Man*

A syllogistic reconstruction of this argument is as follows:

All who are genetically identical individuals raised in disparate environments
are representatives of the only adequate natural experiment for separating
genetic from environmental effects in humans.
All representatives of the only adequate natural experiment for separating
genetic from environmental effects in humans are persons who can command
a sufficient fee from social scientists to lead a life of indolent ease.

All genetically identical individuals raised in disparate environments are
persons who can command a sufficient fee from social scientists to lead a life of
indolent ease.

IX. QUASI-SYLLOGISMS AND SORITES

1. QUASI-SYLLOGISMS

A syllogism with one universal premiss, another premiss stating that a given individual is a member of the subject class, and a conclusion stating that the individual is a member of the predicate class, such as the following, is called a **quasi-syllogism:**

All men are mortal.
Socrates is a man.
Socrates is mortal.

This is obviously an instance of a valid form of reasoning. Strictly speaking, however, it is not a categorical syllogism because sentences such as "Socrates is a man" (called **singular** sentences) are not categorical. Some treatments of syllogistic logic treat this fundamental form of argument by interpreting singular sentences as disguised universal generalizations:

All members of the class in which the only member is Socrates are men.

If the singular sentences are interpreted in this way, the preceding quasi-syllogism becomes an instance of the valid form:

All M are P.
All S are M.
All S are P.

Quasi-syllogisms can also occur with negative universal premisses:

> No whales are fishes.
> Shamu is a whale.
> ─────────────────
> Shamu is not a fish.

The conclusion in this syllogism is interpreted as follows:

> No members of the class whose only member is Shamu are fishes.

Interpreting the singular premiss as in the other quasi-syllogism, this quasi-syllogism becomes an instance of the valid categorical form:

> No M are P.
> All S are M.
> ──────────
> No S are P.

Exercise

Using the Venn-diagram technique, how might you diagram the singular sentences in a quasi-syllogism without transforming this quasi-syllogism to a categorical syllogism?

Hint: Assign a lower-case letter to name the individual in the singular sentence, and treat that letter in the same way as you would the "x" in a Venn diagram. Diagram the quasi-syllogism that argues that Socrates is mortal.

2. SORITES

A **sorites** is an argument with more than two categorical sentences as premisses and from which a final categorical conclusion may be drawn by performing a series of syllogistic inferences. In a sorites with three premisses, the intermediate syllogistic conclusion drawn from a pair of the stated premisses is used as an additional premiss and combined with the third premiss to yield the final conclusion of the argument.

In a sorites with more than three premisses, the process of drawing intermediate conclusions and using them as additional premisses is performed as often as required to reach the final conclusion. This process is limited only by the number of available middle terms. Lewis Carroll, a logician who is best known as the author of *Alice in Wonderland*, discusses this type of argument in his *Symbolic Logic*. All of the following examples of sets of premisses of sorites are taken from this work. Solutions to the first two examples are given. The remaining sets of premisses are intended as exercises.

Examples

A. (i) No ducks waltz.
   (ii) No officers ever decline to waltz.
   (iii) All of my poultry are ducks.

Taking "ducks" as a middle term, the first and third premises can be combined to yield the intermediate conclusion:

(iv) No poultry of mine waltz.

"No officers ever decline to waltz" can be obverted to obtain "All officers waltz." This can then be combined with the intermediate conclusion (iv) to yield the final conclusion:

(v) No officers are poultry of mine.

The conclusion "No poultry of mine are officers," which is equivalent to (v), could also be drawn from the same premises.

B.   (i) No potatoes of mine that are new have been boiled.
       (ii) All my potatoes in this dish are fit to eat.
       (iii) No unboiled potatoes of mine are fit to eat.

Taking "things that are fit to eat" as a middle term, Premises (ii) and (iii) can be combined to provide an intermediate conclusion:

(iv) No unboiled potatoes of mine are my potatoes in this dish.

Before this intermediate conclusion can be combined with (i), the number of terms must be reduced. "Potatoes of mine" is equivalent to "my potatoes." Because "boiled" and "unboiled" are complementary, we will obvert (i), in which "boiled" occurs in the predicate position. Obverting (i) yields

(v) All potatoes of mine that are new are unboiled (potatoes of mine).

Combining (iv) and (v) yields the conclusion:

No potatoes of mine that are new are potatoes of mine in this dish.

Or the conclusion can be stated, less awkwardly, as "None of my new potatoes are in this dish."

Exercise Set 9.7

1. Show that the conclusion "All of my new potatoes are unfit to eat" also follows from the three premises in (B) above.

2. Draw an appropriate syllogistic conclusion from the following three premises:
   a. No one takes in the *Times* unless he is well educated.
   b. No hedgehogs can read.
   c. Those who cannot read are not well educated.

3. Draw an appropriate syllogistic conclusion from the following three premises:
   a. Everyone who is sane can do logic.
   b. No lunatics are fit to serve on a jury.
   c. None of your sons can do logic.

4. Draw an appropriate syllogistic conclusion from the following three premises:
   a. All hummingbirds are richly colored.
   b. No large birds live on honey.
   c. Birds that do not live on honey are dull in color.

5. Draw an appropriate syllogistic conclusion from the following four premises:
   a. No birds, except ostriches, are nine feet high.
   b. There are no birds in this aviary that belong to anyone but me.
   c. No ostrich lives on mince pies.
   d. I have no birds less than nine feet high.

6. Reconstruct Woodward's argument in the following passage as a quasi-syllogism. Is it valid?

   Robert S. Woodward, then president of the Carnegie Institution, reacted with silence to a new archaeology department. He did remark to his colleagues at the institution that archaeology exists to aid museums in the acquisition of collections, and since the Carnegie had no museums, archaeology was therefore not part of the Carnegie's mission.

   —R. L. Brunhouse, as cited by D. R. Givens, *Rediscovering Our Past*

7. Can you construct a syllogism or a sorites on the basis of the following?

   Birdwatchers out for the rare pileated woodpecker . . . [should] search for an aging hardwood tree under which honey mushrooms are growing. Honey mushrooms recognize a weakening hardwood tree and move in to digest its roots. As the fungi digest the tree, carpenter ants move in to excavate galleries beneath the bark, where pileated woodpeckers pick them out for dinner.

   —S. Stein, *My Weeds*

X. REVIEW

An extensive specialized terminology has developed in connection with this subject, which has been studied in classrooms for more than 2,000 years. Although some of this terminology is used predominately in logic classes, much of it has found its way into the everyday vocabulary of educated people. A list of the important terms used in this chapter, with brief definitions, follows.

Categorical Sentence   A type of sentence, having the structure of one of four standard forms. Letting S represent the subject term and P represent the predicate term, these forms are:

1. Every S is P. (universal affirmative, or A sentence)
2. No S is P. (universal negative, or E sentence)
3. Some S is P. (particular affirmative, or I sentence)
4. Some S is not P. (particular negative, or O sentence)

Categorical Syllogism   A type of argument characterized by the following features:

1. Two premisses and a conclusion, each of which is a categorical sentence.
2. Exactly three terms occur in the argument. One of the terms occurs once in each premiss; the other two terms occur once in one of the premisses and once in the conclusion.

Complementary Terms   A pair of terms is complementary when one term of the pair refers to a class and the other term of the pair refers to its complement (the class consisting of all things that are not members of the original class).

Contradictory Sentences   When one sentence in a pair is the negation of the other sentence, the pair of sentences is contradictory. In a pair of contradictory sentences, one is true and the other is false. For categorical sentences with the same subjects and predicates, the A and O sentences are contradictory, as are the E and I sentences.

Contraposition   The contrapositive of an A or an O sentence is formed by exchanging the positions of the subject and predicate terms and replacing each with its complement. Contraposition preserves meaning for A and O sentences but not for I and E sentences.

Contrary Sentences   When a pair of sentences is related in such a way that they could both be false but could not both be true, the sentences are contrary to one another. In the Aristotelian interpretation of categorical sentence forms, the A and E sentences that share the same subject and predicate terms are contraries.

Conversion   Exchanging the subject and predicate terms in a categorical sentence is called *conversion*. Converting I and E sentences yields sentences with the same meaning as the original sentences; converting A and O sentences does not.

Distribution of Terms   When a sentence says something about every member of a class, the term referring to that class is said to be distributed. In universal categorical sentences, the subject terms are distributed; in negative categorical sentences, the predicate terms are distributed. Remember: **USNP**.

Existential Import   When a sentence asserts the existence of some object, the sentence has existential import. Universal categorical sentences, when understood as material conditionals, lack existential import. Particular categorical sentences have existential import.

Fallacies of Distribution   Mistakes in reasoning that occur when a term that is used collectively in the premisses is interpreted distributively in the conclusion (**fallacy of division**) or when a term that is used distributively in the premisses is interpreted collectively in the conclusion (**fallacy of composition**).

Fallacy of the Undistributed Middle   This fallacy occurs in syllogistic arguments when the middle term is not distributed in either premiss.

Figure of a Syllogism   *Figure* refers to the arrangement of the end terms (*S* and *P*) and the middle term (*M*) in the premisses. The four figures are as follows:

MP	*PM*	*MP*	*PM*
SM	*SM*	*MS*	*MS*
SP	*SP*	*SP*	*SP*

Obversion   A categorical sentence is obverted when the quality of the sentence is changed and the predicate term is replaced with its complement. The resulting sentence is a categorical sentence that is logically equivalent to the original sentence.

Quality of a Categorical Sentence   The quality of a categorical sentence refers to whether the sentence is negative or affirmative. The quality of *A* and *I* sentences is affirmative; the quality of *E* and *O* sentences is negative.

Quasi-Syllogism   A three-term syllogism with a universal premiss, a **singular** premiss, and a singular conclusion is a quasi-syllogism.

Sorites   An argument with more than two categorical sentences as premisses and a categorical conclusion that is reached by drawing an intermediate syllogistic conclusion from two of the premisses and then using this conclusion in combination with another premiss to draw a further syllogistic conclusion. This pattern is repeated, using the remaining premisses, until the final conclusion is reached.

Subcontrary Sentences   When a pair of sentences is related in such a way that they could both be true but could not both be false, the sentences are subcontraries. Under the Aristotelian interpretation of categorical sentences, *I* and *O* sentence forms with the same subject and the same predicate terms are subcontraries.

Venn Diagrams   Sets of overlapping circles that can be marked to indicate class membership, class exclusion, and class inclusion. These diagrams exhibit the relationships between classes in categorical sentences and can be used to test syllogisms for validity.

Exercise Set 9.8

PART I. For each of the following incomplete arguments, supply a premiss that will make the argument a valid categorical syllogism or a quasi-syllogism. (Use Venn diagrams, if helpful.)

1. Nuclear plants should not be built because those who live near them pay an unfair cost in health to provide others with cheap electricity.

2. Nuclear power plants should be built because they provide power without increasing greenhouse gases.

3. Austin must be rich, since he drives a Porsche.

4. Female office workers work just as hard as male office workers and are just as productive. Therefore, female office workers should receive the same pay as male office workers in comparable positions.

5. Since Corey's symptoms disappear after the first frost, he must be allergic to pollen.

6. Not all government workers who leak information deserve to be prosecuted, for some of them are merely exposing fraud and waste in the system.

7. Those who do not violate international law need not fear reprisals, so your country shouldn't be afraid of reprisals.

8. Terry is a mathematician, so she must be musically talented.

9. You had no right to take away his gun, because that gun was private property.

10. If you care about the environment, you will use a bike instead of a car whenever possible.

PART II. What syllogistic conclusion, if any, can be validly drawn from the following pairs of premisses? (Venn diagrams will prove helpful.)

1. All dogs are trainable. Some dogs are difficult to train.

2. Some pilots are risk takers. Some risk takers endanger the lives of others.

3. Whoever lives by the sword will perish by the sword. Some soldiers perish by the sword.

4. Whatever goes up must come down. Your untethered balloon is going up.

5. Anything I say can be misinterpreted. Some misinterpretations are harmless.

6. All polynomials are sums of powers. Some mathematical expressions are polynomials.

7. No salt is an element. Some salts are soluble.

8. All metals are fusible. Some conductors are nonmetals.

9. Not all gondolas are boats. Some gondolas have gondoliers.

10. All children are persuadable. Some children can be bribed.

11. All first basemen are athletes. No catchers are first basemen.

PART III. Reconstruct each of the following arguments as a categorical syllogism, supplying plausible premisses when necessary. Test each syllogism for validity, using Venn diagrams.

1. Some valid arguments have false conclusions, but not all syllogisms are valid; so some syllogisms have true conclusions.

2. None but the rich can afford to be idle. Anyone who can afford to be idle is a threat to the Puritan work ethic, so some rich persons threaten the Puritan work ethic.

3. You cannot expect handmade sweaters to be inexpensive because they're labor-intensive and labor is not cheap.

4. Good speakers avoid boring their audiences. No professional politician is not a good speaker. Therefore no professional politicians fail to avoid boring their audiences.

5. Some executives are lazy, but no entrepreneurs are lazy; so some entrepreneurs are not executives.

6. Fallacious arguments are sometimes convincing. None of your arguments are fallacious. Therefore, all of your arguments are convincing.

7. Some professors are ignorant. None who are ignorant are fit to teach college students. So some who are unfit to teach college students are professors.

8. All arts organizations are struggling for funds. Since some organizations that are struggling for funds will go under, some arts organizations will go under.

9. All reporters are aggressive. Only reporters have daily deadlines. So no nonaggressive persons have daily deadlines.

10. Syllogisms all have two premises. Not all syllogisms are categorical. Some noncategorical syllogisms have two premises.

11. Printed newspapers cannot compete with online sources of news, for they are not instantly available. Only instantly available news sources can compete with online sources of news.

12. Science is a vital part of industrial and military production, which is clearly directed at specific values. It follows that science is not value free.

13. The following is an argument against the position that all moral judgments are **subjective**, in the sense of merely expressing personal opinions. It depends on an assumption that an argument between two parties cannot proceed unless there are some premises that both accept.

    Where there is no background of moral agreement, there can be no argument about moral issues. But there are arguments about moral issues. Thus, there is some background of moral agreement.

14. Some moral beliefs transcend the cultural context in which they arise. Beliefs that transcend their cultural contexts are not relative to the culture in which they arise. Therefore some moral beliefs are not relative to the culture in which they arise.

Chapter Ten

QUANTIFIERS AND ARGUMENTS IN WHICH VALIDITY DEPENDS ON RELATIONSHIPS

I. INTRODUCTION

Our examination of sentential arguments and categorical syllogisms shows how deductive validity depends on form. In sentential arguments, validity depends on truth-functional connections between the sentences that make up the argument; in categorical syllogisms, validity depends on logical connections between the class terms (subject terms and predicate terms) within sentences. In analyzing both types of arguments, we ignored content to focus on structural features. We adopted various symbols to help expose the structure of argument forms. Simple sentences in truth-functional arguments were represented by lowercase letters, and special symbols were introduced to represent the truth-functional connectives *and*, *not*, *or*, *if . . . then*, and *if and only if*. Class terms in categorical syllogisms were represented by uppercase letters. In this chapter, we introduce additional symbols and apply similar techniques for analyzing arguments whose validity depends on formal properties of relationships among individuals.

Logicians operate on an assumption that every deductively valid argument is an instance of some valid argument form. As mentioned earlier, the history of logic is the story of continuing investigation of the formal properties of arguments that are intuitively valid. Aristotle's theory of syllogisms was the first formal account of arguments. Soon after Aristotle, the Stoic logicians developed a comprehensive theory of the forms of truth-functional arguments. Only much later did another important type of argument receive formal treatment. The validity of this type depends on formal properties of **relationships**. By studying relational logic, even briefly, we not only see the usefulness of relational arguments in ordinary life, but we also glimpse some of the power of modern symbolic techniques for unifying the study of deductive reasoning.

II. EXAMPLES OF RELATIONAL ARGUMENTS

The following arguments are obviously valid:

1. New Maseratis are more expensive than new Cadillacs.
    New Cadillacs are more expensive than new Fords.
    _____
    New Maseratis are more expensive than new Fords.

2. President G. H. W. Bush served before President G. W. Bush.
    _____
    G. W. Bush did not serve before G. H. W. Bush.

3. One British pint is equal to 570 milliliters.
    _____
    Five hundred and seventy milliliters is equal to one British pint.

If we restrict ourselves to the techniques for analyzing truth-functional logic and syllogistic logic, we cannot represent the forms by virtue of which any of these arguments is valid. In each case, the validity of the argument depends essentially on some formal property of the relationships ("more expensive than," "served before," "equal to") referred to in the arguments rather than simply on truth-functional connections between the sentences in the argument or on categorical connections between subjects and predicates within the sentences.

III. IMPORTANT PROPERTIES OF RELATIONSHIPS

Argument (1) in the preceding section is valid because if one thing is more expensive than a second, and the second is more expensive than a third, it follows that the first is more expensive than the third. In other words, "more expensive than" is a **transitive** relationship. Many ordinary relationships are transitive. Familiar examples of transitive relationships include "older than," "younger than," "prettier than," "equal to," "greater than," "ancestor of," and "descended from." Transitive relationships all share the following property: If the first thing has a relationship to the second, and the second has the same relationship to the third, then the first has the same relationship to the third as well.

Not all relationships are transitive. Some are **intransitive**, and others still are **nontransitive**—that is to say, neither transitive nor intransitive. If the fact that one member of a relationship is related to a second member, and the fact that the second member has the same relationship to a third member rule out the first member standing in that relation to the third, the relationship is intransitive. The following argument is valid because the relationship "mother of" is intransitive:

> Ruth is the mother of Betty.
> Betty is the mother of Claudia.
> _____
> Ruth is not the mother of Claudia.

Other examples of intransitive relationships are "father of" and "twice as large as." In **nontransitive** relationships, if the first member is related to a second member, and the second has that same relationship to a third member, neither of these facts rules out or requires that the first has that relationship to the third. "Cousin of" is a nontransitive relationship. For example, if James is a cousin of Alice, and Alice is a cousin of Richard, James may or may not be Richard's cousin. No conclusion can be drawn regarding the relationship between the first and third members on the basis of a nontransitive relationship between the first and second and the second and third members. Some other nontransitive relationships include the following: "takes a class with," "likes some of the same foods as," "is a friend of," "loves," and "is in a carpool with."

All of the relationships discussed in this chapter relate **pairs** of things or individuals. Such relationships are called **binary,** or two-termed, relationships. The two things that are related by a binary relationship are called the **terms** of the relation. Not all relationships are binary, however. In "Clarissa bought her books from Edward," a relationship connects three terms: Clarissa, her books, and Edward. The following sentence involves a four-term relationship: "Tony gave money to Sally for the hospital fund-raiser." The four terms in that relationship are Tony, his money, Sally, and the fund-raiser. Although constructing English sentences involving relationships with more than four or five terms is awkward, in theory any number of terms can be related. To avoid complexities and to focus on important properties of relationships that relate just two terms, we consider only binary relationships in this chapter.

The relationship "served before" (used in Section II, Argument [2]) is transitive. However, the validity of the argument does not depend on the transitivity of that relationship but on another of its properties. "Served before" is an **asymmetric** relationship. If the first member is related by an asymmetric relationship to the second member, then the second member cannot be related in the same way to the first member. "Greater than," "less than," "weighs more than," and "father of" are familiar examples of asymmetric relationships.

If the fact that the first member has a relationship to the second member implies that the second has that same relationship to the first, then the relationship is **symmetric**. "Equal to," "weighs the same as," "not identical with," and "sibling of" are all symmetric relationships. The validity of Argument (3) in Section II depends on the symmetry of "equal to."

In **nonsymmetric** relationships, the fact that the first member is related to the second member neither implies nor rules out the second member standing in that relationship to the first. For example, "brother of" is a nonsymmetric relationship. Two individuals can be related in such a way that one is the brother of the other but the second is not the brother of the first (when the second is female). In the case of two males, if the first is the brother to the second, then the second is the brother to the first. Because either situation is possible for two arbitrarily selected individuals who can stand in that relationship to one another, "brother of" is a nonsymmetric relationship.

Relationships that relate a thing to itself are called **reflexive** relationships. "Identical with" is a reflexive relationship; everything is identical with itself. Other examples of reflexive relationships include "equal to" and "is the same color as."

Irreflexive relationships are those that no individual can have to itself. Examples of irreflexive relationships are "unequal to," "different from," "not the same as," and "greater than." Some relationships are **nonreflexive**, in which individuals may or may not bear such relationships to themselves. "Loves," for example, is nonreflexive; some persons love themselves, but others do not love themselves.

It might seem odd to think of a relationship as two-termed when the things that are related are one and the same. Nevertheless, it makes good sense to speak of a thing either having or failing to have some relationship to itself. In general, the two terms in any binary relationship need not refer to distinct individuals.

Exercise Set 10.1

PART I. State whether each of the following relationships is:

a. transitive, intransitive, or nontransitive

b. symmetric, asymmetric, or nonsymmetric

c. reflexive, irreflexive, or nonreflexive

1. Hates
2. Wife of
3. Owns
4. Is seated next to
5. More than
6. Is better than
7. Is shorter than
8. Is not identical with
9. Is the same height as
10. Fears

PART II. Name 10 additional binary relationships and categorize each as transitive, symmetric, reflexive, and so on.

IV. USING QUANTIFIERS TO EXPRESS RELATIONSHIPS

Using symbols to display the formal character of arguments is not a new practice. Aristotle used **variables** (letters of the alphabet) to represent class terms when he formulated principles of syllogistic reasoning. As we have seen, using variables in this way simplifies the expression of principles and makes it easier to recognize the formal properties of arguments. The use of letters to represent sentences in truth-functional logic, however, is a twentieth-century innovation. Some grasp of the simplicity gained by applying this technique is evident when the modern formulation of *affirming the antecedent*:

$$p \rightarrow q$$
$$\underline{p}$$
$$q$$

is compared with the formulation of the Stoic logicians:

If the first, then the second.
The first.
Therefore, the second.*

___
*Mates, 1972, p. 214.

When truth-functional argument forms involve numerous simple sentences, the use of sentence letters is even more attractive. (Try to express one of the dilemma forms of argument using expressions such as "the first," "the second," "the third," and so on.)

Twentieth-century developments in the symbolization of logic have facilitated the expression of relationships. The symbolic languages used by modern logicians provide a nonambiguous formulation of categorical syllogisms as well and, by employing symbols common to various types of arguments, clearly show the structural similarities among truth-functional arguments, syllogistic arguments, and relational arguments.

To clarify logical structure, we translate English expressions into artificial symbolic language. These translations are not like translations from English into French, or some other natural language. They cannot capture all of the nuances that could be expressed in natural language. The purpose of these translations is to identify the features of arguments that determine validity. Translations into symbols are designed to preserve meaning only insofar as it is relevant to assessing the validity of arguments.

For any translation to be possible, the symbols of the artificial language must be interpreted. **Interpretations** specify the meanings of the symbols to the extent that they specify truth conditions (the conditions under which sentences in the artificial language are true or false). We have already seen how truth tables can be used to define truth-functional connectives. Because the same connectives are used in this chapter, the following summary is provided. (Here, "p" and "q" are sentence letters, which can be used to represent complex as well as simple sentences.)

1. "$\sim p$" is true if and only if "p" is false.
2. "$p \vee q$" is false only in cases when both "p" and "q" are false; otherwise, it is true.
3. "$p \bullet q$" is true only in cases when both "p" and "q" are true; otherwise, it is false.
4. "$p \rightarrow q$" is false whenever "p" is true and "q" is false; otherwise, it is true.
5. "$p \leftrightarrow q$" is true whenever "p" and "q" have the same truth value; otherwise, it is false.

Other features of interpretations are discussed in context as they arise.

1. SYMBOLIZING THE UNIVERSAL QUANTIFIER

In the universal affirmative sentence form "All S are P," "all" is a **universal quantifier.** In accord with the modern understanding of universal affirmatives, we interpret them as conditionals: If anything is an S, then it is a P. An equivalent conditional formulation is the following: <u>For any individual (person, place, or thing)</u>, if it is an S, then it is a P. In this formulation, the underlined portion represents the universal quantifier. The symbol for the universal quantifier is a lowercase letter enclosed in parentheses. Examples include the following:

(x) Read: "For any x"

(y) Read: "For any y"

(z) Read: "For any z"

In symbolizing the universal affirmative sentence, the same letter that is in the quantifier is used in place of pronouns such as *it* to refer to the same individuals. Thus, to symbolize "For any individual, if it is an S, then it is a P," we write

$$(x)(Sx \rightarrow Px)$$

Parentheses enclose the expression following the quantifier to indicate that the x's in this expression are those referred to by the quantifier that precedes the expression. Lowercase letters that are used in this way are called **individual variables**; the uppercase letters used to represent classes of individuals are called **predicate letters**.

Now, suppose we want to translate the English categorical sentence "All suffragettes are feminists" into a symbolic sentence that represents the meaning of the English sentence as closely as possible. The first step is to specify a **domain of interpretation**, or the set of all individuals that will be referred to in the artificial language. This domain may vary from interpretation to interpretation. In a situation in which numbers are the only individuals referred to, the set of all numbers can be chosen as the domain of interpretation. In another situation, persons may be the only individuals referred to, so the set of all persons can be taken as the domain. In general, the domain of interpretation can be any nonempty set of individuals. To simplify matters for all interpretations in this chapter, unless otherwise noted, the domain of interpretation consists of the set of all individuals. (The members of this domain are all persons, things, numbers, and so on.)

Predicate letters (uppercase letters from the English alphabet) are interpreted as referring to classes (sets) of individuals in the domain. To translate "All suffragettes are feminists," let one predicate letter (S) denote the class of suffragettes and a second predicate letter (F) denote the class of feminists. Then "All suffragettes are feminists" is translated "$(x)(Sx \rightarrow Fx)$."

The universal negative sentence ("No S are P") has a conditional structure similar to the universal affirmative and is written as follows:

$$(x)(Sx \rightarrow \sim Px)$$

(For any individual, if it is an S, then it is not a P.)

To translate the sentence "No Chihuahuas are guide dogs," let the predicate letter G denote the class of guide dogs and C denote the class of Chihuahuas: $(x)(Cx \rightarrow \sim Gx)$, that is, "If anything is a Chihuahua, then it is not a guide dog."

2. SYMBOLIZING THE EXISTENTIAL QUANTIFIER

The quantifier *some* is called the **existential quantifier**. Particular affirmative sentences and particular negative sentences assert both that some individual **exists** and that the individual either has (in the affirmative sentences) or lacks (in the negative sentences) some property. These sentences thus have **existential import**. In the modern interpretation, universal sentences lack existential import because they do not assert the existence of anything.

The structure of *I* and *O* sentences differs from that of universal sentences. Particular generalizations resemble conjunctions rather than conditionals. The *I* sentence:

Some *S* are *P.*

is understood to mean

<u>There is some individual such that</u> it is an *S and* also a *P.*

The *O* sentence:

Some *S* are not *P.*

is understood to mean

<u>There is some individual such that</u> it is an *S and* not a *P.*

In the preceding sentences, the underlined expressions represent the **existential quantifier**. The existential quantifier is symbolized by a backward "E" followed by an individual variable, both enclosed in parentheses: $(\exists x)$.

To symbolize the existential, or particular, affirmative categorical sentence, write the following:

$$(\exists x)(Sx \bullet Px)$$

which can be read: "There is some *x* such that it is *S* and it is *P.*"

To symbolize the existential (particular) negative categorical sentence, write the following:

$$(\exists x)(Sx \bullet {\sim}Px)$$

which can be read: "There is some *x* such that it is *S* and it is not *P.*"

Exercise Set 10.2

Assign predicate letters to classes, and translate the following sentences into symbolic language:

1. Some bands are hot.
2. Some bands are not [hot].
3. No carnivores are vegetarians.
4. All vegetarians are health conscious.

5. There are fanatic vegetarians.

6. Mice are rodents.

7. Not all vegetarians drink milk.

8. All dogs bark, and all cats meow.

9. Some dogs bark, but some do not.

10. Dogs and horses are race animals.

11. If some lions are wild, then some are tame.

12. If no dogs are cats, then no cats are dogs.

13. If anything is a lion then it is not a tiger.

14. There are no vegetarian lions or tigers.

3. SYMBOLIZING RELATIONAL SENTENCES

The symbols used to represent categorical sentences can be adapted to express relationships. The class terms that occur in categorical sentences can be thought of as one-place (**monadic**) predicates. In symbolic language, we indicate that an individual x is a member of a class S by writing a predicate letter followed by a single individual variable: Sx. In a similar manner, binary relationships can be represented by two-place predicates. Predicate letters can be used to indicate that an individual x stands in a relationship R to an individual y by writing that predicate letter between the pair of variables, taken in the proper order: xRy.

Two-place predicate letters are thus interpreted as referring to sets of ordered pairs of individuals who are related by the relationship in question. For example, let the predicate letter L denote the set of all pairs of individuals such that the first member of the pair loves the second member of the pair. In specifying such interpretations, we can use the following notation:

$$L: \underline{\quad} \text{ loves } \ldots$$

Generalizations that involve relationships can be expressed symbolically by using quantifiers, predicate letters, and individual variables. For example, if we interpret L as above, we can translate "Everything loves everything" into symbols:

$$(x)(y)xLy$$

To translate the sentence "Everybody loves everybody," a predicate letter P is used to represent the class of persons:

$$(x)(y)((Px \bullet Py) \to xLy)$$

which can be read: "Given any x and any y, if x is a person and y is a person, then x loves y." Note that if the domain of interpretation is limited to the set of all persons, then "Everybody loves everybody" can be translated as follows:

$$(x)(y)xLy$$

When the domain of interpretation is not limited to persons, the expression

$$(\exists x)(\exists y)xLy$$

can be read "Something loves something."

Again, letting P refer to the class of persons and L to the set of ordered pairs such that the first member loves the second member, "Somebody loves somebody" is translated as follows:

$$(\exists x)(\exists y)(Px \bullet Py \bullet xLy)$$

In contrast to **generalizations** about relations, sentences such as "Ruth is the mother of Betty" state that some specific individual is related to another specific individual. In standard symbolic language, individual variables are lowercase letters from the end of the alphabet (u–z) and specific individuals are represented by letters from the earlier part of the alphabet (a–t). The letters a through t, called **individual constants**, perform the same function in symbolic language as proper names in ordinary language. For example, the sentence "Socrates is mortal" can be symbolized by interpreting s to refer to Socrates and "M" to refer to the class of mortals and by writing the following:

$$Ms$$

Socrates, one of the most influential philosophers of all time, was married to Xanthippe. Interpreting H to refer to "___ is the husband of . . . ," s to refer to Socrates, and a to refer to Xanthippe, then

$$sHa$$

is true, for it says that Socrates is the husband of Xanthippe. Given the same interpretations,

$$aHs$$

is false, for it says that Xanthippe is the husband of Socrates. Because "husband of" is not a symmetric relationship, the order of the individual constants makes a difference in the truth of the sentence.

Using quantifiers, individual variables, and two-place predicate letters, important properties of binary relations can be conveniently and precisely characterized. Let R be some two-place (binary) relationship. Then any of the following properties of R can be expressed symbolically:

    1. R is reflexive: $(x)xRx$

The symbolic formula is read: "Given anything, it stands in relation R to itself."

    2. R is irreflexive: $(x)\sim xRx$

"Given anything, it is not related by R to itself."

    3. R is nonreflexive: $\sim(x)(xRx) \bullet \sim (x)(\sim xRx)$

"It is not the case that R is reflexive, and it is not the case that R is irreflexive." (Or, "R is not reflexive, and R is not irreflexive.")

4. R is symmetric: $(x)(y)(xRy \rightarrow yRx)$

"Given any x and any y (not necessarily distinct), if x bears relation R to y, then y bears relation R to x."

5. R is asymmetric: $(x)(y)(xRy \rightarrow {\sim}yRx)$

"Given any x and any y (not necessarily distinct), if x bears relation R to y, then y does not bear relation R to x."

6. R is nonsymmetric: ${\sim}(x)(y)(xRy \rightarrow yRx) \bullet {\sim}(x)(y)(xRy \rightarrow {\sim}yRx)$

"R is not symmetric, and R is not asymmetric."

7. R is transitive: $(x)(y)(z)((xRy \bullet yRz) \rightarrow xRz)$

"For any three individuals x, y, z (not necessarily distinct), if the first bears relation R to the second, and the second bears relation R to the third, then the first bears relation R to the third."

8. R is intransitive: $(x)(y)(z)((xRy \bullet yRz) \rightarrow {\sim}xRz)$

"For any three individuals x, y, z (not necessarily distinct), if x bears relation R to y, and y bears relation R to z, then x does not bear relation R to z."

Exercise Set 10.3

PART I. Express "R is nontransitive" symbolically, using the previous discussion as your guide. Then interpret in English the symbolic formula.

PART II. Express each of the following in symbols, providing interpretations for symbols when necessary. For example, ___ L. . . : loves and m: Mary. To simplify translations, let the domain of interpretation be the set of all persons.

1. Mary loves everyone.
2. Mary loves no one.
3. Mary loves herself.
4. John loves himself and Mary.
5. Mary loves John.
6. Someone loves Mary.
7. If John does not love himself, then no one loves him.
8. No one loves John except John.
9. Mary loves no one.

10. Everyone loves John, or everyone loves Mary.

11. Not everyone loves himself.

12. Someone does not love himself.

13. Love is not a symmetric relationship.

14. Love is not a reflexive relationship.

4. MULTIPLE QUANTIFIERS

To symbolize most generalizations involving relational properties, more than one quantifier is needed. For example, two universal quantifiers are needed to state that a relationship is symmetric, and three universal quantifiers are required to state the transitivity of a relationship. When multiple quantifiers are all of the same type (all universal or all existential), the order in which they are placed at the beginning of the symbolized expression is irrelevant. Assuming that R is interpreted the same way in each case, there is no difference in meaning among the following:

$$(1)\ (x)(y)(z)((xRy \bullet yRz) \rightarrow xRz)$$
$$(2)\ (y)(x)(z)((xRy \bullet yRz) \rightarrow xRz)$$
$$(3)\ (z)(y)(x)((xRy \bullet yRz) \rightarrow xRz)$$

Likewise, there is no difference in meaning between the following:

$$(1)\ (\exists x)(\exists y)(xRy \bullet yRx)$$
$$(2)\ (\exists y)(\exists x)(xRy \bullet yRx)$$

However, when both existential and universal quantifiers are used in a single expression, reordering the quantifiers can change the meaning of the expression. Consider the sentence "Everybody has a mother."

Limit the domain of interpretation to the set of persons, and assign the predicate letter M to the set of ordered pairs such that the first is the mother of the second:

$$M: \underline{\quad} \text{ is the mother of } \ldots$$

Then the translation of the English sentence is as follows:

$$(x)(\exists y)yMx$$

The symbolic sentence can be read: "Given any x, there is some y such that y is the mother of x." In other words, the sentence says that for any person, there is some person who is the mother.

If the order of the quantifiers is reversed, the symbolic sentence becomes the following:

$$(\exists y)(x)yMx$$

Based on the same interpretation for M, this sentence is read

"There is some y such that given any x, y is the mother of x."

In other words, this sentence says that someone is the mother of everyone. When "someone" occurs at the beginning of the expression, it means "some one person," but no one person is the mother of everyone. When "someone" occurs in the position shown in the first translation, it means "someone or other," and it is true that every person has someone or other as a mother. Thus, although these two symbolic expressions differ only in the order in which the quantifiers are placed at the beginning of the expression, they do not mean the same thing.

Exercise Set 10.4

Using the set of persons as the domain of interpretation and interpreting L as "___ loves . . . ," express each of the following in symbolic language.

1. Everyone loves someone (or other).
2. No one loves everyone.
3. No one loves anyone.
4. Someone loves everyone.
5. There is someone whom no one loves.
6. If everyone loves someone, then no one is unloved.

5. THE FALLACY OF EVERY AND ALL

It is widely believed that nothing happens without a cause. In antiquity, the statement "Everything that happens has a cause" was used as a premiss to infer that there is some "first cause" of everything. If this argument is valid, however, it must be an instance of some form other than the following:

$$\frac{(x)(\exists y)yCx}{(\exists y)(x)yCx}$$

because the above form is invalid. Based on the intended interpretation (C: ___ causes . . .), the symbolization provides a reasonable translation of the argument, as just stated above.

This argument form, however, is shown to be invalid by a counterexample, which is an argument in the form with all true premises and a false conclusion. Using the set of all persons as the domain of interpretation, assign C to the set of all ordered pairs such that the first is the mother of the second:

$$C: \text{___ is mother of . . .}$$

Under this interpretation, the single premiss of the argument is obviously true, but the conclusion is obviously false:

$$\frac{\text{Everyone has a mother.}}{\text{Someone is everyone's mother.}}$$

For an argument form to be valid, it must be valid under any interpretation of the predicate letters.

This fallacious form of argument is called the **fallacy of every and all**. We must remember, however, that an argument that is an instance of some fallacious argument form may not be an invalid argument. An argument is invalid only if it is not an instance of *any* valid argument form. Nevertheless, as with truth-functional arguments that were instances of invalid truth-functional forms, we should at least suspect invalidity when an argument is an instance of an invalid form and when no analysis of the argument is provided to show that it is an instance of some valid form.

Aristotle's argument for the existence of a first cause, or "prime mover," actually involved at least one further premiss, which stated that an infinite series of causes and effects is impossible. We might symbolize Aristotle's rejection of an infinite regress of causes—the claim that there must be some cause that is not the effect of any other cause—in the following:

$$(\exists y)(\exists x)(yCx \bullet \sim(\exists z)zCy)$$

Or, "There is a y such that y causes some x, and there is no z that causes y." The addition of this premiss does not allow us to conclude that there is just one first cause, however, for there may be more than one "uncaused cause." ("Some" means "at least one"; it does not mean "exactly one.")

Aristotle's arguments are difficult to analyze because of problems with translating the ancient Greek language and because the ancient texts, which were essentially lecture notes, suffer from incompleteness and alterations. Many scholars, however, impute the fallacy of every and all to Aristotle in more than one context. In commenting on Aristotle's apparent use of the premiss that every action has a final end to support the conclusion that there is one and the same end to all actions, called the "Supreme Good," a contemporary philosopher has said in defense of the founder of logic:

> This is a type of reasoning [relational logic] that lies beyond the
> reach of his own formal logic. He may, for this reason, have been
> more easily deceived by this fallacy.*

One benefit of modern techniques of symbolization is their ability to expose such fallacious reasoning, thus making it easier to understand and to avoid fallacies.

---

*O'Connor D., 1964

V. SYMBOLIZING ARGUMENTS

Another advantage of modern symbolic languages lies in their capacity to reveal important structural similarities that are shared by various types of arguments. Consider the following quasi-syllogism:

> All princes are handsome.
> William is a prince.
> _____
> William is handsome.

Assign predicate letters and the individual constant b in the following way:

> P: the class of princes
> H: the class of handsome persons
> b: William

Then, the argument can be translated into the following:

> $(x)(Px \rightarrow Hx)$
> Pb
> _____
> Hb

This form is somewhat similar to the form of *affirming the antecedent*, as follows:

> $p \rightarrow q$
> p
> _____
> q

Consider, moreover, that a universal generalization is a sentence that says something about every individual in the domain of interpretation. If what the universal generalization says is true of every individual in the domain, then it must be true of any *particular* individual in the domain. For example, based on the given interpretation, if

$$(x)(Px \rightarrow Hx)$$

is true, then so is the conditional sentence

$$Pb \rightarrow Hb$$

If William is a prince, then William is handsome.

If the first premiss of the original argument is replaced with a particular instance of the generalization ("$Pb \rightarrow Hb$"), then the argument becomes the following:

> $Pb \rightarrow Hb$
> Pb
> _____
> Hb

This argument is an instance of the form of affirming the antecedent and is therefore a valid argument form. The original quasi-syllogism is thus shown to be valid because it cannot have all true premises and a false conclusion. This treatment of singular premises of quasi-syllogisms seems less arbitrary than the treatment that transforms singular sentences to categorical sentences of the *A* or *E* form. There, sentences like "William is a prince" were treated as a type of universal generalization: "All members of the class of which William is the only member are princes," which is strange because universal generalizations lack existential import. The singular sentence "William is a prince," however, is regarded as false if he does not exist.

A detailed discussion of the systems of logic that employ quantifiers is beyond the scope of this text. It is worth noting, however, that all of these systems have a rule of inference that permits inferring particular instances from universally quantified sentences. Additional rules, subject to various restrictions, allow removing existential quantifiers and replacing both types of quantifiers after they have been removed. With this in mind, consider the similarity between one form of a categorical syllogism and the truth-functional form of a hypothetical syllogism:

$$(x)(Sx \rightarrow Mx) \qquad\qquad p \rightarrow q$$
$$\underline{(x)(Mx \rightarrow Px)} \qquad\qquad \underline{q \rightarrow r}$$
$$(x)(Sx \rightarrow Px) \qquad\qquad p \rightarrow r$$

Similarities among categorical syllogisms, truth-functional arguments, and relational arguments also become apparent when this symbolic language is used. For example, the validity of the following argument, "Marcy ran faster than Sam, and Sam ran faster than Carrie; therefore, Marcy ran faster than Carrie," depends on the true, but unstated, premiss that "ran faster than" is a transitive relationship. The argument can be symbolized, using the following interpretation:

$$R: \underline{\quad} \text{ ran faster than} \ldots$$
$$m: \text{Marcy}$$
$$s: \text{Sam}$$
$$c: \text{Carrie}$$

$$(x)(y)(z)((xRy \bullet yRz) \rightarrow xRz)$$
$$\underline{mRs \bullet sRc}$$
$$mRc$$

Replace the first premiss with a particular instance:

$$(mRs \bullet sRc) \rightarrow mRc$$

Again, the symbolism shows the similarity between this form and affirming the antecedent.

The value of symbolic techniques in modern logic should not be underestimated. The development of appropriate symbols has allowed advances in this field that are comparable to the advances in mathematics resulting from the replacement of the system of Roman numerals with the system of Arabic numerals.

VI. REVIEW

Chapter 10 has introduced some relational arguments. Their validity depends on the properties of **binary relationships** referred to in the arguments. Representing these arguments with the symbolic techniques of modern logic facilitates expression of the forms of these arguments and exposes similarities between these forms and familiar truth-functional forms.

Binary relationships fall into the following categories:

1. **transitive, intransitive, nontransitive**
2. **symmetric, asymmetric, nonsymmetric**
3. **reflexive, irreflexive, nonreflexive**

You should review the definitions presented in this chapter of these properties of relationships and be able to categorize examples of binary relationships according to these properties.

In many arguments in which validity depends on some property of a relationship referred to in the argument, the premisses do not say what that property is. You should be able to recognize such unstated premisses and supply them when you reconstruct these arguments.

You should be able to translate from English into logical symbolism both categorical sentences and sentences involving binary relationships. To do this, you need to remember that universal sentences are to be treated as quantified conditional sentences and that existential (particular) sentences are to be treated as quantified conjunctions.

Finally, you should be able to recognize apparent instances in English of the **fallacy of every and all**. This fallacy occurs when sentences containing both universal and existential quantifiers are treated as if truth is always preserved when the order in which their quantifiers occur is exchanged. The ability to symbolize such English sentences helps us to avoid this fallacy.

Exercise Set 10.5

PART I. For each of the following arguments, name the property of the relationship that makes the argument valid:

1. Three of the fastest cars in existence are the McLaren F1, the Ferrari Enzo, and the Jaguar XJ220. The McLaren is faster than the Ferrari, which beats the Jaguar, so the McLaren is faster than the Jaguar.

2. Six is greater than the square root of 34, so the square root of 34 is not greater than 6.

3. Caleb is Cara's twin, so Cara is the twin of Caleb.

4. Marilyn Monroe's hair is the same color as Lady Gaga's, and Marilyn is a blond, so Lady Gaga is a blond.

PART II. Relationships that are transitive, symmetric, and reflexive are called **equivalence relationships**. The relationship "is identical with" is an equivalence relationship. Give three other examples of equivalence relationships.

PART III. Relationships that are transitive, asymmetric, and irreflexive, such as "greater than," are called **ordering relationships**. Give an example of another ordering relationship.

PART IV. When an individual a is related by a relationship R to individual b, then b is said to be related to a by a relationship called the **converse** of R. What is the converse of the following relationships?

1. wife of

2. child of

3. heavier than

4. less than or equal to

5. sold by

6. spouse of

PART V. When a relationship is symmetric, what can we say about its converse?

PART VI. Provide a suitable interpretation of and translate the following into the symbolic language developed in this chapter, using relational predicates when appropriate:

1. McLaren F's are more expensive than Ferrari Enzos.

2. Some Bugatti Veyrons are faster than any Ferrari Enzo.

3. Every sailor fears some storm.

4. Some storm is feared by every sailor.

5. Christopher is Virginia's brother.

6. Not everyone has a cousin.

7. McLaren F1's and Ferrari Enzos are faster than Fords.

8. Snakes eat mice.

9. Not every rich person owns a piano.

10. Some people who are not rich own pianos.

11. Christopher plays pianos.

12. "Fears" is not a transitive relationship.

PART VII. Provide a suitable interpretation of and symbolize all four of the arguments in Part I of this exercise set. Be sure to symbolize the unstated premises in terms of the properties of the relationships involved as well as the stated premises.

PART VIII. G. E. M. Anscombe draws attention to the following argument. What is wrong with it?

> At all times there is a possibility of my abstaining from smoking. Therefore, there is a possibility of my abstaining from smoking at all times.
>
> —G. E. M. Anscombe, *An Introduction to Wittgenstein's Tractatus*, 1959

PART IX. Construct (or find) an example of an argument in English that apparently commits the fallacy of every and all.

PART X. Give an example of a relationship that is symmetric but not reflexive.

Appendix One

PROOF METHOD FOR TRUTH-FUNCTIONAL LOGIC

I. INTRODUCTION

An argument form is valid *if and only if* every consistent assignment of truth to all its premises assigns truth to its conclusion as well. Truth tables, by displaying all possible combinations of truth and falsity for premises and conclusion, provide a mechanical and reliable test for validity of any truth-functional argument form. An argument form is invalid if its truth table contains a row in which all the premises are assigned T and the conclusion is assigned F. Otherwise, the argument form is valid. Truth tables, however, become unwieldy when an argument form contains more than four distinct sentence letters. An argument form with six distinct letters, for example, requires a truth table with 64 rows to show all of the possible combinations of truth values, and each additional letter requires doubling the number of rows. Even the shorter truth-table method is burdensome when arguments have many premises or have complex conclusions that could be false in many different ways. The awkwardness of using truth tables for complex sentential arguments has motivated logicians to devise other methods for proving validity.

Some other proof methods are shorter than truth tables when applied to complex argument forms. Another benefit is that they can be extended to test validity of the more complicated argument forms of class logic and relational logic. Most proof methods taught in introductory logic classes are **natural deduction** systems. These systems contrast with **axiomatic** systems, such as the one you learned in high-school geometry. Axiomatic systems begin with a set of unproven statements (the axioms) and definitions that form a basis for the system. From these first principles, new statements, called "theorems" (conclusions), are derived. The theorems in turn can be used to prove other theorems. Aristotle's treatment of syllogistic logic is an axiomatic system. Aristotle took a small set of intuitively valid first-figure syllogisms as axioms and used such definitional principles as obversion and contraposition to derive all the other valid syllogisms.

Natural deduction systems differ from axiomatic systems insofar as in the former one begins with some premises and a conclusion and then uses a set of rules to work backward to first principles, or axioms. The definitions of truth-functional connectives, plus the understanding that every sentence is true or false and no sentence is both, are the basis of the rules, such as, "Whenever an argument has premises of the form $p \rightarrow q$ and p, infer q." In this case, the valid argument form *modus ponens* (affirming the antecedent) is the basis for a rule that allows drawing the conclusion q from premises $p \rightarrow q$ and p. In a similar manner, other valid forms can be transformed into rules of inference with the goal of providing a set of rules that is *complete,* in the sense that it permits inferring all conclusions—and only those conclusions—that follow validly from a given set of premises.

Some natural deduction systems require ingenuity on the part of the user. Faced with premises, a putative conclusion, and a set of rules, the student must figure out which rules are applicable and in which order they must be applied in order to move in a series of valid steps from premises to conclusion. Failure to derive the conclusion might be the result of a lack of cleverness in using the rules, or it might be because the argument is invalid. Other systems, such as the one presented here, can be applied mechanically. They allow us to break down complicated argument forms into simpler ones by eliminating connectives. In doing so, the goal is to reach argument forms in which the same sentence form appears both as a premiss and the conclusion. Such argument forms are obviously valid.

Our method uses **proof trees** to accomplish this transformation of complex argument forms into simpler ones. It is modeled on a simplified version of proof methods developed by Gerhard Gentzen.[1] This method is simple to use, and it always works—that is to say, for truth-functional argument forms, it always provides an answer to the question of whether a given sentence form (the conclusion) follows truth-functionally from a specific set of sentence forms (the premisses).

We use the logical symbols already introduced for negation ($\sim$), conjunction ($\bullet$), disjunction (v), material conditional ($\rightarrow$), and material biconditional ($\leftrightarrow$). In addition, we use the gate symbol ($\vdash$) to indicate the relationship of **logical consequence,** or **following from**. The conclusion in a deductively valid argument is a logical consequence of, or follows from, the premisses of that argument. In using this proof method, instead of writing an argument form, such as *modus ponens*, in the standard form in which a line separates the premisses from the conclusion:

$$\frac{\begin{array}{l} p \rightarrow q \\ p \end{array}}{q}$$

as we have been doing, we now write argument forms in the following way:

$$p \rightarrow q, p \vdash q$$

Premisses, separated from one another by commas, are written to the left of the gate; the conclusion is written to the right of the gate. The preceding expression, which is called a **sequent**, may be read "q follows from the premisses $p \rightarrow q$ and p."

The strings of sentence forms on the left and the right sides of the gate in a sequent are called **sequences**. In our example, the sequence on the left has two members ($p \rightarrow q$ and p); it is a sequence of "length two." The sequence on the right has one member (q); it is a sequence of "length one." Sequences may be of "length zero," in which case they are called **empty sequences**, or their length may be equal to any positive integer. All sequences are finite in length.

We have seen that when the length of a sequence on the left side of the gate is greater than one, the members of the sequence are separated by commas and each comma on the left is read as "and." (The conclusion of an argument form follows from

[1]See Stig Kanger, "A Simplified Proof Method for Elementary Logic," in *Computer Programming and Formal System,* edited by P. Baffort and D. Hirschberg.

the first premiss and the second premiss and the third, and so forth.) When more than one member of the sequence appears on the right side of the gate, these members are also separated by commas, but each comma on the right is read as "or." For example, we may read the sequent

$$p \vee q, p \rightarrow r, p \rightarrow s, \sim q \vdash r \bullet s, t \rightarrow p$$

as "Either $r \bullet s$ or $t \rightarrow p$ follows from the premisses $p \vee q$, and $p \rightarrow r$, and $p \rightarrow s$, and $\sim q$." Although any argument form has only one conclusion, the rules of deriving the conclusion from the premisses sometimes require moving a sequent from the left to the right of the gate. When this happens, commas can occur to the right.

An empty sequence to the left of the gate indicates a true (although unspecified) premiss. An empty sequence to the right of the gate indicates a true conclusion.

1. Read the following sequent:

$$\vdash p \rightarrow (q \vee \sim q)$$

as "$p \rightarrow (q \vee \sim q)$ follows from any true premiss."

2. Read the following sequent:

$$p, p \rightarrow q, \sim p \vdash$$

as "Any true conclusion follows from p, and $p \rightarrow q$, and $\sim p$."

Remember that since an argument form is invalid only if it can have all true premisses and a false conclusion, any argument form with a conclusion that can only be assigned T is valid as is any argument form with premisses that cannot all be assigned T. In other words, any argument form with a tautological conclusion or with contradictory premisses is valid.

If a sentence form follows from any true premiss, then that sentence form must itself always be true. In other words, a sentence form that follows from any true premiss whatsoever is a **tautology**. Similarly, if a set of premisses deductively yields any true conclusion whatsoever, that set of premisses must be **contradictory**.

II. THE PROOF METHOD

In the following discussion, we use the Roman capital letters "**A**" and "**B**" to refer to sentence forms. The sentence forms thus denoted may be either simple or complex. We use the script capital letters "𝒟," "ℰ," "ℱ," and "𝒢" to denote finite and possibly empty sequences of sentence forms. These letters are useful in applying the proof method because the method proceeds by eliminating one connective at a time. The upper case

Roman and script letters are placeholders for sentence forms and strings of sentence forms that are not being changed in a given operation.

The proof method employs 11 rules, or **postulates**, which include one axiom and 10 rules of inference. Postulates P.1 through P.11 are presented schematically here, with brief comments.

P.1 $\mathcal{D}$, **A**, $\mathcal{E}$ ⊢ $\mathcal{F}$, **A**, $\mathcal{G}$ (axiom)

In this sequent, the same *sentence form* (**A**) occurs both to the left and to the right of the gate; on both sides, it is separated from the other **sequences of sentence forms** ($\mathcal{D}$, $\mathcal{E}$, $\mathcal{F}$, and $\mathcal{G}$) by commas. This means that a **disjunction** that contains **A** is said to follow from a set of premises that includes **A**. Such a disjunction could not fail to follow, for if **A** is a true premiss, then the disjunction contains a true disjunct, and the disjunction is true also. Thus, all the premises cannot be true while the conclusion is false. In our proof method, this instance of the **consequence relationship** is considered to be a fundamentally valid argument form (an **axiom scheme**).

The rules of inference in this proof method are used to eliminate connectives, with the goal of "reducing" the original argument form to a series of simpler forms that are instances of the axiom. Each of the rules of inference (P.2 through P.11) allows us to eliminate a main connective in a sentence form on either the left or the right side of the gate.

P.2 $$\frac{\mathcal{D} \vdash \mathcal{F}, \sim\textbf{A}, \mathcal{G}}{\textbf{A}, \mathcal{D} \vdash \mathcal{F}, \mathcal{G}}$$ (eliminates ~ on right)

P.3 $$\frac{\mathcal{D}, \sim \textbf{A}, \mathcal{E} \vdash \mathcal{F}}{\mathcal{D}, \mathcal{E} \vdash \textbf{A}, \mathcal{F}}$$ (eliminates ~ on left)

P.4 $$\frac{\mathcal{D} \vdash \mathcal{F}, \textbf{A} \cdot \textbf{B}, \mathcal{G}}{\mathcal{D} \vdash \mathcal{F}, \textbf{A}, \mathcal{G} \qquad \mathcal{D} \vdash \mathcal{F}, \textbf{B}, \mathcal{G}}$$ (eliminates • on right)

P.5 $$\frac{\mathcal{D}, \textbf{A} \cdot \textbf{B}, \mathcal{E} \vdash \mathcal{F}}{\mathcal{D}, \textbf{A}, \textbf{B}, \mathcal{E} \vdash \mathcal{F}}$$ (eliminates • on left)

P.6 $$\frac{\mathcal{D} \vdash \mathcal{F}, \textbf{A} \vee \textbf{B}, \mathcal{G}}{\mathcal{D} \vdash \mathcal{F}, \textbf{A}, \textbf{B}, \mathcal{G}}$$ (eliminates v on right)

P.7 $$\frac{\mathcal{D}, \textbf{A} \vee \textbf{B}, \mathcal{E} \vdash \mathcal{F}}{\mathcal{D}, \textbf{A}, \mathcal{E} \vdash \mathcal{F} \qquad \mathcal{D}, \textbf{B}, \mathcal{E} \vdash \mathcal{F}}$$ (eliminates v on left)

P.8 $$\frac{\mathcal{D} \vdash \mathcal{F}, \textbf{A} \rightarrow \textbf{B}, \mathcal{G}}{\textbf{A}, \mathcal{D} \vdash \mathcal{F}, \textbf{B}, \mathcal{G}}$$ (eliminates → on right)

P.9 $$\frac{\mathcal{D}, \textbf{A} \rightarrow \textbf{B}, \mathcal{E} \vdash \mathcal{F}}{\mathcal{D}, \mathcal{E} \vdash \textbf{A}, \mathcal{F} \qquad \mathcal{D}, \textbf{B}, \mathcal{E} \vdash \mathcal{F}}$$ (eliminates → on left)

P.10

$$\frac{\mathcal{D} \vdash \mathcal{F}, \mathbf{A} \leftrightarrow \mathbf{B}, \mathcal{G}}{\mathbf{A}, \mathcal{D} \vdash \mathcal{F}, \mathbf{B}, \mathcal{G} \qquad \mathbf{B}, \mathcal{D} \vdash \mathcal{F}, \mathbf{A}, \mathcal{G}}$$ (eliminates $\leftrightarrow$ on right)

P.11

$$\frac{\mathcal{D}, \mathbf{A} \leftrightarrow \mathbf{B}, \mathcal{E} \vdash \mathcal{F}}{\mathcal{D}, \mathcal{E} \vdash \mathbf{A}, \mathbf{B}, \mathcal{F} \qquad \mathbf{A}, \mathbf{B}, \mathcal{D}, \mathcal{E} \vdash \mathcal{F}}$$ (eliminates $\leftrightarrow$ on left)

When we want to show that one sequence follows from another, we write the premiss sequence, followed by a gate, followed by the conclusion. Then we draw a line below that sequent and construct a "tree" of sequents below it, using the rules of inference (P.2 through P.11). If we are able to construct a tree with an instance of P.1 (the axiom) at the bottom of every branch, the proof has succeeded. If the sequence on the right is a logical consequence of the sequence on the left, we will always be able to construct such a tree. If, after eliminating all connectives in a branch, the branch does not end in an axiom, then the original argument form is invalid.

In addition to the axiom and rules of inference of the proof method, one strategic rule for constructing proofs should be noted. Frequently we may be able to continue a branch of the tree in more than one way because we have more than one main connective to eliminate. When this happens, we always prefer applications of P.2, P.3, P.5, P.6, and P.8 to applications of the other rules. Our preference for these rules will minimize tree branching because these rules themselves do not branch. Before we focus on considering the justification of inference rules, we consider some examples of proofs.

Examples

a. To show that $p \vee q$ follows from p, we construct the following tree:

$$\frac{p \vdash p \vee q \quad \text{(apply P.6)}}{p \vdash p, q \quad \text{(axiom)}}$$

Here, only one main connective (the $\vee$ on the right) can be eliminated. Thus, P.6 is the appropriate rule. In applying P.6 to the sequent on the top line, $\mathbf{A}$ represents p, the sentence form to the left of the connective, and $\mathbf{B}$ represents q, the sentence form to the right of the connective. $\mathcal{D}$ represents the sequence that is to the left of the gate (p). $\mathcal{F}$ and $\mathcal{G}$ are the sequences to the right and to the left of the sentence form $\mathbf{A} \vee \mathbf{B}$, respectively; in this example, $\mathcal{F}$ and $\mathcal{G}$ are empty sequences. In the sequent below the line, the same sequence $\mathcal{D}$ (p) is to the left of the gate. On the right of the gate, the $\vee$ has been eliminated and replaced by a comma. The sequent below the line is an instance of the axiom, for the same sentence form (namely, p) occurs, separated from other sentence forms by commas, on the right of the gate and also on the left. Thus, we have shown that $p \vee q$ follows deductively from p.

b. To show that q follows from $p \rightarrow q$, $\sim p \rightarrow r$, and $\sim q \rightarrow \sim r$, we construct the following tree:

(1)
$$p \rightarrow q, \sim p \rightarrow r, \sim q \rightarrow \sim r \vdash q$$

(2) $\sim p \rightarrow r, \sim q \rightarrow \sim r \vdash p, q$ $q, \sim p \rightarrow r, \sim q \rightarrow \sim r \vdash q^*$

(3) $\sim q \rightarrow \sim r \vdash \sim p, p, q$ $r, \sim q \rightarrow \sim r \vdash p, q$

(4) $p, \sim q \rightarrow \sim r \vdash p, q^*$ $r \vdash \sim q, p, q$ $r, \sim r \vdash p, q$

(5) $q, r \vdash p, q^*$ $r \vdash r, p, q^*$

Line (1) contains the sequent, with the premises on the left and the conclusion on the right of the gate. The only main connectives are $\rightarrow$s to the left of the gate, so the only applicable rule is a branching one, P.9, which could be applied to any of the three sentence forms that make up the sequence on the left.

In this proof, P.9 is applied to the first conditional, $p \rightarrow q$. Thus, **A** is p, and **B** is q. $\mathcal{D}$, which refers to any sequence to the left of $\mathbf{A} \rightarrow \mathbf{B}$, is empty, and $\mathcal{E}$ denotes the sequence $\sim p \rightarrow r, \sim q \rightarrow \sim r$. $\mathcal{F}$ refers to everything to the right of the gate (in this case, q).

Line (2) is the result of applying P.9 to $p \rightarrow q$ in line (1). The right-hand branch ends in an axiom (indicated by the *), with an occurrence of the sentence form q on both the right and the left sides of the gate. That branch is now complete. The left branch is not an instance of the axiom but contains further connectives that may be removed. Again, the only main connectives are the $\rightarrow$s on the left, so P.9 is applicable.

Line (3) is the result of applying P.9 to $\sim p \rightarrow r$ in line (2). Here, **A** is $\sim p$, and **B** is r. $\mathcal{D}$ is empty, $\mathcal{E}$ is $\sim q \rightarrow \sim r$, and $\mathcal{F}$ is the sequence p, q. Neither of these branches is an instance of the axiom, but connectives remain, so each branch is continued.

On the left branch of the tree in line (3), a main connective on the right is a negation sign. Our strategy rule tells us to prefer the application of P.2 over any of the branching rules. Applying P.2 gives us p as **A** and $\sim q \rightarrow \sim r$ as $\mathcal{D}$. $\mathcal{F}$ is empty, and $\mathcal{G}$ is the sequence p, q to the right of $\sim \mathbf{A}$. After applying P.2, this branch ends in an instance of the axiom on the left branch of line (4).

In the right branch of the tree, the only main connective is once more a $\rightarrow$ on the left side of the gate, so that P.9 is applicable. Line (4) on the right gives the result of applying this branching rule. Neither branch ends in an axiom at this stage, so both branches continue.

In the left branch, a negation on the right is eliminated by applying P.2, which results in the branch ending in an axiom on line (5). In the right branch, there is a negation on the left, which is eliminated by applying P.3; that branch also ends in an axiom on line (5).

Thus, each branch of the tree ends in an axiom, and we have succeeded in proving that q is a consequence of $p \rightarrow q$, $\sim p \rightarrow r$, and $\sim q \rightarrow \sim r$.

c. To show that $\sim q$ is not a consequence of $p \rightarrow q$ and $\sim p$, we construct the following tree:

(1) $\qquad \dfrac{p \rightarrow q,\ \sim p \vdash \sim q}{}$

(2) $\qquad \dfrac{p \rightarrow q \vdash p,\ \sim q}{}$ $\qquad$ (P.3 applied to $\sim p$)

(3) $\qquad \dfrac{q,\ p \rightarrow q \vdash p}{}$ $\qquad$ (P.2 applied to $\sim q$)

(4) $\qquad q \vdash p,\ p \qquad q,\ q \vdash p$ $\qquad$ (P.9 applied to $p \rightarrow q$)

In this case, we see two branches on line (4) that do not end in axioms. Whenever at least one branch does not end in an axiom and cannot be extended because no more connectives can be removed, we have a proof that the alleged conclusion does not follow from these premises—that the argument form is invalid.

d. To show that $\sim(p \bullet q) \leftrightarrow (\sim p \vee \sim q)$ is a tautology, we construct the following tree:

(1) $\qquad\qquad \dfrac{\vdash \sim(p \bullet q) \leftrightarrow (\sim p \vee \sim q)}{}$ $\qquad$ (P.10)

(2) $\quad \dfrac{\sim(p \bullet q) \vdash \sim p \vee \sim q}{}$ (P.3) $\quad \dfrac{\sim p \vee \sim q \vdash \sim (p \bullet q)}{}$ (P.2)

(3) $\quad \dfrac{\vdash p \bullet q,\ \sim p \vee \sim q}{}$ (P.6) $\quad \dfrac{p \bullet q,\ \sim p \vee \sim q \vdash}{}$ (P.5)

(4) $\quad \dfrac{\vdash p \bullet q,\ \sim p,\ \sim q}{}$ (P.2) $\quad \dfrac{p,\ q,\ \sim p \vee \sim q \vdash}{}$ (P.7)

(5) $\dfrac{p \vdash p \bullet q,\ \sim q}{}$ (P.2) $\quad \dfrac{p,\ q,\ \sim p \vdash}{}$ (P.3) $\quad \dfrac{p,\ q,\ \sim q \vdash}{}$ (P.3)

(6) $\dfrac{q,\ p \vdash p \bullet q}{}$ (P.7) $\quad p,\ q \vdash p^*$ $\qquad\qquad$ $p,\ q \vdash q^*$

(7) $p,\ q \vdash q^* \quad p,\ q \vdash q^*$

Note that each branch of this tree ends in an axiom. To prove that a sentence form is a tautology, it is sufficient to show that the sentence form follows from any true premiss. Thus, we set up the proof by placing an empty sequence to the left of the gate and the supposed tautology to the right of the gate. If every branch does end in an axiom, we have shown that the sentence follows from any true premiss and that it must itself be true. If some branch fails to end in an axiom and cannot be continued, then the sentence form is not a tautology.

Exercise Set A.1

PART I. Use the proof method to determine the validity or the invalidity of each of the following argument forms:

1. $\dfrac{p \rightarrow q}{p \rightarrow (p \bullet q)}$

2. $\dfrac{p \vee q}{\sim p \vee \sim q}$

3. $\dfrac{p \rightarrow (q \rightarrow r)}{(p \rightarrow q) \rightarrow r}$

4. $\dfrac{p \rightarrow (q \rightarrow r)}{(p \bullet q) \rightarrow r}$

5. $p \rightarrow (q \rightarrow r)$
$(q \rightarrow r) \rightarrow s$
_____
$p \rightarrow s$

6. $p \rightarrow (q \rightarrow r)$
$q \rightarrow (r \rightarrow s)$
_____
$p \rightarrow s$

7. $(p \lor q) \rightarrow (p \bullet q)$
$p \bullet q$
_____
$p \lor q$

8. p
_____
$(q \rightarrow r) \rightarrow p$

9. $((p \lor q) \rightarrow r) \lor ((p \rightarrow r) \bullet q)$
_____
r

10. $(p \lor q) \rightarrow r$
_____
$(p \bullet q) \rightarrow r$

PART II. Use the proof method to determine whether the following sentence form is *tautologous*:

$$(p \rightarrow (q \rightarrow r)) \rightarrow ((p \rightarrow q) \rightarrow (p \rightarrow r))$$

How many rows would a truth table require to show this? How many columns would it take to construct a truth table for this sentence form?

PART III. Use the proof method to show whether the following sentence form is a *self-contradiction*:

$$(p \rightarrow q) \bullet (q \rightarrow r) \bullet p \bullet \sim r$$

III. JUSTIFYING THE RULES OF INFERENCE

It is clear that we can use this set of rules of inference without understanding their justification. A machine could be programmed rather easily to apply the rules to whatever argument forms are fed into it and give the correct answers to whether the forms were valid or invalid. But there is some intellectual value in looking at the justification of each rule.

A deductive rule of inference is **justified** when it can be shown that the use of the rule will never lead from true premises to a false conclusion—in other words, when it can be shown that the rule is **truth-preserving**.

When we remove connectives by using the rules of inference in this proof method, we reduce a complicated sequent (argument form) to a series of **less complicated** sequents, in the sense that each of the sequents below the lines has fewer truth-functional connectives than the sequents above the lines. What we want to show is that the use of any of the rules P.2 through P.11 for eliminating connectives will result in sequents below the line with right-hand sequences that are the logical consequences of their left-hand sequences if and only if the right-hand sequence above the line is a logical consequence of its left-hand sequence.

The rules of inference used in this proof method depend for their justification on:

1. The definition of *logical consequence*, which states that a sentence (or sentence form) **A** is a logical consequence of a set of sentences (or sentence forms) $\mathcal{D}$ if it is impossible for all of the sentences (sentence forms) in the set $\mathcal{D}$ to be true while the sentence (sentence form) **A** is false.
2. The definitions of the **truth-functional connectives** ($\sim$, v, •, $\rightarrow$, $\leftrightarrow$).
3. The understanding that commas to the left of the gate represent "and" and that commas to the right of the gate represent "or."

In each rule, we note that the sequences $\mathcal{D}$, $\mathcal{E}$, $\mathcal{F}$, and $\mathcal{G}$ simply reappear unchanged in the sequents below the line. They are never dropped or modified in any way. For this reason, we can ignore their content in justifying rules P.2 through P.11. In other words, we can simply regard these sequences as empty sequences and focus on how the removal of the connectives that relate **A** and **B** affects the consequence relationship.

Justification of P.2

P.2
$$\frac{\mathcal{D} \vdash \mathcal{F}, \sim\mathbf{A}, \mathcal{G}}{\mathbf{A}, \mathcal{D} \vdash \mathcal{F}, \mathcal{G}}$$
(eliminates $\sim$ on right)

If we regard the sequences $\mathcal{D}$, $\mathcal{F}$, and $\mathcal{G}$ as empty, then the sequent above the line says that $\sim\mathbf{A}$ is a consequence of an empty sequence. This means that $\sim\mathbf{A}$ must be a tautology. Then **A** itself must be a self-contradiction because **A** is equivalent to the denial of $\sim\mathbf{A}$, and the denial of a sentence form that must be true is a sentence form that must be false. But if **A** is a self-contradiction, then any conclusion, including an empty sequence, follows from it. The sequent below the line says that an empty sequence follows from **A**, and this is so if and only if $\sim\mathbf{A}$ follows from an empty sequence.

Justification of P.3

P.3
$$\frac{\mathcal{D}, \sim\mathbf{A}, \mathcal{E} \vdash \mathcal{F}}{\mathcal{D}, \mathcal{E} \vdash \mathbf{A}, \mathcal{F}}$$
(eliminates $\sim$ on left)

Again, we assume that $\mathcal{D}$, $\mathcal{E}$, and $\mathcal{F}$ are empty. Then the sequent above the line in P.3 says that an empty sequence follows from $\sim\mathbf{A}$. Thus, $\sim\mathbf{A}$ is a self-contradiction. But this means that **A** is a tautology, and a tautology follows from an empty sequence. So the consequence relationship holds in the sequent below the line in P.3 if and only if it holds in the sequent above the line.

Justification of P.4

P.4
$$\frac{\mathcal{D} \vdash \mathcal{F}, \mathbf{A} • \mathbf{B}, \mathcal{G}}{\mathcal{D} \vdash \mathcal{F}, \mathbf{A}, \mathcal{G} \qquad \mathcal{D} \vdash \mathcal{F}, \mathbf{B}, \mathcal{G}}$$
(eliminates • on right)

P.4 allows us to eliminate a conjunction (•) on the right side of the gate. If a conjunction follows from any premises—including the **empty set** of premises—then each of the conjuncts separately follows from those same premises. Thus, there are two sequents below the line, and each of these sequents contains one conjunct on the right side of the gate. Conversely, if each of two sentence forms follows from identical sets of premises, then their conjunction follows from that set of premises.

Justification of P.5

P.5

$$\frac{\mathscr{D}, \mathbf{A} \cdot \mathbf{B}, \mathscr{E} \vdash \mathscr{F}}{\mathscr{D}, \mathbf{A}, \mathbf{B}, \mathscr{E} \vdash \mathscr{F}}$$ (eliminates • on left)

P.5 allows us to eliminate a conjunction (•) on the left side of the gate. Consider an argument form with a conjunction with two members (**A** and **B**) as its only premiss. A conjunction is true if and only if both of its conjuncts are true. If the conclusion follows from this premiss, then the conclusion clearly follows from the two premises **A** and **B**. If the conclusion does not follow from **A** • **B**, then it will not follow from the two separate premises **A** and **B**. In P.5, a conjunctive premiss above the line is simply split into two separate premises below the line. (Remember that the comma on the left side of the gate is read as "and.") All other sequences ($\mathscr{D}$, $\mathscr{E}$, and $\mathscr{F}$) are simply carried along without alteration.

Justification of P.6

P.6

$$\frac{\mathscr{D} \vdash \mathscr{F}, \mathbf{A} \vee \mathbf{B}, \mathscr{G}}{\mathscr{D} \vdash \mathscr{F}, \mathbf{A}, \mathbf{B}, \mathscr{G}}$$ (eliminates v on right)

The justification of P.6 is quite obvious if we consider that commas on the right side of the gate are read as "or." To apply P.6, a wedge (v) on the right side of the gate is replaced by a comma. If the disjunction **A** v **B** follows from the premises on the left, then either **A** follows from those premises or **B** does. If the disjunction does not follow, then it is not true that either **A** or **B** follows from the premises.

Justification of P.7

P.7

$$\frac{\mathscr{D}, \mathbf{A} \vee \mathbf{B}, \mathscr{E} \vdash \mathscr{F}}{\mathscr{D}, \mathbf{A}, \mathscr{E} \vdash \mathscr{F} \qquad \mathscr{D}, \mathbf{B}, \mathscr{E} \vdash \mathscr{F}}$$ (eliminates v on left)

To apply P.7, a wedge on the left side of the gate is eliminated by a split. If a conclusion follows from a disjunction (**A** v **B**), the conclusion must be true if either **A** is true or **B** is true. However, this is equivalent to saying that the conclusion follows from **A** and also from **B**. Thus, there are two sequents below the line, and each sequent contains one disjunct as a premiss. Also, if a conclusion follows from either of two premisses considered separately, then it clearly follows from the disjunction of those same premisses.

Justification of P.8

P.8
$$\frac{\mathscr{D} \vdash \mathscr{F}, \mathbf{A} \rightarrow \mathbf{B}, \mathscr{G}}{\mathbf{A}, \mathscr{D} \vdash \mathscr{F}, \mathbf{B}, \mathscr{G}}$$
    (eliminates $\rightarrow$ on right)

If a material conditional follows from some premisses and if all of the premisses are true, then the conditional is also true. But if the conditional is true, then it cannot be the case that its antecedent is true and its consequent is false. Thus, if the antecedent of the conditional is added to the premisses, then the consequent must follow from those premisses supplemented by its antecedent. Similarly, if **B** follows from premisses that include **A**, then the sentence form **A→B** will be true if those premisses (excluding **A**) are all true. This justifies the application of P.8.

Justification of P.9

P.9
$$\frac{\mathscr{D}, \mathbf{A} \rightarrow \mathbf{B}, \mathscr{E} \vdash \mathscr{F}}{\mathscr{D}, \mathscr{E} \vdash \mathbf{A}, \mathscr{F}, \qquad \mathscr{D}, \mathbf{B}, \mathscr{E} \vdash \mathscr{F}}$$
    (eliminates $\rightarrow$ on left)

Consider that **A** $\rightarrow$ **B** is logically equivalent to $\sim$**A** v **B**. If we apply P.7 to the sequent $\mathscr{D}$, $\sim$**A** v **B**, $\mathscr{E} \vdash \mathscr{F}$, we obtain sequents $\mathscr{D}$, $\sim$**A**, $\mathscr{E} \vdash \mathscr{F}$ and $\mathscr{D}$, **B**, $\mathscr{E} \vdash \mathscr{F}$ below the line. If we then apply P.3 to $\mathscr{D}$, $\sim$**A**, $\mathscr{E} \vdash \mathscr{F}$, we obtain $\mathscr{D}$, $\mathscr{E} \vdash$ **A**, $\mathscr{F}$. This sequent and the sequent $\mathscr{D}$, **B**, $\mathscr{E} \vdash \mathscr{F}$ occur below the line in the application of P.9.

Justification of P.10 and P.11

P.10
$$\frac{\mathscr{D} \vdash \mathscr{F}, \mathbf{A} \leftrightarrow \mathbf{B}, \mathscr{G}}{\mathbf{A}, \mathscr{D} \vdash \mathscr{F}, \mathbf{B}, \mathscr{G} \qquad \mathbf{B}, \mathscr{D} \vdash \mathscr{F}, \mathbf{A}, \mathscr{G}}$$
    (eliminates $\leftrightarrow$ on right)

P.11
$$\frac{\mathscr{D}, \mathbf{A} \leftrightarrow \mathbf{B}, \mathscr{E} \vdash \mathscr{F}}{\mathscr{D}, \mathscr{E} \vdash \mathbf{A}, \mathbf{B}, \mathscr{F} \qquad \mathbf{A}, \mathbf{B}, \mathscr{D}, \mathscr{E} \vdash \mathscr{F}}$$
    (eliminates $\leftrightarrow$ on left)

These justifications are left as exercises. In each case, consider that **A** $\leftrightarrow$ **B** is logically equivalent to $(\mathbf{A} \rightarrow \mathbf{B}) \cdot (\mathbf{B} \rightarrow \mathbf{A})$.

It is interesting to note that this proof method may be used effectively even when the user does not understand the justifications of the rules of inference or why they work. The rules work in such a way that machines can be designed to test the validity of argument forms, as well as to test whether sentence forms are tautologous or self-contradictory. If you have some computer experience, you might try to write a program for generating proofs using this proof method.

Exercise Set A.2

PART I. Use the proof method to decide whether the last sentence form is a logical consequence of the remaining sentence forms:

1. $p \rightarrow q$
   $\sim p \rightarrow r$
   $\sim q \rightarrow r$
   $\sim q$

2. $p \rightarrow q$
   $r \rightarrow \sim s$
   $q \rightarrow r$
   $p \rightarrow \sim s$

3. $(p \cdot q) \rightarrow (r \cdot s)$
   $\sim (q \vee s)$
   $t \rightarrow (\sim q \rightarrow (p \cdot r))$
   $\sim t$

4. $p \rightarrow q$
   $r \rightarrow s$
   $\sim s \rightarrow p$
   $q \rightarrow r$
   $\sim s \rightarrow t$

5. $(p \rightarrow q) \vee (r \rightarrow s)$
   $(p \rightarrow s) \vee (r \rightarrow q)$

6. $(p \leftrightarrow q) \rightarrow r$
   $\sim r$
   $\sim p \cdot \sim q$
   s

PART II. Use the proof method to determine which of the following are tautologies. Take care to identify the main connectives correctly.

1. $(p \rightarrow q) \vee (\sim p \rightarrow q)$
2. $(p \rightarrow q) \rightarrow ((r \rightarrow (q \rightarrow s)) \rightarrow (r \rightarrow (p \rightarrow s)))$
3. $((p \rightarrow q) \rightarrow (q \rightarrow r)) \leftrightarrow (q \rightarrow r)$
4. $((p \rightarrow q) \rightarrow r) \rightarrow ((p \rightarrow r) \rightarrow r)$
5. $(\sim p \rightarrow r) \rightarrow ((q \rightarrow r) \rightarrow (p \rightarrow q) \rightarrow r)$
6. $\sim (p \rightarrow q) \leftrightarrow (q \rightarrow \sim q)$

PART III. Using sentence letters to represent simple sentences, translate each of the following English arguments into argument forms. Then use the proof method to determine the validity or the invalidity of each argument form.

1. Either the economy will improve, or the stock market will crash. If the stock market crashes, banks will fail. But banks will not fail. So it is not the case that if the economy improves, the banks will fail.

2. The president is happy if and only if his favorite bills are passed by Congress. If the president is happy, his staff feels good. But if the staff members feel good, they are in no condition to work for the bills, and if that is the case, the president's favorite bills will not be passed by Congress. Therefore, the president is unhappy.

3. If the Republicans choose a good candidate, they will win the election unless there is a split in the party. It is not true that if the Republicans meet in Chicago, there will be a split in the party. But if they meet in Chicago, they will choose a good candidate. So they will choose a good candidate, and they will win the election.

4. If some archaeologists are correct, then the first humans entered North America across the Bering Strait 30,000 years ago. If they crossed the Bering Strait 30,000 years ago, they must have spent time in what is now Alaska. If they spent time in what is now Alaska, they must have left artifacts with radiocarbon dates of about 30,000 years old. If such artifacts are there, they will be uncovered if the archaeologists excavate. So if the archaeologists excavate and if some archaeologists are correct, then they will uncover 30,000 year-old artifacts in Alaska.

Appendix Two

INDEX OF FALLACIES

From the time of Aristotle, fallacies have been studied in both informal and formal accounts of reasoning. In this text, the fallacies have been treated for the most part as departures from correct standards of reasoning. For this reason, they have been introduced in connection with correct patterns of reasoning that they superficially resemble. A more traditional way of handling fallacies is to treat them in a separate chapter, classifying them in three groups: material (for example, the appeal to pity), verbal (for example, equivocation), and formal (for example, affirming the antecedent). This appendix lists the fallacies treated in the text, with a brief explanation of each type. For a more traditional discussion, you can read the brief article entitled "Fallacy" in the *Encyclopedia Brittanica*, which also contains useful references to some of the classical treatments of the subject.

Ad Baculum: (*See* **Appeal to Force.**)

Ad Hoc **Reasoning:** This fallacious form of reasoning occurs when auxiliary hypotheses are rejected (or invoked) merely to save a favored hypothesis. Hypotheses are tested by deriving predictions from them and observing whether the predictions are true. However, deriving predictions requires the aid of additional assumptions (auxiliary hypotheses). These provide the links between the predictions and the hypothesis that is tested. When the auxiliary hypotheses lack independent justification, they are called *ad hoc* assumptions. To invoke such assumptions is to be guilty of *ad hoc* reasoning. For example, auxiliary hypotheses concerning the reliability of observers and instruments of observation are often employed. If an observation fails to support a hypothesis and the blame is laid on a faulty instrument—without any independent evidence that the instrument is at fault—one should suspect the fallacy of *ad hoc* reasoning.

Ad Hominem: (*See* **Fallacious Argument against the Person.**)

Ad Misericordium: (*See* **Appeal to Pity.**)

Affirming the Consequent: This fallacious form of argument resembles the valid form of denying the consequent. Its structure involves a conditional premiss ("If p, then q"), an additional premiss that affirms the consequent (q), and a conclusion that affirms the antecedent (p). The form is fallacious because instances of it can have all true premisses and a false conclusion. A truth table can be used to show that the form is fallacious.

A counterexample with obviously true premisses and an obviously false conclusion can also show that the form is fallacious.

Appeal to Force: This fallacy occurs when a threat of force is somehow put forth as evidence, or taken as evidence, for a conclusion.

Appeal to Pity: This fallacy occurs when sympathy or pity for the circumstances of some person or persons is somehow put forth as evidence, or taken as evidence, for a conclusion.

Begging the Question: This fallacy occurs when some point—which might not be stated—is assumed to be true in the absence of any justification for its truth.

Biased Statistics: Fallacious arguments that depend on biased statistics may have the same structure as correct inductive arguments, but they are based on samples that have not been designed to capture the relevant variety in a population. We have reason to believe that the samples in such fallacious arguments are not representative of the populations from which they are selected.

Black-and-White Thinking: Whenever we neglect to look at a whole range of alternative possibilities and focus only on the extremes (for example, best–worst, priceless–worthless, friend–foe), and when we frame an argument, such as a disjunctive syllogism or dilemma, in terms of the extremes, we commit the fallacy of black-and-white thinking. Other names for the fallacy are **False Dilemma** and **False Choice**.

Circular Reasoning: This fallacy occurs when the conclusion merely restates the premisses of an argument, especially when the premisses are no more plausible than the conclusion that they are supposed to support. If the conclusion of an argument is in doubt, then premisses that are equally dubious give us little reason to believe the conclusion. (Circular arguments are deductively valid because their conclusions cannot be false if all their premisses are true, but the accusation of circularity has to do with how persuasive an argument is in a given context rather than its formal validity.)

Composition: This fallacy occurs when a term that is used distributively (referring to each member of a class or each part of a whole) in the premisses is interpreted collectively (referring to the class or the whole) in the conclusion. In such cases, the term is used in different senses in the premisses and in the conclusion.

Confusing Cause and Effect: This fallacy occurs when insufficient attention is given to causal ordering, leading to misidentification of that which is cause and that which is effect in a causal relationship. Because it is understood that effects cannot precede their causes, many instances of this fallacy result from carelessness in sorting out which event is temporally prior to the other.

Confusing Coincidental Relationships with Causal Relationships (*Post Hoc*): Temporal succession of events is not adequate evidence of a causal relationship between the events; one needs some evidence that the connection is regular. But if an event is unusually interesting or important, we look for its cause and sometimes (fallaciously) identify some pertinent preceding event as "the cause" on grounds of precedence alone.

Confusing the Harm or Benefits That Result from Holding a Belief with Evidence for It: The name of the fallacy describes it. We are in danger of committing this fallacy when our ability to assess evidence for a claim is clouded by a desire to achieve the perceived benefits that would result if that claim were true or to avoid the perceived harms if that claim were false.

Denying the Antecedent: This fallacy occurs when we offer or accept as valid the following form of argument:

If p, then q, but not p, therefore not q.

This invalid form resembles the valid form of denying the consequent.

Division: This fallacy occurs when a term that is used collectively in the premises is interpreted distributively in the conclusion. As in the **fallacy of composition**, the term is used in one sense in the premises and in a different sense in the conclusion.

Equivocation: If the conclusion of an argument depends on a shift in meaning of an ambiguous term, phrase, or grammatical construction in the context of that argument, the fallacy of equivocation is committed. When the middle term in a categorical syllogism is used equivocally, the result is a **fallacy of four terms** (as opposed to the three terms required for a valid syllogism).

Every and All: Sentences that contain both universal and existential quantifiers (*every, all, none, some*) can change meaning when the order of the quantifiers is reversed. For example, *someone* in "Everyone loves someone" means "someone or other," whereas *someone* in "Someone is loved by everyone" means "some one person." The first sentence follows from the second, but the second does not follow from the first. If the conclusion of an argument depends on a failure to recognize such a shift in meaning, the fallacy of every and all is committed.

Fallacies of Distribution: (*See* **Composition and Division**.)

Fallacious Appeal to Consensus: Arguments that offer majority opinion as a reason to believe some claim are fallacious *unless* there is a good reason to believe that the majority opinion on the subject matter of the claim is correct. In general, the mere fact that many people or even most people believe a claim is not good evidence for it.

Fallacious Argument against the Person: An argument that concludes that a claim is false because it was made by a particular person is fallacious *unless* there are good reasons to believe that most of what that person says about the subject matter of the conclusion is false. Sometimes the character of the person is attacked (**Abusive**

ad Hominem), sometimes the person's circumstances are attacked (**Circumstantial ad Hominem**), and sometimes the person is attacked for somehow being associated with the position criticized in the argument (***Tu Quoque***).

Fallacious Argument from Authority: An argument that concludes some claim is true because some authority figure says so is fallacious *unless* (1) the so-called authority is a genuine expert who is speaking in his or her area of expertise, and (2) there is no substantial disagreement among authorities in that subject area.

Fallacy of the Undistributed Middle: In a correct categorical syllogism, the term that occurs in both premises must be distributed in one of its occurrences. If it is not, the fallacy of the undistributed middle is committed.

False Analogy: This fallacy occurs when the relevant dissimilarities between the types of objects mentioned in the premises of an analogical argument are ignored. For example, to argue that the current president of the United States could use the same methods as Franklin Roosevelt to overcome unemployment because the current president has similar powers to create agencies, enact emergency legislation, and so forth, ignores many relevant differences in the economic background of the two eras.

False Dilemma: (*See* **Black-and-White Thinking.**)

Gambler's Fallacy: This fallacy occurs if we interpret what happens "on average" or "in the long run" to mean that departures from what is average will be corrected in the short run. The fallacy is named for the gambler who hopes to overcome losses by betting, for example, that a tail on a coin is bound to come up after a run of heads.

Genetic Fallacy: This fallacy occurs whenever some nonevidential feature connected with the origin of a claim (such as who said it, how it first came to be believed, how old it is) is taken as evidence for or against it. This fallacy is closely related to **Fallacious Appeals to Authority, Fallacious *ad Hominems*,** and **Fallacious Appeals to Consensus,** which can all be considered variants of the genetic fallacy.

Hasty Generalization: This fallacy, also called "leaping to a conclusion," occurs in inductive reasoning when a conclusion is drawn from a sample that is too small.

Ignoring a Common Cause: When we carelessly or without sufficient evidence attribute a direct causal relationship between two events that are only indirectly related to one another through a common underlying cause of both, we commit this fallacy. The fallacy would occur, for example, if we were to argue that red spots on a child cause that child to have a fever, without considering that both features could be symptoms of some underlying cause, such as a measles virus.

Incomplete Evidence: When we construct or evaluate an inductive argument, we must take into account all available relevant evidence that would affect the truth of the conclusion. If we deliberately ignore or carelessly fail to obtain such evidence, we commit this fallacy.

Misleading Vividness: This fallacy occurs when some particularly vivid information is weighted disproportionately so that a substantial amount of statistical support for a conclusion is deemed less important than it really is.

Post hoc: (See **Confusing Coincidental Relationships with Causal Relationships**.)

Slippery Slope: This fallacy argues from the arbitrariness of marking a distinction along some continuum that no distinction is possible. It ignores the fact that numerous small differences can make a big difference and fails to discriminate where discrimination is possible and appropriate. For example, to argue that anyone who takes a sip of wine is bound to become an alcoholic is to commit the fallacy of the slippery slope.

Tu Quoque: (See **Fallacious Argument against the Person**.)

BIBLIOGRAPHY

Anscombe, G. E. M. (1959). *An introduction to Wittgenstein's tractatus* (2nd ed.). New York: Harper and Row.

Aristotle. (1921). *The works of Aristotle.* (W. D. Ross, Ed.). Oxford: Oxford University Press.

Arnauld, A. (1964). *The art of thinking.* (J. Dickoff & P. James, Trans.). Indianapolis: Bobbs-Merrill Co.

Arum, R., & Roksa, J. (2011). *Academically adrift.* Chicago: University of Chicago Press.

Asimov, I. (1960). *The intelligent man's guide to the physical sciences.* New York: Basic Books.

Augustine, Saint. (1951). *The confessions of St. Augustine.* (E. B. Pusey, Trans.). New York: Pocket Books.

Baker, R. (1967). *A stress analysis of a strapless evening gown.* Englewood Cliffs: Prentice Hall.

Bennett, A. (2007). *The uncommon reader.* London: Faber & Faber.

Binford, L. (1981). *Bones.* New York: Academic Press.

Bloom, A. (1984). *The closing of the American mind.* New York: Simon and Schuster.

Bok, S. (1984). *Secrets.* Oxford: Oxford University Press.

Boorstin, D. J. (1983). *The discoverers.* New York: Random House.

Boswell, J. (1917). *Life of Johnson.* (C. G. Osgood, Ed.). New York: Charles Scribner's Sons.

———. (1955). *Boswell on the grand tour.* (F. Brady & F. A. Pottle, Eds.). New York: McGraw-Hill.

———. (1956). *In search of a wife.* (F. Brady & F. A. Pottle, Eds.). New York: McGraw-Hill.

———. (1959). *Boswell for the defense.* (W. K. Wimsatt, Jr., & F. A. Pottle, Eds.). New York: McGraw-Hill.

———. (1963). *The ominous years.* (C. Ryekamp & F. A. Pottle, Eds.). New York: McGraw-Hill.

Braffort, P., & Herschberg, D. (1967). *Computer programming and formal systems.* Amsterdam: North Holland.

Bridgman, P. W. (1927). *The logic of modern physics.* New York: Macmillan.

Campbell, K. (1970). *Body and mind.* Garden City, NY: Doubleday.

Carnap, R. (1962). *Logical foundations of probability.* Chicago: University of Chicago Press.

Carroll, L. (1958). *Symbolic logic.* New York: Dover Publications. (Original work published 1896.)

———. (1962). *Alice's adventures in wonderland/Through the looking glass.* New York: Macmillan. (Original work published 1865/1871.)

Casanova, G. (1966–1971). *History of my life.* (W. R. Trask, Trans.). New York: Harcourt, Brace & World.

Caudwell, S. (1981). *Thus was Adonis murdered.* New York: Charles Scribner's.

Charlesworth, M. (1993). *Bioethics in a liberal society.* Cambridge: Cambridge University Press.

Chernow, R. (2004). *Alexander Hamilton.* New York: The Penguin Press.

Chesterfield, Lord (P. D. Stanhope). (n.d.). *Lord Chesterfield's letters.* New York: A. L. Burt.

Chesterton, G. K. (1951). *The Father Brown omnibus.* New York: Dodd, Mead and Co.

Childs, J. R. (1961). *Casanova: A biography based on new documents.* London: Allen and Unwin.

Cooper, J. F. (1963). *The deerslayer.* New York: The New American Library. (Original work published 1841).

Court, N. A. (2006). *Mathematics in fun and earnest.* Mineola, NY: Dover.

Culbertson, J. T. (1958). *Mathematics and logic for digital devices.* New York: D. Van Nostrand.

Darwin, C. (1903). *The origin of species.* New York: Hurst and Co.

De Beauvoir, S. (1964). *The ethics of ambiguity.* (B. Frechtman, Trans.). New York: Citadel Press.

Descartes, R. (1980). *Discourse on method and meditations on first philosophy.* (D. A. Cress., Trans.). Indianapolis: Hackett Publishing, 1980.

Devlin, P. (1965). *The enforcement of morals.* Oxford: Oxford University.

Dickens, C. (1894). *Our mutual friend.* Boston: Houghton Mifflin.

Doyle, A. C. (1967). *The annotated Sherlock Holmes.* (W. S. Baring-Gould, Ed.). New York: Clarkson N. Potter.

Dunn, L. C., & Dobshansky, T. H. (1946). *Heredity, race, and society.* New York: Penguin Books.

Durrell, L. (1960). *Prospero's cell and reflections on a marine Venus.* New York:

Ehrlich, P. (1968). *The population bomb.* New York: Ballantine.

Eliot, G. (n.d.). *Felix Holt.* New York: John W. Lovell.

———. (n.d.). *Middlemarch.* New York: John W. Lovell.

Fowler, H. W. (1965). *A dictionary of modern English usage.* (2nd ed). Oxford: Oxford University Press.

Fowles, J. (1977). *Daniel Martin.* Boston: Little, Brown and Co.

Frankena, W. K. (1973). *Ethics.* (2nd ed.). Englewood Cliffs, NJ: Prentice Hall.

Frankfurt, H. (1970). *Demons, dreamers, and madmen.* Indianapolis: Bobbs-Merrill Co.

Freud, S. (1956). *The basic writings of Sigmund Freud.* (A. A. Brill., Ed. & Trans.). New York: Modern Library.

Fussell, P. (1983). *Class.* New York: Summit Books.

Galavotti, M. C. (2005). *Philosophical introduction to probability.* Stanford, CA: CSLI.

Galbraith, J. K. (1976). *The affluent society.* Boston: Houghton Mifflin.

George, K. (2001). *Taken.* New York: Delacorte.

Gish, D. (1979). *Evolution? The fossils say no!* New York: Creation-Life Publishers.

Gissing, G. (1971). *The odd woman.* New York: W. W. Norton.

Givens, D. R. (1992). Sylvanus G. Morley and the Carnegie Institution's program of Mayan research. In J. E. Reyman, Ed.). *Rediscovering our past: Essays on the history of American archaeology* (pp. 137–144.) Avebury, England: Aldershot.

Glob, P. V. (1971). *The bog people.* New York: Ballantine.

Goodin, R. E. (1989). *No smoking.* Chicago: University of Chicago Press.

Goodman, N. (1987). *Ways of worldmaking.* Indianapolis: Hackett Publishing.

Gould, R. A. (1980). *Living archaeology.* Cambridge: Cambridge University Press.

Gould, S. J. (1985). *The flamingo's smile.* New York: W. W. Norton.

———. (1981). *The mismeasure of man.* New York: W. W. Norton.

Greene, G. (1978). *The human factor.* New York: Simon and Schuster.

Greene, T. M. (1973). *The arts and the art of criticism.* New York: Gordian Press.

Greenhouse, L. (2005). *Becoming Justice Blackmun.* New York: Henry Holt.

Griffin, J. H. (1977). *Black like me.* (2nd ed.) Boston: Houghton Mifflin.

Guthrie, W. K. C. (1955). *The Greeks and their gods.* Boston: Beacon Press.

Hacking, I. (1975). *The emergence of probability.* Cambridge: Cambridge University.

Hamilton, A., Madison, J., & Jay, J. *The federalist papers.* NY: The New American Library.

Hamilton, E. (1971). *The Greek way.* New York: W. W. Norton.

Harris, M. (1968). *The rise of anthropological theory.* New York: Thomas Y. Crowell.

Hughes, E. R. (1954). *Chinese philosophy in classical times.* London: Dent.

Hume, D. (1970). *Dialogues concerning natural religion.* (N. Pike., Ed.). Indianapolis: Bobbs-Merrill Co.

———. (1888). *A treatise of human nature.* (L. A. Selby-Bigge., Ed.). London: Oxford University Press.

Huxley, A. (1928). *Point counter point.* Garden City, NY: The Modern Library.

Huxley, J. (1957). *New bottles for old wine.* New York: Harper and Brothers.

Jarvie, I. C. (1967). *The revolution in anthropology.* London: Routledge & Kegan Paul.

Jochim, M. A. (1981). *Strategies for survival.* New York: Academic Press.

Johnson-Laird, P. N., & Wason, P. C., (Eds.). (1977). *Thinking.* Cambridge: Cambridge University Press.

Jolly, C., & Plog., F. (1979). *Physical anthropology and archaeology.* (2nd ed.) New York: Alfred A. Knopf.

Jones, P. (1975). *Philosophy and the novel.* Oxford: Clarendon Press.

Kitcher, P. (1982). *Abusing science.* Cambridge: MIT Press.

Koestler, A. (1954). *The invisible writing.* New York: Macmillan.

Laclos, C. de. (1961). *Les liaisons dangereuses.* (P. W. K. Stone., Trans.). Baltimore: Penguin Books.

Lenin, V. I. (1927). *Collected works.* (Vol. 14.). Moscow: V. I. Lenin Institute.

Levi, E. H. (1970). *An introduction to legal reasoning.* Chicago: University of Chicago.

Lewin, R. (1987). *Bones of contention.* New York: Simon and Schuster.

Lip, E. (1998). *Feng shui for the home.* Terence, CA: Heian International Inc.

Livingstone, D. (1992). *The geographical tradition.* Oxford: Blackwell.

Lucretius. (1951). *On the nature of the universe.* (E. E. Latham., Trans.). Baltimore: Penguin Books.

Maalfjit, A. de W. (1974). *Images of man.* New York: Alfred A. Knopf.

MacCullogh, D. (2006). *The reformation.* New York: Viking Penguin.

Machiavelli, N. (1947). *The prince.* Chicago: Great Books Foundation.

Maclean, N. (1992). *Young men and fire.* Chicago: University of Chicago Press.

MacMahon, B., & Pugh., T. F. (1978). *Epidemiology.* Boston: Little, Brown.

MacMahon, B., Pugh, T. F., & Ipsen., J. (1960). *Epidemiologic methods.* Boston: Little, Brown.

Mates, B. (1972). *Elementary logic.* (2nd ed.). New York: Oxford University Press.

Mill, J. S. (1874). *A system of logic.* (8th ed.). New York: Harper and Brothers.

Millett, K. (1970). *Sexual politics.* Garden City, NY: Doubleday.

Morris, H. M. (1975). *Introducing creationism in the public schools.* San Diego: Creation Life.

Morris, H. (1976). *On guilt and innocence.* Berkeley: University of California Press.

Mumford, L. (1966). *Technics and human development.* New York: Harcourt Brace.

Murphy, J. G. (1971). *Civil disobedience and violence.* Belmont, CA: Wadsworth.

Murphy, J., & Coleman, J. (1984). *The philosophy of law.* Totowa, NJ: Rowman & Allanheld.

Murray, G. (1956). *The literature of ancient Greece.* Chicago: University of Chicago.

Newman, J. R. (1956). *The world of mathematics.* New York: Simon and Schuster.

Nietzsche, F. (1954). (A. Apple, Ed.). *The philosophy of Nietzsche.* New York: Modern Library.

Nussbaum, M. C., & Sunstein, C., (Eds.). (1998). *Clones and clones.* New York: W. W.

Nisbett, R., & Ross. L. (1980). *Human inference: Strategies and shortcomings of social judgment.* Englewood Cliffs, NJ: Prentice Hall.

Nordhaus, T., & Shellenberger, M. (2007). *Break through.* Boston, NY: Houghton Mifflin.

O'Connor, D. J. (1964). *A critical history of western philosophy*. New York: Free Press.

Parisi, J., Young, S., & Collins, B. (Eds.). (2002). *Dear editor: A history of poetry in letters*. London: W.W. Norton.

Phillips, G. D. (1975). *Evelyn Waugh's officers, gentlemen, and rogues*. Chicago: Nelson.

Pliny the Elder. (1855). *The natural history of Pliny*. (J. Bostock., Trans.). London: H. G. Bohn.

Polya, G. (1957). *How to solve it*. Garden City, NY: Doubleday.

Radcliffe-Brown, A. (1952). *Structure and function in primitive society*. Glencoe, IL: Free Press.

Reid, T. (1863). *Works*. (6th ed.). (W. Hamilton., Ed.). Edinburgh, Scotland: James Thin.

Renfrew, C., & Bahn., P. (1991). *Archaeology: Theories, methods, and practice*. New York: Thames and Hudson.

Rousseau, J. (1974). *The social contract*. (C. M. Sherover., Ed.). New York: New American Library.

Ruedy, E., & Nirenberg., S. (1990). *Where do I put the decimal point*. New York: Henry Holt.

Russell, B. (1928). *Skeptical essays*. New York: W. W. Norton.

———. (1958). *The conquest of happiness*. New York: Liveright.

———. (1959). *My philosophical development*. New York: Simon and Schuster.

———. (1961). *Religion and science*. New York: Oxford University Press.

———. (2011). *Free thought and official propaganda*. Toronto: University of Toronto Libraries. (Original work published in 1922).

Russo, R. (2001). *Empire falls*. New York: Viking.

Rutherford, J. H. (1992). *The moral foundations of United States constitutional democracy*. Pittsburgh: Dorrance Publishing Co.

Sabloff, J. (1989). *The cities of ancient Mexico: Reconstructing a lost world*. New York: Thames and Hudson.

Salmon, W. (1967). *The foundations of scientific inference*. Pittsburgh: University of Pittsburgh Press.

———. (1983). *Logic*. (3rd ed.). Englewood Cliffs, NJ: Prentice Hall.

———. (Ed.). (1970). *Zeno's paradoxes*. Indianapolis: Bobbs-Merrill.

Scheffler, I. (1982). *Science and subjectivity*. (2nd ed.). Indianapolis: Hackett.

Schiff, S. (2010). *Cleopatra*. Boston and New York: Little Brown.

Shakespeare, W. (1965). *Merchant of Venice*. New York: Airmont Publishing. (Reprint)

———. (1966). *King Lear*. New York: Airmont Publishing. (Reprint)

———. (1966). *Twelfth night*. New York: Airmont Publishing. (Reprint)

Shrader-Frechette, K. (1980). *Nuclear power and public policy*. Dordrecht, The Netherlands: D. Reidel.

Singer, P. (1993). *Practical ethics*. Cambridge: Cambridge University Press.

Singer, P. et al. (1990). *Embryo experimentation*. Cambridge: Cambridge University Press.

Skyrms, B. (1990). *The dynamics of rational deliberation*. Cambridge, MA: Harvard University Press.

Smith, A. H. (1958). *The mushroom hunter's field guide*. Ann Arbor: University of Michigan Press.

Smith, A. (1863). *The wealth of nations*. Edinburgh: Adam and Charles Black.

Storr, A. (2005). *Solitude*. NY: The Free Press.

Strunk, W., Jr., & White, E. B. (2000). *The elements of style*. (4th ed.). Upper Saddle River, NJ: Pearson Education.

Suppes, P. (1970). *A probabilistic theory of causality*. Amsterdam: North-Holland.

Swartz, R. J. (1965). *Perceiving, sensing, and knowing*. Garden City, NY: Anchor Books.

Tannen, D. (1991). *You just don't understand: Men and women in conversation*. New York: Ballantine.

Tatsumi, Y. (2009). *A drifting life*. Montreal: Drawn & Quarterly.

Thompson, J. E. S. (1963). *Maya archaeologist.* Norman: University of Oklahoma Press.

Tierney, P. J. (2000). *Darkness in El Dorado.* New York: W.W. Norton.

Tolstoy, L. (1960). *What is art?* (A. Maude, Trans.). Indianapolis: Liberal Arts Press.

Tuttle, M. (1992). *America's neighborhood bats.* Austin: University of Texas Press.

Twain, M. (1992). *The writings of Mark Twain.* New York: F. Collier and Sons (Original work published 1899).

Van Fraassen, B. (1980). *The scientific image.* Oxford: Oxford University Press.

Wang, W. S.-Y. (Ed.). (1989). *The emergence of language.* New York: W. H. Freeman.

Welch, E. (2005). *Shopping in the renaissance.* New Haven and London: Yale University Press.

Wesley, J. (1974). *The journal of John Wesley.* (P. L. Parker., Ed.). Northbrook, IL: Moody.

Westfall, R. S. (1971). *The construction of modern science: Mechanisms and mechanics.* Cambridge: Cambridge University Press.

White, T. (1980). *Prehistoric cannibalism at Mancos 5MTUMR-2346.* Princeton: Princeton University Press.

Wilde, O. (1980). *The plays of Oscar Wilde.* New York: The Modern Library.

Williams, B. (1972). *Morality.* New York: Harper and Row.

Winchester, S. (1999). *The professor and the madman.* New York: Harper Perennial.

Wootton, B. (1963). *Crime and the criminal law.* London: Stevens.

Xenophanes. (1992). *Xenophanes of Colophon: Fragments.* (J. H. Lesher., Trans.). Toronto: Toronto University Press.

Young, A. (1961). *The men who made surgery.* New York: Hillman Books.

Zakaria, F. (2008). *The post-American world.* New York and London: W. W. Norton.

Zinsser, W. (1980). *On writing well.* (2nd ed.). New York: Harper and Row.

ANSWERS TO EVEN-NUMBERED EXERCISES

Chapter One

Exercise Set 1.1

2. Reports by students who have taken classes from the professor, student surveys, and articles in student newspapers are sources of evidence regarding a professor's reputation. Evidence that is presented in favor of a teacher's greatness includes the ability to inspire students, interesting and lively lecture style, fairness, willingness to help students, and so forth.

4. Possible answers: Comparative literature, political science, economics, legal studies.

6. Ask to see the CARFAX or other vehicle history report based on the automobile's Vehicle Identification Number.

8. a. Dr. Smith asserts that the *Amanita verna* is deadly poisonous. He also asserts that the symptoms are delayed and that applications of first aid are almost useless.

b. The similarity between "store" mushrooms and amanita hides the danger of the latter.

c. No. "Never eat a white *Amanita*" is a warning or a command.

d. It is wise to take the advice of an expert on such matters without seeking further evidence. The taste of a mushroom is not worth risking death.

10. a. "Shallow cultivation" refers to turning over only the top two to four inches of soil when planting seeds or setting out new plants.

b. The reference to experiments is the only statement of evidence.

c. No. Shallow cultivation might work, and it would save money and avoid poisoning the earth.

d. It would be sensible to try to find more evidence for the success of shallow cultivation, or to try it on a limited basis.

12. a. Alcohol kills thousands of Americans each year. (The author does not mention the well-known fact that alcohol can become physically addictive.)

b. No evidence is presented. The author probably assumes that the connection between cigarette smoking and lung cancer is well known.

c. Probably not. That some harmful substances are legal is not a particularly good reason to legalize other substances that are believed (by some) to be less harmful. (But a better argument might be offered for legalizing marijuana.)

14. Lear asks for physical evidence in the form of his daughter's breath.

16. a. Because information about other possible sources of exposure to lead is not mentioned, the evidence for lower classes absorbing less lead than upper classes is not persuasive.

b. Because lower classes were likely to be making, installing, and maintaining products that contain lead, they were probably more susceptible to lead poisoning.

Exercise Set 1.2

PART I

2.   The serious problems the U.S. faces, such as massive debt, poor education, and political impasse, all have solutions.

People who say America is facing inevitable decline as a world power are wrong.

4.   A coin has been tossed 12 times and has shown a head each time.

The next time this coin is tossed, it will also show a head.

6.   We need to be persuaded that something ought to be done before there is any hope whatsoever that it will be done.

Moral philosophy is an indispensable first step in that larger political campaign [for restricting smoking].

8.   In China during the summer, the south winds are refreshing and bring good ventilation or cosmic breath.

A building facing a vacant lot on the south is good geomantically.

10.   Creationism can be discussed effectively as a scientific model.
Evolution is fundamentally a religious philosophy rather than a science.

It is clearly unsound educational practice and even unconstitutional for evolution to be taught and promoted in the public schools to the exclusion or detriment of creationism.

12.   We do actually know, either by reasoning or by experience, that in a hundred or a million throws, an ace is thrown in about one sixth of that number, or one in six times.

In the case of a die [one of a pair of dice], the probability of "An ace is thrown" is one sixth.

14.   People who buy babies don't talk about the practice.
People who buy babies have to buy things (for the baby).

If the baby is alive, she or he got handed over to or is about to be handed over to someone who might buy a stroller or health insurance (for the baby).

PART II

2. The human mind is not the same thing as the human brain for the human body, including the brain, is a material thing and the human mind is a spiritual thing, and because nothing is both a material thing and a spiritual thing.

4. A mortgage-backed security has a prepayment risk because if a homeowner decides to pay off a mortgage ahead of schedule—in other words, to prepay the mortgage—the mortgage-backed security containing that particular mortgage does not receive all the anticipated interest payments.

6. Because Madoff did nothing but lie over the decades while he was committing the fraud, and so why would anyone believe him now? (Note that the conclusion is a rhetorical question.)

8. Because poker involves mathematics, planning, and strategy—all complicated mental processes—and because these are exactly what imparts the benefit of producing more brain neurons, and because poker is novel and mentally challenging, it is one of the finest exercises for keeping gray matter alive.

PART III

2. Argument. In this passage, *For* introduces a reason.

4. *Since* here indicates the passage of time.

6. This passage does not contain an argument. *Thus* introduces examples.

8. This passage is probably best understood as giving a causal explanation for why you are refusing the invitation. You are not trying to prove that you will not attend.

10. Causal explanation. Orest's absence explains why Elektra needs her sister's help.

Exercise Set 1.3

2. a. Publishers are aiming at a national market.

The number one criterion for any textbook is avoidance of controversy.

  b. They (publishers) must respond to a variety of specific criteria from their buyers.

Textbooks have been "dumbed down."

4. In this extended argument, many reasons are given for the need for caution when choosing a therapist who will listen to personal revelations.

  a. Through analytic techniques, etc., self-disclosure is aided and interpreted.
      The therapeutic value of these techniques is not established.

There is a clear need for caution in choosing persons best qualified to listen to self-disclosure.

  b. One cannot trust all who listen to confessions to be either discreet or capable of bringing solace or help.
      The act of confession can increase vulnerability.

Caution in choosing a therapist is well-founded.

  c. Studies have shown that when self-revelation flows in one direction only, it increases the authority of the listener while decreasing that of the speaker.
      In ordinary confiding, the flow is reciprocal.
      In institutionalized practice, there is no reciprocity.
      Therapists and others who receive confidences are taught to restrain themselves from reciprocal sharing.

(Self-revelation to a therapist increases the authority of the therapist while decreasing that of the patient.) This unstated conclusion is another aspect of support for the conclusion stated above in (b), that caution is well-founded.

6. The extended argument traces steps that led to the calligraphic typography used on Mac computers.

   a. I dropped out of college.

   If I had not dropped out of college, I would not have dropped in on a calligraphy class.

   The calligraphy course showed me how to design multiple typefaces and proportionally spaced fonts.

   _____

   This experience influenced the design of the first Macintosh computer.

   b. Windows just copied the Mac.

   _____

   If the Mac had not used multiple typefaces, Windows would not have used them either.

   c. (Conclusion based on both subarguments)

   If I had not dropped out of college, personal computers might not have the wonderful typography that they do.

Exercise Set 1.4

PART I

2. Statistical

4. Statistical

6. Universal (or intended by the author as universal)

8. Statistical

10. Universal

PART II

2.   There is no government plan for the safe disposal of spent nuclear fuel.
     No fuels should be used without a safety plan for disposing their spent remains. (Universal generalization).

     _____

     Nuclear fuel should not be used.

4.   All use of substances that cause people to neglect their duties is wrong.
     People addicted to drugs neglect their duties.

     _____

     Use of drugs is wrong.

The universal generalization seems to be what Bennet assumes, but he needs further (unstated) premises that say the use of drugs is the cause of addicts' neglect of duties, and that all users of drugs become addicts. Is all this plausible?

6.   The current mayor promises to reduce taxes.
     Any incumbent mayor who promises to reduce taxes should be reelected. (Universal generalization—not very plausible, but a statistical generalization with the same subject and predicate would not be plausible either.)

     _____

     The current mayor should be reelected.

8. Tomato growers in Florida were hit by a hard freeze in December.
    Hard freezes generally result in short supplies. (Statistical generalization)
    Short supplies result in higher prices. (Statistical generalization)

    Tomatoes will be expensive in late winter.

10. Your tires have made the coast-to-coast drive six times without trouble.

    Your tires should hold out for this coast-to-coast drive.

No plausible generalization supports this argument. Can you say why this is so?

12. All members of the Amaryllis family (of bulbs) are unattractive to squirrels.
    Snowdrops are members of the Amaryllis family.

    Snowdrops are unattractive to squirrels. (Plausible universal generalization)

Exercise Set 1.5

2. Inflation could be controlled by a sufficiently heavy reduction in the level of demand.
    It could also be controlled with a less drastic reduction if something could be done to arrest
    the interactions of wages and prices or, to speak more precisely, of wages, profits, and prices.

    Both the level of demand and the wage-price spiral are important to inflation control.

Additional Material: In the past, there has been much argument about this issue.

4. People in developing countries live at about one fortieth the consumption level of people in
    the United States.
    The United States population has increased by 135 million people since 1945.
    The entire population of developing countries is 4.2 billion people.
    (Unstated but mathematically true: 135 million × 40 = 5.4 billion)
    Consumption of the additional 135 million people in the U.S. approximately equals that
    of all developing countries combined.

    Population is not the only factor in consumption amounts—lifestyle matters also.
    Background information is provided—along with how population,
    technology, and consumption affect the environment.

6. Envy is noticeable in children before they are a year old.
    The emotion is just as prevalent among adults as among children.

    Envy is one of the most universal and deep-seated of human passions.

Additional Material: Russell elaborates on the form envy takes in children and how it must be handled,
remarking that children are only slightly more open in the expression of the passion than are adults.

8. If humans had stopped emitting greenhouse gases starting in 1998, all the changes today
    resulting from global warming would still be underway.
    If humans stopped emitting new greenhouse gases tomorrow, the planet would continue to
    heat up for several more decades and probably longer.

    As surely as the science of climatology tells us that the warming of the earth is caused by
    humans, it also tells us that a dramatically warmer and transformed climate is almost
    inevitable.

Additional Material: Background information about who investigated the problem and examples of effects of global warming.

10. They [historians] never have access to all the facts anyway, and even those to which they do have access are selected to suit their own purposes.
    There is no history on a mortuary table.
    ___
    The "facts" therefore do not simply "speak for themselves"; the historian manages their performance on the contemporary scene.

Additional Material: The conclusion is also stated in different words as the opening sentence ("Inevitably historians are involved in selecting from the available sources the material they deem significant in light of the problems under scrutiny") and in the final sentence ("Selection, then, is inescapable").

Exercise Set 1.6

2. Argument.

    No man has a natural authority over his fellow man.
    Force is not the source of right.
    ___
    Convention remains as the basis of all legitimate authority among men.

Author assumes that the only basis of legitimate authority is natural authority or convention.

4. Argument.

    Achilles runs 10 times as fast as the tortoise.
    The tortoise has a head start of 100 yards.
    After Achilles runs the first 100 yards, he has reached the tortoise's starting point, but the tortoise has advanced 10 yards.
    When Achilles reaches the 110 yard marker, the tortoise has advanced one more yard.
    When Achilles reaches that point, the tortoise has advanced another tenth of a yard.
    And so on, without end.
    The tortoise always holds a lead, however small.
    ___
    Achillles never catches the tortoise.

Additional information: Achilles was a famous Greek warrior and the tortoise a very slow-moving animal.

6. Adam was led to sin by Eve and not Eve by Adam.
    ___
    It is just and right that woman accept as lord and master him whom she has led to sin.

This argument apparently depends on an implausible missing premise: If the first woman led the first man to sin, then women should accept men as their lords and masters.

8. A long tradition of Christian theological thought emphasizes the primacy of individual conscience.
    A tenet of traditional Christianity is that it is a sin to coerce non-Christians into the Christian Church.
    ___
    It is against Christian faith to use the law to coerce nonbelievers in respect of moral matters.

Background information includes the views of Thomas Aquinas, information about the author's faith and his puzzlement about some Christians believing that they can use the law to impose their morality on non-Christain segments of society.

10. Several arguments are contained in this passage:

1. Concentrations of lead, cadmium, arsenic, and mercury in hair have provided a good record of exposure, according to studies.
   Analysis of lengthwise hair sections can show the approximate time when a short, intense exposure occurred.
   _____
   Hair analysis is a good way to screen large groups of people for exposure to toxic trace materials.

2. The metal grows out with the hair.
   _____
   Analysis of lengthwise sections of hair can show the approximate time when a short, intense exposure occurred.

3. Chromium is essential for the hormone insulin to work properly.
   _____
   It may be that measurements of chromium in hair will be useful in identifying people with diabetes and in monitoring the course of the disease.

An implicit premiss connecting insulin deficiency with diabetes is needed in the third argument.

12. Superior discipline and academic standards in nonpublic schools will cause parents to choose them.
    Tuition tax credits and vouchers for parents will enable them to choose nonpublic schools.
    If there is a large exodus from public schools to nonpublic schools, the system of public education will end.
    _____
    Public schools must improve or face extinction.

Shanker comments also on the danger of tax credits by comparing them to a creeping cancer.

14. [Sense perception] serves as the sole means through which we can gather information about the world around us.
    Knowledge of general laws is posterior, in the empirical sciences, to knowledge of particular instances.
    For the latter, the evidence of the senses is required.
    _____
    Sense perception plays a crucial role in the natural sciences.

16. Stupid savages could not have been the architects and inventors of their admirable and varied languages.
    _____
    There is an eternal and omniscient God.

Unstated premiss: Only God could create the languages that could not have been invented by the humans who use them. This premiss is implausible and has strong racist overtones. Apparently the author of the argument believes that Europeans were clever enough to invent their languages but that indigenous South Americans were not.

18. This passage contains several arguments.

    a. Magic and religion, to many people, are a part of common sense.

    As a part of common sense, it is reasonable for them to hold it.

    b. Part of common sense in our society is being critical towards traditional or received ideas. Once one is critical, and establishes critical standards, it is no longer reasonable to hold onto magico-religious beliefs.

    We are reasonable to accept Western science and not magic.
    Conclusion based on both subarguments: Both author and savage are being reasonable, each within his or her own frame of reference or common sense.

Additional assumption: It is always reasonable to accept what is regarded as common sense within your own cultural frame of reference.

20. a. There were sounds of twigs snapping and leaves rustling. (Description of physical evidence.)

    Hetty was in the forest.

    b. The night was dark and the forest dense. (Again, description of physical evidence.)

    Finding or capturing Hetty in the forest was nearly impossible.
    Assumed premiss: In a dark and dense forest, it is almost impossible to find someone.

Based on these two arguments, plus fear of being captured by enemies, a decision was made to abandon the search and to sail away.

22. Determining the date of Easter was a sign of ecclesiastical authority.
    Accepting the new Gregorian calendar was a matter of accepting papal supremacy.

    The Catholic Church had a deep investment in controlling the calendar.

The passage contains information about the political importance in the sixteenth century of deciding how to set dates of feasts such as Easter, when the old calendar no longer synchronized with the astronomical calendar.

24. Rules are designed to benefit all.
    The punishments for their violation are publicized and the defenses respected.

    In choosing to do an act violative of the rules, an individual has chosen to be punished.

The author of the argument states that the conclusion is plausible in view of the reasons offered but that it is exaggerated. (Obviously one can hope—and even expect—to escape punishments for misdeeds.)

Chapter Two

Exercise Set 2.1

2. Not increasing atmospheric carbon is just one of many criteria for environmental safety.

4. In the first premiss "man" is understood as "human"; in the second it is understood as referring to the male gender.

6. The term "miracle" in the premiss that only God can perform miracles refers to a suspension of natural laws. In the other premiss "miracle" refers to a very surprising or unlikely event.

8. Croesus failed to realize that "a great empire" applied to both Persia and Lydia.

10. Parents ambitious for their child's success would probably understand the teacher's "normal" to mean "average," and would want their child to do better than average.

12. a. ambiguity of "for"

   b. amphiboly

16. "Bits" can refer to small amounts or to units of information.

Exercise Set 2.2

2. b. "Misdemeanor" refers to a minor offense, but "minor" is a relative term. Some laws specify the difference between a misdemeanor (minor offense) and a felony (major offense), such as stating that a theft of less than a certain amount of money is a misdemeanor whereas a theft of that amount or greater is a felony.

2. d. A patriot is someone who supports his or her country, but the term is vague because support can take various forms. People who protest laws that they believe are unjust regard themselves as patriots, but others might not.

4. *Idle* has several overlapping meanings. For example, the term can mean "not engaged in activity" or "not engaged in useful activity."

Exercise Set 2.3

3. b. Too broad—many small animals are not mice.

   d. Too broad—dolphins and seals are also aquatic mammals.

Exercise Set 2.4

2. Yes, because "men" in some contexts refers to all humans and in others only to male humans.

6. "Disorderly conduct" is a criminal charge that is defined differently in different jurisdictions. Use Wikipedia or a similar source to find the definition for your state.

8. Precising definition.

Exercise Set 2.6

1. b. "Public servant" has a positive connotation; "bureaucrat" has a negative connotation.

d. Some believe that "perspire" is a more polite expression—"Horses sweat; people perspire."

f. "Police officer" indicates greater respect than "cop."

h. "Actor" is preferrred because "actress" is considered somewhat sexist.

j. "Estate tax" suggests a tax imposed on the rich; "death tax" suggests a penalty (an additional one) for dying.

l. "Shrink" is more familiar and less respectful than "psychiatrist."

m. "Gentleman" usually implies (perhaps ironically) that a man has special characteristics, such as politeness and grace.

4. "Natural" in these contexts is opposed to "artificial." The term is designed to persuade you that the food or medicine cannot be harmful. The intension of "natural" is "occurring in nature."

6. Persuasive.

Exercise Set 2.7

2. One possible answer; see any dictionary for others: *But* is a coordinating conjunction used to contrast the conjuncts. Example: I am old, but you are young.

Exercise Set 2.8

1. b. "Joan weighs 120 pounds" means that when Joan steps on the scales in her doctor's office, the balance settles at or very near the 120 mark.

   d. When these bandages are stretched they return to the same size they had before stretching.

2. Some possible questions that have been offered as operational tests by such organizations as Alcoholics Anonymous: Do you drink alone? Do you have drinks before a social occasion to "prepare yourself"? Do you have more than two drinks a day? Do you drink in the mornings?

   An operational definition of this type is difficult to formulate because alcoholism takes many different forms and tolerance for alcohol varies. For example, some alcoholics are periodic drinkers who may not have anything to drink for months but who indulge in periodic binges. Some drink relatively small amounts but are nevertheless addicted to alcohol. Some persons who are not addicted to alcohol drink regularly and drink relatively large amounts of alcohol.

Exercise Set 2.9

1. b. "Premiss" is sometimes spelled with a single "s" and a final "e."

1. d. Engravers use "burin" differently from archaeologists.

2. b. No punctuation is needed.

2. d. The Arabic, Roman, and binary representations of the number three are, respectively, "3," "III," and "11."

Exercise Set 2.10

PART I

2. Persuasive: Note the emotional tone of words such as *ruthless*.

4. Verbal extensional.

6. Lexical.

8. Precising.

10. Persuasive.

12. Theoretical.

14. Syntactic.

16. Precising.

18. Theoretical.

20. Persuasive.

PART II

2. A theoretical definition of "nature" is required.

Chapter Three

Exercise Set 3.1

2. We need 20 eggs to make four cakes.

4. The probability of rolling two aces with a pair of fair dice is 1/36.

Exercise Set 3.2

2. Suppose that 13 is not the next prime number after 11.
But 13 is a prime number (it can be evenly divided only by itself and 1). The only whole number after 11 that is closer than 13 to it is 12, but 12 is not a prime number. So the next prime number after 11 is 13.

Exercise Set 3.3

PART I

2. True.

4. True.

6. True.

8. True.

PART II

2. Definitional feature: If a female is the mother of some male, then that male is her son. (We assume that *Michael* is the name of a male—otherwise the definition does not apply.)

4. Structural feature: The set of people who own smart phones includes every senior, so if some individual does not own a smart phone, he is not a senior.

6. Structural feature: If the first, then the second; if the second, then the third; therefore, if the first, then the third.

8. Structural features: In general, not A if B. But in this instance, B. Therefore, in this instance not A.

10. Definitional. What is poisonous is not beneficial.

12. Structural feature: Either the first or the second, but not the first; therefore, the second.

PART III

2. The rule does not say that nonseniors cannot register—just that every senior can. So if every senior registers and places remain, nonseniors may register also.

4. Having the ability to perform well in a class does not mean that one will succeed. Able persons who do not apply themselves sometimes fail.

6. This requires some interpretation as to what is meant by being true to oneself or others. Consider this plausible case, however. You say something you believe to be true when it is in fact not so. (You are being true to yourself.) But the person to whom you are speaking is thus deceived about how things stand. (You are false to the other person.)

Exercise Set 3.4

PART II

2. Premiss: The history of government interventions on behalf of public health, from the construction of sewer systems to the campaign against smoking, is one of consistent, life-enhancing success.

   Conclusion: Government action could help significantly to overcome obesity. (Inductive generalization.)

4. Premiss: Remains of certain plants and fish were found at an archaeological dig.
   Conclusion: The bay near which the plants were found was calmer in the past than in the present.
   This is an argument in which we conclude something about the past on the basis of observations made in the present. (Implicit premiss: The plants and animals whose remains were found required a calm lagoon condition to flourish.)

6. Premiss: In a national sample, one of three Americans over the age of 12 had tried an illicit substance.
   Conclusion: One out of three Americans over the age of 12 has tried some illicit substance.
   This is an argument in which we conclude something about an entire population based on what happens in an observed sample of the population.

8. Premiss: By observing the conditions of the heavens, which are known to affect weather, weather patterns can be predicted.
   Premiss: The conditions of the heavens are known to affect the temperament of humans.
   Conclusion: By observing the conditions of the heavens, human destiny can be predicted.
   This is an argument based on a supposed analogy between weather being controlled by astronomical phenomena and human character or temperament being controlled by astronomical phenomena.

10. Premiss: The *Iliad, Odyssey,* and so on are long and complex poems.
    Premiss: Such complexity can only be the result of many generations of artistic effort using the hexameter metre.
    Conclusion: The *Iliad, Odyssey,* and so on are not the first hexameter poems.
    This argument appeals to causal features, such as the need for preliminary steps to be taken before major hexameter poetry emerges.

Exercise Set 3.5

2. The argument presents two choices (study and social life) as if they were exclusive, but they are not.

4. The person criticizing the governor is using a stereotypic view of women as highly emotional creatures.

6. Here emotions interfere with the president's judgment. It could be understood as an appeal to pity for the accused—the president is saying he knows his aide is a good guy, despite the damaging evidence.

8. "Four" and "fore" sound alike but have different meanings—a kind of equivocation.

Exercise Set 3.6

2. Language is similar to other great human inventions like writing, making pottery, and controlled use of fire, which could have emerged at different places at different times.
   There were many independent human populations from which the emergence of language was possible.
   _____
   Language had several points of origin.

Inductive—the author tells us that his argument is probabilistic and based on similarities between language and other great human inventions.

4. Handling numbers was invented by regular people to make things easy.
   _____
   Handling numbers in daily business has to be easy.

Probably intended as a deductive argument, signaled by "has to." A missing premiss that would make it deductive is "All things invented by regular people to make things easy are easy." This premiss is not obviously true, though.

6. Blacks can "pass" as whites.
   "Looking black" is different from being black.
   _____
   Skin hue is neither a necessary nor a sufficient condition for being classified as black in our culture.

Deductive.

8. Islamic practices of Arab countries cause their economic retardation.
   But other Islamic countries are economically vibrant.
   _____
   Islamic practices cannot be the cause of economic retardation.

Intended to be deductive. Missing plausible premiss: If Islamic practices are the cause of economic retardation, then all Islamic countries will be economically retarded.

10. Within Western civilization, there developed several sources of moral authority.
    Canon Law [based on the authority of God], Roman Law [based on the authority of a perceived natural moral order in the universe], and the social-contract theory [based on the individual in a state of nature concerned primarily about his or her own safety and happiness].
    _____
    Each of these systems of law was based on a different type of ethical system, and each focused primarily on a different facet of human nature.

Intended to be deductive. The conclusion summarizes the information about sources of law in the complex premiss, but it adds a bit in the conclusion about the focus on different facets of human nature.

12. a. Today, the main salmon run up the Bann occurs in midsummer.
        In Mesolithic times, there may have been a late spring run.
        Lower water temperatures make it unlikely that the salmon run would continue beyond
            the fall.
        _____

        Salmon bones indicate summer occupation.

    Inductive, based on what usually happens. Note the use of a causal claim in the third premisses and the tentative nature of the second premiss.

     b. Eels run downstream in the fall.
        _____

        Eel bones indicate fall residence.

Inductive, based on what usually happens.

     c. Hazelnuts are ready for picking by mid-fall.
        Water-lily seeds are best collected in September
        _____

        Hazelnuts and water-lily seeds indicate fall residence.

    Inductive, based on what usually happens.
    The three arguments support the overall conclusion that the site was occupied in the fall and
summer.

14. Mathematics is a language.
     Any meaningful proposition and any generalization about social behavior can be expressed in
        any language. (Implicit premiss—not plausible, unless we mean something like "Any
        language can be developed and refined to express any…" Think of the difficulty, for example,
        of expressing some complex and meaningful mathematical propositions in English.)
     _____

     Any meaningful proposition can be expressed in suitable mathematical form, and any
        generalization about social behavior can be formulated mathematically.

    Deductive, if we include the implausible implicit premiss. Note the appeal to authority (Gibbs)
in the first premiss.

16. Climate has a great influence on bodily functions.
     All of the places in which men of great intellect have been found… have an unusually dry
        atmosphere.
     _____

     Genius is dependent on dry air, and so on.

    Probably intended to be deductive, but the connection between dry air, rapid bodily functions,
and genius has not been established, and no plausible generalization seems to connect them.

18. The majority of the animals painted in the Lascaux cave face right.
     Right-facing is generally preferred by right-handed draftsmen.
     Fossilized rope from the cave was made using the twisting motion natural to the right hand.
     _____

     Paleolithic inhabitants who decorated the cave were predominantly right-handed.
     Inductive, based on what usually happens.

20. Ethiopians make their gods black and mule-nosed.
Thracians say theirs have blue eyes and red hair.

If oxen and horses and lions had hands and could paint with their hands and provide works of art, as men do, horses would paint the forms of gods like horses, and oxen like oxen, and make their bodies in the image of their several kinds.

Inductive, either based on a sample, on what has happened so far, or on similarities.

22. Japanese stocks bounced back after the 1995 earthquake.

Japanese stocks will bounce back after the 2011 earthquake and tsunami.

Inductive, as indicated by the use of "may."

Based on similarities between the two disastrous events in 1995 and 2011. But argument should also take account of any relevant differences between the circumstances surrounding the two disasters.

24. In this country, the essence of government is to preserve the social order.
The well-off benefit from this far more than do the poor.

The well-off ought to pay more.

Intended to be deductive. Implicit premiss, which has some plausibility in this context, is that payment should correspond to benefits received.

26. This passage can be considered an explanation of why the American Dental Association passed a resolution to oppose oral piercing. Their argument in support of the resolution can be reconstructed:

Tongue piercing carries immense risk of disease.
Tongue piercing is embraced by many people. (Implicit, but supported by evidence.)

Tongue piercing is a public-health hazard.

The argument is intended to be deductive. The premisses are designed to show that tongue piercing fulfills the defining conditions for being a public-health hazard.

Chapter Four

Exercise Set 4.1

PART I

2. Reference class: Young people eligible to vote, who are heads of Republican organizations.
Attribute class: Voters in midterm elections.

Weak because of failure to take account of relevant evidence in choosing reference class.

4. Reference class: Americans.
Attribute class: People whose favorite dessert is apple pie.
Strong.

6. Reference class: First recovery years after a recession.
Attribute class: Years in which stocks outperform bonds.

Because the generalization states what "typically" happens, the argument is reasonably strong.

8. Reference class: Students living away from home.

   Attribute class: Students covered by parents' theft-insurance policy.

   Argument is reasonably strong because of "most."

PART II

2.   Eighty-five percent of operations to separate bones in the middle ear result
        in improved hearing.
     The patient's operation will separate bones in the middle ear.
     _____
     The patient's operation will result in improved hearing.

4.   Seventy percent of the area covered by the prediction will experience rain.
     You will be in the area covered by the prediction.
     _____
     You will experience rain.

6.   Most great writers are writers who were not too discouraged by rejections of
        their early work.
     You have had early work rejected.
     _____
     You should not become too discouraged.

   (Note that this argument is weak because the statistical premiss does **not** say that most writers who experienced rejection went on to become great.)

8.   Ten percent of qualified applicants are admitted.
     Implicit premiss: you are qualified.
     _____
     You should not try to be admitted.

   (Argument is weak because conclusion is you should not try, not that you will not be admitted.)

Exercise Set 4.2

PART I

2. Justin Bieber is a pop star.

4. People who have a life-long habit of exercise do not stop just because they are in their seventies. Cher obviously exercises and doesn't fit the usual categories anyway.

Exercise Set 4.3

2. The condition that the authority is speaking in his or her area of expertise is violated because nuclear scientists are not experts on how much risk is socially acceptable.

Exercise Set 4.4

PART I

2.   Two thirds of those polled by the *Washington Post* said that the Afghan war
        was no longer worth fighting.
     My roommate was one of those polled.
     _____
     My roommate said that the Afghan war was no longer worth fighting.

     Reasonably strong statistical syllogism because of the two-thirds figure.

4. Most of what the American Medical Association (AMA) and the American
    Dental Association (ADA) have to say about dental welfare and health is correct.
    The AMA and ADA have endorsed fluoridation of drinking water.

    Fluoridation promotes dental welfare and is not generally harmful to health.
        Correct statistical syllogism (argument from authority).

6. Most presidential economic advisors for the last 30 years have argued that the best way to
    make consumers conserve energy is to increase taxes on gas and oil.

    Raising taxes on gas and oil is the best way to make consumers conserve energy.

    Even though economists disagree about many issues in their field, the agreement in this
    case—among advisors with opposing political views—is impressive. This makes the argument a
    strong argument from authority.

8. *Tu quoque* (You too).

10. The argument appeals to the authority of John Wesley, as one who received benefits from
    folk medicine. But he was not an expert in that field.

12. Most of what North says about his truth telling is false.
    North now says he only wants to tell the truth.

    North is lying now.

    Given North's record of perjury on the same topic, this is a strong argument against the person.

PART II

Gish claims that the objections that evolutionists have to creation science apply equally to evolutionary theory. This is a *tu quoque* form of *ad hominem*.

PART IV

If he is telling the truth, he must be lying, but if he is lying, he is telling the truth.

PART VI

Fallacious appeal to authority.

Exercise Set 4.5

2. My last pair of Brand X running shoes had (unnamed) design, were
    comfortable, gave excellent support, and lasted a long time.
    My new pair of Brand X running shoes have the same (unnamed) design.

    My new pair of Brand X running shoes will be comfortable, give excellent
    support, and last a long time.

    The analogy that makes this argument work (similar design) is not described in enough de-
    tail to assess the strength of the argument. For example, shoes can look similar but differ in fea-
    tures that affect wear, support, and so on. If "same design" includes type of construction and
    materials, however, the argument from analogy is strong.

4. The mansion-to-be is being taxed at the rate of a palatial estate.
    But it is relevantly dissimilar to a palatial estate. It is similar
        to places without plumbing or other amenities.
    _____

    The mansion-to-be should be taxed at the rate of buildings similar to it.

    The relevant disanalogy is pointed out, as is the similarity between this house and others that lack amenities.

6. Chimps have a limited capacity to use tools.
    Other great apes are similar to chimps in intelligence.
    _____

    Other great apes have a capacity for tool use similar to that of chimps.

    The argument from analogy is good and can be strengthened by the implicit premiss that the other apes resemble chimps not only in intelligence but also in body structure and manual dexterity.

8. Laboratory investigations of mice show that mice are more susceptible to bacterial
        respiratory infections after exposure to nitrogen dioxide.
    (Implicit premiss: Young children are similar to mice in relevant ways, perhaps by having
        similarly effective lung-defense mechanisms.)
    _____

    Young children exposed to nitrogen dioxide at home have increased incidence or severity of
        respiratory infections.

    This argument depends on similarities between the respiratory systems of mice and children. The passage also says that studies of human populations were done as well, and these do not depend on analogical reasoning.

10. Men's natural tendency towards goodness is like water's natural tendency to
        find the lower level.
    Water can rise against its nature only if force is applied.
    _____

    Men can be made to do evil against their nature if force is applied.

    The argument depends on whether the tendency of water to seek a lower level is relevantly similar to humans' desire to do good.

    This is a beautiful analogy and bespeaks a faith in human goodness, but the claim that humans are naturally good is not strongly supported.

12. Clinton has lied to or misled his wife and daughter.
    _____

    Clinton would lie to the American public.

    The analogy between lying to one's wife about sexual misconduct and lying to the public about matters of state is not strong.

14. The bending of the twig shapes the tree.
    _____

    The education a person has shapes the person's mind.

    The conclusion is plausible on other grounds, but the degree of relevant analogy between young trees and uneducated minds is not great.

16. Some highly civilized persons today feel about abortion the way some highly civilized persons in earlier times felt about slavery—that it is a normal human institution.
    It would not have been appropriate in earlier times to scorn Jefferson for owning slaves.

    It is not appropriate now for pro-life folk to scorn a woman who terminates a pregnancy by abortion.

There are similarities in the passions felt by abolitionists for their cause and "prolifers" for theirs. However, there are many relevant disanalogies between slavery and abortion. Buckley's argument ostensibly promotes tolerance for abortion, but in reality it condemns abortion by placing it in the same moral category as slavery.

18. A continuous gradation of color patches from yellow through orange into red can be divided into two classes [reddish and yellowish] by choosing some criterion of demarcation in the center of the orange range.
    The fossil record of a sequence of organisms showing gradual changes from reptile to mammal has been divided by taxonomists for convenience into two classes, reptile and mammal.
    It would be absurd to say on the basis of a decision to divide the continuum of color patches that no continuum exists.

    It is absurd to say on the basis of a taxonomist's decision to divide the sequence of organisms into two classes that no continuum exists.

The point that drawing divisions in a continuum does not destroy a continuum is correct, but creationists might not be moved by Kitcher's analogy because they would question the similarity between the continuum found in the color spectrum and the gap-riddled continuum of the fossil record.

20. According to Sir George Baker P, the civil law based on common law in America, Canada, and Australia is permeated with the view that a fetus cannot have a right of its own until it is born and has a separate existence from its mother. English law, like American, Canadian, and Australian laws, is based on common law. So Sir George Baker P uses the analogy between the laws of the various countries to infer that a fetus cannot, in English law, have a right of its own until it is born and has a separate existence from its mother.

Exercise Set 4.6

2. If you legalize marijuana for medical purposes, people will say that it is not harmful.

   If marijuana is not regarded as harmful, people will want to allow its purchase and use for recreation and relaxation.
   If this is allowed, marijuana will be available to everyone.

   If you legalize marijuana for medical use, marijuana will soon be available to everyone.

The slippery slope assumes that any relaxation of treating marijuana as a controlled substance will result in total lack of control. This claim, however, conflicts with the success of controlling other substances (prescription drugs) for medical use.

Exercise Set 4.7

2. In a nationwide poll of registered voters conducted on landline telephones, 60 percent of registered voters said they had voted in the presidential election held the previous day.

    Between 59 percent and 61 percent of registered voters voted in the presidential election.

    Polling based on landline phones is probably biased because many people do not use landlines. Also, although the poll was nationwide, we do not know whether it was sufficiently large to justify the 59 percent to 61 percent conclusion.

4. All members of my fraternity are going to the game.

    The game will be sold out.

    This is an example of fallacious reasoning, based on biased statistics.

6. In a sample of 93 coronary patients, slightly more than half had pets, one third of those without pets died within a year, and only one sixteenth of the pet owners died.

    Pet ownership has a positive effect on the health of humans

    Although the sample is small, the conclusion of the argument is weak, and so the argument is not fallacious. Further background information about whether the pet owners had other properties relevant to longer life would be useful.

8. Statistics collected over a 10-year period show that the bus is the safest form of travel. A recent bus accident took the lives of six people.

    The bus is less safe than an airplane for Jonathan's trip.

Jonathan is fallaciously rejecting a conclusion that is strongly supported by the statistical evidence. He is misled by the vividness of the recent accident.

10. EPA analyses from 12 RadNet monitors showed trace amounts of radioactive elements consistent with the Japanese nuclear incident. The levels at these monitors, though slightly higher than in the weeks before the incident, are far below levels of public-health concern.

    General atmospheric levels of these radioactive isotopes in the U.S. is far below the level of public-health concern.

    The conclusion is not stated, but it is implied by the sampling argument.

    The argument is reasonably strong because the monitors are designed to yield unbiased samples in a wide enough area to support a general conclusion.

12. One of two bats tested for rabies in a lab was rabid.

    Fifty percent of the state's bats are rabid.

    The author of the passage criticizes this inductive generalization because it is based on a tiny sample. The sample is biased as well—bats are not brought in for testing unless they are suspected of being rabid.

Exercise Set 4.8

2. The automated polling technique can eliminate bias that might result from using a variety of different polltakers.

- The use of randomly selected phone numbers in a way that ensures appropriate geographic representation also eliminates bias.
- Calling home numbers at times when most people are at home eliminates another source of bias.
- The processing step is designed to ensure a representative (unbiased) sample of the population.
- Use of census-bureau data and refined census-bureau data to target specific populations is designed to ensure that appropriate reference classes are selected.
- All of the techniques are designed to yield samples that, although relatively small in size, are representative of a very large and diverse population.

4. Parents have the right to share in companionship, care, custody, and
     management of their minor children within the traditional nuclear family.
    Outside the traditional nuclear family, "family-like" relationships—as specified
     in the first premiss—can be maintained.
    The state is severely restricted from interfering with parental rights in the traditional
     nuclear family.
    _____

    The state should be severely restricted from interfering with parental rights
     outside the nuclear family when family relationships are maintained.

    Argument from analogy.

6. This argument is an illegitimate appeal to authority because of the disagreement on the morality of abortion among "experts" in moral matters.

8. This argument is deductive, based on the meanings of sampling results and margin of error.

10. A sample of 36 patients with mild to moderate precancerous lesions in the esophagus had
      biopsies and was given 60 grams of freeze-dried strawberries dissolved in water each day
      for six months.
     At the end of six months, new biopsies were taken, and 29 of the 36 showed improvement.
     _____

     Strawberries can fight cancer.

     This is an argument based on a sample. As the experimenter said, however, a larger
      controlled study is needed to confirm the results.

12. One possible way to select an unbiased sample would be to take a random selection from all the students' ID numbers and interview all of the students whose numbers were selected.

16. The author warns against using a sample that is too small. He uses an argument from analogy to make his point.

18. The author of the letter suggests that the person who wrote the article committed the fallacy of biased statistics (using a sample composed only of men to make a claim about people in general).

20. In the first paragraph, the author refers to several inductive generalizations. In the second paragraph, he discusses an argument from analogy and accepts its conclusion that a ban on the sale or use of tobacco will increase illicit activity and increase contempt for the law.

Chapter Five

Exercise Set 5.1

2. Possible answers: A very large class that meets on Wednesdays in a hall near the food court ends just before noon, or a very popular menu item is available only on Wednesdays.

4. The new phones might share a manufacturer's defect.

6. The students copied their papers from the same paper found in a file of old term papers.

Exercise Set 5.2

2. The company has been granted a new rate increase by the Public Utility Commission. Or, you exceeded your budget amount during the last few months.

4. You ate or drank something unusual at dinner. Or you are particularly worried about some problem.

6. His answer was received before yours. Or the winning entry was selected at random from all of the correct solutions.

8. Something is wrong with the food or with the dog tonight. Or the dog has grown tired of that food.

Exercise Set 5.3

2. a. A cause is sought for the loss of enzyme activity (decreased activity in the cortex) in patients who die of Alzheimer's disease.

b. The five Alzheimer's patients were found in postmortem examination to have a smaller than normal number of cells in the nucleus basalis than the five without Alzheimer's.

c. Joint method of agreement and difference.

d. Reduced number of cells in the nucleus basalis causes loss of enzyme activity, which in turn is suspected of being the cause of brain lesions typical of Alzheimer's.

4. a. Higher rate of beriberi.

b. During a one-year period, half the inmates of the asylum were fed a diet of cured rice; the other half, a diet of uncured rice. Halfway through the year, the patients housed in one ward were moved to the other ward, and vice versa.

c. Joint method of agreement and difference.

d. A diet of cured rice causes a higher rate of beriberi.

6. a. Reduction in alcohol-related deaths of drivers who are less than 21 years old.

b. Laws setting 21 years of age as the minimum age to purchase or publicly possess alcohol are correlated with lower rates of death. States that lowered the minimum legal age for purchasing or possessing alcohol saw rates of crashes and death among youth increase.

c. Joint method of agreement and difference.

d. Raising the minimum legal drinking age to 21 caused a reduction in alcohol-related traffic deaths among young people.

8. a. Relief of joint pain.

b. Study of 1,600 participants with varying levels of joint pain (22 percent with moderate-to-severe pain; 78 percent with mild pain) was divided into two groups. One received Glucosamine/Chondriton supplements; the other received a placebo.

c. Joint method of agreement and difference.

d. Glucosamine/Chondriton supplements cause relief of moderate-to-severe joint pain.

10. a. Increased rate of development of dental caries.

b. A group of 436 patients on a nutritionally adequate diet had a slow rate of caries development over a period of several years. Subsequently, they were divided into nine groups, and sucrose was introduced into their diets in various forms and with varying degrees of frequency of intake. Caries increased significantly, particularly when the ingestion of sucrose was frequent and when the form of sucrose was sticky or adhesive. After two years on the test diets, the control diet was resumed, and the caries activity returned to the slow rate.

c. Method of concomitant variation.

d. Rise and fall of rate of caries development is causally related to rise and fall in amount, frequency, and form of sucrose consumption.

12. a. Increased protection of wine grapes from grape berry moth.

b. Some plots were treated with pheromones. Other plots were treated with insecticide.

c. Joint method of agreement and difference.

d. Treatment with pheromone caused a lower incidence of damage from grape berry moth.

14. a. Increased numbers of migratory birds.

b. Deer were excluded from some four-hectare plots and allowed to enter other four-hectare plots.

c. Joint method of agreement and difference.

d. Exclusion of deer (which destroy plants that provide food and cover for migratory birds).

16. a. Compulsive overeating.

b. Brains of 10 obese people compared with brains of drug addicts.

c. Agreement.

d. Special dopamine receptor causes overeating.

Exercise Set 5.4

2. a. Method of agreement and difference.

b. Not a controlled experiment.

4. Retrospective study.

8. For the retrospective portion of their study, the investigators gathered a sample of $252 + 175$ persons diagnosed with tumors and 822 control subjects, matched only for age and sex. Using interviews, medical records, and examinations, they refined the control group to eliminate controls with tumors and then further refined the match by controlling for socioeconomic status and memory ability. Then, using a smaller but carefully matched number of cases and controls, they did a prospective study monitoring cellphone calls and found no association between cellphone use and risk for the two types of tumors. (This study is typical of many in its effort to construct a good match between subjects and controls—often the most difficult part of an experiment.)

Exercise Set 5.5

2. A sufficient causal condition against a background of accepted, stable, necessary conditions (no unpaid bills, distribution and total credit requirements met, application for graduation completed, and so forth).

4. An agent (arson requires an arsonist) causally responsible for some event.

6. This could be a probabilistic, proximate cause.

8. Lack of *enough* rain is sufficient for poor crops.

10. Sufficient causal condition, proximate cause.

12. Probabilistic cause or, perhaps, a sufficient causal condition against a background of accepted, necessary conditions.

14. Probabilistic cause or, perhaps, a sufficient causal condition against a background of accepted, stable, necessary conditions.

16. The series of accidents was a sufficient cause for the investigation.

18. Sufficient cause against a background of stable, necessary causes.

20. Sperm motility (greater than 20 percent) is a necessary condition for fertility.

Exercise Set 5.6

PART I

2. Ignoring a common cause. According to Reynolds, home ownership, higher education, and middle-class status are all caused by qualities of self-discipline and delayed gratification.

Do you think Reynolds regards these qualities as necessary causes or as sufficient causes?

PART II

2. Confusing cause and effect. Many of the wealthy inherit stocks, bonds, and they like or invest in these because they have surplus income not needed for the necessities of life.

4. Confusing (supposed) consequences of a belief with evidence for (or against) it.

6. Confusion of cause and effect. People did not riot to obtain television sets. The thefts were a result of the conditions of disorder that prevailed during the riots.

8. Ignoring a common cause. Advances in science and technology have both good and bad results.

10. Confusion of cause and effect. Large numbers of passes are frequently a desperate attempt to salvage a game that appears to be lost. A more careful analysis might show that when there is an unusually large number of passes, most of them occur in the final quarter.

12. Fallacy of mistaking some consequence of a belief with evidence for it. The claim that computers think is rejected not on the basis of any evidence but because of a belief that its truth would devalue human worth.

PART III

2. Confusing cause and effect.

4. Confusing cause and effect.

PART IV

2. Confusing cause and effect.

4. Ignoring a common cause.

6. Confusing cause and effect.

Chapter Six

Exercise Set 6.1

2. Use the theorem and the result from Exercise 1 to calculate this:

$$(1 - 1/2) = 1/2.$$

4. The probability of obtaining at least one head is equal to the probability of *not* obtaining all tails. Use the result from Exercise 3 and the theorem:

$$(1 - 1/8) = 7/8.$$

6. The probability of drawing an ace on the first draw is 4/52. The probability of drawing a second ace, given that the first draw was an ace (without replacing the card drawn), is 3/51. Rule (4) applies:

$$4/52 \times 3/51 = 1/221 \text{ (or, } 0.0045).$$

8. a. The combination of a boy and a girl can occur in two different ways: Girl first born and boy second, or boy first born and girl second. Assuming independence and equal probabilites for either sex, Rule (4) applies to each possibility. The probability of girl first and then boy is $1/2 \times 1/2 = 1/4$. Similarly, the probability of boy first and then girl is also 1/4. Because these combinations are mutually exclusive, Rule (3) applies: $1/4 + 1/4 = 1/2$, which is the probability of one boy and one girl in a family with two children.

b. Again assuming independence, the probabilty that the first child is a boy is 1/2, and the probability that the fourth child is a boy, given that the first is a boy, is also 1/2.

$$\text{Rule (4) applies: } 1/2 \times 1/2 = 1/4.$$

10. Assuming independence, Rule (4) applies:

$$0.51 \times 0.51 = 0.26.$$

12. a. The probability that the first person draws a ball of some color is 1. Because the balls are replaced, the probability that the second person will draw the same color is $1/7$; and the probability that the third will also draw the same color is $1/7$. Rule (4) applies:

$$1 \times 1/7 \times 1/7 = 1/49.$$

b. At least two will draw the same color unless none of them draws a color that matches either of the others. Use Rule (4) to calculate the probability of no matches:

$$1 \times 6/7 \times 5/7 = 30/49.$$

(The first draws some color; the second has 6 of 7 chances of not matching the first; and the third has 5 of 7 chances of matching neither the first nor the second.)

The probability that at least two will match is one minus the probability that none will match: $1 - 30/49 = 19/49$.

14. $0.7 \times 0.6 \times 0.5 = 0.21$ (Rule [4]).

Exercise Set 6.2

2. a. The minimum jackpot of $20 million.

b. Personal choice.

c. Dreams about what you would do with the money. Reluctance to risk any amount when the probability of winning is so low. Moral disapproval of gambling.

4. a. Decision under uncertainty.

b. Yes, since the sole purpose is to raise money for charity.

c.

	Rain	No Rain
Indoors	$440	$170
Outdoors	$80	$500

No action dominates. If there is a satisfactory action, it is to have an indoor buffet. If there is no satisfactory action, the gambler would choose the outdoor picnic; the cautious player would choose the indoor supper. The calculator would see that the average utility of the indoor supper is $305 and of the outdoor picnic $290, and would choose the indoor supper.

6. a. Maximize expected utility (decision under risk).

b. It is reasonable to equate units of utility with profits and losses.

Expected utility for new special: $(1/2 \times \$350) + (1/2 \times -\$50) = \$150$.

Expected utility for usual special: $100.

Go for the new special.

8. **States of the World**

	Attend three operas	Attend four operas
Season ticket	$2/3 \times -\$100$	$1/3 \times -\$100$
Pay as you go	$2/3\,(-\$75)$	$1/3\,(-\$100)$

The utilities are based on the cost of tickets only, and the point is to maximize the expected utility. The expected utility of buying a season ticket is −$100, which is what you pay for three, four, or five operas. If the probabilities of attending three or four operas are as given, the expected utility of paying as you go is −$83.33, so it is better to pay as you go. Even if the probability of attending only three operas is 2/3, and the probability of attending all five is 1/3, you would still be better off paying as you go: $2/3 \times -\$75 + 1/3 \times -\$125 = -\$50 + -\$41.33 = -\$91.33$. So if the probability of attending at least four operas is only 1/3, you are better off not buying the season ticket.

10. a. **Pr** (There will be an epidemic) × **Pr** (You will get the flu, given an epidemic and no vaccination) = $0.8 \times 0.6 = 0.48$.

b. The utility of having flu is figured in days lost to illness: −7, and so the expected utility of having the flu is $0.48 \times -7 = -3.36$ days.

c. The expected utility of having the shot is 0.01×-2 days = -0.02 days (or slightly less than minus half an hour).

d. Yes.

12. One way to set up the problem assigns utilities solely on the basis of dollar cost:

States of the World

	Get the Jacket	Miss Out
Actions.		
Buy now	$1\,(-\$100)$	$0\,(-\$100)$
Wait three days	$0.75 \times -\$50$	$0.25 \times \$125$

The expected utility of buying today is −$100, which is today's cost of the jacket.

The expected value of waiting until Wednesday is $(0.75 \times -\$50) + (0.25 \times -\$125) = -\$37.50 + -\$31.25 = -\$68.75$.

To maximize expected utility, wait until Wednesday to buy the jacket.

Chapter Seven

Exercise Set 7.1

2. a. Extensive massaging when applying and removing makeup causes actresses to seek face-lifts at an earlier age than other women.

b. Either a prospective study using a group of actresses who are careful not to massage when applying and removing makeup could be done to observe the results, or a group of nonactresses of similar age and body type who do not wear much makeup could be observed to see whether their faces had "fallen" as much as those of the actresses. Auxiliary hypothesis: The doctor who made the hypothesis has accurate information about the ages of those who seek face-lifts.

c. Alternative hypothesis: Actresses seek face-lifts at an earlier age because their earnings may depend on their looking young.

d. Based on general background knowledge, the prior probability of the alternative hypothesis compares favorably with that of the original.

4. a. Failure to count unemployed 16- to 19-year-olds who have "given up" looking for work is the cause of the relatively low rate of unemployment when New York is compared with cities in the Midwest.

b. A survey of youths without jobs will show that many say they want jobs but have stopped looking because the situation seems hopeless. Auxiliary: Official unemployment figures take account only of those who are actively seeking work. Statistics are accurately reported.

c. Alternative hypothesis: A significant proportion of 16- to 19-year-olds are not interested in jobs because they would prefer to hang out with their friends.

d. Given background information, the original hypothesis has a higher prior probability than the alternative.

6. a. The threat of the death penalty does not lower the rate of homicide.

b. States that abolish the death penalty will show a drop in a higher homicide rates. Auxiliary hypothesis: Accurate statistics can be gathered.

c. Alternative hypothesis: The drop in homicide rates overall is part of a national trend in the U.S.

d. Statistical evidence for drops in homicide rates in other states that have abolished the death penalty supports the original hypothesis. The alternative hypothesis is vague and offers no causal mechanism.

8. a. These bog people died in connection with a midwinter sacrificial ceremony.

b. Other archaeological remains will support the claim that human sacrifices occurred at midwinter ceremonies. Auxiliary hypotheses: Persons to be sacrificed were not fed a special diet but ate whatever fresh foods were available at the time of death. The remains of all foods eaten were equally preserved in the intestines and were found in the examination.

c. The bog people were criminals, were condemned to die, and were fed a special diet.

d. More information is needed to compare the probabilities of the two hypotheses.

10. a. Emotional preparation for surgery aids recovery.

b. Patients who undergo such preparations will suffer fewer postsurgical complications than those who do not receive preparation. Auxiliary: The viewing of videotapes of prior similar operations and conversations with nurses help to prepare patients emotionally.

c. Given the small sample, an alternative hypothesis could attribute the better results in one group to some quirks in the way patients were selected for the experiment. Perhaps it is not emotional preparation per se that accounts for the better result but rather the increased attention to the patients who were interviewed.

d. A higher prior probability could be assigned to the original hypothesis because common sense as well as medical theory supports the view that emotional well-being correlates with physical well-being.

12. a. The red wine that the French drink along with their high-fat diets offer them some protection against obesity and diabetes.

b. The French have lower rates of obesity and diabetes than Americans, who also eat a high-fat diet. Auxiiliary hypothesis: Measures of fat in diets and of obesity and diabetes are accurate. This is probably based on statistics gathered by public-health sources but might be questioned.

c. Alternative hypothesis: Fewer French are obese or diabetic because they consume fewer calories.

d. The red wine hypothesis has some support from controlled experiments of resveratrol's preventive effect against obesity and diabetes in mice. But mice are different from humans, and humans would have to drink 60 liters of red wine daily to get comparable amounts of antioxidant resveratrol. Many other studies have shown that calorie reduction is a good strategy to prevent obesity and diabetes. It seems a higher probability should be assigned to the alternative.

Exercise Set 7.3

2. Hypothesis: Chinese herbs, which prevented replication of the HIV virus in *in-vitro* experiments, are an effective remedy against AIDS.

Disconfirming observation: Many substances that are effective against HIV in a test tube are ineffective or dangerous in the human body.

4. Hypothesis: Hepatiis B vaccine causes or triggers multiple sclerosis in adults.

Disconfirming observation: Clinical and population studies, reviewed by the Institute of Medicine, showed that the hepatitis B vaccine does not cause or trigger multiple sclerosis in adults.

Alternative: The victims of multiple sclerosis who received the vaccine contracted the disease from another source.

Second hypothesis: Hepatitis B virus does not pose a serious enough risk to justify vaccination of infants and young children.

Disconfirming observation: Testimony about the seriousness of the disease, especially for young children, and growing evidence of the benefits of the vaccine.

Alternative hypothesis: No real alternative; claims based on rumor and innuendo.

6. Hypothesis: Photographs of the dead bin Laden would offend viewers and incite reprisals against Americans.

Disconfirming observation: Americans would not be offended because they are used to gruesome pictures. The pictures would be no more inflammatory to the Muslim community than those of the capture and death of Saddam Hussein.

8. Hypothesis: Early humans lived in caves and built campfires for roasting meat in the caves. Plausible on the basis of folklore and tradition.

Disconfirming observation: Huge amounts of ash and other debris in caves.

Alternative: Humans used caves to preserve sources of fire but did not live in them.

10. Hypothesis: Increases in the number of cases of autism in children are caused by widespread use of MMR vaccine. The vaccine contains thimerasol, a mercury compound used as a preservative.

Disconfirming observation: Although Denmark and the U.S. have responded by removing thimerasol from their supply of vaccines, the rate of autism has continued to rise. There is no evidence for an association between thimerasol and increased numbers of autistic children.

Alternative: Better detection and diagnosis of autism, rather than an actual increase in the disease, may account for the rising numbers. Also, some studies show that genetic factors are of primary importance in incidence of the disease.

Exercise Set 7.4

2. a. 1. Use Rule (4). Probability of being an out-of-state resident *and* not having a car: $100/400 \times 25/100 = 1/16$.

2. Rule (4) again: $300/400 \times 200/300 = 1/2$.

3. There are 400 students, and 175 of them have cars: $175/400$, or $7/16$ (0.4375).

b. 1. Use Bayes's Theorem: $\dfrac{\frac{1}{4} \times \frac{3}{4}}{(\frac{1}{4} \times \frac{3}{4}) + (\frac{3}{4} \times \frac{1}{4})} = \dfrac{1}{2}$

2. Because every student with a car is either an out-of-state student or a state resident, the probability that a student who has a car is a state resident is 1 minus the probability that the student who has a car is from out of state:

$1 - 1/2 = 1/2$.

4. a. $1/2$

b. $1/2 \times 1/4 = 1/8$

c. $1/2 \times 1/4 + 1/2 \times 3/4 = 1/2$.

d. 1 minus the probability of drawing a red card, or $1 - 1/2 = 1/2$.

e. Use Bayes's theorem:

$$\frac{\frac{1}{2} \times \frac{1}{4}}{(\frac{1}{2} \times \frac{1}{4}) + (\frac{1}{2} \times \frac{3}{4})},$$

which equals $1/4$.

f. Use Bayes's Theorem:

$$\frac{\frac{1}{2} \times \frac{3}{4} \times \frac{38}{51}}{(\frac{1}{2} \times \frac{3}{4} \times \frac{38}{51}) + (\frac{1}{2} \times \frac{1}{4} \times \frac{12}{51})} = \frac{57}{63} \text{ or } 0.905$$

6. Background information does not favor male or female assignment, but numbers in the population are roughly equal, so a prior probability of $1/2$ ($\Pr(m) = 0.5$) that Tamar is male is reasonable. If Tamar is color-blind, however, the likelihood that Tamar is male is ($\Pr(c\,|\,m) = 0.01$. The likelihood that Tamar is not male, given that Tamar is color-blind, is much lower: ($\Pr(c\,|\,{\sim}m) = 0.0001$. So the posterior probability that Tamar is male, given that Tamar is color-blind, $= 0.50 \times (0.01)/[(0.50 \times 0.01) + (0.50 \times 0.0001)] = .005/[0.005 + 0.00005] = 0.99$.

Exercise Set 7.5

2. a. Use Rule (3): $(0.8 \times 0.5) + (0.2 \times 0.9) = 0.58$.

b. Use Bayes's Theorem:

$$\frac{(0.8 \times 0.5)}{(0.8 + 0.5) + (0.2 \times 0.9)} = \frac{0.4}{0.58} = 0.69$$

4. a. Use Bayes's Theorem: Pr (Brunette is guilty | Witness says so) = 0.12.

$$\frac{(0.20 \times 0.60)}{(0.20 + 0.60) + (0.80 \times 0.40)} = \frac{0.12}{0.44} = 0.27$$

b. Use Bayes's Theorem:

$$\frac{(0.20 \times 0.40)}{(0.20 + 0.40) + (0.80 \times 0.60)} = \frac{0.08}{0.08 + 0.48} = \frac{0.08}{0.56} = 0.143$$

6. A low prior probability is assigned to the smuggling of an asp in a fig basket. A low likelihood is assigned to Cleopatra's dying from an asp bite, given her condition when she was found dead. A higher prior probability is assigned to her using poison, based on knowledge that she had studied the medicines of the time. And a higher likelihood is that she died of poison, given her serene condition in death. But it would be very difficult to assign any numerical probabilities to this problem because of lack of evidence.

Exercise Set 7.6

2. Yes. Remember that the hypothesis being tested is rarely the sole basis for the prediction. If one of the auxiilary hypotheses is false, the prediction could be false as well. Furthermore, some arguments from hypotheses to predictions are inductive rather than deductive. If the reasoning is inductive, true hypotheses can be the basis for false predictions. For example, the true hypothesis that there is a mole involved in some CIA operation could be the basis for a prediction that state secrets are leaked to the enemy. But the prediction could turn out to be false for any number of reasons.

4. When alternatives have the same predictions, their relative standing after a successful prediction is unchanged (though each may have increased its posterior probability). The alternative with the highest posterior probability should be chosen, in any case.

6. Inductive, because an alternative hypothesis that is incompatible with the original hypothesis could support the same prediction.

8. No, because hypothesis testing is embedded in auxiliary assumptions, so a disconfirming observation could mean that *either* the hypothesis being tested *or* one of the auxiliaries was false.

10. If a hypothesis is already very strongly confirmed, then its probability—relative to the available evidence—is very high. If that probability is close to 1, then additional successful predictions cannot increase the probability greatly.

12. No, good scientific hypotheses should lead us to new predictions and new connections with other areas of knowledge.

14. Theoretically, the number of alternative hypotheses that can be devised is unlimited, or limited only by the powers of imagination. But in practice, the number of plausible hypotheses is always limited, and usually is a relatively small number. (This is not to say that an investigator always is able to formulate all the plausible hypotheses that could be tested.)

16. a. This predicted discovery is one of many that constitute confirmation of evolutionary theory. A single instance is not strong confirmation, but the accumulation of such confirmatory instances strongly supports the theory.

b. Alternative nonscientific hypotheses could include a "fortunate accident" or "plan of a clever designer."

18. In the situation described, the prior probability of a mistaken grade is high. Check it out!

20. Because fortune-tellers so often predict what their customers would like to hear, and because they are often clever about obtaining information about what their customers would like to hear, the successful prediction does not raise the probability much, if at all.

Chapter Eight

Exercise Set 8.1

2. If you do not brush your teeth twice a day then you won't please your dentist at your checkups.

4. If you maintain a 3.3 grade-point average you will be eligible for a scholarship.

6. If the teacher asks about her, then (say that) Jane missed the test because she was ill.

8. If a student is graduated, then the student has a grade-point average of C or better.

10. If you ride a bicycle without a helmet, then you care little for your safety.

Exercise Set 8.2

PART I

2. If p, then q.

4. If p, then q.

6. If p, then q.

8. If q, then p.

10. If p, then q.

PART II

1. b. Frank admired Gloria. He met her.

d. Gloria feels the same way about him. ("Frank hopes that" is not a sentence. Nevertheless, "Frank hopes that Gloria feels the same way about him" is a compound sentence because it contains another sentence as a part.)

Exercise Set 8.3

2. If Naomi leaves town, then Ruth will follow her.
    Naomi is going.

    Ruth will follow.

4. If a man cannot own, spend, claim, or want money, then that man cannot be robbed.
    A dead man cannot own, spend, claim, or want money.

    A dead man cannot be robbed.

Exercise Set 8.5

2. If Harry will get the role, then he was trained as a method actor.
    Harry was not trained as a method actor.

    Harry won't get the role.

    Denying the consequent.

4. If you can graduate, then your library fines are paid.
    Your library fines are paid.

    You can graduate.

    Affirming the consequent.

6. If Freud was correct, then morality is nothing but a set of internalized parental commands.
    But it is imbecilic (i.e., it is not true) that morality consists of such commands.

    Therefore Freud was wrong (incorrect) about morality.

    Denying the consequent.

8. If the ability to live a coherent moral life depended on having an intellectual theory of
       morality, most people would not live a coherent moral life.
    (Implied premiss) Most people do live a coherent moral life.

    Living a coherent moral life does not depend on having an intellectual theory of morality.

    Denying the consequent.

10. If two is not a prime number, then there is a positive integer smaller than two and greater
       than one that evenly divides two.
    But there are no positive integers smaller than two and greater than one.

    Two is a prime number.

    Denying the consequent.

12. If we can have all that is written in a language in translation, then we will not
       take the trouble to learn the language.
    We cannot have all that is written in the language in translation (i.e., poetry cannot be
       translated).

    We take the trouble to learn the language.

    Denying the antecedent.

14. If a judgment of acquittal by reason of insanity is inappropriate in the Washington case, then a jury verdict of guilty would violate the law or the facts.
    The jury verdict of guilty does not violate the law or the facts.

    A judgment of acquittal by reason of insanity is inappropriate in the Washington case.

    Denying the consequent.

16. If the simple utilitarian model is correct, then there will be a wide but more or less even pattern of dispersal of axes in all directions from the quarry source.
    There is not a more or less even pattern of dispersal of axes from the quarry source.

    Implicit conclusion: The simple utilitarian model is not correct.

    Denying the consequent.

18. If it wasn't the Major, then it was the Bruce chap.
    It wasn't the Major.

    It was the Bruce chap.
    Affirming the antecedent.

20. If data dictate conclusions, then scientists faced with the same data always reach the same conclusion.
    Scientists faced with the same data do not always reach the same conclusion.

    Data do not dictate conclusions.

    Denying the consequent.

Exercise Set 8.6

PART I

2. Constructive dilemma.

4. Hypothetical syllogism.

6. Not a valid form. If we translate "Either you buy a lottery ticket, or you won't win the lottery" to its equivalent—"If you don't buy a lottery ticket, then you won't win the lottery"—we can see that this is an instance of affirming the consequent.

8. Constructive dilemma.

10. Constructive dilemma, with implied conclusion: Either there will be riots, or there will be intervention.

    This is the sort of situation in which a politician would try to "go between the horns of the dilemma" by not exactly complying with Rome nor standing up to Rome either.

    If there is a third alternative besides complying with Rome or standing up to Rome (i.e., not complying), then the problem might be considered a false dilemma.

12. Disjunctive syllogism—but perhaps black-and-white thinking is involved.

14. Constructive dilemma. Can you state the implicit conclusion?

PART III

The missing premiss of the dilemma is "Either men and women are the same, or they are not the same." The conclusion is "Women should be in the priesthood."

Exercise Set 8.7

PART I

2. $\sim r \rightarrow \sim p$

4. $p \cdot (r \rightarrow q)$

6. $r \lor \sim p$

8. $\sim (p \lor q)$

10. $\sim p \leftrightarrow \sim r$

12. $p \cdot q$

14. $p \cdot (r \rightarrow q)$

PART II

2. It is not the case that logic is easy and symbols can be used.

4. Logic is fun if and only if symbols cannot be used.

6. Logic is easy or fun, but not both.

8. If symbols can be used and logic is easy, then logic is fun.

10. If logic is fun, then symbols can be used, and if symbols can be used, then logic is fun.

PART III

p	q	$p \rightarrow q$	$q \rightarrow p$	$(p \rightarrow q) \cdot (q \rightarrow p)$	$p \leftrightarrow q$	
T	T	T	T	T	T	
T	F	F	T	F	F	
F	T	T	F	F	F	
F	F	T	T	T	T	Equivalent.

PART IV

2. p	q	$\sim q$	$p \rightarrow q$	$p \rightarrow \sim q$	$\sim (p \rightarrow q)$	
T	T	F	T	F	F	
T	F	T	F	T	T	
F	T	F	T	T	F	
F	F	T	T	T	F	Not equivalent.

4.

p	q	$\sim p$	$p \rightarrow q$	$\sim p \vee q$	
T	T	F	T	T	
T	F	F	F	F	
F	T	T	T	T	
F	F	T	T	T	Equivalent.

6.

p	q	$\sim p$	$q \rightarrow p$	$p \rightarrow (q \rightarrow p)$	$p \vee \sim p$	
T	T	F	T	T	T	
T	F	F	T	T	T	
F	T	T	F	T	T	
F	F	T	T	T	T	Equivalent.

Exercise Set 8.8

2. F

4. F

6. T

8. F

10. T

12. T

14. T

16. T

18. T

20. T

Exercise Set 8.9

PART I

2.

p	q	$p \cdot q$	$p \vee q$	$(p \vee q) \rightarrow (p \cdot q)$	
T	T	T	T	T	
T	F	F	T	F	
F	T	F	T	F	
F	F	F	F	T	Valid.

4.

p	q	r	$\sim p$	$p \rightarrow q$	$q \vee r$	$\sim (q \vee r)$	
T	T	T	F	T	T	F	
T	T	F	F	T	T	F	
T	F	T	F	F	T	F	
T	F	F	F	F	F	T	
F	T	T	T	T	T	F	
F	T	F	T	T	T	F	
F	F	T	T	T	T	F	
F	F	F	T	T	F	T	Valid.

Because the conclusion, $\sim p$, is false only when p is true, the shorter truth table consists of the first four rows.

6.	p	q	$\sim p$	$p \to q$	$\sim p \to q$	
	T	T	F	T	T	
	T	F	F	F	T	
	F	T	T	T	T	
	F	F	T	T	F	Valid.

8.	p	q	r	s	$p \to s$	$q \to r$	$p \to (q \to r)$	$r \to s$	$q \to (r \to s)$
	T	T	T	T	**T**	T	**T**	T	**T**
	T	T	T	F	**F**	T	**T**	F	**F**
	T	T	F	T	**T**	F	**F**	T	**T**
	T	T	F	F	**F**	F	**F**	T	**T**
	T	F	T	T	**T**	T	**T**	T	**T**
	T	F	T	F	**F**	T	**T**	F	**T***
	T	F	F	T	**T**	T	**T**	T	**T**
	T	F	F	F	**F**	T	**T**	T	**T***
	F	T	T	T	**T**	T	**T**	T	**T**
	F	T	T	F	**T**	T	**T**	F	**F**
	F	T	F	T	**T**	F	**T**	T	**T**
	F	T	F	F	**T**	F	**T**	T	**T**
	F	F	T	T	**T**	T	**T**	T	**T**
	F	F	T	F	**T**	T	**T**	F	**T**
	F	F	F	T	**T**	T	**T**	T	**T**
	F	F	F	F	**T**	T	**T**	T	**T**

Invalid.

The conclusion, $p \to s$, is false only when p is true and s false. (Shorter table uses rows 2, 4, 6, and 8.)

10.	p	q	$\sim p$	$\sim q$	$\sim p \vee q$	$\sim q \vee p$	$p \leftrightarrow q$	
	T	T	F	F	T	T	T	
	T	F	F	T	F	T	F	
	F	T	T	F	T	F	F	
	F	F	T	T	T	T	T	Valid.

12. Considerations for constructing a shorter truth table:

For this form to be invalid, there must be a row in which the conclusion t is F and all the premisses are T.

Since p is a premiss, assign p the value T. Because t is the consequent in the second premiss, that premiss can be T only when the antecendent $(r \vee s)$ is F. That can happen only when both r and s are F. But if either r or s is false, the first premiss can be T only if $(p \vee q)$ is F—i.e., when p is F and

q is F. But p cannot be assigned F in the first premiss and T in the third premiss, so there is no consistent assignment that will make all the premisses T and the conclusion F.

The form is valid.

Part II

2. p: You can face your problem.

q: You can run away from it.

r: You are brave.

$p \lor q$	p	q	r	$(r \to p)$	$\sim q$	$p \lor q$	$(r \to \sim q)$
$r \to p$	T	T	T	T	F	T	F
$r \to \sim q$	T	T	F	T	F	T	T
	T	F	T	T	T	T	T
	T	F	F	T	T	T	T
	F	T	T	F	F	T	F
	F	T	F	T	F	T	T
	F	F	T	F	T	F	T
	F	F	F	T	T	F	T

Not Valid.

This symbolization of the argument does not recognize that "facing your problem" and "not running away from it" are synonymous.

4. p: The hockey team is winning most of its games.

q: The arena is sold out.

$$p \to q$$
$$\underline{q \qquad}$$
$$p$$

The truth table is that of affirming the consequent.

Invalid.

6. p: I buy a new car.

q: I buy an older car.

r: I'll be broke.

$$p \to r$$
$$q \to r$$
$$\underline{p \lor q \qquad}$$
$$r$$

The eight-row truth table is that of the constructive dilemma.

Valid.

PART III

2. *p*: You have a rival.

q: You must set out to please.

$$p \rightarrow q$$
$$\sim p \rightarrow q$$
$$\underline{p \vee \sim p}$$
$$q$$

Valid instance of a dilemma.

4. *p:* I say I am jealous or unhappy in my marriage.

q: I will admit I am jealous or self-doubting.

$$p \rightarrow q$$
$$\underline{\sim q}$$
$$\sim p$$

Valid instance of denying the consequent.

6. *p*: These pictures are good.

q: They will make their way in spite of objections.

r: They will perish without the aid of objections.

$$p \vee \sim p$$
$$p \rightarrow q$$
$$\underline{\sim p \rightarrow r}$$
$$q \vee r$$

Valid dilemma.

8. *p:* My categories of thought determine what I observe.

q: What I observe provides no independent control over my thought.

$$p \rightarrow q$$
$$\sim p \rightarrow q$$
$$\underline{p \vee \sim p}$$
$$q$$

Another dilemma.

10. Conclusion: Forced unionism is not good for the economy of states.

p: Forced unionism is good for the economy of states.

q: Businesses move to states with forced unionism in great numbers.

Form of the argument:

$$p \rightarrow q$$
$$\sim q$$
$$\sim p$$

Valid, denying the consequent.

12. p: A ruler wants to act honorably.

q: The ruler is surrounded by unscrupulous men.

r: His downfall is inevitable (i.e., he loses his power).

$$(p \cdot q) \rightarrow r$$
$$\sim r \rightarrow (q \rightarrow \sim p), \text{ or } (\sim r \cdot q) \rightarrow \sim p$$

Valid.

14. p: There will be consequences.

q: The man gets out.

$$\sim q \rightarrow p$$
$$\sim q$$
$$p$$

Valid instance of affirming the antecedent.

Exercise Set 8.10

2. No. If an argument has a self-contradictory premiss, then it is impossible for all of the premisses of the argument to be true. Therefore, it is impossible for all of the premisses to be true while the conclusion is false.

4. Yes; if two sentence forms are logically equivalent, then they have the same truth value regardless of how truth values are assigned to their individual components. But then it is impossible for the sentence forms to have different truth values, and so the statement of their material biconditional is itself a tautology.

6. a. $((p \vee q) \cdot p) \rightarrow \sim q$

b. $((p \rightarrow q) \cdot (p \vee r) \cdot r \rightarrow \sim s) \cdot s) \rightarrow q$

c. $(p \vee \sim p) \rightarrow q$

8. a. p: You can win. q: You try to win.

$\sim q \rightarrow \sim p$ (Contingent).

b. p: The rain falls on the rich. q: The rain falls on the poor.

$p \cdot q$ (Contingent).

c. p: It never rains. q: It pours.

$\sim q \rightarrow p$ (Contingent).

d. *p:* You win some. *q:* You lose some.

p • *q* (Contingent).

e. *p:* You really love her. *q:* You tell her you love her.

p → *q* (Contingent).

f. *p:* You are with me. *q:* You are against me.

p v *q* (Contingent). But notice that if "You are against me" is understood to mean "You are not with me," then the form is the tautologous "*p* v ∼ *p*."

g. Perhaps, *p* ↔ *p*.

Translated thus, it is a tautology.

h. *p:* He will win. *q:* He will lose.

p v *q* (Contingent).

i. *p:* You want it. *p* → *p*

(Tautology).

j. *p:* You wait for her at the café.

q: She'll show up.

p → *(q* v ∼*q)* (Tautology).

k. *p:* Determinism is true.

q: Humans have free will.

p → ∼*q* (Contingent).

Chapter Nine

Exercise Set 9.1

PART I

2. All novelists are journalists.

4. Some automobiles are not battery powered.

6. Some electric cars are not battery powered.

8. Some football players are ballroom dancers.

10. Some stockbrokers are not doctors.

PART II

2. Shaq is a short man.

4. Korea's economy is lagging.

6. Dark chocolate is a poor source of antioxidants.

8. When it rains, it drizzles.

10. Parrots are short-lived.

PART III

2. Lemons are not yellow.

4. Some clouds lack silver linings.

6. This jewel does not belong in the Smithsonian.

8. Sometimes it rains without pouring.

10. The polar ice caps are not shrinking rapidly.

Exercise Set 9.2

2. Every electric automobile that will sell has a 40-mile range.

E: Electric automobiles that will sell.

R: Automobiles that have a 40-mile range.

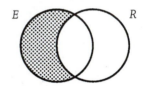

4. Every bride that the sun shines on is a happy bride.

B: Brides that the sun shines on.

H: Happy brides.

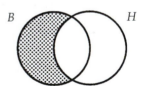

6. Some athletes are not graceful persons.

A: Athletes.

G: Graceful persons.

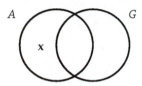

8. All home teams are teams that have the advantage.

T: Home teams.

A: Teams that have the advantage.

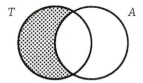

10. Some good singers are not good actors.

S: Good singers.

A: Good actors.

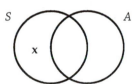

12. Some courses that are easiest are not the courses that are most satisfying.

E: Courses that are easiest.

S: Courses that are most satisfying.

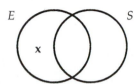

14. Every place where she goes is a place where she brings sunshine.

P: Places she goes.

S: Places she brings sunshine.

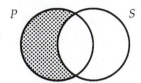

16. Every time like this is a time that tries persons' souls.

T: Times like these.

S: Times that try persons' souls.

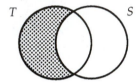

18. Every exercise that is last is an exercise that is best.

L: Last exercises.

B: Best exercises.

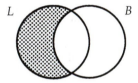

Exercise Set 9.3

PART I

2. *S*: Nonhuman animals; *P*: Things that feel pain; *M*: Thinking things.

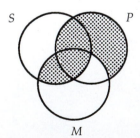

Valid.

4. *S*: Power sources; *P*: Oil reserves; *M*: Unlimited sources.

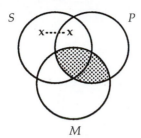

Invalid.

6. *S*: Innovators; *P*: Persons who achieve greatness; *M*: Persons who are not well educated.

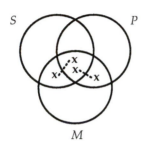

Invalid.

8. *S*: Arguments with two premises; *P*: Valid arguments; *M*: Syllogisms.

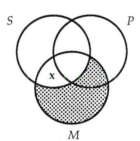

Valid.

10. *S*: Arguments; *P*: Syllogisms; *M*: Invalid arguments.

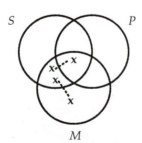

Invalid.

PART II

2. *S*: Good pets; *P*: Rats; *M*: Things with fleas.
No conclusion.

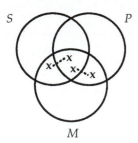

4. *S*: Brave persons; *P*: Fighters; *M*: Soldiers.

No conclusion.

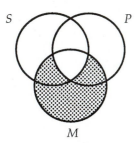

6. *S*: Immunizations at the Health Center; *P*: Valuable things; *M*: Things free of charge.

Conclusion: No immunization at the Health Center is valuable.

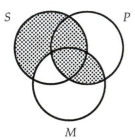

8. *S*: Mammals; *P*: Birds; *M*: Egg-layers.

No conclusion.

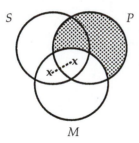

10. *S*: Dinosaurs; *P*: Reptiles; *M*: Things that are cold-blooded.

Conclusion: Some dinosaurs are not reptiles.

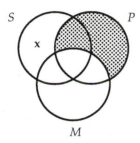

Part III

If a floating *x* remains, the form is invalid because no definite categorical statement can be drawn as a conclusion.

Exercise Set 9.4

2. a. The argument commits the fallacy of division because it argues that what is true of the whole (physical objects) must also be true of the parts (subatomic particles).

b. The fallacy of division. The first premiss states that, collectively, Kyoto has the best tofu in Japan, but the conclusion makes a claim that an individual instance of Kyoto tofu is the best in Japan.

c. Fallacy of composition.

d. Fallacy of composition.

e. Fallacy of division.

4. a. Fallacy of composition.

   b. Fallacy of composition.

Exercise Set 9.5

PART I

2. No persons who aren't trained in medicine are doctors.
    All fortune-tellers are persons who aren't trained in medicine.

    No fortune-tellers are doctors.

    Valid.

4. Some games of Clue are interesting to observe.
    No Monopoly games are interesting to observe.

    Some games of Clue are not Monopoly games.

    Valid.

6. All Mexican recipes are labor intensive.
    Some salad recipes are not labor intensive.

    No salad recipes are Mexican recipes.

    Invalid.

8. All rodents are suitable research animals.
    No capybara is a suitable research animal.

    No capybaras are rodents.

    Valid.

10. Some sofas are not beds.
    Some beds are uncomfortable.

    Some sofas are uncomfortable.

    Invalid.

PART III

If there are two particular premisses, then three possibilities need to be considered:

1. Both premisses are *I* sentences.

2. Both premisses are *O* sentences.

3. One premiss is an *I* sentence, and the other premiss is an *O* sentence.

   If (1), then the syllogism is invalid because the middle term will not be distributed in either premiss.

   If (2), then consider the four figures of the syllogism in which both premisses are *O* sentences:

MP	PM	MP	PM
SM	SM	MS	MS
SP	SP	SP	SP

Because the *O* sentence distributes only its predicate term, in the third figure, the middle term is not distributed, and the syllogism is invalid.

In the Venn diagrams for the other figures, floating xs do not allow any conclusion about the connection between *S* and *P*.

If (3) and the first premise is an *I* sentence and the second an *O* sentence, then in the third and fourth figures, the middle term is not distributed, and the syllogism is invalid. Venn diagrams of the first and second figures contain floating xs, and show invalidity.

Because the order of premises in a syllogism does not affect its validity, reversing the order of the *I* and *O* sentences to make *O* first and *I* second will not affect validity. So, no categorical syllogisms with two particular premises are valid.

Exercise Set 9.6

2. Some engineers are artists.
    All architects are artists.

    Some architects are engineers.

    Invalid. Middle term is not distributed.

4. All amethysts are gemstones.
    Some amethysts are precious.

    Some gemstones are not precious.

    Invalid.

6. All stem-cell research which—involves extractions of stem cells from early-stage human embryos—destroys human life.
    No destruction of human life is ethical.

    No stem-cell research is ethical.

    Valid, if the stem-cell research referred to in the conclusion is the same as that described in the first premiss.

8. No use of human embryos that does not respect their unique moral status is ethical.
    Some use of stem cells from human embryos (that which relieves humansuffering) is not use that does not respect the unique moral status of human embryos.

    Some use of stem cells obtained by destroying human embryos not unethical.

As stated, the syllogism is not valid. If the first premiss were revised as "All use of human embryos that respects the unique moral status is ethical," the syllogism would be valid. Do you think this premiss would be accepted by a person who objects to stem-cell research?

10. No things without parts are things that can perish by dissolution of their parts.
    All souls are things without parts.

    No souls are things that can perish by dissolution of their parts.
    Valid.

12. Every liar is unbelievable.
    No upright person is unbelievable.
    _____
    No liar is an upright person.
    Valid.

Exercise Set 9.7

2. All who take in the *Times* are well educated.
    All who are well educated can read.   _____
    All who take in the *Times* can read.

    No hedge hogs can read.   _____
    No hedge hogs take in the Times.

4. All large birds are birds that do not live on honey.
    All birds that do not live on honey are dull in color.   _____
    All large birds are dull in color. = No large birds are richly colored.

    No large birds are richly colored.
    All hummingbirds are richly colored.   _____
    No large birds are hummingbirds.

6. Institutions that have no museums do not need an archaeology department.
    The Carnegie Institution has no museums.   _____
    The Carnegie Institution does not need an archaeology department.

    The argument is valid, but the truth of the first premiss is based on the mistaken belief that the sole purpose of archaeology is to aid museums in the acquisition of collections.

Exercise Set 9.8

PART I

2. All plants that provide power without increasing greenhouse gases should be built.

4. All who are equally productive and hard working are persons who should be paid equally.

6. No government workers who leak information merely to expose fraud and waste in the system should be prosecuted.

8. All mathematicians are persons who are musically talented.

10. All persons who care about the environment will use bicycles instead of cars whenever possible.

PART II

2. No conclusion.

4. Your untethered balloon must come down.

6. Some mathematical expressions are sums of powers.

8. No conclusion.

10. Some persuadable people can be bribed.

PART III

2. All who can afford to be idle are rich.
    All who can afford to be idle are threats to the Puritan work ethic.

    Some rich persons are threats to the Puritan work ethic.

    Invalid.

4. All good speakers are persons who avoid boring their audiences.
    All professional politicians are good speakers.

    All professional politicians avoid boring their audiences.

    Valid.

6. Some fallacious arguments are convincing.
    No arguments of yours are fallacious arguments.

    All arguments of yours are convincing.

    Invalid.

8. All arts organizations are organizations that are struggling for funds.
    Some organizations that are struggling for funds are organizations that will go under.

    Some arts organizations will go under.

    Invalid.

10. All syllogisms are things with two premisses.
    Some syllogisms are noncategorical syllogisms.

    Some noncategorical syllogisms are things with two premisses.

    Valid.

12. All industrial and military production is directed at specific values (or, by obversion),
    No industrial or military production is value free.
    (Some) science is a vital part of military and industrial production.

    Some science is not value free.

    This seems not to be valid because of more than three terms. The first premiss refers to military/industrial production. The second premiss refers to a part of military/industrial production. We also know that what is true of a whole may not be true of all its parts.

14. No beliefs that transcend their cultural contexts are relative to the culture in which they arise.
    Some moral beliefs transcend the culture in which they arise.

    Some moral beliefs are not relative to the culture in which they arise.

    Valid.

Chapter Ten

Exercise Set 10.1

PART I

2. Intransitive, asymmetric, irreflexive.

4. Nontransitive, symmetric, irreflexive.

6. Nontransitive, asymmetric, irreflexive.

8. Nontransitive, symmetric, irreflexive.

10. Nontransitive, nonsymmetric, nonreflexive.

Exercise Set 10.2

Domain of interpretation: Everything.

B: Bands; *C:* Carnivores; *D:* Dogs; *E:* Horses; *F:* Fanatics; *G:* Health-conscious people; *H:* Hot things; *I:* Milk drinkers; *L:* Lions; *M:* Mice; *N:* Race animals; *R:* Rodents; *T:* Tigers; *V:* Vegetarians; *J:* Things that bark; *K:* Cats; *O:* Things that meow.

2. $(\exists x)(Bx \cdot \sim Hx)$.

4. $(x)(Vx \rightarrow Gx)$.

6. $(x)(Mx \rightarrow Rx)$.

8. $(x)((Dx \rightarrow Jx) \cdot (Kx \rightarrow Ox))$.

10. $(x)((Dx \rightarrow Ex) \rightarrow Nx)$.

12. $(x)(Dx \rightarrow \sim Kx) \rightarrow (x)(Kx \rightarrow \sim Dx)$.

14. $(x)((Lx \text{ v } Tx) \rightarrow \sim Vx)$.

Exercise Set 10.3

PART II

Domain of interpretation: All persons.

m: Mary; *j:* John; *L:* … loves _____; *I:* … is identical with _____.

2. $\sim (\exists x)mLx$.

4. $jLj \cdot jLm$.

6. $(\exists x)xLm$.

8. $(x)(\sim xIj \rightarrow \sim xLj) \cdot jLj$

10. $(x)xLj \text{ v } (x)xLm$.

12. $(\exists x) \sim xLx$.

14. $\sim (x)(xLx)$.

Exercise Set 10.4

Domain of interpretation: Persons.

L: ... loves ____.

2. $(x)(\exists y) \sim xLy$, *or*, $\sim (\exists x)(y)\, xLy$.

4. $(\exists x)(y)\, xLy$.

6. $(x)(\exists y)\, xLy \rightarrow (x)(\exists y)\, yLx$, *or*, $(x)(\exists y)\, xLy \rightarrow \sim (\exists x)(y) \sim yLx$.

Exercise Set 10.5

PART I

2. The relationship *greater than* is asymmetric.

4. The relationship *is the same color as* is transitive. (Note the difference between *is the same color as* and *looks the same color as*.)

PART II

One example: *Is the same age as.*

PART III

One example: *Less than.*

PART IV

2. Parent of.

4. Greater than or equal to.

6. Spouse of.

PART VI

Domain of interpretation: The set of all things.

C: Bugatti Veyron; B: ___ are more expensive than . . .; F: ___fears....

D: Ferrari Enzo; T: ___ are faster than...; S: ___ is the brother of....

G: McLaren F; R: ___ is cousin of....

S: snakes; E: ___ eats.....

M: mice; O: ___ owns....

P: pianos; W: ___ plays....

F: women; c: Christopher.

R: rich persons;   *v*: Virginia.

2. $(\exists x)(y)\,(Cx \bullet (Dy \rightarrow xTy))$.

4. $(\exists x)(y)\,((Mx \bullet Sy) \rightarrow yFx)$.

6. $(\exists x)(y) \sim yRx$.

8. $(x)(Sx \rightarrow \exists y)(My \bullet xEy))$.

10. $(\exists x)\,(\sim Rx \bullet (\exists y)((Py \rightarrow xOy))$.

12. $\sim (x)(y)(z)\,((xFy \bullet yFz) \rightarrow (xFz)$.

PART VII

2. Domain of interpretation: The set of all numbers.

s: 6;   *f*: the square root of 34;   *G*:… is greater than ___.

Implicit premiss: *Greater than* is asymmetric.

> *sGf*
> $\underline{(x)(y)\,(xGy \rightarrow \sim yGx)}$
> $\sim fGs$

4. Domain of interpretation: Persons.

c: Lady Gaga;   *m*: Marilyn Monroe;   *H*:… has the same hair color as ___.

B: blond.

Implicit premiss: *Has the same hair color as* is symmetric.

> *mHc* • *Bc*
> $(x)(y)\,((xHy) \rightarrow yHx)$
> $\underline{cHm}$
> *Bm*

PART VIII

This argument apparently commits the fallacy of every and all.

PART X

One example: Spouse of.

Appendix One

Exercise Set A.1

PART I

2. Invalid.

$$
\frac{\begin{array}{c} p \vee q \vdash \sim p \vee \sim q \\ \hline p \vee q \vdash \sim p, \sim q \\ \hline p, p \vee q \vdash \sim q \\ \hline q, p, p \vee q \vdash \end{array}}{q, p, p, \vdash \qquad q, p, q \vdash}
$$

4. Valid.

$$
\frac{p \to (q \to r) \vdash (p \bullet q) \to r}{p \bullet q, p \to (q \to r) \vdash r}
$$
$$
\frac{}{p, q, p \to (q \to r) \vdash r}
$$
$$
{}^{*}p, q \vdash p, r \qquad \frac{p, q, q \to r \vdash r}{{}^{*}p, q \vdash q, r \qquad {}^{*}p, q, r \vdash r}
$$

6. One branch does not terminate in an axiom; the tree does not need to be completed. Invalid.

$$
\frac{p \to (q \to r), q \to (r \to s) \vdash p \to s}{p, p \to (q \to r), q \to (r \to s) \vdash s}
$$
$$
{}^{*}p, q \to (r \to s) \vdash p, s \qquad \frac{p, q \to r, q \to (r \to s) \vdash s}{p, q \to (r \to s) \vdash q, s \quad p, r, q \to (r \to s) \vdash s}
$$
$$
p \vdash q, q, s \quad p, r \to s \vdash q, s
$$

8. Valid.

$$
\frac{p \vdash (q \to r) \to p}{p^{*}, (q \to r) \vdash p^{*}}
$$

10. Valid.

$$
\frac{(p \vee q) \to r \vdash (p \bullet q) \to r}{(p \vee q) \to r, p \bullet q \vdash r}
$$
$$
\frac{p \bullet q \vdash p \vee q, r \qquad r^{*}, p \bullet q \vdash r^{*}}{p, q \vdash p \vee q}
$$
$$
p, q^{*} \vdash p, q^{*}
$$

PART II

Tautology.

Eight rows (truth table is one line longer).

$$\vdash (p \to (q \to r)) \to ((p \to q) \to (p \to r))$$

$$p \to (q \to r) \vdash (p \to q) \to (p \to r)$$

$$p \to q, p \to (q \to r) \vdash p \to r$$

$$p, p \to q, p \to (q \to r) \vdash r$$

$*p, p, \to (q \to r) \vdash p, r$	$p, q, p \to (q \to r) \vdash r$

$$*p, q \vdash p, r \qquad p, q, q \to r \vdash r$$

$$*p, q \vdash q, r \qquad *p, q, r \vdash r$$

Exercise Set A.2

PART I

2. The last sentence form $(p \to \sim s)$ is a consequence.

$$p \to q, r \to \sim s, q \to r \vdash p \to \sim s$$

$$p, p \to q, r \to \sim s, q \to r \vdash \sim s$$

$$s, p, p \to q, r \to \sim s, q \to r \vdash$$

$*s, p, r \to \sim s, q \to r \vdash p$	$s, p, q, r \to \sim s, q \to r \vdash$

$$s, p, q, q \to r \vdash r \qquad s, p, q, \sim s, q \to r \vdash$$

$$*s, p, q \vdash q, r \qquad *s, p, q, r \vdash r \qquad *s, p, q, q \to r \vdash s$$

4. Consequence.

$$p \to q, r \to s, \sim s \to p, q \to r \vdash \sim s \to t$$

$$\sim s, p \to q, r \to s, \sim s \to p, q \to r \vdash t$$

$$p \to q, r \to s, \sim s \to p, q \to r \vdash s, t$$

$$r \to s, \sim s \to p, q \to r \vdash p, s, t \qquad \text{(other branch to be continued)}$$

$$\sim s \to p, q \to r \vdash r, p, s, t \qquad *s, \sim s \to p, q \to r \vdash p, s, t$$

$$q \to r \vdash \sim s, r, p, s, t \qquad *p, q \to r \vdash r, p, s, t$$

$$*s, q \to r \vdash r, p, s, t$$

Branch continued from above:

$$q, r \to s, \sim s \to p, q \to r \vdash s, t$$

$$q, \sim s \to p, q \to r \vdash r, s, t \qquad *q, s, \sim s \to p, q \to r \vdash s, t$$

$$q, q \to r \vdash \sim s, r, s, t \qquad q, p, q \to r \vdash r, s, t$$

$$*s, q, q \to r \vdash r, s, t \qquad *q, p \vdash q, r, s, t \qquad *q, p, r \vdash r, s, t$$

6. Not a consequence.

$$(p \leftrightarrow q) \to r, \sim r, \sim p \bullet q \vdash s$$

$$(p \leftrightarrow q) \to r, \sim p \bullet q \vdash r, s$$

$$(p \leftrightarrow q) \to r, \sim p, q \vdash r, s$$

$$(p \leftrightarrow q) \to r, q \vdash p, r, s$$

$$q \vdash p \leftrightarrow q, p, r, s \qquad {}^*r, q \vdash p, r, s$$

$${}^*p, q \vdash q, p, r, s \qquad q, q \vdash p, p, r, s$$

PART II

2. Tautology.

$$\vdash (p \to q) \to ((r \to (q \to s)) \to (r \to (p \to s)))$$

$$p \to q \vdash (r \to (q \to s)) \to (r \to (p \to s))$$

$$r \to (q \to s), p \to q \vdash r \to (p \to s)$$

$$r, r \to (q \to s), p \to q \vdash p \to s$$

$$p, r, r \to (q \to s), p \to q \vdash s$$

$${}^*p, r, p, \to q \vdash r, s \qquad p, r, q \to s, p \to q \vdash s$$

$$p, r, p \to q \vdash q, s \qquad {}^*p, r, s, p \to q \vdash s$$

$${}^*p, r \vdash p, q, s \qquad {}^*p, r, q, \vdash q, s$$

4. Tautology.

$$\vdash ((p \to q) \to r) \to ((p \to r)) \to r)$$

$$(p \to q) \to r \vdash (p \to r) \to r$$

$$p \to r, (p \to q) \to r \vdash r$$

$$(p \to q) \to r \vdash p, r \qquad {}^*r, (p \to q) \to r \vdash r$$

$$\vdash p \to q, p, r \qquad {}^*r \vdash p, r$$

$${}^*p \vdash q, p, r$$

6. Not a tautology.

$$\vdash \sim (p \to q) \leftrightarrow (p \to \sim q)$$

$$\sim (p \to q) \vdash p \to \sim q \qquad p \to \sim q \vdash \sim (p \to q)$$

$$p, \sim (p \to q) \vdash \sim q \qquad p \to q, p \to \sim q \vdash$$

$$p \vdash p \to q, \sim q \qquad p \to \sim q \vdash p \qquad q, p \to \sim q \vdash$$

$$p, q \vdash p \to q \qquad \vdash p, p \qquad \sim q \vdash p$$

$${}^*p, p, q \vdash q$$

Part III

2. Valid.

p: The president is happy.

q: His favorite bills are passed by Congress.

r: The staff feels good.

s: The staff is in no condition to work for his bills.

$$p \leftrightarrow q$$
$$p \rightarrow r$$
$$(r \rightarrow s) \bullet (s \rightarrow \sim q)$$
$$\sim p$$

$$p \leftrightarrow q, p \rightarrow r, (r \rightarrow s) \bullet (s \rightarrow \sim q) \vdash \sim p$$

$$\overline{p, p \leftrightarrow q, p \rightarrow r, (r \rightarrow s) \bullet (s \rightarrow \sim q) \vdash}$$

$$\overline{p, p \leftrightarrow q, p \rightarrow r, r \rightarrow s, s \rightarrow \sim q \vdash}$$

$$\overline{{}^*p, p \rightarrow r, r \rightarrow s, s \rightarrow \sim q \vdash p, q} \qquad p, q, p, p \rightarrow r, r \rightarrow s, s \rightarrow \sim q \vdash$$

$$\overline{{}^*p, q, p, r \rightarrow s, s \rightarrow \sim q \vdash p} \qquad \overline{p, q, p, r, r \rightarrow s, s \rightarrow \sim q \vdash}$$

$$\overline{{}^*p, q, p, r, s \rightarrow \sim q \vdash r} \qquad \overline{s, p, q, p, r, s \rightarrow \sim q \vdash}$$

$$\overline{{}^*s, p, q, p, r \vdash s, s} \qquad \overline{\sim q, p, q, p, r \vdash s}$$

$$\overline{{}^*p, q, p, r \vdash s, q}$$

4. Valid.

p: Some archaeologists are correct.

q: The first humans crossed the Bering Strait 30,000 years ago.

r: They spent time in Alaska.

s: They left artifacts with radiocarbon dates of 30,000 years old.

t: Archaeologists excavate.

u: Artifacts with radiocarbon dates of 30,000 years old will be uncovered by archaeologists.

$$p \rightarrow q$$
$$q \rightarrow r$$
$$r \rightarrow s$$
$$(s \bullet t) \rightarrow u$$
$$(t \bullet p) \rightarrow u$$

$$p \rightarrow q, q \rightarrow r, r \rightarrow s, (s \bullet t) \rightarrow u \vdash (t \bullet p) \rightarrow u$$

$$\overline{t \bullet p, p \rightarrow q, q \rightarrow r, r \rightarrow s, (s \bullet t) \rightarrow u \vdash u}$$

$$\overline{t, p, p \rightarrow q, q \rightarrow r, r \rightarrow s, (s \bullet t) \rightarrow u \vdash u}$$

$$\overline{t, p, p \rightarrow q, q \rightarrow r, r \rightarrow s \vdash s \bullet t, u} \qquad {}^*u, t, p, p \rightarrow q, q \rightarrow r, r \rightarrow s \vdash u$$

$$\overline{{}^*t, p, q \rightarrow r, r \rightarrow s \vdash p, s \bullet t, u} \qquad t, p, q, q \rightarrow r, r \rightarrow s \vdash s \bullet t, u$$

$$\overline{{}^*t, p, q, r \rightarrow s \vdash q, s \bullet t, u} \qquad \overline{t, p, q, r, r \rightarrow s \vdash s \bullet t, u}$$

$$\overline{{}^*t, p, q, r \vdash r, s \bullet t, u} \qquad \overline{t, p, q, r, s \vdash s \bullet t, u}$$

$$\overline{{}^*t, p, q, r, s \vdash s, u} \qquad \overline{{}^*t, p, q, r, s \vdash t, u}$$

INDEX